D1241583

THE NEW INTERNATIONAL COMMENTARY
ON THE
OLD TESTAMENT

General Editors

R. K. HARRISON
(1968–1993)

ROBERT L. HUBBARD, JR.
(1994–)

The Book of
PROVERBS

Chapters 15–31

BRUCE K. WALTKE

WILLIAM B. EERDMANS PUBLISHING COMPANY
GRAND RAPIDS, MICHIGAN / CAMBRIDGE, U.K.

Publisher's Note

This commentary was planned and written as a single volume, but its length dictated the need to publish it in two volumes. The reader should note that the Introduction in the first volume covers the entire book of Proverbs; this second volume comprises only commentary on Proverbs 15:30–31:31.

For the reader's convenience, each volume has its own table of contents, abbreviation list, and indexes. Within the text of this volume, references to material in the first volume are made in the form of a roman numeral I followed by a colon and a page number; for example, a reference to page 100 in the first volume will be cited here as I: 100.

© 2005 Wm. B. Eerdmans Publishing Co.
All rights reserved

Wm. B. Eerdmans Publishing Co.
255 Jefferson Ave. S.E., Grand Rapids, Michigan 49503 /
P.O. Box 163, Cambridge CB3 9PU U.K.

Printed in the United States of America

11 10 09 08 07 06 8 7 6 5 4 3 2

Library of Congress Cataloging-in-Publication Data

Waltke, Bruce K.
The book of Proverbs: Chapters 15–31 / Bruce K. Waltke.
p. cm. — (The New international commentary on the Old Testament)
Includes bibliographical references and index.
ISBN-10: 0-8028-2776-4
ISBN-13: 978-0-8028-2776-0 (cloth: alk. paper)
1. Bible. O.T. Proverbs XV-XXXI — Commentaries.
I. Title. II. Series.

BS1465.53.W36 2005
223′.7077 — dc22

2004050609

www.eerdmans.com

Dedicated to
Elaine,
my competent wife,
worthy of praise in the gate

CONTENTS

INDEXES

GENERAL EDITOR'S PREFACE

Long ago St. Paul wrote: "I planted, Apollos watered, but God gave the growth" (1 Cor. 3:6, NRSV). He was right: ministry indeed requires a team effort — the collective labors of many skilled hands and minds. Someone digs up the dirt and drops in seed, while others water the ground to nourish seedlings to growth. The same team effort over time has brought this commentary series to its position of prominence today. Professor E. J. Young "planted" it forty years ago, enlisting its first contributors and himself writing its first published volume. Professor R. K. Harrison "watered" it, signing on other scholars and wisely editing everyone's finished products. As General Editor, I now tend their planting, and, true to Paul's words, through four decades God has indeed graciously "[given] the growth."

Today the New International Commentary on the Old Testament enjoys a wide readership of scholars, priests, pastors, rabbis, and other serious Bible students. Thousands of readers across the religious spectrum and in countless countries consult its volumes in their ongoing preaching, teaching, and research. They warmly welcome the publication of each new volume and eagerly await its eventual transformation from an emerging "series" into a complete commentary "set." But as humanity experiences a new century of history, an era commonly called "postmodern," what kind of commentary series is NICOT? What distinguishes it from other similarly well-established series?

Its volumes aim to publish biblical scholarship of the highest quality. Each contributor writes as an expert, both in the biblical text itself and in the relevant scholarly literature, and each commentary conveys the results of wide reading and careful, mature reflection. Ultimately, its spirit is eclectic, each contributor gleaning interpretive insights from any useful source, whatever its religious or philosophical viewpoint, and integrating them into his or her interpretation of a biblical book. The series draws on recent methodological innovations in biblical scholarship, for example, canon criticism, the so-called "new literary criticism," reader-response theories, and sensitivity to gender-based and ethnic readings. NICOT volumes also aim to be irenic in tone, summarizing and critiquing influential views with fairness while defending their own. Its list of contributors includes male and female scholars from a number of Christian faith-groups. The diversity of contributors and their freedom to draw on all relevant methodologies give the entire series an exciting and enriching variety.

What truly distinguishes this series, however, is that it speaks from within that interpretive tradition known as evangelicalism. Evangelicalism is an informal movement within Protestantism that cuts across traditional denominational lines. Its heart and soul is the conviction that the Bible is God's inspired Word, written by gifted human writers, through which God calls humanity to enjoy a loving personal relationship with its Creator and Savior. True to that tradition, NICOT volumes do not treat the Old Testament as just an ancient literary artifact on a par with the *Iliad* or *Gilgamesh.* They are not literary autopsies of ancient parchment cadavers but rigorous, reverent wrestlings with wonderfully human writings through which the living God speaks his powerful Word. NICOT delicately balances "criticism" (i.e., the use of standard critical methodologies) with humble respect, admiration, and even affection for the biblical text. As an evangelical commentary, it pays particular attention to the text's literary features, theological themes, and implications for the life of faith today.

Ultimately, NICOT aims to serve women and men of faith who desire to hear God's voice afresh through the Old Testament. With gratitude to God for two marvelous gifts — the Scriptures themselves and keen-minded scholars to explain their message — I welcome readers of all kinds to savor the good fruit of this series.

ROBERT L. HUBBARD JR.

AUTHOR'S PREFACE

In a world bombarded by inane cliches, trivial catchwords, and godless sound bites, the expression of true wisdom is in short supply today. The church stands alone as the receptacle and repository of the inspired traditions that carry a mandate for a holy life from ancient sages, the greatest of whom was Solomon, and from the greater than Solomon, Jesus Christ. As the course and bulk of biblical wisdom, the book of Proverbs remains the model of curriculum for humanity to learn how to live under God and before humankind. As a result, it beckons the church to diligent study and application. To uncommitted youth it serves as a stumbling stone, but to committed youth it is a foundation stone.

But, tragically, the church has practically discarded the book of Proverbs, which was written for young people as a compass by which to steer their ship of life (see 1:2-6). Of its 930 ancient sayings many Christians know three — to fear the LORD (1:7), to trust him (3:5-6), and to "train their children in the way they should go" (22:6) — and possibly something about the "virtuous wife" (31:10-31). However, "to fear the LORD" is misunderstood, "to trust him" (3:5) is a platitude divorced from the book, the promise that the child will not depart from childhood rearing raises more questions than solutions, and the poem about the virtuous wife seems out of date.

For some honest readers, as one student confessed, "Proverbs seems banal or wrong." Obviously "a truthful witness gives honest testimony" (12:17), "does not deceive" (14:5), and gives the LORD delight (12:22). For sober theologians the book's heavenly promises of health, wealth, and prosperity are troublesome, and for many saints they seem detached from earth's harsh realities. Some proverbs seem to contradict each other: "Answer a fool according to his folly" (26:4) is followed by "Don't answer a fool according to his folly" (26:5). Moreover, whereas Proverbs affirms a righteous order, Job (9:22) and Ecclesiastes (9:2) deny its reality.

For the logical mind the book seems to be a hodgepodge collection, having no rhyme or reason in its grouping of sayings. They jump from one topic to another like scatterbrains in a living-room conversation. How does one preach and teach such a mishmash?

For the modern mind, the book's cultural setting seems far removed from the twenty-first century. Proverbs puts a high priority on tradition and age, while the modern mind prizes change and youth. Proverbs admonishes parents not to spare the rod, but the state's welfare workers want to jail those who obey it. Its psychology is psychosomatic; modern psychology uses more scientific terms.

Some academics, including evangelicals, have not helped. They are skeptical about the book's claim to Solomonic authorship, substitute trust in man for trust in God, and speak of a world order instead of divine retribution. Instead of accepting its inspired teachings by faith, they call for a curriculum of human rationality and experimentation. Academics have demonstrated that Proverbs is at home in pan-oriental pagan literature but have called into question whether its apparent lack of an Israelite orientation has a home in Israel's covenants and in biblical literature. According to others, compared to Job and Ecclesiastes, Proverbs represents "a single false doctrine."

For Christians, Proverbs seems irrelevant. If Jesus is greater than Solomon, why bother studying and memorizing this ancient book? Besides, "If Solomon was so smart, how come he died such a fool?"

For the translator, Proverbs defies translation. A proverb depends on sound and sense. "A stitch in time saves nine" works because of its alliteration as well as its uncommonly obvious good sense. But the sounds and puns of the biblical proverbs cannot be caught in translation, and so, unlike an English proverb, they are not usually memorable. Moreover, the meaning of what the book calls a proverb is not the commonly accepted English one. In English a proverb expresses a universally accepted truism, but "trust in the Lord with all your heart, and do not lean upon your own understanding" is not a truism that many Americans accept. Americans may claim to trust in God on their coinage, but in fact they teach and preach, "Believe in yourself."

I wrote this historico-grammatical commentary with these issues in mind, hoping to give insight into solutions without necessarily giving "the answer." I addressed some of these problems head-on in the Introduction (found only in vol. 1) and had them in mind in the exegesis of individual verses. The solution for honest readers lies in understanding the profound philosophical and theological insights of this ancient book. The logic of the book has escaped modern readers because they have not understood the poetics used in its composition. The modern mind has to be challenged for its pride and prejudice, and academics must come to realize that their interpretations are often dictated by a "fundamentalistic" historical criticism that is just as rigid as theological fundamentalism. Christians should retain the best of the past in relation to the theological advances in Christ.

The total commentary on Proverbs is divided into two parts: an Introduction (see vol. 1) and an exegesis of the text. The Introduction takes up critical issues of text, authorship, date, and unity in addition to theological and philosophical reflections on the larger issues, such as whether the proverbs are promises or statements of general expectations. In addition, it gives word studies of many wisdom terms in connection with these theological reflections. References to the Introduction in the commentary proper often cite just the first page of their referent in the Introduction.

The commentary portion provides translations of poems and of units of proverbs. If a unit is particularly long, it gives the translation along with its subunits. No accurate translation can provide a word-for-word rendering of the original text. Because the thought patterns and syntax differ between Hebrew and English, accurate communication of the sage's meaning demands constant regard for the contextual meanings of his words and idioms and modifications in sentence structure. Nevertheless, I strove to stay close to the Hebrew text. Where verse numbers in the Hebrew text differ from those in the English Bible, I placed the Hebrew versification in parentheses.

The exegetical comments should be read with translation in hand. I strive first to determine the structure of the poems or the collections, sections, and units through thematic considerations in conjunction with form and rhetorical criticism. I then give exegetical comments on each verse, half-verse, and individual words. However, it is impossible to analyze the structure of the larger groupings without a prior careful exegesis of each verse. Occasionally, I also offer theological reflections. To help out with the matter of sound, I occasionally supply transliterations of the Hebrew word(s). I discuss the meaning of some theologically laden Hebrew words that occur many times in the Introduction and other Hebrew words full of wisdom at their first occurrence, though I may cite only their English glosses. Thereafter I use "see" with cross references to the same Hebrew word, even though the English versions may differ considerably, and "cf." for cross references to expressions in the same semantic domain. I apologize that I sometimes give the same cross references in closely connected verses, but proverbs are meant to be studied both collectively and individually, occasioning their study in isolation.

I intend the footnotes mostly for scholars who want to document a point and/or to research it in greater depth. By contrast, I address the text to the pastor, student, and Bible lover. For this reason I cite German works in my translations of them. Hopefully, my treatments of "the wise and speech" and of "the wise and wealth" in the Introduction will model topical preaching. Expositors should not hesitate to translate the literary forms of Proverbs into the homiletic genre. Just as the Hebrew language must be translated into

English, so also the genres of Proverbs need to be translated into a homily. However, expositors owe it to the inspired sage to be true to his meaning and intention and to consider the larger context. I hope the Contents will enable them to identify that context readily.

Though I wrote the text for the person who had not had opportunity to study Biblical Hebrew, I found it almost impossible to discuss the meaning of the text without appealing to the original Hebrew text. I hope that those readers who do not know Biblical Hebrew will be willing to look over technical terms such as *Hiphil* that nuance a verb's meaning without feeling that they must understand the term just as they can read articles on medicine with comprehension and profit without necessarily understanding their technical terms.

In writing this commentary I also had to face difficult stylistic decisions. I opted to render the Tetragrammaton *(YHWH)* by LORD, not Yahweh, for philological, historical, and theological reasons. God in his providence has not preserved its vocalization, so that its reconstruction by "Yahweh" is in fact speculative. Furthermore, by using the epithet "Lord," not the personal name, God paved the way for the identification of Jesus with the personal name *YHWH.* Verses such as "everyone who calls upon the name of *YHWH*" (Joel 2:32) could easily be applied to the Lord Jesus Christ: "If you confess with your mouth, 'Jesus is Lord' " (Rom. 10:9), "for, 'Everyone who calls on the name of the Lord will be saved' " (Rom. 10:13). In short, I opted for its theological rendering rather than its speculative historical pronunciation.

I also had to face the problem of whether to use A.D. *(anno Domini)* and B.C. (Before Christ) or C.E. (Christian Era) and B.C.E. (Before the Christian Era). I opted for the traditional A.D. and B.C., not for the academic C.E. and B.C.E., because I was writing for the average Bible reader, not for the scholarly community (including notable Jewish scholars), though I attempted to appraise the academic community critically for its strengths and weaknesses.

In contemporary English the third person singular pronoun ("he/she," etc.) is a stylistic bramble patch. Although I desired to use inclusive language as much as possible, I opted to continue to use the third person masculine pronoun as the common pronoun for both genders, hoping that those who choose other options will not take offense. The loss of individualization by shifting from singular constructions to plural constructions is too great a loss in sense, and the loss of agreement between singular subjects and plural qualifiers by grammatical disagreement or by shifting between pronouns or by combining them is too great a stylistic loss.

This commentary has been in the making for over a quarter of a century. In the providence of God, after Derek Kidner and Alan Millard translated Proverbs for the New International Version, I was assigned to the three successive committees of the NIV responsible for its reworking. I am indebted to everyone on those committees. In part the commentary was delayed by the new literary criticism, which has had a profound impact on traditional exegesis and which required my rethinking the entire book. This new approach validates that the proverbs are arranged in a sensible way to protect the vulnerable sayings against misinterpretation and/or to enrich their meanings. In A.D. 2000 the Committee on Bible Translation, of which I am a member, commissioned me to generate proposals for the revision of Proverbs. I am most indebted to the following individuals for the encouragement and instruction I received from that committee: Kenneth Barker, Gordon Fee, Dick France, Karen Jones, Alan Millard, Don Madvig, John Stek, Larry Walker, Herb Wolf, and Ronald Youngblood. I also gladly acknowledge my unending dialectic with the academic community, most of whom are cited in the bibliography. It was a particular delight to use my students' papers and theses. Even those scholars with whom I disagree made the heuristic contribution of challenging my thinking and provoking what I hope is a helpful response.

I could not have worked with more gracious librarians and their staffs than Grace Mullen and Jane Petite of Westminster Theological Seminary; Ivan Gaetz, David Stewart, Joan Pries, Audrey Williams, and Matthew Freeman of Regent College; and John Muether, Dan Wright, and Kevin Nelson of Reformed Theological Seminaries. My talented German students Johannes Kuhhorn and Gabriel Braun helped me with the translation of *Die Sprüche* by A. Meinhold. The Eerdmans Publishing Company and Robert Hubbard patiently allowed me to pursue my research and writing over these many years. Eerdmans editor Milton Essenburg meticulously worked on the clarity, consistency, and correctness of the original manuscript. My students at both Regent College and Reformed Theological Seminary assiduously proofread with loving willingness the Scripture cross-references. The team at Regent, which was led by my multigifted computer tutor, Rob Barrett, were Gay Atmajian, Lane Ayo, Matt Ghormley, Abram Kidd, Allison Koenicke, Max Kuecker, Rod McLain, Stephen Ney, Rosie Perera, and Susan Ting. The team at Reformed Theological Seminary, which was led by my very competent teaching assistant, Scott Redd, were: Guillermo Bernáldez, Jason Foster, Rob Genin, Bryan Gregory, Chris Hackett, Brett Hedgepeth, David Kirkendall, Paul May, Omar Ortiz, Jennifer Redd, Ryan Reeves, Jonathan St. Clair, Cary Smith, Ron Thomas, and Keith Welton.

BRUCE K. WALTKE

ABBREVIATIONS

AB	Anchor Bible
ABD	*The Anchor Bible Dictionary*
ABR	*Australian Biblical Review*
acc.	accusative
act.	active
A.D.	*anno Domini,* in the year of our Lord
AEL	M. Lichtheim, *Ancient Egyptian Literature: A Book of Readings.* 3 vols. Berkeley: University of California, 1973, 1976, 1980
AfO	*Archiv für Orientforschung*
AIR	P. D. Miller Jr., P. D. Hanson, and S. D. McBride, eds., *Ancient Israelite Religion: Essays in Honor of Frank Moore Cross.* Philadelphia: Fortress, 1987
AJSL	*American Journal of Semitic Languages and Literature*
AJT	*Asia Journal of Theology*
Akk.	Akkadian
Amen.	*Amenemope*
ANEP	J. B. Pritchard, ed., *The Ancient Near East in Pictures.* 2nd ed. Princeton: Princeton University, 1969
ANET	J. B. Pritchard, ed., *Ancient Near Eastern Texts.* 3rd ed. Princeton: Princton University, 1969
ANETS	Ancient Near Eastern Texts and Studies
AnOr	Analecta orientalia
AOAT	Alter Orient und Altes Testament
Arab.	Arabic
Aram.	Aramaic
ASTI	*Annual of the Swedish Theological Institute*
ATANT	Abhandlungen zur Theologie des Alten und Neuen Testaments

ATD	Das Alte Testament Deutsch
AUSS	*Andrews University Seminary Studies*
AV	Authorized Version. See KJV
BA	*Biblical Archaeologist*
BARev	*Biblical Archaeology Review*
BASOR	*Bulletin of the American Schools of Oriental Research*
BDB	F. Brown, S. R. Driver, and C. Briggs, *Hebrew and English Lexicon of the Old Testament.* Repr. Oxford: Clarendon, 1959
BETL	*Bibliotheca ephemeridum theologicarum lovaniensium*
BGBE	Beiträge zur Geschichte der biblischen Exegese
BHS	K. Elliger and W. Rudoph, ed., *Biblia Hebraica Stuttgartensia.* Stuttgart: Deutsche Bibelstiftung, 1967-77. *Proverbia* prepared by J. Fichtner
BHT	Beiträge zur historischen Theologie
Bib	*Biblica*
BibAT	*Biblical Archaeology Today: Proceedings of the International Congress on Biblical Archaeology, Jerusalem, April 1984*
BibBh	*Bible Bhashyam*
BibLit	Bible and Literature Series
BibOr	*Biblica et orientalia*
BIOSCS	*Bulletin of the International Organization for Septuagint and Cognate Studies*
BJRL	*Bullletin of the John Rylands Library*
BK	*Bibel und Kirche*
BKAT	Biblischer Kommentar: Altes Testament
BM	*Beth Mikra*
BMB	*Bulletin du Musée de Beyrouth*
BN	*Biblische Notizen*
BO	*Bibliotheca orientalis*
BOAS	*Bulletin of Oriental and African Studies*
BR	*Biblical Research*
BRev	*Bible Review*
BRL	K. Galling, ed., *Biblisches Reallexikon,* Tübingen: J. C. B. Mohr, 1937
BSac	*Bibliotheca Sacra*
BSO(A)S	*Bulletin of the School of Oriental (and African) Studies*
BT	*Bible Translator;* see also *TBT*
BTB	*Biblical Theology Bulletin*
ByF	*Biblia y Fe*
BZ	*Biblische Zeitschrift*

BZAW	Beiheft zur *ZAW*
ca.	*circa,* around
CAH	Cambridge Ancient History
CAT	Commentaire de l'Ancien Testament
CB	Coniectanea biblica
CBQ	*Catholic Bibical Quarterly*
CBQMS	Catholic Biblical Quarterly Monograph Series
CC	The Communicator's Commentary
cent.	century
CESS	Centre d'études supérieures spécialise d'histoire des religions
cf.	*confer,* compare
CG	*Collationes Gandavenses*
ch.	chapter
CHS	Commentary on the Holy Scriptures
CICSB	Congrès international Catholique des science bibliques, *Sacra pagina: miscellanea biblica*
CIS	*Corpus inscriptionum semiticarum*
col.	column
Colloquium	*The Australian and New Zealand Theological Review: Colloquium*
ConBOT	Coniectanea biblica, Old Testament
cons.	construct
CSIC	Consejo superior de investigaciones científicas instituto "Francisco Suarez"
CSR	*Christian Scholar's Review*
CTA	A. Herdner, ed., *Corpus des tablettes en cunéiformes alphabétiques découvertes à Ras Shamra-Ugarit de 1929 à 1939.* 2 vols. Paris: Imprimerie Nationale, 1963
CTJ	*Calvin Theological Journal*
CTM	*Concordia Theological Monthly*
CUASST	The Catholic University of America Studies in Sacred Theology
CurTM	*Currents in Theology and Missions*
DBSup	L. Pirot, R. A. Cazelles, and A. Feuillet, *Dictionnaire de la Bible. Supplément.*Paris, 1928-
DD	*Dor le dor*
diss.	dissertation
DJD	*Discoveries in the Judaean Desert*
DSBS	The Daily Study Bible Series
DTT	*Dansk teologisk tidsskrift*
EB	*Étude bibliques*

EBC	F. Gaebelein, Expositor's Bible Commentary. 12 vols. Grand Rapids: Zondervan, 1979-88
ed.	editor, edited by
EDSS	L. Schiffman and J. Vanderkam, eds., *Encyclopedia of the Dead Sea Scrolls.* 2 vols. Oxford: Clarendon, 2000
EDT	W. Elwell, ed., *Evangelical Dictionary of Theology.* Grand Rapids: Baker, 1996
e.g.	*exempli gratia,* for example
EHAT	Exegetisches Handbuch zum Alten Testament
EHS.T.	Europaische Hochschulschriften: Reihe 23, Theologie
EncJud	*Encyclopaedia Judaica*
Eng.	English
esp.	especially
EstBib	Estudios bíblicos
EstTeo	*Estudios teológicos*
ET	English translation
et al.	*et alii,* and the others
ETL	*Ephemerides theologicae lovaniensis*
EvQ	*Evangelical Quarterly*
EvT	*Evangelische Theologie*
ExpTim	*Expository Times*
fem.	feminine
FOTL	The Forms of the Old Testament Literature
frag.	fragment
FTS	Freiburger theologische Studien
gen.	genitive
GKC	*Gesenius' Hebrew Grammar.* Ed. E. Kautzsch. Tr. A. E. Cowley. 2nd ed. Oxford: Clarendon, 1910
GTJ	*Grace Theological Journal*
GTT	*Gereformeerd theologisch tijdschrift*
GUOST	*Glasgow University Oriental Society Transactions*
HALOT	L. Koehler, W. Baumgartner, et al., *The Hebrew and Aramaic Lexicon of the Old Testament.* Tr. M. E. J. Richardson et al. 4 vols. Leiden: Brill, 1994-99
hap. leg.	*hapax legomenon* (lit. "being spoken once" = unique)
HAR	*Hebrew Annual Review*
HAT	Handbuch zum Alten Testament
HBT	*Horizons in Biblical Theology*
Heb.	Hebrew
HeyJ	*Heythrop Journal*
Holladay	W. Holladay, *A Concise Hebrew and Aramaic Lexicon of the Old Testament.* Grand Rapids: Eerdmans, 1971

HS	*Hebrew Studies*
HSM	Harvard Semitic Monographs
HTR	*Harvard Theological Review*
HUCA	*Hebrew Union College Annual*
IBH	T. Lambdin, *Introduction to Biblical Hebrew*
IBHS	B. K. Waltke and M. P. O'Connor, *Introduction to Biblical Hebrew Syntax.* Winona Lake, Ind.: Eisenbrauns, 1990
IB	G. A. Buttrick et al., eds., *The Interpreter's Bible.* 12 vols. Nashville: Abingdon, 1952-57
ICC	International Critical Commentary
IDB	G. A. Buttrick et al., eds., *The Interpreter's Dictionary of the Bible.* 4 vols. Nashville: Abingdon, 1962
IDBSup	*The Interpreter's Dictionary of the Bible. Supplementary Volume.* Ed. K. Crim et al., 1976
i.e.,	*id est,* that is
IEJ	*Israel Exploration Journal*
impv.	imperative
inf.	infinitive
Int	*Interpretation*
Inter	Interpretation: A Bible Commentary for Teaching and Preaching
ISBE	G. W. Bromiley et al., eds., *The International Standard Bible Encyclopedia.* 4 vols. Rev. ed. Grand Rapids: Eerdmans, 1979-
ISBL	*Indiana Studies in Biblical Literature*
ITQ	*Irish Theological Quarterly*
IW	J. G. Gammie, W. A. Brueggemann, W. L. Humphreys, and J. M. Ward, eds., *Israelite Wisdom: Theological and Literary Essays in Honor of Samuel Terrien.* New York: Union Theological Seminary/Scholars Press, 1978
JA	*Journal of Archaeology*
JAAR	*Journal of the American Academy of Religion*
JAOS	*Journal of the American Oriental Society*
JANES	*Journal of the Ancient Near Eastern Society of Columbia University*
JBL	*Journal of Biblical Literature*
JBR	*Journal of Bible and Religion*
JCS	*Journal of Cuneiform Studies*
JE	*Jewish Encyclopedia*
JEA	*Journal of Egyptian Archaeology*
JESHO	*Journal of the Economic and Social History of the Orient*
JETS	*Journal of the Evangelical Theological Society*

JNES	*Journal of Near Eastern Studies*
JNSL	*Journal of Northwest Semitic Languages*
JOTS	*Journal of Old Testament Studies*
JPOS	*Journal of the Palestine Oriental Society*
JQR	*Jewish Quarterly Review*
JRAS	*Journal of the Royal Asiatic Society*
JSOTSup	*Journal for the Society of Old Testament* — Supplement Series
JSS	*Journal of Semitic Studies*
JTS	*Journal of Theological Studies*
K	Kethib
KAI	H. Donner and W. Röllig, eds., *Kanaanäische und aramäische Inschriften.* 3 vols. Wiesbaden: Harrassowitz, 1962-71
KAT	Kommentar zum Alten Testament
KBL[2]	L. Koehler and W. Baumgartner, *Lexicon in Veteri Testamenti libros.* 2nd ed. Leiden: Brill, 1958
KHCAT	Kurzer Hand-Commentar zum Alten Testament
Lat.	Latin
LB	*Linguistica Biblica*
Leš	*Lešonénu*
lit.	literally
LTJ	*Lutheran Theological Journal*
LUÅ	Lunds universitets årsskrift
LXX	Septuagint (Greek version of the OT)
masc.	masculine
MDB	W. E. Mills, ed., *Mercer Dictionary of the Bible.* Macon, Ga.: Mercer University Press, 1990
mg.	margin
ms(s).	manuscript(s)
MT	Masoretic Text
n.	footnote
NAC	New American Commentary
NASB	New American Standard Bible
NBC	*The New Bible Commentary: 21st Century Edition*
NBD	D. R. W. Wood, ed., *New Bible Dictionary.* 3rd ed. Leicester and Downers Grove, Ill.: InterVarsity, 1996
NCBC	New Century Bible Commentary
NEB	New English Bible
N.F.	Neue Folge, new series
NIB	*New Interpreter's Bible*
NIDOTTE	W. A. Van Gemeren et al., ed., *New International Dictionary*

	of Old Testament Theology and Exegesis. 5 vols. Grand Rapids: Zondervan, 1997
NIV	New International Version
NJBC	R. E. Brown, J. A. Fitzmyer, and R. E. Murphy, eds., *The New Jerome Biblical Commentary.* Englewood Cliffs, N.J.: Prentice Hall, 1990
NJPT	The New Jewish Publication Translation
NLT	New Living Translation
NRSV	New Revised Version
NSBT	New Studies in Biblical Theology. Ed. D. A. Carson
NTD	Das Neue Testament Deutsch
NTS	*New Testament Studies*
OBL	*Orientalia et biblica lovaniensia*
OTL	Old Testament Library
OTM	Old Testament Message
OTS	*Old Testament Studies*
OTSSWL	W. C. Wyk, ed., *Old Testament Studies: Studies in Wisdom Literature*
OtSt	*Oudtestamentische Studiën*
OTWSA	Outestamentiese werkgemeenskap in Suid-Afrika
p.	page
P.	paragraph
par.	parallel
pass.	passive
PEGLMBS	*Proceedings, Eastern Great Lakes and Midwest Biblical Societies*
PEQ	*Palestine Exploration Quarterly*
PIBA	*Proceedings of the Irish Biblical Association*
PJ	*Palästinajahrbuch*
pl.	plural
Pl.	Plate
PNWCJS	*Proceedings of the Ninth World Congress of Jewish Studies: Division A: The Period of the Bible.* Ed. M. H. Goshen-Gottstein. Jerusalem: World Union of Jewish Studies, 1986
prep.	preposition
Presby.	*Presbyterion*
PRS	*Perspectives in Religious Studies*
pt.	part
ptcp.	participle
PTM	Princeton Theological Monographs
PTMS	Pittsburgh Theological Monograph Series
Q	Qere

Qad	*Qadmoniot*
RB	*Revue biblique*
REB	The Revised English Bible
REJ	*Revue des études juives*
repr.	reprinted
RES	*Revue des études sémitiques*
RevExp	*Review and Expositor*
RivB	*Rivista biblica*
RSP	*Ras Shamra Parallels.* 3 vols. Vols. 1–II ed. L. Fisher; vol. III ed. S. Rummel. Rome: Pontifical Biblical Institute, 1968-79
RV	Revised Version
Sagesse	M. Gilbert, ed., *La Sagesse de l'Ancien Testament.* BETL 51. Gembloux, Belgique: Leuven University, 1979
SAIW	J. L. Crenshaw, *Studies in Ancient Israelite Wisdom: Selected, with a Prolegomenon.* Library of Biblical Studies. New York: Ktav, 1976
SBFA	Studium biblici Franciscani analecta
SBFLA	*Studium biblici Franciscani liber annus*
SBL	Society of Biblical Literature
SBLBSP	*Society of Biblical Literature Book of Seminar Papers*
SBLDS	Society of Biblical Literature Dissertation Series
SBT	Studies in Biblical Theology, Second Series
SCS	Septuagint and Cognate Studies
SEÅ	Svensk exegetisk årsbok
SIANE	J. G. Gammie and L. G. Purdue, eds., *The Sage in Israel and the Ancient Near East.* Winona Lake, Ind.: Eisenbrauns, 1990
sing.	singular
SJT	*Scottish Journal of Theology*
SPAW	*Sitzungsberichte der preussischen Akademie der Wissenschaften*
SpT	*Spirituality Today*
StANT	Studien zum Alten und Neuen Testaments
ST	*Studia theologica*
s.v.	under the word
Sym.	Symmachus
Syr.	Syriac Version (Peshitta)
Tar	*Tarbiz*
Targ.	Targum
TB	*Theologische Beiträge*
TBT	*The Bible Today*

TDNT	G. Kittel and G. Friedrich, eds., *Theological Dictionary of the New Testament.* 10 vols. Tr. and ed. G. W. Bromiley. Grand Rapids: Eerdmans, 1964-76
TDOT	G. Botterweck and H. Ringgren, eds., *Theological Dictionary of the Old Testament.* Vols. 1–12. Grand Rapids: Eerdmans, 1974-2001
TEV	Today's English Version
THAT	E. Jenni and C. Westermann, eds., *Theologisches Handwörterbuch das Alten Testament.* 2 vols. Munich: C. Kaiser. Zurich: Theologischer, 1971-76
Theod.	Theodotion
TLH	K. G. Hoglund et al., eds., *The Listening Heart: Essays in Wisdom and the Psalms in Honor of Roland E. Murphy, O.Carm.* JSOTSup 58. Sheffield: JSOT, 1987
TLOT	*Theological Lexicon of the Old Testament.* 3 vols. Ed. E. Jenni and C. Westermann. Tr. M. E. Biddle. Peabody, Mass.: Hendrickson, 1997
TLZ	*Theologische Literaturzeitung*
tr.	translated by
TS	*Theological Studies*
TSJTSA	Texts and Studies of the Jewish Theological Seminary of America
TTT	M. V. Fox et al., *Texts, Temples, and Traditions: A Tribute to Menahem Haran.* Winona Lake, Ind.: Eisenbrauns, 1995
TZ	*Theologische Zeitschrift*
TWAT	*Theologische Wörterbuch zum Alten Testament.* Stuttgart: Verlag W. Kohlhammer
TWOT	R. L. Harris et al., eds., *Theological Wordbook of the Old Testament.* 2 vols.
TynBul	*Tyndale Bulletin*
TZ	*Theologisches Zeitschrift*
UF	*Ugarit-Forschungen*
Ugar.	Ugaritic
UT	C. H. Gordon, *Ugaritic Textbook.* AnOr 38. Rome: Pontifical Biblical Institute, 1965
UUÅ	Uppsala universitets årsskrift
v.	verse
VT	*Vetus Testamentum*
VTSup	Supplement to *Vetus Testamentum*
Vulg.	Vulgate
WBC	Word Biblical Commentary
WIAI	J. Day, R. P. Gordon, and H. G. M. Williamson, eds.,

	Wisdom in Ancient Israel: Essays in Honour of J. A. Emerton. Cambridge: Cambridge University, 1995
WIANE	M. Noth and D. W. Thomas, eds., *Wisdom in Israel and in the Ancient Near East.* Leiden: Brill, 1969
WMANT	Wissenschaftliche Monographien zum Alten und Neuen Testament
WO	*Welt des Orients*
WTJ	*Westminster Theological Journal*
WW	*Word and World*
WWis	J. I. Packer and S. Soderlund, eds., *Way of Wisdom: Essays in Honor of B. K. Waltke.* Grand Rapids: Zondervan, 2000
x	time(s)
ZAH	*Zeitschrift für Althebräistik*
ZAW	*Zeitschrift für die alttestamentliche Wissenschaft*
ZBK	Zurcher Bibelkommentare
ZDPV	*Zeitschrift des deutschen Palästina-Vereins*
ZKT	*Zeitschrift für katholische Theologie*
ZSem	*Zeitschrift für Semitisk*
ZPEB	M. Tenney et al., eds., *Zondervan Pictorial Encyclopedia of the Bible.* 5 vols. Grand Rapids: Zondervan, 1975
ZTK	*Zeitschrift für Theologie und Kirche*

TEXT AND COMMENTARY

B. COLLECTION IIB: THE LORD AND HIS KING (15:30–16:22)

For structure of Collection II, see I: 14-21.

1. Prologue: The Dance between Humanity, the Lord, and His King (15:30–16:15)

30 *The light of the eyes*[1] *makes the heart glad,*
and good news revives the whole person.[2]
31 *The ear that listens to life-giving*[3] *correction*
dwells among the wise.
32 *The person who flouts instruction is one who despises his life,*[4]
but the person who hears correction is one who acquires sense.[5]
33 *The instruction*[6] *that gives wisdom*[7] *is the fear of the* LORD,
and humility [comes] before[8] *honor.*[9]
16:1 *To*[10] *human beings belong the plans of the heart;*
from the LORD *[comes]*[11] *the right answer of the tongue.*[12]

1. The LXX's reading *theōrōn ophthalmos kala* "the eye that sees well" suggests to D. Winton Thomas ("Textual and Philological Notes on Some Passages in the Book of of Proverbs," in *WIANE,* pp. 286-87) the reading *mar'ēh-ʿênayim,* which he interprets to mean "the pleasure of looking at" (see Eccl. 6:9). Since the parallel "good tidings" requires something seen and enjoyed, not the pleasure of looking at something with pleasure, he repoints the form as a *Hophal* ptcp., *môr'eh,* obtaining the rendering of the whole verse: "A fine sight cheers the mind as good tidings make the bones fat." Thomas, however, neither evaluates the paraphrastic nature of the LXX nor explains from a text-critical viewpoint how the alternative readings arose.

2. Lit. "news makes the bones fat."

3. Lit. "to correction of life," a gen. of effect (*IBHS,* p. 146, P. 9.5.2c).

4. Or "himself."

5. Lit. "acquires heart." The LXX reads *agapą psychēn autou* ("loves himself") to create a suitable antithesis to "hates himself" (see 19:8).

6. The emendation of Perles and Humbert (cited by O. Plöger, *Sprüche Salomos (Proverbia)* [BKAT XVII/2-4; Neukirchen-Vluyn; Neukirchener Verlag, 1984], p. 179) and accepted by Fichtner *(BHS)* to read *mûsad* ("foundation") loses the catchword connection with v. 32.

7. Gen. of effect (*IBHS,* p. 146, P. 9.5.2c).

8. The preposition entails a verb of motion (*IBHS,* p. 224, P. 11.4.3d).

9. The LXX *kai archē doxēs apokrithēsetai autę̄* "and the highest honor will correspond with it" may have pointed *ʿnwh* as *ʿanûhā* (A. J. Baumgartner, *Étude critique sur l'état du texte du Livre des Proverbes d'après les principales traductions anciennes* [Leipzig: Imprimerie Orientale W. Drugulin, 1890], p. 151).

10. The original LXX is lacking the first three verses, probably because of the poor state of its *Vorlage.*

11. Elided verb of motion with preposition of motion (*IBHS,* p. 224, P. 11.4.3d.)

12. Note the broken consonance of *l'dm mʿrky-lb wmyhwh mʿnh lšwn.* The first

2 *All the ways of a person [are] pure*[13] *in his own eyes,*
but the LORD is the one who evaluates motives.[14]
3 *Commit*[15] *to the LORD your works,*
and your thoughts will be established.
4 *The LORD works everything to its appropriate end,*[16]
even the wicked person for[17] *an evil day.*[18]
5 *An abomination to the LORD is everyone who is haughty;*
be sure of this,[19] *that person will not go unpunished.*
6 *Through love and faithfulness sin is atoned for,*
and through the fear of the LORD is a departing from evil.[20]
7 *When the LORD takes pleasure in a person's ways,*
he compels even his enemies to surrender to him.
8 *Better a little with righteousness*
than a large income with injustice.
9 *The heart of a human being plans his way,*
but the LORD establishes his step.
10 *An inspired verdict is on the king's lips;*
in giving a judgment his mouth is not unfaithful.

---

verset begins with *l* and the second (not counting the conjunction *w*) with the preposition *m*. These initial consonants are followed in the next two words by *mʿ*, followed by initial *l*. Both versets share the same syntax, and each verset ends with initial *l*.

13. Sing. to agree with collective *kol*.

14. Lit. "spirits." The Targ. and Syr. probably read *ʾorḥôt* and interpreted *tkn* to mean "direct," "order," "establish."

15. The Syr., Targ., and Vulg. read *gal* ("reveal/disclose," *Qal* impv. of *glh*), not *gōl* (*Qal* impv. of *gll*). But *glh* in the *Qal* never occurs with *ʾel*. Ps. 37:5a repeats 16:3b but uses *scripto plena gôl,* supporting the MT.

16. G. R. Driver ("Review of M. Dahood, *Proverbs and Northwest Semitic Philology*," *JSS* 10 [1965] 133) argued that *lammaʿ^{a}nēhû* is a mixed form consisting of *l^{e}maʿ^{a}nēhû* (preposition *l^{e}mʿ^{a}an* + pronominal suffix, "for his own sake") and *lammaʿ^{a}neh* (preposition *l* + definite noun *hammaʿ^{a}neh,* "for a purpose/answer"). This is unlikely because both forms are otherwise unattested; *kōl* calls for a suffix with the notion "for an answer"; and a double determination (an article with a determined gen., including a suffixed pronoun) is unexceptional in West Semitic (M. Dahood, *Proverbs and Northwest Semitic Philology* [Rome: Pontifical Biblical Institute, 1963], p. 36; *IBHS,* p. 249, P. 13.6b; cf. GKC, P. 127i). The article probably protects against the unique reading *l^{e}maʿ^{a}nēhû* (cf. Vulg. *propter semet ipsum,* "all for himself" [KJV]). The Targ. and Syr. curiously read: "to those who respond to him," but the LXX rightly paraphrases: "All the works of the Lord are done with justice."

17. Or "to," parallel to "to its counterpart."

18. With this verse the LXX closes its own series of proverbs.

19. The literal "hand to hand" thoroughly perplexed the ancient translators (see 11:21).

20. The LXX may have this verse after 15:27.

11 *A just balance and hand scale*[21] *are the* LORD*'s;*
all the weights in a pouch are his work.[22]
12 *An abomination to kings is doing*[23] *wickedness,*
because a throne is established through righteousness.
13 *Kings*[24] *take pleasure in righteous lips,*
and whoever speaks[25] *upright things*[26] *he loves.*
14 *The wrath of the king is the messenger*[27] *of death,*
but a wise person pacifies it.
15 *In the light of the king's face*[28] *is life,*
and his favor is like a cloud[29] *of spring rain.*

The first unit of Section B in Collection II introduces the collection by trumpeting its themes. It consists of its own introduction (15:30-33) and a main body pertaining to the LORD's sovereign rule (16:1-9), the first subunit, through his king (16:10-15), the second subunit. The first deals with the LORD's sovereign and righteous rule encompassing human responsibility and accountability (vv. 1-9), and the second to his mediated rule through his righteous king (vv. 10-15). The two subunits are clearly marked off by the repetition of *YHWH* in vv. 1-9 and of *melek* in vv. 10-15. Meinhold notes the many ways in which these two subunits are bound together: (1) the catchwords "abomination" (vv. 5, 12), "favor" (vv. 7, 13, 15), "wicked"/"wickedness" (vv. 4, 12), and, remarkably, *kpr* in the D stem ("to atone"/"pacifies," vv. 6, 14). (2) Both the second from the end of vv. 1-9 (v. 8) and the second from

21. *Peles ûmōʾzᵉnê mišpāṭ* is a cons. override construction with two closely related nouns (*IBHS,* p. 139, P. 9.3b).

22. A similar saying occurs in *Amenemope* (16:22-25): "The Ape sits by the balance, his heart is in the plummet; where is a god as great as Thoth, who invented these things and made them?" (*AEL,* 2:156-57).

23. The Syr. reads, "The kings who do wickedness are abominable," and the Zamora text of the Targ. independently interprets it as the king's own wickedness. But the LXX, Targ., and Vulg. read *ʿōśeh* ("the one who does"), making clear that the wickedness of others, not of the king himself, is in view.

24. Two mss., LXX, Syr., and Targ. read "king," probably to harmonize with the sing. subject of the B verset. The Vulg. rightly retains the pl., which links vv. 12 and 13.

25. The LXX read *dᵉbārîm* and Syr. *ûdᵉbar.* Their facilitating readings conform better with *yᵉšārîm,* which the LXX understood as an attributive adjective ("right words") and the Syr. as a substantival adjective of person ("upright people"), its normal meaning. The Vulg. reads with the MT.

26. Substantival adjective of thing (8:6; Dan. 11:10; see BDB, p. 449). Four codexes read *mêšārîm,* probably to prevent the normal meaning of "upright people."

27. The form is dual.

28. The LXX read *bēn (huios basileōs).*

29. *ʿĀb* is an alternative cons. form (cf. Isa. 18:44; *HALOT,* 2:773, s.v. *ʿāb*).

the beginning of vv. 10-15 (v. 11) lack the keywords of their subunits, namely, *YHWH* and "king." (3) *YHWH,* however, is found in v. 11, and vv. 8 and 11 both pertain to "justice." (4) God expects "righteousness" and "justice" of everyone (v. 8), and the king upholds them (v. 12).[30]

a. Introduction (15:30-33)

The catchwords *šmʿ (yišmāʿ)* ("hears") and *šᵉmûʿâ* (report), the last word of the preceding unit and the first word of 15:30b, assist the transition to the new unit. Its introduction consists of a pair of education quatrains. The first is linked by the catchword *šmʿ,* more specifically the illuminated good news/report *(šᵉmûʿâ)* (v. 30) that revives the heart and the disciple's ear that hears *(šōmaʿat)* (v. 31). It features the bodily organs: eyes, heart, and ears. The second quatrain pertains to "instruction" *(mûsār):* flouted or accepted (v. 32) and elaborated on as "the fear of the LORD" to be humbly received (v. 33). It bears repeating: these proverbs are applicable to many situations (e.g., the "good news" of v. 30 may refer to any good report), but together they also function as an introduction to the following unit. "The good news" of v. 30 in this context refers to the wonderful report that God dances with the pure in heart (16:1-9)! The proverbial pairs are linked by the catchwords "hear correction" *(šômēʿa/šōmaʿat tôkaḥat,* vv. 31, 32).

30 The first pair pertains to good news that the heart receives. The rare metaphor *the light (mᵉʾôr)*[31] *of the eyes (ʿênayim)* connotes the manifestation of the inward vitality and joy of the one bringing good news, as the parallel clause suggests, and is associated with righteousness (13:9). His eyes speak louder than his words (see 15:13). A close synonym, *ʾôr-ʿênay,* also functions as a metonymy for "life" (Ps. 38:10[11]), and the related expression *hāʾîr-ʿênê* ("he gives light to the eyes of"; Ezra 9:8; Ps. 13:3[4]; 19:8; Prov. 29:13) refers to God giving life and joy to human eyes. Proverbs and the rest of Scripture repeatedly associate light with righteousness (13:9; Matt. 6:22-23) and link it with life and good fortune (Job 3:16; 33:28; Prov. 4:18; 6:23; 13:9; 16:15). The New Testament connects light with Christ and his disciples (cf. Matt. 4:16; 5:14-16; John 1:4-5; 12:35-36). Proverbs associates light and life exclusively with the wise, suggesting that illuminated eyes belong to the wise (15:13a). *Makes . . . glad* (*yᵉśammaḥ* [15:20] *the heart* (see I: 90) refers to the disciple's heart, as the parallel clause also suggests. Note the movement from the joy within that beautifies the face (15:13) to the

30. A. Meinhold, *Die Sprüche* (ZBK; Zürich: Theologischer Verlag, 1991), 2:264.

31. *Mᵉʾôr* literally means "luminary" (cf. Gen. 1:14-15) and may function as a metonymy for "light" (cf. Exod. 25:6; Ps. 90:8).

face's illuminated eyes that fill the observer with life and joy. In sum, the sage's life and joy are contagious. *Good* (*ṭôbâ,* see I: 99; 15:23) *news (šᵉmûʿâ)* denotes a verbal report of a recent event that advances life. Outside of Prov. 15:30; 25:25 and Ps. 112:7 *šᵉmûʿâ* is used in the historical and prophetic books mostly of "bad news" about battle reports, but notable exceptions are the message the Queen of Sheba heard about Solomon (1 K. 10:7) and the remnant's report of the Suffering Servant (Isa. 53:1).[32] In this context it functions as a metaphor for the teaching that follows in 16:1-15. *Revives (tᵉdaššen)* paraphrases the verb meaning "to make fat";[33] its passive counterpart "to be made fat," connotes abundance, full satisfaction, and health (11:25). *The whole person* (*ʿāṣem;* see 3:8) paraphrases the noun meaning "bone," a synecdoche for the entire person, both physical and psychical.

31 This verse shifts the focus from the illuminated reporter and the revived heart to the disciple's other receptive organ, *the ear* (see 2:2), a synecdoche for the whole person. If the sage has the student's ear *that listens* (*šōmaʿat;* see 1:5, 8) *to life-giving* (*ḥayyîm;* see I: 104) *correction* (or rebuke, *tôkaḥat;* see 1:23), he has the key to his heart (see 2:2; 15:32b). This uniquely single-sentence proverb in Collection II motivates the disciple to have such an ear, for it *dwells (tālîn) among* (*bᵉqereb;* see 14:33) the honored company *of the wise* (see I: 76, 94). The by-forms *lîn* and II *lûn* occur 68 times in the *Qal* and have the core idea "to remain at night." In poetry they function as a synecdoche for "to remain," "dwell" (Job 17:2; 19:4; 41:22[14]; Prov. 15:31; Isa. 1:21; Jer. 4:14; Zeph. 2:14).[34] Whoever hears the correction of the wise belongs to their community and can start immediately to live with them. This opposite of the solitary mocker (see 15:12) stays close to his source of life, ready to hear correction from evening to evening and morning by morning (cf. Isa. 50:4). The ear characterizes true Israel's relationship with God more than the eye (cf. Rom. 10:5-17). In God's encounters with Israel he is always heard; rarely seen. The hearing ear and the seeing eye are God's handiwork (20:12).

32 The proverb escalates the motivation to accept correction and not

32. According to Y. Ratzhavi ("Clarification of the Blessing Formula in the Lachish Letters," *BM* 33 [1987/88] 454-55), the expression here and in 15:25 (cf. Isa. 52:7) reflects a blessing formula like that at the beginning of several of the Lachish letters; namely, that the LORD causes one's lord to hear tiding of good (= peace). His interpretation finds support in its antonym *šᵉmûʿat rāʿâ* (cf. Ps. 112:7; Jer. 49:23) and reports of defeat associated with being disheartened, troubled, shaken, and fear (Ps. 112:6-7; Jer. 49:23). However, to interpret "good news" always as a blessing formula commits the total transference fallacy, especially since Yahweh is not mentioned here

33. In Sir. 26:13 *dšn* is also parallel to *śimmaḥ:* "A wife's charms delight *(śimmaḥ)* her husband, and her skill puts fat on his bones."

34. *HALOT,* 2:529, s.v. *lyn.*

to rebel by alluding to suicide versus survival (see 8:36; 15:6, 10). *The person who flouts instruction* [see 13:18] *is one who despises* [see 3:11] *his life* (*napšô;* see I: 90). *But the person who hears correction* (*w^e^šômēaʿ;* see 15:5, 31a) *is one who acquires* (*qôneh;* see 4:5; 8:22) *sense* (*lēb;* lit. "a heart"; see I: 90). As *ḥ^a^sar lēb* ("one who lacks heart = sense") denotes one who lacks the essential mental and moral capacity to survive (see I: 115), so *qānâ lēb* ("to acquire a heart") signifies to gain the mental and moral capacity to live, as its chiastic parallel in 15:31a, "life," makes clear. In 19:8 "acquiring a heart" is equated with "loving oneself," the desired antithesis to "hate one's life," as provided by the LXX (see n. 5).

33 The concluding verse of the introduction grounds the instruction in the fear of the LORD and adds the motivation to achieve social honor. The way to wisdom is the fear of the LORD, and the way to honor is humility. All the vocabulary of verset A is found in the book's motto (1:7), and verset B is repeated verbatim in 18:12b. *The instruction* [see 1:2; 15:32] *that gives wisdom* (*ḥokmâ;* see 1:2) *is the fear of the LORD* (see 1:7). Wisdom is a matter of the heart. The disposition of *humility* (*ʿ^a^nāwâ;* see 3:34), which is equated with the "fear of the LORD" in 22:4, brings the disciple into the company of the sage (v. 31) and beyond that into the company of Israel's covenant-keeping God. The original meaning of *ʿnw* is "to be bowed down," "to be oppressed," and then, when affliction has done its proper work, "to be humble." The scoffer and the fool, who despise God's revelation, are the humble person's opposite. *ʿ^a^nāwâ* is a religious term for the quality of renouncing one's own personal sufficiency for life and committing oneself to the LORD, who alone is trustworthy to give instruction leading to life (3:5-7). In this way the disciple integrates himself into the moral order and the realm of life ordained by God and does not lift himself against it. Waving a white flag of surrender to the LORD in this book always [*comes*] *before* [see 8:25] *honor* (see 3:16; 18:12; 22:4). Paradoxically, the one who grants himself no glory before the glorious God in the end is crowned with the glory and wealth that give him social esteem (see 3:16; 8:18; 11:16). This radical humility toward the LORD paves the way for the next subunit contrasting the LORD's freedom with human limits (16:1-9). The key phrase "fear of the LORD" in 15:33 and 16:6 reinforces the connection between the introduction and this body.

b. The LORD's Rule (16:1-9)

The first subunit consists mostly of synthetic parallels and is bound together by the catchword LORD *(YHWH)* in every verse except v. 8. The chiastically arranged *lēb* ("heart")–*ʾādām* ("human being")//*ʾādām-lēb* and the repetition of synonyms for "plan" in 16:1a and 9a and of "establish" in 16:3b and 9b form its *inclusio* and sounds its theme: the LORD's sovereign rule encompasses human accountability.[35] This outer frame is reinforced by an inner frame of *darkê-'îš* ("ways of a person," vv. 2 and 7). Verses 1-3 pertain to the LORD's sovereign rule through human participation, and vv. 5-7 to his sovereign justice in response to human morality. Verse 4 is a janus. Its A verset, asserting that the LORD brings everything to its appropriate destiny, looks back to vv. 1-3, and its B verset, asserting that he matches the wicked with calamity, looks ahead to vv. 5-7.

(1) The LORD's Sovereignty and the Human's Responsibility (16:1-4a)

Divine sovereignty over human initiative pertains both to human speech, the tongue's answer (*ma'ᵃnēh,* v. 1b), and to human work (*ma'ᵃśeh,* v. 3b). The alliteration of *ma'ᵃnēh* and of *ma'ᵃśeh* strengthens this subframe. Sandwiched between this ring, forming an ABA structural pattern, v. 2 asserts the LORD's estimation of human motives behind their words and deeds (v. 2), whereby the LORD determines which to ratify or veto. Presumably only those who are motivated by religious and ethical purity participate in the eternal design. Human beings form, the LORD performs; they devise, he verifies; they formulate, he validates; they propose, he disposes. They design what they will say and do, but the LORD decrees what will endure and form part of his eternal purposes.

1 This verse pertains to human initiative in thought and divine initiative in human speech. Its complementary versets underscore both the necessity and the limitations of human planning; human speech is subject to the divine rule. *To human beings belong* (see I: 89) gives the earthling the first word, but "from the LORD" gives God the last word. The human being's good and effective answer depends both on careful planning, weighing the arguments and arranging them (verset A), and on God's direction to be effective (verset B; cf. Neh. 2:4-5). The meaning of *the plans* (*ma'arkê;* lit. "arrangements") can be deduced from its root *'rk,* signifying either to set things carefully in order, as in setting a battle array (Gen. 14:8), or laying up wood for sacrifice (Gen. 22:9), or "to compare" (by setting things over against each other) (Ps. 40:6[7]) and "to produce a case for justice" (Job 13:18), or "to bring forth words" (Job 32:14).[36] Since *the heart* (see I: 90) is the agent pro-

35. Human thought is represented by "arranging ideas" (v. 1a), motives ("heart"/ "spirits," vv. 1, 5, 9), opinion ("in his eyes," v. 2a), and "thoughts" (v. 3b); human behavior by "ways (vv. 2, 7, 9a), "step" (v. 9b), and "deeds" (v. 3). God's sovereignty is indicated by the keywords "establish/direct" (vv. 3, 9) and "answer" (vv. 1, 4).

36. Its feminine congeners, *ma'ărākâ* and *ma'reket,* also formed by prefixing abstract *mem* to the root, denote respectively "a row," mostly the strategic battle line, and the

ducing the careful and orderly "arrangement," appropriate glosses here are "thought-through plans" or "arguments," not "brainstorming" or "half-baked ideas." The conjunction *wa* means both "and" and "but" because the parallel both complements and contrasts the LORD's activity with that of humans. The context signals its meaning. *From the LORD* (see I: 69-71) casts the ultimate responsibility for good and effective speech on God's grace (cf. 12:18; 15:1, 2; 25:11-12), not on human wit (cf. 1 Cor. 3:6-7).[37] Ringgren rightly restricts *maʿᵃnēh* (see 15:23) to a good and effective utterance, *the right answer.* God does not author an evil and/or ineffective answer. *Of the tongue* (see 15:2, 4) underscores the outward expression, both in its substance and style, of the inward thought of verset A.

2 This verse continues the theme of the LORD's rule over human initiative. It is linked with v. 1 by the catchword "LORD" in their B versets and by the synonyms for the total person, "human being" and "person," in their A versets and for the inner person, "heart" and "motives," in their B versets. The LORD evaluates (v. 2b) the "plans" of the human heart (v. 1a). Since people justify "all their actions" and the LORD evaluates according to truth, conflicts of assessment will arise (cf. 14:12; 15:3, 11; 21:2; 24:12). When a person becomes aware of his impurity, however, he should confess it and so obtain mercy (28:13). *All* [see 15:15] *the ways* (*darkê;* see 1:15) *of a person* (*ʾîš;* see 6:12; 8:4; 12:2) [*are*] *pure (zak) in his own eyes* (i.e., in his deluded opinion, see 3:7; cf. Job 11:4; 16:7; 33:9; cf. Jer. 17:9). *Zak* signifies "pure" in its four references to the cult: of olive oil (Exod. 27:20; Lev. 24:2) and of incense (Exod. 30:34; Lev. 24:7). In its seven uses in the wisdom literature it refers to ethical purity and is sometimes used in association with *yāšār* "upright" (cf. Prov. 20:11; 21:2, 8; cf. Job 8:6). *But the LORD* [see 16:1] *is the one who evaluates (tōkēn). Tkn* means "to measure," "to determine the amount, weight, etc.," "to gauge" (i.e., "to estimate a thing by comparing it with a standard").[38] The metaphor is derived from an ancient Egyptian belief that a person's heart is weighed against truth after death.[39] *Motives* (*rûḥôt;* lit. "spirits"; see I: 92; cf. "heart" in 21:2) may have been chosen to create the paradox, "he weights winds/spirits," that is, the "dynamic vitality" that moves a person, a synecdoche for a person's disposition (Eccl. 7:8, 9; Ezek. 11:19; 18:31; 36:26) or inner life (Job 7:11; Ps. 78:8), including his opinions

---

carefully arranged row or stack of bread set out on the sanctuary table. Its differently formed masculine congener *ʿerek* also refers to a row of bread (Exod. 40:23) but has the other meanings of "equipment or furnishing" (e.g., with clothing, Judg. 17:10), of the table (Exod. 40:4), and of "evaluation" (2 K. 23:35).

37. *Amenemope* 20.5, 6 reads, "If a man's tongue is the boat's rudder, the LORD of All is yet its pilot" (*AEL,* 2:158).

38. B. K. Waltke, *TWOT,* 2.970, s.v. *tkn.*

39. *ANEP,* p. 210, no. 639.

or desires (cf. Ezek. 13:3), mind (Ps. 77:6[7]), will (cf. Prov. 16:32), and motives (cf. 2 Chr. 36:22).[40] The plural, paralleling "ways" argues that complex patterns of behavior depend on complex motives. The disciple should evaluate his motives and conduct against God's revealed standards and not absolutize his own estimation of them (cf. 12:15a; cf. 14:12 [= 16:25]). Nevertheless, since the final verdict as to their purity belongs to the LORD, not the doer, the disciple must not praise himself or decide his reward beforehand. The best he can do is to commit all he does to the LORD and depend on God to make his motives and ways pleasing to God (16:3, 7; cf. Pss. 19:12[13]; 139:23-24; 1 Cor. 4:5-6; Heb. 4:12-13). Moreover, if a person cannot judge his own motives, how much more should he not judge others (Matt 7:1)?

3 This proverb draws the inference of the preceding two proverbs. Since the LORD assumes ownership of the disciple's initiatives (v. 1) and he alone can evaluate the purity of the motives behind them (v. 2), the disciple should commit his planned deeds to the LORD (v. 3a) to establish them permanently, outlasting the wicked person's temporary triumphs (v. 3b). Verse 2 implies that the LORD finds the prepared words and the performed deeds pure; otherwise he would not effect either. When the motives are pure, he will integrate them into his fixed righteous order (10:22; Psalm 127). The admonition *commit to* (*gōl 'el,* lit. "roll to/upon"; cf. Gen 29:3, 8, 10; Ps. 22:8[9], 37:5) connotes a sense of finality; roll it unto the LORD and leave it there. *Gōl 'el* is onomatopoetic; one almost hears the rolling sound of a stone. The indirect object *the LORD*, the subunit's key word, infers rolling away from oneself. *Works* (*ma'ᵃśeh,* from the common root *'āśâ* "to do, make"; see 2:14) refers either to a planned deed (cf. Mic. 2:1) or a performed one (Gen. 44:15). The faithful must not fret or worry about their effectiveness, or even their purity, for that assessment and their achievement depend on God, not on the doer (Pss. 22:8[9]; 37:5; 55:22[23]; 1 Pet. 5:7).[41] Secular man, who feels so self-confident, paradoxically is plagued with fear. Pious people, who know God's sovereignty and their limitations, live in prayer and peace. Conjunctive *and* links "your works" with *your thoughts* (see 12:5) that inform the deed. Verset B emphasizes their personal and subjective element by adding "heart." Plans and deeds performed in conjunction with a total commitment to the LORD *will be established* (see 4:26). What you think in your inner being will become overt historical events as enduring as the elements of the LORD's cosmos (see 8:27-29).

4a *The LORD* (see 16:1-9) brings every word and deed to its appro-

40. Cf. R. G. Bratcher, "Biblical Words Describing Man: Breath, Life, Spirit," *BT* 34 (1983) 204.

41. *Amenemope* (23:10) admonishes: "Settle in the arms of the god" (*AEL,* p. 159).

priate "answer" at the time of judgment. In contrast to the righteous whose plans and deeds are confirmed, the wicked and their deeds will be destroyed. Verse 4a looks back to the sovereignty of the LORD over human initiative in vv. 1-3, and its catchword *ma'ᵃneh* ("answer," v. 1; "counterpart," v. 4) links it to v. 1. *Kōl* ("all"/"everything") brings vv. 1-4a to closure (see 3:15, 17). Verse 4b looks ahead to God's judgment on the wicked (vv. 5-7). The catchword *ra'* "evil" links it to v. 6. *Works* (*pā'al;* see 10:29) means "executes," "puts into action the necessary means to secure the success of the enterprise," and is often used as here of the LORD's sovereign control (Num. 23:23; Deut. 32:27; Isa. 26:12; 43:13). *Everything* allows no exception, no loose ends. Everything will be put to some use and matched with its proper fate. *Its counterpart* (*lama'ᵃnēhû;* see n. 16; 15:1, 23; 16:1) is literally "its (i.e., all things') answer."[42] McKane comments: "Yahweh has made everything in relation to what answers to it ('with its counterpart,' Scott)."[43]

(2) The LORD's Morality and the Human's Accountability (16:4b-7)

4b Providence works to bring *even* [see 14:13] *the wicked person* [see I: 109] *for an evil* [see 1:16] *day* (*yôm,* i.e., "time, a point in time"; see 6:34).[44] The question of when this will happen is left in the hands of God. If even the wicked, who do not entrust themselves to the LORD, will get their "answer," how much more will the righteous, who entrust their planning, speaking, and acting to the LORD, in due course get their right "answer."

Word-initial "abomination" (*tô'ēbâ,* v. 5) and "find favor" *(rāṣâ),* which are stock-in-trade antithetical parallels (see 11:1), frame vv. 5-7. These verses pertain to the LORD's moral sensibilities: the wicked are punished (v. 5), and the righteous triumph over them (v. 7). Sandwiched between this ring — again forming an ABA structural pattern (see vv. 1-3) — v. 6 gives assurance that past sin such as that of v. 6 can be atoned for by serving the community and future sin can be avoided through embracing the fear of the LORD and so finding his favor (v. 7).

5 The wicked of v. 4b are defined more precisely as the haughty in v. 5a, and "the evil day" of v. 4b is clearly identified as the time of punishment in v. 5b. The catchword "all/every" *(kol)* helps the connection. Verse 5 reinforces the judgment of the wicked and grounds the reason for it in the LORD's moral sensibility. Humanity participates with God in creating history, but God establishes only what is pure and purges away the dross. Verse 5b

42. BDB, p. 775, s.v. *ma'ᵃneh; pace HALOT,* 2:614-15, s.v. II *ma'ᵃneh.*

43. W. McKane, *Proverbs: A New Approach* (Philadelphia: Westminster, 1970), p. 497.

44. E. Jenni, *TLOT,* 2:529, s.v. *yôm.*

virtually repeats 11:21, and v. 5a is similar to 11:20a, but substitutes "high" *(g^ebah)* for "perverse" *('iqq^eše).* Since he is *an abomination to the LORD* (see 3:32), the LORD will get rid of him. The topic of this proverb is *everyone* (*kol;* see 15:3) *who is haughty* (*g^ebah-lēb,* lit. "high of heart") *Kol* reasserts the universality of God's rule (vv. 2, 4a). *G^ebah* ("high") is related to the verb *gbh* and the noun *gōbah* ("height"; see 16:18b). All may have a spatial and/or an ethical connotation. For example, the verb is used of an eagle flying high (Job 39:27), and the adjective is used to describe a high tower (Isa. 2:15). Their ethical sense is usually negative. Sometimes the spatial and ethical combine (cf. Prov. 18:11). *Gābōah* is used in connection with one's mouth (1 Sam. 2:3), eyes (Isa. 5:15), and heart (16:5; Eccl. 7:8). When *gābēah* is used of *'ênayim* ("eyes"; Ps. 101:5), *rûaḥ* ("spirit"; Eccl. 7:8), and *lēb* ("heart"; Prov. 16:5), it denotes the arrogant who consider themselves a cut above God and others.[45] People discern the haughty by his raised eyes (6:17). That repugnant disposition precedes its possessor's downfall (11:2; 16:18). Instead of being grateful for his life, the arrogant lifts himself above the Giver and his image bearers and considers his successes his own achievement (cf. Deut. 8:14). "The Hebrew view of man is . . . profoundly humanistic: tremendously enthusiastic about the man God made and the gifts God gave him. But it is also profoundly theistic, for the Israelite was convinced there is one thing man cannot do, and that is replace the God who made him."[46] On the Day of the LORD, when he demonstrates his holiness, the LORD will exalt himself high above all proud people (Isa 5:16; cf. 2 Chr. 17:6; Isa. 52:13).

6 In this sandwiched-between verse, verset A gives a remedy for past sin (v. 5) and verset B presents a preventive against future sin. *Through (b^e) love and faithfulness* (see 3:3) in Proverbs refers to human kindness to the needy, never to divine grace to sinners (cf. Gen. 32:10[11]).[47] The epigrammatic proverb points only to the human virtues that complement the sacrificial system to make atonement (cf. Lev. 1:4; 4:4; 16:21; passim). Unless a person is characterized by unfailing love, the sacrificial system is of no avail (1 Sam. 15:22). The guilty sinner cannot trust himself to the divine

45. *HALOT,* 1.171, s.v. *gābah.*

46. D. E. Gowan, *When Man Becomes God: Humanism and Hybris in the Old Testament* (PTMS 6; Pittsburgh: Pickwick, 1975), p. 91.

47. *Pace* Meinhold, *Sprüche,* p. 267 and R. Van Leeuwen, *The Book of Proverbs* (NIB 5; Nashville: Abingdon, 1997), p. 159. Van Leeuwen believes that "loyalty" and "faithfulness" refer to divine actions because vv. 5-6a "contain clustered terminology drawn from Exod. 34:6-7." However, he overlooks the fact that these attributes are contingent on responsible human behavior. In v. 6 "the fear of the LORD," a genuine expression of one's religion, is parallel to "love and faithfulness," presumably also a genuine expression of the religion to which God extends his favor.

grace mediated through the cultus "if he is not zealous in his relations to his fellowmen, to practice love and truth" (cf. Matt. 6:12, 14-15; Luke 7:47; Jas. 1:26-27; 2:8, 12-18).[48] *Sin* (see 5:22) *is atoned for (yᵉkuppar).* The etymology of *kpr* is uncertain. Some derive it from Arab. *kafāra* ("to cover over/up"), and others from Akk. *kuppūru* ("to clear," "to expiate," "to wipe off," or "to purify [cultically]"). A third possibility is that it is a denominative of *kōper* "ransom" (= to make a ransom; see 6:35). Schenker draws the conclusion that the noun signifies a "placating," a "mollifying," or "a means to mollify or to placate."[49] Maas thinks that it refers here to making "atonement" between people (cf. Gen. 32:20[21]; Prov. 16:14),[50] but "iniquity" refers to misdeeds against God, making "atone" a synonym of "forgiven by God" (cf. Exod. 34:6). *And through the fear of the LORD* (*ûbᵉyir'at YHWH;* see I: 100) *is a departing from evil* (*sûr mērāʿ;* see 3:7), probably, to judge from the parallel "iniquity," a pun for salvation from both the moral aspect of doing evil and its calamitous consequences (see 1:16). "The fear of the LORD," which entails "love and faithfulness" to others, is God's grace to be received by faith, not an independent human effort or something that follows it: "My son, if you accept my words . . . then you will understand the fear of the LORD" (2:1-5).

7 Continuing to use cultic language, v. 7 escalates salvation from the punishment of past sins (vv. 5-6a) and from future sin (v. 6b) to finding God's favor and final victory over the enemy. *When (bᵉ)* shows that the circumstantial situation of verset A (the cause) is simultaneous with the situation in the main clause (the consequence).[51] The assertion that *the LORD* [see 16:1-9] *takes pleasure in* (*rᵉṣôt;* see 3:12; 16:13; cf. Isa. 42:1) *the ways of a person* (*darkê-'îš;* see 16:2) entails that God accepts the person into his beneficent presence (cf. 15:8; 2 Sam. 24:23; Ezek. 20:41) and blesses him (Ps. 44:3[4]). More specifically, *he compels . . . to surrender* (*yašlīm;* see *šālôm* in 3:2), a unique grammatical construction.[52] *Even* (*gam;* see v. 4b) *his ene-*

48. F. Delitzsch, *Biblical Commentary on the Proverbs of Solomon,* tr. M. G. Easton (Grand Rapids: Eerdmans, n.d.; preface 1872), p. 244.

49. A. Schenker, "*Kōper* et expiation," *Bib* 63 (1982) 32-46.

50. F. Maas, *TLOT,* 2:632, s.v. *kpr Piel.*

51. *IBHS,* p. 196, P. 11.2.5cd.

52. The verb *šālēm* in the *Hiphil* occurs in three constructions. (1) In a two-place *Hiphil* with an impersonal direct object such as "plans/wish" it means "to complete, perform, carry out" (e.g., "he carries out the plan of his messengers" [Isa. 44:26; cf. Job 23:14; Isa. 44:28]). With the LORD as agent and a personal object it means "to regard oneself as forced to surrender" ("you compel me to surrender from day to night," Isa. 38:12 [NIV's "you made an end of me" is too free]). (2) In a one-place *Hiphil* governing a prepositional phrase it means "to make peace with someone" (e.g., "the inhabitants of Gibeah made peace with Israel," Josh. 10:1; cf. Deut. 20:12; Josh. 11:19; 2 Sam. 10:19 (= 1 Chr.

mies (*'ôy^{e}bāyw)* entails a wicked person who opposes the one God favors. The enemy can be defined by its descriptive predicates: "oppress" (Deut. 28:53), "persecute" (1 K. 8:37), "smite" (Lev. 26:17; Jer. 30:14), "pursue, persecute" (Hos. 8:3), "deal treacherously with, deceive" (Lam. 1:2). "Furthermore, the proud behavior of the enemies is often mentioned; they exalt themselves (Ps. 13:4[5]), make themselves great (Lam 1:9), scoff and revile (Ps. 74:10, 18; Lam 1:21; Ezek. 26:2), rejoice (Lam. 2:17), open wide their mouths, i.e., rail (2:16), gnash with their teeth (2:16), etc."[53] The book of Proverbs often defines the wicked by these descriptions. This is not a matter of mending a broken relationship with an offended brother but of the wicked person's deep-seated antagonism against the righteous.[54] The righteous do not avenge themselves but depend upon God to vindicate them (see 3:34; 14:19). Through Isaac's willingness to give up his rights to the Philistines and under God's good hand, the Philistines ultimately sought to ally themselves with this man of blessing.[55]

(3) Conclusion (16:8-9)

A qualification (v. 8) and a summary framing statement draw the subunit to its conclusion.

8 This "better . . . than" proverb in its context, like 15:16-17 in theirs, qualifies the assertions in vv. 5-7 of divine punishment on the arrogant and blessings on the virtuous. Several assonances give its synthetic parallels coherence.[56] *Better a little* [see 15:16; 18:12] *with righteousness* (see I: 97) entails that the LORD does not reward piously serving the community with immediate economic prosperity. By contrast, *than a large* [see 5:23] *income* [see 3:9] *with injustice* or "without (*b^{e}lō';* see 13:23) justice (see 1:3)," entailing that the LORD may allow the wicked to enjoy morally ill-gotten gain before he executes his justice (see 10:2, 3). The similarity between 15:16 and 16:8, but with the substitution of "righteousness" in 16:8a for "fear of the

---

19:19). (3) The two-place *Hiphil* of 16:7 combines the last two constructions. The LORD is probably the subject, not "the person" (*pace* McKane, *Proverbs,* p. 491), because the LORD is the subject in the parallel verset and nothing in the syntax signifies a change of subject. Moreover, in this book the sovereign LORD subdues the wicked, not an individual in defense of himself (see 3:5-7; 3:34; 25:21-22).

53. H. Ringgren, *TDOT,* 1:215, s.v. *'āyabh.*

54. *Pace* McKane, *Proverbs,* p. 491.

55. See E. A. Martens, "The Way of Wisdom," in *WWis,* pp. 75-90.

56. Note letter-initial and final *ṭ* and the consonance of the dentals *ṭ d ṣ t* in every word of the first verset and three times in two of four words in the second verset: *ṭwb-m'ṭ bṣdqh mrb tbw'wt bl' mšpṭ;* the assonance of word-initial *ṭôb mērōb;* and the assonance of *m$^{e'}$aṭ* and *mišpāṭ.*

LORD" in 15:16a, suggests that the omission of the LORD is intentional. Perhaps he is uniquely omitted in this one verse of the subunit because he seems absent before he turns the morally upside-down world right-side up (cf. 1 Sam. 2:3-10; Ps. 37:16-17; Luke 1:51-53; 1 Tim. 4:8).

9 This concluding subunit's frame again carefully balances the interplay of divine activity and human initiative (see 16:1-9), giving God "not only the last word but the soundest."[57] *The heart* [see 16:1] *of a human being* (*'ādām;* see 16:1; cf. Ps. 140:2[3]; Prov. 19:21; Isa. 10:7; Jer. 4:14; Ezek. 38:10; Zech. 7:10; 8:17) *plans* (*yᵉḥaššēb;* see 6:3, 18), a poetic word for the result of human thought processes in strategizing that issues in actions. Apart from its four uses in the Psalms, *ḥšb* pertains to negative undertakings (Prov. 24:8; Hos. 7:15) in its other five occurrences. *His way* (*darkô;* see 1:15) extends the frame from his words to his entire life view and behavior. Because *wa* means both "and" and "but," it was left untranslated, allowing the context to signal both senses. *The LORD* (see 16:1-9) both complements and contrasts the LORD with *'ādām* (see 16:1). *Establishes* (or orders, *yākîn;* see 6:8) is one of the meanings of *kûn* in the *Hiphil,* which is glossed "established, established, anchored" in the *Niphal* in 16:4.[58] *His step* (*ṣaʿᵃdô;* see 4:12) denotes metaphorically, as here, the course of one's life, a synonym for "way," its parallel in Jer. 10:31, and of steps *(miṣʿᵃdê)* in Prov. 20:24. The singular suggests that not a step is taken apart from the LORD's superintendence. "A man may plan his road to the last detail, but he cannot implement his planning, unless it coincides with Yahweh's plan for him. He is deluded if he supposes that he has unfettered control and can impose his will on every situation without limitation in order to make his plan a reality."[59] As Shakespeare expressed it: "There is a divinity that shapes our ends, rough-hew them how we will."

c. The Mediatorial King (16:10-15)

The heavenly LORD mediates his justice on earth through his wise and just king (vv. 10-15). This subunit coheres through its use of the keyword "king" in every verse except v. 11 and through the topic of living within the king's rule. The king stands in the place of God, as shown by the many ways vv. 1-9 and 10-15 are bound together (see 15:30–16:15) and by the fact that the LORD could be inserted wherever "king" is found. Every predication of the king demonstrates an aspect of the LORD's own character. These six verses fall into three quatrains: the king's authority to give just verdicts (vv. 10-11),

57. D. Kidner, *Proverbs* (TOTC; Downers Grove: InterVarsity, 1964), p. 119.
58. E. Gerstenberger, *TLOT,* 2:605, s.v. *kûn Niphal.*
59. McKane, *Proverbs,* pp. 495-96.

his moral sensibilities toward justice (vv. 12-13), and climactically his legal performance to effect life and death (vv. 14-15). The catchword "favor" *(rāṣôn)* links the last two (vv. 13a, 15b).

(1) The King's Authority (16:10-11)

The first quatrain is linked by the catchword *mišpāṭ* ("justice"), sounding its theme, and by the assonance of their initial words *qesem* ("inspired verdict") and *peles* ("balance") and their final words *pîw* ("his mouth") and *kîs* ("pouch").

10 The proverb presents the wise king (cf. 14:35; 20:8, 26, 28; 22:11; 25:2-5; 29:4a), not the foolish king (cf. 28:15; 29:4b, 12; 31:3-5), as infallible in administering justice.[60] In this proverb the LORD enacts divine justice (cf. 16:1) through inspiring his wise king to give infallible verdicts that do not betray justice. If pagan kings had the competence to display justice (cf. 31:4-9), how much more the anointed of Israel (cf. 2 Sam. 12:1-14). *An inspired verdict (qesem)* elsewhere refers disparagingly to proscribed pagan divination (Deut. 18:10; 1 Sam. 15:23; 2 K. 7:17; Ezek. 21:18-23[23-28];[61] cf. Num 22:7; 23:23) and false prophecy (Jer. 14:14; Ezek. 13:6). Yet here, to judge from its immediate parallel "justice" and the broader context of this ideal king, it denotes a legitimate method of reaching a verdict in legal disputes. Divination is the art of discerning the mind of the deity to do the right thing at a particular time and in a particular situation. In that light *qesem* is probably used metaphorically here to strikingly denote the Spirit's gifting of the king to reach a swift and correct verdict (see 8:14-16; cf. 1 Sam. 16:13; 2 Sam. 14:17, 20; 16:23; 1 K. 3:16-28; Isa. 11:1-5).[62] *Qesem* in turn suggests that its parallel *b^e^mišpāṭ* means "in making a decision, in giving a verdict/a judgment" (cf. Ps. 105:5), not its other sense "against justice" (see 1:3).[63] *Is*

60. The proverb's halves cohere by: the common topic of *śpty-melek* ("lips of the king") and *pîw* ("his mouth"), giving an inspired verdict *(qesem/mišpāṭ);* by the consonance of *l* (twice in each verset), *m* (twice in each verset), and *p* (three times); and by the assonance of *śpty* and *mšpṭ*.

61. *Pace* E. L. Davies, "The Meaning of *qesem* in Prv 16:10," *Bib* 61 (1980) 554-56. Davies confounds "casting arrows" with the legal method of "casting lots" to solve knotty disputes (Prov. 16:33; 18:18; cf. Lev. 16:8; Num. 26:55-56; Josh. 14:2; 15:1; 19:51; Mic. 2:5; Acts 1:26) and overlooks the fact that Ezekiel links casting arrows with consulting idols and inspecting the liver under the designation of *qesem.* Since the Old Testament proscribes the other two, one should probably assume the same of casting arrows. Van Leeuwen (*Proverbs,* p. 160) similarly holds that it refers to a legitimate means of divination such as with the casting of the Urim and Thummim but is not convincing because he does not clarify what the means is.

62. So also Meinhold (*Sprüche,* 2:269) and R. Clifford (*Proverbs* [OTL; Louisville: Westminster John Knox, 1999], p. 159).

63. *HALOT,* 2:651, s.v. *mišpāṭ.*

on the lips of, and its stock-in-trade parallel *his mouth,* are two common metonymies for speech (see 4:24; 14:3). These inspired verdicts are the inalienable possession *of a king* (see 8:15). In Old Testament theology the divinely endowed king stands as a mediator between God and the people. *Is not unfaithful (yimʿal)* glosses a verb whose basic meaning is "to go astray" (see 4:15; 7:25); when combined with *bᵉ,* it denotes being unfaithful to a legally definable relationship of trust, in this case the king's responsibility to uphold justice.[64] This epigram presents a truth, but not the whole truth, and must be held in tension with other Scriptures that represent the king as in error (Judg. 9:20; 2 Sam. 12:1-14; Eccl. 8:9).[65] When the king betrayed his trust to give justice, the LORD removed him (cf. 2 Sam. 7:14; 1 K. 14:5-11; cf. 1 Kings 21) or at least, as in the case of David, punished him (2 Sam. 12:1-23). In short, the proverb presents the ideal king and anticipates the Messiah (cf. John 5:19-30).

11 The LORD establishes justice on earth by the inspired, infallible verdict of his king in court (v. 10) and through the just weights and measures he ordained for the marketplace and that the king presumably upholds (v. 11). "[The balance and scales] are not something arbitrary which each king can manufacture to suit his convenience. They are fixed by God and delivered into the king's keeping to administer fairly."[66] Standard weights and measures require legal sanction to enforce their authority. According to this proverb, the LORD not only stands behind them (Lev. 19:35-36; Deut. 25:13-16; Prov. 11:1; 20:23; Ezek. 45:10) but owns them (v. 11a) because he made them through human hands (v. 11b; cf. Ps. 139:13). In this chiastically constructed parallelism, the topic of scales and weights constitutes the outer frame and the LORD's ownership of them the inner core. Normally "righteousness" *(ṣedeq)* qualifies just weights (cf. Lev. 19:36; Deut. 25:15; Job 31:6; Ezek. 45:10), but probably its close equivalent *just* (*mišpāṭ;* see 1:3) was chosen as a catchword with v. 10. *Balance* refers to a stationary balance with beams and bolts, *and hand scale* (see 11:1) possibly refers to the handheld balance.[67] They stand as a merism for all weights and measures. *Are the LORD's,* or "belong to *(lᵉ)* [see 16:1] the LORD" (see 16:1-9), for as verset B

64. R. Knierim, *TLOT,* 2:681, s.v. *melek.*

65. Delitzsch (*Proverbs,* pp. 245-46), W. G. Plaut (*Book of Proverbs: A Commentary* [New York: Union of American Hebrew Congregations, 1941], p. 178), and R. N. Whybray (*Proverbs* [NCBC; Great Britain: Marshall, Morgan and Scott and Grand Rapids: Eerdmans, 1994], p. 243) undercut the authority of the proverbs by claiming that this one represents the people's naive and erroneous point of view of the king, not God's authoritative truth about him. Yet the prologue claims that the proverbs represent God's infallible truth.

66. A. Cohen, *Proverbs* (London: Soncino, 1967), p. 105.

67. *ANEP,* pp. 40, 219, nos. 133 and 639.

explains, he made them. The LORD instituted and sustains the means of justice in his everlasting, ordered kingdom, and the king himself is subject to that higher government. *All* undoubtedly refers to the totality of just *weights* (see 11:1). The LXX freely, but rightly, paraphrases "righteous measure," for unjust scales are an abomination to him (11:1; 20:10, 23). *In a pouch,* apart from 1:14, in its three other uses refers to the trader's probably leather pouch in which he stored his weights (see Deut. 25:13; Isa. 46:6; Mic. 6:11). *Are his work* (*ma'ᵃśēhû;* see 16:3) is frequently used for the mighty, just, and praiseworthy acts of the LORD against his enemies (cf. Exod. 34:10; Deut. 3:24; 11:7; Josh. 24:31; Judg. 2:7; Pss. 33:4; 107:24; Isa. 5:19; Jer. 51:10). Job uses it with reference to his noteworthy and praiseworthy work in creation (Job 37:7), and Qoheleth for his mysterious, unfathomable work in history and creation (Eccl. 3:11; 7:13; 8:17; 11:5). The LORD's work is always marvelous. This epigram is not concerned with unjust weights that the LORD detests (see 11:1; 20:23).

(2) The King's Moral Sensibility (16:12-13)

The king's just verdicts (vv. 10-11) and the execution of his sentences (vv. 14-15) are informed by his moral sensibilities (vv. 12-13). This antithetical pair contrasts the wicked deeds the wise king detests with the truthful speech he favors. The pair are also linked by the catchword "kings" (plural), which stands out against the singular form in vv. 10 and 14, and their word-initial, stock-in-trade antonyms "abomination" and "find favor" and "wickedness" and "righteousness." The catchwords "abomination" and "favor" also link his moral sensibilities with the LORD's (vv. 5 and 7), just as "work" linked the divine work through human hands in vv. 3 and 11. In a chiasm the verses begin and end with his moral tastes: "abhors" and "loves."

12 In this synthetic parallelism verset B, asserting that the rule of kings is established through righteousness, validates the moral taste of kings to detest wickedness (verset A). *An abomination* (see 16:5), when used in a positive evaluation in contrast to its negative use with fools (13:19) and the wicked (21:27), usually occurs with "to the LORD" (11:20; 12:22; 16:5), but here uniquely with *to kings* (see 16:10-15).[68] *Doing* (*'ᵃśôt;* see 2:14) *wickedness* (I: 109) may refer to the guilty, antisocial actions of the kings themselves or others such as their officials (cf. 29:12). The revulsion of kings against wickedness identifies them with the moral tastes of Woman Wisdom (8:7) and of the LORD (6:16; 15:9). What is said here of the king could also be said of the LORD (cf. 3:32; 11:1; 15:9; 16:12; 21:3, 15). Verse 12 presents one

68. "Humanity" is the object of *tô'ēbâ* in 24:9 and of "wicked" and "righteous" in 29:27.

of the few sayings that substantiates verset A with *because* (*kî;* cf. 16:26; 21:7, 25; 22:9; 24:5-6; 29:19). *A throne* (*kissēʾ;* see 9:14), which concretizes the ruler and his dominion as well as his place as one of power,[69] *is established* [see 16:3] *through* (*bᵉ;* see 6:6, 8) *righteousness* (see I: 97; cf. 20:28; 25:5; 29:14; Deut. 17:18ff.; Pss. 89:14[15]; 97:2; Isa. 16:5). The Egyptologist H. Brunner shed light on v. 12b from his study of Pharaoh's throne. Parallels with Solomon's throne (cf. 1 K. 10:18-20), particularly the mention of six steps, suggest that Solomon modeled his throne after the pedestal of Pharaoh's throne. The base of that throne took the form of the sign *maʿat,* a hieroglyph standing for justice, order, and proper divine harmony, which can be rendered in Hebrew by "righteousness." By the 19th and 20th Dynasties the throne base, because of its form, was understood as justice or right order.[70]

13 The king's moral sensibilities toward work (v. 12) and speech (v. 13) encompass all activities within his realm. *Righteous* (see I: 97) *lips* and *whoever speaks (dōbēr) upright things* (see I: 98) constitute the inner core of the chiastic parallels. *Kings* [see v. 12] *take pleasure in* (*rᵉṣôn;* see 11:1), by its similarity to v. 7, shows that the LORD mediates his pleasure and acceptance *(rāṣôn)* through his just representative. Together with this clause, *he* [the kings; see n. 24] *loves* (*yeʾᵉhāb;* see 1:22) constitutes the outer frame of v. 13. Collectivity and individuality are achieved by opposing plural "lips" with "one who speaks," "righteousness" with "upright things," and "kings" with "he." 22:11 makes even clearer the high standards demanded of the king's "friends" (i.e., advisers, officials, messengers); they must have a pure attitude before speaking. "This proverb continues to hold up the mirror to princes."[71] His advisers are like Woman Wisdom, who speaks upright things (8:8). Human salvation lies in the King from heaven, the only one who fulfills these proverbs. He does so in part through his Spirit in his church on earth.

(3) The King's Power (16:14-15)

The king's just verdicts and moral sensibilities have little value, however, unless he has the will and power to effect them. The merism of the king's heralds of death (v. 14) and life (v. 15), which bind together this proverb pair, encompasses all his legal enforcement (cf. 19:12).

14 *The* legitimate *wrath* — not an out-of-control rashness (*ḥᵃmat;*

69. M. Metzer, 1985.

70. H. Brunner, "Gerechtigkeit als Fundament des Thrones," *VT* 8 (1958) 426-28; H. H. Schmid, *Gerechtigkeit als Weltordnung* (Tübingen, 1968), p. 61.

71. Delitzsch, *Proverbs,* p. 246.

see 6:34; 15:18) — *of the king* (see 16:10-15) informs his penal execution. This kind of wrath can be appeased. The metaphor *is the messenger of death* (see n. 27; cf. 13:17) is an allusion to a Ugaritic myth, not an allusion to henchmen like Doeg the Edomite (1 Sam. 22:6-19) and Benaiah (1 K. 2:25, 29-34, 46; cf. Esth. 7:8-10; Dan. 2:5-13), because the form is probably dual.[72] In Ugaritic mythology both Baal, the god of life, and probably Mot, the god of death, sent their messengers in pairs. As Mot's messengers heralded death, so the king's wrath presages death (cf. 19:12; 20:2). The LORD is the ultimate Agent who inflicts death on the wicked in an unspecified future, and the just king is his immediate agent (see Eccl. 8:4). Solomon's kingdom is said to be established only after he rid his realm of wrongdoers (1 K. 2:22-46).[73] Unlike the jealous husband, whose anger cannot be appeased (6:34), *a wise* [see I: 94] *person* (*'îš;* see I: 89) *pacifies it* (i.e., the dangerous outburst of royal anger; *yᵉkappᵉrennâ;* see 16:6). The wise person (15:31, 32) appeases the king's wrath against him and/or others (cf. 15:31, 32; 29:8b) through virtues such as humility (15:33), repentance and confession (28:13), renewed community loyalty (16:6), and patience with a gentle answer (15:1; 25:15). For historical illustrations see Num. 25:6-13; 1 Samuel 25; 2 Sam. 22:14-22; Esth. 7:8-10; Dan. 2:5-24; Matt. 22:1-14; Luke 12:5; Rev. 6:15-17.

15 This verse complements the motivation to behave righteously and to speak truthfully in order to escape the king's wrath with the positive motivation to win the royal favor and so promote life (cf. Gen. 40:20-21; Neh. 2:1-8; Esth. 5:2-3).[74] *In* the sphere of *the light* [see 4:18] *of the king's face* (see 6:35) is a frequent metaphor in the Babylonian, El Amarna, and Ugaritic texts to signify the ruler's beneficent favor toward someone. The symbol probably has a solar background in that the king is called "sun" because of his beaming face.[75] The parallel "spring rain" supports this meteorological background. The perceived glow or halo that proceeds from the face of the ruler, which Job associated with a smile (Job 29:24), is here equated with the full and abundant *life* (*ḥayyîm;* 2:19), for they are inseparable (Job 3:16; 33:28, 30; Pss. 56:13[14]; 58:8[9]; Eccl. 6:4). The frequent references

72. H. L. Ginsburg, "Baal's Two Messengers," *BASOR* 97 (1944) 25-30; Dahood, *Proverbs and Northwest Semitic Philology,* p. 36; *pace* Meinhold, *Sprüche,* p. 271.

73. Ahiqar, adviser to the great Assyrian kings Sennacherib (705-681) and Esarhaddon (680-669), warned his nephew, "[The wr]ath of a king, if thou be commanded, is a burning fire. Obey [it] at once. Let it not kindled against thee and cover up the word of a king with the veil of the heart. — Why should wood strive with fire, flesh with a knife, a man with [a king]?" (*ANET,* pp. 428-29).

74. The synthetic parallels partially cohere through *malk* (the original pronunciation of "king") and *malqôš* ("spring rain"), as noted by Clifford (*Proverbs,* p. 159).

75. One Ugaritic text reads: "And the face of the sun (i.e., Pharaoh) shone bright on me" (Dahood, *Proverbs and Northwest Semitic Philology,* p. 36).

to light, lamp, and shine in connection with the LORD show that the metaphor signifies his favor, prosperity, security, victory, and peace.[76] We should assume the same for his king. The connection between the light of God's face to bring life to his worshipers and his king's face to bring life to his subjects once again shows the close connection between the LORD and his mediatorial king. *And his favor* [see 11:1; 16:7, 13] *is like a cloud* that heralds the revitalizing *spring rain.* The early (or autumn) rain, which falls from mid-October to early November, and the latter (or spring) rain, which falls in the first half of April, mark the beginning and end of the rainy season. The early rains prepare the ground for plowing and sowing, and the latter rains provide the last bit of moisture on which the cereal harvest depends. In sum, the Author of life mediates life through his just king (cf. Ps. 72:15-17), whose wrath heralds subsequent death and whose favor heralds subsequent life.

2. Wise and Foolish Speech (16:16-30)

16 *To acquire[77] wisdom, how much[78] better than gold![79]*
And to acquire insight is preferable to silver.
17 *The highway of the upright is turning aside from evil;*
the one who protects his life is one who guards his way.[80]
18 *Before a shattering comes[81] pride,*
and before humiliation, a haughty spirit.

76. Cf. Num. 6:25; Judg. 5:31; Job 17:12; 18:5-6; 22:28; 29:3; 33:30; Pss. 18:28(29); 31:16(17); 36:9(10); 43:3; 44:3(4); 80:3, 7, 19(4, 8, 20); 97:11; 118:27; 119:135; 139:11-12; Prov. 13:9; 24:20; Isa. 9:2(1); 58:8; Jer. 15:9; Amos 5:18, 20; Mal. 4:2(3:20).

77. Instead of pointing *qnh* as the more difficult inf. absolute *qᵉnōh* (cf. the inf. cons. *qᵉnôt* in verset B; GKC, P. 75n), the Syr. and the Targ. read *Qal* ptcp. masc. sing. *qōneh* ("the one who acquires"), and the Vulg. with several mss. read *Qal* imperative, masc sing. *qᵉnēh* ("acquire!" cf. 4:5, 7).

78. It cannot be decided whether the ancient versions deleted *mah* due to haplography with *ḥokmâ* or the MT added it by dittography. The MT represents the more difficult reading.

79. Lit. "To acquire wisdom, how much better than gold!" The nominal exclamation is complex (*IBHS,* p. 681, PP. 40.2.3b).

80. The LXX uniquely reads verset A somewhat differently and expands the proverb by adding versets to both halves and by inserting between them a proverb about teachability: "The paths of life turn aside from evil; and the ways of righteousness are length of life. He that receives instruction shall be in prosperity; and he that guards reproofs shall be made wise. He that keeps his ways preserves his own soul; and he that loves his life will spare his mouth."

81. The temporal preposition "before" implies the verb of motion (*IBHS,* p. 224, P. 11.4.3d).

19 *Better to be lowly*[82] *in spirit with the oppressed*[83]
than to divide plunder with the proud.
20 *The one who pays attention*[84] *to a saying*[85] *finds good,*
and as for the one who trusts in the LORD, *blessed is he!*
21 *The wise of heart is named*[86] *"Insightful,"*
and sweetness of lips increases persuasiveness.[87]
22 *A wellspring of life is prudence to*[88] *those who have it,*
but the discipline of fools is folly.
23 *The heart of the wise causes his mouth to be prudent,*
and on[89] *his lips he adds persuasiveness.*
24 *Pleasant words are overflowing honey,*
sweet to the soul and a remedy to the bones.
25 *There is a way that is right in a person's judgment,*
but the end of it is ways to death.
26 *The appetite of the toiler toils for him;*
surely his mouth[90] *urges him on.*
27 *A troublemaker is one who prepares*[91] *mischief,*

82. A word study shows that the form is the cons. of the adjective *šāpāl* ("the one lowly of spirit"; cf. Prov. 29:23; Isa. 57:15), not *Qal* inf. cons. ("to be low"; cf. Eccl. 12:4), in spite of the parallel *ḥallēq* (*Piel* inf. cons.; *pace* Delitzsch, *Proverbs,* p. 249; *HALOT,* 4:1,631; s.v. *šāpāl*).

83. K reads *ʿaneyîm* ("poor"); Q reads *ʿanāwîm* ("afflicted"; see 14:21).

84. *Maśkîl* may be cons. with the preposition (see *IBHS,* pp. 139-40, P. 9.3a). If so, vv. 20a and 21a share the same syntax (cons. + imperfect + noun).

85. Or "the one who is prudent/competent in speech."

86. Lit. "to the wise of heart it is called." For the indefinite subject construction with passive 3rd masc. sing. see *IBHS,* pp. 70-71, P. 4.4.2a. *Qr'* + *šēm* is a technical term for naming (see C. J. Labuschagne, *TLOT,* 3:1,161-62, s.v. *qr'*). It may have a judicial sense; in other words, this is his official name (cf. 2 Sam. 12:28; Isa. 4:1).

87. And/or "learning."

88. The MT's *beʿālāyw* is a gen. of mediated object; a possessive gen. would be tautologous and jejune. The LXX's *tois kektēmenois* ("to the possessor") may reflect an original *lbʿlyw,* whose initial *lamed* dropped out of the MT by haplography due to the final *lamed* of preceding *śkl.*

89. R. B. Y. Scott (*Proverbs. Ecclesiastes: Introduction, Translation, and Notes* [AB; Garden City, N.Y.: Doubleday, 1965], p. 105), followed by Fichtner *(BHS)* and McKane (*Proverbs,* p. 490), emends *ûʿal* to *ūbaʿal* ("a master of lips" = an expert speaker). The emendation makes sense if *yōsîp leqaḥ* has the same meaning as in v. 21b, but more probably a pun is intended (cf. 10:6, 11). Even though G. André (*TDOT,* 6:123, s.v. *yāsap*) invests v. 21b and v. 23b with the same meanings, he rejects the emendation as unnecessary.

90. The LXX reads *apōleian* ("ruin"), perhaps having read *pîdô* (cf. 24:22). This misreading affected the Syr.

91. The meaning of *kōreh* is uncertain. Traditionally it has been understood as I *krh* "to dig [a hole]," but the other 14 occurrences of this verb always take as its object a

and on his lip[92] *[it] is like a scorching fire.*
28 *A perverse person unleashes conflict,*
and the slanderer[93] *is one who alienates a close friend.*
29 *A violent person entices his companion*
and[94] *leads him in a way that is not good.*
30 *Blinking*[95] *his eyes, he devises*[96] *perversity;*
pursing his lips, he brings evil to pass.[97]

This unit consists of three partial units: an introduction (vv. 16-19) and a main body pertaining to the winsome speech of a good person (vv. 20-24) and the destructive speech of the malevolent (vv. 25-30). The wise teaching now found in the mouth of the disciple (vv. 20-24) is based on his prior lov-

---

word in the semantic domain of a hole (cf. 26:27), not evil, nor is it ever used with reference to that which is dug (*pace* McKane, *Proverbs,* p. 494; Plöger, *Sprüche,* p. 196; Meinhold, *Sprüche,* 2:277) or of cultivating ground (i.e., to labors for a harvest of evil; *pace* Dhorme, cited by McKane). If this root is intended, one must questionably add the object "(pit of) evil" (so C. Toy, *The Book of Proverbs* [ICC; Edinburgh: T&T Clark, 1977], p. 331) and assume that the metaphor signifies entrapping others with an evil plot or stratagem as in 26:7 and Pss. 7:16; 57:7; 119:85. The Targ., Syr., and NIV paraphrase the thought by "plots evil." Gemser emends *krh* to *kûr* "furnace" (Gemser, *Sprüche,* p. 73), and Fichtner *(BHS)* to *qārā'* "encounter/meet" (cf. Fichtner, *BHS*). Dahood postulates a homonym meaning "to cook, to heat" to explain *kûr* and *kîrayim* ("fiery furnace"). His appeal to 2 K. 6:23 is not convincing because III *krh* "to invite to a feast" is used there (*HALOT,* 2:497, s.v. III *krh*). He extends this meaning to "concoct" (so also NRSV). If so, the Hebrew figure is similar to either the English idiom "to cook up" or simply to cook in the sense of prepare. In the final analysis the meaning is not significantly different from the Targ., Syr., and NIV, but this etymology offers a plausible parallel to "a burning fire."

92. K, followed by the LXX, Targ., and Vulg., reads dual (cf. 16:10, 23; 22:18), but Q reads the more unusual sing. (17:4).

93. This is one of the three instances of a small letter, all final *nuns*, in *BHS* (see also Isa. 44:14; Jer. 39:13). The ancient versions were uncertain about the word's meaning: the LXX reads "will kindle a torch of deceit with mischief" (?); the Syr., "persecutes"; the Targ., "querulous man"; the Vulg., "verbose."

94. Probably a *waw* consecutive construction to signify consequence (*IBHS,* p. 525, P. 32.2a).

95. Though *'ṣh* is a *hap. leg.,* an Arabic cognate means "shutting (the eyes) together," and in Sir. 43:7 it is used of the mouth (Gemser, *Sprüche,* p. 112). The ancient versions guessed at its meaning: "fix" (LXX and Vulg.), "wink" (Targ. and Syr.).

96. By smoothing the text to read *yaḥšōb,* the ancient versions obscure the connection of the versets. Driver ("Problems in the Hebrew Text of Proverbs," *Bib* 32 [1951] 196) thinks that the inf. form preceded by *lamed* means "is likely to" in 16:30; 18:24; 19:8, 27; 30:14, but an exceptional meaning is unnecessary.

97. Probably a gnomic perfective as elsewhere in Proverbs, not preterite (*pace* McKane, *Proverbs,* p. 236). The perfective, not imperfective, may have been chosen because the verse is already heavy.

ing and faithful acceptance of the teaching (vv. 16-19). The catchword *ṭôb* ("better"/"good," vv. 19a, 20a) smooths the transition from the introduction to the main body and forms an *inclusio* around the main body, shifting from the good of prudent speech to the not good of malevolent speech (vv. 20, 29).

a. Introduction: Security in Wisdom (16:16-19)

The four-verse introduction to this unit on speech so resonates with the vocabulary of the prologue (cf. 3:13-14; 4:5, 7; 8:10-11, 19) that it can be labeled "a miniature prologue," matching the four-verse introduction of 15:30-33. Verses 16 and 17 link the acquisition of wisdom with being upright, and v. 19 qualifies the assertion in v. 18 that pride precedes a terminal fall by implying that for a time the arrogant plunder the humble and afflicted. The proverbial pair vv. 18-19 subtly develops from the disciple guarding his life (v. 17) to the shattering fall of the proud (v. 18). Verse 19 explains that one protects his way through humility.

16 In the synonymous parallels of the first introductory educational proverb the topic *to acquire wisdom (qᵉnōh-ḥokmâ)/to acquire insight* (*qᵉnôt bînāh;* see 4:5, 7) is claimed to be *better than gold (ṭôb mēḥārûṣ)* and *preferable to silver* (*nibḥār mikkāsep;* see 3:13, 14; 8:10). The exclamation, *how much better! (mah-ṭôb),* not waiting for an answer, gives the comparative degree a superlative force. Wisdom has inestimable superiority to precious metals because it bestows spiritual virtues along with material benefits (see 3:13-18). Wealth without wisdom is vulgar and greedy and/or may be due to ruthless individualism.

17 This verse defines the morally neutral term "wisdom" in terms of ethics.[98] As v. 16 resonates with 4:1-9, so v. 17 echoes 4:10-19. By the imagery of roads, whose synonyms "highway and "way" are its first and last words, it motivates the disciple to opt for ethical integrity. Verset A compares shunning evil, both wrongdoing and its consequences, to a broad, prepared highway leading unimpeded to life. Dorsey explains the imagery. Written and archaeological evidence indicates that in Iron Age Israel (1100-600 B.C.) *the highway (mᵉsillat)* was the main prepared thoroughfare and normally passed by cities, not through them. Those who wished to enter the city by way of an access road "turned aside" to enter it (cf. Judg. 19:11, 12, 15).[99] Here the metaphor depicts the course of life *of the upright* (*yᵉšārîm;* see I: 98), whose geometric root meaning of being straight or level with reference to a fixed line or plane fits the image. Those who steer a straight course

98. According to the Masorah, this verse is at the book's midpoint.

99. D. A. Dorsey, *The Roads and Highways of Ancient Israel* (Baltimore: Johns Hopkins University, 1991), pp. 228-29.

resolutely *turn aside from evil* (*sûr mērāʿ;* see 3:7; 14:16; 16:6), which implicitly likens the corruption and consequences of evil (see 1:16) to a condemned city with its corrupt practices and certain calamity (13:14-15; 15:24; 17:13). By this turning aside from the access roads to the condemned city, the upright stay on the road that is wide enough for all comers and free from all obstacles. Staying within the moral boundaries of this book, they walk confidently without fear of stumbling (4:10-19) and implicitly with the certainty of arriving at their final destination. Verset B escalates the impersonal metaphor of a highway to the dynamic personal metaphor of a journey, the protection and freedom on the journey to preserving life, and the negative of not doing evil to the positive of doing what is right.[100] *The one who protects* (*šōmēr;* see 2:8) signifies that each upright traveler — note the switch from plural to singular — preserves *his life* (*napšô;* see I: 90) as he advances expeditiously and securely without enticement to depart to the right or to the left. That is so because he *is one who guards* (*nōṣēr;* see 2:8) *his way* (*darkô;* see 1:15), which is here used as a synonym of *mᵉsillâ.*[101] The metaphor signifies exercising great care to keep the commandments of this book so as to act in the appropriate manner by paying attention to one's character and conduct in order to be secure and arrive at life.

18 The miniature prologue now shifts its focus from outward ethical behavior to inner spiritual attitudes. Verses 17 and 18 are probably linked by the metaphors of "way/road" (see v. 17) and "stumbling," implicitly of the foot walking on a road. The imagery of v. 18, however, depends on the contrast between high in the sense of pride and low in the sense of abased.[102] Instead of looking where they are going, in defiance of the first principle of wisdom (see 15:33), the arrogant raise their eyes above God and humanity (cf. 30:13) and stumble to their perdition (see the variant proverb in 18:12). The juxtaposition of the upright with the proud suggests that the two verses are antithetical. Inferentially, the upright are lowly and submissive to God and his teachers (see 15:33, "before honor comes humility"), but the arrogant stray from the moral order and stumble to their eternal perdition in the dark, treacherous, and obstacle-filled way they enter (cf. 22:4). The proverb gives the strong impression of saying the same thing twice. Both verse halves begin with *before* (15:33) followed by words denoting ruin and containing the /*š*/ sound (*šeber, shattering;* see 15:4)/*kiššālôn* (*stumbling,* a *hap. leg.* from *kšl;* see 4:9, 12, 16). And they contain the similar-sounding synonyms *gāʾôn* (*pride;* see 8:13) and *gōbah* (*haughty;* see 16:5, whose concrete mean-

100. Verset B is similar to 13:3a; 19:16a; 21:23; 22:5b.

101. Dorsey, *Roads,* pp. 252, n. 8 and 228-29.

102. Clifford (*Proverbs,* p. 160) compares "haughty" (from Fr. *haut* "high") and "humble" (from Lat. *humilis* "low").

ing is "high") *rûaḥ* (*spirit;* see I: 92). In this way its truth is underscored and clarified; the proud are defined more precisely as the haughty in spirit, and the ensuing "shattering" of their body is explained as due to their "stumbling." The fracturing of their limbs that inflicted evil exemplifies the book's principle of divine retribution (see I: 73)."[103]

19 This *better . . . than* (see 12:9; 15:16; 16:8) proverb is linked to v. 18 by the similar-sounding synonyms *kāšal* "to stumble" and *šāpal* ("to be low"), the chiastically arranged *gā'ôn* and *gē'îm* ("pride," vv. 18a, 19b), which derive from the same root (vv. 18a, 19b), and *rûaḥ* ("in spirit," vv. 18b, 19a). Once again the "better . . . than" proverb qualifies the preceding proverb (see 16:8). Before the proud stumble and fall (v. 18) they may trample the oppressed under foot (15:16; 16:8, 19). The proverb teaches the disciple to refrain from unjust acts (16:8, 17) and *to be lowly in spirit* (*šᵉpal-rûaḥ,* 15:33; 22:4; 29:23). The adjective *šāpāl* can have a physical sense (e.g., a "low" vine, Ezek. 17:6; tree, 27:24; kingdom, 17:14). It can also function as a metaphor for one who has been humiliated (2 Sam. 6:22; Ezek. 21:26[31]; 29:14, 15; Mal. 2:9). With "in spirit," however, it has the noble sense of one who through affliction has had his pride knocked out of him and becomes lowly in spirit before God (see 3:34). With such a person God dwells to revive his spirit (Isa. 57:15). The proverb also teaches the disciple to embrace a conscious solidarity *with* [see 13:20] *the oppressed* to whom the LORD gives grace (see n. 83; 3:34). *To divide plunder* (*ḥallēq šāllāl;* see 1:13) is taken from military life (Gen. 49:27; Exod. 15:9; Judg 5:30; 1 Sam. 30:22-24; Ps. 68:12[13]; Isa. 53:12) or from the judicial and other civil injustices of the rich (cf. 1:13; 31:11).[104] The addition *with the proud* (see 15:25) and its parallel, "with the afflicted," show unmistakably their economic prosperity at the expense of the humble and the afflicted. "Poverty and humility are natural allies, and impious pride goes with ill-gotten gain."[105] The proverb's truthfulness depends on the theological conviction that the LORD (see v. 20) stands on the side of the oppressed (3:34) and upholds in an open-ended future his moral order wherein righteousness is rewarded with eternal life (v. 17), and pride, which prompts wrongdoing, is punished with eternal death (see v. 18; cf. 16:8). The LORD looks sympathetically upon the *šāpāl* (Ps. 138:6); he sets them on high (Job 5:11); and they lay hold of glory (Prov. 29:23). The triumph of the *gē'îm* will not be long lasting because the LORD

103. Cf. the Egyptian saying "Pride and arrogance are the ruin of their possessor" (*Papyrus Insinger* 4:22; *AEL,* 3:189), and the Arabic proverb, "The nose is in the heavens, the seat is in the mire" (J. P. Lange, *Proverbs* (CHS; Grand Rapids: Zondervan, n.d.), p.156.

104. Toy, *Proverbs,* p. 329.

105. McKane, *Proverbs,* p. 499.

humiliates them (15:25). In sum, pride leads to plundering the miserable (v. 19) and to its possessor's ruin (v. 18).

b. The Wise Speaker (16:20-24)

Having laid the foundations of wisdom, this subunit develops the societal benefits of prudent speech. Words for speech occur in every verse apart from the center one (v. 22). The broad terms "word" (*dābār,* v. 20, and *'imrê,* v. 24) occur in its outer frame, and within that frame occur the common metonymies for speech, "lips" (v. 21) and "mouth" (v. 23). The unit also coheres by the repetition of the metaphor *mtq,* "sweetness," to depict the winsome character of beneficial speech (vv. 21, 24). Wisdom terms characterize the persuasive speaker: *śkl* "prudent" (vv. 20, 21, 23), *ḥkm-lb* "wise of heart" and *lb ḥkm* "heart of a wise person" (vv. 21a, 23a) and *lqḥ* "persuasive teaching" (vv. 21b, 23b). The first four lines alternate initial *mem* and *lamed.* The pun in v. 20a, whose Hebrew means both "the one who pays attention to a saying" and "the one who is prudent in speech," along with the catchword *ṭôb* ("good"), functions as a transition from the miniature prologue to the body. The rest of the subunit fleshes out "the good" the competent speaker finds: esteem and influence in the community (v. 21); being a well of life (v. 22), increasing persuasiveness in teaching (vv. 21, 23), and being as sweet and healing hurt as a flowing mass of honey (v. 24). The center line, uniquely antithetical and uniquely not mentioning speech, pits the attractive life of prudence against the punishing chastisement of fools.

20 Despite its translation possibilities, the proverb connects good speech with doing well. *Maśkîl 'al-dābār* is probably an intentional pun.[106] Its meaning, *the one who pays attention to a saying* (i.e., a wisdom saying),[107] invests *dābār* with its common meaning in this book (1:6, 23; 4:4; 13:13) and allows *śkl* in the *Hiphil,* meaning "to take note, pay attention" in 21:12, an appropriate sense with "word [of the wise]." Finally, this sense best suits the parallel, *and as for the one who trusts in the* LORD (*bôṭēaḥ baYHWH;* see 3:5; 28:1, 25; 29:25). According to this interpretation, the proverb shows a thematic connection with vv. 16-19 as well as with vv. 21-24. The lowly in spirit will pay attention to the sage's teaching and trust in the LORD who inspired them (3:5), and such a person will himself be recognized as wise in heart and speech (vv. 21, 23). On the other hand, the phrase may also mean *the one who is prudent or competent in speech. Maśkîl* normally means a "prudent person" (see I: 94), and *dābār* commonly means

106. This is a unique occurrence of *'al* with *dābār.*

107. It is unlikely that *dābār* means "matter/thing" or thing in this context on speech and education.

simply "word" or "speech" (10:19; 12:6, 25; 14:15, 23; 15:1, 23). This meaning also fits the references to "the wise of heart"/"heart of the wise" and their ability to speak well (vv. 21, 23). If so, it is also a co-reference to *nābôn* "an understanding person" (v. 21) and *śēkel* *bᵉʿālāyw* ("prudence to its owner"). Verset B then means that prudent speech is inseparable from trust in the LORD. The double entendre functions as a transition from accepting wise speech to giving it. Before a person is competent to win the community's respect by his words (v. 21), he must himself pay careful attention to the words of his inspired teachers. *Finds* [see 2:5; 3:13] *good* (*ṭôb;* see I: 99) lies behind the sage's pronouncement *blessed is he* (see 3:13; 14:21).[108]

21 The imprecise synthetic parallelism suggests that *the wise of heart* (see 11:29) reveals himself in using language that influences people for good. Such a person *is* officially *named* (see n. 86), presumably by the community, *"Insightful"* (*nābôn;* see I: 95), a metaphor signifying his elevated status in the community. *And* adds to the internal wisdom of his heart the external *sweetness* (*meteq;* see 9:17) of his *lips* (4:24). As a metaphor this expression signifies his true — in contrast to the foreign woman's sweet and persuasive but false speech (5:3; 7:21) — and beautiful speech, and as a synecdoche it represents his total gracious deportment. *Increases* (*yōsîp*) may denote adding to the quantity of something (1:5) and/or to its quality (cf. *rōb* in 7:21, depending on *leqaḥ,* which with this verb elsewhere means *learning* the inherited tradition (1:5) and/or *persuasiveness* (see 7:21), probably another pun. The wise in heart teaches the truth winsomely (see v. 13) and thus influences the community for good and wins its respect. The proverb is fleshed out in the life of Christ (Luke 4:22; 19:48; John 7:46).

22 His winsome teaching is now implicitly likened to *a wellspring of life* (see 10:11; 13:14; 14:27). Moreover, "the wise of heart" now becomes *prudence* (*śēkel;* see 3:4) *to those who have it* (*bᵉʿālāyw* = lit. "its possessors"; see 1:17). Those who possess prudence become a life-giving spring that is so attractive that they "turn away" the community from folly to drink from their teachings (see 10:11; 13:14; 14:27). Christians find that Jesus Christ becomes for them a spring of water welling up to eternal life (John 4:14). *But* contrasts the pedagogy of fools (v. 22b) with that of the prudent (v. 22a). The chiastic antithetical parallel to "prudence of its possessor" in the proverb's inner core, *the discipline* (*mûsar;* see 1:2) *of fools* (*ʾᵉwīlîm;* see I: 112), is ambiguous. The meaning of *folly* (see I: 113) rules out taking *mûsar* to denote verbal instruction and "fools" as an objective genitive, for giving instruction to fools cannot be predicated as moral insolence and/or consequent moral ruin. If the genitive is agentive (i.e., "the instruction given by fools"), the otherwise noble *mûsar* is used sarcastically. More probably *mûsar* means here

108. Note the chiastic assonance at the center of the verse: *ṭôb bôṭēaḥ.*

discipline/chastisement as with a rod (1:2) and "of fools" is objective (cf. 7:22 [MT] and 15:5). In that case "folly" refers primarily to the punishing consequences of moral insolence (14:1, 3, 15:20). In sum, the antithetical parallels contrast two forms of pedagogy: the winsome teaching of the wise and the punishment of folly. The imprecise parallelism suggests that the prudent find the former a wellspring of life, but fools must be taught by allowing them to experience the painful, punishing consequence of their folly (cf. 10:13; 13:24; 14:3; 22:15; 23:13, 14; 26:3; 29:15).[109]

23 This proverb reinforces the fact that the winsome teaching (v. 21b) that is a wellspring of life to the prudent (v. 22a) originates in the heart of the wise (v. 21a; cf. Matt. 7:17). *The heart* [*lēb;* see I: 90] *of the wise* [see I: 94] *causes his mouth* [see 2:6] . . . *to be prudent* (*yaśkîl;* see 1:3) *And* in this evaluative +::+ pattern probably functions as an elaboration on verset A. *On his lips* is the stock-in-trade parallel to "mouth" (cf. 4:24). *Yōsîp leqaḥ* repeats 16:21b with its double entendre (n. 87). The phrase defines the meaning of speaking competently in verset A. Thus the proverb motivates the disciple to have "the heart of the wise" through accepting the sage's inspired teachings in love and faith (cf. 2:1-4; 16:16-19). That kind of heart will constantly place the right teaching on his lips to speak in a persuasive way to each new challenging social situation.

24 This verse draws the subunit on competent speech to its climactic conclusion. It compares the extraordinary remedial power of morally and aesthetically pleasing words to overflowing honey. *Pleasant words* (see 15:26) stands in contrast to "evil thoughts" in 15:26, suggesting that the expression denotes a moral as well as an aesthetic quality. According to *HALOT,* the unique compound *ṣûp-dᵉbaš* denotes an *overflowing* mass of *honey* (see 24:13; 25:16, 17; *nōpet ṣûpîm* in Ps. 19:10(11) means "honeycomb" (cf. 5:3; 24:13).[110] The metaphor is explained in verset B: honey uniquely is both sweet and a remedy. *Sweet* (*mātôq;* see 16:21) *to the soul* (*lannepeš;* see I: 90) connotes their pleasing and attractive style to the audience. *And a remedy* (see 4:22) connotes that their substance is an instrument of healing to those hurt by the damaging speech of fools (see 4:22). The synecdoche *to the bones* (see 3:8) refers to the restoration of the entire person or community, both the immaterial and material aspects. Normally medicine is bitter, and what is sweet is not medicinal. Both properties, however, are necessary. Were healing words bitter, the tonic would not be consumed and of no benefit. The metaphor, however, does not walk on all fours. Too much honey makes a person sick (25:16), but not too much good speech.

109. The antithetical proverb also coheres by the consonance of *lamed: śkl [l]bʿlyw . . . ʾwlym ʾwlt.*

110. *HALOT,* 3:1,013, s.v. *ṣûp.*

c. Foolish Speakers (16:25-30)

The catchword "person" *(ʾîš)* gives coherence and focus to this subunit on destructive speech. Verse 25, which explicitly teaches not doing your own thing and implicitly accepting the teaching, introduces the pericope. This janus verse leading from the topic of constructive speech to that of destructive speech is linked by *ʾîš,* the last word of its A verset and the initial word of vv. 27-29, and introduces the four malevolent speakers: a troublemaker (v. 27), the perverse (v. 28a), the slanderer (v. 28b), and the violent (v. 29). Verse 30 modifies the last, the violent person, and so omits it. Verse 26 may have been placed at the seam of the proverb groups pertaining to lips and mouth because it mentions *nepeš* ("appetite") in its A verset, matching *nepeš* in v. 24b, and "mouth" in its B verset, matching mouth and lips in vv. 23, 27, 30. However, in v. 26 mouth functions as an organ to gratify the appetite and not as an organ of speech. The proverb may be included here to safeguard the disciple against the fundamental urge to gratify drives and appetites through the kind of speaking that exploits others without labor. The appropriate means of gratification is painful labor. The catalogue of four malevolent speakers in vv. 27-30 reaches its climax in v. 29 both in its depiction of their character as violent and of their effects as "not good." Verse 30 brings the unit to closure, moving from evil communication to the crime itself. The "evil" *(rāʿâ)* that is planned in v. 27a is finally brought to pass in v. 30b. This *inclusio* is reinforced by "his lips" (vv. 27b, 30b). The catalogue warns the disciple to keep his distance from them (see 4:14-15). The "way" *(derek)* that leads to "death" and is "not good" forms an *inclusio* around the whole (vv. 25b, 29b), recalling that v. 30 belongs with v. 29.

25 This proverb on the lethal danger of deceptive pride recalls vv. 18-19. The repetition of 14:12 here functions to introduce the subunit on bad speech (vv. 25-30).

26 This synonymous parallelism states a toiler's basic drive for food, which serves as an exemplar of all his drives and appetites and goads him on to productive work. *The appetite* (*nepeš;* see 16:24), which also stands in parallel with "mouth" in Eccl. 6:7, refers to the basic desires and drives of all animate beings (see I: 90). The root behind *of the toiler (ʿāmēl)* and *toils (ʿāmᵉlâ)* connotes burdensome labor.[111] Schwertner summarizes its basic meaning here as "the process of work . . . and the trouble that it causes,"[112] and *HALOT* gives as the verb's first meaning "to exert oneself" and of the noun, "trouble."[113] *For him* suggests that the toiler's appetite

111. The gnomic perfective is used to form a paronomasia between the two words.

112. Schwertner, *TLOT,* 2:925, s.v. *ʿāmal.*

113. *HALOT,* 2:845, s.v. *ʿml.*

serves him well. The Suffering Servant will see the rewards of his "toil"/ "work" and be satisfied (Isa. 53:11). *Surely (kî)* indicates that verset B emphasizes and clarifies verset A.[114] *His* (i.e., the toiler's) *mouth* has its rare literal use in this book. In the Hebrew text "his mouth" stands in the outer frame as a parallel to *nepeš ʿāmēl.* The original meaning of *nepeš,* "throat," matches "mouth." *Urges . . . on (ʾākap)* is a *hap. leg.,* but its parallel *ʿāmal* in the proverb's inner core points to its meaning. On the basis of Aramaic cognates, *HALOT* renders it "to press someone hard."[115] *The toiler (ʿāmēl)* stands in marked opposition to the sluggard *(ʿāṣēl),* who also craves but whose appetite cannot overcome his lack of will to work (13:4). Though work is tiring and frustrating in this fallen world, nevertheless the drive to gratify his appetites prods the diligent person to productive efforts. The history of civilization is unimaginable without it.[116] God and the wise do not frustrate these primal, productive drives and appetites by denying them gratification (10:3) or by gratifying them apart from work (cf. 3:27; 10:3a; 1 Thess. 4:11; 2 Thess. 3:10). On the other hand, they frustrate the wicked by not rewarding them (10:3b). The righteous have an appetite for spiritual "meat" (cf. John 6:27).[117]

27 This is the first of three proverbs in the catalogue that begin with *ʾîš*. Each of these malicious persons in his own way overturns the regulations for social order. This proverb identifies the nefarious troublemaker and fortifies the disciple against him (see 6:12-15). Its synthetic parallelism represents this paragon of evil as one who concocts inflammatory speech (v. 27a) and then propagates it (v. 27b). Verset A implicitly compares him to a chef who cooks up a red-hot dish, and verset B explicitly likens his glowing fare to a fire that scorches all faces (cf. Ezek. 20:47[21:3]). *A troublemaker* (see 6:12) is equated with one who *prepares* (*kōreh;* see n. 91) *mischief* (or harm or evil, *rāʿâ,* see 1:16) for others. *And* adds the simile *on his lips (ʿal-śᵉpātō),* suggesting that the preparation of evil pertains to speech. [*It is*] supplies the needed subject for the clause in verset B. *Like* explicitly compares his mischievous speech to *a scorching (ṣārābet) fire* (see 6:27). The meaning of *ṣārābet* can be determined from the verb *ṣārab* in the *Niphal,* "is scorched" (Ezek. 20:47[21:3]) and the *ṣārebet* ("scar") from a burn (Lev. 13:23, 28). The troublemaker is like a flamethrower who scorches others, though the notion that his mischief scars his own lips cannot be excluded.

114. *IBHS,* p. 665, P. 39.3.4e.

115. *HALOT,* 2:845, s.v. *ʿml.*

116. "Hunger! That unwearying good of men, so beneficial to the race, so pitilessly cruel to the individual" (Elmslie, cited by Cohen, *Proverbs,* p. 109).

117. "All other plenty besides my God is mere beggary to me" (Augustine, *Confessions,* bk. 13, ch. 8).

28 This synthetic proverb adds two more to the catalogue of malicious speakers: the perverse person and the perfidious slanderer. The former, who turns the moral order on its head, sets the whole community at loggerheads; the latter, who sullies another's reputation behind his back, alienates his closest friend from himself and from others. Both types distort reality to put others in the worst light (cf. 6:19). The talebearer, however, escalates the social damage in that by sowing suspicion and promoting hostilities he looses the closest ties (cf. 1 Pet. 4:15). *A perverse person* (see I: 110) denotes one who overthrows God's social order. His perversity originates in his heart (6:14; 23:33) and finds expression in his speech (cf. 2:12; 8:13; 10:31, 32; 16:28) and eyes (16:30). He *unleashes conflict* (see 6:14, 19). The Syriac paraphrases verset A: "The wicked threaten justice." *And* adds a third to the evil speakers. *The slanderer* (*nirgān;* see 16:20) glosses a verb that in its one occurrence in the *Qal* means "to find fault, grumble," where it is parallel to "those who are wayward in spirit" (Isa. 29:24). In its two occurrences as a finite verb in the *Niphal* it means "to show oneself (i.e., to behave as) a grumbler." Both refer to Israel's unreasonable and unfaithful murmurings against their gracious God. This kind of murmuring is more clandestine and behind the scene — they murmured in their tents — than *lûn,* which denotes complaining in an open confrontation.[118] This slight datum suggests that the *Niphal* participle (see also 18:8; 26:20) denotes a malicious gossip who misrepresents a situation and by his calumny aims to besmirch and to defame others behind their backs. In 17:9 the talebearer also implicitly repeats a matter without confronting the wrongdoer directly. Both are concerned with garrulous friends who have not learned candor. The result of such behavior is devastating; it decimates even the most intimate relationship. *Is one who alienates* denotes spatial separation and with people may connote social alienation (cf. Gen. 13:9, 11, 14). In Proverbs this connotation comes to the fore (see 18:1; 19:4). The *Hiphil* in 16:28 denotes that *a close friend* (see 2:12) participates indirectly as a second subject in the event.[119]

29 The climactic fourth bad speaker, *a violent person* (see 3:31), denotes a cold-blooded murderer who is motivated by greed and hate and employs as his favorite instrument false accusation and unjust judgment. The predicate now continues the escalation from preparing evil (v. 27), to stirring up conflict (v. 28a), to alienating a close friend (v. 28b), finally to *entices* [see 1:10] *his companion* (*rēʿēhû;* see 3:28), presumably to abet him in his crime (see 1:11-14). *And* signifies the logical consequence (see n. 94). Clines and Gunn argue that "entice" occurs in situations where an attempt to persuade

118. G. W. Coats, *Rebellion in the Wilderness* (Nashville: Abingdon, 1968), pp. 192-93.

119. *IBHS,* pp. 434-35, 27.1d-e.

someone is unsuccessful,[120] but that is not so here. The violent person *leads him* (*hôlîkô;* lit. "causes him to walk") *in a way* [see 1:15] *that is not good* (see I: 98; cf. Ps. 36:4[5]; Isa. 65:2), a litotes signifying "one altogether evil and destructive."[121] The poem in 4:10-19 emphatically warns the disciple to avoid this way because of its tragic consequences.

30 This verse forms a proverb pair with v. 29. Its two participial clauses, modifying the violent person in v. 29, depict him as executing the ruin that he devises by gesturing with his eyes and mouth to his accomplice behind their victim's back (see 6:13). The complementary gestures modify both "to devise perversity" and "brings evil to pass" (cf. 6:13). Within the subunit the final proverb escalates malicious speaking to clandestine sign language and within itself progresses from "devising" evil to pulling it off. *Blinking* (*ʿōṣeh;* see n. 95) *his eyes* recalls the malicious winking *(qōrēṣ)* of the troublemaker's eyes in 6:13 (cf. 10:10). To *devise* (*laḥšōb;* see *maḥšᵉbôt,* 6:18) means "plan creatively," "scheme." *Perversity* (*tahpūkôt;* see I: 110) also connects the violent person with the perverse in 16:28. *Pursing* (*qōrēṣ;* see 6:13) *his lips (śᵉpātāyw)* has no reflex in the catalogue of Prov. 6:12-19 that indexes the behavior of malevolent people. The catchword with v. 27b here functions to communicate by gesturing, not by speaking. *Brings . . . to pass (killâ)* in the *Qal* means "to come to completion, to an end" (see 5:11), and in the *Piel* it has the factitive sense, to make his evil complete by adding to it until it is so full that the evil happens.[122] *HALOT* glosses it "accomplish."[123] The *inclusio evil* has the same nuance as in 16:27a.

3. The Splendid Crown of Old Age through Righteousness (16:31–17:6)

31 *Gray hair is a splendid crown;*
it is found in the way of righteousness.
32 *Better to be a patient person*[1] *than a mighty hero,*
even one who rules over his spirit than one who captures a city.
33 *Into the bosom the lot*[2] *is hurled,*

120. D. J. A. Clines and D. M. Gunn, "'You Tried to Persuade Me' and 'Violence! Outrage!' in Jeremiah XX 7-8," *VT* 28 (1978) 20-27.

121. Delitzsch, *Proverbs,* p. 252.

122. J. Oswalt, *TWOT,* 1:439, s.v. *kālâ.*

123. *HALOT,* 2:477, s.v. I *klh.*

1. The abstract noun "patience" has a concrete meaning when balanced by a concrete noun (M. Dahood, *Psalms III: 101–150* [AB; Garden City, N.Y.: Doubleday, 1970], p. 411).

2. *Yûṭal ʾēt-haggôrāl* is construed an ergative construction (*IBHS,* p. 178, P. 10.3c).

and[3] *from the* LORD[4] *[come]*[5] *all its decisions.*

17:1 *Better a dry piece of bread with peace and quiet*
than a house full of sacrifices with strife.[6]

2 *A prudent slave rules over a shameful son,*
and receives the inheritance in the midst of the brothers.

3 *The crucible is for silver, and the furnace for gold,*
but the one who tests hearts is the LORD.

4 *One who pays attention to a malevolent lip is an evildoer;*[7]
one who listens to a destructive tongue is a liar.[8]

5 *The one who mocks the poor person reproaches his Maker;*
the one who rejoices over calamity[9] *will not escape punishment.*

6 *The [splendid] crown of the aged is children's children,*
and the glorious [crown] of children is their fathers.[10]

The catchword "way" paves the transition between the preceding unit and this one (vv. 29, 31). This unit on old age through righteousness is bounded by the

3. Or "but" (see 16:1).

4. The LXX paraphrases the verse: "All [evils] come upon the ungodly into their bellies; but all righteous things come of the Lord." The Targ. and the Syr. add "oppressor" [*ʿnt*] before "is cast": "Into the lap of the oppressor falls the lot, but from God goes forth his judgment."

5. The preposition entails a verb of motion (*IBHS,* p. 224, P. 11.4.3d).

6. Lit. "sacrifices of strife," meaning that the participants wage war against each other, even as *šaʿarê-ṣedeq* ("gates of righteousness"; Ps. 118:19) means the gates through which the righteous enter and *zibḥê-ṣedeq* ("right sacrifices"; Ps. 4:5 [6]) means sacrifices offered by the righteous. The Targ. takes it as an attributive gen.: "quarrelsome feasts." M. Dahood (*Proverbs and Northwest Semitic Philology* [Rome: Pontifical Biblical Institute, 1963], p. 37) cites U. Cassuto for the analogy in Ugar. *dbḥ dnt,* "a banquet of contention."

7. Or "An evildoer pays attention to a malevolent lip; a liar listens to a destructive tongue." Normally, *mēraʿ* is the predicate stating what the subject is like (*IBHS,* pp. 132-34, P. 8.4.2).

8. Because the abstract noun "lie" is used for a concrete sense (see n. 1), there is no need to emend the text to *šāqqar* (see Gemser, *Sprüche,* p. 73).

9. "Perishing" *(apōllymenǭ)* of the LXX is generally thought to represent *leʾōbēd* ("perishing"; cf. 31:6; Fichtner [*BHS*]) or to interpret the abstract noun for the concrete (Gemser, *Sprüche,* p. 73). However, as with the addition in the Targ., "of his neighbor," "his calamity" may be a paraphrase of the Hebrew. The LXX adds an explanatory addition to the end of the verse. Driver ("Problems in the Hebrew Text of Proverbs," *Bib* 32 [1951] 182) thinks that *ʾēd* is a ptcp. of *ʾwd,* which, according to an Arabic cognate, means "to be burdensome; to be burdened (with trouble)." Hebrew parallelism, however, is not so precise as to demand investing a usual and sensible word with an unattested meaning to form a concrete equivalent to *rāš.*

10. The LXX[B] adds a verse at the end of v. 6: "The faithful has the whole world full of wealth, but the faithless not even a farthing."

inclusio "splendid crown" in 16:31 and 17:6. The frame, entailing an education proverb that introduces the unit, motivates youth to embrace the virtue of these proverbs to win the crown that gives them social splendor. Instead of viewing old age as the time of physical weakness and decline, when virility and fertility have ceased (Gen. 18:11-12; Ruth 1:2; 1 K. 1:4; 2 K. 4:14) and when the aged must resign their authority and hand over power to the new generation, this unit views it as a time of authority, status, and dignity symbolized by a crown. 16:31 ascribes this shining aurora to a person's righteousness, and 17:6 escalates that splendor to future generations. If gray hair by itself crowns a person by displaying he has lived a righteous life (cf. Ps. 92:14[15]; Prov. 20:29), how much more his children to the third and fourth generations, to whom he has successfully passed on the family's testament and secured its heritage into the foreseeable future. The unit first lays the foundations of righteousness in spirituality and theology (16:32–17:3) and concludes by adding two unrighteous speakers under God's judgment, the liar and mocker of the poor, to the catalogue of malevolent persons in 16:17-30.

31 The introductory saying implicitly admonishes the disciple both to respect the authority of gray hair and to win the magnificent crown of beauty, dignity, and authority (v. 31a) through serving others, not self (v. 31b; cf. 23:22; Gen. 47:7-10; Lev. 19:32; Job 12:12; 15:10; Ps. 71:18; cf. Wis. Sol. 4:8-9). The 22 occurrences of *gray hair (śêbâ)* in the Old Testament are associated with "old age" (20:29). It is often considered a blessing (Gen. 15:15; 25:8), but not always (Hos. 7:9), and it is treated with respect (Lev. 19:32). Here it *is* equated with *a splendid crown* (*ʿᵃṭeret tipʾeret;* see 4:9; cf. Isa. 3:5; 9:15), a magnificent adornment to enhance its wearer's beauty and authority (see 4:9; cf. Isa. 3:5; 9:14[15]). Of the 23 references to the "crown," six intensify its beauty and glory by "splendor" (Prov. 4:9; 16:31; Isa. 62:3; Jer. 13:18; Ezek. 16:12; 23:42). *It is found* [see 3:13] *in the way* (*derek;* see 1:15) *of righteousness* (see I: 97) implies that it is attainable for all who seek it in a three-dimensional sense. The proverb presents an essential truth but not the whole truth. Sometimes the righteous die prematurely (cf. Ps. 44:22; Prov. 3:1-12; Isa. 57:1), and old age brings infirmity with it (Eccl. 12:1-8; see I: 108). In modern society the moral value of the gray head is further tarnished in that it is often achieved through amoral and even immoral technology, not through virtue.

32 This "better . . . than" proverb shifts from the exalted teacher, who is to be emulated, to the disciple, reminding him that the foundation of righteousness is his ability to rule his unruly spirit when provoked. "Without the disciplined, wise conquest of oneself, mastery of the external world and its problems — in any area and of every sort — is not possible."[11] More spe-

11. Van Leeuwen, *Proverbs,* p. 162.

cifically it admonishes him to overlook a wrong done to him because it is more beneficial to self and society than the hero who by his physical might conquers an enemy (see 19:11; cf. Judg. 8:1-3; Jas. 1:19, 20). (The proverb is not concerned whether the military hero is good or bad; cf. 21:22; 24:5; 30:30.) Verset A asserts the superiority of the patient person to the hero, and verset B qualifies them as a ruler and a conqueror respectively. *Better . . . than* asserts the utilitarian benefits of spiritual virtue over physical gain without virtue (see 3:14; 8:11, 19; 15:16, 17; 16:8, 18, 19). *A patient person* (see 14:29), who is contrasted with the hothead in 15:18 (cf. 14:17; 29:22), does not retaliate to avenge a wrong. In the parallel he is defined as *one who rules over* [see 12:24] *his spirit* (see I: 92). The spiritual ruler surpasses *a hero* (*gibbôr;* cf. 6:34; 8:14). Kosmala defines *gibbôr* as "a particularly strong or mighty person who carries out, can carry out, or has carried out great deeds, and surpasses others in doing so."[12] The parallel shows that a military hero is in view. He is *one who captures* by force *a city* with its defensive walls (see 1:21) against the opponent's will (*lōkēd;* 5:22). *Even* assumes that verset B stands in apposition to verset A. The proverb entails a battle of inner self; it considers self-control the highest kind of human power (25:28). Abot 4:1, commenting on this verse, says, "Who is strong? He who controls his passions." "The taking of a city is child's play compared with this 'wrestling with flesh and blood.' That is only the battle of a day. This, the weary, unceasing conflict of life."[13]

33 This verse adds a necessary caveat. Ultimately, the LORD, not the disciple's self-possession, rules his destiny, as illustrated by "the lot." Verset A presents its secret handling by people, and verset B the divine judgment behind it. The proverb emphatically matches *in the bosom* (*ḥêq;* see 5:20) and "from the LORD" as the first phrases in the synthetic parallels. *Ḥêq* here denotes the secret holding area in the fold of the garment above the belt where hands were placed and the lot remained covered and uninfluenced (cf. Prov. 17:23).[14] *The lot* (*gôrāl;* see 1:14) was a small stone used to reveal God's selection of someone or something out of several possibilities where he kept people in the dark and desired their impartiality in the selection.[15] *Is hurled*

12. H. Kosmala, *TDOT,* 2:373, s.v. *gābar.*

13. Bridges, *Proverbs,* p. 250.

14. Cf. *HALOT,* 1:312, s.v. *ḥêq.*

15. For example: (1) the distribution of goods or booty (cf. Job 6:27; Ps. 22:18[19]; Nah. 3:10; cf. Matt. 27:35; Prov. 1:14); (2) the order of the priests and their duties (1 Chr. 24:5-19; 26:13-16; Neh. 10:34; cf. Acts 1:26); (3) Saul as king (1 Sam. 10:20-21); (4) the families who had to relocate to give a proper distribution of the populace (Neh. 11:1); (5) warriors for battle where only a percentage was required (Judg. 20:9); (6) the time for action (Esth. 3:7), and (7) the offender out of several (Josh. 7:14-18; 1 Sam. 14:40-42; Jon. 1:7). Sometimes the phrase "before the LORD" was added in partic-

(yûṭal) means to cast someone or something violently away from someone.[16] This unexpected verb contrasts to other texts that use neutral terms for the human manipulation of the lot.[17] The unexpected verb may suggest that the selection of an offender is in view, as the Targ. and the Syr. perceived (see n. 4). However, the proverb should not be restricted to retribution.[18] The lot's selection was final because it was ultimately "hurled down" by God (cf. 18:18). The conjunctive can be glossed by *and* or *but* because verset B both contrasts human and divine activity and combines them (see 16:1). *All* underscores that there are no exceptions. *Its decisions* (*mišpāṭô;* see I: 97) refers back to the masculine topic *gôrāl,* not the LORD, because that would be tautologous. [*Come*] *from the LORD* (see 16:1) traces the mediated action of "hurling (down)" back to Israel's covenant-keeping God. Even when the pagan sailors used the lot, the Sovereign ruled through it (cf. Esth. 3:7; 9:1, 2; Jon. 1:7). After the outpouring of the Spirit the practice of casting lots does not occur in the church. The pagan use of the lot, however, may suggest its appropriate use by the state (e.g., in drafting its warriors) and other secular institutions (e.g., in selecting candidates for organ transplants).

17:1 This *better . . . than* proverb is paired with 16:32 (see 16:31–17:15). As inward control over one's spirit has priority over external military might, so spiritual peace and quiet within a household have priority over its physical feasting (cf. 12:9; 15:16-17; 16:8). Its precise antithetic parallels contrast a dinner party consisting of a piece of bread that had not been dipped into a dish of savory sauce of oil, vinegar or the like (cf. 19:24

---

ularly sacred matters: (8) the allocation of the holy land (Joshua 18–20, e.g., 18:6), and (9) the selection of the scapegoat (Lev. 16:8). (The use of the Urim and Thummim should be discussed separately; cf. Exod. 28:30; Lev. 8:8.)

16. The other 13 uses of the verb occur in situations involving hostility and/or judgment: of Saul's lethal spear against David (1 Sam. 18:11; 20:13), of the LORD hurling Shebna (Isa. 22:17) and Israel out of the land (Jer. 16:13; 22:26, 28; Ezek. 32:4), of a person being overwhelmed by Leviathan (Job 41:9[1]), of a saint stumbling but not being cast down (Ps. 37:24), of the LORD hurling a storm against the sea (Jon. 1:4), and of the sailors' hurling first the cargo into it not only to lighten the ship but also to appease their Sea god (1:5) and then Jonah to appease the LORD (1:12, 15; see J. Sassoon, *Jonah* [AB; New York, London, Toronto, Sydney, Auckland: Doubleday, 1990], p. 94).

17. The other verbs are: *yāṣā'* "to come out" (Num. 33:54; Josh 18:11; 19:1, 17, 24; etc.), *'ālâ* "to come up" (Lev. 16:10; Josh. 18:11; 19:10), *šlk (Hiphal)* "cast" (Josh. 18:8, 10; Mic. 2:5), *ydd* "cast" (Joel 3:3 [4:3] (*Hiphal*?); Nah. 3:10; Obad. 11; and *npl* "fall," in the *Hiphal* (1 Chr. 2:13; 24:31; 25:8; 26:14; Neh. 10:35; 11:1; Esth. 3:7; 9:24; Ps. 22:18[19]; Prov. 1:14; Isa. 34:17) and in the *Qal* (Ezek. 24:6; Jon. 1:7).

18. The lot was used for the selection of an offender after it was decided that a wrong had been committed. It was never used to decide right and wrong, nor to determine the guilt and innocence of an individual (cf. Num. 5:11-31; *pace* Baumgartner, *Critique,* p. 159 and Aitken, *Proverbs,* p. 210).

[= 26:15]), but nevertheless was enjoyed in security, versus unlimited royal banquets plagued with strife. The proverb escalates the two dinners of 15:17. Presumably the quiet harmony and strife were engendered respectively by the love and hate of that proverb (cf. 10:12). *Dry* here denotes the lack of moisture and connotes an undesirable piece of bread (cf. Lev. 7:10). *Piece of bread* (*pat;* see Ruth 2:14)[19] stands as the exact opposite of "full of sacrifices" in its quantity (singular versus "full" + plural) and quality (dry bread versus juicy meat). *With peace and quiet* (see 1:22) infers that carefree security is warranted and that no one was harmed. *House* (see 11:29) is gapped in verset A. *Full of* signifies that a space is filled with as much of something as it can hold. *Sacrifices* (see 7:14) should be distinguished from *ṭbḥ,* which lacks cultic connotations (see 9:2). Bergmann renders *zebaḥ* here "sacrificial meat with strife," though recognizing that some translate "feasting with strife," and notes that the meat was taken home (see 7:14).[20] *With strife* (*rîb;* see n. 6; 15:18) is both a metonymy associating the sacrifice with the conflict of the celebrants (cf. 1 Sam. 1:3-7) and ironic, for a sacrifice was offered to the LORD in joy (cf. Deut. 12:7, 11, 12, 21; Judg. 16:23; 1 Sam. 11:15; 20:6). "The picture is of a 'religious,' wealthy household in which public piety is married to internecine conflict — a topic taken up in the next verse."[21] The proverb instructs the disciple in several ways: (1) to prefer a frugal meal with family concord, not a sumptuous one with discord; (2) to accept a modest lifestyle of having not even sufficient produce and therefore a respect for the produce of others; and (3) to be ready to lower radically his economic expectations, and even his rights, to enjoy a feeling of well-being (cf. 1 Cor. 11:17-34).

2 This proverb, paired with 16:32b, by asserting that *a prudent* [*maśkîl;* see I: 94] *slave* [see 12:9] *rules over* [see 16:32] *a shameful son* (see 10:5) teaches that family leadership depends more on character than on natural birth. *And (û)* introduces the reason for the slave's exalted position. In 10:5 the same juxtaposition of prudence and shame pertained to diligence in contrast to sloth. He *receives* (*yaḥ^{a}lōq* "has primarily the socially defined meaning, '(give or receive) the portion coming to one by law and custom.'"[22] *An inheritance* [see 3:35] *in the midst of* [see 5:14] *the brothers* (see 6:19; cf. 18:24)[23] validates the slave's status as a legal heir of the patrimony. By law and custom the son of the household has every advantage over the menial

19. R. Hubbard, *Ruth* (NICOT; Grand Rapids: Eerdmans, 1988), p. 172.

20. J. Bergmann, *TDOT,* 4:12, s.v. *zebaḥ.*

21. Van Leeuwen, *Proverbs,* p. 166.

22. M. Tsevat, *TDOT,* 4:448, s.v. *ḥālaq.*

23. Note the assonance of *maśkîl yimšōl* in the A verset, and of *yaḥ^{a}lōq naḥ^{a}lâ* in the B verset.

slave, and ordinarily it would be outrageous for a slave from outside the family to take possession of the family's heritage that sustains its life and standing (19:10; Eccl. 10:7). The slave, by contrast, judicially has no control over his fortunes and no hope for his future (see 11:29). However, contrary to judicial law and custom, one's virtue, not the privilege of birth, ultimately counts for more in social and economic standing. The death of the father is presupposed in that his heirs are spoken of as brothers, not as sons, and this infers a long range view of the contest between virtue and rights of primogeniture. The law made no provision for this supplanting of a foolish son by a prudent slave, but it did provide for stoning a rebellious son (Deut. 21:18-21).[24]

3 This verse bases this truth on the omnicompetence of the Tester of character to reward virtue. By the two images of a crucible to test the purity of silver and of a small melting oven to try the genuineness of gold (cf. 27:21), this emblematic parallelism teaches that God strips bare all pretensions and tests all human hearts to determine their genuineness and purity. In treating the LORD's knowing the human heart (15:3, 11; 16:2; 21:2), the author separates appearances and professions from reality.[25] *The crucible (maṣrēp)* occurs only here and in the repetition in 27:21A. *Ṣārap* denotes the process of cupellation, the melting of precious metals to refine and purify them by a technical process (Isa. 1:25; 48:10; Jer. 6:29; Dan. 11:35; Zech. 13:9) and/or "to try/test" them (Pss. 17:3; 26:2; 66:10) and so sometimes "to prove" their purity and value (Ps. 18:30[31] [= 2 Sam. 22:31; Prov. 30:5]; 105:19; 119:140). Here its parallel *bḥn* shows that with *for silver* (*lakkesep,* see 2:4) it means to try and test it, not to refine it (cf. Pss. 11:4-5; 17:3; 26:2; 66:10; and especially Zech. 13:9). The same is true of *and the furnace,* a small melting oven,[26] *for gold* (see 11:22). The melting point of gold is 1,063 degrees Celsius, and of silver, 961 degrees. Some types of smelting furnaces were made of clay, with two small openings at the bottom, one for blowing and fanning the flame, the other for letting off the molten lead at the end of the process. The pure metal was retrieved by breaking the clay. Human be-

24. A slave could inherit the estate of a childless man, and if a slave married the daughter of a free man who lacked a son he became head of the household (1 Chr. 2:35). However, no historical incident precisely matches the proverb. Joseph managed a significant rise from being a slave to becoming a ruler in the household of his owners (cf. 37:26; 39:4, 16; 41:12, 45), and Jeroboam supplanted Solomon's son as ruler over Israel (1 K. 11:28-39). In the New Testament faithful Gentiles, who were without hope, replaced faithless Israel, who was a natural son (cf. Rom. 11:11-21). The sages, however, normally treated the elevation of a slave above a prince with contempt (Prov. 19:10; 30:22, 32; Eccl. 10:7).

25. Plöger, *Sprüche,* p. 201.

26. *HALOT,* 2:446, s.v. *kûr.*

ings can design instruments to tests the purity of silver and gold, *but the one who tests (bōḥēn) the hearts* (see I: 90), none excluded, *is the* LORD (see 17:1). *Bḥn* with God as subject and a human being as object denotes divine examination and divine knowledge and usually does not connect his acquisition of knowledge with any normal activity (cf. 27:21). Both it and *ṣārap* in half of their occurrences "give the impression that one attains knowledge purely intellectually or intuitively."[27] Although outward actions and behavior betray the heart, people also conceal their hearts from others (cf. 1 Sam. 16:7) and even from themselves (Jer. 17:9). The proverb consoles and sobers the disciple with the implicit truth that the omnicompetent Sovereign deals with each person justly according to his ethical purity (cf. Job 23:10; 1 Cor. 4:3-5; 1 Pet. 1:7). It also encourages him to join the psalmist in asking God to expose his heart to himself so that he may see his offensive way and, repenting, he may be led in the everlasting way (Ps. 139:23-24).

4 Like the preceding unit that concluded with four malevolent speakers, so this one concludes with two malevolent communicators: the liar (v. 4), whose speech unleashes misery on the community, and the mocker of the poor, who blasphemes God (v. 5). The omnicompetent LORD will punish them (v. 5), and presumably those who are crowned with old age shun them. The synonymous parallelism of v. 4 underscores the startling truth that the one who listens to lies is himself a liar. The topic is *the one who pays attention* [see 1:24; 2:2] *to a malevolent* (*'āwen;* see 6:12) *lip* (see 16:27), which is a precise parallel to *the one who listens to a destructive* (II *hawwôt;* cf. I *hawwâ* in 10:3) *tongue* (see 10:20/21; 12:19; 31/32). II *hawwâ* denotes here destructive forces that bring ruin.[28] The destructive forces, always plural in this use, are usually evil speech (Ps. 38:12[13]), which in many instances is associated with lies and treachery (cf. Job 6:30; Pss. 5:9[10]; 52:2[4], 7[9]; 55:11[12]; 57:1[2]; 59:11[12]; 94:20). The person who gives his ear to such evil is himself *an evildoer* (*mēra';* see 3:7), more precisely *a liar* (*šeqer;* see 6:27). How one uses his lips and tongue is inseparably connected to that which he inclines his ears. Both the liar and his willing audience have no taste for truth. "Evil words die without a welcome; and the welcome gives us away."[29]

5 The unit concludes climactically before the frame by implicitly censuring *the one who mocks (lō'ēg) the poor person* (see 10:4), such as the one who survives on a dry scrap of bread in 17:1. *Lā'ag* occurs 12 times and means to assail and treat another with ridicule, contempt, and derision as an enemy (cf. 1:26; 2 K. 19:21 [= Isa. 37:22]; Job 9:23; 11:3; 22:19; Pss. 2:4;

27. Tsevat, *TDOT,* 2:70, s.v. *bḥn.*

28. *HALOT* (1:242 s.v. *hawwâ*) glosses the lexeme as "destruction," "threats."

29. Kidner, *Proverbs,* p. 123.

59:8[9]; 80:6[7]). Its parallels include *bûz* "to despise" and *śḥq* "to laugh at" (cf. 1:26). Here its parallel, *the one who rejoices* [see 2:14] *over calamity* (see 1:26, 27), often used for the fate of the wicked, defines the manner of and the reason for the derision. The arrogant rich person, having no sympathy for the poor person's unfortunate situation of being without friends and financial security, regards him as an enemy he vanquished and treats his economic ruin with contempt. His derisive words and mocking gestures, however, *reproach his* [i.e., the poor person's] *Maker* (see 14:31). Because he poured contempt upon the King's image and committed treason against his Sovereign, he *will not escape punishment* (*yinnāqeh,* "be acquitted"; see 6:29), probably a divine passive. The Sovereign made the poor, called him into existence as his image bearer (see also 14:31; cf. Gen. 9:6; Mark 12:16-17), and appointed for him his lowly station, but the haughty mocker supplants God's sovereign control with his superiority over his victims. The Sovereign will treat the one who discredits the pitiful as his enemy and will punish him for his arrogant cruelty. Other proverbs that warn against oppressing the destitute and/or admonish treating them kindly include 14:21; 15:25; 22:16, 22-23, 28; 23:10-11; 30:14. The LXX addition at the end of the verse captures the proverb's intention: "but he that has compassion shall find mercy." Job did not even gloat over the misfortune of those who set themselves up as his enemies (Job 31:29; cf. Prov. 25:21-22). Christians rejoice with those who rejoice and weep with those who weep (Rom. 12:15).

6 This verse, by using the metaphor of the "splendid crown of old age," completes the frame (see 6:31–7:6). Its complementary parallels motivate youth to be righteous (e.g., modest, v. 1; industrious, v. 2; genuine, v. 3; truthful, v. 4; compassionate, v. 5). In the old age bestowed by righteousness they and their children to the third and fourth generations will shine an aurora of glory on each other (cf. 20:29). *The crown of the aged (zᵉqēnîm),* which is "the most common and general term for someone old"[30] and certifies the meaning of *śêbâ* in the parallel of 16:31, *is children's children* (see 13:22), representing the potential limit of living descendants. The proverb pictures them gathered around the aged parent like a crowning diadem. *And* complements the splendor of parents through children with the splendor of children through parents. *The splendid* [*crown*] *of children* [see 4:1] *is their fathers,* not excluding mothers (see 1:8) of each generation (see 4:1-9). The proverb assumes the righteousness of its parallel in 16:31; otherwise the generations would not be compared to glorious crowns. Godless families collapse (17:1), and godless children bring their parents shame (cf. 10:5; 17:2; 19:26). This complementary splendor proves that the family heritage is ancient, enduring,

30. The etymological meaning of *zāqēn* ("beard") is dead, for the term is once used of an old woman.

and true. Israel boasted in their renowned father, Abraham (Matt. 3:9; John 8:33). Ancient Israel regarded children as a mark of divine blessing and reckoned them among the things that gave a man weight and influence in the community (Pss. 127:3-5; 128:3-4; 144:12-15), while childlessness was a curse (Jer. 22:30). By contrast, in the New Covenant dispensation, Jesus Christ, who had no biological children, blessed the church to reproduce spiritually, not physically (see Matt. 28:18-19; Luke 24:50-51; John 20:22; cf. 15:5-8; 1 Cor. 7:8-9, 25-35).

4. A Collection of Proverbs on Fools (17:7-28)

7 *An eloquent*[31] *lip is not fitting for a godless fool;*
how much more unfitting[32] *is a lying lip for a nobleman.*
8 *A bribe is a magic stone*[33] *in the eyes of its owner;*
to whomever[34] *he turns he thinks he will succeed.*
9 *Whoever would foster love is one who covers over a transgression,*[35]
but whoever repeats[36] *a matter separates close friends.*
10 *A rebuke penetrates*[37] *more deeply into a discerning person*[38]
than flogging a fool a hundred times.[39]
11 *An evil person fosters only rebellion,*[40]

31. Gemser (*Sprüche,* p. 73, citing LXX), Fichtner *(BHS),* and *HALOT* (2:452, citing 17:2, s.v. I *yeter*) emend *yeter* to *yōšer* "upright," which Gemser renders as "trefflichkeit" ("excellent"), but this is a meaning of *yeter.* Besides, a fool is incapable of "upright" speech.

32. *Lō'-nā'wâ* is gapped in verset B.

33. The LXX resolved the proverb's superficial moral problem by substituting *paideia* (< *mûsār* "instruction") for *šōḥad* and omitting "magic stone."

34. Indefinite *kol* has the distributive sense "every" (GKC, P. 127c).

35. The normal syntax (*IBHS,* pp. 132-34, P. 8.4.2) is validated by the unambiguous syntax in the parallel 10:12.

36. The LXX and Syr. read *śānā'* ("hate"), a precise but facilitating parallel to "love." Moreover, "to repeat" forms a contrast with "covers a transgression," its true parallel.

37. LXX reads *syntribei* (< *tāḥēt* "to shatter"), a facilitating reading for the relatively much rarer *tēḥat,* the *Qal* imperfect of *nḥt.* "*Ḥtt* with *b* of the object is not Hebr." (Delitzsch, *Proverbs,* p. 258), and the weaker synonym of *nḥt, yrd,* is also used of words descending into a person in 18:8 (= 26:22).

38. LXX reads *kardion phronimou* (< *lēb nābôn,* see 18:15), which is probably due to its misunderstanding of *tēḥat.*

39. The multiplicative numeral, probably with *peʿāmîm* elided (*IBHS,* p. 287, P. 15.4b; cf. Eccl. 8:12). The Targ. uniquely adds "sticks," and Delitzsch (*Proverbs,* p. 258) adds *makkôt* (blows"), as in Deut. 25:3.

40. The LXX, Syr., and Targ., followed by the NASB, Moffatt, et al., understood *meri* as metonymy for a rebellious person and *rāʿ* as an abtract noun ("evil") and object. The

but a cruel messenger is sent[41] *against him.*
12 *Meet*[42] *a she-bear*[43] *robbed of her young by a man,*[44]
but [do] not [meet] a fool in his folly.[45]
13 *As for the one who repays evil for good,*
evil does not depart[46] *from his house.*
14 *The beginning of strife is one who breaks open a dam;*[47]
so before a quarrel breaks out[48] *drop the controversy.*[49]
15 *As for the one who pronounces a wicked person innocent,*
and as for the one who pronounces a righteous person guilty,
both, yes, both of them are an abomination to the LORD.
16 *Why in the world is there payment in the hand of a fool*
to buy wisdom when he has no capacity to learn?[50]
17 *At all times a friend*[51] *is one who loves,*[52]

Vulg., followed by the KJV, NIV, and NRSV, takes *m^erî* as acc. (cf. Deut. 31:27 and Neh. 9:17). The item adverb *'ak* and the meaning of *mry* support this view. The Targ. also misunderstood *mry* as derived from *mrr* ("bitter").

41. A divine passive.

42. The inf. absolute functions as a surrogate impv., as shown by *'al* in verset B requiring a gapped impv. (cf. 12:7; 15:22).

43. An epicene noun (*IBHS,* p. 107, P. 6.5.2a).

44. *Beth* could be adversative "against" (i.e., attacking a man), but were the she-bear attacking someone else she would pose little threat to another person, leaving its sense of agency with the passive as the better option. S. E. Loewenstamm ("Remarks on Proverbs xvii 12 and xx 27," *VT* 37 [1987] 221-24; 1987, p. 222) emends the form to *b^eyē'ūšô* or *b^eyē'ūsa* "in her desperation" to create a fitting parallel with *b^e'iwwaltô* "in his folly." The form is attested only in Mishnaic Hebrew, "where it describes the state of mind of the owner of a lost object, who has given up any hope of retrieving it." The attractive emendation, however, does not change the sense, is unattested in Biblical Hebrew, and is unnecessary.

45. The LXX read verset A as *pāgaš d^e'ābâ b^e'îš śākāl* ("care befalls a man of understanding") and freely paraphrased verset B to match "but fools meditate evil." The Targ. and Syr. also struggled with this verse.

46. K and Q, both reading *Qal,* understood the verb as *mîš* (cf. Ps. 55:11[12]) and *mûš* respectively. *Mîš* provides a better assonance with *mēšîb.*

47. Lit. "the one letting water flow freely."

48. After the *lipnê, hitgalla'* is probably an inf. cons., not a perfective.

49. The LXX read *mlym* ("words") instead of *mayim,* gave *mādôn* an impossible, positive legal sense (= *dikaiosynēs*), and read *n^eṭôš* as *n^eṭûš* (= *stasis kai machē* "sedition"). These errors led to a very different proverb: "Rightful rule gives power to words, but sedition and strife precede poverty." The Targ. and Syr. likewise lost their way.

50. Lit. "wisdom and there is no heart."

51. The article of class designates *hārēa'* as the subject (*IBHS,* p. 130, P. 8.4a).

52. Or "The [true] neighbor is a friend." The LXX uses *philos* in 14:20; 17:17; 21:17; 27:6; cf. 18:24.

and[53] *a relative*[54] *is born for adversity.*
18 *One who claps a palm*[55] *is a human being who has no sense;*[56]
the one who pledges a security[57] *in the presence of his neighbor.*
19 *One who loves strife*[58] *is one who loves transgression,*
and one who makes his doorway high is one who seeks destruction.[59]
20 *A person with a perverse heart*[60] *does not find good,*
and one with a corrupt tongue[61] *falls into evil.*
21 *The one who begets a fool brings himself grief,*[62]
and the father of a godless fool does not rejoice.[63]
22 *A joyful heart promotes healing,*
but a drained spirit dries up the bone.
23 *A wicked person accepts a bribe from the bosom*
to divert the paths of justice.
24 *Wisdom stands ready to serve*[64] *the discerning,*
but the eyes of a fool are [looking] at the ends of the[65] *earth.*

53. Or but.

54. Delitzsch curiously thinks that *'āḥ* is an acc. of state and the subject of *yiwwālēd* ("[The friend] is born as a brother . . ."). He also holds, as does Rashi (M. Lyons, "Rashi's *Commentary on the Book of Proverbs*" [submitted in partial fulfillment of the requirements for the degree of rabbi, 1936], p. 93), whom he does not cite, that "born" "means he then [in adversity] for the first time shows himself as a friend."

55. *Tôqēa'* is the grammatical and conceptual subject (*IBHS,* pp. 132-35, P. 8.4.2). Not every senseless person makes a pledge.

56. A sortal appositional construction (*IBHS,* p. 230, P. 12.3b).

57. Lit. "the one who pledges a pledge," an effected cognate acc. (*IBHS,* p. 166, P. 10.2.1f).

58. Or "One who loves transgression is one who loves strife."

59. The LXX, apparently missing the connection between the versets, combined verset B with v. 16.

60. Abstract for the concrete (see nn. 1 and 8).

61. Lit. "corrupt in the sphere of his tongue."

62. Lit. "to grief," a syntactic equivalent of a predicate nominative (10:1). The preposition *lamed* implies the verb of motion, "bring" (*IBHS,* p. 224, P. 11.4.3d). Fichtner (BHS) believes that it is due to dittography (cf. 10:1) but overlooks the assonance of the line (see n. 110). The Targ., Syr., and Vulg. gloss this relatively rare word (Job 19:2; Prov. 10:1; 14:13; 17:21) as "shame" in 10:1 and 17:21.

63. In addition to some other variations, the LXX adds: "But a wise son gladdens his mother" (cf. v. 25: 10:1).

64. The ancient versions did not understand the complex preposition consisting of *'et* ("with") and *pᵉnê* ("face of"), meaning "before, in the presence" (*HALOT,* 3:941, s.v. *pāneh*).

65. The absence of initial *he* in L and other mss. may be haplography due to final *he* of the preceding *bqṣh.*

25 *A foolish son is a vexation to his father*
and brings bitterness to the one who bore him.
26 *If even*[66] *to fine an innocent person*[67] *is not good,*
how much more flogging nobles is against what is upright.[68]
27 *One who knows knowledge is one who restrains his words,*
and an understanding person is cool[69] *of spirit.*
28 *Even a fool who holds his tongue is thought to be wise;*[70]
one who stops up his lips, to be discerning.

The unit on fools picks up where the *inclusio* of 17:6 with 16:31 left off. It elaborates and expands the catalogue of malevolent communicators (vv. 4-5), mentioning the liar (v. 7), the briber (v. 8), and the gossip (v. 9). Like an overture to a symphony, this introduction sounds themes that will be picked up in the remainder of the chapter: corrupt officials and justice (vv. 7, 15, 26), bribery (vv. 8, 21), and reserved speech and friendship (vv. 9 and 17, 19, 27-28).[71]

The collection of proverbs from 17:7 to 17:28 are mostly synthetic proverbs pertaining to fools (see I: 109). *K^{e}sîl* ("fool") occurs in 17:10, 12, 16, 21, 24, 25; 18:2, 6, 7; *nābāl* ("churl") in 17:7, 21; and *'^{e}wîl* ("fool") in 17:28). Other co-referential terms for fools in synthetic parallels — in contradistinction to antithetic proverbs that mention the wise — occur in vv. 8, 11, 12, 13, 14, 15, 16, 19, 20, 21, 23, 25, and 26. These include three rearing proverbs that introduce the subunits, vv. 10-15, 16-20, and 21-28. In the antithetic parallels, the fool is mentioned in the emphatic B verset (vv. 9, 22), and in v. 10 the order is reversed in a comparative proverb to emphasize the fool's incorrigibility. The friend in the synthetic proverb of 17:17 functions as a foil to the fool in 17:19. The catchword *nādîb* (noble) in vv. 7 and 26 forms an *inclusio* around the unit. Thus the unit begins by cautioning nobles against

66. Initial *gam* in this book always emphasizes the next word and never coordinates clauses (cf. 14:13, 20; 15:7; 17:26, 28; 19:24; 20:11; 22:6; *IBHS,* pp. 662-64, P. 39.3.4c, d; *pace* K. Heim, "Structure and Context in Proverbs 10:1–22:16" (Ph.D. diss., University of Liverpool, 1996), p. 218.

67. *'nš* can occur with acc. of person or with *lamed* and person (*HALOT,* 2:859, s.v. *'nš.*

68. Toy (*Proverbs,* p. 353) corrects the MT to *bal yāšār* ("is not right") on the basis of LXX *oude hosion,* and Gemser (*Sprüche,* p. 75), followed by Fichtner *(BHS),* emends it to *yeter* (= excessively). Neither is necessary.

69. K *w^{e}qar* (so LXX, Syr., Vulg.; cf. 25:25); Q *y^{e}qar* (= rare/precious of spirit); the Targ. read Q but interpreted it to mean "heavy of spirit." The confusion of *waw* and *yodh* is commonplace. Both are *hap. leg.,* but K is more difficult and supported by Egyptian analogies.

70. Acc. of state (*IBHS,* pp. 171-72, P. 10.2.2d).

71. Cf. Meinhold, *Sprüche,* p. 286.

lying and ends with a tyrant who flogs righteous officials! The co-referential terms for the wise in vv. 27-28 stands in striking contrast to vv. 7-26. These synthetic proverbs teach the wise how to cope with the vexation caused by fools.

a. Janus: Catalogue of Fools Expanded (17:7-9)

7 This subunit takes up where the preceding unit left off, returning to the topic of lying. Its synthetic parallels employ the chiastic evaluative pattern - (churl) + (eloquence) // + (nobles) - (lying lip) (see 11:31; 15:11) in an a fortiori argument.[72] The meaning *eloquent* for II *yeter* (see 2:21) is debated.[73] The meaning of II *yeter* can be sketched as "what is left behind, remaining" > "what remains behind" > "excessive."[74] In the last sense it normally refers to quantity, "abundance" (Ps. 31:23[24]; Dan. 8:9; so Targ.). The parallel *šqr* ("false"), however, suggests a notion of quality, not quantity, giving rise to varying interpretations. BDB opts for "arrogant,"[75] and Delitzsch chooses "lofty" in the sense of "superabundant self-consciousness and high pretension."[76] Both glosses of II *yeter,* however, are unattested in Hebrew, and the predicate "not fitting" in the sense of improper is inapposite. Arrogant and pretentious speech match the pariah's character, as Nabal demonstrated (1 Sam. 25:10-11). A fool's eloquence, however, is as grotesque as a ring of gold in a swine's snout (11:22). Probably the lexeme here has its positive sense of "excellent" as in Gen. 49:3 and its Aramaic cognate *yattîr* in Dan. 2:31; 5:12 (so KJV, NASB; cf. "fine" in JB, NRSV). Since the churl is incapable of moral excellence, the Vulg. rightly rendered it *conponita* ("eloquent") and paraphrased *lip* (see 17:4) as "word." *Is . . . fitting,* when modified by *not,* denotes being "beautiful, lovely," and with *for,* "suitable, proper, fitting" (19:10; 26:1; Ps. 33:1).[77] According to Roth, *a godless fool* (*nābāl,* whose root originally meant "tear out") denotes a sacrilegious outcast, the opposite of the "noble" *(nādîb).* The *nābāl* curses God (Job 2:9-10), insults him (Ps. 74:22) and his servants (39:8[9]), and has no regard for his benefits (Deut. 32:6) or judgment (2 Sam. 3:33; 13:13; Jer. 17:11) because he denies that God exists to uphold a moral order (Ps. 14:1). Isaiah describes his unethical behavior against God's image: "[He] speaks folly, his mind is busy with

72. Note the consonance of */l n/: l' n'wh lnbl . . . lndyb.*

73. N. M. Waldman ("A Note on Excessive Speech and Falsehood," *JQR* 67 [1976-77] 142-45) argued for the meaning "false" from an alleged parallel semantic development of Akk. *watāru* "be excessive" to "exaggeration," "falsehood," "untrue things."

74. Cf. *HALOT* 2:452, s.v. II *yeter.*

75. BDB, p. 452, s.v. I *yeter;* so Rashi.

76. Delitzsch, *Proverbs,* pp. 256-57.

77. *HALOT,* 2:657, s.v. *nā'wâ.*

evil; he practices ungodliness and spreads error concerning the LORD; the hungry he leaves empty, and from the thirsty he withholds water" (Isa. 32:6-7). A healthy society regards him as a scamp and a scoundrel (1 Sam. 25:3, 17, 25; 2 Sam. 13:33; Job 30:8; Isa. 32:5). It becomes "one of the strongest possible terms to denote godlessness."[78] *How much more* (see 11:31) introduces the weightier argument (see 19:10). *A lying lip* (see 10:18; cf. 6:17) that deceives to hurt *is not fitting* [see n. 32] *for a nobleman* (*lᵉnādîb;* see 8:16), who is a powerful and respected member of the king's court (cf. 17:26; 19:6; 25:7). Though the fool is sharply contrasted with the pariah (cf. Isa. 32:5-8) and with the needy in Ps. 113:8, the proverb assumes that he is capable of lies. In sum, if the virtue of eloquence in style is unfitting for social outcasts, how much more the vice of lies in substance for nobles!

8 The proverb moves beyond warning the noble against false speech to warning against bribery (cf. 15:27; 17:23).[79] *A bribe (haššōḥad)* "is never used of a disinterested gift" (see *mattān* in 15:27);[80] its 20 other occurrences mostly pertain to a gift that adversely affects the administration of justice (see 6:35; cf. Exod. 23:8; Deut. 16:19; 17:23).[81] This practice is akin to robbery (1 Sam. 8:3; Isa. 33:15), used by the rich to exploit the poor (Ps. 15:5; Isa. 5:23), and will come under God's judgment (Job 15:34; Ps. 26:9-10; Mic. 3:11). *Is a magic stone* (or charm, *'eben ḥēn*) is a *hap. leg. Ḥēn* essentially denotes that which disposes others to favor or accept someone or something (see

78. W. M. W. Roth, "NBL," *JBL* 10 (1960) 407.

79. I am indebted to the excellent discussion on the ethics of bribery by my student, D. J. Montgomery, "A Bribe Is a Charm," in *WWis,* pp. 134-49.

80. Kidner, *Proverbs,* p. 124. Noonan summarizes the difference between a bribe and a gift: "A bribe expresses self-interest, a gift conveys love; a bribe subordinates the recipient to the donor, a gift identifies the donor with the recipient. A gift brings no shame, a bribe must be secret. A gift may be disclosed, a bribe must be concealed. The size of a gift is irrelevant; the size of a bribe, decisive. A gift does not oblige, a bribe coerces" (John T. Noonan Jr., *Bribes* [New York: Macmillan, 1984]).

81. *HALOT* (4:1,457, s.v. *šōḥad*) thinks that it means simply "gift" in 1 K. 15:19; 2 K. 16:8; Prov. 21:14; Isa. 45:13. The "gift" of Prov. 21:14, however, is given in discreet secrecy so that it will not be open to public scrutiny; its negative use of *šōḥad* is consistent with the other proverbs (cf. 6:35; 17:8, 23). Isa. 45:3 pertains to a transactional bribe (i.e., to achieve justice the poor could not have their cases heard at all without the bribe — an effective way of thwarting justice without resort to flagrant illegality; cf. R. L. Langston, "A Biblical Perspective on Bribery and Extortion and Its Implications in the Philippine Context from a Missionary Viewpoint" [D.Miss. project, Trinity Evangelical Divinity School, Deerfield, Ill., 1989]). The two situations in Kings pertain to a gratuity with attendant obligations on the recipient that adversely affect justice. Asa sends a *šōḥad* to Benhadad so that he will break his treaty with Baasha (1 K. 15:19), and Ahaz raided the temple treasury and sent one to Tiglath-pileser to attack Rezin and Pekah and so sealed an unholy alliance with him (2 K. 16:8).

1:9; 3:4). Its parallel supports *HALOT*'s gloss, "magic stone, which provides favor."[82] *In the eyes of* (see 3:7) denotes a fool's state of self-delusion and reliance on his own opinion (cf. 12:15; 16:2; 21:2; 26:5, 12, 16; 28:11; 30:12). Montgomery observes, "The subjects of these verses cover a wide range of 'villains'": the fool (12:15), the sluggard (26:16), the filthy (30:12), and the rich person (28:11).[83] Farmer notes, "The speaker does not ask us to believe that giving bribes *will* guarantee anyone's prosperity"; he merely "*think[s]* this will be the result."[84] *Its owner* (*bᵉʿālāyw;* see 1:19) probably denotes the bribe giver who owns the charm, not the bribe taker who thinks it is his due (cf. 3:27). *To whomever* (see n. 34) refers to the bribe taker who threatens the giver. *He turns (yipneh)* refers to the instigator of the bribe because "stone" is feminine; thus the masculine verbal action with *ʾel* refers to turning toward the threatening person, not a thing.[85] *He thinks* glosses the gapped "in his opinion." *He will succeed* (*yaśkîl;* see 1:3) in perverting justice in this book must be ironic (cf. 17:15), like 9:16; 18:11.[86] This fool's potent instrument succeeds with depraved officials, but not with God and the wise. The lobbyist's momentary success is leading him to eternal doom (see v. 15; cf. 1:20-33). In contrast to pagans, true Israel censured bribery.[87] The law forbade bribery because it opposed God, who shows no partiality and accepts no bribe (Deut. 10:17; cf. Exod. 23:8). The Christian even invites to his table those who cannot repay him (Luke 14:12-14). Felix apparently failed to get a bribe out of Paul; instead he received a message on righteousness, justice, and the judgment to come (Acts 14:24-26; cf. 1 Tim. 5:21; Jas. 2:1).

9 The final malevolent communicator is the gossip (v. 9), who destroys a community already threatened by transgression.[88] The verse also forms a transition to the next subunit on proper responses to fools, laying the foundation in love. The disciple restores a community threatened by wrongdoing by drawing a veil over another's sin to win his friendship and by not re-

82. *HALOT,* 1:332, s.v. *ḥēn.*

83. Montgomery, "A Bribe Is a Charm," in *WWis,* p. 139.

84. K. Farmer, *Who Knows What Is Good? A Commentary on the Books of Proverbs and Ecclesiastes* (Grand Rapids: Eerdmans, 1991), p. 88.

85. *Pace HALOT,* 3:937, s.v. *pnh.*

86. Gemser, *Sprüche,* p. 73.

87. J. J. Finkelstein ("The Middle Assyrian *Shulmanu*-Texts," *JAOS* 72 [1952] 77-80), commenting on cuneiform texts, says that although bribery of judges was regarded at least as a moral offense, "There is no known cuneiform law outlawing bribery specifically." A bribe "was not only a common practice, but was recognized as a legal transaction," and "legal action was taken only if the official did not honor the bribe."

88. Its versets are linked by two *Piel* ptcps., *mkssh/mbqqš,* the repetition of initial *mem* (three times), and the sibilants *s* and *š* (three times); the B verset by the broken consonance of *b/p+dr/rd* in *bdbr mpryd.*

peating his failure to avoid alienation. Verset A essentially repeats 10:12 but substitutes the concrete person for abstract "love" and adds "seeks." "Whereas in 10:12 love — that is, good will or friendship (compare 15:17) — disposes a person to forgive an offence, here the motive for forgiveness is a desire for *future* friendship."[89] If a lover protects an offender, how much more will he promote intimacy among saints. *Whoever would foster* [or seek what seems inaccessible; see 2:4] *love* [see 1:22; 15:17] *is one who covers over a transgression* (see 10:12). *But* marks the contrast. *Whoever . . . separates close friends* repeats 16:28. If gossip spoils a close friendship, how much more does it alienate neighbors. In its six other occurrences in the *Qal* (1 K. 18:34; cf. 1 Sam. 26:8; 2 Sam. 20:18; Neh. 13:21; Job 29:22; Prov. 26:11) *is one who repeats (šōneh)* always refers to doing something once more, a second time, never "again and again," "to harp on." Not even once does he repeat *a matter* (or word, *dābār;* see 11:13) "Matter" is a better gloss than "word" because the parallel is "transgression." The gossip makes future reconciliation impossible. The glory of the wise is that they do not seek vengeance (see 19:11), knowing that God will deal with the guilt of others (Neh. 4:5[6]) and sin will be punished (Prov. 11:21; 17:10, 12, 14).[90]

b. Fools and Their Punishment (17:10-15)

Verse 10 functions as a janus: it both qualifies covering over transgression by calling for verbal rebuke and corporal flogging, and, as an educational proverb, introduces the subunit on how to respond to fools in light of their certain judgment (17:10-15). This subunit also picks up where 16:31–17:6 left off, namely, with the threat of divine punishment (17:5). Moreover, v. 10, calling for a rebuke of the discerning and for the flogging of fools, qualifies the teaching of v. 9, which calls for drawing a veil over wrongdoing. The catchword "seek" in vv. 9b and 11a may serve to link the janus with the preceding subunit. Here is a thematic outline of this partial unit, italicizing catchwords linking the verses:

A Rebuke corrects a discerning person more than flogging a *fool* does. (17:10)
  B Whoever seeks *evil* encounters the cruel messenger. (17:11)
A′ Do not encounter a raging *fool.* (17:12)
  B′ The one repaying *evil* with good, *evil* will not depart from his household. (17:13)

89. Whybray, *Proverbs,* p. 256.

90. Ahiqar (VII) put it this way: "A good vessel that covers a word in its heart, and [not] a broken one that lets it out" (*ANET,* p. 429).

A″ Drop a quarrel immediately. (17:14)
B″ The one acquitting the guilty and the one condemning the innocent, the LORD detests both. (17:15)

The A/A′/A″ verses are admonitions on how to respond to the fool, who is mentioned explicitly in vv. 10b and 12b and implicitly in v. 14b. Versets A of vv. 12 and 14 begin with initial *pe,* alternating with initial *mem* in vv. 13 and 15, and use dramatic metaphor; their B versets use vetive forms. B/B′/B″ are descriptive proverbs that threaten fools with divine retribution. Verses 13 and 15 use initial *Hiphil* participles *(mēšîb, maṣdîq).* The wise know that fools' final punishment lies in God's punishment of them, not in their avenging themselves.

The first pair qualifies the admonition to cover over transgression with an implicit admonition to rebuke the discerning person and to flog the mocker, cautioning that flogging a fool will do little good by comparison (v. 10). God's cruel messenger of death will ultimately punish him (v. 11). The second pair warns against encountering a raging fool (13:12) and escalates both the fool's evil from seeking it to repaying good with evil and his punishment from personal death to ruin for his whole household (vv. 11, 13). The third pair escalates not encountering the raging fool to not provoking his anger in the first place (v. 14), but qualifies that by not perverting justice in acquitting him when he is guilty (v. 15).

10 This verse protects the preceeding saying from the immoral notion that the disciple can sweep sin under the rug. The wise person does not gossip but rebukes a discerning wrongdoer (see 27:5, 6, 9, 19) and flogs a fool. This comparative proverb, whose two halves share the common predicate of "penetrate," contrasts *a* morally indignant *rebuke* (13:1, 8) of *a discerning* (or understanding, *mēbîn;* see 1:2; 8:9) *person* with *flogging (hakkôt) a fool* (*k*ᵉ*sîl;* see I: 112-13). Of the 504 occurrences of *nākâ,* almost all occur in the *Hiphil,* whose meanings range from hitting to killing. In pedagogic texts it refers to flogging (see 17:26; 19:25; 23:13, 14; cf. 23:35 and *mûsār* in 1:2). *Penetrates* (*tēḥat;* see n. 37) represents a rare root that occurs once each in the *Niphal, Piel,* and *Hiphil* and four times in the *Qal* and essentially means to move from a higher to a lower place (cf. Job 21:13; Jer. 21:13). Twice it is used in the context of chastisement with *into* (*b*ᵉ*;* cf. Ps. 38:2[3]), and here in the metaphor of a rebuke descending into a person's inner being. The comparative *more deeply* is demanded by the initial comparative *than (min)* of verset B. Comparative *than* marks the standard to which the success of a rebuke is compared, namely, *a fool* (*k*ᵉ*sîl;* see I: 112-13) physically beaten with the a rod (see 23:13, 14). *A hundred times* (*mē'â;* see n. 39) is hyperbole. In the Egyptian papyrus *Sallier* from the New Kingdom, it signifies a round, exaggerated number, more than twice the 40 blows the law allowed for the worst crimes (Deut. 25:1-3; cf. 2 Cor. 11:14).[91] Measured flogging of the formative child, in contrast to the hardened fool, for wrongdoing will teach him wisdom (see 13:24; 20:30; 23:13-14; see "instruction" in 1:2). If youth would accept the sage's teaching, it would be spared the heartache mentioned in the rest of this unit. Bridges illustrates the proverb: "A word was enough for David (2 Sam. 12:1-7; 24:13, 14). A look entered more in Peter's heart (Luke 22:61, 62), than a hundred stripes into Pharaoh (Exod. 9:34, 35), Ahaz (2 Chron. 28:22), Israel (Isa. 1:5; 9:13; Jer. 5:3)."[92]

11 The fool steels himself against human beatings (v. 10b) and defies God (v. 11a) but cannot withstand the death the LORD sends against him (v. 11b). The synthetic parallels of v. 11, linking the fool's rebellion with God's retribution, are phonetically held together by the broken consonance of their initial phrases, *'ak-m^erî* ("only rebellion") and *mal'āk 'akzārî* ("cruel messenger"). The incorrigible fool is now equated with the morally repulsive *evil person* (*rā';* see 1:16) who *fosters* (*y^ebaqqeš;* see 17:9) *only rebellion* (*m^erî*). The nearly 100 occurrences of *m^erî* refer to people's willful, angry, defiant rebellion against God, though parents may be in view in Deut. 21:18, 20, and its use in Job 17:2 is uncertain. The evil person's defiant deportment pertains to both his attitude toward God, which grieves his Spirit (Isa. 63:10), and his disobedient behavior, which incurs his death sentence (Josh. 1:8). It is used in connection with *m'n* "to resist" and with "stiff-necked" (Deut. 31:27). The LORD equates this rebellion against him with "witchcraft" (cf. 1 Sam. 15:22). The proverb insightfully identifies the person who injures others as one who is totally dedicated to defying God and injuring him (see 14:2; cf. 1 John 3:4). *And* combines his rebellion with God's retribution. The hard-as-flint *cruel* (*'akzārî;* see 5:9; 12:10) matches the evil person's unrelenting, willful rebellion that hurts others and pains God (see 5:9; 12:10). This *cruel messenger* (*mal'āk;* see 13:17) *is sent* (*y^ešullaḥ;* see 6:14) *against him* from the throne of heaven, to judge from the consistent use of "rebellion" as against God and from the alternating structure in which God is the Agent (vv. 13, 15). The messenger is either a metonymy for the Angel of Death (see 16:14; cf. Ps. 35:5-6; 78:49) or, more probably, a personification of death itself (cf. 2:18). The human mediator of God's wrath may be God's just king, who represents him on earth (16:14). In any case, the messenger can be counted on to execute his assignment faithfully (cf. 13:17).

12 Verses 11 and 12 may be connected by the association of bears, who are proverbially notorious for their danger and ferocity (cf. 2 Sam. 17:18; 2 K. 2:23-24; Amos 5:19), with a cruel messenger of death. Verse 12 implicitly cautions the disciple to hand the fool over to this providence by ex-

91. See Meinhold, *Sprüche,* p. 288.

92. Bridges, *Proverbs,* pp. 261-62.

plicitly commanding him not to encounter a raging fool, a situation comparable to meeting a ferocious bear. *Meet (pāḡôš)* signifies to come face-to-face, eye-to-eye, on another in an unavoidable encounter that one or both parties intended. The encounter may be neutral (22:2; 29:13), favorable (Exod. 4:27), or, as here, unfavorable (Exod. 4:24; 2 Sam. 2:13). The command in this emblematic parallel is sarcastic and means "do not encounter." English usage demands interpreting the epicene noun as *a she-bear (dōb),* a biblical symbol for anger and ferocity. The Syrian brown bear *(ursus arctos syriacos)* stands up to two meters high and weighs up to 225 kilograms. "In biblical times the Syrian Bear was found over most of the hilly wooded parts of Palestine. . . . They had become scarce by a century ago. . . . The last bear in Palestine itself was killed in the hills of upper Galillee just before World War II." Her anger and ferocity are exacerbated by the phrase *robbed of her young* (cf. 2 Sam. 17:8; Hos. 13:8). "When accompanied by her cubs the she-bear . . . is more aggressive and potentially dangerous than usual."[93] *By a man* (see 2:12) shows the bear has been bereaved of her young by human action, not by accident, and so is bent on venting her anger and ferocity against the victimizer. Her cubs may have been captured for pleasure. On Egyptian monuments the Syrian as well as the Abyssinian bear appears among the tribute animals. But, in general, ancient bear representations are rather rare. *But* marks the antithetical command in the implicit a fortiori argument. If one should not confront a bear, how much more not a fool. *Do not,* which assumes an elided form of imperative "meet," *a fool* (*kᵉsîl;* see 17:10) *in his folly* (see I: 113), which, answering to "robbed . . . by a man," refers to his paroxysm of anger.[94]

13 The fool's rebellion (v. 11a) is escalated in its parallel (see 17:6-15) as black ingratitude (v. 13a), and the cruel messenger of death sent against him (v. 11b) is replaced by an evil guest who refuses to depart and punishes his host endlessly. Its versets are held together by the logic of cause-result and the assonance of *mēšîb rāʿâ ṭôbâ//tāmîš rāʿâ bêtô. The one who repays* (*mēšîb;* cf. *šûb* in 1:23) glosses a term that literally means "to cause someone or something to turn in the opposite direction." *Evil* here refers to moral insolence that harms (see 1:16), given in payment in exchange *for good* (see I: 98; cf. Gen. 30:15; 44:4; Ps. 38:12[13]). Sometimes paying back evil for good is glaring (cf. 1 Samuel 25; 2 Samuel 10–11; cf. Ps. 38:20[21]). Most times, however, it is so common that it is taken for granted. The fool inflicts evil on God's creation and society, both of whose good he takes for granted (cf. 3:29-30). Children spurn the gifts of their parents; and all humanity, after eating the fruit of the Creator's orchard, spat in his face (Gen. 3:5, 6; Rom. 1:18-32). In verset B *evil* (*rāʿā;* see 1:33; 22:3), now per-

93. G. S. Cansdale, *Animals of Biblical Lands* (Exeter: Paternoster, 1970), p. 117.
94. Delitzsch, *Proverbs,* p. 260.

sonified as a household guest, refers to the consequent harm of insolent behavior. *Not* modifies the whole situation. *Does . . . depart* (see n. 46) entails that a collection of distressing happenings has first been visited upon *his* [the subject of verset A] *house* (see 11:29). Who is the agent? On the human horizon no one is an island; society, especially a close-knit one as in ancient Israel, entangles the individual, his household (cf. 17:6), and others into an inseparable unity of cause-result relationships. The Ultimate Agent, however, upholding the moral order is the LORD (see I: 73). Only God can guarantee that justice will be served. Prov. 20:22 admonishes the disciple not to pay back evil but to wait for the LORD, presupposing the divine responsibility (cf. 3:31-35; 23:17-18; 24:19-20; 25:21-22; Deut. 32:35; Pss. 25:3; 27:14; 37:34; 62:5; Matt. 5:38-48; Rom. 12:17-21; 1 Thess. 5:15; Heb. 10:30; 1 Pet. 3:9). After Nabal, well-named "Fool" (1 Sam. 25:25), paid back the good of David's men with evil (25:21), the LORD smote him and gave his wife to David (25:36-42); after David paid back faithful Uriah with adultery and murder, the LORD took David's child and handed his children over to incest and murder (2 Samuel 11–13; cf. Judg. 8:35; 9:56; Ps. 109:5; Jer. 18:20-23).

14 This verse escalates its parallel imperative, not to encounter a raging fool, to not provoking his pent-up arrogance and anger in the first place. Verset A gives the motivation by a metaphor for literal admonition in verset B. *The beginning* (*rē'šît;* see 1:7) *of strife* (*mādôn;* see 6:14) *is* implicitly likened to *the one who breaks open* (*pôṭēr;* cf. Ps. 22:7[8]) *a dam* or sluice. *Peṭer* denotes the "firstborn" (what first opens and passes through the womb). An Akkadian parallel means "to open a source of water." The metaphor assumes that the "water" in view is that of *a dam* or sluice (cf. Eccl. 2:6-7). The verset likens the beginning of a bitter conflict involving the pent-up arrogance and anger of a fool to a person who digs a hole in a dam or opens a sluice. The seepage starts from a small aperture, but under built-up pressure it quickly bursts open and the small leak turns into a raging, uncontrolled cataclysm that gets out of hand and does irreparable damage. The conjunctive "and" is glossed *so* because verset B logically subordinates the consequence. *Before* (see 16:18) is temporal, and the *quarrel* (*hārîb;* see 15:18) in parallel with *mādôn* refers to an acrimonious controversy. *Breaks out (hitgallaʿ)* occurs only three times, all in Proverbs with reference to strife (see 18:1; 20:3). Its Arabic cognate *(jaliʿa)* means "to show the teeth":[95] "the exposing of the teeth by the wide opening of the mouth, as happens in bitter quarrels."[96] *Drop* (see 1:8) essentially means "to leave someone, something or some situation unattended and uncared for" and here "to desist from," "let alone."[97] If a

95. *HALOT,* 1:194, s.v. *glʿ.*
96. Fleisher, cited by Delitzsch, *Proverbs,* p. 261.
97. *HALOT,* 2:695, s.v. *nṭš.*

quarrel begins at all, processes of reconciliation, such as a gentle answer (15:1), must be brought to bear immediately on the situation to minimize the damage and restore calm for intelligent behavior (cf. 14:29; 15:18; 19:11; 20:3). David exemplifies the proverb. Before those who repaid his good with evil he wisely became as a deaf man who does not hear, and as a mute who offers no reply, but waited instead on the LORD (Ps. 38:12-20[13-21]). By contrast, the fool, who stirs up strife, is labeled a troublemaker (6:12-19), perverse (16:28), wrathful (15:28), angry (29:22), arrogant (28:25), and motivated by hatred (10:12).

15 The second admonition, which draws the subunit on how to react to a fool, balances the preceding. As v. 10 protects "covering over transgression" from the abuse of sweeping sin under the rug, this one protects the admonition to drop a quarrel from the abuse of being indifferent to justice by not finding the wicked fool guilty. Its versets are held together grammatically by the emphatic *yes, both of them,* referring to the two kinds of corrupt judges in verset A. In the Hebrew text verset A presents a terse, chiastic assonance: *maṣdîq rāšāʿ ûmaršîaʿ ṣaddîq. As for the one who pronounces the wicked person* [see I: 109] *innocent* denotes a corrupt judge who esteems and declares the behavior of the guilty as conforming to the divinely established moral order and so acquits them from the punishment of wrongdoing (cf. Deut. 25:1; 1 K. 8:32; Job 27:5). *And* links him as just as guilty with *as for the one who pronounces a righteous person* [see I: 97] *guilty* (see 12:2; cf. 17:26; 18:5; 21:21; 24:23b-25; 28:21; Exod. 23:7-8; Deut. 25:1; 32:4; 1 K. 8:32; Job 34:7; Pss. 45:7[8]; 94:20-21). In the ancient Near East corrupt judges more often acquitted the guilty and simply denied the innocent access to the court (see v. 8; Isa. 5:23; cf. Amos 5:7). The proverb corrects the popular misconception that it is better to set free ten guilty persons than to condemn one innocent person. Both *are an abomination to the LORD* (see 3:32).

c. The Fool versus the Friend (17:16-20)

The catchword "fool" *(kᵉsîl)* in its introductory educational proverb links this subunit with the preceding and following introductions (vv. 10, 16, 21). This subunit is held together and divided by the catchword "one who loves" (vv. 17, 19), contrasting the loving friend with the misanthropic fool who loves strife. Each of these is part of a proverbial pair in which the second saying qualifies the first. The loving neighbor who helps in distress (v. 19) should not be a stupid neighbor who takes on another's debt (v. 20). The misanthropist (v. 19) will fall into calamity through his perverse heart and tongue (v. 20). The first proverb pair is held together by the catchword "friend"/"neighbor" *(hārēaʿ).* The catchword "heart"/"sense" *(lēb)* in every other verse unites the whole (vv. 16, 18, 20). The unteachable heart and the perverse heart frame the incompetent heart sandwiched between them.

16 The introductory proverb implicitly calls on the disciple to accept correction and so have the moral capacity to comprehend the sage's teaching by the dramatic irony of picturing a fool grotesquely coming to the sage with money in hand to buy his wisdom. His rhetorical *why* does not wait for an answer but gives vent to the sage's exasperation at the absurd situation.[98] *In the world* adds an exclamation point to his exasperation.[99] [*Is there*] *payment (m*ᵉ*ḥîr)* denotes the act of giving goods — probably here money (cf. 1 K. 21:2; Job 28:15; Isa. 55:1) — in exchange for goods or services. Three other times (2 Sam. 24:24; 1 K. 10:28 [= 2 Chr. 1:16]) it occurs with *to buy* [see 1:5; 4:4, 5] *wisdom* (see I: 76). *In the hand* (see 6:15) stands in marked antithesis to the inner void *of a fool* (*k*ᵉ*sîl;* see I: 112), who hates knowledge of the moral order and scorns correction. The fool is as grotesque as one coming with fee in hand to acquire a prostitute (cf. Deut. 23:18[19]). Neither wisdom nor true love can be bought. The circumstantial clause *when he has no capacity to learn* (see I: 90 and n. 50) denotes his lack of moral sensibility and so his inability to understand wisdom (see 15:32). He shows his void by taking in wooden literalism the sage's metaphor admonishing the son to buy wisdom (cf. 4:4, 5, 7; cf. Isa. 55:1-3). He cannot interpret figurative language (see 1:6) because he has no heart to understand spiritual things (John 6:53-65; cf. 1 Cor. 2:10-16). Rather, he thinks everything can be had for money, not realizing that wisdom is a free gift of God to the faithful (4:7; 8:9; cf. Isa. 55:1-3; Matt. 13:9; Luke 24:25; 1 Cor. 2:13), and just as wrongly he thinks that the sage is as materialistic as he is. The proverb cannot be used to reconstruct a school situation for the dissemination of wisdom because it is a probably sarcastic literary fiction on the abused metaphor (cf. 14:16). The practice of paying a teacher is unattested before Hellenistic times, and charging tuition is unknown in Jewry down to the Middle Ages.[100]

17 The notion of the second proverb of this subunit resembles that of the second notion of the preceding subunit (17:7), escalating the implicit admonition not to gossip about a neighbor in his moral failure to an admonition to be his constant friend. *At all times* (see 5:19) is placed emphatically up front. *A friend* (*hārēaʿ;* see 3:28) refers to a true or ideal neighbor, like the ideal king in 16:10-16, not a fair-weather friend (cf. 19:4, 6). Since *rēaʿ* conceptually denotes "friend," to avoid tautology *'ōhēb* is best glossed *is one*

98. E. W. Bullinger, *Figures of Speech Used in the Bible Explained and Illustrated* (Grand Rapids: Baker, 1968), pp. 943-56, esp. 956.

99. *IBHS,* p. 323, P. 18.3b.

100. "The Talmudic principle was, "As I (God) taught you gratuitously, so must you teach gratuitously" (Cohen, *Proverbs,* p. 114; Clifford, *Proverbs,* p. 168).

who loves (see 8:17), not "friend" (see 14:20). It signifies the friend's recognition of the inherent worth and dignity of the one with whom he desires to be with at all times in a reciprocal relationship, even in extreme anguish and suffering. The true character of love expresses itself by substantive, unselfish action in adversity, not by outward kisses.[101] Ambiguous *and* could also be glossed "but" (cf. 16:33; 17:3). The parallels both combine one's reciprocal advantage in having a friend and relative and contrast the friend who chooses covenantal solidarity and a relative, who is born into that solidarity (cf. Luke 10:29-37). According to some, *a relative* (*'āḥ;* see 6:19) is an honorable designation for a friend (cf. 2 Sam. 1:26; 1 K. 9:13; Ps. 35:14) and for female correspondences (7:4; Song 4:9-10, 12).[102] However, the first two alleged instances are in direct address, "my brother," and Ps. 35:14 is not convincing. A proper correspondence to the wife as "sister" would be the husband as brother. Finally, Prov. 18:24 and 27:10 distinguish "friend" and "brother." *Is born* means "is brought forth as a child," and *for* represents the purpose of the birth as to help sustain the family in adversity (cf. 2 Cor. 12:14; 1 Tim. 5:8). *Adversity* (*ṣārâ*), a state of extreme and highly possible misfortune (see 1:27), stands in the outer frame with "at all times," contrasting and comparing the spiritual and natural relationships.[103] The friend is represented as always present, in good times and bad; the relative only in adversity. A friend rejoices and weeps with you (Rom. 12:15); a relative functions more as a safety net. But even in adversity the friend's spiritual ties are better and stronger than blood ties (18:24 and 27:10). Though the proverb does not state the nature of the distress, presumably it is not that of a sinner under God's judgment (see 1:22) but of one to whom benevolence is due (see 3:27; 11:8; 12:13). The proverb supports eyeball-to-eyeball charity, not impersonal and institutionalized agencies. While the king and his government assure justice and take care of the needy, he does not administer an impersonal welfare state that has great potential for corruption and despotism (cf. Deut. 24:17-22; Ps. 82:3[4]; Isa. 1:17; Jer. 5:28; 22:1-3).

18 This proverb, which is linked with the preceding by the catchword *hārēa'* ("the friend"/"the neighbor"), qualifies extending charity to the needy neighbor by labeling as sheer stupidity assuming legal responsibility for another's debt.[104] Risking one's present security on the fidelity of the neighbor to pay back his loan and on an uncertain future is the mark of a

101. G. Wallis, *TDOT,* 1:110, s.v. *'āhab.*

102. Meinhold, *Sprüche,* p. 291.

103. R. Whybray, *Wealth and Poverty in the Book of Proverbs* (JSOTSup 99; Sheffield: JSOT, 1990), pp. 23-24.

104. The repetition of *hārēa'* suggests that no difference between "friend" and "neighbor" is intended (*pace* Van Leeuwen, *Proverbs,* p. 168).

senseless person (see 6:1-5). In the chiastic synonymous parallels of v. 18 the subject, *one who claps a palm* (cf. 6:1), is a metonymy for its stock-in-trade parallel, *one who pledges* (see "to go surety," "go bail for" with a personal object in 6:1). *A security* refers to anything a person might put up as collateral, whether property or an oath, in exchange for future payment (22:26; cf. Neh. 5:3).[105] He is classified as *a human being* (*'ādām;* see 11:7; 16:1) *who has no sense* (*ḥ^a^sar lēb;* see I: 115). *In the presence of* glosses now spatial *lipnê,* "before").[106] *Lipnê* never means "for" in the sense of "on behalf of," *contra* all the ancient versions, NIV, NRSV, et al.[107] This meaning suggests that *his neighbor* (*rē'ēhû;* see 6:1; 17:17) refers to a witness to the transaction to make the pact more secure, not to the one to whom the creditor is liable or to the one being secured.

19 This verse continues the theme of neighbors that moves from the good (v. 17), to the stupid (v. 18), to the violent (v. 19). For the first time in this unit the consequence of sin is introduced.[108] "One who loves" links the proverb with v. 17, which presents the opposite kind of "lover" (= friend). In the chiastic, synonymous parallels, the topics "one who loves strife" and "one who makes his doorway high" (i.e., to exalt his mansion above that of his lowly neighbor whom he seeks to exploit; cf. 16:18; 18:12) form the inner core. The predicates, "is one who loves transgression" and "is seeking destruction," constitute its outer frame. The topics move from the consequence of "strife" to its cause of "pride" (see 13:10), but the predicates move from the cause of "transgression" to its consequence of "destruction" (cf. Job 8:4; Lam. 1:14). *The one who loves* (*'ōhēb;* see 1:22) *strife* (see 13:10) in either a verbal battle or coming to blows *is* one *who loves transgression* (see 10:12). *The one who makes . . . high* (*magbîah;* see 16:5) always means "to heighten" someone or something. It often connotes either inaccessibility and so protection, as in the case of an eagle who builds its nest on high (Job 39:27; Jer. 49:16 [= Obadiah 4]), or exaltation in contrast to lowliness (Ps. 113:5; Ezek. 17:24; 21:26[31]). To judge from 16:18 and 18:12 where *gbh,* "to be high," is juxtaposed with *šāber,* "destruction," as here, the latter is in view (cf. 6:17; 29:13). *His doorway (pitḥô)* refers to the opening or entrance wherein the

105. Leslie R. Freedman, "Biblical Hebrew *'rb,* 'to go surety,' and Its Nominal Forms," *JANES* 19 (1989) 25-29.

106. So BDB, p. 816, s.v. *pnh.*

107. The direct acc. is used when "stranger" *(zār)* is secured (11:15; 20:16; 27:13).

108. Almost as if to anticipate the criticism that its halves are disjointed, the parallels are bound tightly together by assonance: *'ōhēb peša' 'ōhēb maṣṣâ//magbîāh pitḥô m^e^baqqeš-šāber.* Seven of eight words have the labial stops /p/ and /b/, three have initially the nasal labial /m/, and the second words of each verset has the two unvoiced /p/ stops initially.

door or gate swung (see 1:21).[109] It functions as a synecdoche for a high house in relationship to the neighborhood, not that this one architectural feature is out of proportion with the rest of it. The LXX rightly paraphrases: "who makes his house high." If so, the high house symbolizes the pride of its owner (cf. 16:5). This arrogant misanthropist *is one who seeks* [see 2:4] *destruction* (see 15:4). He seeks to ruin others in his love to rebel against God, but in truth he is bringing about his own destruction, as did pretentious Shebna (Isa. 22:15-19), Jehoiakim (Jeremiah 13–19), and Haman (Esther). The agent is not stated, but since "transgression" is against God, we may assume that the LORD shatters him and his household.

20 This verse continues the theme of misanthropy but focuses on its dire consequences. The underlying image is of a straight way that a person twists (= "perverse") and overturns (= "corrupted"). *A person with a perverse heart* (see 11:20) is also *one with a corrupt tongue* (*nehpāk bilšônô;* see n. 61; I: 110). *And* combines his perverted heart, the governor of all body members (see 2:2; 4:23), with the commands that emerge from the tongue. The misanthropist's deep-seated, pathological degeneration against what is right works social havoc through his perverse tongue (see 2:12, 14; 8:13; 10:31-32; 16:28, 30). His perdition is certain, as emphasized by the two predicates, matching the negative with its positive equivalent. The heart *does not find good* (i.e., tangible prosperity; see 16:20), but he *falls* (a metaphor for "to perish"; see 11:14) *into evil* (i.e., calamity and a metonymy for pit; see 1:16). The misery he dug for others through his lies recoils upon him (cf. 12:13, 21). The notion, however, that he falls through (cf. 11:5; 13:17; 14:32) the moral evil (see 1:16) he unleashed by his lies cannot be ruled out. Like the "crooked man" in the nursery rhyme, the evil man can walk only a crooked mile. The fool came to the sage hoping to find good, but by his incorrigibility he unwittingly fell into the "calamity" (11:29). Only the righteous find "good" (11:23).

d. The Fool, Injustice, and the Reserved Speech of the Wise (17:21-28)

This subunit can be divided into two parts. Verses 21 and 25 pertaining to the failed rearing of a fool form an *inclusio* around the first subunit. The frame is formed by the catchwords "fool" *(k^esîl),* and in its chiastic structure, participles of the verb "bear" (*yld,* the first word in v. 21a and the last in v. 25b), and "father" (*'āb,* vv. 21b, 25a). Verses 21-22 form a proverb pair. Every verse, except the center, mentions the fool. That center pertains to the injustice of

109. There is no compelling reason, unlike the one in Mic. 7:5 that mentions "high mouth," to take it as a metaphor for mouth (*pace* Lyons, "Rashi's *Commentary,*" p. 94).

the "wicked," the ethical equivalent of fool, as represented by his bribing an official (v. 23). Verse 24 underscores the fool's godless orientation. The second subunit picks up on the theme of injustice. Verse 26, which is related to v. 23 by the stock-in-trade antonyms "wicked" and "righteous," escalates the theme of injustice from bribing officials to punishing righteous officials. Verses 27-28 state how the wise responds to the fool's vexations. The second subunit may be connected by the catchword *gam* (vv. 26, 28). In any case, vv. 27-28 radically alter the wisdom vocabulary from co-referential terms for fools to co-referential terms for being wise. In face of the fool's vexations, the final proverbial pair calls for being forbearing, returning to the need for self-control (16:32).

21 The fool not only brings about his own ruin (v. 20) but also diminishes the vitality of his parents. This proverb implicitly admonishes the disciple to be neither incorrigible nor insensible to God and humanity in order to avoid bringing unmitigated, palpable pain to his parents (cf. 10:1; 17:25; 23:15-16, 24-25).[110] Verse 23 asserts the consequent diminishing of their lives. In the chiastically constructed synonymous parallels of v. 21 the subjects constitute the outer frame and the predicates the inner core. The masculine form *the one who begets* (*yōlēd;* see 17:17; cf. 17:25) intends a metonymy for the father (see 23:22, 24). The incorrigible and misanthropic *fool* (*k^{e}sîl;* see I: 112) does not recognize his elemental solidity with the family (cf. 17:17) and so *brings himself* [i.e., the father against whom the fool acts] *grief* (see 10:1). Conjunctive *and* links the negative predicate in verset B that underscores its positive equivalent in verset A. *The father,* a synecdoche for both parents (see 1:8), is presumably wise because he grieves over his foolish son. *Of a godless fool* (see 17:7) characterizes the fool as a sacrilegious outcast. The father *does not rejoice* (see 5:18) because while he lives his son is a social outcast, squanders the family's inheritance, brings him shame, and offers no hope for the family to enjoy prosperity and social esteem in the foreseeable future.

22 This verse asserts the psychosomatic effects of v. 21 (cf. 14:30; 15:13, 30; 16:24; 18:14). Besides this notional connection, the proverbial pair is also lexically connected chiastically in its inner core by the catchword "rejoice"/"joyful" (*śmḥ,* vv. 21b, 22a) and in its outer frame by the co-referential terms "grief" and "broken spirit" (vv. 21a, 22b). Grief and joy are matters of death and life. Whereas v. 20 connected heart and tongue, this one connects heart and spirit (see 15:13; cf. 12:25; 13:12; 14:30). On its own the proverb admonishes the disciple to live in such a way that he experiences joy that revives and not depression that kills. *A joyful heart promotes healing (lēb*

110. The line also holds together through the assonance of *lamed* attested in every word but one: *yōlēd k^{e}sîl l^{e}tûgâ lô w^{e}lōʾ-yiśmaḥ ʾ^{a}bî nābāl.*

śāmēaḥ yêṭîb gēhâ) essentially repeats 15:13a, but substitutes "healing" for "face," necessitating glossing *yêṭîb* as "promotes," not "makes attractive."[111] The conjunctive functions as an adversative, *but. A drained spirit* repeats 15:13bα. The incomplete metaphor *dries up (t^eyabbeš)* depicts a negative state of perishing to be overcome and may be the result of divine punishment (cf. Job 14:11; Pss. 90:6; 102:11[12]; 129:6; Isa. 40:7; Ezek. 17:10; 19:12).[112] The opposite of a dry bone is a fatty one, full of marrow (3:8; 15:30; 16:24; Isa. 58:11). *The bone (gārem)* is a synecdoche for the whole person (cf. 2 K. 9:13). Its distinction from *ʿeṣem* (cf. 3:8) is unclear. Perhaps *gārem* emphasizes its hardness (see 25:15).[113] If so, then even the most firm and powerful perish when they become depressed. As 15:15 (cf. 18:14) makes clear, the difference between exhilaration and depression depends more on a person's spiritual resources than on his circumstances (cf. Acts 16:25). Depression can be avoided by fearing the LORD (3:7-8; 15:16), wisdom (15:24), hope (13:12), and good news (12:25; 15:30).

23 In the middle of proverbs pertaining to the failed rearing of a fool (vv. 21, 25), the malformed son is named "the wicked person," the ethical equivalent of fool.[114] He is epitomized as one who accepts bribes. *A bribe* (*šōḥad;* see 17:8) is taken out *from the bosom* (*mēḥēq;* see 16:33), where the briber kept it concealed and secret so as not to be seen in an open court with witnesses. *A wicked person* (*rāšāʿ;* see I: 109) is a metonymy for an official who can influence the judicial procedure. *Accepts* glosses *lqḥ,* which is as ambiguous as its English equivalent, "to take." It could mean "to take (i.e., to draw out of the pocket)" with reference to the one who proffers it (cf. 7:20; 20:16; 22:27), or "to accept" with reference to the one who takes it (cf. 1:3; 2:1; 4:10; 10:8). The latter interpretation accords better with 15:27 and Ps. 15:5: "He does not accept *(lāqaḥ)* a bribe against the innocent." Both the briber and the bribed act in order *to divert* (*haṭṭôt;* see 4:27; 7:21) justice. *Naṭâ* in the *Hiphil* with "justice" as object means "pervert," "deny" (see Exod. 23:2, 6; Deut. 16:19; 24:17; 27:19; Song 3:35). With *paths* (*ʾōrḥôt;* see 1:15, 19) it means "to turn aside," "divert from the path" (Num. 20:17; 21:22; 22:23, 26, 33). In this figurative use the path refers to the conditions and

111. *Gēhâ* is a *hap. leg.* The Syr. and Targ., followed by many, read "body," either having read *g^ewiyyâ,* "carcass," or guessed at a connection. Driver ("Interpretation du texte masoret," *ETL* [1950] 344) glosses "face" (cf. 15:13; so also Rashi), after Arab. *jihatun.* Delitzsch (*Proverbs,* p. 265, citing Hos. 5:13, Syr. and Eth. cognates, D. Kimchi, and LXX), BDB, and KBL derive it from the Hebrew verb *ghh,* "to heal," a metonymy of cause for "life" (BDB, p. 155, s.v. *gēhâ; HALOT* [revising *HALOT*^{2}, p. 173], 1:181, s.v. *gehâ).*

112. H. D. Preuss, *TDOT,* 5:378, s.v. *yābēš.*

113. Meinhold, *Sprüche,* p. 294.

114. So Meinhold, *Sprüche,* p. 294.

spheres *of justice* (*mišpāṭ;* I: 97) through which the oppressed poor, who have been sinned against by the oppressive rich, hope to gain access and through those legal procedures to find life (see 18:5). The corrupt official defies God who has placed him over the community to protect the poor. He shows that he is conscious of his guilt by accepting the sly bribe, which is concealed from public scrutiny and opprobrium, but not from God (15:11; 16:2; 17:3; 21:14).

24 The fool fails because he orients himself to distant, godless, and unattainable goals instead of on attainable wisdom that stands nearby ready to serve him well (cf. 8:9; 14:6; Deut. 30:11-13). His looking for godless profit in this verse may be related to his accepting bribes in the preceding verse; it will come to nothing.[115] The imprecise antithetical parallels of v. 24 juxtapose in the outer frame "in the presence of the discerning" with "on the ends of the earth," and in the inner core, "wisdom" and "the eyes of the fool." The imprecision suggests that the eyes of the wise focus on wisdom, which in turn serves them well, but the fool's focus flits from one godless, unattainable thing to another that does not profit him. The complex preposition *stands ready to serve* (or "is always at the service of," lit. "in the presence of"; see n. 64) occurs 32 times for near presence, mostly with reference to the presence of the LORD. It is often used in the context of a covenantal commitment wherein a subordinate stands and/or serves in the presence of an authority figure to be cared for and/or to serve (cf. 1 Sam. 2:11; 1 K. 12:6; Esth. 1:10). Even when it means simply "before/in the presence of" (cf. Gen. 19:13; 1 Sam. 22:4), it connotes that the one in whose presence someone or something exists takes personal responsibility to care for it or him. Here the one served is *the discerning* (*mēbîn;* cf. 1:2; 17:10), and the agent *is wisdom* (see I: 76). The conjunctive functions as an adversative, *but. The eyes of a fool* is a synecdoche for the insolent fool's direction and orientation (see 4:25; cf. Ps. 119:37). His eyes *are* [*looking*] *at* specifies the realm of his orientation. The construction *the ends of the earth* (*qᵉṣēh-'āreṣ)* occurs 24 times. Here it is used as a metaphor for wrong and unattainable goals. To the Israelite the phrase connoted places with ungodly ways far removed from the covenant people (cf. Deut. 13:7[8]; 28:49, 64; Ps. 113:7). David as an exiled king, out of the anguish of his heart, calls to God "from the ends of the earth" (Ps. 61:2[3]). The Syr. and Targ. captured its negative connotation by "depths of the earth."

25 The obvious connections between vv. 25 and 21 suggest that they form an *inclusio* framing this unit on a failed rearing and motivating the son not to be foolish because of his solidarity with his parents (see 17:17). The frame's catchwords are initial *one who begets* (*yōlēd,* masc., v. 21a) and final *one who bore* (*yôladat,* fem., v. 25b), *to* of disadvantage, *father* and *fool*

115. So Heim, "Structure and Context," p. 218.

(kᵉsîl). Verse 25, however, escalates v. 21 by adding the mother and sharpening "grief" to *vexation* (see 12:16a) and "grief" to "bitter affliction." Conjunctive *and* combines the father's grief to the mother's *bitterness* (*memer;* see 14:10). Though *memer* is a *hap. leg.*, its meaning, "bitterness" in the sense of "being grievous, distressful," not in the sense of "being resentful, intensely antagonistic," is not in doubt.[116]

26 This saying thematically escalates 17:23, with which it is partially connected by the stock-in-trade antonyms "wicked" and "righteous"/"innocent," from admonishing magistrates not to deny the innocent justice to not punishing the innocent, turning the judicial system on its head. The tyrant in view is a very high magistrate because he is in a position to flog subordinate nobles in the government's hierarchical structure (cf. Eccl. 5:8[7]). Its synonymous parallels pair two forms of legal punishment, "to fine" and "to flog," for two kinds of virtuous citizens, "an innocent person" and "nobles," and two negative evaluations, "is not good" and "is against what is upright." However, the asyndetic parallels probably intend as well to qualify the noble as innocent. *If even* (*gam;* see n. 66) suggests that an a fortiori argument binds the versets together. *To fine* (*ʿᵃnôš*) is more precise than "to punish" (KJV, NJPS, NIV) because *ʿnš* in the *Qal* means "to impose a fine"[117] (so NRSV). In this context pertaining to legal fines and punishment *ṣaddîq* means *an innocent person* (*laṣaddîq;* see 17:15). The corruption *is not good* (see 16:29) because it establishes tyranny as the coin of the realm. If it is wrong to fine any righteous person, then *how much more* wrong is *flogging* [17:10, 26] *nobles* (i.e., honest officials; see 8:16; 17:7). Corporal beating is more dishonorable and painful than a monetary fine (Deut. 25:1-3). Though nobles could be fools and not merit their honorific title (Isa. 32:5), the parallel "innocent" and the assertion that the flogging is against what is upright show that the nobles in view will not compromise their honor and be corrupted by the system. In 17:7 nobles are the antithesis of fools. *Is against* (*ʿal*) could mean, "on account of," but one then must supply "is not good," an addition not required by "against." *What is upright* (*yōšer;* cf. I: 98) denotes the ethical boundaries within which the community prospers. Thus the proverb admonishes the disciple not to be a tyrant (1 K. 21:11-13; Matt. 26:3, 4; Acts 4:1-3).

27 The preceding sayings explicitly speak of vexation from failed

116. The verb *mrr* in the *Piel* means "make bitter"; in the *Hiphil* "afflict"; in the *Hithpalpel* "become fierce." The noun *mōrâ/morrâ* (Gen. 26:35; Prov. 14:10) means "bitterness, misery." Other derivatives of the root *mrr* are *mārôr, mᵉrōrâ* ("poison," "bile"), *mᵉrērâ* ("bile"/"gall bladder"), *mᵉrîrût* ("agony, bitterness" [*hap. leg.* in Ezek. 26:6(11)]), *mamrôrîm* ("agony, bitterness" [*hap. leg.* in Job 9:18]), *tamrûr* ("bitterness," associated with mourning in Jer. 6:26).

117. *HALOT,* 2:859, s.v. *ʿnš*.

parenting and implicitly from experiencing injustice. The next two sayings, a proverb pair, caution the disciple to respond to provocation with either restrained speech (v. 27) or even total silence (v. 28) (cf. Isa. 53:7). The pair is connected lexically by wisdom vocabulary: "knowledge," "understanding," "wise," and "discerning." The contrast of this vocabulary to that of folly in this unit is striking (see 17:7-28). Verse 27 refers to "words," the product of the mouth, and v. 28 to "lips," part of the mouth. In its synthetic parallelism "one who possesses knowledge" and "a discerning person" are synonyms, but "one who restrains his words" and a "cool spirit" refer to the effect and its cause respectively. *One who knows* as a personal attainment (*yôdēaʿ;* see 3:6) *knowledge* [*dāʿat;* see I: 77] *is one who restrains* [see 10:19] *his words* (*ʾᵃmārāyw;* see 2:1). Conjunctive *and* binds this effect to the cause. *An understanding person* (*tᵉbûnâ;* see I: 96) *is cool of spirit* (*qar-rûaḥ;* see n. 69). The Egyptians used the words "hot" and "cool" in a metaphorical sense of two distinct personality types. The latter represents the ideal person, who is calm and without passion, and the ideal mouth, which speaks prudently.[118] The opposite of the cool spirit in Hebrew, Grollenberg argues, is *ʾîš ḥēmâ,* a person filled with the heated excitement of resentment (see 15:18). *Qar-rûaḥ* is probably the antonym for "quick temper" (*qᵉṣar-rûaḥ,* 14:29), for in 14:29 *qᵉṣar-rûaḥ* is juxtaposed with "understanding" *(tᵉbûnâ),* whereas here *qar-rûaḥ* is equated with it and is probably to be equated with the "patient person." Both the LXX and the Syriac gloss it as "patient." The competent restrain their speech because restrained speech best serves piety and ethics (cf. 14:29; 15:18; 16:32). The measure of the son's wisdom is the extent to which he attains this ideal (cf. Jas. 3:2). The Lord Jesus serves as the example (Isa. 53:7; Matt. 27:14; Mark 14:61; 1 Pet. 2:23).

28 In addition to the thematic links of restrained speech and of wisdom vocabulary binding vv. 27 and 28, they are also linked by the catchword *bîn* (*tᵉbûnâ* "understanding" and *nābôn* "discerning"), and by the broken consonance of */ḥ~ś/š/* in *ḥôśēk* "restrain" and *ḥrš* "keep silent." This phonological binding points up the escalation of the theme from restrained speech to silence. This connection also involves a change of syntax. The expressions for restrained speech are the predicates in v. 27, "is one who restrains his words"/"is cool of spirit," and those for silence are the topics in v. 28, "holds his tongue"/"stops up his mouth." The proverb aims to admonish the disciple to hold his tongue when provoked, not to conceal his stupidity as in the Abraham Lincoln's witticism: "It is better to keep your mouth shut and let them think you a fool than to open your mouth and remove all doubt." The asyndetic structure of its parallels and their synonymity suggest that verset B is in

118. R. P. L. Grollenberg, "A propos de Prov. VIII,6 et XVII,27," *RB* 59 (1962) 40-43.

apposition to A and "is thought" is gapped. If so, "who shuts his mouth . . ." also modifies "fool." There is then an escalation between the parallels marked by *even* (*gam;* see 17:26). *A fool* (*'ᵉwîl;* see I: 112) *who holds his tongue* [see 11:12] *is thought* (*yēḥāšēb;* see 10:19) *to be wise* (see I: 94), the antithesis of a fool (see 10:1). With an impersonal accusative (see n. 70) *ḥšb* "appears to be a fixed idiom meaning 'reckon something (as something) to someone's account.'"[119] *One who stops up,* which is used with "ears" (Ps. 58:4[5]; Prov. 21:13; Isa. 33:15) and as an uncertain architectural term for a closed, barred (?), framed window (1 K. 6:4), is used uniquely here with *his lips* (see 10:19). Such a person is thought *discerning* (*nābôn* or insightful; see I: 95). The proverb mentions the fool, not to rehabilitate him but to argue from the lesser to the greater. Based on the premise that the fool does not have the wisdom imputed to him, he can be thought discerning in the absence of contrary condemning speech. If even the fool, whose mouth is otherwise imminent terror (10:8), whose chatter (10:8) invites a beating (12:16), and who shows his vexation on the same day (12:16), is reckoned as wise for bridling his tongue just once, how much more a wise person (cf. Job 13:5)! However, this proverb pair calling for being self-controlled, taciturn, and forbearing must be held in tension with those calling for confronting the fool's wrongdoing with open rebuke and beatings (cf. 17:9-10; 22:15; 26:5). The wise do not react rashly out of heated passions but speak and act deliberately in full control of their emotions, aiming to restore the erring to friendship, not to defend themselves.

5. The Speech of Fools versus the Speech of the Wise (18:1-21)

1 *The one who separates himself seeks self-gratification;*
against all sound judgment[1] *he starts a quarrel.*
2 *A fool does not delight in understanding*
but in his heart's exposing itself.[2]
3 *When a wicked person*[3] *comes, contempt also comes;*
and with shame is reproach.

119. K. Seybold, *TDOT,* 5:234, s.v. *ḥāšab.*

1. The LXX uniquely translates *tûšîyâ* "at all times," perhaps to match *tō'ᵃnâ.*

2. To account for "foolishness" in the LXX (Syr., Targ.), A. J. Baumgartner (*Étude critique sur l'état du texte du Livre des Proverbes d'après les principales traductions anciennes* [Leipzig: Imprimerie Orientale W. Drugulin, 1890], pp. 167-68), rejecting *bᵉhôllot* (e.g., Fichtner [*BHS*]; cf. Eccl. 1:17), retroverts *bᵉhôlᵉlût* ("madness").

3. Many (e.g., Toy, *Proverbs,* p. 358), probably with Vulg. (= *impius*), emend *rāšā'* to *reša'* ("wickedness") to be consistent with the other abstract nouns (see 11:2). But this emendation overlooks the connection of the wicked person with the misanthropic separatist (v. 1) and the fool (v. 2).

4 *The words of a person's mouth are deep waters;*
the wellspring of wisdom is a rushing stream.[4]
5 *To show favoritism to*[5] *the guilty is not good,*
and so[6] *denies the innocent justice.*[7]
6 *The lips of a fool come*[8] *into controversy,*
and his mouth cries out for beatings.
7 *The mouth of a fool brings terror to himself,*
and his lips are a trap for his very life.
8 *The words of a slanderer are like tidbits;*[9]
they[10] *descend into one's innermost being.*[11]
9 *Even the one who is slack in his work,*
is[12] *a brother of him who destroys.*[13]
10 *The name of the LORD is a fortified tower;*
a righteous person runs into it and[14] *is protected on high.*
11 *The wealth of a rich person is his fortified city,*

4. Lit. "wadi" (i.e., a valley that in winter becomes a torrent valley of water). Several medieval mss. and the LXX read *ḥayyîm* ("life"; cf. 10:11; 13:14; 14:27; 16:22) instead of the unique, and so more difficult, text of the MT, Targ., Syr., and Vulg.

5. Lit. "to lift up the face of."

6. *Lamed* with the inf. cons. is ambiguous. It could be nominative ("to deny"), a parallel to "to lift up," or express purpose ("in order to deny") or explain the circumstances of the preceding action ("denying") (*IBHS,* pp. 604-9, P. 36.2.3b, d, e).

7. Lit. "in [the paths of] justice."

8. The Targ. and LXX translate "bring [him]," perhaps reading *yābîʾû,* but elsewhere in Proverbs the *Hiphil* takes an object (21:27; 23:12; 31:14), which these versions insert here. GKC, P. 145u explains the masc. pl. with the fem. dual subject as due to "the dislike of the 3rd plur. fem. imperf." (cf. Job 15:6; Prov. 5:2; 10:21, 32; 18:6; 26:23)

9. M. Rottenberg ("There Is No Word from the Root *lhm* in the Bible," *Leš* 45 [1981] 153-54), denying that there is a Hebrew root *lhm,* redivides and revocalizes *kmtlhmym* as *kᵉ[dibrê] metel hōmîm — metel* being from *tll* (cf. Exod. 8:29[25]) and *hōmîm* from *hmh* (cf. Jer. 6:23; 50:42). He interprets this to mean, "They sound soft and moderate just like the words of a clown." He is not convincing because, in addition to emending the text, the syntax is unlikely, the connection of a mocker with soft and moderate sounds is implausible, and the comparison in general is not good. The emendations in *BHS, kᵉmamtaqqîm* ("like sweet things") and *makkōt hōlᵉmîm* ("beatings of dreamers") are both unnecessary and the second is infelicitous.

10. Lit. "and they."

11. Lit. "descend into the casket of the belly." The LXX, Targ., and Syr. seem to have read a different Hebrew text.

12. Lit. "even as for the . . . , he is."

13. Lit. "an owner of destruction." In 28:24 the equivalent idiom, *ʾîš mašḥît,* is used.

14. Probably *waw* consecutive.

and like a high city wall in his imagination.[15]
12 *Before destruction a person's heart is high and haughty,*[16]
but before honor is humility.
13 *As for the one who replies before listening,*
it is to him folly and shame.
14 *A person's spirit can endure even sickness,*[17]
but as for a broken spirit, who can bear it?
15 *The heart of the discerning acquires knowledge,*
for the ears of wise people seek knowledge.
16 *A person's gift*[18] *makes room for him*
and leads him before great people.
17 *The first to present his case in a dispute seems right,*
until[19] *his opponent*[20] *comes and cross-examines him.*
18 *The lot puts an end to conflicts*
and separates powerful [opponents].
19 *An offended*[21] *brother is like*[22] *a strong city,*
and conflicts[23] *are like the bolt of a citadel.*

15. The ancient versions misunderstood rare *maśkît.* The Targ. and Vulg. repoint it as *bimśukkātô* ("and his dwelling [lit. 'enclosure'] is high like a wall"). This pointing entails a unique commendation of the "rich person" in this book and misses the otherwise apparent contrast between real security in the LORD and illusory security in wealth. The NRSV replaces "protecting him" of the RSV with the MT's "imagination."

16. Lit. "heart . . . is high" (see 16:5).

17. The LXX uniquely reads *therapōn phronimos,* which, to judge from the use of *therapeuousi* in 19:6 for *yeḥallû,* should be retroverted as *meḥallēhû* ("the one who appeases"). The LXX, however, is an otherwise new verse, and its arbitrary pointing should not be randomly preferred.

18. Fichtner *(BHS)* emends to *mattān,* an unattested cons. form.

19. K (followed by Vulg.) reads *yb',* allowing the audience to supply the logical connection (cf. 28:11). Q *ûba'* supplies either a *waw* disjunctive with a gnomic perfective, "but . . . comes," or, more probably, *waw* consecutive, to denote (con)sequence (see 6:11) to the preceding universal truth.

20. Lit. "neighbor." The LXX also paraphrases by *antidikos.*

21. The ancient versions essentially read, "A brother helped [by a brother]," probably having read *môšîa'* instead of *nipšā',* probably a facilitating reading of the MT *hap. leg.* RSV uniquely followed the versions, but the NRSV follows the MT.

22. The MT, reading *miqqiryat,* probably takes *min* as comparative and supplies a word such as *qāšeh* as having dropped out (= unyielding, NIV; cf. D. Kimchi, cited by Delitzsch, *Proverbs,* p. 275). GB (p. 434, s.v. *min,* citing 1 Sam. 15:22; Job 11:17; Ps. 62:10; Song 5:9; Isa. 10:10; Mic. 7:4) notes that *min* is sometimes elliptical with the dropping out of the main word. But it is better to correct the text with the LXX, Targ., Syr., and Vulg. to *kqryt* because *kaph* and *mem* were sometimes confused in both the angular script and the Dead Sea Scrolls' square script.

23. K reads *mdwnym* and Q *mdynym* with no difference in meaning. The LXX read it as *merômîm* ("high"; cf. Job 16:19; Eccl. 10:6).

20 *From the fruit of a person's mouth his belly is sated,*
[from] the harvest of his lips he is sated.
21 *Death and life are in the power of the tongue,*
and those who love[24] *it, each will eat*[25] *its fruit.*

By mostly synthetic parallels the new unit contrasts in its almost equal subunits the antisocial speech of fools (18:1-11) and the reconciling speech of the wise (18:12-21). Verse 12 also functions as a janus, uniting its two halves.

a. The Fool's Antisocial Speech versus the Defense of the Righteous (18:1-11)

The first subunit's concepts fall into two parts: a description of the fool's antisocial nature, activity, and consequences (vv. 1-9) and the defense of the righteous against him in the LORD (vv. 10-11). The first partial unit continues the topic of the fool, who by co-referential terms is mentioned explicitly in vv. 1, 2, 3, 6, 7, and 8 and inferentially in vv. 5 and 9. Verse 5 speaks of an ordinary person in contrast to the wise. Moreover, v. 5 is the only one containing antithetical parallels to contrast the two. All the rest are synthetic, devoted entirely to the fool.

(1) The Fool's Antisocial Nature, Speech, and Destiny (18:1-9)

The subunit consists of three partial subunits: an introduction (vv. 1-3), a main body (vv. 4-8), and a conclusion (v. 9).

(a) Introduction: The Fool's Alienation from Society (18:1-3)

Verses 1-3 introduce the fool's misanthropy and incorrigibility (vv. 1-2) and his social disgrace (v. 3). In a "scaled" characterization from bad to worse, he is labeled a self-serving loner (v. 1), an incorrigible fool (v. 2), and wicked (v. 3).[26] The fool's garrulous expression of his moral bankruptcy stands in marked contrast to the sage's commendation of restrained speech for the wise and silence for fools (17:27-28).

1-2 By connecting in a proverb pair the fool's incorrigibility with

24. The LXX has *kratountes autēs* (= "rule it" [< *ʼoḥ*^{a}*zêhā*]).

25. The syntactic disagreement in number between the pl. subject and sing. predicate distributes the action to each one.

26. K. Heim, "Structure and Context in Proverbs 10:1–22:16" (Ph.D. diss., University of Liverpool, 1996), p. 221.

his misanthropy, the unit begins typically with an implicit call for being teachable. Verses 1 and 2 are linked thematically and stylistically.[27] In a chiastic pattern the loner and fool are represented as both seeking their own fulfillment (vv. 1a, 2b) and being unrestrained by others (vv. 1b, 2a). The misanthropist gratifies himself while he rails against all sound judgment, and the co-relative fool rejects moral insight while he exposes his malformed thoughts and feelings. In sum, the unfriendly person and the fool are coreferential terms.

1 This synthetic proverb, whose parallels in the Hebrew text share the same syntax (prepositional phrase + verb), sounds the unit's theme and problem: the fool alienates himself from society by his self-indulgent pursuit and bares his teeth against the sage's proficient thinking. *The one who separates himself* (*niprād;* see 16:28; 18:18) "describes the unsociable person."[28] He alienates himself from the community as he *seeks* [or pursues, *yᵉbaqqēš;* see 2:4] *self-gratification* (*lᵉtaʾᵃwâ,* lit. "for gratification"; for the aspirations rooted in his personality, see 10:24). Bent on indulging his cravings, the antisocial person separates himself, and *against all sound judgment* (*bᵉkol-tûšîyâ;* see 2:7) *he starts a quarrel* or bares his teeth (*yitgallāʿ;* see 17:14). The asyndeton between the versets closely connects "for [self]-gratification" and "against all practical thought"; in other words, unfriendliness and unreasonableness are inseparable. Meinhold cites in Midrash Yalkut Schimoni (ca. 1200-1300) a reference to Lot, who separated himself from Abraham in order to go his own way with his possessions (Gen. 13:9, 11), as an example of the separatist.[29] Shakespeare has grim King Richard boast, when told he was born with teeth in his mouth, "And so I was, which plainly signified that I should snarl, and bite, and play the dog. . . . I have no brother, I am like no brother: and this word Love, which graybeards call divine, be resident in men like one another, and not in me; I am myself alone."[30]

2 The second proverb of the introductory pair warns against having a closed mind and an open mouth.[31] In its antithetic parallels, "in understanding" stands juxtaposed to "in his heart exposing itself"; "heart" and "understanding" are also paired in 2:2; 11:12; 15:21; 20:5. The subject "fool" and its predicate "does not delight" is gapped in the B verset, but the restrictive adversative "but" demands that "the fool delights" be supplied. *A fool* (*kᵉsîl;*

27. Stylistically note the assonance of */itgal/* in *yitgallāʿ* ("starts a quarrel") and *hitgallôt* ("exposing itself") in their B versets, and the chiastically patterned synonyms *bᵉkol-tûšîyâ* ("against all sound judgment") and *bitᵉbûnâ* ("in understanding"), involving the loose sequence initial */b t/* and final *â* (v. 2a).

28. Hamilton, *TWOT,* 2:733, s.v. *pārad* I.

29. Meinhold, *Sprüche,* 2:297.

30. Shakespeare, *King Henry VI,* act v, scene 6.

31. Kidner, *Proverbs,* p. 127.

see I: 112) picks up the keyword of the preceding unit (see 17:7-28). *Does not delight* (*lō'-yaḥpōṣ;* see 3:15; 8:11) is synonymous to "reject" (cf. Job 21:14; Isa. 18:10; Jer. 6:20) but emotionally stronger and a litotes for "detest." *In understanding* (see I: 96) entails listening to the sage (2:2: 5:1). The strong adversative *but (kî 'im)* sharply contrasts his incorrigibility with his opinionated garrulity. He takes fatuous pleasure *in his* morally bankrupt *heart's* (see I: 90) *exposing itself* (*bᵉhitgallôt;* see 11:13). He cannot distinguish right from wrong (cf. Sir. 6:32; 15:15; 51:13). The verb occurs in the *Hithpael* elsewhere only in connection with the drunken Noah indecently uncovering himself (Gen. 9:21; cf. Sir. 6:32; 15:15; 51:13).[32] The fool's counter-productive loquacity proceeds from his lack of insight into the damaging effects of his speech (10:8, 10; 14:3; 15:14) and of self-control over his emotions (12:16; 15:2; 17:27) and from his being wise in his own eyes (26:12; see also 12:23; 13:16). Ironically the fool aims to let his heart expose itself, but it exposes what he did not intend, namely, his folly.

3 This proverb adds to the co-referential terms for the antisocial separatist and fool the ethical term *wicked person* (*rāšā';* see I: 109), and in that connection it speaks for the first time of his punishment. The fool's aspiration to indulge himself and his refusal to listen to wisdom lead to his guilt before God for wronging the community and the community's reproach of him. *When . . . comes* (see 1:26-27) denotes the temporal proximity of the cause (the wicked person) and the consequence ("contempt").[33] *Also* logically coordinates the cause-consequence connection, strengthened further by the striking repetition of *comes* and the consonance of initial /b/: *bᵉbô'-rāšā' bā' gam-bûz.* The proverb is ambiguous. Does *contempt (bûz)* refer to the wicked person's inner feeling of holding the innocent vile and worthless (cf. 1:7; 6:30; 11:12) and/or to his evaluation of him (see 12:8; 13:18; 26:1)? Though both are true and may be intended, the parallel favors the latter interpretation. *And* adds to the wicked person's state of disgrace and the community's active reproach. *With* signifies that disgrace and reproach are as inseparable as the wicked and contempt. *Shame* (*qālôn;* see 3:35) refers to social dishonor and disgrace and to the loss of public respect, and gives rise to the *reproach* (or scorn; see 6:33) the community heaps on him. Sometimes the LORD judges the guilty by making them a reproach (cf. Jer. 24:9; 29:18; Ezek. 5:14; Hos. 12:14[15]). Possibly the proverb intends to escalate the dire consequences of the wicked's contempt. His contempt for others leads to the disgrace that he brings upon them, and that in turn to their reproach.[34] But to

32. Some questionably think that Noah did no wrong in exposing his nakedness (see W. Brown, "Noah: Sot or Saint?" in *WWis,* pp. 36-60).

33. *IBHS,* p. 604, P. 36.2.2.b.

34. So Meinhold, *Sprüche,* p. 298.

represent the righteous, who oppose the wicked, as being in disgrace and to give the wicked the last word contradicts the sage's worldview.

(b) Body: The Fool's Perverse Speech (18:4-8)

The introduction's abstract descriptions of the wicked are now narrowed down to specific instances of his misanthropic speech, framed by the *inclusio* "the words of" (vv. 4a, 8a). It escalates the misuse of speech from the concealing speech of the ordinary person (v. 4), to perverse courtroom sentences (vv. 5-7), to slander that sets one person against another (v. 8). Thus this subunit on antisocial fools advances from the alienated fool (v. 1) to the alienated community (v. 8). The perversion of justice, which picks up on a major theme of the preceding unit (cf. 17:8, 23, 26), stands at the center of the partial subunit between obscure speech and slander. Verse 5 condemns the perversion of speech to undermine justice, and vv. 6 and 7, the deadly social consequences of misusing speech implicitly to others and explicitly to himself.

4 The partial subunit begins the topic of bad speech with the concealing speech of an ordinary person, which even he cannot fully plumb because of his depraved motives (cf. 16:2; 20:5). His speech stands in striking contrast to wisdom's open, clear, life-changing, and sustaining speech in an unquenchable supply to serve others, not self (see 8:6-9). However, the LXX, Targ., Vulg., and many commentators essentially render the proverb: "The words of a man's mouth are deep waters [i.e., profound], a gushing torrent and a fountain of wisdom."[35] The lack of disjunctive *waw* (= "but") to introduce verset B favors interpreting the parallels as synthetic descriptions of wisdom's speech.[36] But the meaning of "person" and of "deep waters" favors interpreting the parallels as antithetic (so KJV, NIV, NRSV, and many other commentators).[37] *The words* designates broadly any word (10:19).[38] The unrestricted *of a person's* (*'îš;* see I: 89) denotes the average person, not the wise or the ideal. *Mouth* (*pî;* see 2:6) helps the water imagery by picturing the source from which others drink. *Deep* (*ʿᵃmuqqîm*) occurs 16 times, seven times in Leviticus 13 of a sore that is more than skin deep. Otherwise it is used in poetry of "physical depth(s)," always with the negative connotations of inaccessibility and/or foreboding danger.[39] In that light the "deep water" in

35. For example, Delitzsch, *Proverbs,* p. 269.

36. The versets are bound together by the series of nasals /*m* and *n*/: *mayim ʿᵃmuqqîm dibrê pî-'îš naḥal nōbēaʿ mᵉqôr ḥokmâ.*

37. For example, Meinhold, *Sprüche,* pp. 298-99.

38. Cf. 12:6, 25; 13:5, 13; 14:15; 15:1, 23; 16:20; 17:9; 18:8, 13; 26:22; 29:20.

39. Of a deep cup with a drink that brings scorn and derision (Ezek. 23:32); of the depths of the grave (Job 11:8); of the depths of darkness that must be revealed (Job

18:4 and 20:5 connotes that the person's word and plans respectively are unfathomable, inaccessible, nonbeneficial, and probably potentially dangerous (cf. esp. Ps. 64:6[7]). If they were intended to benefit others, they would be accessible and comprehensible. In 20:5 they are contrasted to the understanding, who can draw them out of someone else. "For words, like Nature, half reveal and half conceal the Soul within."[40] Juxtaposed to the concealing speech of the ordinary person is *the wellspring* (see 5:18), which elsewhere in Proverbs is said to issue life (see 10:11; 13:14; 14:27; 16:22; cf. 25:26). *Of wisdom* (see I: 76) functions as a metonymy for the wise in contrast to the average person. His words are *rushing* [see 1:23] *stream* (or torrent; see n. 4). Verset B mixes the metaphors of "well-spring" with "a torrent valley" to combine the notions of a constant and inexhaustible supply of living water with its ready accessibility and abundance.

5 This synthetic proverb supplements others condemning the miscarriage of justice, adding the injustice of showing favoritism to the wicked at the expense of the innocent (see 17:15, 23, 26; 24:23; cf. Exod. 23:3, 6-8; Lev. 19:15; 1 K. 21:9-13; Isa. 1:23; 10:2; Jer. 22:3; Ezek. 22:12; Amos 5:12). It shares the same syntax as 17:26 and its predicate of declaring injustice "not good." Verset B also shares the same syntax and essentially the same vocabulary as 17:23b, substituting "innocent" for "officials." *To show favoritism* [lit., "lifting the face of"; see 6:35] *to the guilty* (*rāšā'*; see I: 109), which here has its judicial sense (see 17:15; cf. 18:3), *is not good* (see 17:26). The gesture of lifting the guilty suppliant's bowed head is a metonymy for pronouncing him innocent (see 17:15). Verset B probably explains either the purpose/result or circumstances of showing favoritism, *and so denies* [see 17:8, 23] *the innocent* (*ṣaddîq;* see 17:15, 26) in the sphere of *justice* (see 17:23), thereby driving them from the court (cf. Isa. 32:7). Its connection with 17:23 suggests that the magistrate shows favoritism in exchange for a bribe (cf. Exod. 23:8), condemning himself along with the criminal. As 17:15 shows, the proverb indirectly speaks of negative speech for it entails pronouncing judgments in the miscarriage of justice. The New Testament proscribes showing any kind of favoritism (Jas. 2:1-4; 1 Tim. 5:21).

6-7 This proverb pair is tightly linked by the chiastic structure of "lips of a fool/his lips" (vv. 6a, 7b) and "his mouth"/"mouth of a fool" (vv. 6b, 7a) and by the common theme pertaining to the damage of bad speech. Whereas v. 6 refers to the damage the fool's mouth inflicts on himself and

---

12:22); of a cunning heart that plots injustice (Ps. 64:6[7]); of a "deep pit," a metaphor for a harlot (22:14; 23:17). Only in Eccl. 7:24, with reference to the inaccessibility of wisdom (i.e., the scheme of things that Qoheleth cannot fathom), may the connotation of danger be missing.

40. Tennyson, *In Memoriam,* v, cited by Kidner, *Proverbs,* p. 128.

possibly on others, v. 7 focuses only on the former. The pair escalates his afflictions from controversy (v. 6a) to beating (v. 6b) to terror (v. 7a) to death (v. 7b).

6 The fool's misuse of speech foments controversy and conflict, hurting himself and possibly others. In this synthetic parallelism, linked by the word pair "lips"/"mouth" in relation to "fool"/"his," the predicates escalate from verbal damage to physical damage. Though the fool discounts the connection between sin and judgment, *the lips of a fool* [cf. 10:18] *come* [see 18:3] *into controversy* (see 15:18; 17:1, 14). In starting his quarrel he intends to damage others, but in so doing it boomerangs against him. The wise person seeks to avoid conflict (cf. 17:1, 14; 20:3; 30:33) or to resolve it (cf. 15:18; 18:17-18; 25:9; 26:17, 21). In 20:3 avoiding controversy is equated with being held in honor (i.e., enjoying social esteem). McKane explains: "The effect of his speech is always to alienate himself from public sympathy and to attract feelings of hostility."[41] *And his mouth* [see 10:32] *cries out for* [or summons;[42] see 16:21] *beatings* (*mahᵃlūmôt;* 19:29).[43] In view is the flogging of the fool, presumably by order of the court (cf. 10:6, 13, and esp. 19:29, the only other use of *mahᵃlūmôt*). Possibly the fool inciting corrupt officials to flog the innocent is also in view (cf. 6:16-19; 10:11, 18, 23; 14:16; 15:14; 17:12).

7 The proverb now escalates the fool's punishment to his death. The emblematic parallel of a lethal trap (v. 7b) explains the reason for the fool's terror (v. 7a). His lips become unexpectedly and finally a fatal trap that ensnares him. The LORD upholds a moral order wherein those whose mouths devour others are themselves devoured (Gal. 6:6-7). *The mouth of a fool* [see v. 6] [*brings*] *terror* [and ruin; see 10:14] *to himself* [see 13:3], *and his lips* [see v. 6] *are a trap* (or snare; see 12:13) set by God *for his very life* (*nepeš;* see I: 90; not "for himself" because the trap is deadly).

8 This synthetic proverb expands the topic of bad speech in controversy to bad speech in gossip. The proverb again appears in 26:22 in the same context. Proverbs pertaining to controversy (*rîb;* 8:6-7; 26:21) precede them. In 16:18 the connection between controversial speech and gossip is clear: both forms of speech incite people and alienate them from one another, but gossip is a delectable contagion and so more dangerous. The proverb expands the topic of the damaging consequences of the misuse of speech. Un-

41. McKane, *Proverbs,* p. 515.

42. BDB (p. 895, s.v. *qārā'*) invests the idiom with the unique meaning "demand, require."

43. The verb *hālam* occurs nine times with the general meaning "to strike/hit," as with a hammer (Judg. 5:22, 26; 1 Sam. 14:16; Pss. 74:6; 141:5; Prov. 23:35; Isa. 16:8; 28:1 [metaphor]; 41:7).

like the fool's insolent speech that hurts himself in hurting others, gossip destroys the relationship of others, even the closest friends (16:28), and, spreading the controversy (*mādôn* in 26:20) like wildfire, alienates the victim from his community. Verset A likens gossip to a savory morsel, which means, as verset B explains, that others greedily and thoroughly devour it.[44] *The words* [*dibrê;* see 18:4] *of a slanderer* [*nirdān;* see 16:28] *are like tidbits (k^{e}mitlah^{a}mîm),* a *hap. leg.*[45] So *they* shows the cause-effect relationship between the clause situations. *They descend* [*yār^{e}dû;* see 1:12] *into one's innermost being (ḥadrê bāten),* a term found only in Solomonic proverbs (also 20:27, 30; 26:22). According to Shupak, it comes from the Egyptian expression "a casket of the belly," which depicts the belly as a box wherein resides the heart (i.e., a person's mind and thought).[46] "The innermost being" represents the deepest and most complete stratum of a person's psyche. Because slander so thoroughly penetrates a person's thoughts and emotions, it remains indelibly imprinted and effective. Since gossip is so highly contagious because the human heart has no resistance to it, the wise quarantine it by not repeating it (see 16:28; 17:9; 26:20) and by avoiding the company of talebearers (20:19). Jeremiah sets a better model: he ate God's word and delighted in it (Jer. 15:16; cf. Col. 3:12-20).

(c) Conclusion: The Fool Plunders the Community (18:9)

9 This proverb draws the series about the damaging effects of the fool's misuse of speech to its conclusion by implicitly arguing from the lesser to the greater, signaled by *even,* which also typically draws a unit to its conclusion as in 17:28.[47] If even passive lethargy is like a plunderer (v. 9), how much more active gossip (v. 8). Verset A introduces the topic and cause (cf. 3), *the one who is slack (mitrappeh). Rāpā',* like *yārad* (v. 8), essentially means to

44. Note the series of *mems* and the sequence of /*h* and *m*/ in *mitlah^{a}mîm w^{e}hēm,* the chiastic sequence of /*d* and *r*/ in *dibrê . . . yār^{e}dû ḥadrê,* and the alliteration of the initial cons. *dibrê-* and of final *ḥadrê-.*

45. Modern scholarship (cf. *HALOT,* 2:521, s.v. *lhm*) derives its meaning from Arab. *lahima* I, which in Stem VIII means "to swallow greedily," and Eth. *lahama* "to have pleasure." In the *Hithpael* it means "makes itself to be or is swallowed greedily," and the ptcp. is a substantival pl.: "things swallowed greedily" (i.e., "tidbits").

46. He supports his interpretation by arguing that about half of the Bible's characteristic wisdom vocabulary has Egyptian parallels, of which several examples betray direct influence (e.g., *p^{e}rî pî 'îš,* 12:14; 13:2; 18:20) and *tōkēn libbôt* (21:2). N. Shupak, "Egyptians Terms and Features in Biblical Hebrew," *Tar* 54 (1984/85) 475-83.

47. Though not a strict marker, "it can signal a final climax in an exposition . . . and is the only Hebrew adverb that marks a discourse ending — all others mark beginnings or middles" (*IBHS,* p. 663, P. 39.3.4d).

sink down to a lower level (see 4:13; cf. Isa. 5:24). The verb occurs 45 times. Often in the *Qal* it occurs with "hands" (i.e., "the hands drop") to denote discouragement. In the *Hithpael* it means either "to be made slack" (= "to be idle, negligent, careless," Josh. 18:3), or "to be made disheartened" (Prov. 24:10). *In his work (m^ela'ktô).*[48] In Ugaritic *ml'kt* means "trading mision." *HALOT* assigns this narrower meaning to 18:9 and 22:29, and the broader meaning "work" in 24:29.[49] The distinction, however, is arbitrary, for the broader fits all three texts. In practice the slack person is careless and procrastinates like the sluggard (cf. 10:4a; 12:24, 27; 19:15). Verset B presents the consequence by a metaphor. The resumptive pronoun *he* underscores the topic. *A brother* (*'āḥ;* see 6:19) functions as an incomplete metaphor for the indolent's resemblance to a plunderer (= *ḥābēr,* "companion," "partner," in 28:24).[50] The unstated comparison is that the end effect of both lethargy and villainy is ruin. In the idiom, *of him who destroys (l^eba'al mašḥît), mašḥît* occurs 18 times with reference to either "the destroyer" or the act of destroying and/or of effected "ruin."[51] When he does not perform his responsibilities, such as working his fields and tending his animals, which are vital to his interests and his very means of living, his charges languish, rot, decay, and come to ruin just as surely as if someone had set out to plunder them (cf. 6:15; 24:34; cf. Matt. 12:30; 25:14-30).[52]

(2) The Defense of the Righteous in the LORD (18:10-11)

Verses 10 and 11 are a proverb pair linked by their common theme and style. Both pertain to protection and security, the true security of the righteous in the LORD (v. 10) versus the false security of the rich in his wealth. Both use the imagery of fortifications (tower and city) qualified by "strong" *('ōz)* in their A versets and connected with "high" *(śāgab)* in their B versets. The proverb pair mobilizes the disciple to seek protection in the LORD, not in wealth.

10 This verse presents the defense of the righteous against the de-

48. The meaning is derived from its root *l'k* and means "to send," and its bi-form, *mal'āk,* means "messenger."

49. *HALOT,* 2:586, s.v. *m^elā'kâ.*

50. BDB, p. 26, s.v. *'āḥ.*

51. It is used of military plunderers, "raiding parties" (1 Sam. 13:17; 14:15), the destroyer that entered the Egyptian homes on the night of Passover and struck down their firstborn (Exod. 12:23), and the messenger sent to strike down Jerusalem for David's crime (2 Sam. 24:26). It is also used of the effecting and effected ruin in Egypt (Exod. 12:13), in Israel (Ezek. 5:16), in Philistia (Ezek. 25:16). Ezekiel (21:31[36]) speaks of brutal men "who are skilled in destroying" *(hārāšê mašḥît).*

52. Note the series of /m/ in *gam mitrappeh bimla'ktô . . . mašḥît.*

stroyer *(baʿal mašḥît),* the last word of v. 9.[53] Its A verset presents the cause — that is, his defense is "the name of the LORD," which is implicitly likened to "a strong tower" (v. 10a) — and its B verset the consequence — the righteous first runs into it and then is protected (v. 10b). *The name* functions as a character description rather than as merely a label of identification. *Of the* LORD *(YHWH;* see 1:7) refers to Israel's covenant-keeping God who reveals himself through the sages (see 3:5) and signifies his essence (such as personal and spiritual) and attributes (such as powerful and gracious). *Is a fortified* [or strong] *tower (migdāl)* denotes a storehouse, either in the countryside (1 Chr. 27:25) or in the city, that by its strength and height (cf. Isa. 2:15) was firmly fixed and inviolable (see 10:14; 14:26). People fled to such towers when attacked (Judg. 9:46-53; Ps. 61:3[4]). In sum, the sublime nature and character of the LORD who stands behind the book of Proverbs provides for and protects *the righteous* (see I: 97). *Runs* means to move quickly by moving the legs rapidly (cf. 1:16) and connotes acting quickly, decisively, with all diligence (6:18). If there is an antithesis with the slack person of v. 9, there may be an implied alliteration with *ḥārûṣ,* the opposite of being slack (see 10:4). *Into it* refers to the tower under siege. *And is protected on high (wᵉniśgāb)* marks the (con)sequence of his running into the strong tower. *Śāgab* in the *Qal* means "to be very high," and in contexts of attack connotes to be protected. In practice, when attacked by injustice and gossip the faithful gives himself completely to the teachings of this Book, which the LORD promises to uphold (see I: 107).[54]

11 The deluded rich person's false security stands in striking contrast to the righteous person's true security (cf. 11:28, 4, 7; Isa. 25:12). In his delusion, the rich seeks his security and his significance in money (cf. 10:15; 28:11), imagining his wealth to be like "a strong city" (v. 11a) with "a high wall" (v. 11b). The topic "the wealth of the rich man" is gapped in verset B, and the qualifying phrase, "in his imagination," is gapped in verset A.[55] *The wealth of a rich person is his fortified* [or strong] *city* repeats verbatim 10:15a. *And* combines the metaphor "his strong city" with the simile *like a . . . city wall* (see 1:21). In case of an enemy attack, the threatened people retreat to the elevated city behind its walls. *High (niśgābâ;* see v. 10) qualifies the wall as offering maximum protection. From this height the rich thinks that he can beat back off all his attackers. *In* qualifies the area as be-

53. The pair is also linked to v. 9 by the assonance of *mašḥît* ("destroyer") and *maśkît* ("imagination," v. 11).

54. *Papyrus Insinger* (19:12) taught: "The support of the godly man in misfortune is the god" (*AEL,* 3:200).

55. The assonance of /o/ and /u/ binds together *hôn . . . ʿuzzô ûkᵉḥômâ . . . bᵉmaśkîtô* and the series /*ś g~k*/ links together *niśgābâ bᵉmaśkîtô.*

ing the irreality of *his imagination (maśkîtô),* which may be no match for the reality of the *baʿal mašḥît.*[56] In sum, the security of the rich person in his visible wealth is imaginary, as anyone who has faced a terminal illness knows (v. 10), and the security of the righteous in his invisible God is real (v. 11)!

b. Janus (18:12)

Verse 12 is a janus, drawing vv. 10-11 to their conclusion and beginning the introduction of vv. 13-15. Note the conceptual sequence from "destroyer" (v. 9b), to true and false protection (vv. 10-11), to the contrasting destinies of the haughty's destruction and the humble's honor (v. 12). Whereas vv. 10 and 11 are synthetic, v. 12 is antithetic, facilitating linking in the outer frame of the chiasm v. 10 and v. 12b, and in its inner core v. 11 and v. 12a. R. E. Murphy noted, "It is impossible to read 18:11 (and 10:15) without considering the telling points that are made in 18:10, 12."[57] Finally, it is linked with vv. 10-11 by the metaphor of "high," replacing being on high *(niśgāb)* or behind a high *(niśgābâ)* wall with a heart that is "high" *(gābah).*

As 15:33 brought its unit to closure, so this proverb, in which *before honor is humility* repeats 15:33 verbatim, brings the subunit of 18:1-11 to completion. This antithetical proverb contrasts the destinies of the arrogant, who lifts himself up against God and by so much against his community, and the humble, who, renouncing human pride, is a devout worshiper and by so much serves his community (see 22:4). From these contrasting religious roots spring the contrasting behavior of the rich fool (see 21:4) and the pious righteous (see 11:2). Verse 12a matches 16:18a but, after repeating *before destruction,* it substitutes *a person's heart* [see 18:4] *is high and haughty* (*yigbah,* lit. "is high"; see 17:19) instead of "pride" *(gāʾôn),* showing that *gābah* (see 17:19) has its ethical sense of setting oneself up against God and humanity (see 16:5). Probably the change facilitated linking v. 12 with vv. 10-11 by the assonance of *niśgāb[â]* (vv. 10b, 11b) and *yigbah.* In sum, the righteous who sought refuge in the Lord (v. 10), a co-referential term for the humble worshiper in v. 12b, is destined for honor (cf. Isa. 57:15). "Honor is given, not taken."[58] But the rich person (v. 11), who sought refuge in his wealth and is a co-referential term for the arrogant, is headed for the crash he

56. *Maśkit* can denote a literal image (cf. Ezek. 8:12) such as a carved stone, a carved image (Num. 33:52; cf. Lev. 26:1), or a picture (Prov 25:11) or, as here, an image produced by the mind, though "heart" is gapped (Ps. 73:7; Prov. 18:11).

57. R. E. Murphy, "Proverbs 22:1-9," *Int* 41 (1987) 401.

58. Clifford, *Proverbs,* p. 171.

so richly deserves (cf. 11:2; 15:33; 16:5, 8; 17:19; 29:23). "Humility" implies that the LORD is the Agent.[59]

Verse 12 also serves as part of the introduction to the next subunit (esp. vv. 12-15). Stylistically, initial "before" occurs twice in both versets, like the double-initial "spirit" in v. 14 and double-final "knowledge" in v. 15.[60] It is linked with v. 13 by synonyms for temporal "before" (*lipnê,* v. 12 and *bᵉṭerem,* v. 13).[61] In an *inclusio* the proud heart of v. 12 stands in striking contrast to the discerning heart of v. 15. Moreover, v. 12 participates in an alternating structure with vv. 13-15. Thematically, it is closely connected with vv. 13-14 by moving from future honor for the humble (v. 12) and humiliation for the fool to present vitality that restrains sickness for the former and present depression for the latter.

c. The Educated Person's Behavior in Conflict and His Speech (18:13-21)

The new unit no longer focuses on the fool but on the handling of conflict and speech. An educated person is expected to uphold justice, resolve conflicts, and speak powerfully. The unit consists of an introduction, laying the foundation in being teachable (vv. 13-15), and then moving on to a courtroom to deal with settling disputes (vv. 16-19) and to the power of speech (vv. 20-21). The effect of speech is especially noticeable in the courtroom, where the tongue has the power of life and death (v. 21).

(1) Introduction: The Incorrigible Fool versus the Teachable Wise (18:13-15)

This introduction to the second subunit, including the janus (v. 12), has an alternating structure:

59. Aitken (*Proverbs,* p. 114) calls attention to Shakespeare's Wolsey's bitter discovery:

> . . . I have ventur'd,
> Like little wanton boys that swim on bladders,
> This many summers in a sea of glory;
> But far beyond my depth. My high-blown pride
> At length broke under me, and now has left me,
> Weary and old with service, to the mercy
> Of a rude stream, that must for ever hide me.

60. So Meinhold, *Sprüche,* p. 302.

61. Meinhold, *Sprüche,* p. 302.

A Future destruction and honor depending on a person's heart *(lēb-'îš):* v. 12

B The non-listening *(yišmāʿ)* fool: v. 13

A′ Present triumph and depression, depending on a person's spirit *(rûaḥ-'îš):* v. 14

B′ The listening *('ōzen)* wise: v. 15

In A/A′ note that *lēb* ("heart") and *rûaḥ* ("spirit") are sometimes parallel terms (17:22), a connection reinforced by a qualifying *'îš* ("of a person"), and in B/B′ note that *smʿ* ("hear") sometimes qualifies the predicate of *'ōzen* ("ear"; see 20:12; 25:12).

Their topics follow the same sequence as 15:12-14: moral incorrigibility (15:12; 18:13), spiritual fortitude versus depression (15:13; 18:14), and a discerning heart seeking knowledge (15:14; 18:15). As in that passage, the introduction is framed by the incorrigibility of the fool (v. 13), having an evaluative -::- pattern, and the teachableness of the wise (v. 15), having an evaluative +::+ pattern, around a core pertaining to spiritual fortitude and depression, having a +::- pattern in a chiasm with them. The connections suggest that incorrigibility leads to depression and the loss of life, whereas teachableness provides inner heroic strength that enables one to persevere in physical disability. The ear that seeks knowledge in v. 14 is the opposite of the one who replies before listening (v. 13).

13 The fool's arrogance (v. 12a) causes his rude and rash speech (v. 13a), and his future shame (v. 13b) stands in marked antithesis to the coming honor of the humble (v. 12b). This introductory proverb typically pertains to being teachable. Its subject is implicitly the fool who, before the wise has finished speaking, boorishly interrupts him to spout his own opinion (see 18:2). His impertinent and imprudent interruption exposes his folly for all to see and brings him disgrace.[62] *As for the one* renders the focus marker. *Who replies* (lit. "who causes a word to return") is an idiom for "to answer," as in Akkadian.[63] Temporal *before* (see 8:25) infers that he interrupts what he should be listening to. Sir. 11:8 makes the point clearly: "Do not answer before you have heard, nor interrupt a speaker in the midst of his words." *He listens* (*yišmāʿ*; 1:5) means that he hears, usually with the extended meaning to attend closely to, to pay careful attention to, a verbal situation. The interrupted speaker is implicitly wise, for the sage considers it folly and shame to listen attentively to the self-opinionated fool. The interrupter is the fool, who

62. Clifford (*Proverbs,* p. 172) notes, "The sounds in colon A provide unity, *m-š* in the first word is reversed in its last word *š-m,* and the consonantal sequence *b-r* recurs in its two middle words."

63. *HALOT,* 4:1,433, s.v. *šûb.*

is notorious in this book for preferring to spout out his own opinions rather than to listen to wisdom; as a result he receives shame (1:7, 22; 3:35; 12:23; 13:16, 19; 15:2, 5). *It* refers to the circumstance of the preceding clause. *Is to him* denotes the disadvantages that avail against him. *Folly* (see I: 113) denotes intractable moral insolence and possibly by metonymy its negative effects. *And* presents in a unified way a complex situation. *Shame* (*kᵉlimmâ*) denotes degradation both subjectively and objectively. The person to whom the word is applied "is isolated within his previous world, and his own sense of worth is impugned. He becomes subject to scorn, insult, and mockery, and is cut off from communication."[64]

14 Verse 12 contrasted the humble person's hope of honor in the future with the fool's future feeling of shame. This proverb, similar to 15:13 and 17:22, juxtaposes "fortitude (unfolding power)," as Meinhold puts it, in present adversity that leads to triumph against spiritual depression, even without adversity, that leads to defeat.[65] The connection is underscored by the synonyms "a person's heart" (v. 12) and "a person's spirit." Though he is *human* (or anyone; *'îš;* see 18:12), the connection with v. 12 shows that the teachable humble are in view. The antithetical parallel restricts *spirit* (see I: 92) by qualifying it as broken in the depressed. Wisdom produces this spiritual life that *can endure (yᵉkalkēl) sickness* (cf. 15:15). *Kûl* in the *Pilpel* with human beings as objects commonly means "to supply (with food)." With God as object it means "to contain" in 1 K. 8:27. The former and/or the latter shades off into the figurative meaning "to endure, withstand," with the impersonal objects "fire" (Jer. 20:9), "the day of the LORD" (Mal. 3:2), and "sickness" (Prov. 18:11).[66] *Even its own* was added to sharpen the contrast between the A and B versets. *Sickness* (*maḥᵃleh,* masc.) occurs elsewhere only in 2 Chr. 21:15 with reference to an awful, lingering disease of the bowels. Like its feminine by-form, here it probably refers to any sickness (Exod. 15:26; 23:25; 1 K. 8:37 [= 2 Chr. 6:28]). Since a heroic spirit restrains sickness from overwhelming its victim, it implicitly enables its possessor to go from strength to strength and run the race triumphantly. *But* joins two contrasting spiritual states. The rhetorical question *who* involves the disciple in the proverb and, to judge from the positive antithesis, anticipates his negative response, "No one" (cf. 27:3-4). *Can bear it* (*yiśśā';* see 6:35; 9:12; 18:5) pictures *a broken spirit* (see 15:13; 17:22)[67] that has been flogged out of a person as a load or burden to be borne. Since no one can bear a broken spirit,

64. S. Wagner, *TDOT,* 7:186, s.v. *klm.*

65. Meinhold, *Sprüche,* p. 304.

66. Its sense in Ps. 112:5, "your affairs," possibly means exceptionally "to conduct" (*HALOT,* 2:463, s.v. *kûl;* BDB, p. 465, equivocates).

67. Both "it" and "spirit" are feminine; "sickness" is masculine.

it implicitly prevents its possessor from finishing the course and brings him down in an untimely defeat. When the spirit is gone, a person is as good as dead. Therefore psychological depression is worse than physical affliction (cf. 1 Sam. 30:6; Job 1:21; Rom. 8:36-37; 2 Cor. 12:10).

15 This educational proverb on the importance of acquiring knowledge, which is the source of spiritual strength, brings the introduction to its conclusion and sets the stage for the teachings that follow. Its complementary parallels present the inseparable inner and outer receptacles for the acquisition of the sage's knowledge. *The heart* [see I: 90] *of the discerning* [*nābôn* or insightful; see I: 95] *acquires* [see 4:5] *knowledge* [see I: 77], *for the ears* [lit., "and the ear"; see 2:2] *of wise people* [see I: 94] *seek knowledge* (*y*ᵉ*baqqeš-dā'āt;* see 15:14). The heart and ear in view are the inalienable possession of the discerning individual, escalated to wise people (see 8:9). Like the lingering conundrum in Aristotle's ethics that one must be virtuous to become virtuous,[68] so also the sages taught that one must be wise to become wise and to have knowledge in order to strive after it to increase it (cf. 1:5; 1 Cor. 8:2; Phil. 3:10ff.). Inferentially, the Author of virtue must be God, not self. Knowledge comes easily to the elect (14:6), but they must pursue it (cf. 19:20) by going to and listening to the sage who himself knows and therefore reveals the moral connection.

(2) Teachings about Justice and Conflicts (18:16-19)

The setting of vv. 16-19 is the courtroom, and its concern is settling disputes.[69] Verses 16-17 imply the need for an impartial judicial system by exposing the bribe (vv. 16-17), and vv. 18-19 present resolutions in light of the limitations of the best of courts (vv. 18-19).

16 The particular topic of this synthetic proverb is "a person's gifts," gapped in verset B, and the metaphor that it "makes room for him" is interpreted by and escalated to "leads him before great men." *The bribes* (*mattān;* see 15:27), though masculine (see also 21:14), is a by-form of the feminine *mattānâ,* "present gift." In Proverbs these terms, aside from the idiom in 19:6, are used for benefactions given for selfish interests to gain an advantage over others. The NIV glosses it "bribe" in 15:27 and in Eccl. 7:7. In contrast to the poor who are deprived access to the magistrates (17:23; 18:5), the person with a gift gains a hearing and an unjust advantage over them, and as the next proverb asserts, by coming first and without cross-examination he

68. See J. R. Wilson, "Biblical Wisdom, Spiritual Formation, and the Virtues," in *WWis,* p. 298.

69. So also R. Whybray, *The Composition of the Book of Proverbs* (JSOTSup 168; Sheffield: JSOT, 1994), p. 112.

will unjustly appear in the right. *Of a man* (*'ādām;* see I: 89) designates the human being on earth in contradistinction to the Sovereign in heaven. *Makes room (rāḥab)* in its two other uses without an object connotes "to give relief" (Gen. 26:22; Ps. 4:1[2]), a nuance that fits here also. The donor is in distress, and his gift clears the bottlenecks and unlocks doors that normally bar access to people of rank. In each case it is followed by a *lamed* of advantage; here *for him (lô)* entails an unfair advantage. *It leads him* (see 6:22; 11:3) implicitly personifies the bribe as a shepherd that leads the giver safely through snares to the desired goal of presenting his case *before great people* (see 25:6), an adjectival substantive for influential people closely associated with the king (cf. 2 Sam. 7:9; 2 K. 10:6; Neh. 11:14; Jer. 5:5; 52:13; Jon. 3:7; Mic. 7:3; Nah. 3:10). The proverb, like 14:20, lays bare the unvarnished truth about human nature. The selfishly given gift of the donor gives him a free field among those that can assist him in any way, including the judicial process. Gifts should not be necessary to gain access to those who enjoy the public's trust. These transactional gifts secure preferential treatment and by so much adversely affect the administration of justice and the best interests of the community. They inherently favor the rich over the poor and subvert the trust that should accompany public office. This injustice violates the values of this book, namely, "righteousness, justice, and equity" (see 1:3).

17 This verse protects v. 16 against the misinterpretation that the disciple should give gifts to enable him to have a free field with the powerful and influential people of rank. A self-serving gift allows the donor an unjust opportunity to present his case against another without opposition unless the other can also afford to bribe the official. For justice to be served a competent equal must be able to cross-examine a litigant to sift out the evidence. Its synthetic parallels present as narrative a dispute between two litigants. Verset A represents vividly by the definite article *the first* litigant. *In* marks the location of his priority as implicitly *to present his case. A dispute (rîbô)* identifies him as possessor of a case against someone. *Rîb* may denote a controversy outside the judicial sphere (see 15:18; 17:1, 14) or within it (see 22:23; 23:11; 25:9), but *is innocent* (or "righteous"; 18:5) probably has its forensic sense, suggesting a court setting. *Then* marks the temporal sequence of the situation in verset B. *His opponent* (*rē'ēhû;* see 3:28) glosses the word for "neighbor" because in this case the people who have a reciprocal relationship with one another are litigants in a dispute. *Comes* (see 18:3) vividly represents the defendant stepping forward to present his defense *And cross-examines him (waḥ^{a}qārô)* means "to probe" in a purely cognitive and analytical examination and testing[70] and connotes that the search is diligent, penetrating, and difficult because of something hidden

70. M. Tsevat, *TDOT,* 5:149, s.v. *ḥāqar.*

and hard to find (cf. 23:30; 25:2, 27; 28:11).[71] Since the other three pronouns refer to the "the first in his case," presumably the pronoun refers to *him,* as in 28:11, not "dispute" (*rîb;* cf. Job 29:16). In the two other proverbs with personal objects the inferior searches out matters pertaining to the greater: the king of God (25:2) and the poor of the rich (28:11). Here with the first litigant as its object it refers to that which the first and powerful litigant hides in his dispute. The litigant in view is powerful and convincing until his opponent sets forth the other side of the case by forcing the first to reveal data that weaken or negate his position (cf. Acts 24:10). The second must be as competent as the first (cf. Job 29:16). Thus the proverb teaches the equality of disputants and instructs the disciple not only to hear both sides of an argument but to demand direct cross-examination before rendering a decision (cf. Deut. 19:16-18).

18-19 This proverb pair pertains to the resolution of conflicts beyond what an impartial court can achieve. In a chiastic pattern the catchword "conflicts" *(midyānîm)* constitutes the outer frame (vv. 18a, 19b) and the contending opponents the inner core, "powerful [litigants]" (v. 18b) and "an offended brother" (v. 19a). Verse 18 presents the Sovereign's lot to keep powerful litigants from coming to blows. Verse 19 presents the difficulties of reconciling an offended brother.

18 There is a limit to what the judicial procedure of v. 17 can achieve (see 25:8). *The lot* (see 1:14) was used to reveal God's selection of one of several possibilities where people were kept in the dark and needed an impartial verdict (see 16:33). When the guilty party could not be identified, the lot was used to isolate the offender and in that sense decide a person's guilt or innocence (Josh. 7:14-18; 1 Sam. 14:40-42; Jon. 1:7). Albright calls attention to an eleventh-century bronze spatula where *našbît* appears to mean, "Let us *put an end* (*to* our suit at law)."[72] If this is the verb's meaning, *conflicts* (*midyānîm;* see note) is used uniquely here for a lawsuit.[73] Verset B elaborates the situation. *Separates* (see 16:28; 17:9) connotes making a desirable division in contrast to an undesirable alienation. "Between" is left untranslated. The substantival adjective *powerful* [*opponents*] (see 7:26)

71. People search the uttermost recesses of the earth to mine out and to bring to light its most precious, hidden minerals (Job 28:3; cf. v. 11). God even searches out a person's motives (see Ps. 139:1).

72. W. F. Albright, "Some Canaanite-Phoenician Sources of Hebrew Wisdom," in *WIANE,* p. 10.

73. The noun occurs ten times, seven as Q of *mādôn* (see 6:14; 17:14) and three times without a K variant (18:18; 19:13; 21:9). Six times it refers to people who like to quarrel, five of the contentious wife (19:13; 21:9, 19; 25:24; 27:15), and once of a contentious person (26:21). It is also used once of a troublemaker who stirs up strife (6:14) and once of the drunkard's strife (23:29).

probably refers to powerful litigants (cf. Isa. 41:12; so Rashi),[74] and possibly as well their physical might (the common use of *ʿāṣûm*). The context of the preceding proverb pair pertains to courtroom officials (v. 16) reaching a verdict (v. 17), and that of this proverbial pair to "conflicts" involving an offended "brother" (v. 18). The setting is the courtroom, not the battlefield; the issue is legal, not political, disputes. Finally, there is no reason to restrict the use of the lot to strong physical opponents. The lot is used to settle any hidden matter that human beings cannot uncover on their own. Here it is a matter in which both sides have such strong arguments that it is impossible to reach a verdict.[75] It is better to let God, who sees hidden matters, settle a dispute that the judicial system cannot resolve through one throw of a tiny die than to allow any violence, not just extreme violence, be the final argument. Physical force inflicts damage, the one who prevails in its use is not necessarily right, and it does not reconcile the defeated to the victor (see 18:19). For those who abide by its impartial verdict, it adds the spiritual virtues of self-denial, humility, patience, and faith (Josh. 7:14-18; 1 Sam. 14:40, 42; Jon. 1:7).

19 This proverb asserts the difficulty of terminating a dispute and, to judge from the connection with v. 18, specifically through the lot. Its imprecise parallels, "offended brother" and "conflicts," imply that the estranged brother is engaged in the conflict. *Offended* (*nipšāʿ;* cf. 10:12, 19; 12:13; 17:9, 19) glosses a unique *Niphal* of *pšʿ*. R. Knierim defines the verb in the *Qal* as meaning "[it] designates situations involving property offenses or breaks with someone" and glosses its *Niphal* "to suffer loss, to suffer crime, to suffer breach (of a fraternal relationship)."[76] Perhaps this should be reduced to "to sustain a breach (of a brotherhood) through a perceived crime." *Brother* (*ʾāḥ;* see 6:19; 17:2; 18:9) in this context has an extended meaning beyond "relative" by blood to a "brother" by choice (i.e., "a dearly loved companion"; cf. 2 Sam. 1:26; Neh. 5:10). In view is a party in the closest human relation with another, whether by blood or choice, who feels wronged and has cut himself off from the other with a deep sense of personal injury. The difficulty of penetrating beyond the psychological barriers he consciously erects to make himself invulnerable to any and every approach toward reconciliation is presented first by the metaphor *a strong city* (see 18:11). Verset B compounds his resistance by a synonymous simile. *Conflicts* (*midyānîm;* see v. 18) with the offended brother *are like the bolt of a citadel (bᵉrîaḥ ʾarmôn). Bᵉrîaḥ* refers to the strong bolt

74. M. Lyons, "Rashi's *Commentary on the Book of Proverbs*" (submitted in partial fulfillment of the requirements for the degree of rabbi, 1936), p. 98.

75. So also Heim, "Structure and Context in Proverbs 10:1–22:16," p. 228.

76. R. Knierim, *TLOT,* 2:493, s.v. *pešaʿ*.

that secured from within a gate or door (cf. Judg. 16:3; 1 K. 4:13; Neh. 3:3; Isa. 45:2; Ezek. 38:11). The most vulnerable defensive point in a wall was its gate, which had to be secured by a very strong bolt to resist attack. *'Armôn* refers to a strongly fortified place, such as the most massively fortified place of a king's palace (1 K. 16:18; 2 K. 15:25). It is unclear whether the proverb intends to say that the closer the relationship, the greater the alienation when offense occurs, and so the more difficult to effect the reconciliation, as is often alleged. Nevertheless, to judge from v. 18b, unless the conflict is eliminated, the nonreconciled litigants will inflict great damage on one another. Though reconciliation is difficult, the proverb pair asserts that the lot can put an end to the conflict and that "there exists the possibility that confidence will be re-established, injuries forgiven and friendship renewed."[77]

(3) Teachings about the Power of Speech (18:20-21)

This unit's concluding proverb pair is bound together in several ways: by the notion of the certain and abundant effects of good and bad speech, including life and death; by the agricultural metaphors of eating and being sated with fruit and with the harvest; and by the catchword "fruit," the first word of v. 20a and the last of v. 21b in the outer frame and by the organs of speaking in the inner core ("lips," v. 20b; "tongue," v. 21a).

20 This synonymous proverb instructs the disciple that whatever he says to impact others will in fact fully impact him. It pictures one's words as something that people feed on, that influences their behavior (1:31; 8:19; 11:30; 12:14; 13:2; 31:16, 31), and that in turn determines his fate. *From the fruit of a person's mouth . . . is sated* (see 12:14; cf. 1:31) refers to an utterance and its consequence that is either good or bad, even life or death, as the next proverb of this pair asserts (cf. 14:14). *His belly* (*biṭnô;* see 13:25) is a synecdoche for his whole person, both physical and spiritual. [*From*] is gapped in verset B. *The harvest* (*tᵉbû'at;* lit. income; see 3:9, 14; 14:4) changes the metaphor from the orchard to the grainfield (see 14:4), and *of his lips,* the poet's stock-in-trade parallel to "his mouth" (see 4:24), shows that it also refers to speech. "Harvest," too, can be good or bad (3:9, 14; 14:4 versus 10:16; 15:16; 16:18). *He is sated* is repeated for emphasis. Eating one's own fruit (words) is an oxymoron; in other words, to satisfy one's hunger by what comes out of the mouth is an absurdity. The oxymoron forces the thought that whatever a person dishes out, whether beneficial or harmful, he himself will feed on to full measure through what his audience in return dishes out to him.

77. McKane, *Proverbs,* p. 520.

21 On its own this proverb could refer to eating (i.e., taking into one's being) the speech of others, but its close connection with v. 20 suggests that it continues the oxymoron of eating the consequences in an exact correspondence to the way one speaks (cf. 13:3; 15:23; 21:23). By placing in the outer core of its chiastic synthetic parallels word-initial "death and life" (v. 21a) and word-final "fruit" (v. 21b), the proverb clarifies and intensifies the metaphor of "fruit" in v. 20. Its inner core, matching "in the power of the tongue" with "those who love it," clarifies that for speech to effect life or death one must earnestly desire to speak, to pursue it, and to stick with it. This commitment to speech precedes the rewards of v. 20, as eating precedes being filled. The merism *death and life* (see 2:18, 19; 5:5, 6; 8:35, 36; 12:28; 13:14; 14:27; 16:14, 15) comprehends all manner of weal and woe. Speech effects more than clinical death and life. The merism speaks of relationship within community or the lack of it. The deadly tongue disrupts community and by its lethal power isolates its owner from community and kills him. The life-giving tongue creates community and by its vitality gives its possessor the full enjoyment of the abundant life within the community. *Are in the power of* (*b^{e}yad;* lit. "in the hand of") has the metaphorical sense, "in the power/care/authority of" (Gen. 16:6; 39:23; Num. 31:49; 2 Sam. 18:2; Job 1:12).[78] *Of the tongue* is another common metonymy for good or bad speech in this book (10:20; 12:18; 15:2, 4 versus 12:19; 17:4, 20), complementing "mouth" and "lip" in the proverb pair. *And* adds the parallel that qualifies verset A. *Those who love it* (i.e., "the tongue" [= speech];[79] see 1:22) designates people who "are in love with language; they use it fastidiously, they search for chaste expression and precise meaning, and they have an end in view which they will reach because they know what language is for and how it can best be used to achieve its purpose."[80] Their objective may be good (i.e., producing life; cf. 4:6; 8:17; 12:1; 13:24; 16:13; 22:11; 29:3) or bad (i.e., producing death; cf. 1:22; 8:36; 17:19; 20:13; 21:17).[81] *Each one will eat* (*yō'kal*) *its fruit* (*piryāh;* see v. 20).[82]

78. BDB, p. 391, s.v. *yād.*

79. *Lāšôn* is mostly masculine but sometimes feminine (15:2).

80. McKane, *Proverbs,* pp. 514-15.

81. It is also true that the speech of the wise or of the fool is effective only to the extent that the audience "loves it" and "eats it" (cf. 12:18; 15:4; 26:28; Jas. 3:5).

82. *Any* (7.7-11) noted the negative: "A person may be ruined by his tongue; beware, and you will do well" (*AEL,* 2:140).

6. Wealth and Wisdom in the Court and in the Home (18:22–19:23)

22 *One who finds*[1] *a wife*[2] *finds good,*
and so obtains favor from the LORD.[3]
23 *The poor speaks pleadingly,*
but the rich answers rudely.
24 *A person*[4] *who has unreliable companions is about to be*[5] *broken,*[6]
but there is a friend who sticks closer than a brother.
19:1 *Better is a poor person who walks in his integrity*
than one who twists his lips,[7] *for*[8] *he is a fool.*[9]

1. The LXX reads *hos heuren* ("who has found" < *mōṣēʾ,* not *māṣāʾ).*

2. The addition of "good" in the LXX, Syr., Vulg., and one medieval Heb. ms., but not in the Targ., represents a tautologous interpretive gloss.

3. The LXX adds, "He that puts away a good wife puts away a good thing, and he that keeps an adulteress is foolish and ungodly." The Syr. adopted the first half of the addition, and the Vulg. the whole of it.

4. The *Sebirin* (i.e., "supposed" readings in the Masorah to give the expected form of a word but that are in fact not part of the tradition and have no binding force) equate the form *ʾîš* with *yēš,* "there are," citing 2 Sam. 14:19 and Mic. 6:10 as parallels. C. D. Isbell ("Initial *ʾaleph-yod* Interchange and Selected Biblical Passages," *JNES* 37 [1978] 227-36) argued for the *ʾ/y* shift on other grounds as well. However, the form in 2 Sam. 14:19 and Mic. 6:10 is defective *ʾiš.* Moreover, the text in Mic 6:10 is corrupt (see B. Waltke, "Micah," in *The Minor Prophets: An Exegetical and Expository Commentary,* ed. T. E. McComiskey [Grand Rapids: Baker, 1993], p. 738). According to Healey, *ʾyt* of the Targ. and Syr. corresponds to the MT's *ʾîš.*

5. *IBHS,* p. 610, P. 36.2.3g.

6. The Targ., Syr., and Vulg. either misunderstood *lhtrʿʿ* or read *lhtrʿôt* from II *rʿh* ("to make oneself a companion"; see 22:24): "There are friends to be companions" (i.e., social fellows for sociable occasions). The Vulg. rendered it by *ad societam: vir amiculus ad societam magis amicus erit quam frater* ("an amiable man will be a greater friend than a brother"), an obviously free paraphrase based on a misunderstanding of the verse. The Hexapla (F. Field, *Origenis Hexaplorum Quae Supersunt* 2:349) reads *anēr hetairion tou hetaireusasthai* ("A man of companionships [is a man] for getting companions"). The KJV renders, "A man *that hath* friends must show himself friendly." G. R. Driver ("Problems in the Hebrew Text of Proverbs," *Bib* [1951] 183), to avoid altering the MT, derives the same meaning from the Heb. *rûaʿ* ("to shout") in the weakened sense of Syr. "chattering," so that the clause may be glossed, "A man of (many) friends (is a friend only) for chattering together." The NRSV reads, "Some friends play at friendship." However, this is not the meaning of the *Hithpōlēl* of *rʿʿ,* the Aramaic equivalent of *rṣṣ* ("to be broken asunder"; see Delitzsch, *Proverb,* p. 278; BDB, p. 950, s.v. II *rʿʿ; HALOT,* 3:1,270, s.v. II *rʿʿ*), probably in the sense of either "makes himself to be broken" by acting against himself or, more probably, "made to be broken" by an unspecified agent. The inf. cons. with *lamed* probably has its immanent sense (*IBHS,* p. 610, P. 36.2.3g; GKC, P. 114i).

7. Many Heb. mss. and retroverted Targ. and Syr. read *dᵉrākāyw* ("his ways"), probably a harmonization with 28:6 and a facilitating parallel to "walk" in verset A. Re-

2 *If even desire*[10] *without knowledge*[11] *is not good,*
how much more[12] *will the one who hastens with his feet*
miss the way.[13]
3 *The folly of a human being overturns his way,*
but his heart rages against the LORD.
4 *Wealth attracts many companions,*
but as for the poor person, his close companion[14] *separates*
himself.
5 *A perjurer will not escape punishment,*
and a witness to lies[15] *will not escape.*
6 *Many seek the favor of a nobleman,*
and the generous person has everyone for a companion.[16]
7 *Every one of the poor person's brothers hates him,*
how much more his close companion becomes distant[17] *from*
him.
Though he pursues them with pleadings, they are
not to be found.[18]

---

markably the LXX, which does not retain 19:1, has *plousiou pseudous* ("a rich liar") in 28:6b, which seems to recall *š^epātāyw* ("lips") of 19:1.

8. Lit. "and" (see *IBHS,* p. 649, P. 39.2.1c).

9. Toy (*Proverbs,* p. 368), Fichtner *(BHS),* et al. emend the text with the Syr. to *ʿāšîr* to harmonize it with 28:6, but the imprecise antithesis of the MT cannot be explained away.

10. Some English versions uniquely, unnecessarily, and paraphrastically render *nepeš* by "zeal," which is not in the LXX, nor does the UBSNT regard it as the basis of Rom. 10:2.

11. According to the conjunctive accent, *nepeš* is best construed as an epexegetical gen. ("a without knowledge appetite"; *IBHS,* p. 151, P. 9.5.3c). Were it an objective gen. ("without knowledge of his person/appetite"), one would expect *h^ayôt b^elōʾ-daʿat napšô* ("his being without knowledge of his person/appetite").

12. A gloss for "and." In Hebrew *gam* in verset A or *ʾap kî* in verset B (see 19:7) may signal the a fortiori argument. English may use both.

13. Or "is a sinner." *Ḥṭʾ* means "miss the mark"; in that sense it never takes an impersonal object such as goal or way.

14. *Mērēʿhû* of L could be construed as either "from his companion" (cf. Eccl. 4:4; so LXX) or "his close companion" (cf. Gen. 26:26; so Targ. and Vulg.). Most manuscripts of the MT, however, read *m^erēʿhû* as in 17:4, removing any ambiguity. In any case, "close companion" forms a better contrast with "many companions."

15. See 6:19.

16. Lit. "the entirety (i.e., 'all,' 'the whole') of companions" (GKC, P. 127b), the comprehension of the individuals of the genus. The LXX *pas hos kakos* pointed *hāraʿ* "every bad person," and influenced the Syr. and Targ. but not the Vulg.

17. An ingressive, adjectival stative perfective in a gnomic situation (*IBHS,* pp. 491-92, P. 30.5.3a, c).

18. Lit. "pursuing with words, they are not." Q, against all ancient versions,

8 *The one who gets sense is one who loves his life;*
the one who heeds understanding will soon find[19] *what is good.*
9 *A perjurer*[20] *will not escape punishment,*
and a witness to lies[21] *will perish.*
10 *Luxury is not fitting for a fool;*
how much more [unfitting] for a slave to rule over princes.
11 *A human being's prudence yields patience,*[22]
and his splendor is to pass over transgression.

---

reads *lô,* not *lō':* "He chases after words — they that are to/for him." Rashi interprets this to mean "who pursues words to his benefit" (M. Lyons, "Rashi's *Commentary on the Book of Proverbs*" [submitted in partial fulfillment of the requirements for the degree of rabbi, 1936]. p. 101). Many think that so-called v. 19c (actually v. 19b in the MT), a unique phenomenon in Collection II, is incomplete, an unintelligible fragment. Toy contends that it is impossible to recover the original text. The LXX uniquely adds: *ennoia agathē tois eidosin autēn engiei, anēr de phronimos heurēsei autēn. Ho polla kakopoiōn telesiourgei kakian, hos de erethizei logous* [> *logois*], *ou sōthēsetai.* Delitzsch (*Proverbs,* p. 283) showed that *hos de erethizei logous* renders *mrdp 'mrym,* which Gemser (*Sprüche,* p. 77) completed by a retroverting *yimmālēṭ* (cf. 28:26) where the LXX renders *hemma* as *sōthēsetai.* Gemser's complete retroversion is: *śēkel ṭôb yiqrab lᵉyōdᵉʿāyw wᵉʾîš tᵉbûnâ yimṣāʾennû. marbeh habbîyaʿ yᵉkalleh rešaʿ ûmᵉraddēp ʾᵃmārîm lōʾ yimmālēṭ* (= "Good insight is near to those who know, and a man of understanding will find it. Whoever speaks much perfects wickedness, and whoever chases after words will not escape"). The LXX, however, is creative, adds proverbs of its own, and is distant from the Hebrew. McKane (*Proverbs,* p. 527) comments, "In these circumstances the enterprise of using the additional Greek text to reconstruct a non-existent Hebrew one has little value." The Vulg. reads, "He who pursues only words will have nothing," which it adds to v. 8, but "will have nothing" violates Hebrew syntax and its connection with v. 8, the received tradition. The MT reads literally, "He who pursues with words they are not," which occasions various nonconvincing interpretations. For example, Martin Buber paraphrased, "He chased after the formerly spoken words, but this is no longer valid." Meinhold, preferring Q, explains, "The poor longs after the friendly words which were addressed to him in better times among his brothers and friends." However, one expects disjunctive *waw* for this meaning. The NJPS glosses, "He who pursues words — they are no avail." If one looks to Job 6:21; Ezek. 21:32 for the meaning of "no help" for *lō',* let it be noted that their syntax differs. Many (e.g., KJV, NASB, NIV) essentially paraphrase according to the text.

19. There is no need to smooth the inf. into the finite verb *yimṣā'* with the ancient versions. *Lamed* with the inf. expresses immediacy here (cf. 18:24; see *IBHS,* p. 610, P. 36.2.3g; GKC, P. 114i).

20. See 12:17.

21. See 6:19.

22. Lit. "relaxes his face." The MT reads *heʾᵉrîkᵉ* ("[Prudence] causes him to be patient"). The Syr., Aquila, and Theod. read *haʾᵃrîk* ("[Prudence] consists in having patience"), a more facilitating reading because it agrees with the parallel *Qal* inf. cons.

12 *The roaring as of a lion*[23] *is the fury of a king,*
but like dew on vegetation is his favor.
13 *A foolish son*[24] *is destruction*[25] *for his father,*
and a wife's quarrelings[26] *are a leaky roof that drips constantly.*
14 *A household and wealth are an inheritance from fathers;*
but from the LORD *is a prudent wife.*[27]
15 *Laziness casts [one] into a deep sleep,*[28]
and a slack person hungers.
16 *The one who keeps a commandment is one who preserves his life,*
but the one who despises[29] *his ways*[30] *will die.*[31]

23. Gemser (*Sprüche,* p. 112) notes the proposal by Seeligmann (*VTSup.* I, p. 164, after Ehrlich) to read *kakkōper,* "like frost," instead of *naham kakk^{e}pîr,* forming a better parallelism with *k^{e}ṭal.* The emendation fails to note, however, that the parallelism of "lion" and "dew" precisely matches that of Mic. 5:7-8(6-8) and more closely resembles Prov. 16:14, 15.

24. See 10:1.

25. Abstract pl. (see 17:4). Possibly the pl. is countable to match the countable pl. "strifes." The Targ uniquely has ". . . like sour wine."

26. Elsewhere (21:9, 19; 25:24; 26:21; 27:15) *'ēšet midyānîm* ("quarreling wife"). Conceivably *midy^{e}nê 'iššâ* is also an abstract pl. with a gen. of genus (= "a quarrelsome wife"), but why the different construction here especially when it is in parallel with a gen. of species? The LXX has a different second half: "Vows paid out of the hire of prostitutes are not pure." Perhaps it read *neder,* not *tōrēd* and *nādān/niddâ, 'etnān, māḥîr* (Lagarde), not *mdyny* (A. J.. Baumgartner, *Étude critique sur l'état du texte du Livre des Proverbes d'après les principales traductions anciennes* [Leipzig: Imprimerie Orientale W. Drugulin, 1890], pp. 176-77) and was influenced by Deut. 23:19.

27. The LXX, Targ., and Syr. read *mśklt* as a passive (i.e., is made competent) and so interpreted verset B to mean that God suits the wife to the husband.

28. The LXX has "Cowardice possesses the effeminate man," curiously rendering *tardēmâ* by *androgynos* because "*radham* puzzled the Greek translators to such an extent that they did not know quite what to make of it" (J. G. Thomson, S.S., "Sleep: An Aspect of Jewish Anthropology," *VT* [1955] 422). The LXX presents a curiously similar variant in 18:8.

29. It is tempting to add disjunctive *waw* with the ancient versions and explain its omission as haplography due to *napšô,* but parallel v. 8, although a synonymous parallelism, suggests that the lack of the disjunctive may be deliberate.

30. Toy (*Proverbs,* p. 375), Fichtner *(BHS),* et al. emend *drkyw* to *dbr* ("the word"). The emendation can be defended by noting that *bzh* occurs with *dbr* three times (Num. 15:31; 2 Sam. 12:9; 2 Chr. 36:16), always of "the word of the LORD," never with *drk,* and the verb's by-form *bāz* occurs with *dbr* in 13:13. Also, in wisdom literature the object of *bzh* is always a person (14:2; 15:20; Eccl. 9:16), never a thing. Finally, *dbr* forms a better parallel with *miṣwâ.* Moreover, the MT can be explained — i.e., the suffix is due to dittography with *ywmt,* and the transposition of *b* to *k* and the metathesis of *b* and *r* are common scribal errors. On the other hand, the MT has the support of all the ancient versions. Though difficult, it is not too difficult; *bzh* may take an impersonal object (Gen.

17 *The one who shows grace to the poor is one who lends to the*
LORD;
and as for his deeds, he will repay him.
18 *Discipline your son, for surely*[32] *there is hope,*
and to killing him[33] *do not set your desire.*
19 *A hothead*[34] *is one who incurs a penalty;*
surely if you deliver [him], you will do so again.[35]

25:34; Esth. 3:6), and the idea of despising one's ways is conceptually the same as loving death (8:36) and an apt conceptual antithesis to guarding his way (16:17). Moreover, K's *ywmt* may be due to dittography from *drkyw.* J. Emerton ("Notes and Studies on Some Passages in the Book of Proverbs," *JTS* n.s. 20 [1969] 208) defends the MT differently. He argues that the form is an abbreviation of *drky YHWH.* This is plausible because "the ways of the LORD" is a common syntagm for living the way the LORD prescribes (Deut. 8:6; 12:1; passim). Also, his proposal defends Plöger, who interpreted "his ways" as a reference to the LORD to form a link with the following Yahweh saying, against the objection that the suffix would be uniquely cataphoric to the next verse. It is also explains K's divine passive "will be put to death." Though plausible (see Waltke, "Micah," p. 625), it involves emending final *waw* to *yodh* and is unnecessary.

31. K, Syr., and Vulg. read *yûmat* ("will be put to death"), but Q and Targ. read *yāmût* ("will die"). The *Hophal* of *mût* is common in the legal literature (Exod. 21:12, 15-17, 29) but never occurs in wisdom literature, whereas *Qal* is common in the latter (Prov. 5:23; 15:10; 23:13; cf. 10:21; 30:7). It would be astonishing to find a saying prescribing a death sentence in wisdom literature. Moreover, Q forms a better parallel with "preserves his life." The son must choose for himself either life or death. The transposition of the two middle letters was facilitated in K by dittography with the preceding suffix (see the preceding note).

32. Lit. "your son — surely." Although many (e.g., AV, NJPS, REB, NASB, NRSV, and NLT) think *kî* with *yēš* is temporal (= "while"), that meaning cannot be defended from usage (see Job 11:18; 14:7; cf. Gen. 33:11; 2 Chr. 15:7; 16:9; 25:8; Job 28:1; Eccl. 2:21; Jer. 31:6, 16; Mic. 2:1). The LXX renders it *gar houtōs* ("for so").

33. The LXX (cf. Syr. "to his shame") reads *eis hybrin* (= "[do not rouse yourself] to passion/wanton excess"), assuming hubris refers here to violence, not pride as in 1:22; 8:13; 11:2; 16:18; 18:10. Lagarde relates the word to Aram. *hmywt* (cf. Isa. 14:11; cf. Baumgartner, *Critique,* p. 178). Gemser (*Sprüche,* p. 77), though not ruling out the MT, obtains a similar thought by reading *ḥēmôt* ("anger"), but as McKane (*Proverbs,* p. 524) notes, "to lift up the soul" means "to aspire to." The Targ. and Vulg. read the MT. D. W. Thomas ("Some Passages," p. 288) questionably thinks that the MT is hyperbole, meaning no more than "to chastise excessively," but, as Gemser (*Sprüche,* p. 77) notes, "weakens the text."

34. Lit. "great of wrath," reading Q *gdl ḥēmâ,* "great of wrath" (cf. "great of wings" (Ezek. 17:3, 7), an epexegetical gen. (*IBHS,* p. 151, P. 9.5.3c) and an abstract for the concrete (see 12:24, n. 31). Kethib *gōral* "lot" is unintelligible, unless it represents an otherwise unattested Hebrew adjective related to Arab. *jarila* "stony ground," in turn related to "lot." Scribes commonly confused *d* and *r.* Fichtner *(BHS)* questionably thinks that the LXX (cf. Targ. and Syr) *anēr* represents *geber.*

35. The *Hiphil* of *ysp* commonly adds *'ôd;* here, however, it elides *l'śwt* (see BDB, p. 415, s.v. *ysp*).

20 *Listen to counsel and receive discipline*[36]
so that you may be counted among the wise in your final destiny.[37]
21 *The plans in the heart of a person are many,*
but as for the counsel of the L*ORD*,[38] *it will take place.*
22 *What people desire*[39] *in a human being*[40] *is his*[41]
unfailing kindness;[42]
better is a poor person than a liar.
23 *The fear of the* L*ORD is surely life;*
fully satisfied, he dwells not met with harm.[43]

36. "Discipline" was chosen rather than "instruction" to preserve the connection with *yassēr* in v. 18 (see 1:2).

37. The Syr. reads *b'wrḥtk* (< *bᵉ'ōrᵉḥōtêkā,* "in your paths"), perhaps a facilitating reading for the more difficult MT.

38. Nominative absolute construction for emphasis (*IBHS,* pp. 76-77, P. 4.7a-c).

39. For *ta'ᵃwat* the LXX has *karpos* (< *tᵉbû'at* "the gain, yield"; see 3:14; 14:4). On this basis McKane (*Proverbs,* p. 532) renders verset A: "A man's productivity is his loyalty," which he explains to mean, "Productivity should be measured in terms of loyalty rather than wealth," but his interpretation is forced. The text could mean, however, "The revenue to a man is his kindness," but this too is unnecessary and not a good parallel to verset B. The rendition, "The desire of a human being is his [doing] kindness," is also forced (Toy, *Proverbs,* p. 378). It is unclear how the Vulg. got *homo indigens misericors* ("A needy man is merciful"). Nevertheless, verset A is neither hopeless nor incapable of being brought into natural connection with B (*pace* Toy, *Proverbs,* p. 378).

40. Semantic pertinence favors taking *'ādām* as gen. of a mediated object, if *ḥasdô* is the correct text (see *IBHS,* p. 146, P. 9.5.2b). Rashi (Lyons, "Rashi's *Commentary,*" p. 103) takes it as an objective gen.: "People desire a person because of his kindness," which is not grammatically possible for the predicate nominative *ḥasdô.* Verset A, however, could also mean, "What a human being desires is kindness to himself" (cf. Saadia, cited by Toy, *Proverbs,* p. 378), taking the suffix as an objective gen. This seems less natural and does not offer as good an antithetical parallel with verset B as the proposed text.

41. Possibly the suffix is due to dittography with following *wᵉ.* If so, *ḥesed* is probably a subjective gen., "The desire of a human being is *ḥesed*" = "What a human being desires is kindness" (cf. NIV). The difference in meaning from the received text is slight. The received text looks at the human being from without, the emendation from within.

42. Or "A person's self-gratification is his shame." *Ḥesed* is a homonym meaning both "unfailing kindness" and "disgrace, shame" (*HALOT,* 1:336, s.v. I *ḥesed* and II *ḥesed*). Since both interpretations of *ḥesed* are feasible, probably the pun is intentional. Clifford (*Proverbs,* p. 178) and most English versions prefer the text, while Van Leeuwen (*Proverbs,* p. 181), REB, NJPS and NIV [note] prefer the alternative.

43. Verset B regards "the fear of the LORD" as an abstract for the concrete, "the one who fears the LORD" (see 12:24).

The unit 18:22–19:23 pertains to wealth and poverty in the court and in the home. Its three subunits (18:22–19:7, 8-15, 16-23) are crocheted together in intricate embroideries. The catchwords "finds good" *(mṣ' ṭôb)* that connect "acquire" *(qōneh)* a wife and sense (18:22; 19:8) link the introductions to their first two units. These two units also take up the problem of a "false witness" (*'ēd šeqer* and *yāpiaḥ kᵉzābîm,* 19:5, 9), shifting from a potentially corrupt official (19:6) and veiled references to the LORD (19:3, 5) and his righteous prince/king (19:10, 12) who "will not acquit" (*lō' yinnāqeh,* 19:5, 9) the perjurer. After their introductions (18:22, 19:16) the first and third subunits begin with reference to the poor (*rāš/dāl,* 18:23; 19:17) and use "better . . . than" proverbs to assert that the poor person *(ṭôb-rāš)* is better than a liar (19:1, 22). This unit that begins looking for the rare friend that sticks closer than a brother (18:24) appropriately ends with educating the son to be kind to the needy (19:16-23) and climaxes with the promise of eternal life for the one who fears the LORD (19:23).

Meinhold perceived the connection between the introductions to the second and third subunits (19:8 and 16). Both use *Qal* active participles to denote both the condition of keeping the sage's teaching and the consequence of preserving one's life *(napšô)*. Moreover, with reference to the former they escalate from the positive "one who acquires" (*qōneh,* 18:22; 19:8a) "sense" (19:8a) to "one who keeps" *(šōmēr)* "understanding" (19:8b)/"a commandment" (19:16a). The four versets of these two introductions form a chiasm, matching in their outer frame the positive "one who acquires" (v. 8a) with its negative ("one who despises," v. 16b), and in their inner core the synonyms "one who keeps *(šōmēr)* understanding" (v. 8b) with "one who keeps *(šōmēr)* a commandment" (v. 16b), reprising the escalation from acquiring to keeping also observed in 3:13, 18, and 20. The first two subunits chiastically consist of two partial units pertaining to the spheres of the court (19:5-7 and 9-12) and of the family (18:22; 19:13-15). The second qualifies that the wife in view in 18:22) is a prudent wife from the LORD, not a quarrelsome wife that drives him from his home. Agur, in a unified numerical proverb, also shifts from the body politic to the home (30:21-23).

a. Poverty, Wealth, and Companions (18:22–19:7)

After an introductory proverb about the closest of human relationships, that of a man and his wife (18:22), 18:23–19:7 are about the moral ambiguities of wealth. The rich attract companions, but the poor person loses them. Words for the poor person (*rāš* and *dāl*) occur at the seams of this unit: *rāš* in 18:23 and 19:7, forming an *inclusio* around it, as well as in 19:1 that introduces the subunit of 19:1-3, and *dāl* in 19:4 that introduces the subunit 19:4-7. The other keyword is "companion" (*rēa',* 18:24; 19:4a) or "close companion" (*m*ᵉ*rēa*ʿ, 19:4b, 7b). The unit begins with the poor person's supplications (18:23) and ends with the assertion that they are of no avail (19:7). After the introductory proverb the unit falls into three subunits. The first pertains to failed companions: the supplications of the poor person (18:23a) and the implied failure of companions (v. 24a). The second (see 19:1-3) concerns ethics and wealth: to walk with moral integrity in spite of poverty (v. 1) and not to hasten after wealth (v. 2) because the LORD will punish folly (v. 3). The third has to do with the moral ambiguity of wealth and companions in court: wealth adds companions in court (vv. 4a, 6) and the poor person loses them (vv. 4b, 7), but perjurers will not escape punishment. The connection of these sub-units suggests that the companions in view are not wise; they can be bought (18:23; 19:1-3, 4-7), and it is folly to depend on them (18:24). The poor person's only hope is "a friend that sticks closer than a brother" among the wise. The reference to currying favor with a ruler in v. 6 prepares the way for the next unit on "wisdom in the court and in the home" (19:8-15).

(1) Introduction (18:22)

The unexpected shift of topic to the wife in the middle of proverbs pertaining, superficially at least, to speech (18:20-21, 23) again signals the introduction to a new unit (see 11:16, 22; 12:4). Its initial *mem,* linking it with initial *mem* in vv. 20-21, and the personification of the tongue as a woman smooth the transition between the two units. It is entirely fitting that a unit on social relationships should begin with the most intimate relationship of a spouse. Verse 22a echoes and 22b repeats the words of Woman Wisdom in 8:35: "The one who finds me finds life and obtains favor from the LORD." Aitken comments, "As if to say that finding a good wife is on a par with finding wisdom."[44] If this intertextual play is intentional, v. 22 may function as an educational proverb, encouraging the disciple to attain the sage's wisdom in order to obtain the LORD's favor in the form of a wife (see 11:1; 12:2; 19:14; 31:10-31). The proverb assumes that God is good and rewards the man who fears him with a wife equal to him (see 31:10, 30).[45] Moreover, the echo may presume that the good wife, like Wisdom, has to be sought from the LORD (see 8:34; 19:14). In its synthetic parallels the finding of a wife is affirmed as a "good" situation (v. 22a), and its source and cause are the LORD's favor (v. 22b).[46] In this asyn-

44. Aitken, *Proverbs,* p. 153.

45. Delitzsch (*Proverbs,* p. 277) cites a Talmudic tradition (Yebamoth 63b) where the rabbinate in Palestine asked when someone married: Is it *māṣāʾ* ("finds" as in Prov. 8:12) or *mōṣēʾ* ("finds" as in Eccl. 7:26)?

46. The assonance of /*a*/ in the MT and consonance of /*ʾ*/ in *māṣāʾ ʾiššâ māṣāʾ ṭôb* is obvious; note also the loose series of fricatives *(ṣ, š, ṭ)* and interdental explosives. The consonance continues in *rāṣôn,* which has assonance of /*ō*/ with *ṭôb.*

detic conditional clause *the one who* is indefinite[47] and the verb *finds* (see 1:28; 2:5; 3:4, 13) entails his attainment of a goal that he has pursued diligently, unlike the poor person's quest that ends in failure (19:7).[48] The English idiom requires the gloss *wife ('iššâ),* not "woman" because the man finds/obtains her (see I: 118). Leaving aside references to the "the harlot wife" (2:16; 6:24, 26, 29; 7:5, 10), the wife is often qualified by an attributive adjective construction pertaining to the semantic fields of *good* (see I: 98; 11:16; 12:4; 14:1a; 19:14; 31:10, 30) or bad (cf. 12:4; 14:1; 19:13b; 21:9, 19; 25:24; 30:20; 31:3). The epexegetical *waw* consecutive *(and so)* continues the apodosis, the consequence of finding a wife. The grammar disallows the interpretation that he seeks a wife to elicit God's favor. *Obtains favor from the LORD* (see 8:35) through the metonymy of "favor" identifies the LORD as the source of the good (cf. Jas. 1:17). There may also be an intertextual play with Gen. 2:18, where a man without a wife is pronounced "not good," a litotes for bad. As with the first man, the Creator gives each fractured male with whom he is pleased one wife to complete the abundant life he intended. The apostle Paul, however, commends a better way of being single to be fully engaged in the LORD's business (1 Corinthians 7).

(2) Wealth and Failed Companions (18:23-24)

23 The proverb turns from the intimate relationship of husband and wife to the polar relationships of rich and poor. In the Hebrew text the chiastic, antithetic parallels, marked by *but,* place in their inner core the topics *the* undeservedly *poor person* (see 13:8) and *the* materially *rich* but spiritually poor *person* (see 1:28; 10:15; 14:20; 18:11). In the central position occur the complementary verbs *speaks* (see 2:12) and *answers* (1:28; 15:28; 16:1), and in the outer frame the antithetical adverbs *pleadingly (taḥ^{a}nûnîm)* and *brazenly ('azzôt). Taḥ^{a}nûnîm* derives from the root *ḥnn,* "to be gracious," "to show favor," and means in essence "cries for favor." "*Taḥ^{a}nûnîm* are the expressions of a mind beset with terror which do not have established formulations."[49] By contrast, *'az,* which usually means "strong, powerful, mightily," can also mean "fierce" (or "insolent"), "impudent," or "shameless" (cf. Deut. 28:50; Dan. 8:23).[50] The line between strong and shameless is often attenuated. In the former sense it may connote "unyielding" (Song 8:6). It is parallel to "cruel" *(qšh)* with anger (Genesis 49), both with reference to a king

47. *IBHS,* pp. 70-71, P. 4.4.2; p. 636, P. 38.2a.

48. The suffix conjugation represents the situation as hypothetical (*IBHS,* p. 493, P. 30.5.4b; Delitzsch, *Proverbs,* p. 277).

49. *HALOT,* 4:1,719, s.v. *taḥ^{a}nûnîm.*

50. Note all three words in verset B begin with *'ayin.*

(Isa. 49:17), and to "ruthless" *(ʿārîṣ)* with reference to a nations (Isa. 25:3). Other proverbs condemned the rich person for making wealth his "strong" city (10:15; 18:11); this one implicitly censures him for his "strong" (i.e., shameless, unyielding) response to the poor man's cries and his brushing him aside (see 14:20-21). These are not unrelated. Since the rich person's own sense of security depends on his wealth, not on the LORD, he must defend "his city" against their cries. The poor have no choice but to speak pleadingly, but the rich have an option how to answer and so are accountable. A Jewish proverb says, "In order to chase away beggars one needs a rich person."[51] By contrast, God hears the pleas of the needy (Pss. 28:2, 6; 34:6[7], 15[16]; 116:1), and the New Testament teaches that only the merciful obtain mercy (Matt. 5:7). Once again a proverb links poverty with innocence and prosperity with baseness (see I: 108).

24 The proverb now focuses on the relationship of companions. Its antithetical parallelism draws a line between the topics, companions (i.e., run-of-the-mill friends) versus a true friend, and their respective predicates, "about to be shattered" versus "who sticks closer than a brother." This last, imprecise antithesis implies that the man of typical "friends" is about to be ruined because he lacks one true friend in adversity; and the man with one true friend is not about to be ruined.[52] Sirach (6:10) puts the contrast this way: "There is a friend who is a table companion but will not stand by you in your day of trouble." *A person who has unreliable companions* glosses the unique expression *ʾîš rēʿîm* (lit. "a person of neighbors"; see 3:28). *Rēaʿ* is glossed "neighbor," "another," or "companion" when it refers to a neutral or somewhat negative relationship and by "friend" when it refers to a positive relationship (17:17; 22:11; 27:9-10, 14[?]). In 17:17; 22:11 "the friend" is qualified by *ʾōhēb,* ("a lover [i.e., a true friend]"). The absolute plural found here is used four other times: of superficial sexual partners (Jer. 3:1) versus true ones (Song 5:1), of companions attracted to wealth (19:4), and of falsely denounced neighbors (Job 17:5). Here also companions (i.e., partners who fail to come through in adversity) are in view. (1) With them one is on the verge of being shattered. (2) They are contrasted with the *ʾōhēb* (the singular true friend; cf. 17:17; 22:11). (3) The *rēʿîm rabbîm* of 19:4, 6, who also belong to this unit, are also pseudo, for they rally to the rich and abandon the poor. (4) This interpretation admirably suits the next unit warning against the folly of hastening after money. The person who has these fair-weather friends is a rich person according to 19:6, linking v. 24 to v. 23. The gloss *about to be*

51. *Die ganze Welt,* pp. 116-17, cited by Meinhold, *Sprüche,* p. 309.

52. In *ʾîš rēʿîm lᵉhitrōʿēaʿ wᵉyēš ʾōhēb dābēq mēʾâ* note the assonance of /ē/ in six of its seven words; the loose sequence of gutturals *ʿ, h, ʿ;* and the alliteration between *rēʿîm* and *lᵉhitrōʿēaʿ.*

[or is soon] *broken* (*l^ehitrōʿēaʿ;* see n. 6) is disputed. II *rʿʿ* in the *Qal* is used of breaking iron and bronze (Jer. 15:12) and twice of shattering enemies (Job 34:24; Ps. 2:9), and, in its other use in the *Hithpael,* of the earth being rent asunder (Isa. 24:19). Thus the lemma connotes being shattered, being broken into pieces, and of the many synonyms for "to destroy," it was probably chosen for its assonance with *rēaʿ*.[53] The infinitive construct with *l^e* signifies an event that is ready to happen (see 17:17). Prov. 25:19 likens the fair-weather friend to an unreliable bad tooth and a lame foot, and 11:13; 25:9 show that misplaced trust can be misused in gossip (11:13; 25:9). *But (w^e)* contrasts that situation with *there is* [see 3:28] *a friend* [see 14:20]. *One who sticks (dābēq)* mixes both an essentially psychological stative notion of clinging with the activity of adhering tightly to someone or something (cf. Deut. 4:4), so closely that even death could not separate them (Ruth 1:14-17).[54] The comparative *closer than a brother* (*mē'āḥ;* see 18:19) uses the blood relative as a basis of comparison for sticking to someone through thick and thin but which the subject has to an even greater degree (see 17:17).[55] Economic survival was precarious in ancient Israel, and one needed the "insurance" of a true friend. One also needed such a friend in court. The similar proverb in 17:17 shares with this proverb three keywords, "friend" *('ōhēb* and *rēaʿ)* and "brother" *('āḥ).* A friend more loyal than a brother is needed because even a brother inwardly "hates" a poor relative (19:7). The friend in view is a wise person who belongs to the community of the faithful and/or possibly God. The significance of friends is found in their quality, not quantity. Thus, the proverb implicitly warns the disciple against pursuing wealth and having pseudo-friends, or of belonging to their company, but exhorts him to pursue wisdom and pick his friends among the wise (cf. 12:26; 13:20; 22:24; 28:7; 29:3). The friend whose loyalty transcends the solidarity of blood is realized in Jesus Christ (cf. John 15:12-15; Heb. 2:11, 14-18).

(3) Wealth and Ethics (19:1-3)

The unit now turns from the friendless poor person to the worse-off unethical rich person, escalating the latter's wrongs against his neighbor (his lies, v. 1, and his greed, v. 2), to his overthrow by the LORD and his continued impiety (v. 3). This subunit is framed by the *inclusio* "fool" and "folly" (vv. 1, 3). It is connected by intellectual terms in the semantic domain of fool: "fool" (v. 1),

53. For example, cf. E. W. Goodrick and J. R. Kohlenberger III, *The NIV Exhaustive Concordance* (Grand Rapids: Zondervan, 1990), s.v. "destroy." Note the sequence of consonants */r ʿl* in *rʿym lhtrʿʿ*.

54. *IBHS,* p. 369, P. 22.3k.

55. *IBHS,* p. 264, P. 14.4d.

"without knowledge" (v. 2), and "folly" (v. 3) and by the metaphor of a journey, referring to "walks" (v. 1), "feet" and "misses the way" (v. 2), and "way" (v. 3). Verses 1-2 are a proverb pair further connected by the theme of what is "not good," involving the catchword *ṭôb,* by characterizing the rich sinner by his misuse of his dual body parts "lips" and "feet," and by the assonance of *rāš* ("poor") and *'āṣ* ("one who is hasty").

1 This proverb continues the topic of the *rāš* (the poor man) and his speech (see 18:23), but turns from his failed social relationships to his successful ethics. Through a *better . . . than* proverb (see I: 44), it asserts that the poor person's impeccable walk in the sage's teachings (cf. 19:22), in spite of the social liability of his poverty, is a better situation than being a liar. Even though his pilgrimage crosses through the twisted speech of a liar who plunders him, he is better off because the LORD will punish the liar (19:3). The proverb has the evaluative pattern of A (negative, the poor man) plus B (positive, who walks in his blamelessness) :: C (negative, who twists his lips) plus D (negative, for he is a fool). We may presume that since C normally refers to material advantage, "the one who twists his lips" enriches himself at the expense of the poor. The outer core, *a poor person* (see 13:8; 18:23) versus *a fool* (*k^{e}sîl;* see I: 112) consists of imprecise, antithetical parallels, inferring that the poor person is wise and the fool is rich. The Syriac version and the synoptic proverb 28:6 replace "fool" with "a rich person" (see n. 9). The inner core of this chiastic parallelism, *who walks* (*hôlēk;* see 1:15) *in his integrity* (or "blamelessness," *b^{e}tummô;* see I: 99) versus *who twists* (*ʿiqqēš;* see 2:15) *his lips* (18:20), entails that the former speaks the truth and that the latter despises wisdom. Even though the rich person answers him rudely (18:23) and the poor person is on the verge of ruin (18:24; 19:7), the poor person's way is better because it is blessed (20:7) and secure (cf. Job 4:6). On this eternal way the LORD is his shield to protect him (2:7); his way is like a mountain fortress (10:29); and, with full confidence that he will never lose his relationship with God and the community of the faithful, he can walk securely in it (10:9). By contrast, the twisted person will not find good and is headed for calamity (17:20; cf. 22:5). Once again a proverb correlates poverty with piety and wealth with impiety (see I: 108). The poor may be miserable for the moment, but the unethical rich are miserable for eternity. Thus the proverb teaches the pilgrim to walk by faith, not by sight.

2 The second proverb of the pair escalates the rich fool's lies to defraud his neighbor to his intentional pursuit to gratify his greed. The particle *if even* (see 17:28; 18:9) signals that the proverb employs an a fortiori argument, reasoning from the lesser to the greater. Its synthetic parallels escalate moral ignorance to deliberate disregard of moral consequences, internal desire to actions by the feet, and "not good" to "misses the way/sinner." If even *desire* [or appetite, *nepeš;* see I: 90) *without* [see 13:23] *knowledge* [see

I: 77] is *not good* [see I: 99], *how much more* [see n. 12] *will the one who hastens . . .* [*to make money*] *('āṣ).* The verb *'ûṣ* denotes forcing others or oneself to act quickly (Exod. 5:13; Josh. 10:13). In Proverbs it always occurs as a *Qal* substantival participle to denote a person who acts without regard to moral consequences, especially in order to make money ((21:5; 28:20; 29:20).[56] The connection of v. 2 to v. 1 makes that sense probable here. *With his feet* is added in this proverb pair to form a link with "who walks" (v. 1a) and "his lips" (v. 1b), to couple greed for money (v. 2a) with feet that carry it out (v. 2b), and to intensify haste (cf. 1:16; 6:18), not to refer to sexual activity.[57] The gloss *misses the way* (*hôṭē';* lit. "is one who misses"; see 1:10) assumes that with rushing feet *ḥṭ'* retains its basic meaning "to miss the way or goal" (see Judg. 20:16; Job 5:24; Prov. 1:10). The missed way or goal here is a figure for a lifestyle that fails the standard of conduct demanded by God, a crime that incurs his punishment (i.e., "to sin"; see 11:31; 13:6; 14:22). In Prov. 20:2 the consequence that one forfeits his life through sin stands in the forefront. In that light, how much better is the poor person who walks in his total dedication to the LORD and his teachings than the condemned sinner who enriches himself through lies. Verset A alerts the disciple to curb his appetite by his moral knowledge of the deed-destiny nexus, and verset B cautions him against the inevitable judgment of hastening to gratify his desire for money. Paradoxically, the spiritually rich, though materially poor, person departs from the morally bankrupt rich person lest he be infected by his contagion (14:7).

3 The rich fool's sinful behavior of lying (v. 1b) and his drive to become rich (v. 2b) are now escalated climactically to "human folly," which signifies the earthling's intractable moral insolence even when the LORD judges him. In this antithetical, chiastic parallelism, the topics *the folly* (see I: 113) *of a human being* (*'ādām;* see I: 89) and *his heart* (see I: 90) stand in the outer frame and shed light on each other. The imprecise antithetical predicates *overturns* [*t^esallēp;* see 13:6] *his way* (see 1:15) and *rages (yiz'ap) against the LORD* (see I: 67) form its inner core. They, too, shed light on each other: the intractable, arrogant fool elevates himself as the ruler of the universe and rages against its Moral Governor for turning his sinful way, which he hoped would continue forever, on its head. *Zā'ap* denotes an emotional state of extreme anger (cf. Isa. 30:30) against someone leading to hostile action against the antagonist (cf. 2 Chr. 26:19). Its by-forms are used exclusively of the emotions attributed to kings (1 K. 20:43; 21:4; 2 Chr. 16:10; 26:19; Prov. 19:12) and of God (2 Chr. 28:9; Isa. 30:30; Mic. 7:9; Jon. 1:15, where the sea is personified as a deity). Instead of repenting of the sins that

56. "A characteristic of money-making people" *(HALOT,* 1:23, s.v. *'wz).*
57. *Pace HALOT,* 1:23, s.v. *'wz.*

prompted the Lord to ruin him, the earthbound creature is so convinced that his sinful way of life is right that he storms against the Lord, holding him accountable for not granting what he thought, planned, and willed. His absurd raging against the Lord implies that he experienced ruin before reaching his goal and has recognized his misfortune.

(4) Wealth and Companions in Court (19:4-7)

The final subunit returns to the moral ambiguity of companions and wealth with a particular focus on the court. Verse 6 elaborates the notion of v. 4a that wealth attracts pseudo-friends, and v. 7 the notion of v. 4b that the poor lose even their close companions. Verse 6 splits apart the *rēʿîm rabbîm* of v. 4a into *rabbîm* (v. 7a) and *hārēaʿ* (v. 7b), and v. 7aβ repeats *mᵉrēʿîm* of v. 4b. In that light it becomes clear that vv. 6 and 7 are an antithetic proverb pair, an antithesis underscored by the repetition of *kol* in v. 4b and v. 7aα. Meinhold suggests that by placing the divine threat of punishing the perjurer (v. 5) between vv. 4 and 6, the proverb may imply the life-threatening danger confronting the poor person who lacks a true friend in court.[58]

4 This antithetical parallelism presents the socioeconomic limitations of human friendship untouched by wisdom, juxtaposing (1) *wealth* (*hôn;* see 3:9) with *as for the poor person* (*dāl;* see 10:15); (2) *many* (*rabbîm;* see 4:10) *companions* (*rēʿîm;* 18:24) with *even* (*ad sensum*) *his close companion (mērēʿîm);* (3) and *attracts* (*yōsîp;* lit. "adds"; see 1:5) with *separates himself* (see 18:1). Typical neighbors, not spongers or sycophants, are in view. *Mērēaʿ* is never used of close friends in the covenant community.[59] The same harsh reality about merely human friendships is also accentuated in 14:20 and 19:7. The everyday, run-of-the-mill "friends" crowd around wealth, hoping to enrich themselves through it. The Romans quoted the proverb, *Ubi amici, ibidem opes* (= "Where there are friends, there is wealth").[60] Even the bosom companion takes the initiative to dissolve the relationship when the demands made on him become too burdensome. Thus the proverb cautions the disciple about the dangers of wealth and friendships outside the community of faith. Although it is a crowd, each one forms the friendship out of what he can gain, not for what he can give. The proverb anticipates the Lord's teaching on the use of money to win friends and an eternal reward in the kingdom of God (Luke 16:1-9).

58. Meinhold, *Sprüche,* p. 313.

59. *HALOT* (2:637) glosses *mᵉrēaʿ* as "bosom friend." It is used in conjunction with *ʾāḥ* ("brother"/"relative") in 2 Sam. 3:6; Prov. 19:7 and of Samson's Philistine friends at his wedding (Judg. 14:20; 15:2, 6), of Abimelech's personal adviser (Gen. 26:20), and of Abner's friends in Saul's house (2 Sam. 3:6).

60. Cited by Plaut, *Proverbs,* p. 202.

5 This proverb applies the principle of v. 1 to the courtroom, the setting of this proverb as suggested by the courtly term "seek the favor of a nobleman" in the following proverb and the concern for giving false testimony in this one. By a rare, precise synonymous parallelism, this proverb emphatically warns the perjurer against the lure of money, for he will not escape punishment (see vv. 1-3). The seriousness of the warning is further underscored by its repetition in v. 9. *A perjurer* (*ʿēd šeqārîm;* see 12:17) *will not escape punishment* (see 6:29). *And* links the two synonymous parallels into one complex statement. *A witness to lies* (*yāpîaḥ kezābîm;* see 6:29) *will not escape (yimmālēṭ),* which in its one other use is also a parallel to *yinnāqeh* (11:21), confirms that the escape is from punishment and suggests that it, too, is a legal term. In light of this reality and since one cannot depend on even the closest friend to save him in court, the Agent who unmasks the perjurer and exacts his punishment must be the LORD (see 16:1-9; 19:1-3; Eccl. 3:16-17). *Amenemope* (14.2) agrees: "God hates the falsifier of words."[61] Moreover, the predicted punishment must transcend clinical death, for the truthful witness does not escape the grave any more than the false (Ps. 49:10[11]), nor does he necessarily enjoy a longer life (see I: 104).

6 The setting of this proverb is still the courtroom, and in that context it warns against the moral dangers of wealth and so-called "friends." It is not wrong for the needy to seek the favor of the nobleman (cf. 1 Sam. 25:1-9; Job 11:19; Ps. 45:12[13]); Mal. 1:9), but the relationship between the petitioner and nobleman is fraught with the moral danger of serving self, not justice. Verset A points to the moral danger at the beginning of the courtly ceremony. *Many* (*rabbîm;* see 19:4) shades off into the "all" in the parallel. According to Seybold, *seek the favor of* (*yeḥallû penê;* lit. "to make the face pleasant")[62] "refers to the introductory act of a ceremony defining the fundamental relationship that commonly issues in a petition" (Exod. 32:11; 2 K. 13:4ff.; Ps. 119:58; Zech. 7:2).[63] The subject performing the action declares a subordinate position to the one whose favor is sought: wealthy officials to the queen (Ps. 45:12[13]), priests to God (Mal. 1:8-9); the lay judge to the "great" (Lev. 19:15), and a litigant to a *nobleman* (see 8:16; 17:7). The subject performing the action is himself privileged to have access to the one whose favor is

61. *AEL,* 2:154.

62. The phrase occurs 16 times, 12 times with God as the object (Exod. 32:11; 1 K. 13:6 [2x]; 2 K. 13:4; 2 Chr. 33:12; Ps. 119:58; Jer. 26:19; Dan. 9:13; Zech. 7:2; 8:21, 22; Mal. 1:9) versus 4 times with human beings (Lev. 19:15; Job 11:19; Ps. 45:13; Prov. 19:6). The etymology of this idiom, which always involves the *Piel* of *ḥlh* followed by *pānîm* "face," is opaque, but it probably derives from a root *ḥlh* "be sweet, pleasant" *(Qal),* "adorn, bedeck" *(Piel),* not from I *ḥālâ* "to be weak/sick" (cf. 23:35; K. Seybold, *TDOT,* 4:407; BDB, p. 318; *pace HALOT* 1:316-17, s.v. *ḥlh*).

63. K. Seybold, *TDOT,* 4:408, s.v. *ḥālāh.*

sought. This introductory act cannot be visualized further, but probably it entailed the giving of a gift or gifts to incline the official to bestow the soon-to-be-asked-for benefaction. *And* unites the parallel situation that expands on the situation of verset A. *The generous person has* (*lᵉʾîš mattān;* see 18:16) glosses a conventional idiom for a person who has the nature, quality, character, or condition of "gift-giving"; the parallel suggests that many petitioners are in view. *Everyone* (*kol;* see 17:8, n. 34) *for a friend* (*hārēaʿ;* see 19:4), according to the parallel, includes the official and, in this context, the eyewitnesses. The generous benefactor is in a position to attach to his person or cause the beneficiary through his munificence. The connection with vv. 5 and 7 suggests that justice on behalf of the poor is not being well served, and v. 5 takes on new urgency. In other words, the gift is in danger of becoming a bribe (see 17:8, 23; 18:16). By contrast, the wise care for the poor (14:21) and are free from moral jeopardy because they depend on the LORD for his benefactions. Sometimes the disciple has to stand apart from the masses.

7 As v. 6 expands the thought of v. 4a that wealth adds everyone as a "friend," v. 7 develops the antithesis of v. 4b that the poor person loses everyone as his "friend" (cf. 14:20). The catchword *kol* (vv. 6b, 7aα) strengthens the semantic antithesis between vv. 6 and 7. Verses 7 and 4b are linked by the catchword *mᵉrēʿēhû,* "his close companion," but v. 7 escalates v. 4b. First it adds *every one (kol) of the brothers* (*ʾaḥê;* see 6:19; 18:24), who were born into covenantal soliditary with the family to provide for each other's needs in adversity (17:17), *of a poor person* [see 13:8] *hates him* (see 1:22). The addition of v. 7aα now becomes the premise of v. 7aβ as it drives home the poor person's alienation by the a fortiori argument. *How much more* [see 11:31; 19:10] *his close companion* (*mᵉrēʿēhû;* see 19:4) *becomes distant* [or far in tangible space and felt emotions] *from him.* If all his relatives, whose obligations to help him are based on blood, internally feel like ridding themselves of the burdensome relative so as not to hear his pleas for help, how much more will his close companion, who is not constrained by the primary and inescapable bonds of blood, set up barriers in order not to hear his supplications (cf. 14:20; 19:4b). Verset B clarifies the poor person's plight in both relationships. *He pursues* (see 11:19) to overtake them to satisfy his cravings *with pleadings* (*ʾămārîm,* "words"; i.e., the external expression of his felt needs; see 1:2; 15:26; 16:24; 17:27; 18:23) *that are of no avail* (*lōʾ-hemmâ;* see n. 18). However, a longtime friend of the family is better than a relative far away (27:10).

b. Wisdom in the Court and in the Home (19:8-15)

In addition to the noted links between the introductions to the first two subunits (18:22; 19:7) and the repetition of v. 5 in v. 9, the juxtaposition of "hate" at the end of the first (19:7) and of "love" at the beginning of the second (v. 8) also ties them together. Although the poor man is hated by everybody and not presently experiencing "good," yet by keeping these teachings he will preserve his life and is about to find good (cf. 19:1).

(1) Introduction (19:8)

The parallels of v. 8 are not precise, and its versets must be extended to one another.[64] Their topics, *the one who gets* [or acquires] *sense* (see 15:32) and *the one who heeds* [see 2:8; 19:16] *understanding* (see I: 96), are connected phonologically, syntactically, and semantically. Together they yield the thought that one acquires the mental and moral capacity to live by carefully observing and obeying the insights into piety and ethics taught in this book. In 15:32 one acquires sense by heeding correction, the opposite of flouting instruction (cf. 19:16). The predicates express the logical entailment. Such a person is *one who loves* [see 1:22; 8:17; 12:1] *his life* (*napšô;* see I: 90), a unique expression in Proverbs (cf. 29:24). Since "love" means to desire something so strongly that one faithfully strives to be with it, the expression means to preserve one's life (cf. 19:16). Because Jonathan loved David as much as his own life *(nepeš),* he made an oath to protect David (1 Sam. 20:17). Beyond finding life, such a person *will soon find* [see n. 19; 3:13] *good* (see I: 99). The person who heeds the sage's teachings is destined to preserve an abundant life in an open future.

(2) Wisdom in the Court (19:9-12)

Verses 9-12 pertain to the public arena, beginning with the punishment of the perjurer and ending with the king's wrath and favor toward all (v. 12). Verses 11 and 12 are a proverb pair commending patience and forbearance with wrath. Verses 9 and 10 are linked by *lōʾ* and pertain to three things that are not fitting: perjurers are *not* acquitted (v. 9), fools do *not* live in luxury (v. 10a), and indentured slaves do *not* rule princes.

9 Perjury is the first folly that must not be tolerated to acquire good, as underscored by repeating v. 5 with the exception that it replaces the negative "will not escape punishment" with the positive *will perish* (see 10:28). The contexts of the subunits probably assume that God is the ultimate Agent who upholds justice (v. 5) through his surrogate the king (v. 9), reprising the sequence of 16:1-9 and 10-15.

64. The consonance of the labial stops, /*b* and *p*/ and the assonance of /*e* and *o*/ in *qōneh-lēb ʾōhēb napšô šōmēr tᵉbûnâ limṣōʾ-ṭôb* give the verse coherence, and the consonance of the interdental stops /*ṣ* and *ṭ*/, followed by /*ō*/ link the last two words.

10 In 30:22 Agur essentially repeats the second and third instances of folly, of what *is not fitting* (see 17:7). First, *luxury (taʿ^{a}nûg)* is not fitting *for a fool* (*lik^{e}sîl;* see I: 112). *Taʿ^{a}nûg* denotes "good (or luxurious, rich) living, a life of pleasure and luxury."[65] In 30:22 it is equated with being sated with food. In an upside-down kingdom the incorrigible fool lives the good life at the expense of the righteous and so validates his impiety toward God and his unethical behavior toward people. In 26:1 a fool held in honor is as unfitting and damaging as snow in summer and as rain in harvest. Tragically, as the story of Nabal illustrates, this failed way too often prevails; but God's established order is righted eventually (cf. 1 Sam. 25:2, 25, 37). *How much more* introduces the weightier argument to be drawn from the premise of verset A (see 19:7) and shows that "the fool" and "the slave" are not coreferential terms, unlike the "slave" and the "outcast" in 30:22. The predicate nominative *(is not fitting)* is gapped (cf. 19:7). *For a slave* [see 12:9] *to rule over* [see 12:24] *princes* (see "rulers" in 8:26) entails the incompetence of the former to govern subordinates (12:24) and the competence of the latter to maintain their positions through wisdom (see 8:26), not by unfounded revolution (cf. 1 K. 16:9; 2 K. 9:31). The proverb does not envision either the competent royal servant (14:35) or the prudent household slave (17:2). Whereas the comfortable fool is merely validated in his incorrigibility, the incompetent slave afflicts the entire community through his insubordination to wise rulers. Moreover, to judge from 30:22-23, the slave, who is incompetent both by disposition and training, will be drunk from the feeling of power and his rulership will develop into unbearable despotism. The consequences

65. *HALOT,* 4:1,769, s.v. *taʿ^{a}nûg;* cf. Gemser, *Sprüche,* pp. 76-77; Plöger, *Sprüche,* p. 222). *Taʿ^{a}nûg* is an abstract noun, which in its other four uses occurs as a masc. or fem. pl. of intensification, with no difference in meaning, and always in cons. It is related to an Arabic verb that means in I stem "coquetted" and in II "fondled" and to the Heb. verb that in the *Pual* means "to be soft, effeminate" in connection with "lovely" (Jer. 6:2) and in the *Hithpael* "to be of dainty habit [of a woman]" (Deut. 28:56), "to satisfy one's desire [in]" (Isa. 55:2), "to refresh oneself" (Isa. 66:11), and "to make merry over" (Isa. 57:4). Its nominal by-forms are *ʿōnēg* "delight/desire" (Isa. 13:22) and *ʿānōg* "to be fastidious/dainty" (Deut. 28:54). But D. W. Thomas ("Notes on Some Passages," p. 400) and independently G. R. Driver ("Problems in the Hebrew Text of Job," *VTSup* 3 [1969] 84) derive the noun from an Arabic cognate meaning "to draw, pull" (e.g., camel's head by means of the halter). In its IV stem it means "arranged with a rope," "ordered affairs in a good man" and its noun means "rope, cord, management." According to them, *taʿ^{a}nûg* in Prov. 19:10 means "control," "administration," a sense determined by the parallel, "to rule." However, 30:22 places in parallel as things under which the earth trembles (i.e., as not fitting) "a slave when he becomes king, and a fool when glutted with food." This association of rule and luxury validates the traditional association of *taʿ^{a}nûg* with the several Hebrew words, and not with an Arabic cognate that is otherwise unattested in Hebrew.

for the community are only incompetence, mismanagement, abuse of power, corruption, and injustice; in brief, social chaos (cf. Eccl. 10:5-7).

11-12 Verses 11 and 12 pertain to avoiding "anger," both subjectively within oneself (v. 11) and objectively from the king (v. 12; cf. 16:14).

11 This proverb, which teaches the prudent to forgo anger and to forgive sin, nuances the punishment motif that frames the partial subunit. Its complementary parallels match cause with consequence both with reference to their subjects ("the prudent human being" with "his splendor") and with reference to the predicates ("has patience" with "to overlook offenses"). *The prudence* [*ṣēkel;* see I: 94] *of a human being* [see I: 89] *yields patience* (lit. "to cause the face to be long" [= to relax the face"; see n. 22; 14:29]). Such a person rules over his spirit and his natural inclination to seek revenge (16:32) and calms controversy (15:18). To get into a storming rage because of crimes is understandable, but not necessarily less destructive than being a hot-tempered person who promotes strife and discord, not peace and well-being (cf. 14:29; 17:27). *And* combines the synthetic parallels. *His splendor* (*tip'artô;* see 4:9) implicitly likens the prudent person's forgiveness of sin to some attractive adornment he wears. *To pass over* [lit. "to pass along by," a figure meaning "to forgive"][66] *transgression* (see 10:12) causes people to delight and rejoice in him and wins him more fame, honor, praise, and distinction than a warrior (cf. 16:32; 20:3). Although the proverb does not specify whether the offense is against the prudent person himself or others, one should probably assume that the offended overlooks all sorts of irritating and offensive violations of his rights. Prov. 10:12, 19; 17:9 attribute the covering over of offenses to love. In this ability to forgive sin, the prudent person reflects the glory of Israel's God, who "forgives iniquity" and who does "not retain forever his anger because he is one who delights in unfailing love" (Mic. 7:18; cf. Amos 7:8; 8:2) and models the Christian disciple (Luke 11:4).

12 The second proverb of the pair contrasts the unrestrained fury of the king with the restrained patience of the prudent who forgives. Its antithetical parallels pit the king's fury against his favor, and contrast respectively their malevolent and benevolent effects by the imagery of the lion's roar and of dew on rich vegetation (cf. Mic. 5:7-8[6-7]). Roaring *(naham)* occurs elsewhere in the Old Testament only in 20:2.[67] As of a lion *(k^{e}pîr)* originally meant a "young lion," who goes out on his own in search of prey. The lion as a proud sovereign tramples its victims into subjection, and tears them fatally

66. BDB, p. 717, s.v. *'ābar.*

67. The verb *nāham* denotes "a lion's roar" (Prov. 28:15; Isa. 5:29, where it is parallel to *šā'ag* "to roar"), and the cry of a sufferer (Prov. 5:11; Ezek. 24:23). Its feminine by-form refers to the raging of the heart, which causes one to roar (*šā'ag,* Ps. 38:8[9]) and of the sea (Isa. 5:30).

with no one to deliver. From antiquity lions have been used to represent the strength and ferocity of rulers (30:30; cf. Gen. 49:9; Judg. 14:5-7; 1 Sam. 17:34-47; 2 Sam. 1:23; 17:10; 23:20; Rev. 5:5). Its roar is even used to represent God (Isa. 31:4; Jer. 2:30; 25:30, 38; 49:19; 50:44; Hos. 5:14; 13:7-8; Joel 3:16[4:16]; Amos 3:8). They are also agents of God's judgment, man eaters sent by the LORD (1 K. 13:24-28; 20:36; 2 K. 17:25-26; Isa. 15:9; cf. Dan. 6:27[28]). Israel's poets and prophets often use lions in simile and metaphor to represent enemies who are hungry, lie in wait, roar, and tear their prey (Pss. 7:2[3]; 10:9; 17:12; 22:13[14]; 57:4[5]; Isa. 5:29; Jer. 2:15; 4:7; 50:17; 51:38; Ezek. 32:2; Joel 1:6; Amos 3:12; Zech. 11:3). *Is the fury* [see 19:3] *of a king* (see 14:28; 16:12-15) refers to justified fury, not unjustified as in 28:15, assuming his favor in verset B is based on merit (cf. 16:14; 20:2; 25:4-5; 2 Sam. 12:5-6).[68] To be hot tempered, however, is always wrong (14:17, 29; 15:18; 26:21; 29:11, 22). The king's unrestrained fury is as dangerous and dreadful as that of a roaring lion who seizes its prey, and no one can deliver it (20:2; cf. Isa. 5:29). Prov. 20:2a substitutes "terror" for his "fury," and 20:2b explains the metonymy, namely, that its target will forfeit his life. The wise person appeases this messenger of death (16:14). *But* joins the two contrasting attitudes of the king with their two effects on his subjects (cf. 16:14, 15). The simile *like dew* [see 3:20] *on vegetation*[69] depicts his favor (see 11:1; 14:35) as being life-giving, salubrious, pervasive, penetrating, beneficent, refreshing, reviving, mysterious, and heavenly (cf. 2 Sam. 23:3, 4; Hos. 14:5). Dew, which in the climatic conditions of Palestine was essential to the survival of vegetation in the hot, dry summer, is a gift from God that he could either confer on his people or withhold from them (cf. Deut. 33:28; 1 K. 17:1; Hos. 14:5[6]; Hag. 1:10; Zech. 8:12). The proverb instructs the disciple to avoid the king's fury and to seek his favor (cf. 16:10-14).

(3) Wisdom in the Home (19:13-15)

Verse 13 may be connected to v. 11 by the contrast between the patience of prudence and the strife of the quarrelsome wife and to v. 12 by the motif of

68. *Zaʿap* (see 19:3) occurs seven times to refer both to the despotic rage of Asa and Uzziah (2 Chr. 16:10; 26:19) and to the violent anger of God against sinners (2 Chr. 28:9; Isa. 30:30; Mic. 7:9) and of the sea personified as a deity against Jonah (Jon. 1:15).

69. "Vegetation" *(ʿēśeb)* and "vegetation of the field/earth" refer to feed/pasturage for animals (Gen. 1:30; Deut. 11:15; Ps. 106:20; Prov. 27:25; Isa. 42:15; Jer. 14:6), to food for people, both as vegetables and cereals (Gen. 3:18; Exod. 9:22, 25; 10:12, 15; Job 5:25; Ps. 104:14; Jer. 12:4; Amos 7:2; Zech. 10:1); "vegetation" refers to plants in general, as here, and to food for people and for animals (Gen. 2:5; 9:3; Deut. 29:23[22]; 32:2; Ps. 105:35; Mic. 5:7[6]). It is a picture for transitoriness in Ps. 102:4[5], 11[12], but here and in Pss. 72:16; 92:7[8] for rich growth.

water: dew (v. 12) and constant dripping (v. 13). However, the setting shifts from the public arena (vv. 9-12) to the private home (vv. 13-15). Once again, the mention of the wife occurs at a seam between units and/or subunits (cf. 18:22). Moreover, these "three sayings are rife with vocabulary that echoes the introduction to the antithetical collection (10:1-5)": *bēn kᵉsîl* ("foolish son"), *hawwat/hawwōt* ("craving"/ "destruction"), *'āb* ("father"), *rā'āb* ("hunger"), *maśkîl/maśkālet* ("prudent"), *nirdām/tardēmâ* ("sleep"), *rᵉmîyâ* ("slack"), *nepeš* ("appetite"/"person").[70]

Verses 13-14 pertain strictly to the home: son and wife (v. 13), chattel and wife (v. 14); they are also linked by "father(s)" in their A versets and "wife" in their B versets. Verse 13 presents the dysfunctional home: a foolish son, a man's closest male companion (10:1; 12:1; 15:20; 17:21, 25), and a quarrelsome wife (v. 13), his closest female attachment (see I: 118; cf. 21:9, 19; 25:24; 27:15). Verse 14 presents a functional home: his household and property and a prudent wife. The son who squanders the family's inheritance (v. 13a) and the contentious wife (v. 13b) stand juxtaposed to the father's inheritance and the prudent wife (v. 14b).

13 The synthetic parallels link by *and* the foolish son who from beneath undermines the father's household (v. 13a) and the nagging wife who from alongside him drives him out of it (v. 13b).[71] *A foolish son* [see 10:1] *is destruction* (*hawwôt;* see 17:4) *for his father* (see 17:25) because the father is left without a "staff" to sustain him in his old age or one competent to preserve the family's inheritance after his death. The reference to the son suggests that *'iššâ,* which generally refers to "woman" or *femina* (2:16), here refers more specifically to the *wife's* [see I: 118] *quarrelings* (*midyᵉnê;* see "conflicts," 6:14; 18:18). In bitter irony the many conflicts she stirs up are likened to *a leaky roof (delep),* which occurs elsewhere only in Prov. 27:15.[72] The man's very place of refuge, peace, and hope has turned against him and failed him. *That drips constantly (ṭōrēd)* also occurs elsewhere only in Prov. 27:15.[73] Roofs were made out of layers of wooden boards and sticks arranged crosswise and overlaid with a layer of clay, water, chalk, and chaff. In heavy rain they were prone to leak. "Among the Canaanites, so an old folk tale tells us, repairing the roof in wet weather was one of the most highly prized virtues in a good son."[74] "Incessantly dripping eaves" invites the pun "inces-

70. Van Leeuwen, *Proverbs,* p. 180.

71. Verset A coheres by consonance of the labials /*w* and *b*/: *hawwōt lᵉ'ābîw bēn kᵉsîl,* and verset B by the interdentals /*d* and *ṭ*/: *delep ṭōrēd midᵉynê.*

72. The meaning of *delep* is derived from Arab. *dalf* "leaky roof," and from the verb I *dālap,* "be leaky" (of a house [Eccl. 10:18]), and "weep, shed tears" (Job 16:20; Ps. 119:28); see *HALOT,* 1:223, s.v. *delep.*

73. It is related to Arab. VIII *ṭarada* "flow or do something constantly."

74. Farmer, *Proverbs and Ecclesiastes,* p. 152.

santly dripping Eves." The last place the man expects an attack is from his wife (see 25:24), from whom he hoped to find good (18:22). Yet right under his own roof he is being constantly assaulted by a nagging woman who never lets up. He cannot escape the torment except by abandoning his house altogether.[75]

14 By contrast, the functional family successfully passes on its household and wealth through the generations, and the wife competently manages it. The chiastic parallels of v. 14, which is marked by *but,* contrast and escalate in their outer frame *household* [see 11:29] *and wealth* (see 3:9) with *a prudent* [*maśkālet;* see I: 94] *wife* (see 19:13) and in their inner core *are an inheritance* [see 17:2] *from fathers* (see 4:1-3) with *is from the LORD* (see I: 118). She searches out wealth, adds to it, and manages it (31:10-31). Although the successful passing on of the inheritance from father to son through the generations assumes the successful rearing of the sons — the point of v. 13 — that factor is not in view here. Plöger rightly argues that verset A has in view the established laws of inheritance (cf. 17:2). To be sure, the inheritance from the father surely submits also to the variables of life, but it is a factor with which one can reckon. The matter, however, is very different with regard to the wife. A man's fortune depends on her moral competence to grasp the problems involved in running a household and their solutions and to throw all her energies into their successful management (see 1:3; 12:4; 14:1; 18:22). Normally a wife was selected by the parents (Gen. 24:3-4; 38:6), though Samson is a tragic exception (Judg. 14:2). However, in spite of all human activity in this connection, the wise know that success in this attempt and fortune in life do not depend on humans but on divine providence. It is not carefully planning that brings it to pass, as the story of Ruth illustrates. Wisdom, says Plöger, loves to bring things that lie at the limits of what can be calculated into relation with the LORD; one compares, for example, the expression about the decision of the lot in 16:33 or about the preparation for battle in 21:31.[76] God, however, is faithful and just, not fickle and capricious. Thus the proverb instructs the disciple to look to God (15:8, 29; 16:3; cf. Gen. 24:14) and find his favor through wisdom to obtain from him a competent wife (8:35; 18:22). "A good wife is a great blessing; she will be granted among the blessings of the man who fears the LORD" (Sir. 26:3). As a result, when a man has a competent wife, he praises God, not himself.

15 The foolish son (v. 13) who destroys the father's inheritance (v. 14) is now concretized as having a slack hand (cf. 10:1, 4-5; 6:6-11 and

75. An Arab proverb says that three things make the house intolerable: "*âlṭaḳḳ,* the trickling through of rain; *âlnaḳḳ,* the contention of the wife; and *albaḳḳ,* bugs" (cited by Delitzsch, *Proverbs,* p. 285).

76. Plöger, *Sprüche,* pp. 223-24.

24:30-34). The root *rdm* of *tardēmâ* "deep sleep" (v. 15a) and of *nirdām* "sleeps" with reference to the foolish son (10:5), along with the numerous other connections between 19:13-15 and 10:1-5, supports this inference. A foolish son shows his moral degeneracy by his laziness (cf. Eccl. 10:18). In 6:6 the sluggard is admonished "to become wise," the antithesis of being a fool; in 24:30 the sluggard is said to "lack sense"; and in 26:12-16 the sluggard is said to be more despicable than a fool. In other words, this partial subunit escalates his being a fool (19:13) to his being a sluggard (19:15). The synthetic parallels present a cause (v. 15A)-effect (v. 15b) relationship.[77] Personified *laziness*[78] [see I: 114] *casts* [*one*] [see 7:26] *into a deep sleep* (*tardēmâ;* cf. 6:10), suspending all sensibility to one's situation.[79] *Rādam* describes a heavy, deep sleep: "The sleeper is closed against the outer world. His organs of sense perception are, for time being, stopped up or shut; and it was felt that neither *nûm* ['to be drowsy, slumber'] nor *yāšēn* ['to sleep'] was adequate to describe this rarer sleep phenomenon."[80] *And* combines the physical consequence with the spiritual cause. *A slack* (*r^emîyâ;* see 10:4) *person* (*nepeš;* see I: 94) *hungers* (see 10:3). None of his drives and appetites are satisfied (10:3), especially his need of food (see 6:30; 20:13). Note his progressive deterioration from static laziness to deep sleep that has a tendency to death (21:25), to hunger (see 19:23-24). Laziness plunges him into a state of being so deep in sleep that he is totally unconscious of his situation. Unaware of his tragic situation and unable to arouse himself, the sluggard neglects his source of income and so hungers. His fate is similar to that of drunkards and gluttons (23:21).

c. Educating the Son to Show Kindness to the Needy (19:16-23)

The educational proverbs, vv. 16 and 23, frame the third subunit, though v. 23 also introduces the next unit. Both frames mention the reward of life (vv. 16a, 23a), but v. 23 escalates the father's command (v. 16a) to the fear of the LORD (v. 23a). The subunit's core (vv. 18-21) consists of two pairs of rearing proverbs. The first, in a rare direct address in this collection, admonishes the father to discipline *(ysr)* his son and not aspire *(nś' npš)* to kill him (v. 18) and then, also partially in direct address, teaches him not to ease *(nś')* the penalty incurred by a hothead (v. 19). The second proverb pair also be-

77. The consonances of the interdental stops /*t, d,* and *ṣ*/ and of the liquids /*l* and *r*/, along with the assonance of final /*ā*/ in every other word, give the verse coherence.

78. Although *'aṣlâ* is a *hap. leg.,* its meaning is certified by *'āṣēl* ("sluggard"; see 6:6-9), *'^aṣaltayim* ("lazy," Eccl. 10:18), and *'aṣlût* ("sluggishness," Prov. 31:27).

79. *Nāpal* is used five times with *tardēmâ:* in the *Qal* (Gen. 15:12; 1 Sam. 26:12; Job 4:13) and in the *Hiphil* (Gen. 2:21; Prov. 19:15).

80. Thomson, "Sleep," p. 423.

gins with the rare imperative, admonishing the son to accept the father's discipline *(mûsār,* from *ysr)* and counsel (*ʿēṣâ,* v. 20a), which is implicitly escalated to the LORD's immutable counsel (*ʿēṣâ,* v. 21b). This collection should not be regarded as introductory rearing proverbs. Whybray comments, "The fact that the father is first addressed and then the child shows that this not an 'Instruction' in the proper sense, but a collection of proverbs on a single theme."[81] Sandwiched between the frame and core in a chiastic pattern are two proverbs relating to the poor *(rāš* and *dāl):* first an instruction to be kind to the poor (v. 17) and then an instruction to show unfailing love; better to be poor than a liar (v. 21). To reach that pedagogic goal requires hard discipline (vv. 18-19). The unit is punctuated with sayings about the LORD (vv. 17, 21, 23), who upholds a moral order that rewards the kind with abundant life (vv. 17, 23) and that punishes the unkind with death (see I: 73). Education in kindness to the poor is a matter of life and death.

(1) Introduction: Keep the Father's Commandment to Live (19:16)

Both catchwords, "the one who keeps" *(šōmēr)* and "his life" *(napšô),* link this introductory rearing proverb to the preceding introduction (v. 8), and *nepeš* ("person"/"life") also connects it to the last verse of that subunit. That catchword profiles the contrasts between the irresponsible (v. 15b) person and the responsible person (v. 16a). The proverb's antithetical parallels contrast the one who scrupulously obeys the parents' commandment (3:1) with the one who treats his conduct and its outcome with contempt, implying that "commandment" pertains to one's way of life (cf. 13:13-14). It also juxtaposes "one who preserves his life" with "dies," showing that the wise preserves his life from death. *He who keeps* (*šōmēr;* see 2:8) *the commandment* [see 2:1] *is one who preserves* (or keeps; *šōmēr;* 2:8) *his life* (*napšô;* see I: 90). An obvious pun on *šāmar,* captured also by English "keep," meaning both to "heed scrupulously" and "to protect scrupulously," links the versets (see 2:8 and 11).[82] The unique expression *the one who despises* [see 1:7] *his ways* (*dᵉrākāyw;* see 1:15) means that he treats with contempt his character and conduct and their consequences. "His" grammatically refers back to "the one who despises," not the implied wisdom teacher or the LORD, for they lack an antecedent (see n. 30). *Will die* (*yāmût;* see n. 31) signifies a severance of what should be an unending relationship in love and loyalty with God and his people.

81. Whybray, *Proverbs,* p. 283.

82. The nasals /*m* and *n*/ and sibilants /*ś* and *š*/ dominate verset A: *šmr mṣwh šmr npšw.*

(2) The LORD Will Reward Kindness to the Poor (19:17)

This proverb turns to the unit's goal in the son's education: to esteem the powerless poor person as worthy of favor, active acceptance, and acts of charity because the LORD will reward him (cf. 14:21, 31; 22:9; 28:27). The disciple stands apart from the crowd on the side of the poor who otherwise stands alone, without a friend (see 19:7). The inner core of the proverb's chiastic parallels present the topic, *the one who shows grace* (*ḥônēn;* see 14:31; cf. 14:21) *to the poor* (*dāl;* see 10:15) and its abstract equivalent, *as for his deeds* (*g^e^mûl;* see 12:14). Its outer frame gives the synthetic predicates, *is one who lends* (*malwēh;* cf. 22:7; Deut. 28:12; Isa. 24:2) *to the LORD* (see I: 73) and *he* [the LORD] *will repay him* (see 11:31). *And* joins these synthetic predicates stating the cause-effect relationship.[83] The one who gives generously to the destitute figuratively gives a loan to the LORD presumably because the LORD's honor is tied up with the poor, for he made them and they, too, are his image (14:31; 17:5; 22:2). Their just and gracious Creator takes it on himself to assume their indebtedness, and so he will repay the lender in full (cf. 3:27-28; 11:17, 25; 14:21; 22:9, 22-23; 25:22-23; Pss. 41:1-3[2-4]; 112:5; Matt. 25:34; Luke 6:38; Jas. 1:27). By contrast, if one oppresses the poor he will have to contend with God as their Defender (21:13; 22:22-23; 28:27).

(3) Admonitions to the Father to Discipline His Son and the Hothead (19:18-19)

18 Unlike most rearing proverbs, which are addressed to the son and assume that the father instructs his son, this one does not make that assumption. In the chiastic parallels of this proverb the outer frame presents the command to the father and the inner core, the motivation. Verset A presents positively both the command (aα), *discipline* [see 1:2; 9:7; 23:13; 29:17] *your son* (see 1:8), and the motivation (aβ), *for surely there is* [see n. 31] *hope* (see 10:28). To be sure, timely pedagogy is necessary (Eccl. 3:1-8),[84] but the accent here is on the promise of pedagogy. *And* now combines the negative command and motivation to underscore and clarify the positive

83. The parallels also cohere by the loose sequence of /*m* and *l*/: *malwēh YHWH ḥônēn dāl ûg^e^mûlô y^e^šallēm-lô.*

84. "The (callow) youth has reached the age where intentional choice becomes possible. Indeed, only in youth can one's direction for life be set. In youth, one has the potential for the fundamental ethically meaningful choice, What sort of character do I commit myself to developing?" (B. Kovacs, "Sociological-Structural Constraints upon Wisdom: The Spatial and Temporal Matrix of Proverbs 15:28–22:16" [Ph.D. diss., Vanderbilt University, 1978], p. 505).

command of verset A.[85] Kovacs comments: "The child's life seems to be patterned rather than determined" (see I: 118).[86] In the motivation (bα), *to* marks the goal or termination of "to lift up the soul" and is part of that idiom. *Killing him* (see n. 33) refers to causing the son to participate in experiencing an eternal death severed forever from a relationship with the living God and his people (see 5:23). *Do not* signals the negative command that shifts from the external act of discipline to the inward disposition. *Set your desire* (lit. "lift up your soul") is a figure to express directing the desire (*nepeš;* see I: 90) toward someone or something, "to long for," with the nuance of dependence on the person or thing.[87] The imprecise antithetical parallels imply that the father's hope in discipline is to impart to his clinical offspring eternal life, the opposite of death, and that a failure to discipline the son is tantamount to participating in killing him (cf. 11:7, 23; 13:24; 20:30; 22:6, 15; 23:13, 14; 29:15). Psychologically healthy parents do not consciously desire to kill their children. But if they do not employ the God-given means of verbal reproof to prevent acts of folly and corporal punishment to prevent their repetition, they are in fact unwittingly party to the worst punishment, his death (5:23).[88] The proverb assumes both that folly is bound up in the heart of the child, and that the rod of discipline will drive it far from him (22:15).[89] In Proverbs discipline is based on love, never on an intention to harm (cf. 3:12; 4:4; 13:24).

19 The second proverb of the pair continues the theme of pedagogy through punishment in the style of direct address and is linked

85. Verset A coheres by the loose sequence of /y + sibilant/ in initial aα and aβ *(yassēr . . . kî-yēš)* and the assonance of /a/ in their final syllables, *binkā . . . tiqwâ.* Verset B coheres by the sequence /' + l/ in the initial words of Ba, Bb: *'el . . . 'al.*

86. Kovacs, "Sociological Structural Constraints," p. 505.

87. Several times in their petitions worshipers make the LORD the object of their intense desire (Pss. 25:1; 86:4; 143:8; cf. Lam. 3:41 [= "lift up our hearts"]), not an idol (Ps. 24:4). The poor urgently desire and count on their wages (Deut. 24:15). In Hos. 4:8 the priests are denounced for desiring to feed on the people's iniquities.

88. R. D. Branson, *TDOT,* 6:132, s.v. *yāsar.*

89. Rashi and several later expositors (e.g., Plöger, *Sprüche,* p. 224) understood verset B to mean that the father should not smite him a mortal blow. The NEB arbitrarily renders "to kill him" by "to flog him to death." Meinhold argues against this on historical grounds. According to him, in early times, before the state existed, the *paterfamilias* had the right even to kill a daughter or a son in cases of severe crimes (cf. Gen. 31:32; 38:24). However, the stipulations regarding the family in Exod. 21:12, 15-17 show already that this right was taken away from the family and placed into the judicial sphere of the village (cf. Exod. 21:13-14). Later Deut. 21:18-21 establishes that the father and mother (!) have to hand over a incorrigible son to the judicial sphere of the village when he should be put to death. Meinhold concludes that none of these cases is present here (*Sprüche,* p. 322). Proverbs 23:13 strongly supports our interpretation.

chiastically to the preceding pair by the catchword *nś'* (vv. 18b, 19a). It begins as a saying and ends in direct address. The proverb shifts the one punished from the son (v. 18) to the hothead, a specific type of fool to which the untutored son is liable. In the outer frame of these imprecise, chiastic parallels, "the hothead" is expanded to "you will do so again" (i.e., he will again vent his heated emotions intentionally against the perceived offender and unintentionally against himself). In the inner core, "one who incurs a penalty" is expanded antithetically to "surely if you deliver him," implying that deliverance from his just penalty is in view and that it does not work.[90] The hothead is characterized by a heated excitement of resentment against a perceived offender, not by love for him (see 19:11). The proverb teaches that baling him out of trouble is counterproductive. *A hothead* (see n. 34; cf. 6:34; 15:1, 18; 16:14) refers to his tendency to respond with ungovernable passions of resentment against a perceived offender, not by love (cf. 19:11), making his behavior irrational.[91] *Is one who incurs* (*nōśē'*; see 9:12) *a penalty* (*'ōneš;* see 17:26) implies that the hothead must make amends by paying compensation in some way to repair and make good the damage he has done in his fervid agitation. *Surely* subordinates the clauses of verset B to that of A. *If* (see 1:10), which envisions a real possibility, *you deliver* (*taṣṣîl,* see 2:12), continuing the direct address to the father, *you will do [so] again* (cf. 1:5; 19:4), Whereas the son is corrected by parental discipline, the hothead must be corrected by allowing the consequences of his own foibles to punish him. The wise father does not interfere in the operation of the cause-consequence of the divinely established penal and remedial moral order. Ironically, the person who "rescues" the hothead becomes caught in the unhealthy dynamics of his way.

(4) Admonitions to the Son to Accept His Father's Discipline and Counsel (19:20-21)

20 The first proverb of this pair continues the style of direct address but turns from addressing the father to addressing the son, matching the admonition to the father to discipline (*yassēr,* v. 18a) his son with the admonition to the son to accept the discipline (*mûsār,* v. 20a).[92] Verset A sets forth the condition. *Listen to* (see 1:5, 8), another rare imperative in Collection II,

90. There is a loose sequence of /n, o, and ś~š/ in *nōśē' 'ōneš* and of /t, ṣ/s, i/ in *taṣṣîl . . . tôsip.* The assonance of /i/ also in *kî 'im* also binds together verset B.

91. *Gᵉdol-ḥēmâ,* lit. "a person of great wrath," is probably a synonym of *qᵉṣar-'appayim* (14:17), *qᵉṣar-rûaḥ* (14:29), and *'îš ḥēmâ* (15:18).

92. The line coheres phonologically through the consonance of the fricative gutturals /' and ḥ/, which occur eight times; the voiced in the first two words, and the unvoiced in the last two.

counsel (see 1:25), for it shapes character and quells waywardness. *And* joins the second imperative *receive (qabbēl)* to the first to intensify the command by repetition and to escalate from outward "hear" to inward "receive" in deliberate and spiritual taking in of *discipline* (see n. 36).[93] This education must be accepted willingly for the pedagogue's desired goal to be achieved. Verset B asserts the motivating consequence. *So that* (*lᵉmaʿan;* see 2:20; 15:24) marks this logical progression; it does mean "for," "on behalf of."[94] *You may be counted among the wise* [see I: 94] *in your final destiny* (*bᵉʾaḥᵃrîtekā,* lit. "in your afterwards"). *ʾAḥᵃrît* occurs 13 times in Proverbs and refers to the final outcome of a way of life (cf. 5:4, 11; 14:12 = [16:25]; 14:18; 20:21; 23:32; 24:20; 25:8; 29:21; cf. Deut. 32:29). Here with *bᵉ* it refers to the time of the end, the future hope that will not be cut off by anything, including death; it does not mean merely that after receiving the instruction he will become wise.[95] The LXX renders it by *ep' eschatōn sou* ("your latter days"). The proverb motivates the son to internalize the teaching with the certain hope that he will enjoy all the benefits of being wise in a future that outlasts death itself (see I: 104; cf. 23:18; 24:14; cf. 1 Tim. 4:8; 1 Pet. 4:2). A person does not control his future, but with this hope he can face it without anxiety and apprehension. Verse 27 will make clear, however, that one must persevere in the teaching to guarantee this outcome.

21 The second proverb of this pair, but in the form of a saying, implicitly gives the reason for heeding the parental instruction. The LORD's purpose informing their instruction will prevail over human schemes to subvert the teaching (see 16:1-9). The catchword "counsel" *(ʿēṣâ)* links the authoritative counsel of the parent (v. 20a) with the LORD's (v. 21b). The pair is also linked by the concept that God's counsel will stand forever (v. 21b) and that those who follow parental counsel will be wise in a final and eternal destiny (v. 20b). In this proverb's chiastic antithetical parallels, the topic "human plans" over against the "LORD's counsel" forms the inner core, and the predicate "many" versus "it will stand," its outer frame. *The plans* [see 6:18] *in the heart* [see I: 90] *of a person* (*ʾîš;* see I: 89) refers to creative calculations within the human thought processes, weighing matters first this way and then that. *But* strikes the antithesis. *As for the counsel* [see 19:20] *of the LORD* (see I: 67), which is emphasized by the syntax (see n. 38), refers to God's immu-

93. *Qbl* occurs 11 times in the *Piel* and is an Old Hebrew word that was replaced by *lāqaḥ* ("take/accept"; see 2:1), and was again used under the influence of Aramaic (cf. 1 Chr. 12:18[19]; 2 Chr. 26:16; 29:22; Ezra 8:30; Esth. 4:4; 9:23, 27; Job 2:10; Prov. 19:20). See also E. Jenni, *Das hebräische Piʿel: Syntaktisch-semasiologische Untersuchung einer Verbalform im Alten Testament* (Zürich: EVZ, 1968), p. 240.

94. *Pace* the NIV and NRSV.

95. *Pace* Toy, *Proverbs,* p. 377.

table will (see 1:25). The juxtaposition *are many* (see 7:26) with *it* [i.e., "counsel"] *will take place* (*tāqûm;* see 15:22; cf. Isa. 40:8) contrasts the many human plans that may or may not occur in historical reality with God's single plan that will happen (cf. 6:1).[96] The manifold images developed in the human thinking organ are one thing, but what finally transpires as a reality is another. God can make them successful or cancel them (2 Sam. 15:30–17:14) or bring about the reverse of what people intended (cf. Gen. 45:4-8; 50:20; Exod. 1:8-12, 20; Job 23:13; Ps. 2:1-6; Prov. 20:24; 27:1; Isa. 45:9; Acts 2:23; 4:27-28; 23:11-15). Even the best human plans and efforts cannot stand before him if he does not will it (Prov. 21:30-31; cf. Ps. 33:11; Isa. 7:7; 14:24; 46:10). In sum, the wise son can count on God to bring to pass his good and moral pleasure regardless of what ungodly people intend, including the promise that those who take care of the poor will enjoy a happy ending (v. 20).

(5) The Poor Desire Unfailing Kindness, Not Selfishness (19:22)

22 Sandwiched between "Yahweh proverbs" (vv. 21, 23) and rearing proverbs (vv. 18-21, 23) and matching its counterpart to be kind to the poor (v. 17), this proverb by a pun instructs the son specifically to show unfailingly kindness to the needy, and not to be selfish. Verset A lays down both truths by a pun on the homonym *ḥesed* (see n. 42). According to the first interpretation, *what people desire* (*ta'ᵃwat;* lit. "the desire of"; see n. 39; 10:24) *in a human being* (*'ādām;* see n. 40; I: 89) *is his unfailing kindness* (*ḥasdô;* see 3:3; 11:17; 14:22; 16:6).[97] The pronominal suffix shows that others directed their expectations for help toward him. People desire this virtue because it favorably affects them (cf. 20:6). According to the second interpretation, *the self-gratification* (*ta'ᵃwat;* see 18:1) *of a human being* (*'adam*)[98] *is his shame* (*ḥasdô;* see 14:34). *And* combines verset B to A in order to underscore both truths. With reference to the first truth, *better a poor person* [see 19:1] *than a liar* (*mē'îš kāzāb;* cf. 6:19), the imprecise antithetical parallels "unfailing kindness" and a "liar" suggest that one in need had counted on the liar to help him. In that sense it is better to be a destitute person from whom no one expected help (see 13:8) than a liar, who is like a bad tooth and a lame foot (25:19). Isaiah, using the same vocabulary as Prov. 19:20-21, contrasts the faulty "unfailing kindness" (*ḥasdô* = "its kindness") of humanity with the

96. The LXX adds *eis ton aiōna menei* "will abide forever."

97. S. Romerowski ("Que signifie le mot *ḥesed?*" *VT* 40 [1990] 99), who challenges N. Glueck's influential thesis that *ḥesed* means "covenant fidelity," grants that in this text that notion is a most defensible meaning; it is opposed to lying.

98. Now a gen. of inalienable possession (*IBHS,* p. 145, P. 9.5.1g).

reliability of the LORD's word (Isa. 40:6-8). The former fades like the flower of the field; the latter stands (*yāqûm,* see v. 21) forever. This proverb, however, is not so pessimistic but encourages the disciple to conform his life to the LORD's teaching, for his word stands forever. According to the second interpretation, the imprecise parallels suggest that a selfish person lies to gratify his greed. Since that is shameful, it is better to be poor than corrupt (see 19:1). Whybray is more specific. He notes that *kāzāb* elsewhere in Proverbs (6:19; 14:5, 25; 19:9; 21:28) refers to perjury. "If this is implied here, the point of this line is that it is better to remain poor than to seek to gain an advantage by perjury."[99]

(6) Conclusion (19:23)

The unit's concluding proverb, also a frame with v. 16, sets forth the sublime benefit of *the fear of the LORD* (see I: 100). Verset A, a variant of 14:27, summarizes the benefit by the emphatic equation *is surely life* (*ḥayyîm;* see I: 104). Explicative *wᵉ* (not translated) introduces verset B, which explains the full life as abundant provision and sure protection (cf. Lev. 26:6; Deut. 11:15).[100] The emphatic *fully satisfied* (see 1:31) depicts him as being full of something to a consummate measure. His every need, especially as symbolized by food, is fully sated. *He dwells* (*yālîn;* see 15:31) probably entails its primary notion of "to remain at night," the time of danger, a synecdoche for all the time (see 15:31). The asyndetic clause introduced by *not* (*bal;* see 9:13) functions adverbially to modify *lîn. Met (yippāqed)* is one of several meanings of *pqd* in the *Niphal. HALOT* glosses it broadly here by "to be called to account, be afflicted, be punished," and, specifically, "to be met by trouble."[101] The passive is best construed as a divine passive: "*Pqd* ni. rarely refer[s] to negative experiences that do not originate with Yahweh. . . . In Prov. 19:23, fear of Yahweh protects against being affected (*pqd* ni.) by disaster."[102] *With harm* interprets *rāʿ* as having its physical, not moral, sense (see 1:16; 3:7; cf. Isa. 29:6) because the parallel is physical. In other words, the proverb encourages the disciple to embrace with a whole heart the father's teachings in order to enter into covenant blessings and to avoid its curses (cf. Leviticus 26; Deuteronomy 28). The proverb looks to the ultimate end of the matter and in that light asserts that the God-fearer does not hunger or suffer calamity (see 10:3).

99. Whybray, *Proverbs,* p. 284.
100. *IBHS,* p. 649, P. 39.2.1b.
101. *HALOT,* 2:957, s.v. *pqd.*
102. W. Schottroff, *TLOT,* 2:1,029, s.v. *pqd.*

7. The Pedagogue and Punishment of Fools (19:23–20:11)

24 *The sluggard buries his hand in the pan;*[1]
to his mouth he does not return it.
25 *Flog*[2] *a mocker, and the gullible will become prudent;*[3]
and if one corrects[4] *the insightful, he discerns knowledge.*
26 *The one who ruins [his] father, driving*[5] *out [his] mother,*
is a shameful and disgraceful[6] *son.*
27 *Cease,*[7] *my son, listening*[8] *to instruction*
in order to stray from the words of knowledge!
28 *A corrupt witness mocks at justice,*

1. For a history of interpretations of *ṣallaḥat* see D. Winton Thomas, "Notes on Some Passages in the Book of Proverbs," *VT* 15 (1965) 272-73. Rashi says, "And I have heard (that) *bṣlḥt* means the tear of the shirt . . . , that is to say, he hides it in his bosom" (M. Lyons, "Rashi's *Commentary on the Book of Proverbs*" [submitted in partial fulfillment of the requirements for the degree of rabbi, 1936], p. 103). Note its assonance with *ʿāṣēl* ("sluggard"). *Ṣallaḥat* occurs four times: 19:24 (= 26:15), 2 Kgs. 21:13, where it is wiped dry and turned upside down, and 2 Chr. 35:13 in connection with pots and cauldrons.

2. The imperfect represents either the volitional mood of instruction (*IBHS,* p. 510, P. 31.5c) or, possibly, an elliptical condition (see 25:4, 5). In either case, the situation is represented as real.

3. See 15:5, n. 1.

4. An asyndetic hypothetical perfective (*IBHS,* p. 493, P. 30.5.4b; see 9:12) with an indefinite subject (*IBHS,* pp. 70-71, P. 4.4.2), not an infinitive, for it lacks the expected *lamed* expressing the gerundive idea, "by correcting" (*IBHS,* p. 608, P. 36.2.3e). The LXX supplies the conditional particle *ean.*

5. The LXX and most English versions add "and" without textual or philological warrant.

6. See 10:5; 13:5.

7. Read *ḥ*ᵃ*dal,* not *ḥadal,* an error in L (see *BHS*). Numerous alterations of the text have been proposed because of a failure to reckon with the proverb's sarcasm. The LXX read a participial form + subject *huios apoleipomenos* (< *ḥādēl bēn,* "a son who ceases"), but in this book "my son" is normally vocative with an impv. The Targ. (cf. Syr.) resolves the problem by "Refrain, my son, and hear correction and do not deviate . . ."; and the Vulg. by "Cease not . . . , and be not ignorant." Rashi turned the two inf. cons. around: "Cease, my son, to stray from words of knowledge, in order to listen to instruction!" (Lyons, "Rashi's *Commentary,*" p. 104). Delitzsch (*Proverbs,* p. 291, citing Oetinger), arbitrarily paraphrases: "Cease from hearing instruction if thou wilt make no other use of it than to depart." Saadia, Ibn Ezra, and the KJV render, "Cease . . . to hear the instruction that causeth to err," but *mûsār* never has a negative sense. The proposal of Cohen (*Proverbs,* p. 130), "Cease, my son, to obey discipline . . . , it is to stray from the sayings of knowledge," is the best alternative to sarcasm, but it questionably emasculates the impv. force entirely, reducing it to a conditional particle, "if you cease" (cf. 2:1; 25:4, 5).

8. Gerundive *lamedh* with the inf. cons. (*IBHS,* p. 608, P. 36.2.3e).

and the mouth of the wicked swallows[9] *iniquity.*
29 *Punishments*[10] *are established for mockers,*
and beatings for the back of fools.
20:1 *Wine*[11] *is a mocker and beer is a brawler;*[12]
and everyone[13] *who staggers by them is not wise.*
2 *The roaring as of a lion*[14] *is the terror*[15] *struck by the king;*
whoever angers[16] *him forfeits his life.*

9. *Yᵉballaʿ* is traditionally interpreted as the *Piel* of I *blʿ* ("to make swallowed"), which suggests that the "mouth" is an orifice for ingesting rather than an orifice for words to come forth that is favored by the parallel "witness." The LXX has *katapietai* ("drinks down"). Toy (*Proverbs,* p. 282, citing Frankenberg), Fichtner *(BHS),* et al. emend the text to *yabbîaʿ* ("utters"; cf. 15:28). G. Boström (*Paronomasi i den äldre hebreiska Maschallitteraturen* [*LUÅ,* N.F., Avd. 1, Bd. 23, Nr. 8; Lund, 1928], p. 178), however, rightly objects: "*yblʿ* is an unmistakable allusion to *blyʿl,* which the Frankenberg-Toy proposal of *ybyʿ* overlooks." *HALOT* (1:135, s.v. II *blʿ*) achieves the same sense as Frankenberg-Toy without emendation by regarding the verb as belonging to II *blʿ,* which is attested in the Arabic root *balaġa* ("to be eloquent") and in IV stem "to report" and possibly in Biblical Hebrew *Pual* "to be communicated" (2 Sam. 17:16; Job 37:20). J. Schüpphaus (*TDOT,* 2:138, s.v. *blʿ*), who rejects this root in 2 Sam. 17:16 and Job 37:20, favors the *yabbîaʿ* emendation, ignoring the tagging paronomasia. E. Jenni (*Das Hebräische Piʿel: Syntaktisch-semasiologische Untersuchung einer Verbalform im Alten Testament* [Zürich: EVZ, 1968], p. 246) does not find the Arabic derivation "very clear." Moreover, one reluctantly accepts an Arabic homonym for a word that occurs frequently in Biblical Hebrew with a sensible, usual meaning. Also, this interpretation leaves the condition of verset A (i.e., mocking justice) without a negative moral consequence unlike the rest of the proverbs in the subunit. However, it may be that in this proverb pair, v. 28 represents the cause and v. 29 the consequence. Nevertheless, although *HALOT*'s interpretation cannot be ruled out, it seems best to retain the traditional meaning and to regard the expression as a double entendre and an oxymoron.

10. The LXX, adopted by Toy (*Proverbs,* p. 382) et al., reads *mastiges* "scourges," "lashes" (< *šôṭîm* or *šᵉbāṭîm* ["rods of correction"; cf. 10:13b; 26:3; cf. 14:3]), which superficially affords a better parallel with "beatings." But *šebeṭ* is always sing., and the MT is intelligible and richer, matching divine with human punishment.

11. L erroneously reads *hayyayn* for *hayyayin.*

12. Lit. "one who is turbulent."

13. Before the sing. noun, *kol* distributes the aggregate of the group in view to each individual of it.

14. See n. 54.

15. Since synoptic proverbs often vary, there is no need to emend *ʾêmat* to *ḥᵃmat* to come closer to 19:12. LXX *apeilē* ("threat") is no nearer to the one than to the other.

16. Lit. "the one who makes him to show himself angry" (see 14:16). On the basis of Arabic and Syriac cognates G. R. Driver ("Hebrew Notes on Prophets and Proverbs," *JTS* 41 [1940] 174) proposed with a slight emendation interpreting the text to mean "He that is negligent is as one that sinneth." But why emend and interpret an acceptable Hebrew text by Semitic cognates and not by Hebrew usage?

3 *Abstaining*[17] *from strife brings*[18] *glory to the individual,*
but every fool starts a quarrel.
4 *A sluggard does not plow*[19] *from winter*[20] *on;*
then[21] *he asks for [a crop] in the harvest, but there is none.*
5 *The counsel in a person's heart is deep waters,*
but an understanding person draws it out.
6 *As for*[22] *many human beings, each person proclaims his unfailing kindness.*
But a conscientious person who can find?
7 *As for one who walks in his blamelessness as a righteous person,*[23]
blessed are his children after him.
8 *A king is one who sits on a throne of judgment,*
winnowing all evil with his eyes.[24]

17. Or "ceasing." *Šebet* is either a verbal noun of *šbt* ("to cease"; cf. 18:18; so Syr., Vulg.) or a substantival infinitive of *yšb* ("to sit"; so Targ.). The LXX curiously derived it from *šûb.* The nominal is otherwise surely attested only in Exod. 21:19 with the sense "to be quiet, inactive," which meaning could belong to either root. L. Kopf ("Arabische Etymologien und Parallelen zum Bibelwörterbuch," *VT* 9 [1959] 258) prefers *yšb* in light of Arab. *qaʿada* "to sit" and *qaʿada ʿan* "to abstain from." Its use in Exod. 21:19 also favors the *yšb* derivation. Finally, "abstain from" forms a better antithesis to "starting a quarrel."

18. The verb of motion is inherent in *lamed* (*IBHS,* p. 224, P. 11.4d).

19. The Targ. and Syr. (cf. LXX) understood *yaḥărōš* from II *ḥrš Hiphil* ("to be silent").

20. The LXX (cf. Targ.) reads *oneidizomenos* (< *meḥōrāp, Pual* ptcp. of *ḥrp* "reproach"), occasioning its other departures from the MT. It also misunderstood in vv. 6a, 25b, and 30, puts v. 10 after v. 22, and lacks vv. 14-19. The Syr. likwise misunderstood verset A.

21. K = *yišāʾal;* Q = *wešāʾal* (*waw* consecutive with suffix conjugation denoting sequence; *IBHS,* pp. 526ff., P., 32.2.1c).

22. The syntax of verset A is difficult. The Targ., Syr., and Vulg. render "many men are called 'merciful,'" but this facilitating reading repoints the verset as *yiqqārēʾ ʾîš ḥesed* (or *ḥāsîd*). Delitzsch (*Proverbs,* p. 295) renders, "Almost every man meets a man who is gracious to him," understanding the verb as a bi-form of *qrh* and the pronominal suffix as objective gen. But he must invest *ḥesed* with the exceptional connotation, "not reliable." Toy (*Proverbs,* p. 384) renders literally, "Many men proclaim every one his kindness," apparently taking *ʾîš* as in apposition to *ʾādām.* But the appositive should immediately follow the lead word. Probably *rob ʾādām* is an emphatic nominative absolute (*IBHS,* p. 76, P. 4.7b).

23. Or "one who walks in his blamelessness is a righteous person" (cf. *IBHS,* pp. 132-34, P. 8.4). However, taking verset A as a nominative absolute with apposition provides a clearer connection between the cause (20:7a) and the consequence (20:7b). *Ṣaddîq* is best construed as an acc. of state modifying the subject (*IBHS,* p. 171, P. 10.2.2.d) (cf. Delitzsch, *Proverbs,* pp. 295-96).

24. Or "every evil person," but see the pl. for the concrete sense in 20:26.

9 *Who can say, "I have cleansed my heart;*
I am pure from my sin"?
10 *As for diverse weights [and] diverse ephahs —*
indeed, both of them are an abomination to the LORD.
11 *Even a youth in his evil deeds dissembles.*
So is his conduct pure, or[25] *is it upright?*[26]

The new unit on the pedagogue and the punishment of fools, which is introduced by an implicit admonition to fear the LORD (19:23), consists of two subunits. The first presents a catalogue of fools in need of correction and/or punishment (19:24–20:1).[27] The second pertains to cleansing the kingdom of fools (20:2-11).

a. Introduction (19:23)

Verse 23 functions as a janus between units. On the one hand, this educational proverb forms an *inclusio* with v. 16 and, in its connection with the preceding unit (18:22–19:23), suggests that the one who cares for the needy will himself be fully sated and protected by the LORD. On the other hand, the educational proverb also introduces the new unit.

b. A Catalogue of Fools and Their Punishment (19:24–20:1)

The seven-verse first subunit (19:23–20:1) after the introduction follows an alternating pattern of failed rearing types with the appropriate punishment for fools. This catalogue of fools escalates from the sluggard, who damages and punishes himself (v. 24), to the shameful son, who destroys the family (v. 26), to corrupt witnesses, who destroy the social order by their false witness (v. 28), to the brawling drunkard, who endangers everyone (20:1; 26:9). The shameful son may also be a sluggard (see 10:5). If so, the catalogue escalates the sluggard's damage from himself to his family. The punishment and correction of fools begin with flogging the mocker so that the gullible

25. In Job 6:12, *'im . . . 'im* is also used for two synonymous questions.

26. The traditional rendering, "A child is known by his deeds," fails. (1) It cannot explain cogently *gam* "even." (2) It uniquely invests *ma'ᵃlāl* with reference to human beings with a nonmoral value. (3) It uniquely interprets *yitnakker* as a reflexive of the *Hiphil,* not the *Piel.* (4) One expects *rš'*, not *yšr.* The proposal by Toy (*Proverbs,* p. 388) to emend *yšr* to *rš'* is ill founded. (1) It lacks textual warrant. (2) It fails to take account of the almost identical parallel *zak yāšār po'ᵒlô* in 21:8b. (3) It misinterprets *ma'ᵃlālāyw* to mean "his [neutral] deeds," not "his [evil] deeds." (4) It expects both of these antonyms to match the antithetical parallels.

27. I am indebted in part for this analysis to Meinhold, *Sprüche,* 2:325.

will learn (v. 25) and end with divine punishments and human beatings for the mocking revolutionary. With regard to being teachable, note the anabasis from the impressionable gullible becoming prudent by punishing the mocker and the discerning gaining knowledge by being corrected (v. 25) to the intractable mockers and fools being brought into line by penal, not remedial, punishments and beatings (v. 29). Sandwiched between them stands the sober warning to the son not to neglect his parents' teaching (v. 27). The mad drunkard is transitional to the subunit pertaining to cleansing the realm of fools. The catchword *bēn* ("son") links the proverb pair of vv. 26-27, and the catchwords *lîṣ* ("mock") and *špṭ* ("judgment"/"punishment") link vv. 28-29. Indeed, the catchword *lîṣ* ("mock") tightly binds together the whole subunit (19:25 [*lēṣ*], 28 [*yālîṣ*], 29 [*lēṣîm*]; 20:1 [*lēṣ*]). The broken consonance of *ṣ* and *l* in *ʿṣl* "sluggard" also binds v. 24 into the subunit's paronomasia.

24 The escalating catalogue of tragic failures in education begins with the sluggard. In a smooth transition between the introduction and the catalogue, it contrasts the sated God-fearer with the starving sluggard, though he is surrounded with food. The contrast exposes the sluggard as one who does not fear the LORD (see 19:15). Proverbs about the sluggard immediately before (v. 15) and after the rearing proverbs of vv. 16 and 23 may form an *inclusio* around the preceding unit on the goal of education.[28] *The sluggard* (*ʿāṣēl;* see I: 114) *buries* [*and hides*][29] *his hand* [*and forearm*] [see 6:5] *in the pan* (see n. 1). BDB refers *ṣallaḥat* to an Aramaic cognate meaning, "a flat dish." If so, a flat saucer, a metonymy for the food in it, would require the least effort in dipping out food. Orientals dispensed with spoons and forks, dipping their hand into the dish to take their portion. *Gam* has its emphasizing adversative function (= "yet"; cf. Job 18:2; Ps. 129:2; Ezek. 18:11) but is best left untranslated.[30] *To* marks either the direction "toward" or the goal or termination "to." *His mouth* functions here as an orifice for food, not as usual for words (see 2:6; 11:9). *He does not return it* glosses the more literal, "He does not cause his hand to participate in the act of returning" (see 15:1; 18:13). The antithetical parallels are structured chiastically by the verb forms "buries and hides" and "does not return," constituting its outer core. The inner core develops an antithesis revolving around an eating scene. In the center stands a pan, out of which the diner takes pieces of food or into which he dips into the sauce (cf. 17:1; Sir. 31:14; Mark 14:20). In verset A

28. So Meinhold, *Sprüche,* 2:325.

29. *HALOT* (1:377, s.v. *ṭmn*) glosses *ṭmn* by (1) "to hide"; (2) "to fix secretly," but here gives the ad hoc meaning "to dip." More specifically, the verb means "to hide by burying": of a carcass (cf. Exod. 2:12), of a treasure (Josh. 2:6; 7:21-22), of stones (Jer. 43:9), and of the dead (Job 40:13). This normal sense with b^e fits here.

30. *HALOT,* 1:196, s.v. *gam.*

the sluggard puts his forearm and hand into the pan and hides it there. In verset B he is too lazy, as the parallel in 26:15 makes clear, to bring it back to his mouth. The sarcastic proverb teaches that the sluggard starves in spite of opportunity. Although he may even make a promising start to satisfy his longing (see 13:4), for the life of him he lacks the spiritual energy to effect it. Bridges applies the proverb: "A religion without sacrifice, without diligence, will never open a way to heaven."[31]

25 The catalogue of failure in education now escalates to the intractable mocker, but, paradoxically, it offers a pedagogic corrective to wrong behavior.[32] Both versets consist of a condition (i.e., a pedagogical situation) and the consequences (i.e., a moral education), for the gullible (v. 25a) and for the discerning (v. 25). *Flog* [see 17:10, 26] *a mocker* (see I: 114) represents the condition or situation as real (see n. 2). *And* introduces the apodosis, the consequence. In this way the basic need of the uncommitted *gullible* (see I: 111) will be achieved; he *will become prudent* (*ya'rīm;* see I: 95); cf. "become wise" in synoptic 21:11). For the mocker flogging is penal (i.e., to satisfy the demands of justice), and for the impressionable gullible remedial (i.e., to satisfy the rules of pedagogy). In contrast to the intractable mocker (9:7; 13:1; 14:6; 15:12), the impressionable gullible learns by the salutary example of physically punishing the mocker. Inferring that the same punishment will be inflicted on him for folly (v. 25a), he becomes alert to his situation and the outcome of his waywardness (cf. Deut. 13:11[12]; 17:13; 19:20; 21:21 and 1 Tim. 5:20). On the other hand, the person who has a discerning disposition gains insight into the divine moral order through merely a word of correction (14:6; 15:5; 17:10). *And* now functions to both compare and contrast the pedagogy of the gullible and of the discerning. [*If*] *one corrects* [see 3:12] *the insightful* (*nābôn;* see I: 95), who already discerns the moral cause-effect reality, represents the verbal situation as hypothetical (see n. 4), in contrast to the very real possibility of flogging a mocker. *He discerns* (*yābîn;* see 1:2) *knowledge* (see I: 77) may have as the subject's antecedent either the one who corrects, for he does not waste his time on mockers (see 9:7-8), or, more plausibly, the "insightful," for he is easily corrected and gets more knowledge (see 1:5). According to the latter interpretation, the hand blows used to impress the gullible are contrasted with the sufficiency of verbal correction for the insightful (see 9:9).

31. Bridges, *Proverbs,* p. 328.

32. This proverb is essentially the same as 21:11, suggesting that the following pairs are synonyms: *ya'rīm* ("to become prudent") and *yeḥkam* ("to become wise"); *nābôn* ("a discerning person") and *ḥākām* ("wise person"); *hikkâ* ("to strike/flog") and *'ānaš* ("to beat/flog"); *yābîn dā'at* ("to discern knowledge") and *yiqqaḥ dā'at* ("to accept knowledge").

26-27 The catchword "son" links this proverb pair. According to v. 26, the son's failed rearing brings ruin on his parents and shame on the family (see 10:1; Exod. 20:12). According to v. 27, the cause of his failed rearing is the son's failure to persevere in his parents' teaching (cf. 3:21). The pair is linked to v. 25 by "knowledge," the last word in each proverb pair. According to v. 25b, verbal reproof gives the discerning knowledge; according to v. 27, ceasing to listen to instruction leads to the loss of knowledge.

26 This chiastic proverb escalates the topic of failed rearing to the shameful son. It frames the family members, father, mother and son, with the participial modifiers of the son: "the one who ruins" and "shameful and disgraceful."[33] It consists grammatically of the topic (or cause, v. 26a) and a predicate (or consequence, v. 26b). *The one who ruins* [see 11:3] [*his*] *father* (see 1:8) points to the father as the ultimate object of the foolish son's wrongdoing; the immediate object is probably the father's property. The gloss, *driving out,* is in agreement with the other biblical uses of *brḥ* in the *Hiphil* (cf. 1 Chr. 8:13; Neh. 13:28; Job 41:20[12]).[34] The asyndetic imperfect probably represents a circumstantial situation, suggesting that the forcible eviction of the mother is an attendant circumstance to the violence done to the father. When the father and his household lie in ruin, the *mother* (see 1:8) is left in a tragic situation without the provision and protection of her husband. By ruining his father, the imbecile (cf. 17:2) leaves his mother almost like a defenseless widow. The ingrate *is a shameful* [see 10:5] *and disgraceful* [see 13:5] *son* (see 17:2). He brings public opprobrium on his parents for their failed venture in raising him and possibly also on himself (see 10:5, n. 18). How he destroys the father is not stated. It could be by passive sloth (10:5), actively squandering the family fortune in riotous living (29:3), and/or by the overt crime of plundering the father and evicting the mother to seize the inheritance (20:20 [cf. Exod. 21:17; Lev. 20:19]; 28:24; 30:11, 17; cf. 2 Sam. 15:1-14). In the latter scenario, the LORD

33. The verse coheres phonologically by the consonance of the initial nasal /m/ in the first *(mšdd)* and the last two words of the verse *(mbyš mḥpyr)* and final /m/ in the last word of verset A *('ēm)* and of nasal /n/ in *bēn,* and of the labial stops /b/ in four words and of /p/ in the final word: *mšdd-'b ybryḥ 'm bn mbš wmḥpyr.*

34. The connection of *brḥ* with *šdd* suggests to some that this is a unique instance of a homonym related to the Arab. *baraḥa* "to be annoyed, suffer," and so they gloss the verb "to injure" (*HALOT,* 1:156, s.v. *brḥ*). H. Graetz retains the traditional meaning by emending *mšdd* to *mᵉnōdēd,* and D. W. Thomas ("Textual and Philological Notes on Some Passages in the Book of Proverbs," in *WIANE,* p. 289) relates *mšdd* to Eth. *sadada* "expel, eject," supposing that the two words should be synonymous. However, "There is no compelling reason why they [*šdd* and *brḥ*] must be synonymous" (McKane, *Proverbs,* p. 532). Indeed, the syntax, wherein the asyndetic imperfective seems to function as a circumstantial clause, suggests that the forcible eviction of the mother is an attendant circumstance to the violence done to the father (Cohen, *Proverbs,* p. 130).

himself, who has the power of life and death, will avenge the wronged parents (cf. 20:20). In any case, the son's crime was especially heinous in antiquity because there was no other form of caring for the aged (cf. Sir. 3:11-13). The proverb assumes that for some unknown reason the parents do not have the power to turn the profligate over to the elders of the village for stoning to protect themselves (Deut. 21:18-21). Tragically, God himself raised profligate children before the appearing of his beloved Son (Isa. 1:2).

27 The son's failure to persevere in his parent's instruction leads to his becoming shameful (cf. 1:8b). Plöger comments: "It seems to me that v. 27 wants to give a reason, in an unusual form, for the shameful behavior of the son as it is pictured in v. 26."[35] The son's progressive hardening in sin develops from his holding himself back from his parents' instruction (v. 27a), to straying from wisdom (v. 27b), to crime against his parents (v. 26). The proverb consists of a protasis stating the cause of the son's apostasy in the form of an imperative, "cease . . . ," and an apodosis stating the purpose of becoming morally derelict in the form of a purpose clause, "to stray. . . ."[36] *Cease* [or refrain from; see 10:19] . . . *listening* [see 1:5, 8] *to instruction* (see 1:2) so obviously contradicts the teaching of this book (see 1:8, 10, 15; 2:1; 3:1, 11, 21; 4:10, 20; 5:1, 20; 6:1, 3, 20; 7:1) that the sage felt he could safely use sarcasm (see I: 40). Jerome captured the intention by negating the imperative, "do not cease listening . . . ," the NIV by a conditional sentence: "cease listening . . . and you will stray . . ." (see n. 7). The vocative *my son* is unique in Collection II (but cf. 23:15, 19, 26; 24:13, 21; 27:11). *In order to stray* (see 5:19) unconsciously like sheep *from the words* [see 1:2; 2:1] *of knowledge* (see 19:25). Without constant attention to wisdom depraved human beings unconsciously stray from it. Even Solomon, ancient Israel's paragon of wisdom, strayed when he ceased listening to his own proverbs (see I: 36).

28-29 These verses also form a proverb pair. Their A versets are linked by the catchwords *yālîṣ/lēṣîm* ("mock"/"mockers") and *mišpāṭ/ šᵉpāṭîm* ("justice"/"penalties"). Note the */ṣ š/* sequence binding these words together in both versets. Verse 28 identifies the revolutionary as the cause of injustice, and v. 29 asserts flogging as the appropriate pedagogic and penal response.

28 This proverb escalates the catalogue of failed rearing to the corrupt witness, the revolutionary who aims to dissolve society by treating the legal system with contempt.[37] *A corrupt* (*bᵉliyyaʿal;* see Prov. 6:12; 16:27)

35. Plöger, *Sprüche,* p. 227.

36. The verse coheres phonologically by the alliteration of *lišmōaʿ mûsār* (v. 27a) and *lišnôt mēʾimrê* (v. 27b).

37. The verse coheres phonologically by the sound pattern between the second words from its beginning and end, *bᵉlîyyaʿal* and *yᵉballaʿ,* which underscore the thought

witness (see 12:17), an implacable revolutionary against the good of society who either has firsthand knowledge of an event or a report of it, *mocks* [see 3:34] *at justice* (*mišpāṭ;* see I: 97). The perjurers in the lawsuit against Naboth are called *beliyya'al* (1 K. 21:10, 13), a story that illustrates the lying witnesses' lethal power (cf. Prov. 18:21). *And* joins the synonymous subject and a synthetic predicate to verset A. *The mouth* denotes the orifice as the instrument from which words emerge (see 2:6; 11:9) and that ingests food (see 19:24). The plural *of the wicked* (see I: 109), assuming that it is synonymous with the "corrupt witness," escalates the more than one witness who has incurred guilt by freeing himself from God's rules that serve society's best interest to serve self (see 2:22; 10:2, 3). The figure *swallows* [see n. 9; 21:20] *iniquity* (see 6:12) may be a double entendre and/or an oxymoron. As a double entendre it means that the corrupt witnesses greedily savor and devour the trouble they are making by their lies as a tasty tidbit[38] and/or they literally consume the exquisite food their lies in court give them (cf. 1:12; 4:17; 21:20; Job 16:5, 20:12-15). On the other hand, it could be an oxymoron, picturing the lying mouth as having to swallow the harmful consequences of its lies (see 1:31; 10:6; 14:14; 16:4; 18:20).[39] McCreesh says: "The false witness mocks justice by bringing forth words from his mouth, but by acting in this way he is really swallowing evil."[40] According to Deut. 19:16-21, justice is worked out by due process of law, but here, because the judicial system has failed, it looks to God to match misdeed with misdeed (16:4).[41] All three interpretations are viable options.

29 The noted catchwords linking vv. 28 and 29 show that this proverb sets forth the God-ordained punishments established for the corrupt witnesses that mock justice (see v. 28). Whereas there was some ambiguity whether v. 28b dealt with the negative consequences of being a corrupt witness, there is no doubt whether v. 29 presents their punishments. However,

---

(see T. McCreesh, O.P., *Biblical Sound and Sense: Poetic Sound Patterns in Proverbs 10–29* [JSOTSup 128; Sheffield: Sheffield Academic, 1991], pp. 75-77). The evildoer will swallow his own evil. McCreesh also notes chiastic phonic sequences that are evenly divided between subject and predicate in verset A:

'd bly'l ylyṣ mšpṭ
d bly l yl pṭ

Note the chiasim of the sequences of the labial stops */b, p/*, the dentals */d, ṭ/* plus */y/* and */l/*. Note, too, the consonance of *ṣ* and *š* in the predicate. He notes this sequence in verset B: *wpy rs'ym ybl' 'wn p ' b '.*

38. Delitzsch, *Proverbs,* p. 291.

39. Meinhold (*Sprüche,* p. 327) accepts both interpretations.

40. McCreesh, *Biblical Sound and Sense,* p. 86.

41. *Amenemope* (14.2) says, "God hates him who falsifies words" (*AEL,* p. 154).

the sapiential terms "mockers" and "fools" (see 1:22) do not restrict their wrongdoing to the courtroom or even to speaking. In its chiastic parallels the subjects "punishments" and "beatings" constitute its inner core, and the predicates "established for mockers"/"for backs of fools" the outer frame.[42] The 16 occurrences of *punishments* (*šᵉpāṭîm;* see 1:3) are always plural with reference to God's acts of judgment. These dreadful acts are penal, not remedial, to satisfy God's justice. The LORD of hosts inflicts them through his creation (cf. Exod. 6:6), through human armies (2 Chr. 24:24; Ezek. 16:41) and/or through both. Ezek. 14:21 specifies as his agents the sword, famine, wild beasts, and plagues. *Are established* (*nākônû;* see 16:4) denotes that the punishments are part of God's fixed, immutable, eternal order (see 12:3; cf. Job 15:23) *for mockers* (see I: 114). The article may refer back to the mocking witnesses (v. 28). *And* combines the synthetic parallels pertaining to mockers and fools. Providence fixes the acts of judgments against mockers, though they may be mediated through human hands, but human hands inflict *beatings* [see 18:6] *for the back* [see 10:13] *of fools* (*kᵉsîlîm;* see I: 112). Both punishments are penal to satisfy the demands of justice, not remedial, for both mockers and fools are intractable. In the process, however, the gullible become prudent (cf. 19:25; 21:11).

20:1 The drunkard draws the catalogue of failed rearing begun in 19:23 to its climax. The catchwords *lēṣ* ("mocker," v. 20a; see 19:24, 28, 29) and *šāgâ* ("stray"/"stagger," 19:27; 20:1b) link it to the catalogue. It adds to the theme of mocking, which began with the miscarriage of justice (19:28) and the earning of just penalties (19:29), a potential cause of mocking, namely, intoxicants. The drunkard lacks consciousness and self-control, and in dissolute madness breaks the bounds of sanctity, morality, and propriety. In verset A the intoxicants "wine" and "beer" are personified as villains to warn the son in verset B that they destroy wisdom and life. Their personification represents liquor's bad characteristics to bring to the fore its danger of transforming people into the failed rearing types that mock at virtue (cf. Hos. 7:5) and justice (19:27) and behave in a turbulent manner. *Wine* [see 3:10; 9:2] *is a mocker* (see 19:25). Of the 22 occurrences of *beer (śēkār),* 20 occur with "wine," either favorably or unfavorably. It denotes any alcoholic beverage, not just barley beer, that is a light intoxicant, about 7-10 percent alcoholic content, by comparison with modern strong drinks.[43] Beer *is a brawler* (see 7:11; 9:13; cf. Ps. 46:3[4]; Zech. 9:15) is a co-reference with "wine is a mocker," for both almost always occur together, and in the parallel the singular pronoun ("through it") has both as its antecedent. The sort of person in

42. The line coheres phonologically through the consonance of /l/: *llṣym . . . mhlmt lgw ksylym.*

43. R. L. Harris, *TWOT,* 1:376, s.v. *yayin.*

view is mocking, noisy, and restless; he disturbs the peace and perverts justice (cf. 19:28; 31:4-5). *And* joins the consequence and conclusion of verset B to the cause of verset A. *Everyone* (*kol;* see n. 13) *who staggers* (*šōgeh;* see 19:27; cf. "intoxicate" in 5:19: Isa. 28:7) *by them* [i.e., the co-references] *is not wise* (see I: 94). Lacking the essential virtue for life, they die. The epigrammatic nature of the proverbs in general concentrates the negative side of wine and beer in this proverb. In 21:17 and 23:19-21, addiction and/or overindulgence in drink or in olive oil and/or meat leads to drowsiness and/or poverty; in 31:4-5 to the miscarriage of justice. On the other hand, in 3:10 and 9:6 wine and beer function as symbols of prosperity and the good life. The same ambivalence is found elsewhere in the Old Testament. On the one hand, wine and beer are prohibited for those situations demanding sharp discretion (Lev. 10:9; cf. Isa. 5:11-12, 22) and for the Nazirite who is separated to God from earthly joys (Num. 6:3). It is also symbolic of self-indulgence (Isa. 28:1-5; Amos 6:6). (The Rechabites refused wine not on account of its threat to wise living in general, but to preserve their nomadic way of life by not being bound to the land by planting vineyards and building houses [Jer. 35:6-7].) On the other hand, wine and beer are the tokens of God's blessings (Gen. 27:28; Exod. 29:40; Deut. 14:26). Jotham praises it as the elixir of gods and people (Judg. 9:13). "These two aspects of wine, its use and its abuse, its benefits and its curse, its acceptance in God's sight and its abhorrence, are interwoven into the fabric of the OT so that it may gladden the heart of man (Ps. 104:15) or cause his mind to err (28:7), it can be associated with merriment (Ec. 10:19) or with anger (Is. 5:11), it can be used to uncover the shame of Noah (Gn. 9:21) or in the hands of Melchizedek to honor Abraham (Gn. 14:18)."[44] The proverb protects itself against contradicting this favorable side of wine and beer by restricting it to the inebriated.

c. The Righteous King and Fools (20:2-11)

The ten-verse second subunit pertains to the righteous king's cleansing the realm of all fools. It can be analyzed as having two partial subunits. The first begins with the righteous king's powerful roar, threatening judgment on the wicked (v. 2), and ends with the king's divine authority as he cleanses his realm of all evil (v. 8). Power without authoritative justice is tyranny, and justice without power is weak. Sandwiched within this *inclusio* is a second catalogue of fools (vv. 3-7) to qualify the first, tempering punishment and universal justice with the reality of universal human depravity (vv. 9-11). The two partial subunits are crocheted together by initial *mem* in vv. 7, 8, and 9, by negative rhetorical questions in vv. 6, 9, and 11, and by an alternating struc-

44. F. S. Fitzsimmonds, *NBD,* p. 1255, s.v. "Wine and Strong Drink."

ture. The first two rhetorical questions pertain to the extent of human depravity, escalating its extent from the few conscientious people to none who are pure; the third rhetorical question pertains to its duration — even youths are sinful. The structure alternates between the king's justice (v. 8) and God's (v. 10), tempered by the reality of universal human depravity (v. 9) from youth (v. 11). An "even" *(gam)* proverb concludes the subunit, the only coordinating adverb that functions like this (see 17:26; 18:9). A rearing proverb (v. 12) introduces the next unit.

(1) The Righteous King Roots Out All Evil (20:2-8)

Sandwiched within the royal framework (vv. 2, 8) is the second catalogue of fools, who are now contrasted with the wise in vv. 3, 5, and 6: the quarreling fool (v. 3), the deluded sluggard (v. 4), the conniver (v. 5), and the hypocritical masses (v. 6). Verse 7 both qualifies v. 6 and contrasts the LORD's favor to the conscientious person's descendants with the king who roots out the future offspring of evildoers in v. 8. The catchword "person" (*'îš;* vv. 3, 5, and 6) crochets the partial subunit together. The discerning person in v. 5 finds concrete expression in the discerning king (v. 8).

2 The brawling drunkard, along with the other types of fools in the first catalogue (19:24–20:1), is now handed over to the king, God's surrogate (see 16:1-9, 10-15). This royal proverb sets forth the fatal and imminent danger of incurring the king's wrath. *The roaring as of a lion is the terror struck by the king* repeats 19:12a, except that the king's "fury" *(zaʿap)* gives way to his victim's "terror" *('ēmat).* The 16 occurrences of *'ēmâ* denote a sharp, intense, overmastering fear, such as fell on Abraham in his concern for Israel's bondage in Egypt (Gen. 15:12) and later fell on the Egyptians at the Red Sea (Exod. 15:16; cf. Josh. 2:9; Ezra 3:3; Job 9:34; 13:21; 20:25; 33:7; 41:14[6]; Pss. 55:4[5]; 88:16[17]; Isa. 33:18). The young lion claimed its prey by roaring (Ps. 104:21), and no one can deliver it (Isa. 5:29). Verset B, unlike the parallel in 19:12, reinforces his roar by explaining the metaphor. *Whoever angers him* [i.e., makes the king flare up; see 14:16] *forfeits his life* (*ḥôṭē' napšô;* lit. "to miss his life"; see 11:31) or "who wrongs or sins against himself" (see I: 90; 6:32; 8:36). The two interpretations do not differ significantly because sin entails the loss of life (see 10:16; cf. Hab. 2:10).[45] The parallel, roaring lion, suggests that death is in view. The dreadful "roar" is no empty threat. The other royal proverbs in Collection II suggest that the surrogate's roar is in fact God's roar against fools that threaten his kingdom (see 16:10-15; 19:12; 20:8, 28). Fools would be well advised to appease the surrogate's roar immediately, but they have no sense (cf. 16:14).

45. *HALOT,* 1:305, s.v. *ḥṭ'.*

3 As the king's anger and patience were joined in 19:11-12, so again the king's wrath is moderated by forbearance in 20:2-3. Though the king's anger is justified, stirring up conflict is not. As the brawler ended the catalogue of fools at the end of the first subunit, the contentious person now heads the list in the second catalogue. Verset A presents social weight as the reward of abstaining from strife, and verset B describes every fool as one who starts a quarrel. *Abstaining* (*šebet;* see n. 17) *from strife* [see 15:18] *brings* [see n. 18] *glory* [see 3:16] *to a person* (*ʾîš;* see I: 89). *But* joins the antithetical parallels that characterize this second catalogue. *Every* [see 20:1] *fool* (*ʾewîl;* see I: 109) *starts a quarrel* (*yitgallāʿ;* see 17:14; 18:1). The semantically antithetical parallels "abstaining from strife" and "starting a quarrel" are fairly precise antonyms, but "every fool" and "glory to the individual" are not, suggesting that the fool has no social weight, and the one who has gravitas in a community is no fool. Society grants honor to the one who is able to pacify a situation by not participating in the strife. Paradoxically, the way to honor is to abstain from defending one's honor. Contrast Gideon's humility, when he was contended against, which healed society (Judg. 8:1-3) with his revenge when he was the contender (Judg. 8:7-21), showing how complex in fact an individual can be. The wise are more concerned to bring peace than to be right, but the fool cannot restrain himself and at the first opportunity explodes and shows his teeth. This demeanor to forgo defending one's pride when insulted demands that one be humble and submissive, not a rash hothead who trumpets his refusal to submit to anyone (cf. 10:12; 12:16; 14:29; 15:18; 17:27, 28; 19:11; 29:11; cf. Jas. 3:13-18).

4 The second fool is the *sluggard,* who headed the previous catalogue (see I: 114). What is said of the shameful son in 10:1-5 is transferred here to the sluggard. In 10:5 the lazybones is said to endure public shame (10:5), not honor, and this may provide a connection with the contentious fool who also lacks honor in 20:3. In the parallels of v. 4, the situation of the sluggard "from winter on" (v. 4aα) is contrasted with "in harvest" (v. 4bα), and the predicate "he does not plow" (v. 4aβ) is matched with "but there is not" (v. 4bβ). These seven Hebrew words move from winter to harvest. According to Isa. 28:24, *plow* (cf. 3:29) refers to the arduous work of both opening and breaking up the ground and of harrowing it.[46] The plow was a wooden-frame plow to which a metal point (copper, bronze, and later iron) was attached, pulled by a team of animals, usually oxen or donkeys (Deut. 22:10; 1 K. 19:19).[47] The Palestinian farmer encountered many hardships, such as a rainy season limited to mid-October to April, fluctuations in precipitation, and the rocky and hilly nature of most of the terrain. Nevertheless, by

46. H. Ringgren, *TDOT,* 5:221, s.v. *ḥāraš.*

47. O. Borowski, *ABD,* 1:97, s.v. "Agriculture."

the careful selection of grains, hard work, and Palestine's fertility, agriculture was the economic backbone of ancient Israel, practiced by both city dwellers and villagers. Egyptian records from the Old, Middle, and New Kingdom recognize Canaan's agricultural richness, making it a target for invading armies. Israel's most common cereals were wheat, emmer, barley, and millet; its legumes were lentil, broad bean, chick pea, pea, and fenugreek; its spice plants were black cumin, cumin, and coriander; other plants were flax and sesame. Plowing began about December. Assuming temporal *from,* it may or may not include the beginning point named.[48] *Winter* designates the Palestinian rainy season from mid-October to April. It includes the ninth month (Chislev [= November-December]; Jer. 36:22), and according to the rabbinical division of the year winter extends from December to January.[49] The Gezer calendar inscription (10th cent. B.C.) reads: "two months of ingathering [olives], two months of sowing [cereals], two months of late sowing [legumes and vegetables], a month of hoeing seeds [for hay], a month of harvesting barley, a month of harvesting [wheat] and measuring [grain], two months of grape harvesting, a month of ingathering summer fruit."[50] Thus two months were devoted to sowing cereals and two more to the late sowing and planting of legumes and vegetables. Since no sowing could have been done without plowing, the farmer waited for the first autumn rains to soften the ground. The sluggard, however, lacks the industry to plow from winter on, the only time that matters. In the synthetic parallel *then* (*w^e;* see n. 21) adds the (con)sequential situation. Ironically — as is always the case with the sluggard — he stands by idly watching while others are busy plowing their fields, yet turns up at harvest time demanding a crop. "The fellow lives in cloud-cuckoo land!"[51] The verb glossed *he asks (šā'al)* — with no one in particular in mind — occurs 171 times with two related meanings, "to ask" and "to request/beg," which maintain themselves about equally. The two images are not separated so that its range of meanings includes to beg (Ps. 109:10), to petition (1 K. 2:16), to borrow (2 K. 4:3), to demand (2 Sam. 3:13).[52] Here he demands a yield *in the harvest* (see 6:8). *But there is none* (see 13:4), for in God's moral laws of reciprocity neglect leads to loss, just as sin leads to death and selfishness to self-victimization. God will not be mocked. An aftergrowth from the fruit of the unworked field is not in view (Lev. 25:6-7). By failing to reap a harvest, he deprives himself of life immediately, and should he survive the first winter, he still lacks the seed to plant a crop for the

48. *IBHS,* pp. 212-13, P. 11.2.11c.
49. E. Kutsch, *TDOT,* 5.205-6, s.v. *ḥrp* I.
50. *ANET,* p. 320.
51. Aitken, *Proverbs,* p. 119.
52. G. Gerleman, *TLOT,* 2.1282-83, s.v. *šā'al.*

following year that would guarantee his continued existence (cf. 12:11; 28:19). Malbim applies the proverb: "Similarly, youth is the time to prepare the seed-bed of one's character for moral wisdom to take root."[53]

5 The second catalogue of fools now advances to the conniver, but he cannot outsmart the wise (v. 5). In the Hebrew text, the antithetical topics "the counsel in a person's heart" and "an understanding person" constitute the inner core, and its predicates, "are deep waters" versus "draws it up," constitute the outer frame. Heretofore in Proverbs *counsel* referred to the counsel from the wise to the disciple (1:25, 30; 8:14; 12:15; 19:20) or of the immutable will of the LORD (see 19:21). But hereafter it has the weakened sense of "advice" from a peer or an inferior (20:18; 21:30) or *in a person's heart* (see *b^eleb-'îš;* see I: 89, 90; cf. 27:19). The pejorative metaphor, *deep waters* (see 18:4) signifies that the latter counsel is paradoxically unfathomable, inaccessible, nonbeneficial, and potentially dangerous (see 18:4; 21:30; cf. Job 10:3; 18:7; 21:16; 22:18; Pss. 1:1; 106:43; Isa. 29:15). *But* combines the antitheses. *An understanding person* [see 10:23] *draws it up (yidlennâ). Dālâ* in the *Qal* denotes "to draw water" (Exod. 2:16, 19; Prov. 20:5) and in the *Piel* "to draw up (from the deep) to save" (Ps. 30:3[4]). Here the metaphor represents the competent person's ability to draw up skillfully to the surface the conniver's unfathomable counsel from beneath its verbal surface. The heart of the ordinary person, in contrast to the understanding, is conniving, not genuine (cf. Jer. 17:9), just as his hand is closed, not open. The hidden counsels of his heart in his self-talk do not aim to serve the community but himself. As a result, "He keeps it secret, conceals it carefully, craftily misleads those who seek to draw it out."[54] The insightful person, however, by his piety toward God, his purity of ethics, and his perception of the moral order, is not deceived (cf. Isa. 11:1-5). And if the aim of the hostile counsel "is pernicious to him, he meets it in the process of realization."[55] Sick David, for example, perceived that behind the empty words of his visiting enemies their hearts were gathering mischievous gossip to be used against him (Ps. 41:6[7]; cf. 64:5-6[6-7]; 119:28; Matt. 12:25; Mark 12:15; Luke 5:22; 6:8; 11:17; John 2:24-25; 13:11).

6 The third kind of fool is now escalated to a group, the many hypocrites (cf. 12:9; 25:14; 27:5-6). The proverb is linked with v. 5 by the unnecessary twofold repetition of "person" *('îš)* in its inner core. In v. 5 the hidden and dangerous depths of the human heart are contrasted with the understanding

53. M. L. Malbim, *The Commentary of Rabbi Meir Leibush Malbim on the Book of Proverbs,* based on the original draft by Avival Gottlieb Zornberg (Jerusalem: Feldheim, 1973), p. 204.

54. Delitzsch, *Proverbs,* p. 295.

55. Delitzsch, *Proverbs,* p. 295.

person's insights. In v. 6 the proclamation of many about their universally applauded virtue of loyal kindness (see 19:22; cf. 25:14) is contrasted with the rare and precious conscientiousness of the person who truly acts in time of need. Implicitly, the majority who ponder dark counsel within (v. 6a) profess kindness without (v. 7a); and the insightful person (v. 6b) is conscientious (v. 7b). In the antithetical parallels of v. 6 the outer frame presents the topics, the many hypocrites versus the one very rare and precious reliable person, and the inner core presents the predicates, "proclaims his kindness" versus the "conscientious person" who performs it. "The antithesis," says Clifford, "is not . . . between being loyal and being trustworthy but between having a reputation for a virtue and actually practicing it, between untested and tested friendship."[56] The nominative absolute construction represented by *as for* (see n. 22) underscores the contrast between normative human nature and the exceptional individual. *As for many* [see 5:23] *human beings* (*'ādām;* see I: 89), *each person* (*'îš*), which distributes the "many" to each individual and provides a keyword connection with vv. 3 and 5, *proclaims* [see 1:21] *his unfailing kindness* (*ḥesed;* see I: 100). *But* introduces the antithesis (see 20:5b) between profession and reality, not between kindness and *a conscientious person* (*'ᵉmûnâ;* or trustworthy; see I: 99). The rhetorical negative *who can find* (see 1:13; 3:13) implies the answers, "no one" or, as here, "hardly anyone" (see v. 7). With this meaning the object frequently precedes the question (cf. 24:22; 31:10).[57] His rarity is viewed within the background of a general human evaluation. Thus the proverb gives the son insight into the hypocrisy of human nature and aims to instruct him to seek diligently the rare friend who has the rocklike quality of being conscientious in unfailing kindness and to be one himself.

7 This synthetic proverb nuances the pessimism of v. 6 by implying that a few conscientious folk exist, identifying them by the co-referential terms "blameless" and "righteous." It both further characterizes this exceptional person, the cause (v. 7a), and presents his reward, the consequence (v. 7b). Such a person shows unfailing kindness to the community as part of his total dedication to the LORD and his teachings (v. 7a). As a reward, his offspring realize life to its fullest as the Creator intended it to be experienced (cf. Gen. 18:22; Pss. 25:12, 13; 37:26; 112:2). *One who walks* about (see 6:22) *in his blamelessness* (*bᵉtummô;* see I: 99) is characterized as *a righteous person* (*ṣaddîq;* see n. 23; I: 97). Verset B draws his descendants into the beneficiaries of his good behavior (cf. 13:22; 14:11, 26; 17:6). *Blessed* [see 3:13] *are his children* [see 4:1; 5:7; 14:26; cf. 13:22; 17:6] *after him,* referring to his immediate lineal descendants.[58] His blessed future

56. Clifford, *Proverbs,* p. 182.

57. BDB, p. 567, s.v. *mî.*

58. *IBHS,* p. 192, P. 11.2.1a, n. 17.

stands in contrast to that of the king's enemies whom he roots out of the land (v. 8), which gives him the last word over the apostate son who ruins his parents (19:26). The righteous person dies in peace, knowing that his family's spiritual and economic patrimony has been securely transmitted to the immediately succeeding generations. "The branches fare better for the sap of grace in the root."[59] God promises to show unfailing kindness to a thousand generations of those who love him and do not apostatize. Whereas God interdicts punishment after three or four generations, he never of his own initiative prohibits his unfailing kindness to those who love him (Exod. 20:5-6; cf. Prov. 13:22; 14:26). However, a child may hate the LORD (cf. Ezek. 18:20), and it cannot be concluded that every foolish child is unwise because of a parent's lack of righteousness (cf. 5:12-13; 10:1; 17:21, 25; 19:13, 27; 20:20; 28:7; 30:17).

8 The closing frame around the partial subunit of evildoers again presents *a king* (see 1:1; 14:28; 20:2) — "a righteous king" as LXX paraphrases — judicially ridding his realm of them. Though they connive to deceive him (v. 5), he ferrets them out. Verse 2 presented his awesome power to execute judgment, now v. 8 presents his heavenly authority and his universal justice. The synthetic parallels of this royal proverb modify the topic by two participial phrases, "who sits . . . ," scenically depicting his authority to judge, and "who scatters . . . ," presenting his justice as universal both in space and time. No evil survives to take root again. *One who sits* (see 3:29; 9:14) denotes the king's shift to a lasting or even permanent state. *A throne* (see 9:14) "is undoubtedly the most important symbol of royal authority"[60] and is associated with justice (2 Sam. 15:2-4; 1 K. 7:7; Ps. 122:5; Isa. 16:5) and God's presence. In Israel, the LORD is the authentic initiator and guarantor of enthronement (cf. 2 Sam. 7:13, 16; 1 K. 1:13, 17; 2:24), and his spirit of justice rests on his anointed king (Isa. 11:1-5; 28:6; cf. Ps. 122:5). *Of judgment (dîn)* has its original meaning; it "embraces all individual acts of supportive or punitive justice."[61] *Dîn* refers to the formal judicious process as a whole; its synonym "*špṭ* denotes first of all the act of arbitration, the legal decision."[62] In sum, verset A presents the king as God's vice regent in administering justice (cf. Ps. 72:2; Prov. 20:8; 31:5, 8, 9; Jer. 21:12; 22:16). His sharp, discerning eye perceives all that is morally corrupt and socially disruptive to the well-being of God's kingdom, and his binding decisions are so ef-

59. Bridges, *Proverbs*, p. 340, citing Sinnock's *Christian Man's Calling*, p. 383.

60. T. Ishida, *The Royal Dynasties in Ancient Israel* (BZAW 142; Leiden: Brill, 1977), p. 104.

61. M. Görg, *TDOT*, 6:430, s.v. *yāšab*. In Prov. 22:10, where *dîn* appears in parallelism with *mādôn* "strife" and *qālôn* "abuse," it has almost lost its juridical sense and simply means "quarreling."

62. V. Hamp, *TDOT*, 3:188, s.v. *dîn*.

fective that not a trace of evil is left to take root again. *Winnowing* (*m^{e}zāreh,* from I *zrh;* cf. 1:17; 15:7) means to separate and drive off in various directions (cf. 20:26; Lev. 26:33; 1 K. 14:15; Pss. 44:11[12]; 106:27; Jer. 49:32, 36; 51:2). With peoples, *zārâ* pictures a defeat so devastating that no one survives to resist the victor to take root again. This notion may be intensified by the addition of "to the winds" (e.g., Jer. 49:32, 36; Ezek. 5:10, 12). *With his eyes* (see 3:7) is added because the assessment of what is evil depends on one's taste, expressed in Hebrew by "in one's eyes." His keen discernment, a gift from God (1 K. 3:9-12, 16-18), immediately discerns *all evil* (see 1:16), a metonymy for all people whose behavior is morally corrupt and who destroy the kingdom (cf. Ps. 5:5[6]; Heb. 4:13). During the monarchy Israel's judicial system extended from the elders in the gate to the king on his supreme throne in the Hall of Judgment (2 Sam. 14:4-11; 15:1-6; 1 K. 3:16-28; 7:7; 2 K. 8:1-6). His judgment seat was situated at the right hand of God's throne in the temple, at the heart of which stood the Ten Commandments. Righteousness at the top was necessary to undergird the whole judicial system.

(2) Justice Tempered by the Reality of Human Depravity (20:9-11)

Verse 8 may be rightly regarded as a janus, forming an *inclusio* with v. 2 and sharing an alternating structure with vv. 8-11:

A The king's justice (v. 8)
  B Universal human depravity (v. 9)
A′ The LORD's justice (v. 10)
  B′ Human depravity from youth (v. 11)

The alternating structure of vv. 8 and 10 shows that God stands behind his surrogate king's judgment, for the LORD detests deceit (see 16:1-9, 10-15). The omniscient God sees all evil, and his anointed king's eyes search it out (vv. 5, 8). In spite of human cleverness, no one escapes. The universal justice of the LORD and his king, however, is tempered by the hard reality of universal human depravity (vv. 9, 11). The negative rhetorical question in v. 9, "Who can say, 'My heart is pure *(zikkîtî)*'?" corresponds to the negative rhetorical question in v. 11, "Is his conduct pure *(zak)* or upright?" The activity of the righteous king to cleanse his realm of evil (v. 8) must be tempered by the reality that no person is free from sin (v. 9). So also the LORD's revulsion against fraud and deception (v. 10) is tempered by the reality that human beings practice deceit from their youth (v. 11). The extent of the king's justice in space (all evil) and time (rooting out the descendants, v. 8) is matched by the extent of human depravity in space (v. 9) and time (v. 11). By alternating the proverbs in this way, the collection implicitly matches justice with grace. Van Leeuwen comments: "We are morally ambiguous creatures, and inevitably we are implicated in society's immorality. None of us will be whole until Christ makes humanity whole. . . . The line between wisdom and folly, good and bad, cuts through the heart of us all. What matters is that one is on the road of progressive righteousness and wisdom" (see 4:18).[63] In addition to these semantic connections, the catchword *zākak* ("cleanse"/"pure") links v. 11 with v. 9, a pun on *gam* ("indeed"/"even") links it with v. 10, and vv. 9a and 11b in a chiastic pattern use negative rhetorical questions.

9 This factual proverb, asserting humanity's moral impotence and bondage to sin, is not concerned with why a person is ethically impure or how one might proceed to purify himself, but to qualify vv. 7 and 8. Blamelessness (v. 7a) does not mean sinless perfection. Moreover, although the ideal king rids his realm of all evil (v. 8), the compassionate also recognize that no human being can cleanse his heart of sin (v. 9). The conceptual connection between "evil" and "sin" is validated textually in Prov. 1:10-16, where the feet of *"sinners"* (v. 10) "run to *evil*" (v. 16). The tension between practical blamelessness and rooting out evil, on the one hand, and the recognition of human depravity, on the other, can be resolved by 28:13: "The one who confesses and forsakes transgression obtains mercy." "The compassionate man will try to understand the humanity of weakness and the weakness of humanity," says Plaut.[64] The impossibility is underscored by the rhetorical question, *Who can say?* (cf. 1:11), anticipating the answer, "No one" (see 20:6b). Its first object is the clause, *I have cleansed (zikkîtî) my heart* (see I: 90). *Zākâ* and its by-form, *zākak,* with no difference in meaning, mean "to be pure, unadulterated." Aside from Exod. 27:20; Lev. 24:2; Job 15:4; 25:5; Lam. 4:7, where its meaning is more literal, the passages exhibit a metaphorical sense with religious and ethical force, as the parallel terms demonstrate. In three passages the adjective *zak* is used in combination with *yāšār,* "upright" (Job 8:6; Prov. 20:11; 21:8b).[65] Verset B gives the second object. The synthetic parallel adds to the ingressive state the durative situation. *I am pure* [see 15:26] *from my sin* (see 5:22; 16:26) refers to "moral purity" as in the other wisdom literature (Job 4:17; 14:4; 17:9; 25:4; Prov. 30:12; Eccl. 9:2). The proverb drives home its point by using the first person, which the Hebrew text underscores by the assonance of terminal *î.*[66] When profiled against God, who alone can

63. Van Leeuwen, *Proverbs,* p. 189.

64. Plaut, *Proverbs,* p. 210.

65. A. Negoita and H. Ringgren, *TDOT,* 4:63, s.v. *zākhāh.*

66. *Zikkîtî libbî ṭāhartî mēhaṭṭā'tî* (cf. Ps. 51:3a[5a]). Note, too, the broken sequence of final /*tî*/ along with /*ṭ*/ in *ṭāhartî mēhaṭṭātî.*

truly assess the situation (15:3, 11; 17:3; 20:27; 21:2; 22; 24:12), all human beings are found lacking in moral purity (cf. Gen. 6:5; 8:21; 1 K. 8:46; Job 15:14-16; Pss. 14; 19:12[13]; 32; 51:5-6[7-8]; 143:2; Eccl. 7:20-29; Jer. 17:9; Ezek. 18:31; Rom. 3:9-19).[67] In sum, vv. 7-8 combine ethical purity with compassion, which rid the kingdom of evil and begets forbearance. The proverb engenders humility and implicitly instructs one to throw himself on the mercy of both God and his king (see 15:3, 11; 16:10-15). The final court of appeal is God's throne (see v. 10), which is a throne of grace (Heb. 4:16). "And truly, if none can *say — I have made my heart clean,* myriads can witness to the blood of him who is the Son of God, cleansing it from guilt (1 John 1:7), and to the mightiness of the Creator to renew it unto holiness."[68]

10 This proverb puts the full weight of God's moral sensibility and justice behind the king's throne (v. 8; cf. 16:1-9, 10-15) and keeps the compassion of the preceding proverb from being abused. Abominable weights and measures, which represent all forms of fraud and deceit, are concrete expressions of the abstractions "evil" (v. 8) and "sin" (v. 9). Sir. 26:29 pessimistically states that a trader cannot be free from sin, suggesting a link with v. 9. A clearer connection, however, pertains to the "abomination to the LORD" formula. Since the iniquitous stone and ephah are an abomination to him, he will rid his realm of them and of those who use them. Standard weights and measures require legal sanction to enforce their authority. The righteous LORD stands behind them (Lev. 19:35-36; Deut. 25:13-16; Prov. 11:1; 16:11; 20:23; Ezek. 45:10). In practice the king (2 Sam. 14:26) and the priests (Exod. 30:13) set the standard. Behind the blessedness of the righteous family, who do not commit this kind of wickedness (v. 7), and behind the just king who cleanses his realm of evil (v. 8) — while tempering it with mercy (v. 9) — stands the LORD, who enforces ethical purity (v. 10). The proverb emphatically censures diverse weights and measures by the nominative absolute construction, glossed *as for,* wherein both are mentioned in verset A and repeated chiastically and emphatically by the resumptive "them" at the end of the proverb (cf. 17:15; 20:12; 29:13; cf. 22:2; 30:15-33). *Diverse weights* (see 11:1; 16:11) pertain to measuring by a scale. *Diverse ephahs* have to do with the largest dry measure of a container in antiquity.[69] According to the

67. The Sumerian poem "Man and His God" (ca. 1700 B.C.) also expresses this conviction: "Never has a sinless child been born to its mother. . . . A sinless workman (?) has not existed from of old" (S. N. Kramer, "'Man and His God': A Sumerian Variation on the 'Job Motif,'" *VTSup* 3 [Leiden: Brill, 1955], p. 179).

68. Bridges, *Proverbs,* p. 343.

69. The word *ephah* was a loanword from Egyptian that probably meant "basket" (cf. Zech. 5:5-11) and secondarily a basket's capacity (i.e., "basketful"). "In the OT, it was a standard unit of dry measure in grain commerce (Mic 6:10; Amos 8:5). An omer (i.e.,

rabbis, the ephah contained 22 liters.[70] The phrases "diverse weights" and "diverse ephahs" for two kinds of weights and measures occurs also in Deut. 25:14, 15, where the explanatory words "large and small" are added.[71] *Indeed, both of them are an abomination to the LORD* (see 17:15b). Traders used the scanty weights and measures for selling and the large ones for buying. Significantly, all the proverbs that denounce false scales and measures explicitly link the LORD's name in the abomination formula with them (11:1; 20:10, 23; cf. also 15:25; 16:11). The demand for honesty among traders is consistent with other Old Testament theologies (Lev. 19:36; Deut. 25:14-15; Ezek. 45:10; Amos 8:5; Mic. 6:10).

11 As noted above, the LORD's revulsion against deceit (v. 10) is now tempered by the reality that human beings are deceitful from youth (cf. Gen. 8:21). In the Hebrew text, the antithetical parallels place "in his evil practices" and "his conduct" in the outer frame and juxtapose "fakes" with "pure" and "upright," in the inner core, having "youth," the topic, at the center. *Even* (*gam;* see 17:26, 28; 18:9 and 19:2) introduces the a fortiori argument, drawing the subunit to its conclusion. If even *a youth* (see 1:4; 22:6, 15; 23:13) practices or can practice fraud and deception (cf. v. 10), how much more a grown person (cf. v. 9). In 37 of the other 40 occurrences of the phrase *by his evil deeds (bᵉmaʿᵃlālāyw)* the verbal noun, always plural, refers to the evil deeds of people.[72] This use of the noun is consistent with its verb, "to indicate the exercise of power over another person, generally in a bad sense, hence meaning to maltreat."[73] In that light, the noun probably denotes here the evil deeds of youth, not a unique use for deeds in general.[74] *Dissembles* means either "to make oneself unrecognizable" (1 K. 14:5-6) or "to act

---

'ass load') was one-tenth of an ephah (Exod. 16:36; Ezek. 45:11). The fact that an ephah equaled the liquid measure *bat* ('bath'; Ezek. 45:11, 14) provides the only clue to its quantity. Jars marked *bt* (ca. 8th cent. B.C.) found at Tell Beit Mirsim and Lachish had an approximate capacity of 22 liters (5.8 U.S. gallons) or one-half to three-fifths of a bushel. Thus, the ephah would have weighed about 29 (U.S.) pounds" (R. L. Hubbard, *The Book of Ruth* [NICOT; Grand Rapids: Eerdmans, 1988], p. 179).

70. Meinhold, *Proverbs,* p. 336.

71. Note the assonance of initial /'/ along with the labial-dentals /*b* and *p*/, voiced and unvoiced respectively.

72. Eleven times with *rōaʿ* "evil" (nom.), two times with *rāʿîm* "evil" (adj.), 12 times from context alone; once with *hērēʿû* "to make [deeds] evil," five times with *hêṭîbû* (= "amend [your deeds])," once with *lōʾ-ṭôbîm,* "not good," five times with "the fruit of your deeds," a figure for punishment; and three times, in a striking contrast, to the LORD's renowned and/or righteous deeds (Pss. 77:11[12]; 78:11; Mic. 2:7). Its by-form *ʿᵃlîlâ* is used in sharply contrasting the wicked actions of men with the renowned and righteous acts of God (see Carl Schultz, *TWOT,* 2:671, s.v. *ʿᵃlîlâ*).

73. C. Schultz, *TWOT,* 2.671, s.v. *ʿālal.*

74. *Pace* BDB, p. 760, s.v. *maʿᵃlāl.*

as a stranger [not to make known oneself]."[75] Delitzsch objects to the meaning "dissembles" because that statement "is not justified by experience." Did he have children? Clifford translates the verb as "fake."[76] Verset B underscores verset A by the polar rhetorical question *Is . . . or . . .* that again demands negative answers (cf. Job 6:12).[77] *His conduct (po‘^{o}lô)* looks back to his youth. *HALOT* gives the meaning "acting, conduct" here and in 21:8. It is used in connection with the moral quality of good or evil in Job 34:11; Prov. 24:12, 29; of evil in Job 36:9; Ps. 28:4; Isa. 59:6; Jer. 25:14; 50:29; and of good in Prov. 20:11; 21:8.[78] The parallel *b^{e}ma‘^{a}lālāyw* reveals his character as depraved; *po‘^{o}lô* leaves it unknown. *Pure* (see 16:2; 20:9), or is it — *po‘^{o}lô* is gapped in these terse questions — *upright* (*yāšar;* see I: 98) is antithetical to "[evil] deed." Thus the proverb again instructs the disciple both to abhor sin and to show mercy to the sinner and, when he commits evil and acts hypocritically, as he certainly will, to throw himself through the purple veil upon the heart of God.

8. Speech and Commerce (20:12-19)

12 *As for the hearing ear and the seeing eye,*
indeed, both of them the LORD has made.[79]
13 *Do not love sleep lest you become poor.*
Open your eyes and be filled with food.
14 *"Bad, bad," says the buyer —*
and when he has it in hand,[80] *then he boasts.*
15 *There is gold and an abundance of corals,*
but a precious vessel is lips that speak knowledge.
16 *Take away his garment when one becomes surety for a stranger;*
and for an outsider[81] *impound it.*[82]

75. *HALOT* (2:699-700, s.v. *nkr*) gives these meanings for *nkr* in the *Hithpael* in contradistinction to the *Hiphil yakkîr,* "to recognize" (Gen. 42:7). But these uses make unlikely the opposite meaning given in *HALOT,* "to make oneself recognized" (Prov. 20:11). That meaning is also undermined by Arab. *tankar* ("to make oneself unknowable"). Moreover, the context, asserting universal depravity (v. 9) and deception (v. 10), suggests that *nkr Hithpael* probably has its usual meaning, "to make oneself unrecognizable, to dissimulate, to dissemble." Finally, the otherwise unattested meaning, "to make oneself recognized," delivers a more jejune, platitudinous proverb.

76. Clifford, *Proverbs,* pp. 183-84.

77. BDB, p. 50, s.v. *'im.*

78. *HALOT,* 3:951, s.v. *pō‘al.*

79. For the syntax of this verse see v. 10.

80. Or "when he goes away."

81. K and Vulg. read *nokrîm* ("foreigners"), but Q and Targ. (cf. Syr.) read *nokrîyâ* ("a foreign woman"), probably motivated by the otherwise synoptic 27:13. The

17 *Food gotten by deceit*[83] *is sweet to the person,*
but afterward his mouth is filled with gravel.
18 *Plans are established with counsel,*
so[84] *with guidance make*[85] *war.*
19 *He who goes about as a slanderer divulges secrets,*
so do not get involved[86] *with a silly chatterer.*

This unit consists of four proverb pairs. The first is a pair of rearing proverbs matching the LORD's making of the human receptors of wisdom, the ear and the eye (v. 12), with the human responsibility to "open your eyes" (v. 13). The second matches the common business practice of lying to haggle down the price and impious boasting (v. 14) with the rarity of knowledgeable lips, which do not lie or boast (v. 15). Moreover, Van Leeuwen notes: "Taken together, the two sayings present an ironic contrast between the goods for which one haggles and priceless wisdom (see 3:15; 8:10-11)."[87] The third links the imprudent business practices of going surety for another (v. 16) and being deceptive (v. 17) by a play on I *'ārab* ("to go surety") and III *'ārab* ("to be sweet"). The fourth pair admonishes the need for taking counsel (v. 18) but not with a gossip (v. 19)! These two proverbs share the unusual syntax of making a statement in verset A that provides the premise for the admonition in verset B. In sum, the unit consists of an introduction to accept the wisdom tradition in conjunction with being alert (vv. 12-13) and a conclusion to accept wise counsel from one's peers (vv. 18-19), sandwiching between them the body that deals with imprudent business practices. The body escalates from bargaining lies (v. 14), to the risk of putting up security for somebody else (v. 16), to outright deception (v. 17).

original reading may have been *nokrî-m* with enclitic *mem,* a morpheme for emphasis or for indetermination not understood by the Masoretes (see *IBHS,* p. 759, P. 9.8b).

82. The Targ. reads a substantive, "his pledge." Delitzsch (*Proverbs,* p. 300) cites as a parallel of this *Qal* impv. *ḥannēnî* (Pss. 9:14; 80:16).

83. The gen. is ambiguous. The text interprets it as a gen. of instrument (cf. 10:2; 23:3; *IBHS,* p. 144, P. 9.5.1d). Gemser (*Sprüche,* p. 79), appealing to 18:8, thinks that it is an appositive gen. (i.e., the bread is deception is itself), and Van Leeuwen (*Proverbs,* p. 187) believes that it is an attributive gen. (i.e., the bread proves deceptive). But nothing in this context suggests that the bread is wicked.

84. Lit. "and."

85. The Targ. and Syr. read passive (< *Niphal tē'āśeh,* which may be explained as the MT having lost initial *t* through haplography due to the final /*t*/ of *wbthblwt,* or as having read *'ś'* as the *Qal* inf. absolute *'āśōh* (A. J. Baumgartner, *Étude critique sur l'état du texte du Livre des Proverbes d'après les principales traductions anciennes* [Leipzig: Imprimerie Orientale W. Drugulin, 1890], p. 187). While the passive form offers a better parallel to *tikkôn,* the parallel in 24:6 favors retaining the MT.

86. Injunctive imperfect (*IBHS,* p. 509, P. 31.5b).

87. Van Leeuwen, *Proverbs,* p. 186.

The introduction and body are linked by asserting that there is a right and wrong way to obtain food (*leḥem,* vv. 13, 17). The body and conclusion are linked by a wordplay on yet another homonym of *ʿārab,* II *ʿārab,* "to get involved with someone," the final word in v. 19. III *ʿārab* ("to be sweet"), the initial word in v. 17, occurs only one other time in the Old Testament, suggesting that the play is intentional. Aside from the introduction, the other pairs feature terms pertaining to the semantic domain of speaking: "says" (v. 14a), "boasts" (v. 14b), "lips" (v. 15b), "mouth" (v. 17b), and "lips" (v. 19b).

a. Introduction and Janus (20:12-13)

12 This introductory rearing proverb also functions as a janus between the preceding unit and the new unit. It continues the alternating pattern of vv. 8 and 10 by leaping back to v. 10. Both are sayings about the LORD, and in the Hebrew text both begin with initial *aleph* in segholate nouns (*ʾeben,* "weight," and *ʾōzen,* "ear") and terminate with *indeed, both of them* (*gam-šᵉnêhem;* see v. 10). Finally, its syntax also resembles v. 10, consisting of a nominative absolute construction in verset A glossed by *as for,* resumed by the pronoun "them" in verset B. In addition, the janus proverb may be related to v. 8 by the catchword "eye," making the king's winnowing eye God's creation. It is also related to vv. 9 and 11. To correct humanity's moral disability (vv. 9, 11) the LORD created two receptive organs that inform the wise heart for good (see 2:2; 4:21; 24:32). Through them the son can succeed, not fail; live, not die. In this book *ear* almost always connotes being teachable,[88] and the 30 occurrences of *hear[ing]* (or listen) almost always connote "to listen and obey."[89] In that light the phrase, though absolute without specification, probably connotes hearing instruction from the wise and as such functions as an introductory educational proverb. *And* joins with the teachable ear the *seeing eye.* "Eye" is used in many different ways in this book.[90] "To see" by it-

88. See 2:2; 4:20; 5:1, 13; 15:31; 18:15; 22:17; 23:9, 12; 25:12; 28:9, but once with reference to compassion (21:13) and once to a dog's ear (26:17).

89. With reference to being teachable apart from the participle 20 times (1:5, 8; 4:1, 10; 5:7; 7:24; 8:6, 32, 33; 5:13; 12:15; 13:1, 8(!); 18:13, 19:20, 27; 22:17; 23:19, 22; 28:9) and as a participle seven times (1:33; 8:34; 12:15; 15:31, 32; 21:28; 25:12). But once each it is used with reference to a confidence (25:10) and an oath (29:24) and to God hearing prayer (15:29).

90. With reference to the physical organ alone (23:29); to sight in general with the verb "to see" (20:12; 23:33; 25:7; 29:13); to sight of a bird (1:17), of God (5:21; 15:3; 22:12), of God and/or humanity; for "opinion" (3:4; 6:4, 13; 7:2; 10:26; 20:13; 21:10; 27:20); of human teachability and/or wisdom (3:21; 4:21; 15:30; 20:8; 22:9; 23:26; cf. 4:25); of self-delusion and of fools in the phrase "in one's own eyes" (3:7; 12:15; 16:2; 17:8[!]; 21:2; 26:5, 12, 17; 28:11); and of their misuse in connection with evil (6:13, 17; 10:10; 16:30; 17:24; 21:4; 23:5, 6; 28:22, 27; 30:12, 17). The verb in this book never refers to seeing temptation.

self refers to moral discernment (see 6:6; 7:7; 22:3; 24:18 [of God]; 27:12), but with "eyes" it signifies the ability to see in general (23:33; 25:7; 29:16), and in conjunction with v. 13 it connotes to be awake and alert. In sum, the two phrases together connote that in order to be useful the learned tradition must be combined with diligent application. *Has made ('āśâ)* is a frequent term in the Old Testament for God's creative achievements (see 8:26) and is a synonym of *bārā'* ("create"; cf. Gen. 1:1 and Exod. 20:11; Gen. 1:16 and Ps. 148:3, 5; Isa. 40:26). Unfortunately, the fool misuses God's good creation of the receptors that could make him wise to salvation (17:24; 23:9). In sum, the point of the proverb is not a jejune statement of fact that the eye and ears can be trusted; rather, it is prescriptive, calling for their proper use to see and to hear. Listening and observing are important qualities of a good disciple, and the sage regularly calls on him to use them to read and hear his teaching.[91]

13 This proverb, binding itself to the preceding proverb by the catchword "eye," explains what is meant by "the seeing eye" and balances the divine initiative with human responsibility. The Creator gave humans the receptive organs, but humanity must use them. It should now be clear that vv. 12 and 13 are a rearing proverb pair. The superficially antithetical parallels of v. 13 are in fact synonymous, matching the negative threat and motivation, not to sleep to not become destitute (v. 13a), with their positive counterparts, to stay awake to be enriched (v. 13b). The repetition emphasizes human responsibility. The rhetorical imperative, *do not love* (cf. 1:22), aims to effect this in the audience. *Sleep* can be a beneficent gift (see 3:24) or, as here, a bane (see 6:9, 10; 19:15). *Lest* [see 30:9] *you become poor* gives the negative motivation for heeding the admonition.[92] The point is not that people become "poor" through loss of domestic animals and other property, but rather that they suffer from a general loss, an overall reduction, affecting human beings, their domestic animals, and their other possessions as a whole.[93] *Open* occurs 19 out of 20 times with "eyes," as here, *your eyes* (see v. 12a). With the one exception with reference to ears (Isa. 42:20), the idiom always denotes to leave a state of unconsciousness to one's situation to become awake and vigilant with respect to someone or something.[94] Clifford thinks that the impera-

91. So L. Boström, *The God of the Sages: The Portrayal of God in the Book of Proverbs* (ConBOT 29; Stockholm: Almqvist & Wiksell, 1990), p. 65.

92. Although the verb is formally the *Niphal* of *yrš* ("dispossess"), its meaning is more closely related to the group of words deriving from *rôš,* "to be poor" (see 10:4).

93. N. Lohfink, *TDOT,* 6:373, s.v. *yāraš.*

94. Six times (2 K. 19:16 [= Isa. 37:17]; Job 14:3; Jer. 32:19; Dan. 9:18; Zech. 12:4) it is used in an anthropomorphism of God opening his eyes and so becoming attentive and aware of a need. Four times it is used of God supernaturally opening human eyes to spiritual realities (Gen. 21:19; 2 K. 6:17) and of giving sight to the blind (Ps. 146:8). Likewise in the *Niphal* it refers to spiritual sight (Gen. 3:5, 7) or to the eyes of the blind

tive *be filled with food* (see 12:11) is humorous. "'Open your eyes and eat!' The readers perhaps expects the idiomatic phrase 'Open your eyes and see!'" (cf. Gen. 21:19; 2 K. 6:20; Isa. 37:17).[95] The imperative loses its purely volitional force and expresses an assurance of the promise given as a consequence of heeding the admonition (see 19:27).[96] The prudent worker must contend against the ever-threatening impending chaos to create and sustain life just as God did at the beginning of creation (see 3:19-20; 8:22-31). Without wisdom death overwhelms life (see 6:9-11; 24:30-34). As a result, within the moral reciprocity ordained by God, neglect inevitably leads to loss, and the sins of omission lead to death just as certainly as the sins of commission (cf. Jas. 4:17). Untimely sleep entails the omission of the good deeds that sustain life. The wise perceive this, but sluggards are motivated to untimely sleep because they seek to avoid hard work (cf. 12:11; 28:19). Other Scriptures warn against untimely work (cf. Ps. 127:2).

b. Body: Imprudent Speech in the Marketplace (20:14-17)

14 The unit now moves from losing property through spiritual apathy (v. 13) to gaining property through active wickedness. Perhaps it begins with masking speech because of the references to deceit at the conclusion of the last unit (see vv. 10-11). It consists of two synthetic parallels. Verset A, which commences the transaction, dramatically quotes the buyer as emphatically insisting that the product is inferior, and verset B, which completes the transaction, pictures him with his purchase in hand gloating.[97] The masking lie *"bad"* (*raʿ;* see 1:16) is underscored by the repetition of *"bad." Says* [see 1:11] *the buyer* (*haqqôneh;* see 4:5) assumes his expectation that the seller will lower his price by the persistent haggling. *And when* represents the participle as a circumstantial clause to the predicate. *He has* glosses the more literal, "[goes over] to him." *It in hand (ʾōzēl)* glosses a verb that occurs four times with the intransitive senses of either "to be gone," "to go away," "to disappear" (Deut. 32:26; 1 Sam. 9:7; Job 14:11) or "to go about" (Jer. 2:36). It

being opened (Isa. 35:5). Four times it is used of the LORD's agents giving sight supernaturally: of Elisha (2 K. 4:35; 6:20[2x]), and of the Anonymous Servant (42:7). Only one other time is it used of awaking from the unconscious state of sleep (Job 27:19).

95. Clifford, *Proverbs,* p. 184.

96. *IBHS,* p. 572, P. 34.4c.

97. Note the syntax and phonology that give the verset coherence. In each verset two words, "bad, bad" and "and-when-it-goes-over to-him," precede the two words of the subject and predicate: "the-buyer says" and "then he-boasts." Moreover, *rʿ* occurs twice in verset A, and *ʾz* occurs twice in verset B (cf. *ʾōzēl . . . ʾāz*). Finally, the consonant /l/ is repeated four times in verset B, with every word except *ʾāz,* which is unnecessary and thus emphatic (cf. Meinhold, *Sprüche,* 2:337).

could modify either the buyer (i.e., "when the buyer goes away")[98] or what the buyer called "bad." *HALOT* favors the latter, giving the meaning "is transferred by purchase."[99] *Then* (see 3:23) refers with some emphasis to a future situation relative to the transaction.[100] *He boasts* (*hithallāl;* cf. 25:14; 27:1; 31:30) occurs 21 times in the *Hithpael* but only twice in the reflexive sense of to praise oneself, "to brag" (cf. 1 K. 20:11).[101] Self-centered praise or boasting about someone or something other than the LORD is not good, but making one's boast in the LORD is fitting (cf. 1 K. 20:11; Pss. 49:6[7]; 52:1[3]; Prov. 20:14; Jer. 9:23-24[22-23]; 27:1; 49:4). According to many commentators, this proverb is only a humorous depiction of the normal and necessary trading practices in oriental bazaars, without moral evaluation. The seller, it is assumed, overprices his product, and the sharp buyer has to take time and use his wit to depreciate it in order to knock the price down. On reflection, however, the buyer is both a deceitful liar and an impious boaster. He is lying because he would buy and/or boasts about his purchase as if in fact he considered it bad. His lies are not violent like those of waylaying thugs (1:10-19), but he aims to advantage himself at the expense of the seller through deceit just as much as through violence or dishonest measures (see 20:9). For the sage, lies and impiety are no laughing matter. Abraham bargained with God, who graciously lowered "the price," but he neither lied nor boasted (Gen. 18:22-33). Ephron as a seller probably lied to Abraham in offering him his field for nothing in an example of reverse bargaining, but Abraham did not bite (Genesis 23).

15 The bad speech in the marketplace of v. 14 gives way to a proverb commending knowledgeable speech in general in part to protect v. 14 from the common misinterpretation that because lies and bragging are so common in the oriental bazaar they are acceptable. Whybray notes v. 15 comments on v. 14: "that which is most valuable cannot be obtained 'over the counter' or through sordid deals."[102] In this comparative parallelism the fantastic material wealth in verset A is compared with wise speech in verset B and found wanting. Unlike the "better . . . than" proverbs, which compare

98. According to this interpretation, *lô* is a *lamed* of interest signifying that the buyer has disassociated himself from his surroundings (*IBHS,* p. 208, P. 11.2.10d).

99. *HALOT,* 1:26, s.v. *'zl.*

100. BDB, p. 23, s.v. *'āz.*

101. In addition, *hithallāl* occurs once with its passive sense (Prov. 31:30), 16 times with *bē* for the object of praise: seven times "of the LORD" (Pss. 63:11[12]; 97:7; 105:3 [= 1 Chr. 16:10]; Isa. 41:16; 45:25; Jer. 4:2), nine times of something else (wisdom, riches, strength, valleys, evil, gifts, or tomorrow [Ps. 52:1(3); Prov. 25:14; 27:1; Jer. 9:22 (cf. Ps 49:7), 23; 49:4]), and four times absolutely: two times of the LORD, which is gapped (Pss. 64:10[11]; 106:5).

102. Whybray, *Proverbs,* p. 295.

that which is bad to that which is worse (cf. 16:8), this one compares that which is good to that which is better. It does not aim to disparage possessing wealth but to set it within a framework of values (cf. 3:14-15; 8:10-11; and 16:16).[103] *There is* [see 11:24] *gold* (see 11:22), which from earliest times was valued for its metallurgical and aesthetic qualities, is escalated to *and an abundance* [see 5:23] of *corals* (see 3:15), which designates a vast amount of the precious material used for jewelry. *But* introduces the antithetical comparative parallel. *A precious* (see 3:15) restricts the all-purpose word *vessel,* which refers to material objects and finished products. The phrase, to judge from the parallel, here refers to a beautifully finished piece of jewelry perhaps made of gold and coral for the face (cf. 25:11). The metaphor expresses the unstated thought that *lips* [see 5:2] *that speak knowledge* (see I: 77) are extremely valuable and aesthetically pleasing and the unstated feeling that they are earnestly desired. Although comparative particles are missing (cf. 11:31), the precious vessel is implicitly better than gold and corals because, beyond consisting of these most precious materials, it is finely wrought and exquisitely manufactured. Thought-through speech that conforms to God-established morality presupposes the long, hard work of education that is finally more precious than all possible materials.[104] It is incomparably superior to any treasure because, as 3:15 makes clear, it brings riches, honor, long life, and peace.[105]

16 Putting up security for another is yet another expression of imprudence in speech and in business (see 6:1-2). This sarcastic proverb is repeated almost verbatim in 27:13. It envisions four participants: (1) the addressed audience; (2) a debtor who is a stranger; (3) the creditor who is also an outsider to the covenant community, and (4) a guarantor who stands behind the stranger's debt. The synonymous imperatives in the outer frame of its chiastic parallels ("take his garment" and "seize it in pledge") are rhetorically addressed to the audience, and the garment is that of the guarantor. The inner core gives the reason: the guarantor has pledged himself for the debtor (v. 16a), and the disciple must impound the guarantor's garment to pay back the creditor (v. 16b). In other words, the guarantor has in effect already handed himself over to the creditor. The fictive command *take away* (*l^eqaḥ;* cf. 1:3; 11:30) means to get something into one's possession and control, with the nuance here of being against its owner's will.[106] *His garment (bigdô)* can refer to

103. So McKane, *Proverbs,* p. 542, followed hesitantly by Meinhold (*Sprüche,* p. 539).

104. So Meinhold, *Sprüche,* p. 338.

105. The Egyptian sage Ptah-hotep (line 58, ca. 2200 B.C.) taught, "Good speech is more hidden than the greenstone, but it may be found among maids at the grindstones" (*AEL,* 1:63).

106. *HALOT,* 2:534, s.v. I *lqḥ.*

any kind of garment or covering, from a widow's garb (Gen. 38:14) to ceremonial dress (Exod. 28:2). Here it probably refers to a person's basic possession: "his clothing by day, his covering by night [cf. 1 Sam. 19:13; 1 K. 1:1]."[107] A person left this most personal and/or last possession as a pledge to symbolize his whole body (6:1-5; Exod. 22:25-27[24-26]; Amos 2:8). *When* (see 11:15) introduces the foolish situation. *One becomes security* (*ʿārab;* see 6:1; 11:15) *for a stranger* (*zār;* see 6:1). *Zār* sometimes has the weakened sense of "another" (see 6:1; 11:15; cf. 27:1), but in parallel with *nokrî* it means "stranger" (i.e., outside of family and community; cf. Job 19:27; Ps. 69:8[9]; Prov. 5:10; Obadiah 11).[108] *And* links the two synthetic parallels. *When he has done it* is supplied on the assumption that *kî ʿārab* is gapped in verset B. He does it *for* the benefit (lit. "surrounding in protection of"; see 6:26)[109] *of an outsider* (*nokrî-m;* see n. 81; 2:16; 5:20), the customary parallel of *zār* (cf. Job 19:15). The creditor outside of the community will demand as payment from the debtor or the guarantor the shirt off his back. *Impound* means "to take or to require in pledge" (cf. Exod. 22:26[25]; Deut. 22:6[2x], 17; Ezek. 18:16; Amos 2:8) or, as here and probably in Job 22:6; 24:3, 9, "to seize it in pledge." The parallel suggests that the antecedent is "his garment." The TEV captures the thought well: "Anyone stupid enough to promise to be responsible for a stranger's debts ought to have his own property held to guarantee payment." The admonition to the disciple to foreclose on the guarantor is rhetorical sarcasm, not a real command (see 19:27). The disciple has no vested interest in the other three participants, and it is imprudent to meddle in their business (26:17). Rather, the proverb emphasizes the stupidity of risking one's life for an unknown creditor by becoming security for a stranger.[110]

17 The theme of foolish speech in the marketplace is escalated from implied rash and imprudent speech (v. 16) to false speech (v. 17). The two proverbs are also linked by the homonyms I *ʿrb* ("becomes surety") and III *ʿrb* ("to be sweet").[111] Van Leeuwen thinks that the wordplay suggests that "someone can be enticed by a 'sweet deal' and swallow a bad deal."[112] The

107. Plaut, *Proverbs,* p. 211.

108. *HALOT,* 1:279, s.v. *zār;* 2:700, s.v. *nokrî.*

109. *HALOT,* 1:141, s.v. *baʿad.*

110. McKane (*Proverbs,* p. 339) takes it as a real command and thinks that the gist of the instruction is, "If you are to have dealings with a person who is a bad risk and is liable for dubious debts, secure yourself immediately." This interpretation is unlikely. (1) It is folly to do business with a bad risk in the first place. (2) Almost every collection of the book of Proverbs proscribes without qualification putting up security for another's debts (6:1-5; 11:15; 17:18; 22:26-27; 27:13). (3) The command violates the law that prohibits taking a person's garment overnight in pledge (Exod. 22:26).

111. *HALOT,* 2:876-77, s.v. I *ʿrb,* III *ʿrb.*

112. Van Leeuwen, *Proverbs,* p. 187.

personal subject of its antithetical parallels is the liar and/or cheat. The imprecise parallels of its first and last words, "sweet" and "gravel," suggest that the deceiver's present, delightful, and satisfying rewards seem to have no negative consequences and that its future, painful, and deadly consequences have no sweetness (see Job 20:12-29). Elsewhere *food* (see 9:5), a necessity for life, is to be obtained through labor and merit (cf. 12:9; 20:13). Here, by the nature of a proverb, it may stand as well for satisfying any drive and appetite, including sex (see 9:17).[113] *Gotten by deceit* (see n. 83) refers generally to something that appears differently than it actually is and hurts others (see 6:17), and here probably through deceptive speech, as suggested by its parallel "mouth" and its customary use in this book, apart from 11:18 (a "deceptive" wage) and 31:30 (deceptive charm).[114] *Is sweet,* which occurs elsewhere only in Song 2:14 with reference to the delight and desirability of a "sweet voice," was probably chosen to form a verbal link with *ʿārab* in v. 16, instead of its synonym *mtq* (9:17; 16:21; 27:9). *To the person* (*lāʾîš;* see I: 89) may be definite to designate the liar, not the audience that devours his speech like tidbits (18:8; 26:22). His jaded moral taste savors obtaining his food without effort and overreaching his neighbor (cf. 10:23a). *But* joins the antithetical parallel. Temporal *afterward* (lit. "behind") starkly contrasts the before and after scenes of this proverb and infers their cause-consequence connection. *His mouth,* probably as in 19:28, functions both as an orifice for producing his false speech and for ingesting food, a metaphor for his having "to eat" the results of his deceptive speech. The expanded metaphor *is filled* (*yimmālēʾ;* see 1:3; 3:10; 12:21) signifies that he is so completely pervaded that there is room for nothing else and connotes his final unrelieved and awful pain. *With gravel* completes the metaphor, and, to judge from its only other occurrence, connotes to break the teeth so that the liar can no longer speak and eat but comes to an awful end. In poetic justice, the deceptive fare the liar and cheat dished out to others now turns around and deceives him (10:2a). Sin is pleasant to the sinner for a season, but it ultimately proves fatal (cf. Prov. 9:17-18; 23:31-32). By contrast, holiness is sweet both along the way and in its final end (cf. 10:23).

113. So M. Lyons, "Rashi's *Commentary on the Book of Proverbs*" (submitted in partial fulfillment of the requirements for the degree of rabbi, 1936), p. 106; Farmer, *Proverbs and Ecclesiastes,* p. 58.

114. Cf. a "lying" tongue (6:17; 12:19; 21:6; 26:28), one who testifies to "lies" (6:19; 14:5; 25:18), "lying" lips (10:18; 12:22; 17:7), a "perjurer" (12:17; 19:5, 9), a "false" word (13:5; 29:12), a person who boasts of gifts "he does not give" (25:14).

c. Conclusion: Accepting Wise Counsel (20:18-19)

18 This verse could be connected phonologically with v. 17 by the assonance of *leḥem* ("food") and *milḥāmâ* ("war"). More importantly, however, it forms a pair with v. 19. Together the proverbs teach, seek counsel before making war (v. 18) but do not engage a babbler (v. 19). Verse 18 pertains to being teachable. Sensible people give weight to the opinions of the wise — that is, they take "counsel" before taking action and accept "rebuke" after a mistaken action (cf. 11:14; 15:22; 24:6).[115] In the inner core of its chiastic parallels are "with counsel are established" and "with guidance make," and in its outer frame the pair "plans" and "war." Aside from "counsel" and "guidance," the semantic parallels are not precise, moving from cause to effect, from plans to war itself. The descriptive cause, "plans [for war] are established through counsel," leads to the prescriptive admonition, "so make war with guidance."[116] *Plans are established* [see 16:3] *with counsel* (see 1:25; 19:21), that is, informed by the sage's teachings and backed up by the LORD; otherwise they would not stand the test of time (see 19:21). *So* paratactically combines the versets, but the connection is logical. *With guidance* [see 1:5] *make* (*ʿ^{a}śēh;* see 10:4) *war (milḥāmâ).* The 319 occurrences of *milḥāmâ* in the Bible always refer to conflict carried on by force of arms between nations or parties.[117] The disciple is envisioned as a king, for making war belongs to kings (cf. 24:5-6; Eccl. 9:13-18). However, the language of war is probably metaphorical for any leader confronting hostility (cf. 21:22; Luke 14:31-33); by its inherent nature a proverb is a paradigm for many situations (see 1:6). In this context it is germane to business leaders. The proverb, which assumes that there is no alternative to war (cf. 20:3; 25:7b-8; cf. Ps. 120:7), admonishes the wise son that before employing force to bend the will of his evil enemies, he should be certain that his goal and methods are consistent with the teachings of this book. Only when the king was in unison with the will of the LORD was God on his side. The fate of the nation or of the community depends on his seeking the previous counsel of his pious and ethical friends before engaging in battle (see 11:14; 15:22; 24:6; cf. 10:8; 12:15; 13:10; 21:5), not his genius alone. A mistake could lead to the defeat of the righteous (cf. Eccl. 4:13-14).

115. So Farmer, *Proverbs and Ecclesiastes,* p. 89.

116. The transliterated verse reads: *maḥ^{a}šābôt b^{e}ʿēṣâ tikkôn ûb^{e}taḥbulôt ʿ^{a}śēh milḥāmâ.* The versets cohere by the assonance of */ôt/* and the consonance of */ḥ, b, t/* in their first two words and by the consonance of */ʿ, ś~ṣ/* in their second words (i.e., *b^{e}ʿēṣâ* and *ʿ^{a}śe*).

117. Gemser (*Sprüche,* p. 79) thinks that it refers to "den Lebenskampf" (= "the battle of life"), citing Pss. 27:3; 35:1; 52:2-3; 120:7; 140:3, but he misunderstands the extensive royal orientation of the psalter (J. Eaton, *Kingship and the Psalms* [SBT 32; Naperville, Ill.: Alec R. Allenson, 1976], pp. 1-26).

19 The syntax of the unit's final proverb is similar: a description of the foolish situation, followed by an admonition. The inveterate gossip divulges secrets, so do not get involved with loose lips. The prohibition comes climactically as the final word of the proverb. Verset A repeats almost verbatim 11:13a except that it describes the reverse, *He who goes about as a slanderer (hôlēk rākîl) divulges secrets (gôleh-sôd),* not "a slanderer is one who. . . ."[118] Moreover, 11:13 is antithetic, contrasting the betrayer with the one who speaks discreetly from a faithful spirit, but 20:19 is synonymous, equating "the slanderer who divulges secrets" with "a silly chatterer" — that is, one who handles words in a careless, not thoughtful and unguarded way.[119] *So* [see 20:18] *do not*[120] *get involved with* (*tit'ārāb lᵉ,* from II *'rb;* see 14:10), which is the third homonym of *'rb* in this unit. The command is ironic, for it requires the son not to associate with one who destroys community. *HALOT* glosses the phrase *pōteh* [cf. 1:4, 10] *śᵉpātāyw* [see 4:24] *a silly chatterer.*[121] Although gossiping may be compulsive and careless, not a malicious calumny, idle speech springs from the immoral flaw of unfaithfulness. The result of indiscreet speech can be as fatal as that of a rash commitment or of a lie (see v. 17). The gossip lacks wisdom because he lacks love (cf. 1 Tim. 5:13). Sir. 8:17 likewise proscribes intimate talk with a fool because he cannot keep a secret.

9. Trusting the LORD to Avenge Wrongs through His Wise King (20:20-28)

20 *As for the one who curses his father and his mother,*
his lamp will be snuffed out in pitch[122] *darkness.*
21 *As for an inheritance gained in haste*[123] *at the beginning,*

118. 20:19 replaces the *Piel* participle *mᵉgalleh* of 11:13 with the *Qal gôleh,* probably to create an assonance with the parallel *pōteh* ("silly").

119. The parallels cohere phonologically by the consonance of /l/ in all of the three accented words of verset A and in two of four in verset B; by the assonance of /o/ in its first three words and in two of four in verset B; by the consonance of /t/ in three words of verset B, and by the assonance of *gôleh/pōteh* in the first two words of each verset.

120. *Lō',* not *'al,* probably to create the assonance of /ō/ sounds in the aphorism.

121. *HALOT,* 3:984, s.v. *pth.* This meaning is derived principally from its use with a dove (= "silly," a parallel to "lacking sense," *'ên lēb;* Hos. 7:11). But the root is probably II *pth* "to be open," attested in Mishnaic Hebrew, not I *pth* "to be gullible" (cf. with heart (= "to be simple > enticed," Deut. 11:16; 31:27), and of an envious person (= "gullible," parallel to "fool," *'ᵉwîl;* Job 5:2). If so, it means literally "one who is open of lips."

122. K, LXX, Syr., and Vulg. read *bᵉ'îšôn* ("in the pupil"); Targ. and Syr. read *k,* not *b,* before *'îšôn.* Q reads *be'ᵉšûn,* questionably meaning "with the approach of" (see 7:9).

123. K reads *mᵉbuḥelet,* which may mean, according to an Arabic cognate, "gotten avariciously" (BDB, p. 103, s.v. *bāḥēl*); cf. Gemser (*Sprüche,* p. 79), who renders K "despised." The ancient versions and most editors favor Q, *mᵉbōḥelet* (see 13:11).

in its latter end it will not be blessed.[124]

22 *Do not say, "I will repay evil!"*
Look expectantly to the LORD, and he will avenge you.

23 *An abomination to the LORD, are diverse weights,*
and deceptive balances are not good.

24 *From the LORD are the steps of a man;*
and as for a human being, how can he understand his way?

25 *A trap for a human being is one who says rashly,*[125] *"Consecrated,"*
and after [making] the vows to examine [them].

26 *The wise king winnows the wicked,*
and brings back the cartwheel[126] *over them.*

27 *The words of a human being are the lamp*[127] *of the LORD,*
shedding light on his innermost parts.

28 *Kindness and reliability guard*[128] *the king;*
he upholds his throne with kindness.[129]

124. The subject in verset A is displaced to precede the clause, being separated from it by a conjunction (see *IBHS,* p. 77, P. 4.7c).

125. *Yālaʿ* is either *Qal* or *Hiphil* imperfect of either I *lûaʿ* or *lāʿaʿ* "to talk rashly" (Job 6:3) or of II *lûaʿ* or *lāʿaʿ* "to drink" (Obad. 16). The KJV, following Jerome, "devotare sanctus," renders v. 25aβ "to devour the holy," referring to the prohibition against eating holy food. Jerome either invested II *lûaʿ* or *lāʿaʿ* with a unique meaning or arbitrarily read *ylʿ* or *blʿ*. But the parallelism demands I *lûaʿ* or *lālaʿ*. "The LXX hits the true meaning with rare success" (Delitzsch, *Proverbs,* p. 304): *pagis andri tachy ti tōn idiōn hagiasai* ("It is a snare to a person to hastily consecrate some of his own [property]").

126. Fichtner *(BHS),* following Graetz (cited by Gemser, *Sprüche,* p. 79) unnecessarily emends *ʾôpān* to *ʾônām* ("their iniquity") on the basis of Ps. 94:23. The REB's "wheel of fortune" is based on the gratuitous suggestion by G. R. Driver ("Problems in the Hebrew Text of Proverbs," *Bib* 32 [1951] 184), who draws attention to a Sophocles fragment that reads, "Fortune revolves on the frequent wheel of the god."

127. Fichtner *(BHS)* emends *nēr* to *nōṣer* ("protects") because it is used as a description of divine solicitude for humanity in Job 7:20; Prov. 24:12 and provides a better assonance with parallel *ḥōpēś*. S. E. Loewenstamm ("Remarks on Proverbs xvii 12 and xx 27," *VT* 37 [1987] 221-24) takes up the suggestion of M. Seidel to parse *nēr* as ptcp. of the verb *nîr* "to break up, freshly till by plowing," rendering the proverb: "God ploughs and examines the soul of man, searches all the innermost chambers" (cf. Jer. 17:10). Loewenstamm also questionably argues that *ḥpś* means here "to dig," but that meaning is unknown to *HALOT.* Both suggestions are gratuitous and destroy the felicity of the parallelism between "lamp" and "search out."

128. Fichtner *(BHS)* emends *yiṣṣᵉrû* to *yiṣṣōr* either to conform the verse to 16:6 or to make the king the subject, but see 3:3; Ps. 40:11[12] for the pl. verb with these subjects.

129. Gemser (*Sprüche,* p. 79) et al. follow LXX, which reads *en dikaiosynē* (< *bṣdq*), but the LXX is probably under the influence of 16:12; 25:5. Moreover, the alteration, by obliterating the reference back to *ḥesed* in verset A, opens the proverb to the misunderstanding that verset B refers to the LORD's attribute.

This unit consists of an introduction (vv. 20-21), a body (vv. 22-25), and a conclusion (vv. 26-28). Its introductory proverb pair typically pertains to the parent-son relationship, a warning not to curse parents and not to seize one's inheritance, implying the son's need to honor and so obey his parents (cf. 30:17). The law (Lev. 20:9) regarded cursing one's parents as tantamount to blasphemy "because the parents represent God's authority to the child."[130] The body, which is linked to the introduction by the catchword "LORD" in vv. 21-23, consists of an admonition not to seek revenge but to trust the LORD (v. 22), for he is just (v. 23) and sovereign (v. 24). In this regard, it is imprudent to make rash vows to consecrate something to God because the future, which is not at human disposal to direct, may make it difficult or even impossible to fulfill them (v. 25). Verses 26-28 conclude the unit with the reward and the punishment. God's surrogate king will unfailingly repay the wicked (v. 26) and show kindness to the needy (v. 28) because, in addition to being moral and just, he is omniscient (v. 27). The body pertains to the LORD and human beings, and the conclusion to the king and his subjects. "Lamp," a metaphor for human life in the introduction (v. 20) and escalated to human discernment in the conclusion (v. 27), forms an *inclusio* around the unit. The metaphor highlights the admonition of the unit not to avenge oneself (v. 22). The human spirit is the LORD's lamp inside the very core of a human being guaranteeing perfect justice.

a. Introduction: Honoring Parents (20:20-21)

20 The introductory proverb casts its theme to respect parents by the negative not to curse them in order to forge a link with the theme of bad speech in the preceding subunit (vv. 14-19). In contrast to that subunit, in which conjunctive "and" *(waw)* introduces the B versets, this introductory proverb pair uses the nominative absolute construction glossed by "as for" in the A verset and a resumptive pronoun ("his"/"its") in the B verset, matching the syntax of the educational proverb that introduced the preceding unit (v. 12). Semantically, verset Aa presents the cause of cursing one's parents, and verset B, the consequence of an untimely death. The verb glossed *the one who curses (meqallēl)* in the *Qal* means "to be slight, trifling," and in the *Piel,* used here, "to make of no account" by declaring the person such.[131] The law interprets this to mean that he has his blood on his head (Lev. 20:9). *His father and his mother* entails a foolish son (see 10:1). By publicly de-

130. G. J. Wenham, *The Book of Leviticus* (NICOT; Grand Rapids: Eerdmans, 1979), p. 279.

131. Jenni, *Das hebräische Pi'el,* p. 41; *IBHS,* pp. 402-3, P. 24.2f.

faming his parents the fool aimed to harm them, perhaps, to win his inheritance prematurely (see 19:26; 20:21). Instead he wins a premature death. *His lamp will be snuffed out* (see 13:9) metaphorically depicts the foolish son's untimely and unfortunate death. The metaphor extended to *in pitch darkness* (*beʾěîšôn,* lit. "in the pupil of darkness"), which may mean "the center of darkness,"[132] or "thickest darkness,"[133] or "midnight darkness,"[134] intensifies the son's untimely death as tragic and hopeless. If the Q reading, "at the approach of darkness," is correct (see n. 122), the proverb refers to the fool's hopeless situation "when evil comes."[135] As he cursed his parents, the LORD curses him (Deut. 27:16; cf. Sir. 3:16). The gnomic proverb asserts a universal truth: the law puts the cursing son's blood into Israel's hand to avenge (Exod. 21:17; Lev. 20:9). The proverb expresses the reverse side of the first commandment with promise: "Honor your mother and father, that your days may be long in the land . . ." (Deut. 5:16; Eph. 6:1-3; cf. Jer. 35:1-10).

21 Saadia,[136] Plöger,[137] and Whybray[138] connect the hasty son (v. 21) with the cursing son (v. 20). The proverbs' sharing the same syntax and together presenting the antonyms of word-initial "to curse" (v. 20) and word-final "to bless" (v. 21) validate their interpretation. Its pairing with v. 20 suggests that the son hastened the demise of his parents or got his hands on his legacy by some misdeed (see 19:26). His ill-gotten inheritance will come to the same unfortunate and untimely end (v. 21b) as the cursing son (v. 20bβ; cf. 13:11; 15:27; 2 Sam. 15:10 and 18:9-17; 1 K. 1:5-9; 2:25; 16:8-22; 21:1-15, 19; Job 15:29; 20:18; Amos 6:4-8; 1 Tim. 6:9, 10). Human hands put the cursing son to death; providence removes the divine blessing from his inheritance. Juxtaposed chiastically at the core of v. 21 are two temporal antonyms, "at the first" (v. 21a) and "in its latter end" (v. 21b). The scenes shift from the beginning, when the greedy and ungrateful son lays hands on the family fortune prematurely (v. 20a), to the climactic end, when he loses his fortune (v. 21b). *An inheritance* (see 17:2; 19:14) refers to the family patrimony that is handed down as a parental legacy, not by children grabbing for it. *Gained rashly* (*m*ᵉ*bōḥelet;* see n. 123) derives from a verb that may have originally meant "to be breathless,"[139] and in the *Piel* "to make breathless" > "to make haste." In the *Pual,* which is used here, *bḥl*

132. Delitzsch, *Proverbs,* p. 302.
133. Gemser, *Sprüche,* p. 78.
134. Toy, *Proverbs,* p. 390.
135. Lyons, "Rashi's *Commentary on the Book of Proverbs,*" p. 106.
136. Cited by Toy, *Proverbs,* p. 391.
137. Plöger, *Sprüche,* p. 237.
138. Whybray, *Proverbs,* p. 299.
139. Jenni, *Das hebräische Piʿel,* p. 230.

means "gained hastily."[140] In Esther (2:9; 6:14; 8:14) *bāḥal* in the D stems *(Piel, Pual,* and *Hithpael)* may have a favorable sense, but in the wisdom literature it connotes to act rashly, without wisdom (28:22; Eccl. 5:2[1]; 7:9; 8:3). Here it probably refers not to the person who makes a fortune quickly by unscrupulous means (cf. 13:11; 15:27), but to the one who in some way lays hands on the family fortune prematurely (cf. Luke 15:11-16).[141] If K (see n. 123) be read, it may mean, "gotten by greed" (cf. Leviticus 25; 1 Kings 21; Isa. 5:8-9; Matt. 21:33-46). *At the beginning* (see 18:17) refers here to first in time of a definite series. *In its* [i.e., "the inheritance"] *latter end* (see 5:4) refers to the end or ultimate issue of a course of action, "the result of a matter"[142] (cf. Prov. 5:4; 14:12; 16:25; 25:8). *Will not be blessed* (see 10:6) is a divine passive because blessings ultimately come from God (cf. Ps. 128:4). God will not grant him the auspicious powers he had hoped to get by seizing the inheritance, such as long life, descendants, prosperity, success, and power. Quite the contrary, he will be cursed by God.

b. Body: Trust God, Not Self, to Avenge Wrong (20:22-25)

The body reasserts truths about the Lord found in 16:1-9. It escalates from a proverb rejecting self-vengeance (v. 22a), to looking to the Lord for help (v. 22b), to an assertion that he detests human injustice (v. 23) and has the final say in every human being's life (v. 24), underscored by the imprudence of making rash vows (v. 25).

22 This proverb in its antithetical parallels proscribes foolish speech to respond to the bad speech of fools such as that articulated in vv. 14-20, and prescribes in verset B the wise response based on faith in the Source of all blessings (see v. 21). It juxtaposes both the negative admonition "do not say," to self and/or others, with "look expectantly to the Lord," and the assertion "I will repay evil" with "the Lord will avenge you." The last, an imprecise parallel, suggests that the Lord will help the disciple by compensating him justly for the wrong done to him. The Helper will both compensate the damage and punish the wrongdoer. Its verb forms exhaust the register of volitional forms: negative jussive (or prohibition, "do not say"), cohortative (or resolve, "I will repay"), imperative (or command, "look to") and positive jussive ("he will avenge"). Thus it admonishes in the strongest terms not to

140. In the *Niphal* it means "to make haste," presumably from "hasten oneself" (Prov. 28:22; Eccl. 8:3); in the *Piel,* "to make haste" (Esth. 2:9; Eccl. 5:2[1]; 7:9) or perhaps, more precisely, "to make breathless" (*HALOT,* 1:111, s.v. *bḥl*). With this meaning it is the Aramaic equivalent of Heb. *mahēr,* to which it is parallel in Eccl. 5:1[2].

141. McKane, *Proverbs,* p. 539.

142. *HALOT,* 1:36, s.v. *'aḥ^{a}rît.*

respond to fools with human vengeance but with faith in divine avenging (see 24:29; cf. 17:13; 24:17-18). *Do not say* (cf. 1:11) refers to a communication between the disciple and himself and/or an indefinite other. *I will repay* (see 11:31) to achieve compensation and satisfaction for *evil* (*rāʿ;* see 1:16), both moral evil, a social wrong against the disciple, and physical damage. *Look expectantly* (*qawwēh,* traditionally "hope") is related to *qaw,* "tense string," and depicts expectation and hope as a tense attitude with reference to a specific goal. The disciple looks to God to right wrongs no matter how long he must wait for divine intervention (Pss. 25:3; 27:14; 37:34; 39:7[8]; 62:5[6]; Matt. 5:38-48; Luke 18:7, 8; 1 Pet. 2:23; 4:19). The repetition of "to" with *to the LORD (laYHWH)* and *to you (lāk)* suggests the close bond between Israel's covenant-keeping God and his son (see Prov. 30:4b-5). *He will avenge* (*yōšaʿ;* see 28:18; cf. 1 Sam. 25:26, 31, 33) is closely related to legal terms and "implies bringing help to those in trouble rather than rescuing them from it," an interpretation that gives a better parallel with "to repay" than "to save, to deliver."[143] A wrong done against the son is a wrong against God (Deut. 32:43). Vengeance belongs to the LORD, not to the one who suffered wrong (cf. 16:7; Deut. 32:35, 43; 2 Sam. 3:39; Rom. 12:17-21; 1 Thess. 5:15; Heb. 10:30), because the omniscient, impartial LORD can mete out perfect justice, unlike the restricted earthling, who may also be blinded by lust and prejudice. The self-avenger expresses a lack of faith in the LORD to protect his own kingdom (8:14-17).[144] Proverbs and Scripture in general, however, do not exclude judicial procedures for justice. God-ordained government is necessary to uphold the moral order (see Prov. 16:10-15; 20:2; Rom. 12:17–13:7).

23 The context gives this proverb, which restructures 20:10 and resembles 11:1, its distinctive nuance. Garrett says, "This verse is . . . an assurance that the reader can trust God to punish; one need not extract personal revenge."[145] Commenting on vv. 22-23, Malbim says, "If you have been cheated in business, do not be tempted to cheat in turn and thus even things out. The example given here is of being sold merchandise by false weight: you may be tempted to use false weights yourself next time in order to get your own back; resist the temptation, as any tampering with scales is hateful to the Almighty."[146] If you respond to a fool as a fool, "even you" will become a fool (26:4). The proverb's chiastically formed parallels complement one another; its compound subject, *diverse weights* [see 20:10] *and deceptive*

143. J. F. Sawyer, *TDOT,* 6:445, s.v. *yāšaʿ.*

144. The *Teaching of Any* (8:14-17) says similarly, "Don't rush to attack your attacker, leave him to the god; report him daily to the god, tomorrow being like today, and you will see what the god does, when he injures him who injured you" (*AEL,* 2:142).

145. Garrett, *Proverbs,* p. 178.

146. Malbim, *Proverbs,* p. 212.

balances (see 11:1), in its inner core, and their predicates, *an abomination to the LORD* (see 20:10) and *are not good* (see 16:29), in its outer frame. Since according to 16:11 the LORD created the weighing apparatus, every deceitful practice touches him. Moreover, it also touches him since he is intimately involved with his son. Life in the marketplace and religion are inseparable.

24 The third of the *YHWH* proverbs now moves from his moral sensibility to his sovereignty, a common truth in Proverbs (e.g., 16:9; 19:21; 21:30), but this one takes its distinctive texture from vv. 22 and 23. The son looks to the LORD for help rather than avenging himself (v. 22) because the LORD in his outrage will certainly punish any wrongdoing (v. 23), and in his sovereignty he directs the steps and the destiny of everyone, thereby enveloping each in mystery (v. 24). In other words, the LORD's sovereignty (v. 24) executes his justice (v. 23). The parallels of v. 24 are linked by the a fortiori argument. If even a strong and powerful man cannot determine his steps, how can any human being discern the way his steps take? The similarity between *from the LORD* and "to the LORD" (see vv. 22-23) identifies the just God as the ultimate author of *the steps* (see 16:9[147]), a metaphor for every decision and activity *of a man* (*geber,* referring to the male in his strength; see 6:34). *And* joins the synthetic parallels. *As for a human being* (*'ādām;* see I: 89) shifts the focus from humanity in its strength to humanity in its earthbound limitations (see 3:13; 20:6), highlighted by the nominative absolute construction. The rhetorical *how* qualifies *can he understand* (see 1:2) as an impossibility.[148] The parallel to "step," *his way* (*darkô;* see 1:15), moves from his individual decision to his entire direction and the destiny within which he acts. People do not understand their ways because God makes the actual direction and destiny of their free actions subservient to his plan. The earthling has the responsibility for the choice of his way (i.e., the direction and orientation of his life) and for his steps (the decisions and actions he takes), but the LORD determines the realization and the attaining of his goal. Therefore, the wise look to the LORD, not to their own hands, to work out the course of justice in their narratives, validated by the narrative of Israel's history (cf. Gen. 24:27; Exod. 2:1-5; Esth. 6:6-13).

25 Since a mortal does not rule his future (v. 24), it is imprudent to consecrate impetuously someone or something to God in a future not under the mortal's absolute control (v. 25; cf. 27:2).[149] The catchword *'ādām* re-

147. *Miṣ'ād,* a by-form of *ṣa'ad* (see 16:9), occurs elsewhere only in Dan. 11:43 (= "train") and was probably chosen for the consonance of /m/ with *mēYHWH* and *'ādām mah,* making the nasal-labial prominent in the first two words of the Hebrew text of each verset.

148. BDB, p. 553, s.v. *mah.*

149. So also Whybray, *Proverbs,* p. 298.

inforces the linkage of this proverb pair, and "vows" implies the LORD, linking it to vv. 22-24. Its syntax tersely and emphatically places the predicate nominative *a trap* [see 12:13] *for a human being* (*'ādām,* v. 25aα; see I: 89) before the topic (v. 25aβ-25b), consisting of the antithesis of first speaking rashly (v. 25aβ) and afterward reflecting on it.[150] The subject is the indefinite *one.*[151] *Says rashly (yāla')* glosses a *hap. leg.* probably related to Arab. *laġā* "to blab" and Eth. Tigr. *lā'le'a* "to speak animatedly." *"Consecrated"* (*qōdeš;* see 9:10) is a metonymy for anyone or anything set apart from the profane as God's property. By the performative speech-act "consecrated [is this or that]" — like "I baptize you," and "I pronounce you husband and wife" in English liturgy — one sets apart someone (cf. Judg. 11:30; 1 Sam. 1:11) or something (cf. Lev. 27:10, 33; Num. 18:17; 30:1-16[2-17]) to belong to (or is reserved for) the cult and so as God's property.[152] *And* links the two chronologically successive situations of these synthetic parallels as signified by *after.*[153] *Making the vows* (see 7:14) refers in general to any kind of votive offerings or promised gifts to the LORD and expresses strong piety. Beforehand the petitioner promised God gifts for answering prayer because he wanted God to know the sincerity of his petition, hoped to move God to act, and recognized that nothing short of a gift would suffice to express his appreciation (see 31:2; 1 Sam. 1:11; Jon. 1:16; Matt. 15:5; Mark 7:11; Acts 18:18; 21:23-24; etc.). *To examine* occurs five times and essentially means "to look carefully after or into [someone or something]" (Lev. 13:36; 27:33; 2 K. 16:15; Ps. 27:4; Ezek. 34:11). *HALOT* glosses *bqr* here as "to reflect,"[154] and McKane as "to seek ways and means" to fulfill his obligations.[155] To examine vows entails thinking through carefully whether one has the ability and the means to pay them and how it will affect others. After making the vow it is already too late to investigate these matters. Unless the vower has counted the cost and is fully prepared to pay them, at the time payment is due he will find that his situation is like that of a witless animal entering a trap (cf. Judg. 11:30, 35). Scripture cautions against needlessly shackling oneself with this manacle. One is at full liberty not to make them, but having vowed, one is bound to pay them exactly (Deut. 23:21-23[22-24]; Eccl. 5:1-6[4:17–5:5]). Meinhold says that this is necessary because God must have been reckoned

150. Note the sequence /š/ and the assonance of /ō/ in the first and last words of verset A, *mōqēš . . . qōdeš,* and the sequence final /r/ the words of verset B: *'aḥar neḏārîm lebaqqēr.*

151. *IBHS,* pp. 70-71, P. 4.4.2.

152. *HALOT,* 3:1,076, s.v. *qōdeš.*

153. Probably an item, not clausal, adverb (*IBHS,* pp. 656-57, 659, PP. 39.3.1d; 39.3.2).

154. *HALOT,* 1:151, s.v. *bqr.*

155. McKane, *Proverbs,* pp. 242, 538.

as of secondary importance if the word given to him could be neglected without penalty.[156] Rash religious excitement that leads to hasty vows is no substitute for a solid character that thinks soberly with well-balanced judgment.

c. Conclusion: The King Judges the Wicked and Protects the Needy (20:26-28)

The subunits now shift from the relationship between the LORD and the mortal to the king and his subjects. The LORD's wise king under the omniscient God (v. 27) administers his kingdom by judging the wicked (v. 26) and by protecting the needy (v. 28).

26 The piety of trusting the LORD to avenge wrongs now gives way to the king functioning in God's place (cf. 16:1-9, 10-15; Rom. 12:17-21; 13:1-7). As in 20:8, the unit begins to come to closure with the king judging the wicked by using the agricultural imagery of threshing to picture him ridding his kingdom of them. *A wise* [see I: 94] *king* (*melek;* see 14:28) is the topic of both versets, and their predicates pertain to his condemning sentence and to his extinguishing the wicked. The metaphor *winnows* [see 20:8] *the wicked* (see I: 109) signifies that he rids the earth of the guilty. (Con)sequential *and* represents verset B as occurring after the scattering, but in fact the threshing precedes the scattering.[157] The dischronology underscores in the emphasizing B verset that in the judicial process the wise king thoroughly separates the wicked from the righteous — an escalation of v. 8 from his discerning eye to his action — so that when he scatters them shortly thereafter he will have disposed of all of them. *He brings back* (lit., "causes to return"; see 1:23) represents the wheel of the cart going over the heads of grain many times to thresh it thoroughly. The *wheel ('ôpān)* always refers to the wheel of a vehicle (cf. Exod. 14:25; 1 K. 7:30; Isa. 28:27; Ezek. 1:15).[158] The verses' agricultural imagery points to the heavy cartwheel rolled over the grain to thresh it (Isa. 28:27).[159] Franzmann supports the agricultural imagery from a study of the Ode of Solomon 23:11-16, where the Ode associates the wheel with the concepts of kingdom and of rule/government.[160] The threshing cart,

156. Meinhold, *Sprüche,* p. 344.

157. This pattern of sequential inversion attested elsewhere (cf. Job 4:20; Y. Hocherman, "Etymological Studies in Biblical Language (15)," *BM* 34 (1989-90) 131-37 suggests that the situation of verset B is pluperfect (*IBHS,* p. 552, P. 33.2.3).

158. D. Snell ("The Wheel in Proverbs XX 26," *VT* 39 [1989] 503-7) interprets the wheel on the basis of three Hittite texts as a torture wheel in the judicial process, but he admits that the Hittite material is far from clear.

159. L. Alonso-Schökel and J. Vilchez, *Proverbios* (Madrid, 1984), pp. 392-93.

160. Majella Franzmann, "The Wheel in Proverbs 20:26 and the Ode of Solomon 23:11-16," *VT* (1991) 121-23.

whose rollers were fitted with sharp iron cutters, cuts the sheaves when it is driven over them time and again on the threshing floor and separates the chaff and husks (cf. Isa. 28:27). *Over them* implicitly likens the wicked to chaff and husks, which is first threshed with the cartwheel and then scattered to the wind with fork and shovel. The wheel depicts the sharp and vigorous separation of the godless, not torture. Both the separation and extinction of the wicked are necessary. Extinction without separation is unjust, and separation without extinction is worthless. As a result of his thorough separation of the wicked (v. 26b) and of his complete removal of them (v. 26a), nothing remains of the wicked in his realm (cf. v. 8; Ps. 1:5). This proverb finds its fulfillment in the messianic kingdom of the eschaton. It is the King of kings alone who can make this separation complete (cf. Mal. 3:2; Matt. 3:12).

27 Sandwiched between royal proverbs pertaining to the king's execution of justice against the wicked (v. 26) and his unflinching loyalty to the righteous (v. 27), v. 27 assures perfect justice by asserting the very close connection between the LORD and every human being. Also, it relativizes the power of the king, for he, too, is under God's scrutiny. The LORD, who inspires his king (16:10) and guides him (21:1), knows every human thought and motive. The catchwords *LORD (YHWH)* and *human being ('ādām)* connect it to vv. 24-25. The disciple can trust the LORD to help him and not to avenge himself (v. 22) because the LORD, in addition to being moral (v. 23) and sovereign (v. 24), is also omniscient (v. 27). All three attributes are essential for the LORD to execute perfect justice. Verset A represents his omniscience by the metaphor of a lamp, and verset B gives the interpretation. The proverb makes best sense by construing "breath" *(nišmâ)*[161] as a metonymy for *words* (or speech), just as *rûaḥ* "wind/spirit," a synonym of *nišmâ* (see Job 33:4), connoted "thoughts" > "words" in 1:23b (cf. Job 26:4; 32:18). Van Leeuwen comments, "Breath typically goes in and comes out of a person, giving life; but it also comes out as wisdom and words."[162] The metaphor *are the lamp* refers to both human life (see 20:12) and to illumination (see 6:23). The parallel, "searching out," which modifies "lamp," focuses on the latter notion. To continue this connotation, *shedding light on* glosses the metonymy of adjunct to "searching out" *(ḥōpēś),* which in the *Piel* refers to the result of making a thorough search (cf. Gen. 31:35; 44:12) and in the *Qal*

161. *Nišmâ* occurs 23 times: five times as an anthropomorphism for God's use of strong, atmospheric wind, a blast (2 Sam 22:16 [= Ps. 18:15(16)]; Job 4:9; 37:10; Isa. 30:33); 11 times, especially in the Deuteronomist, as a synecdoche for the life of human beings and/or animals with a connotation of their mortality (Gen. 7:22; Deut. 20:16; Josh. 10:40; 11:11, 14; 1 K. 15:29; 17:17; Job 26:4; 27:3; Ps. 150:6; Isa. 2:22; Dan. 10:17); and six times, including this proverb, with reference to the LORD who gives human beings their breath (Gen. 2:7; Job 32:8; 33:4; 34:14; Isa. 42:5; 57:16).

162. Van Leeuwen, *Proverbs,* p. 188.

to the performance of the act.[163] *All (kol)* emphasizes the entirety of the measured thing, *of one's innermost parts* (*ḥadrê-bāṭen,* lit. "chambers of the belly"; see 18:8; 20:29), an Egyptian expression to denote the human heart as the hidden place where in the deepest layer of human existence the truth about a person is to be found. In sum, a person's speech associated with his breath serves as the LORD's flashlight to expose human thought, inclination, and will in the darkest recesses of a person's life. The context of vv. 26 and 28 suggests to Bridges, "We are placed under a solemn dispensation of Divine government. An infallible judgment is in constant exercise, discerning our principles, estimating their standard, and pronouncing sentence."[164] The proverb consoles the righteous and sobers the wicked (cf. 15:3, 11; 16:2; 17:3; 22:12).

28 The catchword "king" *(melek)* matches his judgment on the wicked (v. 26) with his *kindness and reliability* (*'emet;* see I: 99) to his helpless covenant partner in need of being avenged (see v. 22), bringing the unit on trusting the LORD, not self, to a conclusion. Verset A personifies these virtues as guardians protecting the king. The plural verb *guard* (*nṣr;* see 2:8) personifies these distinct virtues as also protecting the one who commissions them to serve the needy. *And* combines with the cause of verset A a further clarification of the personified consequence. *He upholds (sā'ad)* looks back to the king as its subject, and the verb means "to maintain someone or something by supplying it with things necessary for existence," such as food for the heart (Gen. 18:5; Judg. 19:5, 8; 1 K. 13:7; Ps. 104:15). In that light, *with kindness* — "and reliability" is gapped (cf. 20:6) — is essential for the existence of *his throne* (*kis'ô;* see 9:14; 20:8), symbolizing his royal authority and dominion. According to other texts, the LORD supports his anointed king and keeps him safe (cf. 2 Sam. 7:15; Pss. 18:35[36], 20:2[3]; 41:3[4]; 89:33[34]; 119:117; Isa. 9:6[7]). In sum, the LORD sustains his king, an exemplar for all leaders, by empowering the king to support, uphold, and maintain his throne by helping the deserving helpless in their need. Should the son be in a position such as a king to provide help to the needy, he should exercise this option and thereby on the LORD's behalf deliver the oppressed. The proverb finds its final fulfillment in Jesus Christ (see Ps. 72:1, 2, 4; Isa. 16:4b-5).

163. Jenni, *Das hebräische Pi'el,* p. 130.
164. Bridges, *Proverbs,* p. 361.

10. Doing Righteousness and Justice (20:29–21:31)

29 *The splendor of choice young men is their strength,*
and the majesty of the aged is their gray hair.
30 *Bruising wounds scour*[1] *away evil,*[2]
and blows [polish] the innermost being.
21:1 *The king's heart in the* LORD*'s hand is a channel*[3] *of water;*
on all who please him, he turns it.
2 *Every way of a person may seem upright in his own eyes,*
but the LORD *is the one who evaluates hearts.*
3 *To do righteousness and justice*
is more desirable to the LORD *than sacrifice.*
4 *A haughty look and an audacious heart —* [4]
the unplowed field[5] *of the wicked — produce sin.*
5 *The calculations of the diligent lead*[6] *only to profit,*

1. K and Vulg. read *tamrîq* ("scours"); Q reads *tamrûq* ("rubbing"). With the latter one expects the objective gen. *ra'* (= "rubbing/scouring away of evil"). *Rûq* is used elsewhere only of massages with perfumes and other cosmetics (Esth. 2:3, 9, 12) and may ease the syntactic disagreement between the pl. subject and sing. predicate. K can be defended: (1) the sing. after *peṣa'* is unexceptional (GKC, P. 146.1a). (2) The verb may be transitive with the preposition *b^e* (*IBHS,* pp. 163-64, P. 10.2.1b). The LXX invents *synantai kakois* "befalls evil men."

2. Possibly *b^e* signifies "with" or "by," not transitivity (cf. Job 31:12; Jer. 42:20[Q]), but it is unlikely that the proverb intends that "evil" or an "evil person" cleanses a person's inner being. The emendation to *rēa'* ("thoughts"; so *BHS;* cf. Ps. 139:2, 17) forms an attractive, synonymous parallel to "innermost being," but the text of the MT and of all ancient versions provides the expected moral reason for the wounding.

3. *Palgê* may a countable pl. ("streams"), as probably in 5:16 (see 5:17), or a pl. of extension to indicate that the channel is inherently large and/or complex, as probably in the case of the one tree in Ps. 1:3 (*IBHS,* p. 120, P. 7.4.1c).

4. Lit. "the height/loftiness of the eyes and breadth/width of heart."

5. The homonym *nîr* occurs eight times, four of I *nîr* "light/lamp," the preferred meaning here according to BDB (p. 633, s.v. *nîr*) and *HALOT* (2:697, s.v. *nîr*). But I *nîr* is otherwise restricted to the metaphor for David's offspring (1 K. 11:36; 15:4; 2 K. 8:19 [= 2 Chr. 21:7]). The ancient versions and many manuscripts probably read *nēr* ("lamp"; see *BHS*), a metaphor for "life." II *nîr* ("unplowed field"; see Prov. 13:23; Jer. 4:3; Hos. 10:12) is more difficult, but not too difficult, and the more common *nēr* is "lame and obscure" (W. McKane, *Proverbs,* p. 559). An "uplowed field" is a fitting metaphor for the arrogant and the wicked. These incorrigible people are not amenable to moral instruction (cf. 13:23) and produce bad moral fruit (cf. 13:23). There is no need to interpret *nîr* as "branding mark" after Arabic and Ethopic cognates (so the REB; *pace* Driver, "Problems in the Hebrew Text of Proverbs," *Bib* 32 [1951] 185). The expected Hebrew word for this meaning would be *'ôt* ("sign"; Gen. 4:15; Exod. 13:9).

6. *Lamed* implies a verb of motion (*IBHS,* p. 224, P. 11.3.4d).

but everyone who hastens [to get rich] comes only to lack.[7]
6 *The acquisition*[8] *of treasures by a lying tongue*
is the windblown[9] *breath of those seeking*[10] *death.*
7 *The violence of wicked people drags them away*
because they refuse to do justice.
8 *The way of a guilty*[11] *person is crooked;*[12]
but as for the pure, his deed is straight.

7. There is no need to emend v. 5b in order to obtain the more pedestrian antithesis of diligence and laziness (*pace* Toy, *Proverbs,* p. 399, who reads *darkê ʿāṣēl* ["the ways of a sluggard"]). Also, it is unnecessary to add *maḥšᵉbôt,* for antithetic parallels are often not precise. The Targ. read *wkl* as *rgl* ("foot"), the Syr. read *ʾṣ* as *ʾāwen* ("iniquity"), and Jerome read it as *ʿāṣēl* ("sluggard") (= "and those of the wicked"; see A. J. Baumgartner, *Étude critique sur l'état du texte du Livre des Proverbes d'après les principales traductions anciennes* [Leipzig: Imprimerie Orientale W. Drugulin, 1890], pp. 191-92).

8. The LXX and Vulg. read *pōʿēl* ("the one who procures") with a focus on the doer, not on the deed. These versions, but each in its own way calling their witness to an original text into question, transform *hebel niddāp* into personal performance. The metaphor "windblown breath" of the MT can also refer to the actor (cf. Jas. 1:6). The MT speaks of the perishing of both the treasures and the wicked, but the LXX and Vulg. only of the latter.

9. The LXX uniquely reads *diōkei* (< *rōdēp,* "one who pursues"). The Vulg. reads . . . *est vanus et inpingetur* . . . ". . . is vain and stumbles. . . ." Both readings may be explained as having been influenced by reading personal *pōʿēl* and/or by investing *hebel* with its common meaning, "vanity," and/or not understanding the difficult syntax of verset B.

10. Although the syntax of *mᵉbaqšê* is difficult, it can be explained as a gen. after an absolute, even though GKC (P. 128c) tries to explain away the more than 12 instances of this construction as textual corruptions. But one can more readily explain away *moqᵉšê* ("traps") of the LXX, Vulg., and several Hebrew mss, as a facilitating reading due to the rare syntax, than explain away the more difficult text substantiated by the great majority of Hebrew mss., Targ., Syr., and Symmachus.

11. The emendation to the common noun *kāzāb* (cf. *BHS*) ignores the alliteration between *wāzār and wᵉzak* (so T. McCreesh, O.P., *Biblical Sound and Sense: Poetic Sound Patterns in Proverbs 10–29* [JSOTSup 128; Sheffield: Sheffield Academic, 1991], pp. 58-59).

12. The ancient versions, each in its own way, reflect an inferior oral tradition for v. 8a to the MT. The Targ., Syr., and Vulg. derived *wāzār* from the conjunction *w* and *zār* "strange" (cf. AV, "The way of a man is froward and strange") against the Hebrew syntax. The rare word *wāzār* was probably chosen to play with its similarity in sound with *wᵉzak* ("and pure") and should not be deleted on the supposition that it is a dittography of *wzk.* Driver, "Problems," p. 185) reconstructs *ʾys hpkpk darkô zār,* deriving *zār* from Arab. *zawira* I "inclined; was crooked-breasted," II *zawwara* "falsified" (= "the man whose way is crooked is false"). The more difficult MT, however, is perfectly good Hebrew (Delitzsch, *Proverbs,* pp. 311-12) and exhibits the alliteration of *ʾyš wzr wzk yšr* (McCreesh, *Biblical Sound and Sense,* p. 59).

9 *Better to dwell on a corner of the roof*
than in a house shared[13] *with a contentious wife.*[14]
10 *A wicked person craves evil;*
his neighbor does not find favor in his eyes.
11 *Through fining a mocker, the gullible becomes wise,*
and through paying attention to a wise person[15] *he*[16] *gains knowledge.*
12 *The Righteous One*[17] *is the one who pays attention to the household*[18] *of the wicked person;*
the One who casts down wicked people[19] *to calamity.*

13. The KJV renders *hāber* "wide" (i.e., "spacious"), which involves an arbitrary transposition of consonants into *rḥb.*

14. Lit. "than a contentious wife and house of association."

15. This translation invests *haśkîl lᵉ* with the same value as in 21:12 (so BDB, p. 968, s.v. *śākal*). *HALOT* (3:1,328-29, s.v. *śākal*), Delitzsch (*Proverbs,* p. 313), et al. interpret it to mean "to instruct a wise person," but as *HALOT* recognizes this interpretation entails emending the text to *haśkîl ḥākām,* for with this meaning *śākal* (*Hiphil*) takes a direct object (1 Chr. 28:19; Neh. 9:20; Dan. 9:22). But the Targ. and Vulg. support the given translation, and the LXX can just as well be explained as haplography for the same reason. With the meaning "to pay attention to [someone/thing]," *haśkîl* can take the acc. (Deut. 32:29; Job 34:27; Pss. 64:10; 106:7) or a preposition: *'el* (Neh. 8:13; Ps. 41:2), *bᵉ* (Ps. 101:2; Dan. 9:13), *lᵉ* (Prov. 21:12; see the next note), and *'al* (Prov. 16:20). Moreover, the alternative confounds whether the gullible or the wise person is the subject of "he gains" (see the next note). Another possible interpretation is "through the prudence of the wise person (lit. 'with reference to' the wise)," but in that case the preposition *lᵉ* is unnecessary and awkward.

16. The Targ. and Vulg. also make "gullible" the subject of "he gains." But the LXX makes "wise person" the subject, which entails explaining away *lᵉ* before *ḥkm* as dittography due to homoioteleuton from *bhškyl* (so Fichtner [*BHS*]). But this reading destroys the unity of the verse (so Plöger, *Sprüche,* p. 246), and the omission of *lᵉ* may be due to haplography.

17. Although *ṣaddîq* elsewhere in this book always refers to a human being, here it refers to God because it is in apposition to "the one who casts down the wicked," who can only be the LORD. The same adjective is used for the LORD in Isa. 24:16 (cf. Job 34:17), and similar substantival adjectives occur in Gen. 18:25; Job 6:10; Isa. 40:25; Hab. 3:3 (cf. E. Bullinger, *Figures of Speech Used in the Bible Explained and Illustrated* [Grand Rapids: Baker, 1968; originally published in 1898], p. 495 and many commentators beginning with Rashi [Lyons, "Rashi's *Commentary,*" p. 109]). The KJV (cf. Ibn Ezra, cited by Greenstone, *Proverbs,* p. 225) makes "righteous man" the subject of verset A by arbitrarily adding God as the subject of verset B. Some commentators think that a righteous judge overthrows the wicked, but that would be a unique thought in this book.

18. The LXX, followed by the Syr., reads *kardias* (< *libbôt*).

19. Garrett (*Proverbs, Ecclesiastes, Song of Songs,* p. 181, n. 386), to mitigate the difficult interpretation of *ṣaddîq,* emends to *mᵉsallepet riš'â* after *riš'â tᵉsallēp* (13:6). But he offers no explanation for the more difficult, but not impossible, MT. Gemser (*Sprüche,* p. 81) notes that the LORD is the subject of *slp* also in 22:12 and Job 12:19.

13 *As for whoever stops his ear to*[20] *the cry of the poor,*
indeed, he himself will also cry out and not be answered.
14 *A gift given*[21] *in secret subdues*[22] *anger;*
even a bribe in the bosom[23] *pacifies*[24] *strong wrath.*
15 *The doing of justice brings*[25] *joy to the righteous person*[26]
but a terror[27] *to those who do iniquity.*
16 *A human being who strays from the way of being prudent*
will come to rest in the congregation in the realm of the dead.
17 *The one who loves pleasure is*[28] *a destitute person;*
the one who loves wine and olive oil will not become rich.
18 *A wicked person is a ransom for the righteous,*
and a treacherous person comes[29] *in the place of the upright.*
19 *Better to dwell in a desert land*
than to dwell with[30] *a contentious and vexing*[31] *wife.*
20 *A desirable supply of food*[32] *and oil*[33] *are in the dwelling place of*

20. Lit. "from" (= from [hearing]); cf. Isa. 33:15.

21. The preposition *b*ᵉ implies the verb (*IBHS,* p. 224, P. 11.4d).

22. Or "averts" (see Delitzsch, *Proverbs,* p. 314; *HALOT,* 2:492, s.v. *kph*). In cognate Semitic languages *kph* means "bend." Instead of the MT's *hap. leg.* the Targ. and Sym. may have read the common verb *y*ᵉ*kabbēh* ("extinguishes"). The LXX reads *anatrepei* ("calms down").

23. The LXX, followed by the Syr., reads *dōrōn de ho pheidomenos . . . egeirei* ("but he that turns away from gifts stirs up . . .), reading *šoḥad* as *šōmēr* or *ḥōśēk* and creating an antithesis to *anatrepei* (cf. Baumgartner, *Critique,* p. 193).

24. R. Nogah ("A Proposition Which Is Clarified by a Parallel Proposition: The Twenty-Second of the Thirty-Two Hermeneutical Principles," *BM* 34 [1988-89] 241-49) notes that Abraham ibn Ezra took special interest in the twenty-second of Rabbi Eliezer's 32 hermeneutical principles — that usage in one clause may be extended to the following one. The supplied verb was varied to match normal variation in Hebrew and English verse.

25. Lit. "is."

26. The NIV (cf. NRSV) renders, "When justice is done, it brings joy to the righteous," to safeguard against the interpretation "It is a joy to the just to do judgment."

27. The KJV makes *m*ᵉ*ḥittâ* subject (= "destruction shall be to"), but the antithetical parallel favors taking it as the object of gapped "doing of justice."

28. The Targ. and Syr. interpret verset A as part of the compound subject of "will not become rich."

29. The preposition presupposes the verb of motion (*IBHS,* p. 224, P. 11.4.3d).

30. "To dwell" is gapped, and the implied preposition is also added in the Syr.

31. Lit. "a contentious wife and/with vexation."

32. Lit. "supply/treasure" (see *'ôṣār,* 21:6), whose precise identification is uncertain.

33. Though *wāšemen* overloads the line, it should not be omitted because it clarifies the meaning of *'ôṣār,* makes the connection with v. 17, and/or is stylistically poignant (see commentary). Eitan (adopted by McKane, *Proverbs,* pp. 244, 552-53 and followed by the REB) points *šāmîn* after Arab. *tamīn* ("expensive").

the wise,
but a fool gulps his down.
21 *The one who pursues righteousness and kindness*
will find life, prosperity,[34] *and honor.*
22 *The wise scales the city walls*[35] *of warriors,*
and pulls down its[36] *strong security.*[37]
23 *He who guards his mouth and his tongue*
is one who guards his life from distresses.
24 *The insolent, presumptuous person — "Mocker is his name" —*
is one who behaves with insolent[38] *fury.*
25 *The craving of the sluggard kills him,*
because his hands refuse to work.
26 *All day long he*[39] *craves greedily,*
but the righteous gives without sparing.[40]
27 *The sacrifice of wicked people is an abomination;*[41]
how much more[42] *[when] he brings it with evil intent.*
28 *A false witness will perish,*
but a person who listens well will testify[43] *successfully.*[44]

34. The same word is glossed "righteousness" in verset A.

35. The English idiom demands adding "walls."

36. The 3rd fem. sing. suffix is also without *mappiq* in Isa. 23:17, but the Cairo Geniza mss. and some Tiberian mss. have it.

37. The NIV helpfully paraphrases *'ōz mibṭeḥâ* by "the stronghold in which they trust."

38. Lit. "fury of pride." *HALOT* (2:782, s.v. *'ebrâ*) glosses *'ebrâ* "outburst, excess" in Prov. 21:24; 22:8; Isa. 1:6; Jer. 48:30, but Driver ("Problems," *Bib* 32 [1951] 185-86) restricts this meaning to Prov. 21:24 and Isa. 16:6. However, the normal semantic domain of "rage" fits these two passages as well. The NIV and the NRSV gloss it as "insolence" (i.e., insultingly contemptuous in speech and/or conduct) in Isa. 16:6 and Jer. 48:30, and as "fury"/"anger" in 22:8. The NRSV glosses it as "outbursts" in Job 40:11, but the NIV as "fury."

39. The LXX probably reads *asebēs* without reflecting *ta^a'wâ* through its moralizing tendency (McKane, *Proverbs,* p. 557), and "through misunderstanding the proverb; the subject is the *'āṣēl* of ver. 25 carried through into ver. 26" (so G. R. Driver, "Hebrew Notes on the Prophets and Proverbs," *JTS* 41 [1940] 174).

40. Lit. "and does not hold back."

41. The LXX adds *kyriǭ,* probably from 15:8.

42. All the ancient versions neglect *'ap,* rendering only causal *kî.*

43. The NEB interpreted *y^{e}dabbēr* (see 18:23), on the basis of Arab. *dābir* and Sir. 41:5 (LXX) *tekna,* to mean, "to leave children behind" (cf. Gemser, *Sprüche,* p. 113), but the REB does not follow. J. Emerton ("The Interpretation of Proverbs 21:28," *ZAW* 100 [1988] 164) objects that *a verb* with this meaning is unattested. Dahood proposed on the basis of an Akkadian cognate to repoint the text as *y^{e}dubbar* (= "will be pursued"; cf. NIV, "will be destroyed"), but Emerton ("Proverbs 21:28," p. 165) objects that the meaning is

29 *A wicked man becomes brazen,*
but as for the upright, he discerns[45] *his way.*[46]
30 *There is no wisdom, and there is no understanding,*
and there is no counsel that can stand[47] *before*[48] *the* LORD.

---

not securely established in Hebrew. Emerton ("Proverbs 21:28," pp. 168-69) emends the form to *Hiphil* (cf. Pss. 18:48; 47:4) or invests the *Piel* with exceptional meaning — he admits that the text of 2 Chr. 22:10 is insecure — and glosses "will overthrow." But he must interpret "he who listens" with the exceptional additional meaning, "and as a result detects the inconsistencies and other weaknesses in his [the false witness's] words," and follow Thomas in his questionable interpretation that *laneṣaḥ* is a superlative (= "completely"; see the next note).

44. The phrase *laneṣaḥ* occurs 31 times, always in poetry, apart from *hᵃlaneṣaḥ* in 2 Sam. 2:26, which may be a proverbial saying. Twenty-six times it means "forever" in conditioned contexts, unlike Prov. 21:28: eight times in a question (Pss. 49:9[10]; 68:16[17]; 74:1, 10; 49:5; 89:46[47]; Jer. 3:5; Lam. 5:20), 13 times with a negative (Pss. 9:18[19]; 10:11; 44:23[24]; 74:19; 77:8[9]; 103:9; Isa. 13:20; 28:28; 33:20; 57:16; Jer. 50:39; Amos 8:7; Hab. 1:4), and six times in the context of "endless ruin/destruction" (Job 4:20; 14:20; 20:7; Pss. 9:6[7]; 52:5 [7]; 74:3). Moreover, although the notion of speaking endlessly can be defended from 12:19, "to speak forever is something which would not naturally be said of (or desired for) any man, good or bad, in court of law or elsewhere" (Toy, *Proverbs,* p. 411). Interpretations retaining the sense "forever" are unconvincing. "It has been suggested that the meaning is that people will always listen to such a person (Wisemann), that he will always be able to speak, either without having to become silent or because what he says is valid permanently (Delitzsch), or even that he 'goes on repeating his story' (Scott), but all such interpretations are forced explanations of 'will speak for ever'" (Emerton, "Proverbs 21:28," p. 162). D. W. Thomas ("The Use of *neṣaḥ* as a Superlative in Hebrew," *JSS* 1 [1956] 106-9) argued that the phrase sometimes has a superlative sense other than the temporal in Pss. 74:10; 79:5; 89:47, but *HALOT* (2:716, s.v. II *nṣḥ*) invests it with its normal temporal sense in these passages. In the four positive passages, like Prov. 21:28, *laneṣaḥ* connotes "victoriously," "successfully," "prevailingly" (Job 23:7; 34:36; 36:7; Isa. 25:8; cf. also Hab. 1:4), especially in legal contexts. Job 23:7 matches Prov. 21:28, "There an upright man could present his case before him, and I would be delivered successfully [*laneṣaḥ*] from my judge" (cf. M. Pope, *Job* [AB15; Garden City, N.Y.: Doubleday, 1979], p. 170). In Job 34:36 Elihu calls for a trial that will prevail over Job. The notion of winning a case fits this antithetical parallelism nicely; it also fits the idea of triumphing over the cheeky (v. 29) and of the victory that comes from the LORD, not from human skill (vv. 30-31). The ancient versions (Vulg., Aquila, Sym., Theod., et al.) have similar readings (Emerton, "Proverbs 21:28," pp. 162-63).

45. K, Syr., Targ., and Vulg. read *yākîn* ("fixes"); Q, LXX, and one medieval ms. read *yābîn,* "gives thought to."

46. K, LXX, and Syr. read *dᵉrākāyw* ("his ways"); Q, one ms., Targ., and Vulg. read *darkô* ("his way").

47. "That can stand" is implied by the preposition *lᵉneged* (*IBHS,* p. 224, P. 11.4d).

48. The Vulg. renders by *contra,* but the Targ. and Syr. interpreted, "in comparison of, in the face of, like."

31 *A horse is prepared for the day of war,*
but success belongs to the Lord.

The theme of trusting the Lord, not self, to avenge wrongs against oneself (20:19-28), which drew to a conclusion with the motif that the king will protect the needy, is now qualified by a unit on doing righteousness and justice, which is framed with another focus on the Lord and his king. The new unit follows the pattern of an introduction (20:29–21:2), a main body (21:3-29), and a conclusion (21:30-31).

The introduction consists of two proverb pairs. The first is the typical education proverb commending the teaching (vv. 29-30). The second, an *inclusio* with the concluding pair (21:30-31), sets the teaching within the thematic frame of the Lord's sovereignty exercised through his king (21:1-2) and the lexical frame of unique references to the Lord, apart from the janus in v. 3. Both introductory pairs pick up on the preceding unit. The catchword *ḥadrê-bāṭen* ("innermost being," v. 27b) links the first proverb pair with v. 27, and the second pair matches the same notions of the Lord's rule over humanity through his king asserted in 20:8, 24; 20:26-28. The teaching of the main body, to do righteousness and justice, must be interpreted within the grid that the Lord ultimately is the sanction that rewards the righteous (vv. 1-2) and prevails over the wicked (vv. 30-31). The janus (21:3) introduces the unit's theme: exploring human behavior with reference to righteousness and justice. The body employs the metaphor *derek* ("way") in all its subunits (vv. 2, 8, 16, 29). The gullible, for whom in part the book was compiled (1:4), is never lost sight of. He needs the correction of being beaten with hard blows (20:29-30) and of observing the righteous rewarded and the wicked fined (21:11-12). The descriptive statements about doing righteousness and justice aim to wake him up to the reality that the Lord rewards the righteous but punishes the wicked (cf. 21:11). The startling and unexpected transitional verses about the dangers of the contentious wife (vv. 9, 19), which divide the main body into its subunits, hit like hammer blows the need of having a wise wife.

a. Twofold Introduction (20:29–21:2)

The educational introduction focuses on the pedagogical relationship of the older generation (i.e., the wise) to the younger (i.e., the strong youth), implying that the wise need to educate virile youth. Hard blows, their pedagogical method, rather than verbal rebukes, may be featured here because the main body pertains mostly to wicked types who need hard blows in their youth to save them from final death (cf. "unplowed field" in v. 4). Verse 29 presents the mutual dependence of the generations on each other by featuring their splendors, the strength of youth and the wisdom of the aged. Verse 30 admonishes that the misdirected virility granted youth must be purged by therapeutic wounds.[49]

(1) Introduction: Education (20:29-30)

29 Synthetic parallels surprisingly juxtapose *choice young men* (*baḥûrîm;* see 1:29) with *the aged* (see 17:6). The former conveys a stereotyped meaning that can be derived from its root meaning, to make a well-thought-out choice according to the principle of their natural strength (cf. Exod. 18:25; 17:9; Josh. 8:3). The parallels also juxtapose the characterizing distinctives: *their strength* (i.e., their vital power; see 5:10) of the former, and *their gray hair* (see 16:31, their wisdom) of the latter. Though contrasting the generations, the parallels are synthetic, signaled by conjunctive *and,* because they do not represent the generations as rivals but celebrate their adornments that reveal the generations are mutually dependent on each other. The strength of youth is their *splendor* (*tip'eret;* see 4:9; 19:11), which is often used of a crown. The aged wear their wisdom in *majesty* (*hᵃdar;*[50] see 14:28), validating the way of wisdom, for it is won through a righteous life (16:31; cf. 17:6) and the fear of the LORD (cf. 10:27). According to Pirqe 'Abot 5:24, thirty-year-olds stand out through the unfolding of their power, and seventy-year-olds are connected with gray hair. The proverb is concerned not with deficiencies such as defacing immaturity or even the wanton abuse of power by the strong and the pathetic decrepitude of old age (cf. Eccl. 1:17). Though weak, the aged lay down the tracks along which immature youth through their power advance the faithful community's rich inheritance in everlasting life (cf. 2 Cor. 4:16-18).

30 The synthetic parallels have as their synonymous subjects, "bruising wounds" and "blows." The complementary predicates, "scour away evil" and "polishes the innermost being" teach that outward, corporeal chastening therapeutically purges evil from *the innermost being* (see 18:8; 20:27), leaving the core of the personality brilliantly polished. Both *bruising*

49. Verses 29 and 30 are phonetically linked by the consonance-sequence */h~ḥ d r/* in *hdr* "majesty" (v. 29b) and *ḥdry* "innermost" (v. 30b) and by the broken sequence */b ḥ r/* in *baḥûrîm* ("choice young men," v. 29a) and *ḥabburôt* ("wounds," v. 30aα). The latter may also serve as a link with the following pericope by their repetition in *nibḥār* (21:3) and *rᵉḥab* (21:4). The sequence of */ṭ n/* in *bāṭen* and *yaṭṭennû,* the last words of 29:30 and 21:1 respectively, link the two introductions.

50. The term is used to characterize the magnificence and eminence of something like a luxurious tree (Lev. 23:40; cf. Isa. 35:2), a firstborn bull (Deut. 33:17), or a king's rule over a multitude (Prov. 14:28; cf. Isa. 5:14). Several times it is used metaphorically of being arrayed in a magnificence that sets one apart and above others (Ps. 104:1; Prov. 31:25; Jer. 16:14).

(peṣaʿ) and *wounds (ḥabbūrôt),* though distinct concepts (Gen. 4:23; Exod. 21:25 [twice]; Isa. 1:6), refer to body wounds (cf. Isa. 1:6) that are inflicted by an adversary or by a friend for a partner's good (Job 27:6). *Ḥabbûrâ,* the welts on the body, are probably left by a whip or rod; they can fester and stink (Ps. 38:5[6]). *Peṣaʿ* may also be inflicted by strokes (1 K. 20:7), but here they qualify the wounds (or stripes) as contusions and/or bruises. The singular verb *scours away* (*tamrîq;* see n. 1) puts the emphasis on the singular genitive.[51] *Rîq* means to remove dirt and patina from vessels such as bronze spears and pots through hard rubbing (Lev. 6:28[21]; 2 Chr. 4:16; Jer. 46:4). The metaphor implicitly compares moral *evil* (see 1:16) to tarnish. *And* joins the synthetic parallels. *Blows (makkôt),* though a synonym of *ḥabburâ* and *peṣaʿ,* is distinct from them (Isa. 1:6), probably meaning either "blows" received in a beating (cf. Deut. 25:3) or "wounds" (cf. 1 K. 22:35). *Polish* is gapped in the Hebrew text.

(2) The Framing Introduction: The LORD's Sovereignty (21:1-2)

The introductory framing pair presents as the Sanction behind this instruction "the LORD," who works salvation through his "king" (21:1-2). Here the king, not parents as often elsewhere (cf. 13:24; 19:18; 22:6; 23:13, 14; 29:17), is represented as the wise pedagogue in the LORD's hand. This pair is linked chiastically in their outer frame by the catchwords *lēb* ("heart") and *YHWH* ("the LORD") (vv. 1a, 2b), and in their inner core by *kol* "all" (vv. 1b, 2a). It may also be linked by the alliteration of *melek* ("king," v. 1) and *derek* ("way," v. 2) as well as by the references to body parts: "hand" (v. 1), "eyes" (see also v. 4), and "heart" (v. 2). Verse 1 pertains to the LORD's sovereignty over the king in his pedagogical bestowing of blessings, and v. 2 to his omniscience over every human being, implying the king's ability to reward and punish justly. The catchwords *derek ʾîš* ("way of a person," vv. 2a, 8a) and *yāšār* ("upright," vv. 2a, 8b) tie together the last verse of the introduction and the last verse of the next subunit.

1 This proverb features the LORD's sovereign benediction on those who please him through his anointed magistrate. Verset A presents the king's heart both as under the LORD's sovereign control and as the source of the people's life. God's inscrutable mastery extends to kings, the most powerful of human beings, and to the heart, their most free member. The LORD rules even the most free and powerful of all human beings (see 16:14-15; 19:12; 20:2). Verset B restricts the Sovereign's benefits to those who please him. As the heart of the individual determines and directs his every move, *the king's* [see 14:28] *heart* (see I: 90) determines the nation's direction and well-being (see

51. GKC, P. 146.1a.

vv. 10-15). *In the LORD's hand* (*b^{e}yad-YHWH,* cf. 18:21) could restrict the heart to one that submits itself to the LORD's power, care, and/or authority (see 18:21), but the parallel infers that it is nonrestrictive, referring to every king's heart. God's inscrutable mastery directs the king, who has in his hands the life and death of his subjects (16:10-15). Here the anthropomorphism teaches that God steers the king's heart according to the LORD's good pleasure. The metaphor *is a channel of water* (*palgê-mayim* or canal; see 5:16; cf. Sir. 48:17) denotes a decision that blesses, not curses, the people. Water is especially precious in the parched Near East. Aside from Lam. 3:48 and Ps. 119:136, which use the phrase in a hyperbole for tears, it always connotes positively the channeling of abundant, gladdening, life-giving water in an otherwise dry place. Whereas a river *(nāhār)* might run wild and a wadi *(nāḥāl)* run dry, the artificial stream of water provides a steady, directed, full supply of refreshing, living-giving water. However, it takes great skill and power to direct water's chaotic nature. *On* [see 17:8] *all* refers to everything in the garden needing water, and its interpretation applies to every needy person in his realm (see 20:28). *Who please him* (or whom he delights in; cf. 18:2) "denotes the direction of [God's] heart or passion. . . . The basis of God's delight or lack of it revolves around human obedience (cf. Ps. 37:22, 28, 34, 38),"[52] restricting his benedictions to the faithful. The LORD has no emotional pleasure in fools and wickedness (cf. 3:32; 8:7; 11:1, 20; 12:22; 13:19; 15:8, 9, 26; 16:5, 12; 17:15; 20:10, 23; 24:9; 28:9; 29:27). The parallel "LORD's hand" implies that the LORD is the subject and the king's heart the object of *he turns it* (see 2:2). Farmers in Mesopotamia and Egypt divert the water by putting up dams and other obstructions in the stream's flow to direct the water to their fields and gardens. Palestinian farmers depended on rain (cf. Deut. 11:10-12), but must have captured and directed the water to where it was most needed. Natural streams are not meant, because their direction is fixed. The LORD is the Farmer; the king's heart is the flexible channel; and his well-watered garden is the pious and ethical needy. In Isa. 32:2, each ruler is compared to a "stream of water in a dry place," a reference to salvation from oppressive government. Their governments included sages who provided guidance. The proverb instructs the audience to be those who please the LORD in order to receive his favors through his king (16:15; 19:12; cf. Gen. 20:6; 41:37-45; Ezra 1:1; 6:22; 7:27; 9:9; Ps. 106:46; Dan. 2:48; 3:30; 6:1-3, 28). It may also instruct them to pray for God's blessing through the king (Neh. 2:4-5; 1 Tim. 2:1-2), and perhaps cautions the king against arrogance, for he functions according to providence (cf. Isa. 44:28; Jer. 25:9; Acts 4:27-28).

2 This synoptic variant of 16:2 again teaches that, since people

52. D. Talley, *NIDOTTE,* 3:232, s.v. *hpṣ.*

may justify all their motives and actions and only the omniscient Sovereign rightly assesses them (cf. 15:11; 17:3; 24:12), conflicts of assessment arise. ("May" in the translation is rhetorical.)[53] Verset A uses *way* (sing.) to represent each way individually in contrast to "ways" (pl.; 16:2) and represents ethical conduct by the more common and literal adjective *upright* (see I: 98) instead of the more rare metaphor "pure." These two variants, in addition to the catchword *ʾîš* ("person"), link this introduction to the last verse of the main body (v. 29, reading *darkô* with K) and its next subunit (v. 8). Verset B uses *hearts* (see I: 90) instead of *rûḥôt* ("winds"/"motives") as one of the three catchwords linking this introductory proverb pair. Verse 1 emphasizes God's sovereign power to bless; v. 2, his moral omniscience. Whereas in 16:2 the conflict of assessment pertains to the planner and doer of an action (16:1, 3), here it has to do with the recipient of the LORD's blessing through his king. God will not divert life-giving water on those who act according to their own value system. Self-distrust must be matched by bold confidence in the LORD, who keeps his promises to bless the upright (see 3:5; 16:3).

b. Body: On Doing Righteousness and Justice (21:3-29)

The main body, vv. 3-29, consists of a janus introduction stating the unit's theme (v. 3), followed by three subunits (vv. 4-8, 10-18, 20-29) separated by the refrain about the "the contentious wife" (vv. 9, 19; cf. 19:13, 14). Once again a reference to the wife functions as an organizing principle in Collection II. Its first subunit focuses on the defeat of the wicked; the middle, on the triumph of the righteous over them; and the last, on the lasting gratification and establishment of the righteous and the demise of the wicked. The keyword "wicked" forms an *inclusio* (21:4b, 29a).

(1) Janus: The LORD's Desire for Righteousness and Justice (21:3)

Verse 3 forms a janus between the introduction and the main body (vv. 4-29). The catchword YHWH ("the LORD") unites it with vv. 1-2 and "to do righteousness and justice" with the body's three subunits (cf. 7b, 15a, 21; cf. v. 25). The saying about the LORD's omniscience (v. 2) prepares the way for this saying about his delight in people; it is based on his perfect knowledge of them. The janus maxim sets forth by positive comparisons the standard for measuring what counts before God. Verset A represents the topic, *to do* [see

53. This repetition suggests to D. C. Snell (*Twice Told Proverbs* [Winona Lake, Ind.: Eisenbrauns, 1993]) that variants from 16:2 may be the result of oral composition and/or transmission that do not demand mechanized learning processes, but more importantly they are repeated to enrich different literary contexts.

10:4] *righteousness and justice* (see 1:3), as the quality carefully chosen by the LORD. Verset B represents the predicate, the thing compared, to show that the subject *is more desirable* [see 1:29] *to the LORD (laYHWH) than sacrifice* (see 7:14; 15:8). The comparative does not exclude sacrifice as a good (see 12:9). Both ethical behavior and cultic actions, such as fine-sounding hymns and well-phrased prayers, are important and desired by the LORD, but he prefers ethics over the cult (cf. 15:8; 20:25). Verse 7 juxtaposes to this desired conduct that of the wicked, who refuse to seek the well-being of all the citizens under the heavenly King's rule. They divorce ethics and cultus and are repugnant to him. The last subunit intensifies the point: "The sacrifice of wicked people is an abomination [to the LORD]" (v. 27). The sluggard is wicked because he refuses to do anything; how much less, righteousness and justice (see v. 25). The priority of ethics over ritual was taught by Moses. He ratified the moral law before being giving any cultic instructions (Exodus 24). This teaching of the prophets (cf. 1 Sam. 15:22; Ps. 50:7ff.; Isa 1:11-14; Hos. 6:6; Amos 5:21; Mic. 6:6-7) "lost none of its force with the sages" (cf. 15:8, 29; 21:27; 28:9, 13; 1 K. 3:4; 8:64)[54] or in the teaching of Jesus (Matt 23:23; Mark 12:33-34). The New Testament disposed of some cultic laws (cf. Matt. 12:7; Acts 10:34, 35), but none of the moral (Matt. 22:37-39). Although this is not the way human beings often see it (see v. 2), in common grace Egyptian literature taught the same value.[55]

(2) An Analysis of the Wicked Person's Pursuit of Wealth (21:4-8)

The body's first subunit, which analyzes the wicked, is connected in its opening verse with the introduction by the catchwords "heart" (vv. 1, 4) and "eyes" (vv. 2, 4) and in its closing verse by the catchwords "upright," "person," and "way" (vv. 2, 8). The same three words are repeated in the concluding verse of the body (21:29). The abstract term "wicked" (vv. 4b and 7a) and the elaboration of "sin" (v. 4b) as "refuse to do justice" form a frame around vv. 4-7 in their escalating analysis of the wicked person's pursuit of wealth. The antithetical parallelism of v. 8 sums up the section by contrasting the devious behavior of the guilty with the straight conduct of the pure. Within the *inclusio* of vv. 4 and 7 the wicked are broken down into several self-serving types by the motif of their body parts: "lofty of eyes" and "audacious of heart" (v. 4a) and "lying tongue" (v. 6a). The partial subunit escalates both their sin and their judgment. With regard to the former it escalates their arrogant attitudes expressed in their eyes that derive from their unrestrained heart

54. Toy, *Proverbs,* p. 399.

55. "More acceptable is the character of one upright of heart than the ox of the evildoer" (Merikare, 129; *ANET,* p. 417).

(v. 4a) and lack of discipline (v. 4b) to their "haste [to make money]" (v. 5b) expanded to "acquiring treasures through lying lips" (6a), escalated to "violence" (v. 7a) to their refusal to repent (v. 7b). They condemn themselves by their "labyrinthine course" to escape detection (v. 8a). So also there is an escalation in their judgment from the evaluation that they are sinners, implying the LORD's judgment (v. 4b), to their "lack" (v. 5b), to their becoming "driven-away breath among those seeking death" (v. 6b), to their being dragged away (v. 7), to a summarizing burden, "guilty" (v. 8a).

4 Verse 4 now turns to the megalomaniacs who do not do righteousness and justice. Verset A breaks down the wicked individually into their psychosomatic components, their outward, haughty eyes and their inner, audacious hearts; and verset B presents the wicked as a group, comparing them to an unplowed field that yields this sin. *Haughty (rûm) eyes* (see n. 4) is a semantic equivalent to "rising eyes" (i.e., "haughty eyes"; see 6:17) and "raises its eyes" (see 30:13). This looking down on others symbolizes impious and unethical haughtiness. *Rûm* ("height"), apart from its literal use in 25:3, is always a metaphor for censured pride.[56] God and Woman Wisdom detest haughty eyes (6:16, 17; 8:13). *And* probes beneath the arrogant eyes. Haughty eyes peer out of an *audacious* (*r^{e}ḥab;* lit. "wide of"; see 18:16) *heart* (see I: 90). *Raḥab* with concrete nouns denotes breadth or width (e.g., of land, Exod. 3:8; of a wall, Jer. 51:58; etc.), but in construct with psychosomatic words it pejoratively denotes unrestraint, immodesty: with *nepeš,* an unrestrained appetite (see 28:25; cf. Ps. 101:5); with *lēb,* of unrestrained thoughts, ambitions, plans, and so on. This heart, recognizing no boundaries to curb its aspirations, behaves as if it were God. Verset B now explains the cause and consequence of this "megalomaniac aberration which can be equated with the intellectual pride of *hubris*."[57] The metaphor *an unplowed field* (cf. 13:23) underscores and explains their arrogance. As an unplowed field yields inedible growth because it is uncultivated and not sown with good seed, so *the wicked* (see I: 109) are not amenable to moral discipline, for they lack good instruction. The moral intention of the metaphor is clarified by *produce* [lit. "is"] *sin* (see 1:10). Guilty before God for their impiety and unethical activity, they deserve death (cf. 16:5, 18; 18:12; 29:23; 30:13-14).

56. Twice as an absolute (Isa. 10:2, 17); once in cons. with "his heart" (*libbô,* Jer. 48:29); twice in cons. with "eyes/his eyes" (Isa. 10:12, where it is parallel with "greatness [= arrogance] of heart," *gōdel l^{e}bab,*" similar to Prov. 21:4, "audacious of heart," *r^{e}ḥab-lēb*). In these five instances it occurs in parallel or in combination with other words for pride: from *gbh* (see 16:5, 18): *gāb^{e}hût* (Isa. 2:11, 17) and *gābah* (Jer. 48:9); from *g'h: gā'ôn, gē'eh, ga'^{a}wâ,* and *gōdel l^{e}bab.* In Isa. 10:2 this symbolic look qualifies "vainglory" (*tip'eret rûm 'ênāyw,* "the vainglory of his haughty look."

57. McKane, *Proverbs,* p. 559.

5 The arrogant wicked are now defined more precisely in the antithetical parallels of v. 5 as those hasty to get rich.[58] The antithetical parallels *the calculations* (*maḥšᵉbôt;* see 6:18) *of the diligent* (*ḥārûṣ;* see 10:4) and *who hastens* [*to get rich*] (see 19:2) are imprecise, implying that the hasty act without moral reflection to avoid the hard discipline of diligence. We should assume that the diligent creatively plan within the framework of God's revealed will and by nature act accordingly, *but,* marking the antithesis, the one who hastens to get rich acts without reckoning with the divine order. "In monetary matters, haste connotes greed (28:20; cf. 11:24), and haste in speech connotes a lack of reflection (29:20)."[59] Elsewhere the diligent person stands over against the lethargic sluggard (10:4; 12:24, 27; 13:4), but here he stands opposed to the rash and imprudent. The lazy are defective in action; the hasty, in thought. The prudence of the diligent now consists in his wise planning in contrast to ill-conceived and misdirected actions (cf. 11:24-28). Rashi rightly defined the diligent as "a righteous man who goes in truth and with clear-cut judgment."[60] *Everyone,* allowing no exceptions, is probably gapped in verset A, for one should not suppose that some of the diligent do not make a profit. The consequences of these two lifestyles are precisely antithetical. The former *lead only to profit* (*môtār;* cf. 14:23), and the latter *comes only to lack* (*maḥsôr;* see 11:24; 14:23). "Only" refers to an unexpected conclusion. Contrary to the expectations of those who do what is right in their own eyes (see 21:2), the restrained diligent surprisingly gain only more than they invested (cf. Rom. 2:7; Heb. 6:12), and the unrestrained hasty person loses only what is essential to life. The plans and ways of God are higher than human ways and thoughts (Isa. 55:6; cf. 11:24).

6 The "hasty" of v. 5b are now described procuring treasures by deceptive speech, and their "lack" is escalated to "the blown-away breath of those pursuing death." Like vv. 3-5, verset A presents the topic, the foolish situation: *the acquisition of* (*pōʿal,* see 20:11)[61] *treasures* (*'ôṣārôt;* see 8:21; 10:2) *by a lying tongue* (*lᵉšôn šāqer;* see 6:17). Their antisocial speech falsifies facts to fill their vaults with stores of food and/or precious metal at the community's expense. Verset B presents their ill-fated consequences by a metaphor in apposition to the ill-gotten treasures. *Windblown* is used of a leaf (Lev. 26:36; Job 13:25), a dried-up plant (Isa. 19:7), chaff (Isa. 41:2), and breath (Prov. 21:6) to connote that they are no more. Visible *breath* is the

58. The juxtaposition between the versets is underscored by the sound patterns: /*ṣ + 'ak-lᵉmôtār* :: *ṣ + 'ak-lᵉmaḥsôr*/, and the threefold repetition of /*k, l*/: *'k-lmwtr, wkl, 'k-lmḥswr.*

59. Van Leeuwen, *Proverbs,* p. 192.

60. M. Lyons, "Rashi's *Commentary on the Book of Proverbs*" (submitted in partial fulfillment of the requirements for the degree of rabbi), p. 108.

61. BDB, p. 821, s.v. *pōʿal.*

consistent meaning of onomatopoetic *hebel,* which connotes being transitory and fleeting.[62] Ironically, the treasures procured through deception are themselves deceptive; they are as insubstantial as breath. *Of those seeking* (*m^ebaqšê;* see n. 10; 2:4) *death* (see 10:2) refers to the end of the treasures so sought, and of those who so seek them (cf. 10:2; 11:4; 20:21; 28:20, 22). Instead of procuring the fortune and life they hoped for, deceivers find that they were actually seeking death and so lose everything (cf. 13:11; 20:17).

7 As v. 6 elaborates and escalates v. 5, so v. 7 expands v. 6b, again teaching that the opposite of what the wicked strove for unexpectedly comes to them. The fraudulent acquisition of treasures by a lying tongue (v. 6a) entails violence (v. 7aα), and the wicked's loss of life and property (v. 6b) is pictured as their being netted like fish (v. 7aβ). Verset A asserts their sin and its consequence, and verset B the cause.[63] *The violence* (*šōd;* cf. 11:3) *of wicked people* (see 21:3) may be an intentional pun on sin and its consequences. On the one hand, *šōd,* like Eng. "destruction," denotes either the social sin of wanton acts of destroying (= "oppression," "violence") or the fact or condition of being violated (= "devastation," "havoc," "ruin"). The genitive "of" can be either agentive (i.e., the wicked commit violence) or objective (the wicked experience ruin). BDB[64] and *HALOT*[65] assign the first sense to 21:7, but the second sense cannot be ruled out. *Drags them away*[66] compares the wanton and bloody violence of tyrants against their victims to drag-netting fish, but it boomerangs against them so that they themselves are caught (cf. 1:17, 19; 11:3, 5, 6b, 8, 18; 12:13, 26; 13:21; 14:14; 15:6). This is their fate *because* [see 16:26] *they refuse* [see 1:24] *to do* [see 10:4; 21:3] *justice* (I: 97). The *inclusio* with 21:3a suggests that the LORD is the Agent of their being dragged away (see 21:3b). The proverb assumes, but does not explain how, the wicked had opportunity to repent (cf. 1:20-33).

8 This verse brings the body's first subunit to its conclusion, loading the arrogant (v. 4), the hasty (v. 5), the deceiver (v. 6), and the violent (v. 7) with God's evaluation, "guilty," entailing their judgment.[67] They are recognized by their crooked way (v. 8a; cf. Isa. 53:6); indeed, a straight way is an abomination to them (v. 8b; cf. 29:27b). *But* marks the antithesis. Using the

62. K. Seybold, *TDOT,* 3:315, s.v. *hebel.*

63. *Šōd-r^ešā'îm y^egôrēm* coheres by the consonance of /š/ and /r/ and by the assonance of /ō/.

64. BDB, p. 994, s.v. *šōd.*

65. *HALOT,* 4:1,418, s.v. *šōd.*

66. *Y^egôrēm,* without doubling the first root radical, occurs elsewhere only in Hab. 1:15 [= "catches," NIV), where it seems to signify the operation of dragging the net through a stretch of water to catch fish.

67. Possibly *derek 'îš* and *yāšār* function as a link with v. 2 and *pō'al* as a link with v. 6.

metaphor of "way," implied by "straight" in verset B, the antithetical parallels juxtapose chiastically the topic *wāzār wᵉzak* "guilty versus pure" in the inner core with the predicates "crooked" and "straight."[68] The imprecise parallels *the way of* (*derek;* see 1:15) and *his deed* (*poʿᵒlô;* see 21:6) inflate the latter with the notions of character and consequence and highlight the notion of conduct in the former. *A guilty person* (*ʾîš wāzār*) is a *hap. leg.* whose meaning is derived from Arab. *wazara* ("to burden oneself with a crime") and *wazira* ("to be burdened with guilt.") But it could also mean "to be wrong, dishonest" according to Arab. *zawira* (see n. 12).[69] The imprecise parallels "guilty" and *pure* (*wᵉzak;* see 16:2) show that the motives of the former are not free of moral dirt and that the latter are free of judgment. *Crooked* (*hᵃpakpak*) is also a *hap. leg.;* its meaning is derived and interpreted from the verb *hāpak* ("to overturn," "to change"; cf. 12:7). This unusual form probably was chosen over *tahpukôt* (cf. 2:12, 14; 6:14; 8:13; 10:31, 32; 16:28, 30; 23:33), for its soundplay with *zak,* and possibly with *derek.* In keeping with wisdom thinking, like its antithetical parallel *straight* (*yāšār;* see 1:3; 3:6; 11:3; 14:12), the adjective has both physical and moral connotations. Instead of running a "labyrinthine route,"[70] the pure keep a straight, moral course. Transparently sincere and untainted by duplicity, they can be counted on (8:7-9; Rom. 16:10, 11; Phil. 2:19-22; Tit. 1:15).

(3) Janus: The Contentious Wife (21:9)

By the dramatic switch from wicked types of men to the wicked (i.e., quarrelsome) wife a sharp division is formed between the body's subunits (see 11:16, 22; 12:4; 18:22; 19:13; 21:19). Selfishness destroys the closest relationships, both of husband and wife (v. 9) and of neighbors (v. 10). In that light v. 9 emerges as a janus linking the preceding and following sub-units about the wicked. This *better . . . than* (see I: 44; 12:9; 15:16, 17; 16:8) proverb, which is repeated in 25:24, evaluates the solitariness, discomfort, and privation of *dwelling* [see 3:29] *on a corner* [see 7:8, 12] *of the roof* (*gāg*). *Gāg* can refer to any flat surface, such as of an altar (Exod. 3:3), a tower (Judg. 9:1), or a gate (2 Sam. 18:24). The solid, flat roof supported people (Deut. 22:8; cf. Judg. 16:27; 2 Sam. 11:2; 16:22; 18:24), and Ps. 129:6 assumes that they had grass (cf. 2 K. 19:26). Though one slept overnight in summer on the Palestinian flat roofs (1 Sam. 9:25-26), this "better . . . than" proverb does not envision a balmy evening or an upper chamber such as is mentioned in 2 K. 4:10. Ac-

68. The versets also cohere phonetically: /k/ of *hpkpk drk* is picked up by *wzk,* and the /r/ of *drk* is echoed by *wzr* and *yšr* (McCreesh, *Biblical Sound and Sense,* pp. 57-59).

69. *HALOT,* 1:259, s.v. *wāzār.*

70. McKane, *Proverbs,* p. 562.

cording to the synoptic parallel in 21:19, where roof is replaced by desert and the other "better . . . than" proverbs comparing the contentious wife to a leaky roof (19:13; 27:15), the proverb envisions being exposed to all kinds of weather.[71] But this negative physical situation for living, to judge from its contrast, implies the positive spiritual condition of peace and quiet (see 17:1). As verset A presents the negative physical state of having no better hiding place from the storms of heaven than the narrow corner in which the parapet walls of the flat roof meet (Deut. 22:8), verset B presents the worse spiritual state of being *in a house* [see 19:14] *with* [see n. 14] *a contentious wife* (see 18:18, 19; 19:13; 26:21). The meaning of *shared (ḥāber)* is debated. A good argument can be made for "and a noisy house (family)."[72] Also, "woman" is ambiguous, for it could refer to another woman in the household, such as a mother, grandmother, mother-in-law, or daughter (cf. 11:16, 22); but the wife (12:4; 19:13-14) is more probably intended, as 18:22 validates. The NRSV revises "woman" (RSV) to "wife." Ironically, her lord *(baʿal;* cf. Gen. 18:12; 1 Pet. 3:6) lives alone on its outer extremity, unprotected from storms and possibly from a fall, while the one created to help him lords over it securely within (cf. Gen. 2:18). The proverb, which expresses contempt for a brawling wife, not for generic woman (cf. 31:10-31),[73] instructs the son to be the kind of person who finds the LORD's favor in a wife who in mutual love submits to him and builds up the household (see 12:4; 14:1; 18:22; 31:12; cf. Deut. 24:1; Matt. 5:31-32; 19:1-12; 1 Cor. 7:10-16; Eph. 5:21-33). No Scripture instructs the husband to control his wife.[74] The proverb also indirectly admonishes the wife

71. The LXX renders *gāg* by *hypaithrou* ("in the open air"); cf. Plöger, *Sprüche,* pp. 245-46.

72. *Ḥeber* is a homonym derived from three Semitic roots denoting (1) the concept of color or brightness and thus joy; (2) "to unite, be united," and (3) "to tell, report," which suggests some kind of audible phenomenon (H. Cazelles, *TDOT,* 4:193, s.v. *chābhar*). BDB and *HALOT* recognize only the second root, which they gloss here "association" (i.e., "share a house with . . . ," NIV; cf. NRSV) (BDB, p. 288, s.v. *ḥeber; HALOT,* 1:288, s.v. *ḥeber*). Others connect it to Akk. and Ugar. *bt ḥbr,* "storeroom, granary." S. B. Gurewicz ("Some Examples of Modern Exegeses of the OT," *ABR* 11 [1963] 22-23), who also finds this root in Job 40:30 for a granary guard, glosses here: "than to be a great owner of many granaries, and have a brawling wife." The Ugaritic data, however, are inconclusive (McKane, *Proverbs,* p. 554). J. J. Finkelstein, followed by Cazelles (*TDOT,* 4:196, s.v. *chābhar*), connects it to "tell," the third root, more specifically to Akk. *ḫabāru* "to be noisy, to make noise," and glosses *bêt ḥāber* "a noisy household." However, the notion of sharing the comforts of being inside the house offers a better contrast to being exposed to the elements on a corner of a roof and has the support of a known Hebrew word (see Prov. 28:24), not solely of a Semitic cognate.

73. *Pace* C. Osiek, "Inspired Texts: The Dilemma of the Feminist Believers," *SpT* 32 (1980) 140.

74. B. Waltke, "The Role of Woman in the Bible," *Crux* 31 (1995) 29-40.

to submit to wisdom and cautions her against pride, for only with pride is there strife (13:10).

(4) The Righteous Triumph over the Wicked (21:10-18)

Verses 10-18 continue the theme of doing justice but pertain more specifically to the triumph of the righteous over the greedy and merciless wicked, now, however, treated as individuals, not as a group. The subunit is framed by the *inclusio* "wicked" (*rāšā'*, vv. 10a, 18a), which also functions as a catchword with the preceding and following subunits (cf. vv. 4, 7, 29). Unlike vv. 4-8, where the righteous are never mentioned, in this subunit and the next the wicked are contrasted with the "righteous" *(ṣaddîq)* and "wise" *(ḥākām)*. Meinhold helpfully observes the mention of *ṣaddîq* as the second word in every third verse between vv. 10 and 21 (vv. 12, 15, 18; cf. 21), but he probably errs in extending the subunit to v. 21.[75] Since v. 19 forms a divide between the subunits (vv. 10-18 and 20-29), v. 20 shows strong links with the latter, and the abstract form *ṣ*ᵉ*dāqâ* occurs twice in v. 21, it is best to regard *ṣ*ᵉ*dāqâ* as a catchword linking the subunits (vv. 10-12, 13-15, 16-18). In that light, the concluding refrain of the three proverbs predicting the triumph of the righteous can be analyzed into three partial subunits. The theme of the triumph of the righteous over the wicked commences with the Righteous One himself overthrowing them (v. 12). It is developed by noting that the doing of justice (v. 15; cf. v. 3) gives sheer joy to the R/righteous but fills the doers of malevolence with terror (v. 15). The subunit comes to a climax by promising that the wicked will be popped into the death they intended for the righteous (v. 18).

10-12 The repetition of "wicked[ness]" *(rš')* and of "evil"/"calamity" *(rā')* in vv. 10 and 12 forms an *inclusio* around vv. 10-12. In dramatic irony, the one who craved doing evil *(rā')* gets "evil" (*rā'*; see 1:16)! Verse 10 sounds the theme, identifying the wicked person's problem with his evil craving, to which v. 13, the introduction to vv. 13-15, adds that he is without mercy. A pun on the catchword "pay attention to" *(haśkîl/maśkîl l*ᵉ*)* links vv. 11 and 12. The Righteous One (cf. Job 34:17) "pays attention to" the house of the wicked and overthrows them. However, by paying attention to God's punishment of mockers and his showing favor to the wise, the gullible find a way out from the greed of the wicked (v. 10) and from their punishment (v. 12).

10 This verse locates the source that pollutes the wicked person's outlook in his depraved appetite. Its synthetic parallels represent two sides of the coin: on the obverse, his craving for evil (v. 10a) and on the reverse his poor and needy neighbor who finds no favor in his eyes. The impressive

75. Meinhold, *Sprüche,* 2:352.

paronomasia of *rāʿ* (an abstract for many *evil* acts) and *rēʿēhû* (*his neighbor;* see 3:28) at the ends of its versets helps give the verse coherence, playing on both sound and sense. *A wicked (rāšāʿ) person* functions as a catchword with vv. 4 and 7. *Person* (*nepeš;* see I: 90) connotes his passions and commonly occurs with *craves* (see 10:3). Because *in his eyes* (see 3:7) no one is worthy of his esteem and acceptance, his neighbor does not *find favor* (*lō'-yūḥan,* i.e., any acts of kindness; see 14:21). The gnomic situation of craving evil in verset A is broken down into the individual situations of mercilessness in verset B. Delitzsch thinks that the notion of finding favor in his eyes refers to the glow in the eyes that accompanies acts of charity in contrast to the wicked person's steely look that shows no compassion to the needy (cf. 3:4; 23:23; Isa. 13:18). Instead of helping his neighbor, he brutalizes him (see 1:11-14; 4:16-17). Wisdom changes this hard appearance (Eccl. 8:1). The next proverb gives an insight into how to escape this condemnation (21:12; cf. Matt. 12:33-35).

11 According to this proverb, a gullible person is saved from greed through a successive twofold educational process. The proverb assumes the punishment of mockers and the prosperity of the wise, but it relates them to their pedagogic effect on the weak-willed and easily influenced simpleton. In its synthetic parallels, joined by *and, through fining* [see 17:26] *a mocker* (see I: 114) is complemented by *through paying attention* (*haśkîl;* see 1:3) *to a wise person* (see n. 15; I: 94; 20:26), *the gullible* [see I: 111] *becomes wise* (see 6:6), which is advanced to *he gains* (*yiqqaḥ;* see 1:3) *knowledge* (see I: 77). First, through the fining of the mocker he learns the connection between crime and punishment (cf. 19:25). Second, having entered the ranks of the wise, he pays attention to the wise and accepts with approval the connection between virtue and its rewards. Reproving the incorrigible mocker is folly (9:6-7; 14:16; 15:12); even beating him is worthless. But imposing a monetary penalty on him has the value of educating the receptive gullible.

12 This verse escalates the magistrate's penalty of fining mockers to the LORD's toppling all the wicked.[76] Its synthetic parallels escalate the LORD from the *Righteous One* (*ṣaddîq;* see n. 17; 1:3; 10:2) who *pays attention to* [see 21:11] *the household* [see 11:29] *of the wicked* person (see 21:10) to *the One who casts down* [i.e., "to subvert and ruin"; see 13:6] *wicked people* (see 21:4, 7), shifting the focus from each household to the group. The addition *to calamity* (*lārāʿ,* i.e., physical evil; see 1:16) is unnecessary and added for em-

76. Even as the initial participles in each verset, *maśkîl* and *mᵉsallēp,* answer to each other, so also their final *lᵉ . . . rāšāʿ* ("to the wicked individual") and *lārāʿ* ("to calamity [lit. "evil"]) match in alliteration and thought: the wicked are bound for physical evil.

phasis (cf. 13:6; 19:3; 22:12). The LORD is represented as the Righteous One because as King of his community he must uphold its best interest by ridding it of the wicked, who oppresses the pious and ethical.

13-15 The motif of judgment forms an *inclusio* around this partial unit in which the wicked who refused to do justice (v. 13b) will be terrified when ironically justice is exacted of them (v. 15b). Its initial proverb escalates that of the preceding in that "[the wicked person's] neighbor does not find favor in his eyes" (v. 10b) escalates to "[he] stops his ears to the cry of the poor" (v. 13a). These introductions to the partial subunits may also be connected by *nepeš* (lit. "throat"; v. 10a) and "cries out" (v. 13b), creating a chiasm between vv. 10a and 13b as well as between vv. 10b and 13a. Verse 14 escalates the wicked's evil craving to his accepting the bribe that perverts justice. The wicked misuse both their ears (v. 13) and their bosoms (v. 14); they callously close their ears to the cry of the poor and weakly open their bosoms to the bribe. The concluding refrain of justice triumphing over the wicked reinforces the subunit's theme.

13 Verse 13a specifies the wicked person's lack of righteousness, justice, and mercy (cf. vv. 3, 10b) by describing him as the one who *stops* [see 17:28] *his ear* [see 2:2] *to* [lit. "from"] *the cry (mizzaʿ*^{a}*qat) of the poor (dāl,* see 10:15), implying his cruelty and/or insensibility to justice (cf. 24:7; 1 Sam. 25:10-11; Job 31:13-40; Neh. 5:1-11). *Z*^{e}*ʿāqâ* refers to poor's "loud and agonized 'crying' out in acute distress, calling for help and seeking deliverance with this emotion-laden utterance."[77] The cry of distress serves as an accusation or appeal; someone who is threatened or has been assaulted calls with utmost urgency for assistance (2 Sam. 13:19; Job 17:7; Neh. 5:1, 6; Isa. 5:7; Jer. 20:8). "When the heart is hard, the ear is deaf" (1 Sam. 25:10-11; cf. 3:27-28; 18:23; 24:11-12; Job 22:7; 29:14-16; 31:16-17). Verset B of the synthetic chiastic parallels answers this "active inactivity" with the lex talionis consequence: the wicked person's own cry for deliverance at his time of need (cf. 1:28) will not be answered. The emphatic coordinator *indeed* has a distinctly logical force[78] linking the consequence to the cause, and so it makes perfectly plain that the antecedent of the pronoun *himself (hûʾ)* is "the one who shuts his ear," not "the poor." *Will also [ad sensum] . . . cry out (yiqrāʾ;* see 16:21) probably has the more specific connotations attached to *zʿq/ṣʿq* "a cry for help" (1:28; cf. Pss. 3:4[5]; 4:1[2], 3[4]; Mic. 3:4). *And not be answered* (cf. 1:28; 16:1) by the LORD (21:3, 7, and 12) or by his surrogate king at the time of judgment (see 20:8, 26; cf. Exod. 22:22-24[21-23]; Judg. 1:6-7; 1 Sam. 15:33; Luke 18:21-35). The Syr. and Aram. Targ. add "God" to relieve the ambiguity. The merciful obtain mercy (3:3-4; 19:17; Matt. 5:7;

77. G. Hasel, *TDOT,* 4:115, s.v. *zāʿaq.*

78. *IBHS,* p. 663, P. 39.3.4d.

Luke 6:38), but the callous will not pitied (cf. Ps. 109:6-20; Matt. 18:23-35; 25:31-46; Jas. 2:13).[79]

14 This proverb escalates the wickedness of the impious and ethical in perverting righteousness and justice from callously resisting the cry of the poor (v. 13) to capitulating to bribes (v. 14; see 15:27; 17:8, 23; 18:16; 19:6). Whereas they could resist the cry of the poor for mercy and justice, they cannot resist compromising gifts, even when they are filled with indignation against wrongdoers. The self-serving *gift* (see 15:27) is matched by the justice-perverting *bribe* (6:35; 17:8; cf. Exod. 23:8). *In secret* (i.e., in unrighteous concealment; see 9:17; cf. Deut 13:6[7]; 27:15) is defined as *in the bosom* (see 17:23), probably of the briber or possibly of the bribed (cf. 16:33). The outward expression of *anger* (see 14:17) is complemented by the *strong* (see 10:15) inward *wrath* (6:34) of the bribed for a perceived wrong by the briber. In this synonymous parallelism verset B emphasizes and/or concretizes verset A.[80] This precise parallelism suggests that *subdues* (or pacifies; see n. 22) is gapped in verset B. The bribe's wickedness is symbolized by its having to be carried in the breast pouch and given in discreet secrecy to avoid public scrutiny (cf. 21:8). Although the turning away of wrath through virtue is positive (cf. 15:1; 29:8), the turning away of righteous indignation (cf. 24:8) by a bribe is negative.

15 After the two negative proverbs about injustice — that is, refusing to hear the cry of the poor (v. 13) but being pacified by a bribe (v. 14) — v. 15 draws the second partial subunit to its conclusion by returning to the positive theme of the unit. Justice will be done, bringing joy to the righteous and terror to the wicked. As the topic "the way of the LORD" in 10:29a was gapped in 10:29b so here the topic *doing justice* (see 21:3, 7) is gapped in verset B. The parallels are precisely antithetical: *joy* [see 10:28] *to the righteous person* (see I: 97) versus *terror to those who do iniquity* (see 10:29b). Verset A may be an intentional pun. It can mean, that the Righteous One feels joy in doing justice, striking terror in evildoers (v. 12). It certainly means that joy comes to the righteous in the finished product of justice that guarantees their victory over the wicked. By contrast, evildoers, who use violence and deception against society's weaker members, will be filled with terror when the finished process of justice throws them into the destruction that they themselves had done. "In the final analysis it has to be said that 'from the LORD a man gets justice' (29:26; [cf. 21:12])."[81]

79. *Papyrus Insinger* (33:15) contains a similar proverb: "Whoever leaves the weak alone in his need will break out in loud cries, when he himself will no longer be protected" (*AEL*, 3:211).

80. Note that the first three words in verset B have the unvoiced guttural /*ḥ*/ and the last word its voiced equivalent /*ʿ*/.

81. Farmer, *Proverbs and Ecclesiastes,* p. 87.

16-18 The final partial subunit is linked with the first (vv. 10-12) by the paronomasia on "prudence" (i.e., *haśkîl,* v. 11b; *maśkîl,* v. 12a; *haśkēl,* v. 16a) in reversing the direction from becoming prudent to abandoning it. Once again its final line represents the triumph of the righteous over the wicked (vv. 12, 15, 18). It is bound to the second partial sub-unit (vv. 13-15) by co-referencing the death of evildoers (v. 15b) with apostates (v. 16). Whereas the second partial subunit elaborated on the injustice and callousness of the wicked in v. 10b, the third develops in its center the wicked person's craving for pleasure in v. 10a. The concentric circle forming the resulting frame around this center sounds the grim warning that a lover of pleasure will find death instead. Instead of the pleasure he sought at the expense of others, he finds death (v. 16), poverty (v. 17), and the miseries he inflicted on others to gratify his lust (v. 18).

16 Using the metaphor of "way," verset A presents the foolish journey of *a human being* (*'ādām;* see 3:13; 16:1) *who strays* (*tô'eh;* see 7:25; 10:17; 14:22) *from the way* (*midderek;* see 1:15) *of being prudent* (*haśkēl;* see I: 94; 1:3; 21:12). As every motion has an end, so every journey has a goal (cf. 2 Pet. 2:21). Ironically the apostate rebelled to settle down in final peace and victory, but he *will come to* his final and irretrievable *rest* [see 14:33][82] *in the* hapless *congregation* (*biqhal;* see 5:14) *in the realm* (lit., of the realm) *of the dead* (*rᵉpā'îm;* see 2:18)! Isaiah sharply contrasts the death of the *rᵉpā'îm,* who while living were tyrants, with the death of the LORD's saints. Of the former he predicts: "They are now dead *(mētîm),* they live no more; those *rᵉpā'îm* do not rise. You punished them and brought them to ruin; you wiped out all memory of them" (Isa. 26:14). Of the latter, however, he sings: "But your dead *(mēteykā)* will live; their bodies will rise. You who dwell in the dust, wake up and shout for joy. Your dew is like the dew of the morning; the earth will give birth to her *rᵉpā'îm*" (Isa. 26:19). Many think "come to rest" denotes a premature death, but the point of the proverb is that the apostate's goal and terminus is death, not life (see I: 104; cf. 10:17; 11:19; 12:28; 13:13, 14; 14:12 [= 16:25, 27; 15:24; 19:16; 22:4]).

17 Verses 15 and 17 contrast two kinds of pleasure, that which is

82. In its comprehensive sense *nûaḥ* means "to be at rest/at peace/undisturbed/quiet," as shown by its connection with *šqṭ* "to be undisturbed/at peace" (see Job 3:13, 26; Isa. 14:7), *yšn* "to sleep" and *škb* "to lie" (Job 3:13; cf. Isa. 57:2), and *šlh* "to have rest" (Job 3:26), the opposite of *rgz* "to be in turmoil" (3:17). This rest describes different situations: cessation from work on the Sabbath (Exod. 20:11; 23:12), the situation of those freed from oppression by an enemy who enjoy peace (Neh. 9:28; Isa. 23:12), and the state of the dead (Job 3:17). All these nuances are favorable, but here they are ironic. "Every word in the second line is charged with irony. The rebel, who must roam at will, is only hastening to lose his mobility (*shall rest,* RV), his independence (*in the congregation,* KJV, RV), and his life *(of the dead)*" (Kidner, *Proverbs,* p. 144).

the reward of virtue versus the love of it. Sandwiched between this frame that grimly warns of final death (vv. 16, 18), this proverb warns against the love of pleasure because it leads to perpetual loss on the way to the grave. In dramatic irony, the person who chases after the pleasures of life comes only to lack what is desirable and necessary to life (*contra* 10:22; cf. Luke 6:24; 16:25). Its chiastic synonymous parallels match, in its inner core, the topic and cause *the one who loves* [see 1:22] *pleasure* (or "joy"; see 10:28), which the parallel concretizes as *the one who loves wine* [cf. 9:2, 5; 20:1] *and olive oil* (see 5:3). The outer frame predicates the negative consequences — that is, *is a destitute* [see 11:24] *person* (*'îš;* see I: 89) and *will not become rich* (see 10:4). The movement from a nominal clause, expressed by "is," to a verbal clause, expressed by "become," creates a sense of movement, but the opposite movement used here from a verbal to a nominal clause feels more settled (cf. Lam. 5:19). This construction projects the lover of pleasure, who should be equated with "one who hastens to get rich," into an endless cycle of poverty (21:5). Both wine and oil symbolize festive pleasure: the wine for drinking, the oil for anointing the body (27:9; 2 Sam. 14:2; Song 1:3; Amos 6:6). Among other uses, wine heightens joy at festive celebrations (cf. Gen. 21:8; 1 Chr. 12:39[40]).[83] Oil is a symbol of God's rich blessings (Deut. 33:24) and is associated with joy. It was used in cosmetics and perfumery, often in connection with festivities. The phrase "oil of joy" (Ps. 45:7[8]; Isa. 61:3) symbolizes religious joy.[84] But when one chases after these pleasures as ends in themselves, they become vices. As the result of virtue, pleasure is a token of God's blessings and a source of positive emotion (cf. 10:28; 12:20; 15:23; 21:17). But apart from virtue, where pleasures are loved rather than God (cf. 2 Tim. 3:4), they lead to unrelieved grief (cf. 14:13; 15:21).

18 The partial unit vv. 16-18 again draws to a conclusion by asserting the triumph of the righteous over the wicked. As in vv. 13-15, this positive proverb follows two negative ones. *A wicked person* [see 21:10, 12] *is a ransom* [6:35] *for the righteous* (21:12, 15). *Even* represents verset B as underscoring and clarifying verset A. *The treacherous person* [*bôgēd;* see I: 110] *comes in the place of the upright one* (see I: 98). This commercial imagery escalates the ruin of the lover of pleasure. The wicked person not only does not get rich but finds himself a "ransom," facing death. The metaphor

83. Wine was used for nourishment (Gen. 14:18; 27:25) and comfort (Prov. 31:6-7; Zech. 10:7) as well as for pleasure (Judg. 9:13; Ps. 104:15; Eccl. 2:3; 9:7; 10:19 [W. Dommershausen, *TDOT,* 6:62, s.v. *yayin*]).

84. Olive oil was also used in lamps (Exod. 25:6; 27:20); for food, such as shortening in cooking (1 K. 17:12-16); in sacrifices and worship (Lev. 2:16; 8:26); in various consecration ceremonies, such as the anointing of the king (1 Sam. 16:13; 1 K. 1:39), and in the consecration of the tabernacle and its contents (Lev. 8:10).

"ransom" designates compensation money to pay a penalty to free a prisoner and save his life (cf. Exod. 21:29-30; Prov. 13:8; Isa. 43:3). Certainly literal "ransom money" is not intended because the righteous has no debt to pay. The metaphor represents the righteous as in the place of the penalty (i.e., distress) because the wicked plotted it, not because the righteous deserved it. But the wicked comes in his stead into the place of distress, and the righteous go free (see 11:8). The metaphor connotes that the wicked, not the righteous, are the expendable members of society.[85] The metaphor should not be pushed to walk on all fours by asking to whom the ransom is paid (cf. 6:35; 13:8).[86] The proverb teaches that the merciful Righteous One (v. 12) turns the tables against the expendable wicked and pops them into the place of the righteous whom they oppress, not that sinners pay the debt of the righteous (cf. 21:12; Ps. 49:7-9[8-10], 15[16]). Rashi illustrates the truth by pointing to Haman taking the place of Mordecai (Esth. 7:10).[87]

(5) The Contentious Wife (21:19)

19 The "better . . . than" structure of this proverb — its thought of a contentious wife destroying the closest social relationship, and its function of dividing units — repeats v. 9. However, its verset A escalates *to dwell* on a corner of a roof to the solitariness, discomfort, danger, and privation of living *in a desert (midbār) land,* an uncivilized land where one can barely eke out an existence.[88] This portrayal of the nagged husband is similar to Job's depiction of the oppressed poor who go about their labor of foraging food as wild donkeys in a desert (*bammidbār,* Job 24:5). Here he is drenched by mountain rains and hugs the rocks for lack of shelter (cf. Job 24:8). Such a lonesome, dangerous experience is preferable to the closeness of a *contentious wife* (see 21:9) and the anger that she unleashes. Moreover, "with a shared house" in v. 9b is escalated to *vexing* (lit. "and/with vexation"; see 12:16). Since "contentious" denotes stirring up conflicts with others, *kāʿas* refers to the provocation she incites in her husband (17:25), not to her own irritation (cf. 12:16).

85. Kidner, *Proverbs,* p. 144.

86. Delitzsch (*Proverbs,* p. 316) thinks that the righteousness of God is satisfied by passing the righteous and demanding it of the wicked, and Garrett (*Proverbs,* p. 182) supposes that the wicked is a ransom payment for the sins of the righteous.

87. Lyons, "Rashi's *Commentary,*" p. 109.

88. *Midbār* describes three kinds of land: pastureland (Ps. 65:12[13]; Jer. 23:10; Joel 2:22), large areas of land in which oases or cities and towns exist here and there (Josh. 15:61), and uninhabited and/or uninhabitable land (Deut. 32:10; Job 38:26; Jer. 9:2[1]).

(6) The Endurance of the Righteous versus the Death of the Wicked (21:20-29)

This subunit contrasts the eternal endurance of the righteous with the death of the wicked. It consists of two partial subunits, vv. 20-23, and 24-29. As the "better . . . than" proverb of v. 9 is drawn more closely to v. 10 than to v. 8, so also v. 19 is tied more narrowly with vv. 20ff. by the motif of dwelling place and perhaps by the reference to *ṣᵉdāqâ* "righteousness" in v. 21, the third verse after the pattern of vv. 12, 15, and 18.

20-23 These four proverbs feature the wise/righteous. After an exceptionally unbalanced antithetical parallel in v. 20, placing heavy weight on the wise over against the fool, the remaining three synthetic parallels set forth the advantages of the wise/righteous. He finds, among other things, "a supply of grain and oil" (v. 20a), life (v. 21b), victory over evil and the wicked (v. 22), and security (v. 23). The partial subunit assumes that the Covenant Keeper supplies these blessings. The wise and righteous are brought together by the concentric circles of "wise" (vv. 20a, 22a) around "one who pursues righteousness" (v. 21a). Right thinking, not brains as such, characterizes the wise. In sum, the subunits have moved from accenting the wicked and their punishment (vv. 5-7), to the punishment of the wicked and the triumph of the righteous (vv. 10-18), to the enduring prosperity of the righteous (vv. 20-21) in their triumph (vv. 22-23). As noted above, the last two are linked by the refrain using *ṣedeq* as their second word with reference to the triumph of the righteous. This keyword also binds this subunit to the whole (see v. 3). Moreover, the final subunit is bound to the first by the catchword *'ôṣār* ("treasure"/"supply," vv. 6, 20) and to the second by *šemen* ("oil," vv. 17, 20) and the motif of greed (v. 20b). These links assert that the righteous come to possess the treasure and oil that the wicked crave.

20 The catchword "oil," the symbol of wealth and luxury, links v. 20 with v. 17, juxtaposing respectively the wicked person's loss with the wise person's gain. The proverb is also connected with v. 19 by comparing and contrasting dwelling in a desert with dwelling in a "pasture." Its antithetical parallels, juxtaposing "wise" and "fool" in its inner core, contrast the wise person's continual abundance (3:16; 8:18, 21; 10:4; 12:11; 24:4; 28:19) with the fool's desire for instant gratification. The extremely heavy Hebrew construction of four more words in verset A versus one more in verset B (i.e., "gulps it down") underscores the contrast between endurance and brevity. *A desirable* [see 1:22] *supply of food* [see n. 32; 21:6] *and oil* [see n. 33; 21:17] *are in the dwelling place* [lit. "in the pasture"] *of the wise* (see 21:11). The zoological metaphor "pasture" connotes provision, security, and peace.[89] Ol-

89. *Nāweh* (masc. in sing.) and *nᵉ'ôt* (fem. in pl.) occur 45 times to denote literally animal "pasturage": for jackals (Isa. 34:13); for flocks (2 Sam. 7:8); for camels (Ezek.

ive oil here refers to both its utilitarian and its aesthetic values and together with grain represents the year-round agricultural cycle. Grain was harvested in the spring, and the olive oil pressed in the fall. *But* sets up the antithesis with *a fool* (see 15:20). *Gulps his down* (*yᵉballᵉʿennû;* lit. "gulps it down") signifies "to snatch with the mouth and to gulp down through the esophagus."[90] The masculine suffix, glossed "his," refers to the merism "supply and oil" as a unity. To refer it to the wise person and treat "gulps him down" as a metaphor for "to plunder" gives the fool the last word, contradicting the book's theology. Gulping food probably connotes greedily eating before anyone else and a lack of restraint in instant consumption. It is tempting to think of the fool as one large digestive tract.

21 Verse 21 elaborates the reward of the wise (v. 20a), explaining in verset A why the wise person's dwelling place is filled endlessly with grain and oil, and escalating this reward to life, prosperity and social honor in verset B (cf. 3:2, 4, 6, 8, 10; 8:18; Matt. 5:6; 10:41, 42; Luke 6:38; Heb. 6:10). A pun on *ṣᵉdāqâ* ("righteousness/prosperity") underscores the connection of the cause of spiritual virtue with the consequence of material benefit (cf. 2:1-11 with 3:1-10; 13:21). The "wise," who encompasses this proverb (vv. 20, 22), is now defined by the metaphor *the one who pursues,* as in a chase (see 11:19; 15:9), *righteousness* [see I: 97] *and kindness* (see I: 100), an unusual compound used instead of the customary "righteousness and justice" (see 21:3) or "kindness and reliability" (see 3:3). But in his intense pursuit, as a serendipity he comes on something else; he *finds* [see 3:13] *life* (see I: 104), *prosperity* (*ṣᵉdāqâ,* a metonymy for the tangible results of righteousness; see 8:18), and *honor* (see 3:16), three benefits that express the comprehensive and high gain that only the LORD can grant.[91]

22 The proverb escalates the material gain of *the wise* (*ḥākām;* see v. 20) through spiritual virtue (v. 21a) to a climactic assertion: nothing and no one can stop his triumph over evil and wicked men. Implicitly likening him to a warrior, the wise, who may have been poor and despised at first (cf. Eccl. 9:16), is stronger than a multitude who lack his spiritual virtue (cf. Pss. 18:29[30]; 144:1). In narrative form, marked by narrative *and,* the synthetic parallels represent first his attack, represented by "to go up," and then his subsequent victory, represented by "he brings down." Both aspects of the height and depth imagery underscore the seemingly impossible achievement

---

25:5). It is used figuratively for the dwelling place of human beings (Prov. 21:20; 24:15; Isa. 32:18) or the nation Israel (Jer. 23:3; 50:19), or of God in Jerusalem (2 Sam. 15:25; Isa. 33:20) or in heaven (Jer. 25:30), or of God himself (Jer. 50:7).

90. J. Schüpphaus, *TDOT,* 2:139, s.v. *bālaʿ.*

91. "To find," notes Meinhold (*Sprüche,* p. 357), "plays a role at important passages in connection with valuable goods in the Book of Proverbs (2:5; 3:4, 13; 4:2; 8:17, 35; 16:20; 18:22; 19:8; 21:21; 24:14)."

of the wise. In verset A he *scales* (*ʿālâ;* lit. "to go up") the high *city* (see 1:21), entailing its high *wall,* and single-handedly overpowers its mighty *warriors* (*gibbōrîm;* see 16:32; cf. Isa. 21:17; Jer. 48:41; Ezek. 39:20; Joel 2:7; 3:9 [4:9]), who try to defend their city by pouring down a hail of arrows, heavy stones, and various arms against him. In verset B the solitary warrior pulls down the city's formidable walls and towers that seemed so invincible and impregnable that its citizens felt unconcerned. *Pulls down* (*wayyōred;* lit. "causes to go down"; see 1:12) in the *Qal* essentially signifies the direction of movement from above to below, the common antonym of *ʿālâ,* and in the *Hiphil* of its object (e.g., demolishing a fortress; Amos 3:11).[92] *Strong* (*ʿōz;* see 10:15) qualifies the source of security as so formidable that it seems impregnable and invincible. *Its security* (see 14:26), a metonymy for the city's protection, such as its defensive wall and tower (cf. Amos 3:11), denotes the source or ground of feeling so secure and confident that one can be unconcerned. The concentric circle "wise person" (vv. 20, 22) surrounds "one who pursues righteousness and kindness" (v. 21), and its proverbial match (v. 23) is about guarding one's speech. The point of the figurative proverb is that the wise through spiritual virtue overcomes his enemies and surmounts every evil (14:26), not that "brains are more important in war even than picked troops and fortified positions."[93] The proverb represents the final superiority of spiritual virtue over vices such as intimidation, censure, systematic spreading of lies, murder (cf. 2 Cor. 10:4), and trusting in one's own might (3:7; 16:32; 24:5; Eccl. 9:16). In spite of insurmountable odds, including famine, nakedness, the sword (Rom. 8:35), and spiritual forces of evil in heavenly places (Eph. 6:12), Christ builds his church through saints who wear God's armor (Isa. 59:17; Eph. 6:10-18).

23 Verses 22 and 23 are linked by military motifs, moving from the offense of the wise against evil to his defense against it. Verse 23 explains that the wise escape the distresses that the wicked implicitly design for them through guarding their speech. Right speaking is connected with wisdom (vv. 20, 22) and righteousness (v. 21). Its parallel versets represent the subject (i.e., the cause) and its predicate (i.e., the consequence), the same as in v. 21, but whereas that verse also pertained to the pursuit of virtue, this verse deals with the defense of virtue. *He who guards* [2:8] *his mouth* [see 13:3] *and his tongue* (see 21:6) is highly emphatic. These common metonymies for speech normally occur in parallel (cf. 10:31; 15:2; 31:26), but here they are exceptionally compounded to stress the necessity of guarding one's speech. The syntax of its synthetic parallels requires interpreting verset B as the predicate of this nominal clause, demanding that *is* be supplied to join the subject and

92. G. Mayer, *TDOT,* 6:316, s.v. *yārad.*
93. McKane, *Proverbs,* p. 551.

predicate. The person who is careful about his speech is *one who guards (šōmēr) his life* (*nepeš;* see I: 90) *from distresses* (*miṣṣārôt;* see 1:27). The unique plural suggests the manifold miseries that result from rash speech. The pun "one who guards" (which first accents "to be on the lookout" and then "to preserve"; see 2:8) links the cause and consequences as "righteousness" did in v. 21. The one who observes carefully his mouth and tongue and exercises great care to defend them against evil speaking also protects his life against extreme necessity and/or misfortune, which produce anguish (see I: 101; cf. 10:19; 11:12; 12:23; 13:3; 15:28; 29:20; Jas. 3:5-8).[94] Some people have tongues long enough to cut their own throats.

24-29 The final subunit draws 20:29–21:29 to a conclusion with a catalogue of wicked types of people (vv. 24-29), matching the series of wicked types in its body's first subunit (cf. vv. 4-7): the proud (21:4, 24), the sluggard contrasted with the diligent (21:5, 25-26), the liar (21:6, 28), and, climactically, the brazenly wicked (v. 29). These four wicked types — the arrogant and sluggard (vv. 24-26), and the liar and brazenly wicked (vv. 28-29) — form a concentric circle around the hypocritical worshiper in v. 27. The catchword "sacrifice" links the subunit to verse 3, which sounds the broad unit's theme. The catchword "to work" (*ʿaśôt)* in v. 25 also links the subunit with v. 3. Several antithetical parallels contrast these failed inferior types of people with the righteous/the upright, who do not lack (v. 26) but endure forever (vv. 27, 28).[95]

24-26 On the lexical level the first pair of inferior types are paired by the catchword *ʿśh,* "acts" (v. 24), "work" (v. 25). The pun points to their semantic connection. Both destroy the community: the former by his aggressive destructive acts, the latter by his refusal to work. Verses 25-26 are linked by the catchword *ʾwh,* which also points up their semantic connection — that is, the craving of the sluggard.

24 The topic shifts dramatically from the wise (vv. 20-23) to his antagonist, the mocker, who heads the list of wicked types. All the terms applied to the mocker entail *aggressive* pride, suggesting a connection with the military imagery for the wise in vv. 23-24. By his spiritual virtue the wise overcomes him, and by his prudent speech he defends himself against him. Like v. 23, this proverb is a single nominal clause, presenting the subject in verset A and the predicate in verset B. The two halves cohere by the consonance of *zēd* ("insolent") and *zādôn* ("fury and pride"). To say that the proud

94. Ahiqar (7.98) taught: "More than all watchfulness watch thy mouth. . . . For a word is a bird: once released no man can recapture it" (*ANET,* pp. 428-29).

95. A whole series of catchwords and phonological patterns link the subunit: *ʿśh* (vv. 24, 25), *taʾawat* (vv. 25, 26), *ršʿ* (vv. 27, 29), the alliteration of *temîtennû* and *yebîʾennû* (vv. 25, 27), the sequence */z b/* in *zebaḥ* and *kezābîm* (vv. 27, 28), and *ʾîš* (vv. 28, 29).

act with pride is not tautology (a logical problem), but a rhetorical means of intensification, as in "boys will be boys."[96] The proverb does not aim as much to define the mocker as to explain that his fury against God and humanity stems from his exaggerated opinion of his self-importance. *The insolent*[97] and *presumptuous person*[98] describes him as one who disregards God, the wise and revealed truth. *"Mocker* [see I: 114; 1:22; 21:11] *is his name"* (see 10:27) refers to his character description (see 18:10). He *is one who behaves* [see 13:16] *with insolent* [see n. 38] *fury* ("fury of pride," his exaggerated opinion of his importance; see 11:2; 13:6),[99] underscoring pride as the spiritual source of his antagonism against the wise. Sir. 10:7 (cf. 10:7-18) also links arrogance with injustice. The only way to rid the community of strife and shame is to banish the mocker (22:10).

25-26 This proverb pair is linked both by the chiastically arranged catchword and topic *ta'ᵃwâ* ("craving"), the first word in v. 25a and the last in v. 26a (= "greedily"), and by the syntax of sluggard (v. 25a) functioning as the antecedent of "he craves" in v. 26 (see n. 39).[100] The connection with the unit's theme and tincture is clear. The craving sluggard is lumped with the

96. So Van Leeuwen, *Proverbs,* p. 194.

97. *Zēd* occurs 13 times, otherwise always in pl., and, possibly apart from Ps. 19:13(14), of insolent people. Malachi (3:15) uses the adjective with reference to "evildoers" and "those who challenge God." The psalmist uses it to refer to those who attack him (86:14), mock the pious without restraint (119:51), forge lies (119:69), and dig pits (119:85); he prays that God will put them to shame (119:78) and not let them oppress him (119:122). Jeremiah (43:2) uses it of those who reject his prophecy. The LORD is said to rebuke them (Ps. 119:21), and he will cause their arrogance to cease (Isa. 13:11; cf. Mal. 4:1 [3:19]).

98. *Yāḥîr* occurs otherwise only in Hab. 2:5 with reference to a tyrant. In Hab. 2:5 the LXX glosses it by *kataphronētēs* ("contemptuous") and the Syr. by *maraḥa* ("willful," "presumptous," "headstrong"), but here the LXX renders it by *alazōn,* "swaggering, boastful, braggart," and the Syr. omits it.

99. *HALOT* glosses *'ebrat* as "outburst" in Job 40:11 (see 11:4, 23); Prov. 21:24; 22:8; Isa. 16:6; Jer. 48:30. Driver ("Problems in the Hebrew Text," *Bib* 32 [1951] 185) questionably limits this meaning to Prov. 21:24 and Isa. 16:6. The NIV and NRSV gloss it as "insolence" in Isa. 16:6; Jer. 48:30 and as "fury"/"anger" in Prov 22:8. The NRSV renders *'ebrôt 'appekā* (Job 40:11) as "overflowings of your anger," but the NIV as "fury of your anger," and Pope (*Job,* p. 316) as "your furious wrath." Instructively, in these passages, aside from Prov. 22:8, it is used in conjunction with pride. "Fury" nicely suits this text as well. In sum, in its clear uses *'ebrâ* always means "fury/wrath," and in a few ambiguous uses it questionably means "excess," making "overweening" (NIV) and "arrogant" (NRSV) unlikely interpretive options.

100. So the majority of commentators; but Meinhold (*Sprüche,* 2:360) holds that the subject is the indefinite "one" (= "people"; *IBHS,* p. 72, P. 4.5b). "Sluggard," however, is more natural, and because he is wicked it forms a better antithesis to "righteous" in verset B than neutral "one."

wicked, who craves for himself without sharing, in contrast to the righteous, who rejoices in doing mercy and justice (see vv. 3, 15a, 26b; cf. 11:24-26; 14:21; 19:17; 22:9; Ps. 37:21-26). The insolent mocker plunders the needy; the sluggard is passive. He is no better than a bandit (cf. 6:11).

25 The sluggard, the subject of both synthetic parallels, stands opposed to the diligent in v. 5. Instead of "doing" *(ʿᵃśôt)* righteousness and justice, the theme of the unit (vv. 4, 7, 15), he refuses to "do" *(ʿᵃśôt)* anything (cf. vv. 7, 15). The relatively rare tactic of introducing verset B with "because" and sporting the only other occurrence of "refuse" *(mēʾᵃnû)* in Collection II links it even more closely with v. 7b. The connection suggests the sluggard's connection with the "wicked" in v. 7a. This parasite on society (see 6:6), on account of laziness, his fatal spiritual flaw, obviously does not do justice (see 19:15). "Craving" also links the proverb with another accent in this unit (see vv. 10, 20). Verset A links the cause, *the craving* (*taʾᵃwâ;* see 10:24) *of the sluggard* (see I: 114) with its consequence, *kills him* (see 19:18; i.e., he loses a relationship forever with the living God in addition to undergoing clinical death). Verset B, marked by *because,* substantiates verset A (see 21:7). *His hands* [see 6:10] *refuse* [see 21:7] *to work* (*laʿᵃśôt;* see 21:3, 7, 15). Craving refers to aspirations rooted deeply within his personality, but its unclear objects could be his inordinate desire to do nothing but sleep or, more probably, his passion for the necessities of life such as food and drink. The substantiating parallel, "because his hands refuse to work," implies that his cravings could be fulfilled by work (see 13:4; 19:24). The appetite keeps normal people alive by driving them to work to satisfy it, but it kills the sluggard because his hands refuse to satisfy it. His unfulfilled craving kills him both by starvation and frustration (13:12).

26 The addition to the chiastically arranged noun *taʾᵃwâ* (vv. 25a, 26a) of the verb *ʾāwâ* ("to lust/crave/desire") in v. 26a underscores the sluggard's greed. The consequence of the sluggard's ungratified craving implicitly escalates from his own death (v. 25b) to his having nothing to share with the needy and thereby to save their lives (v. 26b). The antithetical parallel, "the sluggard" versus "the righteous," and its predicates, "craves" and "gives," are imprecise, implying that the sluggard is not righteous but wicked, while the righteous gives to others without himself lacking. The emphatic qualifiers "greedily" for self and "without holding back" from others are fairly precise. *All day long* (lit. "the whole of the day") shows that he constantly, without any relief, *craves* (or "lusts," *hitʾawwâ;* lit. "lusts for himself"; see 13:4). To this temporal intensity both the grammatical form of the verb, "he lusts for himself,"[101] and the syntax *greedily (taʾᵃwâ)* add a qualitative intensity to his greed. *But* introduces the antithesis. *The righteous* [see

101. A benefactive *Hithpael* (*IBHS,* p. 430, P. 26.2e).

10:3; 21:3, 12, 15, 18] *gives* (see 1:4) refers here to his gracious bestowal of the basic necessities for which the wicked crave. *And* adds the emphatic qualification *without sparing* (lit. "he does not restrain" or hoard; see 10:19; 11:24).

27 The hypocritical worshiper, who stands in the middle of the pairs of nefarious types, is labeled "wicked," a term applicable to all four, and clearly connects him with them. Verset A repeats 15:8a with the exception that "abomination" is absolute, not qualified by "to the LORD" (see n. 41). Nevertheless, since the sacrifice is offered to the LORD, we should assume that it is an abomination to him. Verset B, through its use of the a fortiori argument *how much more* (see 11:31; 19:7), escalates the certainty of the LORD's rejection of the sacrifice, *when,* which is elided, the hypocrite manipulates the cult to abet his nefarious plan against the community. *He brings it* is the common idiom "to bring (an offering, to sacrifice)" (Gen. 4:3; Num. 15:25; Mal. 1:13);[102] *with evil intent* (*b*^{e}*zimmâ;* see 10:24) denotes a crass plan to hurt the community. "The *a fortiori* construction is directed towards a special intention of deceit or malevolence connected with the bringing of the sacrifice."[103] This is not about a damaged sacrifice (Mal. 1:8, 13-14) or even a sacrifice by one who is otherwise unethical (Gen. 4:5 [cf. 1 John 3:12]; Prov. 15:8; Isa. 1:10-17), but about a sacrifice calculated to make God a minister of sin. One can think of pretending a special piety aimed to lead others astray and make them their easy prey (cf. 2 Sam. 15:7-13; 1 K. 21:9-12; Prov. 7:14-15; Matt. 23:14).

28-29 The last pair in this catalogue of wicked men are linked both by unique constructions involving the catchword *ʾîš* ("person") with a narrower determination, "listening" (v. 28b) and "wicked" (v. 29a), and by alliteration of initial *ʿēd* ("witness," 28a) and *hēʿēz* ("make firm," v. 29a). In this way the false witness is linked with the wicked and represented as audaciously and boldly asserting his lies. This brazenness brings the catalogue to a climax.

28 The imprecise antithetical parallel of v. 28, "false witness" and "one who listens," suggests that the false witness is not a reliable listener whereas the true witness listens attentively and critically (cf. 14:5, 25). Likewise the imprecise antithesis of their predicates (or the consequences) implies that the former "perishes [and does not have the last word]" and the latter "tes-

102. *HALOT,* p. 114, s.v. *bôʾ.* Delitzsch (*Proverbs,* p. 319, citing Hitzig), interprets *b*^{e}*,* not as circumstantial, qualifying the situation of sacrifice, but as *beth pretti* ("in exchange for") the price paid in exchange for the villainy. However, one expects the verb *kpr* "to make atonement" (see 16:6) for that meaning, and it does not work well with the a fortiori argument.

103. McKane, *Proverbs,* p. 560.

tifies successfully [and does not perish]." The unique expression *a false witness (ʿēd-kᵉzābîm),* which is elsewhere expressed by *ʿēd-šᵉqār[îm]* (6:19; 12:17) and its equivalent, *yāpîaḥ kᵉzābîm* (6:19; 14:5), may be due to the desire for alliteration with initial *hēʿēz* in v. 29 and for the consonance of /d/ with *yōʾbēd* (*will perish;* see 10:28 and esp. 19:9). The three synonyms refer to a witness (see 12:17) who consciously aims to deceive and disadvantage another. A witness is one who has firsthand knowledge of an event or who can testify on the basis of a report that he has heard (Lev. 5:1). Verset B assumes that this connection between knowledge and testimony for the true witness, who has listened attentively and soberly, will prevail. *But* introduces the antithesis. *A person who listens well* is a unique construction in the Old Testament (cf. 8:34) to underscore that the individual in view is characterized as a listener. He knows how to listen attentively and critically so that his judgment is sound and his testimony reliable. Even God listens in this way (15:29). The false witness either cannot or will not listen to the report objectively because he has a hidden agenda that distorts the truth and so is unable to give trustworthy testimony. By contrast, the true witness, who loves reality, listens attentively and critically to the evidence and so is able to give credible testimony. Such a person *will testify* [see n. 43; 18:23] *successfully* (see n. 44). Though for a moment the false witness has his word, in the final analysis he will be destroyed and the true witness will have the last word. The Ultimate Agent, without excluding a court decree (Deut. 19:19) vindicating the true witness and silencing the false, is the God of truth.

29 The effrontery of the wicked person, an abstraction for the liar and probably all the inferior types in this subunit, brings the catalogue to a climactic conclusion. No righteousness, justice (21:3), or mercy (21:10), the concerns of this unit, can be expected from the brazenly wicked. This antithetical proverb contrasts the subjects — "a wicked person" and "the upright" — and their behavior, that is, impudent, cheeky, shameless behavior versus a cautious consideration to pick the way that leads to life, not death. *A wicked person* (*ʾîš rāšāʿ;* see I: 109) is a unique construction (cf. 11:7), suggesting a deliberate connection with v. 28b. *Becomes brazen* (see 7:13) means that he becomes impudent, cheeky, and shameless in his behavior. 'Abot 5:23 says that an impudent face is destined for Gehenna. If the *Kethib* is followed, verset B means that the upright unswervingly follows righteousness and justice (cf. 4:26-27). *But* marks the antithesis. To *as for the upright* (see I: 98) emphatic *he* is added to heighten the antithesis to the wicked and his behavior.[104] The MT and the versions vary between "fixes" (*yākîn,* i.e., goes on his way unwaveringly, see 6:18)[105] and *discerns* (*yābîn,* he picks his

104. *IBHS,* p. 295, P. 16.3.2d.
105. *HALOT,* 2:465, s.v. *kûn.*

steps with nice moral discrimination, see n. 45; 14:8).[106] Although "fixes his steps" offers an antithesis to "fixes his face," "to discern" more subtly offers a better antithesis to the picture of effrontery.[107] The texts and versions (see n. 46) also vary between singular *his way* and "his ways," with little difference in meaning; both refer to all the decisions and the entire direction and destiny of his life.

c. Conclusion: The LORD's Sovereignty over People and Kingdoms (21:30-31)

To be sure, the wicked impudently defy God and his wisdom (v. 29), but no human power can stand before the LORD (vv. 30-31). This proverb pair is linked by the keyword "LORD," by the soundplays between *ḥokmâ* ("wisdom," v. 30) and *milḥāmâ* ("battle," v. 31), and between *t^{e}bûnâ* ("counsel," v. 30) and *t^{e}šû'â* ("success," v. 31) and by the similar syntax of two nominal clauses in each verse. Together with the introduction (21:1-2) this conclusion forms a chiastic frame affirming the LORD's sovereignty over humanity in general (vv. 2, 30) and over kings and their armies in particular (vv. 1, 31). Behind the victory of the righteous/wise over the wicked/fool stands the invincible LORD.

30 Verse 30 protects against misinterpreting v. 29b to mean that a human being, even the upright, has the power to consummate his journey independently from the LORD. The LORD has the final word in realizing the goal. Everything in this proverb stops at the divine name. Phonologically, the first three phrases begin with the alliteration of the negative existential particle *'ên* (*there is no;* see 13:4; 17:16) at their beginnings and of the assonance of feminine /*â*/ at their end: *ḥokmâ* (*wisdom;* see 1:2), *t^{e}bûnâ* (*understanding;* see 2:2), and *'ēṣâ* (*counsel;* see 1:25; cf. 2 Sam. 16:23). The third spills over into the B verset, creating an exceptional AaaB pattern (see also 23:3, 4) and a powerful anaphora. This all comes to a complete halt in the last phrase. The audience is fully expecting *w^{e}'ēn,* ("and there is no"), not *l^{e} neged* (*that can stand before,* i.e., in opposition to his will; cf. *l^{e}neged* in Num. 22:32), and a feminine wisdom noun, not *YHWH* (*the LORD*; see 1:7). These literary effects stop the forward momentum of the repetition and so give God the full majesty and weight due his name. By the triple anaphoric hammer blows "there is no," the proverb drives home the vast and unbridgeable gulf between the best of human wisdom and the LORD's sovereignty. "Wisdom" and "counsel" are used in battle imagery in 2 K. 18:20 and Isa. 10:13, and probably all three words refer explicitly to human military strategy as suggested by 21:31 (cf. 24:5). Obviously the sage's wisdom, counsel, and understanding are not in view, for the LORD begot them and they stand forever

106. McKane, *Proverbs,* p. 562.
107. Toy, *Proverbs,* p. 411.

(8:22-31). The proverb pair of vv. 30-31 does not negate human wisdom but puts it into perspective. Before the LORD, who is infinite in his omniscience and omnipotence, human ability fails to even raise its head above the plain of human folly. Without him, and how much more against him, these significant skills on the human axis do not even exist on the vertical axis (cf. 16:1, 9; 19:21; 20:24; 24:5-6; 27:1; Deut. 32:30; Job 5:13; Ps. 33:10-11; Isa. 8:10; 14:27; 24:29; 46:10; Matt. 2:8, 16; Acts 2:23; 4:27-28; 1 Cor. 1:18-25; 3:19). "The best laid scheme o' mice an' men gang aft a-gley" (Robert Burns).

31 Verset A presents the warhorse, a military innovation that gave the armies using it a surpassing advantage, as a concrete military example of human wisdom. Verset B complements and contrasts this human initiative with the LORD's final word. The difference between the initial human word and the LORD's final word is so great in achieving victory, not necessarily in content, that the conjunction binding the parallels is best glossed *but,* even though the parallels are essentially synthetic, not antithetic. This proverb presupposes that *a* war *horse* that draws the chariot (cf. Ps 20:7[8]; Mic. 5:10[9]) *is prepared* [see 6:8] *for* [the purpose of][108] *the day of* (see 16:4) hand-to-hand fighting in *war* (see 20:18).[109] The warhorse, which functions as a synecdoche for all the paraphernalia of war, was used to pull the war chariot because of its agility, speed, and endurance; it can cover up to 100 kilometers per day.[110] Solomon introduced it to the army as a principal weapon of war (1 K. 10:26-28). He also served as a middle merchant in their trade from Egypt to the Hittites and to the Arameans (1 K. 10:29). In the battle of Qarqar (853 B.C.) against Shalmaneser III, King Ahab of Israel presented the largest contingent of war chariots in the anti-Assyrian coalition.[111] Verset B, however, implicitly warns the king and his counselors against trusting horses and chariots (Ps. 20:7[8]). Something, or better Someone else, is more decisive. *Success* [see 11:14][112] *belongs to*[113] *the LORD* (see 21:1, 30). The secular capability of the warhorse threatened Israel's faith in the LORD and drew heavy theological criticism (cf. Deut. 17:16; Isa. 31:1; Hos. 1:7; Zech. 9:10). Mic. 5:10-16(9-15) equates trust in military hardware with idolatry and witchcraft. This proverb was part and parcel of the king's godly guidance before battle (Prov. 20:18; 24:6; cf. 2 Chr. 32:2-8). The two words of verset B function as a doxology in Jon. 2:9(10), but here the words are reversed, perhaps to make "success" the final word in this unit on the triumph of doing righteous and justice (20:29–21:31).

108. BDB, p. 517, s.v. *l^e*.
109. *HALOT,* 2:589, s.v. *milḥāmâ.*
110. Meinhold, *Sprüche,* 2:362.
111. *ANET,* p. 279.
112. *HALOT,* 4:1,801, s.v. *t^{e}šûʿâ.*
113. BDB, p. 513, s.v. *l^e*.

11. Wealth and Moral Instruction (22:1-16)

1 *A good*[1] *name is more desirable than great riches,*
and to be esteemed is better[2] *than silver and gold.*
2 *Rich and poor meet together;*
the LORD is the Maker of them all.
3 *The shrewd sees evil and hides himself,*[3]
but the gullible pass on and pay the penalty.[4]
4 *The wage*[5] *for humility — the fear-of-the-LORD sort —* [6]
is[7] *riches, honor, and life.*

1. The LXX and Vulg, not the Syr., add "good," but it is uncertain whether they rightly interpret *šēm* or their *Vorlage* had *ṭôb.* In any case, "The usage permits, and the rhythm rather favors, its omission" (Toy, *Proverbs,* p. 420).

2. The text could be read "good favor" (KJV), but this is awkward and rejected by all the ancients.

3. Q reads *wᵉnistār* (= *waw* consecutive + suffix conjugation signifying sequence ["and so"] with the value of the gnomic perfective [see *IBHS,* p. 530, P. 32.2.3a]). K reads either *wᵉyissātēr* (= conjunctive *waw* + habitual imperfect, allowing the logic of the verbs to denote consequence, or *wayyissātēr* (= *waw* consecutive with prefix conjugation, carrying on the gnomic force of the preceding perfective [*IBHS,* p. 555, P. 33.3.1b]). The Q may be due to a desire to harmonize the text with the synoptic parallel in 27:12, and the grammatical parallel *wᵉneʿᵉnāšû* in 22:3b. The LXX (cf. Syr.) may have interpreted 22:3a according to 21:11: "An intelligent man, seeing a bad man severely punished, is himself instructed" (< *ʿārûm rāʾâ rāʿ mᵉyussar nōsar*).

4. The *waw* may be consecutive with the suffix conjugation. In any case, the logic of the lexemes is one of cause and effect.

5. According to D. W. Thomas ("Textual and Philological Notes on Some Passages in the Book of Proverbs," in *WIANE,* p. 289), followed by the REB, "the LXX's *genea* 'offspring' goes back to the Arabic *ʿqb* 'son, offspring,' literally 'that which follows, results, issues.'" But why create a homonym for *ʿqb* when its normal meaning is consistent with the theme of this unit?

6. A sortal appositional construction (*IBHS,* p. 229, P. 2.2c; see v. 5 for the same construction). Plöger (*Sprüche,* p. 251) renders the construction "Demut, (nämlich) der Yahwefurcht"). The emendation of compounding the two religious terms by adding *waw* (so Gemser, *Sprüche,* p. 82; cf. NIV) is pedestrian. If "the fear of the LORD" and "humility" stand in apposition here, as W. J. Dumbrell (*NIDOTTE,* 3:463, s.v. *ʿānāw*) also contends, then they probably also stand as appositional parallels in 15:33, not as distinct virtues. Whybray (*Proverbs,* p. 319) explains *ʿᵃnāwâ* as a scribal gloss to define the fear of the LORD. But of the 14 occurrences of *yirʾat YHWH* in this book, why would a scribe add a unique explanatory gloss here?

7. Semantic pertinence demands taking verset B as the predicate of this nominal clause. Some scholars think that "the fear of the LORD" begins the predicate in verset A. But this is less apposite, for it makes the reward of a spiritual virtue another spiritual virtue plus tangible benefits.

5 *Snares,*[8] *the bird-trap sort,*[9] *are in the way of the perverse;*
the one who would preserve his life keeps far from them.
6 *Dedicate*[10] *a youth*[11] *according to what his way dictates;*
even when he becomes old,[12] *he will not depart from it.*[13]
7 *The rich person rules over poor people,*
and the borrower is a slave to the lender.[14]
8 *The one who sows injustice will reap*[15] *empty deception,*
and the rod he wields in his fury will fail.[16]

8. The meaning of *ṣēn* is uncertain, prompting many emendations and/or conjectures for each of its two or three occurrences (see *HALOT* 3:1,037, s.v. *ṣēn*). Fichtner *(BHS)* cites Toy's emendation to read *ṣammîm* "traps" (cf. Job 18:19) and Dyseinck's *ṣᵉpûnîm* "hidden." The Vulg. (cf. Syr.) reads *arma* (< *ṣnh*) "shield." The LXX glosses it as *triboloi* ("prickly plants") and attests "and" with *pagides* "thorns and snares." This interpretation is probably based on reading *ṣᵉnînîm* "thorns" in Num. 33:35 and Josh. 23:13, but it demands adding "and" ("thorns and snares"), for "bird traps" can scarcely be in apposition with "thorns." Besides, "thorns and snares" is an improbable combination. Moreover, Hebrew has other words for "thorns" (cf. 15:19; 24:31). G. R. Driver ("Problems in the Hebrew Text of Proverbs," *Bib* 32 [1951] 186), on the basis of Arab. *ṣinnu* "basket-shaped vessel covered with a lid" and of the glosses in the Targ. and Syr., plausibly believes that it means "[basket] trap." In Job 5:5 it refers to some sort of defense that the rich use to protect their fields against the poor. Its fem. pl. equivalent in Amos 4:2 refers to an instrument to carry people away and is parallel to "fishhooks." This, too, makes good sense. In sum, whatever may be the derivation, "trap/snare" seems a safe guess without emending the MT. The asyndetic apposition, "the bird-trap sort," narrows the *ṣînnîm* down to this category of traps.

9. The LXX, Syr., and Vulg. add "and."

10. The Vulg. renders *proverbium est adulescens* ("it is a proverb: a young man"), perhaps because the first word was missing from its *Vorlage.*

11. *Lamed* marks the direct object (*IBHS,* pp. 210-11, P. 11.2.10g).

12. The *Hiphil* prefix conjugation of *zqn,* attested otherwise only in Job 14:8 with the same ingressive sense, is probably the counterpart to the *Qal* suffix conjugation, which occurs 24 times (see 23:22). The *waw* relative with the prefix conjugation occurs in the *Qal* in 2 Chr. 24:15 but has the same preterite value as the suffix conjugation.

13. The verse is omitted in the LXX.

14. The LXX changes the sense of the verse by making *ʿebed* the subject ("and the servant will lend to the lender"), having read *l'yš lwh,* not *lwh l'yš,* and seeing in these words the designation of a master who borrowed money from his servant (A. J. Baumgartner, *Étude critique sur l'état du texte du Livre des Proverbes d'après les principales traductions anciennes* [Leipzig: Imprimerie Orientale W. Drugulin, 1890], pp. 198-99). The Targ., probably under the influence of the LXX, also reads thus but interprets the verse as a gnomic truth. The Syr. further modifies verset A by reading passive, "will be ruled." The Vulg. and moderns read the MT and interpret it as gnomic.

15. K reads *yiqṣôr,* but Q reads *yiqṣor* in proclisis with *ʾāwen.*

16. Because Gemser (*Sprüche,* p. 82), followed by Fichtner *(BHS)* and McKane (*Proverbs,* p. 570), wrongly interprets *ʿbrtw* as "hubris," as in 21:24, he also thinks it nec-

9 *As for the generous,*[17] *he will be blessed*
because he gives from his food to the poor.[18]
10 *Drive out the mocker so that*[19] *contention might depart,*
and[20] *strife and disgrace might cease.*[21]
11 *As for the one who loves*[22] *a pure*[23] *heart,*

---

essary to emend *yikleh* to *yakkēhû* ("strikes him") for a better antithesis. The REB accepts the emendation but retains the meaning "fury" by interpreting "his" as God's fury. The LXX uniquely reads *'brtw* as *ergōn autou,* "his works," leading Toy (*Proverbs,* p. 421), following Frankenberg, to emend *šēbeṭ* to *šeber* ("and the produce of his work will come to an end," but, says McKane (*Proverbs,* p. 570), "This is weak and, moreover, the meaning 'produce' is not attested for *šeber.*" The LXX adds an extra verse after v. 8: "God blesses a cheerful and liberal person; [a person] shall fully receive the vanity of his works." Verset A is a variant of v. 9a (cf. 2 Cor. 9:7), and verset B is similar to v. 8b.

17. Lit. "the good of the eye."

18. The LXX has here another verse: "The one who gives liberally secures victory and honor; but he takes away the life of them that possess [them]." Its A verset adds to v. 9a, but it is difficult to explain the connection of its B verset to A.

19. In the sequence imperative + *waw* + imperfect, the second clause usually expresses a purpose or result (*IBHS,* p. 119).

20. Epexegetical *waw* (cf. KJV, "yea").

21. Driver ("Problems," p. 186) retroverts the first two words of verset B with the LXX and Syr. as *yēšēb bêt dîn* and follows Wolfson ("Notes on Proverbs 22:10 and Psalms of Solomon 17:48," *JQR* n.s. 37 [1947] 87) in emending the third word as *wᵉyaqlennû* so that the sense reads, "And, if he sits in the courthouse, he dishonours it." But Gemser (*Sprüche,* p. 82) rejects the proposals as not apt for verset A, and McKane (*Proverbs,* p. 567) rejects them as textually unsatisfying in contrast to a textually satisfying MT. Moreover, Zeitlin, in an earlier study (1946), "showed that in all the eight instances in this book in which LXX has the word *synhedrion,* as well as in all other places in Hellenistic and Tannaitic literature prior to the destruction of the Temple, the term is never used in the sense of a court-of-law, but rather in the sense of council or conference" (Greenstone, *Proverbs,* p. 236).

22. Not grasping the nominative absolute construction, the LXX, Syr., and Targ. insert "the LORD" from v. 12, making him the subject of *'ōhēb.* But v. 11b without emendation does not syntactically admit of this addition. McKane ("Textual and Philological Notes on the Book of Proverbs with Special Reference to the New English Bible," *GUOST* 24 [1974] 80) calls this use made of the ancient versions by the NEB "a lapse of judgment." Toy (*Proverbs,* p. 418), Driver ("Problems," p. 186), and McKane (*Proverbs,* p. 568) transpose *melek* to verset A: "The king loves. . . ." Driver explains: "[*Melek*], having ing accidentally dropped out of its proper sense, was put in the margin and then added *contra sensum* at the end of the line." To make sense of verset B, Driver has to emend *rēʿēhû* to *rēʿāhû* (= "makes himself friendly to him"). To get around this otherwise unattested and unlikely causative *Piel* from *rāʿâ,* McKane follows Toy and arbitrarily emends to *rᵉṣônô* (= "[and grace of lips] meets his approval"). The enjambment of the MT, however, is acceptable Hebrew poetry (see v. 16) and makes perfectly good sense.

23. K reads the cons. as *ṭᵉhôr* (cf. Hab. 1:13), and Q as *tᵉhor-* (but as *ṭᵒhor* in Job 17:9).

whose[24] lips are gracious, the king is a friend of his.
12 *The eyes of the* LORD *protect knowledge,[25]*
and so he subverts the words of the treacherous.
13 *The sluggard says,[26] "A lion is outside.*
In the midst of the plaza[27] I will be as good as murdered."[28]
14 *A deep pit is the mouth of the unfaithful wife;[29]*
the one cursed by[30] the LORD *falls into it.[31]*
15 *Folly is bound up in the youth's heart,*
but the rod of discipline[32] removes it far from him.
16 *He who oppresses[33] the poor to increase[34] [riches][35] for himself[36]*
[and][37] he who gives gifts[38] to the rich come[39] only to lack.

24. The marker of the relative clause is commonly elided in poetry; the pronoun of *śᵉpātāyw* assumes it (see *IBHS,* p. 338, P. 19.6).

25. D. Winton Thomas ("A Note on *dāʿat* in Proverbs xxii.12," *JTS* 14 n.s. [1963] 93-94), followed in the REB, gratuitously invests *dāʿat* with the meaning "lawsuit" by looking away from the common Hebrew word to an Arabic cognate, *daʿa* ("sought, desired, asked, demanded").

26. The perfective denotes instantaneous action with *verba dicendi* (*IBHS,* p. 488, PP. 30.5.1d). The ancient versions add varying glosses here: Targ., "in his laziness"; Syr., "when he is sent"; LXX, "makes excuses."

27. See I: 20, n. 3.

28. Probably because *rṣḥ* elsewhere has human beings as the agents of murder, the LXX rendered verset B: *en tais plateiais phoneutai* ("in the streets are murderers").

29. The LXX reads *stoma paranomou* ("mouth of a transgressor"). Did the translator read *zār* or *zārîm?*

30. The Targ. reads *zōʿēm* ("the one who blasphemes"). "Targum, wishing to avoid the implication of God being just, creates a reason for God's wrath referring to the blasphemy" (J. Healey, *The Targum of Proverbs* [The Aramaic Bible 15; Collegeville, Minn.: Michael Glazier, 1991], p. 49).

31. The LXX adds "three tedious moralizing lines" after v. 14 (Delitzsch, *Proverbs,* p. 328).

32. Gen. of effect (i.e., the rod that brings discipline [*IBHS,* p. 146, P. 9.5.2c]).

33. The unambiguous parallel *nōtēn* shows that the ambiguous form is a *Qal* ptcp. (BDB, p. 798, s.v. *ʿāšaq; HALOT,* 3:897, s.v. *ʿšq*), not the noun "oppression" (*pace* REB).

34. McKane (*Proverbs,* p. 572), following Ringgren, interprets *lᵉ* to mean "is likely to," appealing indefensibly to its use in 16:30. Delitzsch (*Proverbs,* p. 328) achieves a similar sense by curiously rendering the purpose infinitive "it is gain." This grammatically unjustified rendering leads Kidner (*Proverbs,* p. 149), in a rare lack of judgment, to the morally questionable interpretation, "More can be squeezed from the poor than wheedled from the rich."

35. The Targ. and Syr. add "evil" but have to interpret the infinitive as a finite verb. Moreover, it forms a poor parallel to "lack."

36. So the ancients (LXX, Sym., Vulg.; cf. also the Syr.) and most English versions (NASB, NIV, NRSV; cf. NLT).

37. The insertion of "and" assumes that the compound subjects are linked asyndetically, as also in the enjambment of v. 11. The oppressor and the self-aggrandizer could

The theme of the LORD's sovereignty over kingdoms and peoples in 21:30-31 paves the way for the specification of that theme to the LORD's sovereignty over wealth in the first subunit (22:1-9) of the final unit of Collection II. The final unit can be analyzed as having two halves: the LORD's sovereignty over wealth (vv. 1-9), of which v. 1 functions as an introduction to the whole unit, and the need for moral instruction in connection with wealth (vv. 10-16), of which vv. 15-16 also function as a conclusion to the whole. Actually the LORD's sovereignty over wealth is part of the argument supporting that theme. In addition to this thematic unity the unit also exhibits lexical unity. The key root *ʿšr* "rich" is found in vv. 1a, 2a, 4a, 7a, and 16b) and forms an *inclusio* around the whole (vv. 1, 16); the catchword "the LORD" (vv. 2, 4, 12, and 14) punctuates the whole. The refrain "gives" and "poor" *(dāl)* occurs in concluding verse of each half (vv. 9, 16). Within the macrostructure of its two halves, the microstructure linking vv. 6 and 7 with 15 and 16 gives the unit an educational character. Verses 6 and 15 are linked by the admonition to the father to discipline his son, by the catchwords *naʿar* "a youth" (vv. 6a, 15a), *rḥq* "to be far/to remove far" (vv. 5b, 15b), and by the related prepositional phrases *mimmennâ* "from it" (v. 6b) and *mimmennû* "from him" (v. 15b); the former looks back to *mēhem* "from them" in v. 5b. Verses 7 and 16 pick up the key root and catchword *ʿāšîr* "rich person." Garrett[40] and Heim[41] justly urge taking these verses as a double *inclusio* framing vv. 7-14. But they fail to take account of data supporting the analysis of the contended-for macro-structure, and their treatment of vv. 7-14 as a potpourri, what Garrett labels as "various proverbs," as a subunit is not satisfying. The connection of vv. 6-7 with vv. 15-16 is better treated as foreshadowing the emphasis on moral instruction that draws the unit and the Collection to its conclusion. Verse 6 calls for correcting youth's innate depravity as soon as possible, and v. 15 for severity. Chapter 5 similarly mixes the call for moral instruction with the lesson. Finally, as will be argued, vv. 14-15 form an *inclusio* with the prologue.

---

be the same person or different people. Scott (*Proverbs,* pp. 128-29) and the NAB ("He who oppresses the poor to enrich himself will yield up his gains to the rich as sheer loss") interpret verset B as the predicate of verset A (see the next note). McKane (*Proverbs,* p. 571) rightly judges it "a forced translation."

38. The LXX renders both the inf. *lhrbwt* and the ptcp. *ntn* by finite verbs: *poiei . . . didōsi de* ("increases . . . yet gives"). The Vulg. likewise makes *nōtēn* the finite predicate: *dabit ipse ditiori* ("shall himself give to one that is richer"), but then has to interpret *ʾak* as a conjunction, *et egebit* ("and shall be in need").

39. The verb of motion is entailed in the preposition (see *IBHS,* p. 224, P. 11.4d).

40. Garrett, *Proverbs,* p. 187.

41. K. Heim, "Structure and Context in Proverbs 10:1–22:16" (Ph.D. diss., University of Liverpool, 1996), pp. 290-91.

a. The LORD*'s Sovereignty and Wealth (22:1-9)*

R. E. Murphy recognized that 22:1-9 constitute a pericope, but he failed to take note of the *inclusio* in v. 16.[42] The subunit coheres by key terms, a common theme, a distinct structure, and phonetic consonance.[43] The key root *ʿšr* occurs as "riches" (vv. 1, 4) and as *ʿāšîr* "a rich person" (vv. 2, 7). Its antonym *rāš* "poor" occurs in vv. 2 and 7, and its synonym *dāl* in v. 9. Other financial terms are "to be fined" (v. 3), "wage" (v. 4), "generous" (v. 9), and "the one who sows injustice will reap an empty deception" (v. 8), which by standing opposed to "generous" suggests that the metaphor pertains to the oppressive rich of v. 7. If so, every verse, except the partial subunit of vv. 5-6, contains terms pertaining to wealth. This subunit teaches that the LORD pays back virtue but punishes vice. Israel's Sovereign is mentioned explicitly in vv. 2 and 4 and implicitly by "blessed" in v. 9. In the light of his moral government, the subunit aims to sober the rich, to console the poor, to warn the oppressor, and to comfort the oppressed (see v. 7).

The subunit consists of an introduction asserting the priority of a good name to wealth (v. 1) and two partial subunits of three verses each around a middle subunit of two verses. Thematically, the first of these combines the LORD's sovereignty (v. 2) with human accountability (vv. 3-4), the third asserts the LORD's retribution (vv. 7-9), and the middle pertains to education (vv. 5-6). The outer two partial subunits begin by juxtaposing initial "the rich" with "the poor" (vv. 2 and 7),[44] and the first is linked to the introduction by *ʿšr.* These framing partial subunits assert the equality of rich and poor before the LORD in heaven (vv. 2-4) and their inequality on earth (vv. 7-9). Each in its own way seeks to heal the natural social rupture between the classes that destroys the community's peace.

(1) Introduction: A Good Name Is Better than Wealth (22:1)

The subunit typically begins with a motivation to acquire wisdom. This introduction ushers in the unit's topic of wealth by relativizing its value compared

42. R. E. Murphy, "Proverbs 22:1-9," *Int* 41 (1987) 398-402.

43. The consonant /ʿ/, the initial consonant of *ʿāšîr,* occurs 22 times in nine verses, averaging about 2.3 times per verse: once in vv. 1, 5, and 9; twice in vv. 6 and 7 (both initially in its verset); three times in vv. 2, 4, and 8; and four times in v. 3. The consonant /r/, the final consonant of the key root, occurs 24 times, on average about 2.6 times per verse: once in v. 9; twice in vv. 2, 4, and 7; three times in vv. 1, 5, 6, and 8; five times in v. 3. In the preceding pericope of 31 verses /ʿ/ occurred 32 times for an average of about once per verse, even though its key terms included *ršʿ* "wicked" and *ʿśh* "do," and /r/ occurs about 46 times for an average of 1.15 times per verse.

44. Note the broken sequence of /š, r/ in *ʿāšîr* and its antonym *rāš.*

with a good name. Social favor with God and people, founded on esteem and trust, is better than material wealth. *A good name (šēm)*[45] and *to be esteemed* (*ḥēn,* lit. "grace," "favor"; see 3:4 — note the assonance with *šēm*) function as metonymies of wisdom's effect. A good name represents a person's good character and his memory (see 10:7; 18:10; 21:24) and depends on his wisdom (3:1-4). Moreover, other texts present wisdom, a co-referential term for a "good name," as having priority to riches (2:4; 3:14; 8:10-11, 19; 16:16). According to 13:15a social favor is effected through good insight, and according to 3:3-4 through reliable goodness (see also 11:27; 12:8). In sum, a good name is the outward expression of the person's inner wisdom. In this chiastic, synonymous parallelism the comparatives *is more desirable* (see 21:3) and *is better* (see 2:20) form the outer frame. The topics "a good name" and "esteem" form its middle elements;[46] and *than great* [see 7:26] *riches* (see 3:16) and its specific equivalents, *silver* [see 2:4] *and gold* (*zāhāb;* see 17:3; cf. 3:14), the inner core. "Its [gold's] possession is the preeminent mark of wealth and — often in combination with silver — becomes practically synonymous with riches (Gen. 24:53; Prov. 22:1; Eccl. 2:8; Sir. 19:11)."[47] In this positive comparison, material wealth is esteemed as good, but the social quality of a good reputation and its causes is better (cf. Eccl. 7:1; Sir. 41:11-13; Abot 4:17). The value of social favor can be gauged by considering the value of gold. "It is a mark of independence (1 K. 20:3, 7) and signifies the honor of princes (Job 3:15) and kings (1 K. 10:14; Ps. 72:15). It is the most precious of gifts (Gen. 24:22; 1 K. 10:2), the currency of political bribery (1 K. 15:19), tribute levied for an offense (2 K. 18:14; 23:33), and coveted booty (Josh. 7:21; 2 S. 1:24; 2 K. 25:15). . . . It is 'means' in the strict sense of the word: it provides power (Ezr. 1:6; Sir. 40:24)."[48] Wealth can be obtained apart from virtue (see 11:16, 28), but not a good name. Wisdom gives both (see 3:14). Moreover, wealth can pass away unexpectedly and quickly (23:4-5), but a good name endures (10:7; cf. 2 Sam. 18:18; Luke 7:4, 5; Acts 9:36-39). The rest of the unit defines a good name as being generous to the poor, not striving to become rich at their expense (22:2, 4, 7, 9, 16).

45. In this comparative clause *šēm* has its more specific sense "a good reputation," "fame," precisely the same as in Eccl. 7:1 (*HALOT,* 4:1,459, s.v. *šēm*).

46. Note the consonance of /*r*/ in verset A and the broken sequence of /*š, m*/ in *šēm mē'ōšer.*

47. B. Kedar-Kopfstein, *TDOT,* 4:38, s.v. *zāhābh.*

48. Ibid.

(2) The LORD's Sovereignty over Wealth and Human Accountability (22:2-4)

While material possessions create distinctions among human beings, v. 2 teaches that rich and poor meet on common ground before the LORD: he made both of them, thereby instructing the rich and poor to remember this basic item of human equality (cf. 19:17). Verses 3 and 4 protect this saying against fatalism. By prudence, as opposed to being gullible, one can avoid being "fined," and the "wage" from the fear of the LORD is wealth, honor, and life (v. 4). "Fined," the last word of v. 3, and its antonym, "wage," the first of v. 4, occur back-to-back. The initial consonant of each verse is /ʿ/, giving the partial subunit phonological coherence.[49]

2 This initial proverb asserts the LORD's sovereignty over rich and poor.[50] Although the proverb could mean that the Sovereign created a social order of economic gradations entailing the rich at one extreme and the pathetic poor at the other, that interpretation seems unlikely. Proverbs does not treat the rich person sympathetically but portrays him as impious (see 18:11; 28:11) and tyrannical (14:31; 17:5; 18:23; 29:13). By contrast, it treats the poor with compassion, for they lack the necessary subsistence to maintain their lives in spite of their virtue (cf. 19:1, 22; 28:6). Sin, not the LORD, creates an order of economic oppression (e.g., 21:4). Rather, the proverb means that rich and poor have a common Maker and so a common humanity and value. Verset A pictures this common ground by asserting that *rich* (*ʿāšîr;* see 10:15) *and poor* (*rāš;* see 10:4; 13:23) *meet together* (*nipgāšû;* see 17:12) in an unavoidable, face-to-face, eye-to-eye encounter. The expression could be literal, "to meet one another in hostility." Because of their economic disparity, on the human level they naturally meet each other at the city gate to settle their disputes in hostility, disturbing the peace of the community. More probably, however, it is a figure, as in the other two uses of the *Niphal* of *pgš* (cf. Ps. 85:10[11]; Prov. 29:13), to signify that rich and poor, oppressed and opressor, meet in a common bond. Verset B, as in the parallel proverb, 29:13, explains the point of the similitude; the LORD grants both their existence. *The LORD* (*YHWH;* see I: 67) *is the Maker* [or Creator;[51] see 17:5] *of them all* (see 8:9), signifying that no one is excluded. In his sight they are all of equal value and dignity and should be respected as such (cf. 14:31; 17:5; 29:13; Job 34:19). Boström, citing Doll, rightly comments, "The saying reminds both parties of the fact that they are God's creation and as such have both rights

49. Cf. *ʿāšîr* (v. 2), *ʿārûm* (v. 3), *ʿēqeb* (v. 4).

50. Its versets cohere by the consonance of /š/ in its first four words and by using verset B to explain verset A.

51. *HALOT,* 2:890, s.v. *ʿśh.*

and responsibilities."[52] The reminder is necessary, for, as Meinhold comments, the rich deals with the poor in an intolerable way and/or the poor brings to expression his despising of the rich man and/or revolts against him. Both can silently or expressively deny the dignity of the other.[53] The rich should remember that his treatment of the poor is equated with his treatment of their Maker (17:15), and the poor should learn not to despise, envy, or revolt against the rich (3:31), or sycophantically to ingratiate himself with him or compromise his conscience to get his smile. Rather, he should both respect him and yet evaluate him as merely God's creature. Both must bear in mind that the LORD gives wealth and poverty, and according to his moral order he will ultimately redistribute it (1 Sam. 2:7-8; Prov. 15:25; Sir. 11:4, 14).

3-4 The consonant initial *ʿayin* of *ʿārûm* ("shrewd," v. 3) and *ʿēqeb* ("wage," v. 4), the back-to-back antonyms of *ʿnš* "fine (or penalty)" and of *ʿēqeb* "wage," and the theme of human accountability bind vv. 3-4 together as a proverb pair. These financial metaphors, pertaining to human accountability, move from avoiding a terrifying fine to gaining an immense wage. Together the proverb pair protects v. 2 from misinterpretation.[54] The Sovereign indeed creates both rich and poor (v. 2), but human folly leads to impoverishment, be it one's own (v. 3) or others' (v. 4). The connection with v. 2 suggests that the Agent of the legal "fine" (v. 3b) is the LORD, who enriches or impoverishes people according to human accountability, making "is fined" a divine passive.

3 *Penalty* (*neʿᵉnāšû;* lit. "are fined"; see 17:26) refers to the legal imposition of a monetary payment. Its financial concept and broken sequence with *ʿšr* link the proverb with the keyword "riches," *ʿšr* (vv. 1, 2, and 4). In striking symmetry its antithetical parallels juxtapose (1) the topic, *the shrewd* (see I: 95) versus *the gullible* (see I: 111) — the plural suggesting that they are more numerous (see 20:15); (2) the predicates, *sees* with moral discernment (*rāʾâ;* see 20:12) the connection between *evil* and its misery (*rāʿâ;* see 1:15 — note the assonance) versus *pass on* (or keep on going, *ʿābᵉrû;* see 4:15); (3) and the consequences, *and hides himself* from the LORD's just scourge (see n. 3)[55] versus "and so is fined"

52. L. Boström, *The God of the Sages: The Portrayal of God in the Book of Proverbs* (ConBOT 29; Stockholm: Almqvist & Wiksell, 1990), p. 66.

53. Meinhold, *Proverbs,* p. 364.

54. The repetition of the proverb in 27:12 suggests its one-time independent existence; its insignificant variants are probably due to oral reformulation and/or transmission.

55. As a reflexive *Niphal str* occurs 17 times. Apart from a metaphorical reference to God hiding himself from prayer in Ps. 89:47, it always occurs with reference to a mortal who conceal(s) himself so as not to be seen, and with the possible exception of Jer. 23:24, to avoid a terrifying threat from an angry God (Gen. 4:14; Job 13:20; 34:22; Amos 9:3) or a tyrant (1 Sam. 20:5, 19, 24; 1 K. 17:3; Ps. 55:12[13]; Prov. 28:28; Jer. 36:19) or

(w^e^ne'^e^nāšû).[56] *Rā'* refers to moral evil and physical calamity because "sees" refers to moral discernment, and "hides himself," in opposition to being fined, refers to harm. Although the first antithesis is precise, the next two are not. The shrewd does not pass along and the gullible lack the moral insight to see evil, and, by hiding himself, the shrewd protects himself from serious loss that the gullible could have avoided had they hid themselves. If the gullible do not develop moral astuteness when scoffers are fined (21:11), they too will suffer a painful financial pinch. A distinctive characteristic of the shrewd in this book is his ability with keen moral discernment (13:16; 14:8, 18) to pick his steps cautiously (14:15), including taking cover (13:16) to avoid evil and its consequences (22:3). He protects himself both by not participating in evil and by taking preventive action against the anticipated judgment. The context implies that the shrewd by faith discern the connection between generosity and enrichment and between tyranny and impoverishment. The incautious and morally dull gullible fail to see this connection and so act precipitously without regard to moral law (cf. 7:21-23) and take no precaution to find salvation while they can (1:32; cf. Isa. 26:11).

4 Verse 4a offers the cure whereby the gullible and fools can become shrewd, and its synthetic parallel, the palpable benefits spelling out *the wage ('ēqeb).*[57] The remedy is *humility* (see 15:33), a religious term denoting the renunciation of human sufficiency (see 15:33), of the sort associated with *the fear of the LORD* (see I: 100). The failure of the gullible to spot danger arises from their arrogant refusal to submit to God. The wages of pure religion are *riches* [see 3:16] *and* with it *honor* (*kābôd;* see 3:16; 15:33; 18:12), *and,* bringing the compound predicate to its fitting climax, *life* (see I: 104). Without this last benefit, riches and its honor are a vapor. Paradoxically the person who walks humbly before God will find honor among people (cf. 1 Pet. 5:5-6). According to 1 K. 3:12-14, after Solomon's request for an obedient heart, the LORD promised him wealth and honor, but conditioned prolonging his days (see 3:2) on his continued obedience to the covenant.

---

an overwhelming scourge from the LORD (Deut. 7:20; Isa. 28:15). In that light Prov. 22:3a and its synoptic parallel in 27:12 probably imply that the shrewd perceive the LORD's scourge against the wicked through the very evil they plotted against others.

56. The parallels cohere phonetically by the consonance of /r/ in each word of verset A and of /'/ in two of those plus another guttural /'/ in the third, and in verset B the repetition of /r / and in *'āb^e^rû* and of /'/ in it and *ne'^e^nāšû.* This consonance continues into its pair, v. 4, which has /'/ in the first two words of verset A and /r/ in *yir'at,* with both consonants being found in *'ōšer,* the first word of verset B.

57. According to *HALOT* (2:873, s.v. *'ēqeb*) its original meaning "the very back," "the end" (Ps. 119:33, 122) led to the derivative meaning "wages" (Ps. 19:12), and that in turn to the idiom with *'al,* "on account of" (Ps. 40:15[16]).

(3) Center: Educating Youth in the Right Way (22:5-6)

The center of the subunit on the LORD's sovereignty over wealth and poverty (22:1-9) does not mention the topic as such but focuses on the need for educating youth in the way that leads to true riches. The concept of paying attention to one's way (vv. 3-4) and the need to orient youth to the right way (vv. 5-6) link the partial subunits. The relatively rare sortal apposition constructions (i.e., "humility — the fear-of-the-LORD sort," and "snares, the bird-trap sort") further unites them. The middle pair's metaphor "way" in their A versets and the complementary notions of staying far away from the wrong path and of starting youth out on the right way in their B versets bind together the middle pair. The repetition of "from" (i.e., "from them" and "from it") tightens this linkage. One protects the youth from the deadly way of the perverse by dedicating them at the start of life to the opposite of their natural folly.[58]

5 This proverb escalates the preceding pair from the gullible who do not watch where they are treading to the perverse who tread a road infested with moral dangers. The line between the two foolish types becomes attenuated, for both implicitly fail to attain the goal of life for which they hoped. By contrast, the shrewd, by keeping himself far from these traps, protects himself and thereby guarantees the happy wages of v. 4. Word-initial *snares* is the subject of verset A and the antecedent of "from them," the last word in verset B. Verset A presents the danger. *Snares* (see n. 8), narrowed down to *the bird-trap sort* of nets used by fowlers (see n. 9; 7:23), by design aim to deceive the unwary in order to capture and destroy them. The metaphor refers to temptations such as easy sex and easy money that tempt youth. The morally degenerate tread a dangerous road infested with snares. They are found *in the way* (*bᵉderek;* see 1:15) *of the perverse* (see 2:15). Verset B presents the defense (see 16:7). *The one who would preserve* [or protect; see 2:8] *his life* (*napšô;* see I: 90) *keeps far* [see 19:7] *from them,* looking back to snares/bird-traps, the only plural antecedent.

6 While the proverbs are addressed to youth (1:4-5), now at the end of Collections I-II the wise pedagogue is admonished to reorient the youth away from the folly of his endemic selfishness (vv. 6, 15). Verse 5 implicitly admonished the youth to stay clear from the sinister road the perverse travel; now its pair implicitly admonishes the educator, especially the parent (see 10:1), to start him on the right way to steer him clear of danger.[59] The prov-

58. It may be connected to v. 4 by the unusual grammatical construction of an asyndetic sortal apposition.

59. For other interpretations of the proverb see T. Hildebrandt, "Proverbs 22:6a: Train Up a Child?" *GTJ* 9 (1988) 3-19, to whom this study is indebted. However, the data does not confirm his unique views that (1) *ḥānak* refers "to the inauguration process . . . as

erb's topic, the early moral education of youth, is stated in verset A and referred to by the neuter pronoun "it" that closes verset B. Verset A presents the admonition (i.e., the cause), and verset B the reason (i.e., the consequence). The relatively rare imperative *dedicate (ḥᵃnōk)* means to start the youth off with a strong and perhaps even religious commitment to a certain course of action.[60] Dommershausen says arbitrarily, "In this context, *ḥānak* means continual 'training,'" but Clifford argues that it has this meaning in rabbinic Hebrew (B. T. Nazir 29a).[61] To be sure, dedication entails continual training, but the almost ubiquitous translation "train up" misses the lexeme's emphasis on inauguration and possibly consecration. In the book of Proverbs, Israel's moral primer (see 1:2-6), this initiative refers to religious and moral direction, not professional activity. Although the age of *the youth* (*naʿar;* see 1:4) can vary from infancy to adulthood, a child is certainly in view in 20:11 and probably implied in the verb "dedicate." He can be molded by verbal instruction (1:4; 23:13; 29:15) and, according to its parallel in 22:15, by corporal punishment. Since he is still teachable, the dedication must take place while there is still hope (23:13; cf. 19:18). The uniquely definite construction "the

---

a consequence of having completed an initiation process"; (2) *naʿar* refers to a young squire; and (3) "according to his way" means "according to the standard and status of what would be demanded of the *naʿar* in that culture."

60. In its two or three other occurrences, the verb *ḥnk* refers to dedicating a house (Deut. 20:5 with acc.), a temple (1 K. 8:63; 2 Chr. 7:5 with *ʾet*), and "youth" (Prov. 22:6 with *lamed* + personal object). "Arabic *ḥanaka* (cf. *ḥanakun,* 'gums') has the primary meaning of rubbing the gums of a newborn child with the juice of dates or with oil, hence 'initiate' (including 'initiate into something') and 'make experienced'" (W. Dommershausen, *TDOT,* 5:19-20, s.v. *ḥānak*). Its etymology with an impersonal object was probably "initiate," "inaugurate," "put into use for the first time" and with personal objects, "accustom." In biblical usage, however, the verb and noun mean "dedicate" and "dedication." The temple was "inaugurated" by offering a mass sacrifice, and the notion of cultic initiation/dedication is also found in the eight uses of the noun form *ḥᵃnukkâ* in connection with cultic objects: the temple (Ps. 30:1 [title]), altars (Num. 7:10, 11, 84, 88; 2 Chr. 7:9), and Nehemiah's wall (Neh. 12:27). The Feast of Hanukkah commemorates the rededication of the desecrated temple by Judah Maccabeus by means of legitimate sacrifices on the 25th of Kislev, 167 B.C., after it had been defiled by Antiochus Epiphanes by means of pagan sacrifices three years earlier to the day. It is unclear whether there is a cultic connotation (= "to consecrate") with reference to dedicating one's house or a youth. In postbiblical Aramaic the term is used of the high priest, who was inaugurated, and of Isaac, who was initiated *(ḥānak)* into the covenant on the eighth day. The meaning of *ḥᵃnîkāyw* in Gen. 14:14 is disputed. In Prov. 22:6 it is used, perhaps metaphorically, with reference to the education of the youth and signifies "to initiate," and perhaps "consecrate," and so orient and commit him in the appropriate moral correction that his innate folly dictates. (Hannah's so-called dedication of Samuel is used appropriately to illustrate the early dedication of a child, but in 1 Sam. 1:28 she says, "I lent him *(hišʾiltīhû)* to the LORD.")

61. Clifford, *Proverbs,* p. 196.

youth" may imply that he must be assessed individually to design personally the appropriate moral initiative. *According to* (lit. "according to the mouth of") refers to what someone or something dictates.[62] Here *his way* dictates the orientation of his dedication.[63] The nature and/or the moral content of "way" depends on its possessor, be it God (Prov. 8:22), the wise (11:5; 14:8; 16:7), human beings in general (16:9; 20:24), or fools (19:3). Although outside of Proverbs the gloss "according to the way" can refer to "according to the nature of" (cf. Gen. 19:31; Isa. 10:24) — here it would mean dedicating the child according to the physical and mental abilities of the developing youth (Saadia,[64] Malbim,[65] Delitzsch[66]) — the construction is *kᵉderek* in those passages outside of Proverbs, not *ʿal-pî* ("according to the dictate of"). The other six references to *naʿar* univocally characterize his way as foolish. He is grouped together with the gullible in 1:4, is said to lack sense in 7:7, to have folly bound up in his heart in 22:15, to dissemble in his evil deeds in 20:11, and so to be in need of correction in 23:13. Left to himself, he will disgrace his mother (29:15). Grammatically and rhetorically, as in 19:27, the command could be sarcastic (i.e., "Dedicate a youth according to his foolish way, and when he grows old he will not depart from it!").[67] However, the proverb would then assume that the youth attained old age in his folly. In this book the wise, not fools, are crowned with the gray hair of age (20:29). In sum, the proverb implies that the religious and moral initiation of the youth should be oriented from the first to counteract his foolish way: "The fool's mouth cries out for a beating" (18:6). This instruction and discipline must not be withheld from him (cf. 13:24; 19:18; 23:13, 14; 29:15, 17).

The consequence of this strong spiritual initiative is that the dedicated youth will never depart from the original initiative. *Even* (see 14:13) probably aims to prevent the misinterpretation that there may be a moral lapse between the dedication and old age. The point is that even when the youth at-

62. *ʿal-pî* can mean, in cons. with a personal gen., "the command of" (Gen. 41:40) or "evidence of" (Deut. 17:6), or, in cons. with an impersonal gen. as here, "the measure of," "in accordance with," whether the standard be questions (Gen. 43:7), words of the covenant (Exod. 34:7), or the decisions and teaching taught by the priests (Deut. 17:10, 11). In both constructions, however, it refers to what someone or something dictates.

63. The metaphor *darkô* occurs seven other times in the book. The gen. is always possessive or a gen. of inalienable possession, and the metaphor "way" always refers to the context and conduct of someone. *Derek* is neutral without qualifiers, whether positive ("goodness," 2:20; "life," 6:23; "insight," 9:6, "righteousness," 16:31) or negative ("evil," 2:12; "wicked," 4:19).

64. Plaut, *Proverbs,* p. 228.

65. Malbim, *Proverbs,* pp. 229-30.

66. Delitzsch, *Proverbs,* p. 324.

67. Cf. Plaut, *Proverbs,* p. 228; so Clifford, *Proverbs,* p. 197.

tains old age, he will not turn off from the chosen course. *When* shows that the two situations of verset B (i.e., becoming old and not departing) are contemporary.[68] *He grows old* (see 17:6) refers to beginning and continuing in the state of being aged; the majesty of the aged is their grey hair (20:29). *He will not depart* [see 3:7] *from it* (a neuter feminine pronoun) refers to his not turning aside from the situation formulated in verset A. The proverb, however, must not be pushed to mean that the educator is ultimately responsible for the youth's entire moral orientation. "Rather, it gives a single component of truth that must be fit together with other elements of truth in order to approximate the more comprehensive, confused patterns of real life."[69] Other proverbs recognize the youth's freedom to choose sin (cf. Ezek. 18:20) and apostatize by taking up with villains (Prov. 2:11-15) and whores (5:11-14). The book is addressed to youths, not parents. Were the parents ultimately responsible for his moral choice, there would be no point in addressing the book to youth (see 1:4). Moreover, Solomon himself stopped listening to instruction and strayed from knowledge (19:27). In sum, the proverb promises the educator that his original, and early, moral initiative has a permanent effect on a person for good. But that is not the whole truth about religious education.

(4) The LORD Punishes the Rich and Rewards the Generous (22:7-9)

The subunit again returns to the topic of virtue and wealth, with a focus on its unequal distribution. The partial subunit opens with reference to the word-initial "rich person" and closes with word-final "poor person." Heim contrasts "the domination of the rich over the poor in verse 7" with "the benevolence shown to the poor in verse 9."[70] Verses 7-8 reject the dominion of the tyrannical rich over the poor, and v. 9 advances generosity. Verse 7 states the harsh reality that the perverse rich enslave the poor; v. 8, that wickedness will be punished; and v. 9, that the generous will be rewarded.[71] Garrett notes: "While the wicked sow injustice, the righteous share the end product of their literal sowing and harvesting, their bread, with the poor. In light of v. 8 (also vv. 7, 15), the crop the wicked sows is oppression of the poor. The industry and generosity of the righteous is implicitly contrasted with the 'industry' of the oppressor."[72]

68. *IBHS,* p. 643, P. 38.7a.

69. Hildebrandt, "Proverbs 22:6a," p. 16.

70. Heim, "Structure and Context," p. 291.

71. The stanza also coheres by the consonance of /ʿ/, initially in v. 7 and as the first consonant of the second word in vv. 8-9. This seems intentional because *ṭôb-ʿayin* is a hapax.

72. Garrett, *Proverbs,* p. 189.

7 The synonymous parallels of v. 7 match "the rich person" with "the lender" in the outer frame, "the poor" (pl.) with "the borrower" (sing.), and the verb "rule" with the noun "slave" (cf. the matching of the noun "youth" with the verb "to grow old" in v. 6).[73] *The rich person* [see 10:15; 22:2] *rules over* (or lords it over, *yimšôl;* see 12:24) the oppressed *poor people* (*rāšîm;* see 10:4; cf. 2 K. 4:1; Neh. 5:5; Amos 2:6) is explained in verset B as due to his enslaving them with loans.[74] *And* joins the clauses of the two versets to make a compound sentence. *A borrower* [see 19:17] *is a slave* (*'ebed,* i.e., one who has lost his freedom and is responsible to his master, though the term allows for latitude in the precise relationship between master and subject; see 11:29; 14:35) *to the lender* (*'îš malweh;* cf. 19:17). The proverb does not elaborate on how the creditor enslaves the debtor. Many think that the poor, who is here represented as a debtor, is finally forced to sell himself and/or his children into slavery to the rich person, who is represented as a moneylender (cf. 2 K. 4:1; Neh. 5:1-5; Amos 2:6). But for that notion one expects, "The debtor [not the borrower] is a slave to the creditor." Moreover, the law allowed an honorable person to buy a slave for six years, freeing him with generous gifts on the seventh (Exod. 22:1-4[21:37–22:3]; Deut. 15:12-15). More probably, the proverb is a metaphor picturing the one rich person, who has more than sufficient means for his own subsistence, charging interest from the poor borrower, who otherwise cannot maintain his life, and so in effect making him his slave. Charging interest from the poor was forbidden in the law (Exod. 22:25[24]; Lev. 25:36-37; Deut. 23:19[20]), preached against by the prophets (Ezek. 18:8, 13, 17; 22:12), and censured in Prov. 28:18.[75] Charging enslaving inter-

73. Note the alliteration of *'āšîr* and *rāšîm,* and of *lōweh* "borrower" and *malweh* "lender" in verset B. Moreover, all three words in verset A contain /*š*/, and a broken sequence of /*š*/ and /*m*/ occurs in *bršym ymšwl.* The parallels cohere phonologically by the consonance of initial /*'*/ in each verset, of /*l*/ at the end of verset A and in the last three words of B, and of /*m š l*/ in their final words: *ymšwl . . . l'yš mlwh.* "The phonic association suggests what the actual juxtaposition of the cola is also intended to convey, that the 'lender rules'" (T. McCreesh, O.P., *Biblical Sound and Sense: Poetic Sound Patterns in Proverbs 10–29* [JSOTSup 128; Sheffield: Sheffield Academic, 1991], p. 67).

74. The word "mortgage" derives from the two Latin words "mort" (death) and "gage" (cf. pledge), resulting in a word literally translated "death pledge."

75. Exacting usury from the poor was allowed everywhere in the ancient Near East except in Israel. The Code of Eshnunna (ca. 1925 B.C.), just before the Code of Hammurabi, from the Old Babylonian Period, is the earliest extant legal source and begins a 4,000-year history of legislation on interest taking to protect the widow and the fatherless against the rich man. The law codes from the Old Babylonian period limit the rate of interest to 20 percent for money and 33⅓ percent for grain, and the later Assyrian laws allowed interest at 25 percent for money and 50 percent for grain. These rates aimed to protect the borrower against the greed of moneylenders, who were notorious for their avarice! Robert P. Malroney ("Usury and Restriction on Interest-Taking in the Ancient Near

est is not a natural social law created by God but the social product of depraved greed. The unit's refrains ensure that this harsh enslavement will be reversed. The proverb must be held in tension with the theology of Deuteronomy, which regards Israel's ability to grant loans to the heathen as a sign of their God-given prosperity (Deut. 28:12) and Israel's need to borrow from them the absence of God's blessing (28:44).

8 This verse points beyond this harsh reality to the LORD, who will end the wrong, and v. 9 points to the generous, who remedy it immediately and receive the LORD's reward for doing so. The synonymous parallels of vv. 8aα and 8bα match two metaphors, "sowing injustice" and "rod of fury," to depict the rich person as an unsympathetic tyrant exercising cruel misconduct toward a neighbor, and Ab and Bb assert that the tyrant's iron rod will come to an end. *The one who sows* [see 11:18] . . . *will reap* is used metaphorically to describe the connection between an action and its consequences (cf. Job 4:8; Hos. 8:7; 10:12-13; Gal. 6:7). The etymology of *injustice* (*ʿwl;* cf. 29:27) "apparently goes back to an objective category, that of the in-*correct,* which is then complemented by the legal component of the il-*legal. ʿwl* would then be a term for 'to behave incorrectly' or 'to pervert, falsify.'" It occurs predominantly with verbs of "doing" *(ʿśh* and *pʿl)* with reference to "a concrete juristically definable illegal act" ("to do an injustice"). In a legal proceeding the injustice can be committed by the judge (Lev. 19:15) or by the accuser (Job 5:16; 6:29; 13:7; 27:4; Ps. 71:4), or it can result in a judicial verdict. Where the nature of the transgression is perceptible, "it consistently involves crimes of a social, property or commercial nature,"[76] and it may result in the death of innocent victims. Although the noun glossed *empty deception (ʾāwen)* elsewhere in this book means the abuse of power to harm and destroy (see 6:12), it can also be used for "deception," "nothingness."[77] The malevolent use of power is often associated with "deception" and "lying," and this metonymy occasions the transition to the less frequent concept of "nothingness," "vanity."[78] The proverb, however,

---

East," *CBQ* 36 [1974] 5) notes, however: "Money-lenders, . . . knew how to get around the law. A greedy lender could set the date for repayment very early . . . and set a high penalty in case of default. . . . [Moreover,] borrowing ordinarily took place when prices were high (because of the scarcity) and repaying occurred when prices were low (because of the abundance created by the harvest), so that the lender (besides the interest he gained legally) could actually buy much more low-priced grain with the money repaid him. . . ." Also, "Usurers were not above falsifying contracts or records" (Mulroney, "Usury," p. 9).

76. R. Knierim, *TLOT,* 2:849-50, s.v. *ʿāwel.*

77. *HALOT,* 1:22, s.v. *ʾāwen.*

78. K. H. Bernhardt, *TDOT,* 1:142, s.v. *ʾāwen.* It is used with *hebel* "vapor" (Zech. 10:2), *šāwʾ* "vain/worthless" (Isa. 1:13; Hos. 12:11[12]), and *tōhû* "empty" (Isa. 59:4 [cf. *šqr* in Ps. 7:10[11]) plus *ʾepes* "nothingness" and *rûaḥ* "wind" (Isa. 41:29). "Will become *ʾāwen*" in Amos 5:5 is parallel to going into exile.

could mean that the unjust will reap the malevolence of those he abused, and by their revolt the rod of his fury comes to an end (so Malbim).[79] Ironically, the unjust sowed a crop of injustice hoping to reap more than his investment, but the riches he gets in return are a delusion, for they will come to nothing. In verset A he loses his property; in verset B his power. *And* introduces the synonymous parallel. *The rod* (see 10:13) may be figurative or literal. Perhaps it symbolizes the authoritative power of the unjust oppressor and his powerful means to beat down the oppressed. But Clifford thinks that in parallel with an agricultural metaphor it may be another agricultural metaphor referring to a flail for threshing (cf. Isa. 28:8).[80] *He wields in his fury* (lit. "of his fury"; see 21:24) refers to the motivation of the agent who wields the oppressive rod, and the pronoun refers back to the one who sows injustice. If referred to God, that antecedent would have to be expressed. The parallel, "nothingness," supports the MT's reading *will fail* (see n. 16; 5:11; cf. Isa. 10:25; Ezek. 5:13). In sum, divine retribution demands that those who abuse their power will in the end be utterly and eternally disappointed (cf. 10:28; 11:7, 18, 19; 12:3; 13:9, 25; 21:12; 24:19-20; 28:22).

9 *As for the generous* (lit. "the good of eye")[81] sharply contrasts the generous with the tyrant (v. 8). In 'Abot 2:12 the "good eye" "is the good way to which a man should cleave," and in 'Abot 5:22 it is one of the three virtues, along with lowliness and humility, that characterize Abraham's children. Verset B defines him best. *He gives* [see 1:4] *from* [i.e., some of] *his food* of cereal and meat (see 9:5) that he set aside for himself *to the poor* (see 10:15) without expectation of repayment. The tyrant out of his excess uses his power to exploit the weak and powerless, who cannot maintain their life, but the generous sacrificially shares his food to feed and sustain them. As in 21:7, verset A presents the consequence, and verset B the cause, marked by *because.* The resumptive pronoun *he* links the main clause stating the consequence, *will be blessed* (see 20:21), to the generous. The LORD, from whom all blessings flow, rewards the generous from his auspicious powers to grant

79. Malbim, *Proverbs,* p. 230.

80. Clifford, *Proverbs,* p. 197.

81. *Ṭôb-ʿayin* is glossed "bountiful" (BDB, p. 744, s.v. *ṭôb-ʿayin*), "friendly" (*HALOT,* 2:818, s.v. *ʿayin*). "Good" denotes the desirable quality of being useful and advancing life (see 4:25), and "eye" reveals a person's character and disposition (see 6:17; 21:4; cf. 21:10). Its antonym, "evil eye" (*raʿ ʿāyin;* see 23:6; 28:22), is glossed "niggardly one" (BDB, p. 744, s.v. *ṭôb-ʿayin*), "grudging" (Kidner, *Proverbs,* p. 151), "avaricious" (Scott, *Proverbs,* p. 128), "stingy" (NIV, NRSV), "envious" (LXX), "resentful" *(HALOT,* 2:818, s.v. *ʿayin*). It is used in 23:6 to describe a hypocrite who feigns hospitality but resents it, and in 28:22 he is identified as "one who hastens [i.e., acts rashly apart from wisdom] to get wealth" (cf. 20:11). The generous, in contrast to the selfish, does not hasten to advance his own life but that of his neighbor (see 3:27).

prolonged life, progeny, property, and power (cf. 10:6-7; 11:24-26). Dependence on the LORD excludes dependence on the mortal. The generosity of the blessed entails his prior painful labor to work his land, harvest his crops, tend to his animals, and slaughter them. Garrett notes, "The industry and generosity of the righteous is implicitly contrasted with the 'industry' of the oppressor."[82] Whybray adds: "This [proverb] clearly reflects the economic situation of the giver, who is able to spare something for the truly destitute, but from a limited budget rather than from great wealth."[83] Other proverbs relate such donations as giving to the LORD, who in his humility obligates himself to repay the sacrificial "loan" (see 14:31; 19:17; 21:6b). Paradoxically the greedy loses his property and his power, and the liberal participates in a cycle of endless enrichment. From his increased wealth "he will surely give still more liberally" (Nachmias; cf. Soṭah 38b).[84] In sum, instead of becoming professional moneylenders who enslave the poor, the unit instructs the audience to give to the hapless poor generously (3:26-27; 28:27; cf. Deut. 15:10; Neh. 5:16-18; Job 31:17; Ps. 34:10[11]; Isa. 32:8; 58:7; Ezek. 18:7, 16; Matt. 25:31-46; Luke 14:13; 2 Cor. 9:6; 1 Tim. 6:17, 18).[85]

b. Wealth and Moral Instruction (22:10-16)

The second subunit consists of three proverb pairs: an introduction regarding the king's friends (vv. 10-11), a body containing warnings against the deceptive speech of the sluggard and of the unfaithful wife (vv. 12, 13-14), and a conclusion pertaining to wealth and moral instruction (vv. 15-16). Verse 12 functions as a janus between the introduction and the body. The concluding verse explicitly mentions "the poor" *(dāl).* This conclusion complements v. 9, matching the LORD's blessing on the generous, "who gives from his food to the poor," with "the one who oppresses the poor" and "gives to the rich" (v. 16). Verses 10-12 and 15 pertain to moral instruction, the other theme of the unit. The reference to gracious lips (v. 11b) and treacherous words (v. 12b), exemplified in the speech of the sluggard (v. 13) and unchaste women (v. 14), seems out of place until it is remembered that both threaten the family's economic future (cf. 10:1-5; ch. 5). They are probably both reintroduced at the end of Collection II to form an *inclusio* with Collection I, where she played a prominent role (2:16-19; 5:3-6; 6:24-25; 7:5-27) and he a minor one (6:6-11). Verse 15 with its insistence on the need for strict disci-

82. Garrett, *Proverbs,* p. 189.

83. Whybray, *Proverbs,* p. 320.

84. Greenstone, *Proverbs,* pp. 235-36.

85. "Do not eat bread while another stands by without extending your hand to him" (*Any* 8:3; *AEL,* 2:141).

pline to correct youth's folly binds the unit's two subunits but also Collections I and II. Whybray agrees: "In their present juxtaposition these two verses [vv. 14-15] may be said to epitomize the teaching of the final edition of the Instructions of chapters 1–9. . . . The fact that these verses occur at the end of the section supports this view."[86]

The subunit's introduction indirectly motivates the youth to accept the parents' teaching by commanding rulers to evict mockers and by asserting that the pure and understanding have the king for a friend. Verse 12 links the introduction with the warnings against easy money and easy sex by asserting that the LORD infallibly protects the moral order upheld by the ideal king (cf. v. 12a) through frustrating treacherous words (v. 12b) such as those of the sluggard (v. 13) and the unchaste wife (v. 14). The subunit is drawn to a conclusion by implicitly instructing the father to drive folly, such as laziness and promiscuity, from the son's depraved nature.

(1) Introduction: The King's Friends (22:10-11)

The first proverb pair (22:10-11) juxtaposes the mocker, whom kings evict (v. 10), with the pure and gracious whom he welcomes.[87] Although v. 10 is probably addressed to the king (see v. 11), it concerns the youth, who wants the king's friendship, not eviction. Kings evict mockers because they disrupt the community's peace, but welcome the pure because they promote peace. Verses 10-12 share the evaluative pattern +::+ in contrast to the -::- pattern of vv. 13-14.

10 As in v. 6, in this synonymous parallelism the condition, expressed as a command, "drive out the mocker" (10aα), is followed by the motivating result, strife ceases (10aβ, b). *Drive out* denotes interrupting an existing relationship forcibly in order to deprive those being chased away from a situation they cling to (cf. Gen. 3:24; 4:14; Exod. 23:29, 30; Josh. 24:18; Ps. 78:55).[88] Since *the mocker* (see I: 114) clings to feeding his ego by debunking others and shaming them, an authority must forcibly expel him. Verse 10aβ gives the reason (*so that;* see n. 19) by personifying *contention* (*mādôn;* see 6:14) as a twin that *departs* (see 12:13) with the evicted mocker. Verse 10b clarifies v. 10aβ, marked by epexegetical *and* (*wᵉ;* see n. 20). *Strife* (*dîn,* see 20:8) *and disgrace* [see 3:35] *cease* (or come to an end; Gen 8:22; Job 32:1). If the mocker were teachable, one could endure him in hope of improvement, but since he is not (see 9:7-8), he must be ban-

86. Whybray, *Proverbs,* pp. 321-22.

87. They may be phonetically related by the assonance of /ē/: *gārēš lēṣ wᵉyēṣēʾ* (v. 10a); *ʾōhēb tᵉhor-lēb ḥēn śᵉpātāyw rēʿēhû* . . . (v. 11).

88. H. Ringgren, *TDOT,* 3:68, s.v. *gāraš.*

ished to protect the community from his baneful effects. Van Leeuwen comments: "The matter of boundary definition, of inclusion and exclusion . . . is crucial, for without it no group, even the family of God, can have identity with integrity."[89] And Kidner says, "What an institution sometimes needs is not reform, but the expulsion of a member" (cf. Gen. 21:10; Deut. 7:17; 13:6-11[7-12]; Psalm 101; Matt. 18:17; 1 Cor. 5:1-13; 1 Tim. 1:20; Tit. 3:10, 11; 1 John 5:16).[90] The proverb neither clarifies the social context[91] nor explains how this should be done.

11 As the focus marker in v. 9 functioned to sharply contrast the oppressor (v. 8) from the generous (v. 9), so the nominative absolute glossed by *as for* contrasts sharply the kind of person a ruler expels with the kind of person who shares his friendship.[92] The nominative absolute that entails an enjambment of v. 10a and v. 10bα by characterizing the person states the spiritual cause, and the main clause of v. 10bβ the blessed consequence. He is *one who loves* [see 1:22] *a pure* [see 15:26] *heart* (see I: 90), a synecdoche for the person. Verse 10a features the heart purity of the king's friend within, and v. 10b his gracious, amiable speech without: *whose* [see n. 24] *lips* [parallel with "heart" also in 10:8; 16:21; 24:2; cf. Job 33:3; Ps. 21:2(3)] *are gracious* (see 1:9). Heart purity, which belongs to the regenerated person, not the natural (cf. Matt. 12:33-34), is put first to protect elegant speech from being a mere facade (cf. 26:25). In fact, his attractive speech is a moral necessity of a pure heart, and winning the king's friendship is a necessary moral consequence of a righteous king (see 16:13). *The king* [see 14:28] *is a friend of his* (see 3:28). If the more technical use of "friend" for the king's confidant, such as Hushai, David's friend (2 Sam. 15:37; cf. 1 K. 4:5), were in view, one would expect, "He is the friend of the king." As in 16:10-15, an ideal king is in view. An upright attitude and high competence in speech are the prerequisites for a career in the palace (cf. 25:5; Gen. 41:37-45; 1 K. 18:3, 12; 2 K. 13:14; Ezra 7:6, 21-25; Dan. 6:1-3[2-4], 28[29]), but the proverb by nature pertains to any moral leadership.[93]

89. Van Leeuwen, *Proverbs,* p. 198.

90. Kidner, *Proverbs,* p. 148.

91. The LXX adds *ek synedriou* ("from the council").

92. Both nominative absolutes also employ the rarer epexegetical gen.s ("good of eye" and "pure of heart"; *IBHS,* p. 151, P. 9.5.3c).

93. By inserting LORD (= "the LORD loves a person to be sincere"; see n. 23) and making verset B a separate clause (= "by attractive speech a king's friendship is won"), the REB implies a contrast, leading to the perverse notion that flattery and eloquence are more sure routes to advancement than sincerity and truth.

(2) Body: The LORD Upholds Truth and Subverts Treacherous Words (22:12-14)

12 As elsewhere in Proverbs, this janus verse puts a Yahwistic saying back-to-back with a royal one (cf. 14:27-28) and continues to nerve youth to obey the faithful teaching and not to place unwarranted confidence in false doctrine. Supporting his king, the LORD upholds knowledge (or truth; v. 12a). At the same time, by asserting that he subverts treacherous words (v. 12b), it forms a transition to the treacherous words of the sluggard (v. 13) and unchaste wives (v. 14). The cause, the moral awareness of "the eyes of the LORD" (v. 12a), guarantees the consequence, the treacherous reprobates will "be cursed by the LORD" (v. 14b). *And so* marks the logical connection. The parallels are also antithetic. "The eyes of the LORD protect" and "he subverts" are relatively precise antonyms, but "knowledge" and "words of the treacherous" are not, suggesting that "knowledge" refers to the words of his faithful teachers and "words of the treacherous" deny them. The anthropomorphism *the eyes of the LORD* (see 5:21; 15:3) is also a synecdoche for the LORD himself who *protects* (*nāṣ*ᵉ*rû;* see 2:8; 3:1, 21) and so preserves *knowledge* (see I: 77). Since "knowledge" derives from the LORD (2:5-6), his eyes guard what belongs to him.[94] To protect his knowledge, *he subverts* [see 13:6] *the words* (*dibrê;* see 10:19) *of the treacherous* (see I: 110) and brings them to a dead end so that his truth alone endures.

13-14 The second proverb pair of the subunit exemplifies two kinds of words by the treacherous, namely, that of the sluggard (v. 13) and that of the harlot (v. 14). The sluggard will be tempted to find easy money, and the harlot offers easy sex.

13 The sluggard by his refusal to work undermines righteousness (see 10:4-5). In this synthetic parallelism the dramatic and revealing speech of the sluggard (see 19:15), formally introduced in v. 13aα, is begun in v. 13aβ and explained in v. 13b. *The sluggard* [see I: 114] *says* (*'āmar;* see 1:11), *"A lion* [*'ᵃrî;* cf. 22:13; 26:13; 28:1] *is outside* [*ḥûṣ;* see 1:20]. *In the midst of* [see 4:21] *the plaza* [see 1:20] *I will be as good as murdered"* (*'ērāṣēaḥ* — note the consonance with *'ᵃrî* and with *ḥûṣ). Rāṣaḥ* elsewhere denotes taking innocent human life from another human being, either intentionally (= murder) or unintentionally (= manslaughter; Exod. 20:13; Num. 35:6, 11, 16, 30). Here it is uniquely used of an animal, probably as a hyperbole and/or a metonymy. The former depicts the enormity and horror of the wrong done to him as an innocent victim; the latter means that the one forcing him into the plaza is guilty of murdering him. *As good as* represents his figurative language. By absurdly claiming that there is a lion in the street that

94. Meinhold, *Sprüche,* 2:370.

will kill him, he excuses himself from leaving the amenities of his home and his free meals, which others have provided, to venture the hard work that builds a community. To judge from the several words for lions in the Old Testament, in ancient times lions were plentiful in the forests.[95] But they were not found in the streets of Israel's fortified cities, and especially not in the fortified plaza area bustling with soldiers, merchants, administrators, and common people. Thus as in the semantically similar, but less detailed, satire at the beginning of a series of proverbs about the sluggard (26:13-16), the sluggard is represented as finding fantastic and preposterous excuses to demonstrate that no idea is too odd or fantastic to keep him off welfare. His life and that of the community are not in danger from his phantom lion in the streets but from his lazy lifestyle.

14 In 23:27, the only other passage outside chs. 1–9 that mentions "the unfaithful wife," the whore herself is the deep pit. But here "her mouth" is the pit, probably to link the proverb with "words" in 22:12. The femme fatale, who loomed so large in Collection I (2:16-19; ch. 5; 6:20-35; ch. 7; 9:13-18), is again represented as a huntress waiting to trap her prey (6:26 and 21:23), especially young people who are under the power of youthful lusts (2 Tim. 2:22). She is probably met here for the first time at the close of Collection II for two reasons. First, sexual immorality is God's judgment on the unfaithful (cf. n. 30; cf. Ps. 81:11-12[12-13]; Rom. 1:18-32). The gullible, not the pious and ethical, who obey the sages' teachings and have the godly king for a friend, fall into her trap (see v. 12). Second, her introduction forms a fitting conclusion to the Collection by matching it to that of the prologue (chs. 1–9). Now, however, the singular unfaithful wife gives way to the plural, "unfaithful wives." If the victims of one harlot are many (see 7:26), those of several must be a multitude. The proverb's synthetic parallels complement each other in a sustained metaphor. "Deep pit" and "fall there" constitute the outer frame, and "mouth of unfaithful wives" is juxtaposed with "cursed by the LORD" in its inner core, showing that their "mouth" is God's instrument to punish the unwary cursed (see v. 3). *A deep* [see 18:4] *pit* (*šûḥâ;* cf. 23:27, both times of the harlot) connotes danger and death. As in Jer. 18:20, 22, *šûḥâ* probably refers to a trap hunter's dig in contrast to *šaḥat,* the common word for the pit of the grave (Ps. 28:1; Isa. 14:15; 38:18; Ezek. 32:18), though they derive from the same root *šûaḥ* "to sink down." The metaphor

95. In prose lions are noted for their strength (Judg. 14:5-7; 1 Sam. 17:34-47; 2 Sam. 23:20) and as man eaters (1 K. 13:24-28; 20:36; 2 K. 17:25-56; Isa. 15:9; Dan. 6:27-28). Israel's psalms often use lions in simile and metaphor to represent one's enemies (Pss. 7:2[3]; 57:4[5]). These forces are likened to lions who are hungry, lie in wait, roar, and tear their prey (Pss. 10:9; 17:12; 22:13[14]; 57:4[5]). In prophetic literature rulers and nations that oppose Israel are likened to lions who roar and growl (Isa. 5:29; Jer. 2:15; 4:7; 50:17; 51:38; Ezek. 32:2; Joel 1:6; Amos 3:12; Nah. 2:11-13[12-14]; Zech. 11:3).

represents *the mouth,* certainly a metonymy for speech and perhaps also connoting her vagina (cf. 5:3; 9:17; 23:27; 30:20), as a hidden trap of foreboding danger and irretrievable ruin (see 2:19; 23:27). Seductive speech is part and parcel of stolen sex (5:3). To judge from the descriptions in the prologue, *of unfaithful women* (*zārôt;* see 2:16) designates unfaithful wives who stalk the streets to seduce young men. Unlike the sluggard's fantasy of a man-eating lion roaming the city streets, these harlots are very real, deadly predators in the streets. God proscribed adultery in the Ten Commandments (Exod. 5:20), but this proverb asserts that adulterers already stand under his curse. The verb glossed *the one cursed (zeʿûm)* may have originally meant "to snap at in anger, to scold strongly."[96] Usually the verbs associated with the noun *zaʿam* have a clear judgment aspect (cf. Ps. 69:24[25]; Ezek. 21:31[36]; 22:31; Zeph. 3:8), and the LORD's *zaʿam* finds expression in human pain and suffering (Pss. 38:3[4]; 69:24[25]; 78:49; 102:10[11]; Jer. 15:17).[97] The cursed *by the LORD* (see 1:7; 16:1-9; 22:12) realizes his damnation by the fact that he *falls* [see 11:5] *into it* (lit. "there," i.e., the harlot's "mouth"). Though in 23:28 the imagery changes from the hunter to the robber, both images represent the man who falls into her clutches as stripped of everything he has, even of his very life (see 5:10-11; 6:32-35; 7:23).

(3) Conclusion: Moral Instruction and Wealth (22:15-16)

The youth's folly includes his propensity for easy money (vv. 7-8, 13) and easy sex (v. 14). Verse 15, matching v. 6, escalates the admonition to start the son off on the right way to using the rod to keep him on it. Verse 16 returns to the unit's theme of the LORD's sovereign control over rich and poor.

15 To protect youth against the LORD's curse of casting them into the whore's deep pit, the educator must severely discipline them to drive their innate folly from them. The synthetic parallels present the reason — what Whybray describes as "the doctrine of 'original folly'"[98] (v. 15a) — and the rod as the means of effective discipline (v. 15b). *Folly* (see I: 113), not purity, *is bound up* [see 3:3; Gen. 44:30] *in the heart* [see 2:11] *of a youth* (see 1:4; 22:6). *The rod* [see 22:8] *of discipline* (*mûsār;* see 1:2) *will remove it far* [see

96. C. A. Keller, *TLOT,* 2:1,143, s.v. *qll.* The noun *zaʿam,* used of the LORD, speaks of his burning wrath, as its synonyms confirm: *ʾap* (Isa. 10:5, 25), *ḥᵃrôn ʾāp* (Isa. 13:9), *ḥēmâ ʾap* (Isa. 66:15); *ḥēmâ* (Ps. 38:1 [2]), *ʿebrâ* (Isa. 13:9), *qeṣep* (Jer. 10:10).

97. The verb with a human subject means "to speak curses," "do injury to someone by cursing" (cf. Num. 23:8; Prov. 24:24). In connection with God this is the verb's probable meaning in Num. 23:8; Mic. 6:10, but in Isa. 66:14; Zech. 1:12; Mal. 1:4 it is not easy to decide between the meanings "be angry" and "curse." Since the context of Prov. 22:14 features speech, the notion of "cursed" fits well (cf. B. Wiklander, *TDOT,* 4:107-10, s.v. *zaʿam*).

98. Whybray, *Proverbs,* p. 125.

19:7] *from him* (see 22:5, 6). Youth's intractable insolence and his immoral propensity for laziness (v. 13), lust (v. 14) and greed (v. 16) are tightly bound within his very constitution (v. 15a; cf. Gen. 8:21; Job 14:4; 25:4; Ps. 51:5[7]; Isa. 48:8), but the father's disciplining rod breaks folly's hold and frees him (v. 15b). Since folly incurs the LORD's curse (v. 14b; cf. Eph. 2:3), this proverb seeks to protect the youth from eternal death through the father's relatively light sting. Prov. 20:30 called for bruising wounds to scour defiled humanity generally; 22:15 applies that truth to depraved youth particularly. Bodily harm without heals the moral rot within. Whereas most proverbs call for the youth to give an attentive ear, moral education calls for physical punishment along with sharp reproof for wrongdoing (29:15). The father must not underestimate the difficulty of his task, for he does battle with an innate recalcitrance and perversity. He must both tear down and build up; eradicate and implant.[99] The English proverb "Spare the rod and spoil the child" was probably derived from Proverbs (cf. also 10:13; 13:24; 23:13-14; 29:15).[100]

16 The unit's keyword, *ʿāšîr* ("rich"), forms an *inclusio* with v. 1, and the catchword *dāl* binds this conclusion of the second subunit with that of the first (v. 9). The last word of Collection II aptly pertains to social justice toward the poor, forming an *inclusio* with the first lecture of Collection I (see 1:8-19) and the first subunit of Collection II (10:1-5). The first admonition of the next collection after its prologue (22:17-21) again picks up this theme: "Do not plunder the poor *(dāl)*" (22:22). The parallels *he who oppresses the poor* (see 14:31) in v. 16aα and *he who gives gifts* [see 3:28; 5:9; 6:31; 30:8] *to the rich person* (see 22:1, 7) are two methods of self-aggrandizement. "Gifts were made to the rich not out of love, but to secure their favor," says Toy.[101] In this enjambment *to increase* [*riches*] (see 6:35; 13:11) *for himself* in v. 16aβ is gapped in v. 16bα. The predicate *come only to lack* (see 11:24; 14:23; 21:5) censures grinding down the poor and currying favor with the rich. The oppressor and self-aggrandizer unexpectedly suffer(s) the loss of what is essential to life (cf. Luke 14:12-14). The giver to the rich is unrighteous, for when the righteous give, they enrich (22:9), not diminish (see 21:26).[102] The juxtaposition of one who takes money from the poor, who needs it, with the one who gives to the rich, who does not need it, points up the folly. For example, "It happens when executives are paid exorbitant sums . . . and overwork their re-

99. McKane, *Proverbs,* pp. 564-65.

100. Aitken (*Proverbs,* p. 145) cites an Egyptian counterpart: "Boys have ears on their back sides," and Delitzsch (*Proverbs,* p. 328) cites Menander (*Monost* 422): "He who is not flogged is not educated."

101. Toy, *Proverbs,* p. 420.

102. Garrett (*Proverbs,* p. 188) refers the giver to the borrower in v. 16, but were that connection intended, one would expect the catchword *lwh* "to lend," not *ntn* "to give" (see v. 9).

maining employees."[103] This unit makes clear that the paradoxical outcome for the oppressor and self-aggrandizer is due to the eyes of the LORD, who protects his moral imperium (see I: 73; 14:31; 15:25; 17:5; 22:12, 23).

III. COLLECTION III: THE THIRTY SAYINGS OF THE WISE (22:17–24:22)

For demarcating the Thirty Sayings of the Wise as the Third Collection and for its structural analysis, see I: 21-24.

The external evidence of the Egyptian *Instruction of Amenemope* (ca. 1186-1069 B.C.) confirms the internal evidence that the Thirty Sayings of the Wise is a distinct anthology of wisdom sayings. Most scholars believe that the Thirty Sayings of the Wise shows a *creative* use of *Amenemope.*[104] The structural model for this collection, "Do I not write for you thirty sayings?" derives from the last chapter of *Amenemope* (27:6): "Look to these thirty chapters." In Egypt, and we should probably assume the same about this collection, the holy number "thirty" symbolizes a complete and perfect teaching. But its material dependence on *Amenemope* extends only for the first eleven sayings (22:16–23:11). The next saying introduced by the educational saying at 23:12 that separates it and the next unit of the Thirty Sayings is common to the Aramaic Ahiqar. The saying against debt surety finds thematic analogy in the Aramaic and Akkadian wisdom tradition, but not in the Egyptian. The lampooning saying against drunkenness (23:29-35) descends from the Egyptian tradition, but not from *Amenemope.*[105]

A. PROLOGUE: SAYING 1 (22:17-21)

17 *Incline your ear and hear the sayings of the wise,*[106]

103. Van Leeuwen, *Proverbs,* p. 200.

104. For a full account of the scholarly discussion of this relationship — namely, whether the Hebrew depends on the Egyptian, or vice versa, or both depend on some no longer extant earlier work, see G. Bryce, *A Legacy of Wisdom: The Egyptian Contribution to the Wisdom of Israel* (Lewisburg: Bucknell University, 1979). For a judicious evaluation of the dependence of Prov. 22:17–24:22 on *Amenemope,* see Washington, "Wealth and Poverty," pp. 207-11.

105. D. Römheld, *Wege der Weisheit: Die Lehren Amenemopes und Proverbien 22:17–24:22* (BZAW 184; Berlin: de Gruyter, 1989), p. 37.

106. The text of v. 17a is uncertain. The LXX of v. 17a reads *logois sophōn paraballe son ous, kai akoue emon logon* (= *d^ebārâ?*), "Incline your ear to the words of the wise, and hear my word." This variation from the MT might suggest that "words of the

and pay attention to[107] *to my knowledge,*[108]
18 *because [it is] lovely when you keep them in your belly,*
[when] they are fixed together[109] *on your lips.*
19 *In order that your trust may be in the LORD,*
I teach you[110] *today, even you!*[111]

---

wise" was originally a heading that became glossed into the text of the LXX and of the MT in different ways, necessitating other adjustments. Since 22:17–24:22 is a distinct collection, one expects a heading matching 10:1; 24:23; 25:1; 30:1; 31:1. More specifically, the heading in 24:23, "These also belong to the wise," begs for an earlier heading such as "the sayings of the wise." Moreover, v. 17 is now a heavy tricola in the MT, and for the resulting bicola to have "ear" and "heart" in parallel is normal. Accordingly, even Meinhold (*Sprüche,* p. 378), a most conservative text critic, thinks that the original text of v. 17a may have read after a superscription, "Incline your ear and hear my sayings." However, the parallels in the MT, the "sayings of the wise" and "my knowledge," make clear that Solomon has adopted and adapted the sayings of other wise men. The connection between a heading, "the sayings of wise men" and "my sayings," nevertheless, is unclear. Moreover, the change from "the sayings of the wise" to "my word" in the LXX is consistent with its other changes to purge the text of authors other than Solomon. But there is no motive for the MT to drop this one heading since it preserves others that make clear that Solomon did not author their collections. The MT makes plain that Solomon functioned as an author-editor of 22:17–24:22, but infers that he is only the copy editor of 24:23-30. A superscription at 22:17 would strongly suggest a different author than Solomon for the Thirty Sayings of the Wise and confusingly orphan the "my" of its prologue (22:17-21).

107. Lit. "set the heart to" (see *HALOT,* 4:1,485, s.v. *šît;* BDB p. 1,011, s.v. *šît*). The common idiom suggests that *libb^{e}kâ* is the object, not the subject.

108. The LXX reads *l^{e}da'tî* as an infinitive "to know," making *kî-nā'îm* its object (= "to know that they are good"), but Toy (*Proverbs,* p. 423) objects that the proper object of "know" is "instruction" (1:2; 4:1).

109. On the basis of "mooring peg" in the putative parallel *Amenemope* (3:16), Gemser *(Sprüche)* et al. reconstruct *b^{e}yātēd* or *k^{e}yātēd* "with/like a wooden peg." Plöger (*Sprüche,* p. 262) rightly rejects the suggestion because *Amenemope* has in view a storm of words requiring appropriate silence. Meinhold (*Sprüche,* p. 379) thinks that the Egyptian perceives in the tongue a ship and at its end a peg or a pole so that it is able to remain immovable in the storm of words, the dispute. By contrast, Prov. 22:18 does not aim for silence.

110. A performative perfective, signifying that the situation occurs at the moment of speaking (*IBHS,* p. 489, P. 30.5.1d).

111. Instead of *'ap-'āttâ,* LXX^{SA}, followed by Gemser (*Sprüche,* p. 84) et al., reads *tēn hodon autou* (*'orḥôteyw* "his ways" [cf. Pss. 25:4; 103:7]). Gemser notes that in Egyptian wisdom the "way of God" is equivalent to "the will of God" over against "the fear of God" (cf. 22:23; 23:11, 18; 24:3-4, 6, 12, 14, 18, 20, 22). Some interpreters emend "today even you" to *'orḥôt ḥayyîm* "the way of life" (cf. *Amenemope* 1.7; 16.8; Prov. 2:19; 5:6; 10:17). Plöger (*Sprüche,* p. 262) dissents from following the LXX. He prefers the application made in the MT and understands the LXX as supplying an expected object of the verb "to cause to know." Indeed, the LXX probably had "even you" in its *Vorlage* but confounded it with v. 20 since it begins that verse with *kai sy.* Toy (*Proverbs,* p. 425) wrongly believes that the LXX interpreted an impossible Hebrew expression (cf. 26:4).

20 *Have I not written*[112] *for you thirty sayings,*[113]

112. Probably not a performative perfective. The sage now teaches what he formerly wrote down (see 2:1). The LXX translator read "you write," erroneously thinking the son ought to write these good doctrines. He was puzzled by his unique *Vorlage,* but guessed from the root *šlš* "three" that the son should write them *trissōs* "in a threefold manner." The other ancient translators, although reading "I write," also associated the disputed word with *šālōš* (see G. Bryce, *Legacy of Wisdom,* pp. 226-27, n. 53). This reading comports better with the emendation proposed in the next note than with K and Q, which they obviously did not read. Instructively, the Vulg.'s reading *tripliciter* shows that this was the reading of the Hebrew text in Palestine as late as the fourth century A.D. Rashi (M. Lyons, "Rashi's *Commentary on the Book of Proverbs*" [submitted in partial fulfillment of the requirements for the degree of rabbi, 1936], p. 113) also associated the word with "three" and referred it to the three parts of the Tanak.

113. "Thirty" *(šl[w]šym = šᵉlôšîm)* represents an emendation of both *šlšwm* (= *šilšôm* "formerly"; so K) and *šlyšym* (= *šālîšîm,* glossed "noble things"; so Q). Contemporary lexicographers agree that Q represents III *šālîš.* This word in its other 13 or 14 uses always means "adjutant, a military officer of some kind" (2 K. 7:2, 17, 19; 9:25; 15:25) or "officers" (Exod. 14:7; 15:4; 1 K. 9:22 [= 2 Chr. 8:9]; 2 K. 10:25[2x]; Ezek. 23:15, 23; and 1 Chr. 11:11 Q), but 2 Sam. 23:8 shows a similar confusion as Prov. 22:20. Admittedly these references are all in prose, but a lexical jump from a military officer to "noble sayings" even in poetry is fanciful. The appeal by Delitzsch (*Proverbs,* p. 332) to *nᵉgîdîm* in Prov. 8:6 is not convincing because the reading "what is straightforward" is not fanciful and the text is doubtful. In prose, K's reading *šilšôm* occurs 24 times and always in conjunction with an initial *tᵉmôl/tᵉmōl* or its variants *'etmôl* and *gam-tᵉmôl gam-šilšôm,* "yesterday (and) the third day" (i.e., "formerly"). In poetry this notion, with reference to either the immediate or remote past, is expressed by the abbreviated forms *'etmôl* (Ps. 90:4; Isa. 30:33; Mic. 2:8) or *tᵉmôl* (Job 8:9), never by *šilšôm.* Indeed, from a phonological point of view the dental /t/ of the attested form would form a nice consonance with *kātabtî, mô'ēṣôt,* and *dā'at,* whereas the /š/ of *šilšôm* has only a limited, sibilant correspondence with /ṣ/ of *mô'ēṣôt.* In sum, it is unreasonable to suppose that K means "formerly" and represents the original text. Admittedly "formerly" makes a nice contrast with "today" in v. 19, but this unique meaning does not fit well in a prologue introducing a new collection of Proverbs. "This rendering is improbable, for the reason that it introduces a strange contrast between the instruction now given to teach trust in Yahweh, and that formerly given to impart the capacity of answering (v. 21)" (Toy, *Proverbs,* p. 423). The K and Q readings of the MT and a similar confusion in 1 Chr. 11:11 show that excessive confidence cannot be placed in the MT as regards these unsatisfying readings. By contrast, the striking affinities of the prologue and admonitions in Prov. 22:17–23:11 with ch. 1 of *Amenemope* plausibly support the emendation to *šᵉlôšîm* "thirty [sayings]." The conclusion of the alleged Egyptian counterpart enumerates its content as consisting of 30 chapters. From a text-critical viewpoint, this emendation is most plausible. Against this reading, however, originally proposed by Erman (1923) and adopted by the majority of subsequent scholars, it is objected that Hebrew grammar expects some specification of the thing enumerated, e.g., *dᵉbārîm* "sayings" or *'ᵃmārîm* "words." However, Hebrew grammar commonly omits "certain specifications of *measure, weight* or *time* after numerals" (GKC, P. 134n). Although GKC limits his examples to these categories, one can easily extend the point of

as[114] *advice*[115] *and knowledge,*
21 *to teach you to be honest*[116] *in speaking reliable words,*[117]
to bring back reliable[118] *reports to those*[119] *who commission*[120] *you?*

---

grammar to "sayings" (cf. 22:17) because the constraints of poetry demand it, and it causes no ambiguity. In 2 Sam. 24:11 the numeral is used absolutely with reference to "three [options]." R. N. Whybray ("Structure and Composition of Proverbs 22:17–24:22," in *Crushing the Boundaries: Essays in Biblical Interpretation in Honor of Michael D. Golder,* ed. S. E. Porter, P. Joyce, and D. E. Orten [Leiden: Brill, 1994], p. 87) objects that "Prov. 22:17–24:22 is *not* a single work and does *not* comprise thirty proverbs." Following A. Niccacci ("Proverbi 22:17–23:11," *SBFLA* 29 [1979] 93), he holds that 22:17–24:22 contains three independent units: 22:17–23:11; 23:12-25; and 23:26–24:22. To be sure, this division is legitimate, but Plöger (*Sprüche,* p. 266) and Meinhold (*Sprüche,* p. 374) are on firmer ground when they recognize the existence of three sections, while still maintaining that the whole is a collection of 30 proverbs. The other collections also contain several sections with unique introductions, but they are gathered into broader collections according to editorial superscriptions (e.g., 10:1a; 24:23a; 25:1; 30:1; 31:1), a prologue (22:17-21), or both (1:1–9:18). Scholars differ in their precise analysis of the material from 23:12 onward after the agreed-upon ten "sayings" that are preceded by an introduction in 22:17–23:11, in part because they fail to recognize that its prologue (22:17-20) is the first saying (see p. 23). Bryce (*A Legacy of Wisdom,* p. 85) comments: "The fact that the book can be generally divided into thirty small sections, dealing with approximately twenty-four to twenty-eight subjects, provides a general guide for understanding the way in which the composition has been shaped around the number of sayings."

114. *Beth essentiae* (*IBHS,* p. 198, P. 11.2.5e).

115. Grimme (see D. Herzog, "Die Sprüche des Amen-em-ope und Proverbien 22:17-24, 35," *ZSem* 7 [1929] 148; cf. Fichtner [*BHS*]), emended *bmʿṣwt* into *bm ʿṣwt* "in them are (wise) "counsel" to eliminate the negative connotation attached to the word *mʿṣwt* ("advice"). Since the noun always occurs in the pl., the pl. may specify the quality of "counsel," not the number (*IBHS,* p. 121, P. 7.4.2a). The following sing. supports this interpretation.

116. Toy (*Proverbs,* p. 425) et al. eliminate *qōšṭ* as a gloss explaining *ʾimrê ʾemet* to late readers more familiar with Aramaic than with Hebrew. Cody ("Notes on Proverbs 22,21 and 22,23b," *Bib* 61 [1980] 418) objects. "Since a late reader able to use the Hebrew text in the first place should not have found the words *ʾimrê ʾemet* puzzling in themselves, *qōšṭ* would seem to be not a gloss but original." Cody (p. 419) et al. with more probability explains away *ʾimrê ʾemet* "reliable words" as a scribal gloss to correct the enclitic *mem* constuction *ʾamārîm ʾemet* in v. 21b that then slipped into the text in the wrong place. But he is unconvincing when he explains the resulting brevity of verset A from the fact that the gloss replaced something else that was loss.

117. An accusative of specification (*IBHS,* p. 173, P. 10.2.3a).

118. Attribute gen. after enclitic *mem* (see *IBHS,* pp. 158-60, P. 9.8).

119. Or "him . . . commissions," a pl. of majesty (see GKC, P. 124k).

120. Or "who have sent you." The independent relative ptcp. by itself expresses neither time nor aspect (*IBHS,* p. 623, P. 37.5e). Delitzsch (*Proverbs,* p. 332) et al. prefers to read *lešōleḥeykā* "to those who ask you." (Rashi [Lyons, "Rashi's *Commentary,*" p. 113] also

The prologue (22:17-21) shows affinities with the first "chapter" of the Egyptian exemplar as well as with its last chapter and preamble, and picks up the direct address of the father to the son (1:8), using the pronouns "I" and "you" in v. 17.

The prologue consists of two quatrains (vv. 17-18, 20-21) around a center line (v. 19). Verses 17-18, which pertain to the son, contain the typical admonition to accept wholeheartedly the adjusted sayings of the wise (v. 17) with motivation (v. 18). Verses 20-21, which pertain to the father, define his sayings (v. 20) and his purpose in writing (v. 21). The center line janus, with its focus on the son in v. 19a and on the father in v. 19b, founds their theological intention on trust in the LORD. The framing quatrains follow a main cause (MC) subordinate clause (SC) pattern, but the center line reverses this pattern so that the prologue is stitched together by an MC:SC//SC:MC// MC:SC pattern. In sum, Solomon aims through these thirty sayings to ground the character and social structure of Israel by inculcating these sayings that demand trust in the LORD into the belly of Israel's covenant sons and placing them on their lips (v. 21).

A complex pattern of catchwords stitches these stanzas together. The Hebrew pronoun *kā* ("your") occurs in every verset except v. 20b. The root *yd'* ("know") occurs in every verse except v. 18: *da'tî* ("my knowledge," v. 17), *hôda'tîkā* ("I cause you to know," vv. 19, 21), *da'at* ("knowledge," v. 20). Verse 19 is stitched together with v. 18 by the paronomasia between the final words of the A versets, *b^ebiṭnekā* ("your belly") and *mibtaḥekā* ("your trust"). The synonyms *dibrê* "sayings" (v. 17) and *'imrê* "words" (v. 21), with reference to the same content, form an *inclusio* around the prologue.

1. Motivating the Son to Hear (22:17-18)

Verses 17 and 18 are bonded together syntactically by the subordinating conjunction "because" and by the pronoun "them," having "sayings of the wise" as their antecedent. Imagery of organs associated with the learning process — ear, heart, belly, and lips — bind together the admonitions to accept and memorize the sayings (v. 17) with motivation (v. 18). The learning process, as also in Egyptian wisdom literature (see I: 65; 4:20-27), progresses from

---

interpreted the MT in this way.) They appeal to the LXX reading *proballomenois soi* "to those who question you." The interpretation of *proballein* has been influenced by its rendering of *l^ehāšîb* as *tou apokrinesthai* ("to answer"). Cody ("Notes on Proverbs 22,21 and 22,23b," p. 419), however, objects: "The verb *proballein* does not mean 'to ask' a question requiring a truthful or accurate answer. In the middle voice, with a dative and without a direct object, it means 'to accuse someone,'" a meaning that Heb. *šā'al* does not have. Cody also notes that the Coptic verb that means "to send" was used in translating the Gk. *proballein*. Finally, "v. 21b (MT) makes perfect good sense" (McKane, *Proverbs*, p. 377).

the outward *ear* that acquires the sayings (v. 17a), to the interior *heart* set on their acquisition (v. 17b), to preserving them in the *belly* that is thought to house the heart, to the outward *lips* that represent them to others (cf. 4:20-27).[121]

17 The synthetic admonitions, which escalate from *incline your ear* (see 4:20) to *and hear* (see 1:8) and *pay attention to* (see n. 107), emphatically admonish obedience to the inherited wisdom and unbroken concentration on it (see I: 62). The ear is the exterior organ that receives the information, and the heart is the interior organ that directs the whole body (4:20-27). According to 2:2, a listening ear entails an adaptable heart. The parallels, *the sayings of the wise* (see 1:6) and *to my knowledge* (see I: 77), infer that Solomon is adopting and adapting the sayings of his sage-peers.

18 The medial emphatic *because* motivates the son to accept the twofold admonitions with their twofold results, and logically motivates the son by imaging the carefully preserved saying in the heart and forever fixed firmly on his lips as something exquisitely pleasant or charming. *It is lovely* (i.e., possessing the quality of exceeding beauty that appeals to the heart as well as to the eye)[122] qualifies the two following parallel circumstances of having tenaciously and accurately memorized the sayings within and being able to reproduce them readily and articulately as the occasion demands without. The metaphor *when you keep them* (*tišmᵉrēm;* see 2:8) means "exercise great care to protect them" and entails memorizing them forever.[123] *In your belly* may be a shortened form of the Egyptianism "in the casket of your heart" (see 18:8; 20:30). *When,* to judge from the asyndetic construction, is gapped in the B verset. *They are fixed* (see 4:18) connotes to be "lasting," "safe," so that they endure (see 12:19) as well as being ready. *Together on your lips* (cf. 4:24) both collectivizes the sayings and individualizes them (cf. Exod. 19:8) to be spoken at the right time.

121. N. Shupak, "The 'Sitz im Leben' of Proverbs in the Light of a Comparison of Biblical and Egyptian Wisdom Literature," *RB* 94 (1987) 98-119.

122. *Nāʿîm* occurs 13 times in the Bible: as an epithet of beloved heroic fighters (2 Sam. 1:23), of the beloved's lover (Song 1:16), of David, as the beloved singer of Israel's songs (2 Sam. 23:1), of a melodious harp (Ps. 81:2[3]), of verbal compliments (Prov. 23:8), of treasures (24:4), of the pleasant circumstances when brothers live together in unity (Ps. 133:1), of praising God (135:3; 147:1), and as a substantival adjective of delightful places (16:6), eternal pleasures (16:11), and years of prosperity (Job 36:11). Its synonyms are *šāpār* "to be beautiful" (Ps. 16:6), *yāpeh* "fair"/"handsome," *neʾhābîm* "loved" (2 Sam. 1:23), *ṭôb* "good" (Job 36:11; Ps. 133:1), *nāʾwâ* "fitting" (Ps. 147:1), *yāqār* "rare/precious" (Prov. 24:4). Though the verb *nāʿam* occurs in Prov. 2:10; 9:17, the adjective occurs only in this collection (22:18; 23:8; 24:4; cf. 24:25).

123. In *Amenemope* (22:15) the metaphor means to keep them locked up from too free an access to the lips: "Better is a man whose talk (remains) in his belly than he who speaks it out injuriously" (*AEL,* 2:159).

2. Center Line: Theological Motivation (22:19)

The prologue now shifts from the son's role in the learning process to that of the sage and, more importantly, adjusts the adopted sayings of the wise to faith in Israel's covenant-keeping God. Beyond making the son charming to others, the sayings enable him to realize a dynamic, trusting relationship with Israel's covenant-keeping God. That your trust (see 3:5) *may be in the LORD* modifies the main clause of v. 19b and entails that Israel's God inspired his sage in writing them down and teaching them (see I: 80) so that the believer may have a relationship with God. Through the mediation of the sage's inspired, and thus trustworthy, teachings, the son has the LORD as his object of trust and seat of authority. *I cause you to know* (*hôdaʿtîkā;* see 1:23) represents the son as taking an active part in internalizing the inspired sayings.[124] Even the most brilliant moral sayings are powerless without personal application. *Today* refers to each day of the son's life because he is to have them always ready on his tongue (cf. Heb. 3:13; 4:7 with Ps. 95:7). The daily calling to mind of the collected sayings becomes the "today," not just one day in the past when they were first memorized. It entails the contemporary relevance of these ancient sayings for each day into the indefinite future. Emphatic *even* [125] and the tautological personal pronoun *you* concentrate the application of the sayings on the son. This active trust in the LORD, who reveals his will through the adjusted sayings, entails a constant commitment to the LORD and his words, not an autonomous reliance on oneself (cf. 3:5-7) or a passive resignation to fate. This faith distinguishes Solomon's sayings from those of his peers in the ancient Near East.

3. The Father's Purpose (22:20-21)

A purpose phrase subordinates v. 21 to v. 20.

20 The synthetic parallels of v. 20 qualify the sayings externally as being 30 in number and written down (v. 20a) and as belonging to the sphere of moral knowledge (v. 20b). *Have I not written* expresses a strong asseveration (i.e., "I certainly"; see 8:1; 14:22) to preserve the sayings accurately (see I: 62). *For you* emphasizes the father's personal effort on behalf of his son. Bryce explains, without demonstration, the number, *thirty sayings* (see n. 113), as a reference to a "revered tradition of Egyptian wisdom, which was mediated through the wisdom schools of Palestine, to give to his book the authority and weight of tradition."[126] Verset B qualifies the sayings as authoritative, unshakable advice, having an insight into the moral deed-destiny nexus. *As* (see n. 114) marks the state or condition of the sayings. Of the seven uses

124. *IBHS,* pp. 434-35, P. 27.1d, e.

125. *IBHS,* pp. 362-63, P. 39.34a-d; *HALOT,* 1:76, s.v. *ʾap.*

126. Bryce, *Legacy of Egypt,* p. 86.

of *advice (môʿēṣâ)* in the Bible, only here it has its positive sense of being definite, unchangeable, authoritative (see 1:31; 22:20), not "an [insidious] plan, decision." Its combination with *knowledge* (*dāʿat;* see I: 77) may constitute a hendiadys, "knowledgeable advice."[127]

21 The 30 sayings also aim to make the son reliable to those who commission him. Verset A specifies the development of his character as a trustworthy speaker, and verset B specifies those to whom he reports. Through these sayings, the king insures that the entire chain of command within his administration will be honest, making its decisions on the basis of truth, not distortion, intrigues, and misrepresentations. *To teach you* (see v. 19) links vv. 19-21. *Honesty (qōšṭ)* is a *hap. leg.,* but an Aramaic cognate and the use of its denominative verb in post–Biblical Hebrew shows that the term has the sense of right, justice, rectitude, and aptness, not just truth (*pace* NIV). Cody says, "*Qōšṭ* here is the quality of a man whose speech and actions conform to what reality is and requires. In that sense it comes close to Egyptian *maʿat,* 'truth, justice, righteousness, correctness, order, proportion', whose implications for social justice remind us of what is to follow in the entire section running from 22:17 to 24:22."[128] Possibly *qōšṭ* is a metonymy for the 30 sayings, and *reliable* [or truthful, *ʾemet;* 3:3] *words* (*ʾimrê;* see 1:2) functions as a sortal apposition. But that interpretation results in a semantically inapposite parallelism. A connection between honest teachings and honest reports seems less cogent than connecting the formation of an honest character to giving honest reports. If *qōšṭ* refers to human character, "reliable words" is best understood as an accusative of specification (= "with regard to truthful words") glossed *in speaking reliable words.*[129] *To bring back* (*lᵉhāšîb;* see 1:23; 15:1) expresses the purpose of the teaching. The emphatic repetition *reliable reports (ʾamārîm ʾemet)* firmly links verset B with verset A in this synthetic expansion of his purpose. On the bases of the parallels in *Amenemope* 1.6 and the extant Coptic versions of this verse, Cody thinks that *ʾamārîm* more specifically means "reports."[130] Indeed, this is also the meaning of both *dābār* and *ʾamārîm* with personal accusative.[131] The verse does not identify *to those who commission you* (see 10:26; cf. 13:17; 15:23; 26:6). Some exegetes think that tuition-paying parents or guardians, who have sent their sons to school and desire an account of their progress, are in view, and so gloss the independent relative, "to those who sent you." Toy says that this is the only possible meaning of the MT![132] But the evidence

127. Gemser, *Sprüche,* p. 84.
128. Cody, "Notes on Proverbs 22,21," p. 424.
129. *IBHS,* p. 173, P. 10.2.3a.
130. Cody, "Notes on Proverbs 22,21," p. 423.
131. BDB, p. 999, s.v. *šûb.*
132. *Toy,* Proverbs, p. 424.

points to home schooling in ancient Israel (see I: 62). Thus the genre points to commissioners to whom the son is accountable. Cody comments, "The general purpose of the *genre* 'instruction' in Egypt and in Israel leads us to see the man who 'sends' as one of those important persons in whose service receiving the instruction of Prv 22:17–24:22 was likely to be engaged, a man who tells his councillors, diplomats, emissaries, to look into various situations on which he expects reliable reports."[133] The use of the equivalent form in 10:26 and 25:13 validates his interpretation. Perhaps Solomon adopted an earlier collection addressed to a go-between on behalf of his principles.[134] But proverbs typically function as exemplars for numerous applications. Honesty and reliable reporting are moral prerequisites for employment in many businesses.[135]

B. SECTION A: A DECALOGUE OF SAYINGS ABOUT WEALTH (22:22–23:11)

22 *Do not rob a poor person because he is a poor,*
and do not crush the afflicted in the gate;
23 *because the* Lord *will plead their case,*
and so he will despoil those that despoiled them of life.
24 *Do not associate with a hothead,*
and with a wrathful[136] *person do not get involved;*
25 *lest you learn his ways,*[137]
and so you fetch a snare for your life.
26 *Do not be among those who strike a palm,*
among those who pledge securities[138] *for loans.*
27 *If you do not have the means to repay,*
why[139] *should your very bed be taken*[140] *from under you?*

133. Cody, "Notes on Proverbs 22,21," p. 423.

134. The prologue to *Amenemope* similarly reads: "Knowing how to answer one who speaks, to reply to one who sends a message" (1.5, 6) (*AEL,* 2:148).

135. The verse seems to be an adjustment of the prologue of *Amenemope* (1:1-6): "very rule for relations with elders,/For conduct toward magistrates;/Knowing how to answer one who speaks,/To reply to one who sends a message."

136. Abstract pl. (*IBHS,* pp. 120-21, P. 7.4.2a).

137. Q is pl.; K, sing.

138. The form is definite, though the expected form is *bāʿōrᵉbîm* (cf. *bᵉʿereb* in 7:9) (cf. *IBHS,* p. 238, P. 13.3c).

139. The LXX, Syr., and Targ. (apart from the Zamora ms.) do not render *lmh.* Gemser (*Sprüche,* p. 84) explains the MT as due to dittography from the preceding *lšlm.* This would explain the *lm* but not the final *h.* More probably, the ancients were confused by its interruption of the logical connection between the protasis and the apodosis.

140. *IBHS,* pp. 70-71, P. 4.4.2a.

28 *Do not move an ancient boundary*
that your ancestors have set.
29 *Do you see a person who is skillful in his commission?*
He will present himself before kings;
he will not present himself before obscure people.
23:1 *When you sit down to eat with a ruler,*
mark well what[141] *is before you;*
2 *and place a knife*[142] *in our gullet*
if you are a glutton.[143]
3 *do not crave*[144] *his delicious morsels,*
for[145] *that is deceptive food.*
4 *Do not become weary to make yourself rich;*[146]
stop trusting in your own insight.[147]
5 *Will you let your eyes*[148] *glance*[149] *at riches?*
If you do, they[150] *are not.*
Surely, without question[151] *they will make a set of wings for themselves;*
like an eagle they will fly[152] *toward the heavens.*
6 *Do not insist on eating the food*[153] *of a begrudging host,*[154]

141. Or "who."

142. Stumped by two *hap. legs.*, the LXX renders "and apply your hand" (cf. A. J. Baumgartner, *Étude critique sur l'état du texte du Livre des Proverbes d'après les principales traductions anciennes* [Leipzig: Imprimerie Orientale W. Drugulin, 1890], p. 204).

143. A rare instance when Eng. "gullet" and "glutton" catch the assonance of Heb. *bl'* and *b'l-nepeš.*

144. K reads *tit'āw* and Q, *tit'āyw,* with no difference in meaning.

145. Lit. "and" (see *IBHS,* p. 635, P. 38.1g; p. 649, P. 39.2.1c).

146. The LXX, Syr., and Targ. point *lᵉhaʿᵃšîr* as *lᵉheʿāšîr* "rich person." The external evidence favors the MT (cf. *IBHS,* pp. 24-28, P. 1.6.3).

147. Lit. "Cease from your own insight."

148. The pl. subject *ʿêneykā* could be the subject (cf. 1 Sam. 4:15), but the construction would be unusual.

149. Reading tolerative *Hiphil tāʿîp* with Q, not *Qal tāʿûp* with K (see *IBHS,* p. 446, P. 27.5c).

150. Lit. "riches and they."

151. Toy (*Proverbs,* p. 432) emends *ʿāśōh* to *ʿōšer,* "wealth," but the subject is inherent in *haʿᵃšîr* of v. 4.

152. Reading *yāʿûp* with Q, not *waʿᵉp* of K. I *ʿēp* means "to be tired." II *ʿēp* can be a bi-form of II *ʿûp* "to be dark," but neither meaning fits the context. Some mss. read *wāʿûp* "and it will fly," but the syntax militates against this reading. It is one of ten words registered in the Masora with initial *yodh* to be read instead of *waw* (Delitzsch, *Proverbs,* p. 338).

153. The ancient versions and one medieval Hebrew ms. omit *leḥem.* Driver

do not even[155] *desire*[156] *his delicious morsels;*
7 *because as he calculates*[157] *within himself, so is he.*
"Eat and drink," he says to you, but his heart is not with you.
8 *As for the piece of food that you will have eaten, you will vomit it;*
and[158] *you will have wasted your pleasant words.*
9 *In the ears of a fool do not speak,*[159]
because he will show contempt for your prudent words.
10 *Do not move the ancient boundaries;*
and do not enter the fields of the fatherless.

("Problems in the Hebrew Text of Proverbs," p. 187) deletes or transposes *leḥem* and understands *'et* as the preposition "with." But *'et* can be used with an indefinite direct-object acc. (*IBHS,* p. 180, P. 10.3.1b). The more difficult MT should be retained.

154. Lit. "the evil person of eye" (see 22:9).

155. Interpreting *waw* as an epexegetical conjunction.

156. See n. 156.

157. The LXX and the Targ. misunderstood the *hap. leg.* that is preserved in the MT. The LXX (cf. Syr.) rendered *šāʿar* as *tricha* "hair" (< *śēʿār*), and the Targ. as "high gate" *(šaʿar)*. McKane (*Proverbs,* p. 385; cf. REB) favors the LXX because a hair in one's throat fits the notion of vomiting. L. Durr ("Hebrew *nepeš* = Akkadian *napistu* = Gurgel, Kehle," *ZAW* 43 [1925], pp. 262-63) suggested from a line in *Amenemope* (14.7) that it means "blocking" and emended *bᵉnapšô* to *bᵉnepeš* without the suffix, yielding "an obstacle in the throat." Because *Amenemope* compares the stingy man to a storm within one, Plöger (*Sprüche,* p. 263) et al. emend the text to *śaʿar* "storm." *HALOT* (4:1,613-14, s.v. I *šʿr*) follows a lexicon tradition to render I *šʿr* "calculate, reckon," appealing to post-Biblical Hebrew and Jewish Aramaic and to the later Aramaic noun meaning "interest, market price." They (4:1,618, s.v. II *šaʿar*) further argue that the nominal form occurs in Gen. 26:12 with the meaning "measure," agreeing with this meaning for the verb. Most English versions accept this tradition (AV, ASV, NASB, JPS, GNB, JP, NAB, NIV, NRSV, NLT). M. Dahood (*Proverbs and Northwest Semitic Philology* [Rome: Pontifical Biblical Institute, 1963], p. 47) agrees but restricts the meaning to "arrange, serve (food)," rendering the line, "like one serving his own appetite, such is he!" K. L. Barker ("Proverbs 23:7 — 'To Think' or 'To Serve Food'?" *JANES* 19 [1989] 3-8) agrees with this derivation and sense but renders the line "for as he serves food (i.e., 'puts on a feast' within himself)." While it is true that in Ugaritic the verb may denote "serve food, set tables," it is also used in Ugaritic for "arrange balances," as J. Gray (*Legacy of Canaan: The Ras Shamra Texts and Their Relevance to the Old Testament* [VTSup 5; Leiden: E. J. Brill, 1965], p. 266) noted. The notion "arrange (thoughts)" is also in keeping with the cognate languages and yields a better sense than "puts on a feast within himself."

158. The Masoretic accents represent the situation as conjunctive, not successive (*IBHS,* p. 520, P. 32.1.1b).

159. Toy (*Proverbs,* p. 432) et al. emend the text to *'almānâ* because of the frequent collocation of the terms "widows and orphans" (Deut. 10:18; 14:29; Job 22:9; 24:2, 3; Ps. 146:9; Jer. 7:6). Possibly *gᵉbûl ʿôlām* influenced 23:10. If so, the corruption is early because the ancient versions support the MT.

11 *Because their Defender is strong,*
he[160] *will plead their case against you.*

The first saying of the Decalogue forbids enriching oneself through unjust acts. An *inclusio* unit ends with a single verse, having the prohibition in verset A and the motivation in verset B. An *inclusio* proscribing taking advantage of the poor (22:22) and of the fatherless (23:10), along with threats that the LORD will plead their cause (22:23; 23:11), frames the Decalogue (see I: 22). Whybray observes, "The first and last admonitions in this section are the only ones that have a specifically religious reference."[161] Recall that it is precisely at 23:11 that material dependent on *Amenemope* disappears. This *inclusio* sounds the Decalogue's dominant theme. Apart from Saying 9 (23:9) before the concluding frame, all the sayings pertain to wealth. Sayings 1-4 prohibit illegitimate forms of moneymaking (22:22-28); Sayings 6-8 escalate these prohibitions against overt acts to prohibitions against greed (23:1-8). At their center, Saying 7 strikes at the heart, the desire to become rich (23:4-5). Only the positive fifth saying presents a legitimate form of success, and that to serve kings, not to make money for self (22:29). The ninth saying (23:9) forms an inner frame with the second (22:24-28); both pertain to avoiding socializing with fools. The ninth forbids speaking to fools to convert them, preparing the way for the second unit of the Thirty Sayings.

As in the prologue (Collection I) and in Collection II (1:8-9; 10:1), so also in Collection III, an admonition to hear (1:8-9; 10:1; 22:17-21) is followed by teaching against illegal gain based on the principle of retribution (1:10-19; 10:2-3; 22:22-31; see I: 73). Pride of place is given to these prohibitions, for the love of money is the root of all sorts of evil. Material gain is the bottom line of the masses' values. Other sayings pertaining to care for the poor are 14:21, 31; 15:25; 17:5; 22:28; 23:10-11; 28:3; 30:14.

All these prohibitions are expressed by *'al* + jussive ("do not"). At the center of these seven prohibitions against wrong ways of increasing one's wealth, the fifth saying, the only positive saying in the subunit, prescribes diligence to serve kings as the legitimate form of making money. Reckoning the tenth saying as a recapitulation of the first four sayings leaves the remarkable symmetrical arrangement of four prohibitions before and after this central saying. Even this saying, however, contains the rare negative *bal.* In that light all ten sayings contain a negative form of expression. The ninth saying

160. M. Dahood ("The Divine Designation *'hû'* in Eblaite and the Old Testament," *Annali* 43 [1983] 193-99) argued for the presence of Eblaite *hû'* as a divine appellative and suggested a larger presence in the Bible as well (Deut. 32:39; Ps. 102:28; Prov. 21:29; 23:11; Isa. 41:4; 43:10, 13, 25; 46:4; 48:12), but he has not been followed.

161. Whybray, "Structure and Composition of Proverbs 22:17–24:22," p. 92.

pertains to speech and so thematically stands apart. It proscribes casting one's pearls before swine. Nevertheless, it is connected with the eighth saying; both warn against wasting one's energy in words that will be lost. It, too, contains *'al* + the jussive, but not initially.

1. Saying 2 (22:22-23)

The first four sayings forbid the son to enrich himself through injustice. Prohibitions forbidding the exploitation of the weak (the poor and the widow) frame them. Instructively, Job 24:2, which combines in a single verse robbery and moving boundary stones, is similar the two commands, "Do not rob a poor person" (22:22) and "Do not remove an ancient boundary" (22:28). The two middle sayings of this unit prohibit association with the antisocial hothead (vv. 24-25) and becoming surety for another's debts (vv. 26-27). The outer two pertain to gaining property through folly; the middle two, to not losing it through folly. The instruction genre commonly follows a prohibition with a motive clause.[162] The first three sayings house the prohibition in their first verse and the motivation in their second verse. Verse 23 is linked to v. 22 by the logical conjunction "because," its pronouns "their" and "them" looking back to "poor" and "afflicted" in v. 22.[163] The first exhortation not to rob the poor *(dāl)* functions as a catchword link with the last and framing proverb in Collection II (22:16), pointing to one author/editor who interfaced the two collections and established Solomon as their author. The motivation in v. 23 to trust in the LORD couples this first saying with the prologue (3:5). The saying is also connected with the next saying by warning against a threat to "life" *(nepeš),* the final word of 22:23, 25.

22 The synthetic parallels of v. 22 prohibit robbing the poor.[164] Verset A explains the temptation as due to their vulnerability.[165] Lacking financial resources to protect their legal rights, they are a tempting target for the sharp practices and blatant injustices of their rich and powerful neighbors. *Do not* (*'al-* with the second-person jussive) reflects an urgent, personalized prohibition in contrast to *lō'* with the imperfect, which expresses legislation.[166] (It per-

162. R. Murphy, "Proverbs," in *Wisdom Literature* (Grand Rapids: Eerdmans, 1981), p. 74.

163. Note the consonance of */nb~pš/* in the versets' final words: *'ny bšʿr* and *npš.*

164. *Amenemope* 4.4-9 prohibits the same injustice in its second saying: "Beware of robbing a wretch,/Of attacking a cripple;/Don't stretch out your hand to touch an old man,/Nor open your mouth to an elder./Don't let yourself be sent on a mischievous errand,/Nor be friends with him who does it" (*AEL,* 2:150).

165. Verset A coheres phonologically by the consonance of */l/* in *'l-tgzl-dl ky dl.* The B verset, by the repetition of the gutturals */'/* and */ʿ/*: *'l-tdk' 'ny bšʿr.* The two versets cohere by the repetition of initial *'al.*

166. *IBHS,* p. 567, P. 34.2.1b.

sonalizes the negative command.) *Rob* (cf. 4:16) refers to taking something from someone else by unlawful force and to continue forcibly and illegally to withhold it from its rightful owner.[167] *A poor person* (*dāl;* see 10:15) is so destitute of material resources that he is unable to protect himself against an oppressor. *Because* means here, "Do not take advantage of his weakness and inability to resist (Rashi)."[168] *He* refers back to the poor person. The adjective *is poor (dal)* is now used in its nonsubstantival sense. By definition "poor" entails being vulnerable to an economic predator. Verset B elaborates verset A by picturing robbing the poor as pulverizing them and by pointing to the rich merchants, who manipulate the economy, in cahoots with just as corrupt magistrates, who deprive the poor of justice when they plead their case in the gate (cf. Exod. 23:1-9 [esp. v. 6] etc. and Exod. 22:21-22[20-21], 25-26[24-25]; Lev. 19:13; Deut. 27:25; Ezek. 18:7ff.; Mic. 2:1-11; 3:1-12; 6:9-16; 7:1-6; etc.). Meinhold suggests that the metaphor *do not crush* (or pulverize)[169] depicts the extinction of their status as free citizens; they are brought to a state of inability to pay and

167. J. Milgrom (*Leviticus 1–16* [New York: Doubleday, 1991], p. 335) notes that Tannaitic law distinguishes *gāzal* "to rob" and *gānab* "to steal," "the difference being that robbery is committed openly by force whereas theft is by stealth." In Lev. 5:20-26 Milgrom notes that the robber, in contrast to a thief, is always identifiable (*Leviticus,* p. 336). He further observes that *gāzal* and *ʿāšaq* alike refer to open force, but they differ in that with *ʿāšaq* the acquisition is legal, whereas with *gāzal* it is illegal. The verb occurs 29 times in the *Qal,* usually either with an inanimate direct object or with a personal indirect object. For example, illegally seized inanimate objects include a well (Gen. 21:25), a donkey (Deut. 28:31), a spear (2 Sam. 23:21 = 1 Chr. 11:23), a field (Mic. 2:2), houses (Job 20:19), flocks (24:2), women and fatherless children treated as objects (Gen. 31:31; Judg. 21:23; Job 24:19), unspecified items (Lev. 5:23; cf. Mal. 1:13), figuratively of justice (Isa. 10:2) and skin (Mic. 3:2), and with cognate accusatives (Ezek. 18:7, 12, 16, 29). With personal objects, as here and at Prov. 28:24, it does not specify what is forcibly and illegally taken, but the stated objects in other texts are suggestive (Lev. 19:13; Deut. 28:29; cf. Judg. 9:25; Pss. 35:10; 69:4[5]; Jer. 21:12).

168. Lyons, "Rashi's *Commentary,*" p. 113.

169. *Dk'* occurs 18 times in the Bible. It is found only in poetry and only in the factitive D stems, except for the *Niphal* ptcp. in Isa. 57:15, and only figuratively. It is always applied to people in general, except for Rahab in Ps. 89:10[11]. H. F. Fuhs (*TDOT,* 3:196, s.v. *dākhāʾ*) notes that the following roots appear in parallelism with or as synonyms of *dk'* in the Old Testament: *ṭaḥan* "to grind" (Isa. 3:15), *šābar* "to break in pieces, break, crush" (Pss. 34:18[19]; 51:17[19]); *nākâ* "to smite" (Isa. 53:4 — in the sense of a very serious injury); *nagûaʿ* "to strike, smite" (Isa. 53:4); *ḥālal* II "descrate, defame" (Isa. 53:5), *ʿāšaq* "to oppress" (Ps. 72:4); *ʿānâ* II "to oppress, humble" (Ps. 94:5; Isa. 53:4); and *šāpal* "to bring low, humble" (Isa. 57:15a — twice). Fuhs (p. 199) also notes that an examination of the nouns built from the verb forms of the roots *dk* and *dq* sheds light on the semantic difference between *dk',* *dkh, dk(k),* and *dwk* on the one hand, and *dqq, dq,* and *dwq* on the other. "If a form of *dk* is used as a verbal phrase in a sentence, a personal term usually appears as its subject, referring to a small, specifically defined group" (Fuhs, *TDOT,* 3:204).

pressed into a state of dependence (see v. 7).[170] The personal subject and object of the verb stand in well-established relationships: enemies against people/individuals; the LORD against enemies; and finally the LORD against people/individuals. Here it entails the son becoming an enemy of the oppressed class. *The afflicted* (or oppressed; see 3:34) denotes the economically disadvantaged and often occurs in parallel with *dāl* (Job 34:28; Ps. 82:3[4]; Isa. 10:2; 11:4; 26; Amos 2:7). *In the gate* (see 1:21) is a metonymy for the rulers, elders, and merchants who carry on the economic, social, and political life of the community. In the Ugaritic text II Aqht, 5.4, Danel sits at the entrance of the gate where "he judges the case of the widow, adjudicates the cause of the fatherless." Cullen Story says, "The 'gate' in a peculiar sense was the place of legal tribunals (cf. Deut. 16:18; 21:19; 25:7)."[171] Amos illustrates how one can rob even a destitute person. He condemns those who callously take the last garment of the poor, which they had to give up as payment for a debt (cf. Exod. 22:26-27[25-26]; Deut. 24:12-13; Amos 2:6-8). Landlords can strip the poor, who cannot afford decent housing, by taking their last cent to live in rabbit warrens. The destitute renter has no other choice.

23 *Because* now signals the reason for this prohibition. "Robbers" deceive themselves if they think the poor have no protector. The Protector of the poor is none other than *the LORD* himself (see I: 67), who *will plead* (*yārîb;* see 3:30) *their case* (*rîbām;* see 15:18). All who belong to the class of the representative poor person in v. 22 can bring to the LORD's heavenly court their claim for what is right to defend them against their oppressors (cf. 23:10-11). *And so* marks the (con)sequence of their committing their case to their Prosecutor to his becoming the Judge handing down a death sentence, exacting life for life.[172] The root of *will despoil* (or plunder, *qāba'*) is a synonym of "rob" *(gāzal).*[173] *Those that despoil them (qōbᵉʿêhem)* refers to the plunderers and the plundered respectively, and the cognate accusative underscores the notion of poetic justice. The complement accusative, *of life* (*nepeš;* see I: 90), may mean "those who despoil them of life," but it certainly means "will despoil of life" the robbers because the focus of the verse is on punishing them. Also, this interpretation better satisfies its connection with

170. Meinhold, *Sprüche,* p. 381.

171. C. Story, "The Book of Proverbs and Northwest Semitic Literature," *JBL* 45 (1936) 326.

172. The versets syntactically cohere by the *waw* consecutive and by both having a cognate accusative.

173. *Qbʿ* occurs only four other times, all in Mal. 3:8-9. G. R. Driver ("Problems in 'Proverbs,'" *ZAW* 50 [1932] 145) recalls Arab. *qabaḍa* "to seize, take, grab" and draws the conclusion, "If these two words are cognate, *qābaʿ* is simply an Aramaism for the well-known *qbṣ* 'gathered' used in the special sense of 'removed.'" Unlike the Arabic verb, however, the Hebrew verb takes a double accusative.

v. 25. The poetic justice envisions the seizure of the very source that finds delights in satisfying its drives and appetites. When Israel's judicial system fails in the city gate, the insulted Maker of the poor (14:21; 17:5) takes their brief, gives voice to those too weak to have a voice, and avenges them in the heavenly court (cf. Exod. 22:22-24[21-23]; Deut. 10:17-18; Psalm 72; Isa. 1:23; 10:1-2; 11:4; 25:4; Jer. 5:28; Amos 2:6; 4:1; 5:12; Mic. 3:11; cf. Prov. 15:25) in an indefinite future. As the robbers dealt out death to the defenseless, the Protector of the poor, who has in his hands the life and death of all people, will hand down a death sentence on the contemptible offenders.

2. Saying 3 (22:24-25)

The prohibition against associating with a hothead (v. 24) with the motivation not to lose one's life (v. 25) is tightly linked by the logical particle "lest" and by the broken sequence of /*t b~p* ʾ/ in the last word of v. 24 (*tbʾ* "involve") and the first of v. 25 (*tʾlp* "learn"). Associating with a hothead is as self-destructive as robbery, but whereas the LORD upholds the death sentence against the robber of the poor, he has built in the hothead's ways his own self-destruction (cf. 1:16; 29:6).[174]

24 The chiastic parallels of the prohibition put the negative commands in the outer frame and the forbidden affiliation in the inner core.[175] *Do not (ʾal) associate yourself* [cf. 13:20] *with (ʾet) a hothead* (*baʿal ʾāp;* lit. "a master, possessor of a nose whose physical characteristics express anger"; cf. 14:17; 15:1), whose judgment is clouded by irrational thought and who loses all sense of proportion, acts impetuously, often in a terrifying way, and is incapable of measured utterance. The quick-tempered is like a bomb with a short fuse, ready to explode at any moment with devastating consequences. The father emphasizes the prohibition by using a rare, precisely synonymous parallelism down to the preposition *ʾet: with a wrathful person* (*ʾîš ḥēmôt;* cf. 29:22)[176] *do not get involved.*[177] However, *ʾāp* (lit. "nose") points to the phys-

174. *Amenemope* (11.12–12.11) commands: "Do not befriend the heated man, Nor approach him for conversation. . . . Swift is the speech of one who is angered, More than wind [over] water. He tears down, he builds up with his tongue, When he makes his hurtful speech. He gives answer worthy of a beating, For its weight is harm. . . . He is the ferryman of snaring words, He goes and comes with quarrels" (*AEL,* 2:153). Brunner says, "The one who knows how to remain silent in the right way, who keeps quiet according to Maʿat [the order] . . . is the ideal of the one who remains silent to God's order. 'The quiet one' accepts circumstances, is modest also in his everyday life and does not urge God" (cited by Meinhold, *Sprüche,* p. 382).

175. The verse coheres phonologically by the broken sequence of /*l*/ and /ʾ~ʾ/. In verset A each word, counting the proclisis construction as one word, begins with /ʾ/; verset B also begins with /ʾ/, and its final two words end in /ʾ/.

ically visible state of excitement of an individual breathing heavily as a consequence of anger, while *ḥēmâ* emphasizes more the inner emotion, the inner fire of anger.[178] *Get involved* (*tābô';* see 1:26) glosses the common root *bô'* ("come," "enter"), which takes on this particular nuance with the prepositions *'et.*[179]

25 *Lest* expresses a situation to be avoided or requiring caution and introduces the rationale behind the emphatically repeated prohibition. The habits of the hothead are both infectious (verset A) and lethal (verset B). The root behind *you learn (te'ᵉlap)* occurs only in wisdom literature (here and at Job 15:5; 33:33; 35:11), and its Aramaic, Arabic, and Ethiopic cognates suggest that it means "to be accustomed to" (cf. *'allûp* in 2:17). This meaning nicely fits "to associate with" (v. 24). The metaphor *his ways ('ōrᵉḥōtāw;* see 1:19) signifies the behavior patterns of the hothead.[180] In addition to involving his companions in deep trouble, the hothead conforms them to his image. *And so* introduces the inevitable consequences of taking to oneself the underhanded dangers of that lifestyle. *Fetch* [see 1:3] *a snare* (see 12:13) signifies lethal hidden danger. By associating with the hothead, one becomes fatally involved even before he becomes aware of it himself. *For your life* (*lᵉnapšekā;* see I: 90) shows that the trap is lethal. The metaphor is ironic. One avoids traps to save one's life, not fetches them to kill oneself.

3. Saying 4 (22:26-27)

Saying 4, which again consists of a prohibition ("do not," v. 26) and motivation (v. 27), forbids becoming surety for another's debts (see 6:1-5; 11:15; 17:18; 20:16; 27:13), continuing the theme of wise stewardship. The catchword *lāqaḥ* ("to fetch) in verset B of the motivating verse binds it with the preceding saying.

26 *Do not be* here connotes the idea of becoming, "to exist and to abide, remain, continue,"[181] nuanced by the spatial *among* designating the sphere of existence. *Those who strike a palm* (see 6:1) refers to the gesture that seals the guarantee. The cataphoric article of *among those who become*

176. A precise syntactic equivalent of *ba'al* + attributive genitive *('āp).*

177. The meaning of *bô'* with *'et* (*HALOT,* 1:113-14, s.v. *bô' lō'* with the imperfective of prohibition) in this chiastic construction functions as a synonym of *'al* + jussive in verset A (cf. *IBHS,* p. 510, P. 31.5c; *pace* GKC, P. 109d). *'îš ḥēmâ* and *ba'al ḥēmâ* are both lexical and syntactic equivalents (cf. *IBHS,* p. 149, P. 9.5.3d; Prov. 29:22).

178. *TWOT,* 1:58, 374; 2:808, s.v. *'āp, ḥēmâ, qeṣep.* The abstract pl. *ḥēmôt* is the semantic equivalent of the sing. in the same idiom in 15:18.

179. *HALOT,* 1:113-14, s.v. *bô'.*

180. Cf. *HALOT,* 1:59, s.v. *'lp.*

181. BDB, p. 226, s.v. *hāyâ.*

surety (*bā'ōrᵉbîm;* see n. 138; 6:1) looks back to "those who strike a palm." Elsewhere the prohibition against becoming surety is restricted to foreigners; a nonrestricted use would be exceptional. *For loans* derives from the verb I *nś'* "to lend on interest" and so means "a contractual loan" (i.e., the debt contracted on the guarantee.[182]

27 The sage motivates the son by threatening him with the loss of all his valuable possessions. Although at the time of becoming the surety he may have had the financial means to risk becoming guarantor, future financial reversals may expose him to losing everything he owns. *If* introduces the protasis of real condition.[183] *You do not have* [*the means*] glosses the idiom "there is non-existing belonging to you" (see 13:3). *To repay* (see 6:31) must be supplied from "loans" in v. 26b. The hypothetical deprecation *why* (see 5:20) implies criticism and censure. The independent question breaks the syntax, leaving the protasis of verset A without a proper apodosis, but implying it. The LXX probably omits the interrupting question to reconstruct a nonelliptical syntax. *Should your very bed* [see 7:17] *be taken* [see "fetch," 22:25] *from under you?* dramatically represents the consequence of defaulting on payment and presumes that the son is a person of means. Ordinary people slept on the floor in their garments or under blankets (Judg. 4:18). *Very* represents the bed as his last valuable possession. All of a sudden, if at the time of payment he lacked the money, he will find himself on the floor. The *Instruction of Amenemope* has no comparable saying.

4. Saying 5 (22:28)

Saying 5 draws the first section of the Decalogue to a close with a single line and returns to the theme of not violating the property rights of the poor. Verset A prohibits violating ancient landmarks, and verset B gives the reason that they were sacred and inviolable by reason of their antiquity (cf. Judges 11; 1 K. 21:4). *Do not* [see vv. 22, 24, 26] *move* [see 14:14] *an ancient* [see 8:23] *boundary* (see 15:25) refers to the time when Joshua distributed the land by casting the sacred lot (Joshua 14–19). Elsewhere in the ancient Near East boundaries stood under the protection of the god of the land,[184] but within the territories of Israel's tribes set by the sacred lot, the first generations in the

182. The pl. does not signify extreme carelessness for assuming a number of debts but complements the pl. "those who pledge."

183. *IBHS,* p. 636, P. 38.2d.

184. M. Ottosson, *TDOT,* 2:366, s.v. *gᵉbûl.* The parallel to 22:28 and 23:10-11 in *Amenemope* is its ch. 6, which begins, "Do not move the markers on the borders of fields" (7.11) and goes on to specify "nor encroach on the boundaries of a widow" (7.15). In Prov. 23:10-11 Israel's covenant-keeping God protects the boundaries, but in *Amenemope* the moon god Thoth does (7.19; *AEL,* 2:151).

land effected the family boundaries. The Mosaic law protected them (Deut. 19:14; cf. Deut. 27:17). The boundaries of private land were marked out by stone pillars or cairns erected between property to mark legal ownership. The relative pronoun *that (ʾăšer)* further qualifies the boundary and contains the reason.[185] It was rendered sacrosanct by its sacred origin and antiquity, as Jephthah argued (Judg. 11:14-17). The parallel admonition in 23:10 is followed in v. 11 by the causal "because." *Your ancestors* refers to the first or the former generations who marked out the boundaries of their families when they settled the land. Elsewhere in Proverbs *ʾāb* ("father") occurs in the singular with reference to the son's immediate father (cf. 1:8 and passim) as both the begetter and the head of the family. In the plural it denotes these senses plus the broader sense of "ancestor," "forefather." The historical activity of these begetters and heads at the beginning of the family's settlement in the land is denoted by the broad and common verb *have set* (*ʿāśû;* lit. "have made"; see 13:16, having the additional nuance "to put into effect").[186] Throughout the ancient Near East people had great respect for private and tribal boundaries so essential for a family's life. Without this understanding, every field would be up for grabs and anarchy would ensue. Unfortunately, the crime was easy to accomplish and difficult to prove. Probably the boundary stone was moved annually only about an inconspicuous half-inch, which in time could add up to a sizeable land grab. The book of Proverbs is concerned with protecting the fields of the widows and the fatherless (see 15:15; 23:10; cf. 14:21, 31; 17:5; 30:14) because the economically disadvantaged, who had limited financial resources and no one to represent them in legal disputes, were most vulnerable to this high-handed, greedy transgression of their rights (cf. Job 24:3). As the era of the monarchy progressed, the powerful class seized the ancestral lands of their subjects (1 K. 21:4; Isa. 5:8; Hos. 5:10), causing the prophets to envision a new covenant whereby human nature was regenerated to effect a real change in Israel.

5. Saying 6 (22:29)

Saying 6 stands apart from the rest of the Decalogue in its positive modeling of "success" and from the preceding subunit by being a so-called tricola, actually an extended A (Aa and Ab) + B.[187] Its antithetical parallels implicitly contrast the fortunes of the skillful and the unskillful person. The didactic saying, not an admonition, aims to motivate the son to become competent in

185. *IBHS,* p. 640, P. 38.4a.

186. *HALOT,* 1:890, s.v. *ʿśh.*

187. Probably it uses the negative *bal* "not," not the expected *lōʾ,* as a paronomasia with *ʾal* "not" of the preceding admonitions.

whatever commissions he receives in order to rise to his greatest social and economic potential in the service of kings.

29a The question "do you see" (Aa) presents the condition, namely, keeping a sharp lookout for a competent person to emulate, and Ab the consequence, that such a person will confidently present himself before a number of kings who covet his services. The polar question, expecting a positive answer, glossed *do* is not formally marked in Hebrew but demanded by sense.[188] *You see (ḥāzîtā),* in contrast to its broader synonym *rā'â* "to see," is predominantly a technical term for a form of revelation to the prophet consisting of a perception of God's voice in a vision or deep sleep. However, the word is used in Proverbs (22:29; 24:32; 29:20), as in Pss. 11:4 and 17:2, to connote a sharp inspection.[189] The illocution could call on the son to inspect or test the skill of a person, but the parallels in 26:12 and 29:20 suggest a rhetorical question that aims to motivate the son to keep a sharp lookout for *a person* (*'îš;* see I: 89). *Skillful (māhîr)* occurs three other times in the Bible (Ezra 7:6; Ps. 45:1[2]; Isa. 16:5). Its meaning is often sought in the verb *māhar* "to hasten," and the adjective is even glossed "speed" in Isa. 16:5 (NIV). Barr, however, cites this as an etymological fallacy.[190] Cognates in Syriac and Arabic mean "able, skillful"; in Old South Arabic "craftsman" and in Ethiopic "experienced, learned."[191] A related proverb (14:35) uses *'ebed maśkîl* ("a prudent servant"). Although the adjective in Ps. 41:1(2) and Ezra 7:6 modifies "scribe" and the parallel in *Amenemope*[192] suggests that notion here, in Isa. 16:5 it refers to the king and thus *in his commission* (see 18:9) should not be restricted to a scribe. *He will present himself before* means "to take one's stand (firmly) before."[193] All the verb's uses pertain to firmly presenting oneself to engage in a mission, such as a fight or a commission. It is never used of taking one's stand after fulfilling an assignment. To present oneself firmly, boldly, and confidently to receive a commission is appropriate, but risky, with *kings* (cf. Prov. 16:10, 12-15; 19:12; 20:2; 21:1). The plural suggests that this proficient person enjoys an international reputa-

188. *IBHS,* p. 316, P. 18.1c, n. 1.

189. A. Jepsen, *TDOT,* 4:289, s.v. *chāzāh.*

190. J. Barr, *Comparative Philology and the Text of the Old Testament* (Oxford: Clarendon; repr. with additions; Winona Lake, Ind.: Eisenbrauns, 1987), p. 295.

191. *HALOT,* 2:552, s.v. *māhîr.*

192. The final saying in *Amenemope* is: "The scribe who is skilled in his office, he is found worthy to be a courtier" (27.15-16; *AEL,* 2:162).

193. *HALOT,* 2:427, s.v. *yṣb.* Outside of this verse, *yṣb* in the *Hithpael* occurs with locative "before" seven times. Five times it is used in contexts "to stand up against" or "to confront an enemy" (Exod. 8:20[16] = 9:3); Deut. 9:2; Josh. 1:5; 24:1; cf. Job 41:10[2]), and in the other two, "to present oneself [before God]" (Josh. 24:1; 1 Sam. 10:18]), also a risky thing to do.

tion. He takes his stand firmly because he has no fear of bungling his assignment and bringing disgrace on the king.

29b Verset B gaps the situation of Aa and presents the contrast to Ab. The capable person "will not bury his talents in the service of obscure and mediocre principals."[194] The chiastic juxtaposing of "before kings" with *before obscure* [or "low"] *people (ḥᵃšukkîm)* in its outer frame and the negative repetition *he will not* (*bal;* see 10:30; 12:3; 19:23) *present himself* emphatically contrast his commissions.[195] Since poor people do not give commissions, obscure people refers to low officials in contrast to kings with their rank and visibility. By receiving this endless supply of royal commissions and successfully fulfilling them, he earns himself an international reputation and a handsome profit. In a parable about the kingdom of God and the eschaton, Jesus taught that the one who is trustworthy in the small matters of this world will be entrusted with ten cities in his coming kingdom (Matt. 25:14-30; Luke 19:11-27; cf. John 12:26).

6. Saying 7 (23:1-3)

The Decalogue reverts to prohibitions. Its next three sayings (23:1-3, 4-5, 6-8) pertain to greed. Sayings 7 and 9 form a frame by the catchwords "Do not crave his delicious morsels" (vv. 1a, 6b), "food" (vv. 1a, 6a) and *nepeš* (untranslated, v. 2b, and "himself," v. 7a) and by the theme of prohibiting greed at table with a superior. Both warn the son not to mistake the invitation to dine with him as a sign of his friendship, for he is not merely giving food.[1] The seventh saying warns about the greed of the gluttonous guest and the ninth saying about the greed of the stingy host. At their center stands the eighth saying, prohibiting the quest for riches, for they are a false security. All three sayings warn that things are not as they appear. The superior's food is not a sign of friendship, and riches are not a sign of security. What appears to be desirable for advancing the potential of a fuller life veils harsh realities that hinder its full enjoyment. The wise govern their lives by these insightful teachings, not by external appearances.

194. McKane, *Proverbs,* p. 380.

195. The *hap. leg. ḥᵃšukkîm* probably derives from the root *ḥšk* "to be dark" and, with the infixed pattern of *qatul,* signifies "dark(ened) ones." In Middle Hebrew the adjectival substantive denotes miserable men, and in Jewish Aramaic, obscure *(HALOT,* 1:362, s.v. *ḥāšōk).*

1. 'Abot (2:3) similarly cautions agains the selfish motivation of those in authority. "Be ye cautious regarding those in authority, for they permit not a man to draw nigh unto them but for their own purpose."

The seventh saying is linked with the sixth (22:29) by the catchword "before" and by the notions of "to present oneself before kings" and of "to dine with a ruler." The saying's three verses are formally bound by "his" (v. 3a), looking back to the "ruler" (v. 1a), and by the consecutive "and" (v. 2a), linking the two admonitions of vv. 1 and 2. Semantically they are linked by three relational admonitions. The first two, "to discern the true intention of the food" (v. 1) and "to cut your throat if you are a glutton" (v. 2) are interpretative of the climactic third, "do not crave the food."

The saying is not concerned primarily with gluttony, as is the case in 23:20-21, but with dining with a superior. The ruler's invitation to dine with him presents an unusual opportunity for success or failure, for his host can influence his career for good or ill. The official may not be testing the young man, but he will take note of the glutton, detest him, and wreck his career.[2] Dining with a ruler is the moment to display the "well-proportioned behaviour and self-control" of a model statesman.[3] The stakes are high — so much so that, if the subordinate knows he has trouble restraining his appetite, he should abstain altogether.

1 Verset A of the synthetic parallels of the first verse presents the situation: *When you sit down* [see 9:14] *to eat* [see 4:17] *with* [see 13:20] *a ruler* (see 6:7) assumes that the son has a close enough social relationship to a ruler for the latter to invite him to dine with him, but it does not concern itself with the reason for the meal. Verset B presents the emphatic admonition, *Mark well* (or "carefully discern," *bîn tābîn;* see 1:2) The gloss *what* (*ʾᵃšer;* or "who") interprets, along with all the ancient versions, the ambiguous relative as referring to the food, not the ruler, for though that sense fits 22:29, nevertheless one expects "him" (*ʾôtô,* not *ʾᵃšer*). Some think that this refers to the food for you, matching *Amenemope*'s "Look at the bowl that is before you." But to restrict one's attention to something is not equivalent to discerning what it is. Verse 2 clarifies that he should discern that the food *before you* (cf. 22:29; Gen. 18:22) is deceptive. The ruler's dainties test one's mettle, not merely feed someone.

2. Sirach (31:12-18) illuminates its meaning: "Are you seated at the table of a great man? Do not be greedy at it. . . . Remember that a greedy eye is a bad thing. . . . Do not reach out your hand for everything you see, and do not crowd your neighbor at the dish. . . . Eat like a human being what is set before you, and do not chew greedily, lest you be hated. Be the first to stop eating, for the sake of good manners, and do not be insatiable, lest you give offense. . . ." Egyptian parallels are also instructive: Kagemani admonished, "When you sit with company, shun the food you love; restraint is a brief moment, gluttony is base and is reproved" (*AEL,* 1:59-60). Amenemope (23.13-20) taught, "Do not eat in the presence of an official. . . . Look at the bowl that is before you, and let it serve your needs. An official is great in his office, as a well is rich in drawings of waters" (*AEL,* 2:160).

3. McKane, *Proverbs,* p. 381.

2 *And* denotes a logical sequence that connects the second command with the first. Chiastically, however, their outer frame presents the conditional situations (vv. 1a, 2b) and their inner core the admonitions (vv. 1b, 2a). The hyperbole *place*[4] *a knife* [or dagger][5] *(śakkîn) in your gullet*[6] drives home the need for total abstinence, not merely to curb the appetite, like Eng. "Bite your tongue" and Jesus' command, "Pluck out your eye." Conditional *if* introduces the complementary situation when dining with a ruler. *You* [see 22:19] *are a glutton* (*baʿal nepeš;* see I: 90), though referring here narrowly to food, can be interpreted broadly with reference to all appetites. Total prohibition is necessary for a person who cannot control his appetites; the disciple can give no place to lust (cf. Matt. 5:29-30).

3 The sixth saying is now brought to its climactic admonition. Verset A of its synthetic parallels presents the prohibition. *Do not crave* [see 10:24; 13:4] *his delicious morsels (maṭʿammôtāyw). Maṭʿammîm* occurs six times besides 23:3, 6 as a key word to point up Isaac's character flaw of loving tasty food (Gen. 27:4, 7, 9, 14, 17, 31). Verset B gives the reason. *For* [lit. "and"] *it is* groups the various tasty morsels into a whole. *Deceptive* [see 6:29] *food* (lit. "food of lies"; see 6:26) may mean that the morsels cause the subordinate who is not used to such rich fare to suffer from insomnia, vomiting, and stomachaches (Sir. 31:20). Or, the tidbits do not have a really solid, saturating effect (but the use in Genesis calls this interpretation into question). More probably, it means that being wined and dined, which seems to be the intention of the banquet, is in fact a test of the subordinate's character. Proverbs is concerned with moral character, not with gastronomy; so are the Egyptian parallels.

7. Saying 8 (23:4-5)

Meinhold notes that thematically this is the focus of the subunit (22:22–23:11). He schematizes their themes as follows:

A Illegitimate (and legitimate) forms of moneymaking (1/3/4/5)
  B Greed at the occasion of dinners with superiors (6)
    C Greed for wealth (7)
  B′ Greed at the occasion of dinners with superiors (8)
A′ Illegitimate form of moneymaking (10)[7]

4. *HALOT,* 3:1,322-23, s.v. *śym, śwm.*

5. *HALOT,* 3:1327, s.v. *śakkîn.* The *hap. leg. śakkîn* is connected with Aram. *sakkin,* Arab *sikkin.* A more precise definition than "knife" is not possible. *Maʾᵃkelet* is a large knife (Gen. 22:10; Judg. 19:29; Prov. 30:14) and *taʿar,* a small shearing knife (Num. 6:5; cf. Jer. 36:23).

6. The *hap. leg. lōaʿ* is connected with the verbal by-form II *lʿʿ* "to slurp" (cf. Arab. *luʿat* "gulp" and probably Akk. *luʾu* "gullet").

7. Meinhold, *Sprüche,* 2:386.

The two verses of the seventh saying are linked grammatically by the pronouns "they" in v. 5 with reference to riches in v. 4 and logically by the motivation in v. 5 for the prohibition in v. 6. Verse 5b pictures the truth of v. 5a. The saying finds a striking parallel in ch. 7 of *Amenemope* (10.4-5): "Ill-gotten riches made for themselves wings like geese and flew away to the sky."[8] Jesus likened money to becoming moth-eaten and rust-riddled if a thief does not get to it first (Matt. 6:19). Here one notes the escalation by a wordplay on "fly" *(ʿûp)*. First the eye "flies" to the riches, and then the riches "fly away" to the sky.

4 In the chiastic synthetic parallels of v. 4 the imperatives form the outer frame around an inner core linking "to make oneself rich" with "your own insight." *Do not become* physically *weary* by toiling[9] *to make yourself rich* (*leḥaʿăšîr;* see 10:4). *In your own insight* (or cleverness, *mibbînāteḵā;* see 1:2; 3:5) marks the human being as the authority from whom the standard of moral behavior originated apart from trust in God (see 3:5).[10] *Stop* [*trusting in*] (*ḥădāl;* see 10:19) "refers to human withdrawal or withdrawal from or cessation of a particular activity." Here it probably means "refrain from" in the sense of "not even beginning to do something" (cf. Num. 9:13; Deut. 23:22[23]; Amos 7:5). In this construction it may be "used in the second member with a main verb understood, in which case it serves primarily as a term of negation." That is the sense here, with "trust" being understood.[11] While the verset should be understood universally as a prohibition against the employment of one's mental faculty without trust in God (see 3:5), the chiastic parallel shows that it has particular reference to the inherent human trait of seeking security in money. When wealth is acquired through wise effort such as diligence (10:4) and modesty (21:17) and given by the LORD, it is a positive blessing (see 3:16; 8:18; 10:22; 12:27; 14:23, 24; 22:4; 28:20). But when acquired impiously, riches are a curse (10:2; 11:4, 18; 20:17; 22:4; 28:20). Derived independently from trust in the LORD that leads to acts of righteousness toward the poor and needy, money is associated with self-ambition and envy, and that in turn leads to disorders such as anxiety, discontent, and all sorts of evil practices (Eccl. 5:8-12[7-11]; 1 Tim. 6:6-10; Jas. 3:13-16).

8. *AEL,* p. 152.

9. "In Hebrew usage of the verb [*yāgaʿ*] and various derivatives, the primary emphasis is on the basic meaning 'be/become weary' [in the objective sense of bodily fatigue]. Extended semantic fields arise from the effort exerted while being or becoming weary, so that one 'toils' or 'labors'" (G. Hasel, *TDOT,* 5:387-88, s.v. *ygʿ*).

10. *IBHS,* p. 303, P. 16.4d.

11. "The Pentateuch uses *chādhal* three times (with either *min* or *le*) in the sense of refraining from some religious or moral obligation. In these legal texts, *chādhal* takes the place of the negative particles *lōʾ* and *ʾal*" (see Exod. 23:5; Num. 9:13; Deut. 23:22[23]). D. Freedman and J. Lundbom, *TDOT,* 4:216, s.v. *chādhal.*

5 This verse gives the reason behind the admonition of v. 4. Its chiastic parallels picture the son letting his eyes fly on riches (v. 5aα) and the riches as flying away (v. 5bβ). Verset A consists of the condition of the son glancing coveteously at riches (aα) and a staccato consequence (aβ): they are gone! The rhetorical question signaled by *will* involves the son in the argument. *You let your eyes* [see 3:7] *glance (tāʿûp)* represents the activity as acceptable to the son but not to the father (see above, p. 226 n. 149), and "glance" paraphrases the metaphor "let fly," the meaning of *ʿûp,* which is normally used with winged creatures. Eyes reflect the son's character and disposition (see 15:30), which the preceding verse clarifies as a disposition of coveting. (The metaphor may have been evoked by the idiom "wise in your own eyes," and is equivalent to "your own insight" [see 3:5, 7].) *At riches* (lit. "on it") with eyes is idiomatic for "to look for" (Job 7:8); the antecedent "riches" is implied in the verb "make yourself rich" (v. 4a).[12] To smooth the broken syntax of the Hebrew text (cf. 22:27) *if you do* is added. The terse one-word clause *they are not (ʾênennû;* see 13:4) matches their nonexistence. Verset B underscores that truth as emphatically as possible by two emphatic adverbs, *surely* and *without question,*[13] by the metaphor *they will make* (see 20:12) *for themselves a set of wings* (*k*ᵉ*nāpayim;* see 1:17) in 5bα, and by intensifying the metaphor to that of the swift and powerful eagle flying off into the heavens in v. 5bβ. According to Q, *like (k*ᵉ) is an item adverb and marks agreement in kind between the wings and the eagle (i.e., wings like the eagle, and they will fly), but according to K it is a clausal adverb modifying verset A (so the text).[14] *They will fly (yāʿûp,* Q) constitutes a paronomasia with "glance" *(tāʿûp)* in v. 5aα and *toward the heavens (šamāyim),* the last word ofv. 5bβ, has an assonance with *k*ᵉ*nāpayim,* the last word of v. 5bα. The addition adds to the metaphor of the swift and powerful eagle that he outstrips all attempts to capture him. Riches will certainly disappear, and once gone, they are gone forever.

8. Saying 9 (23:6-8)

The connections of the ninth saying with the seventh were noted above. It is connected with the eighth saying by the catchword "eye" (vv. 5a, 6a), the theme of money, and a similar syntactical pattern. Both begin with a twofold admonition (vv. 4a, 6a) followed by motivation (vv. 5, 7-8). However, it es-

12. The LXX, Syr., and Targ. referred it to "rich person" because they read "rich person" in v. 5a, but that is not as cogent as the MT, for it makes the rich person flying off, for which they had to accommodate the text in other ways.

13. Glossing the inf. absolute *ʿāśōh.*

14. See *IBHS,* pp. 655-60, PP. 39.3.1; 39.3.2.

calates the pattern. Verse 5b contained an elaborate figure; v. 7 contains an elaborate quotation followed by further evaluation of the situation (v. 8). The reprise again turns to greed at the dining table. A greedy guest will displease his host (v. 3), and dining with an unwilling host is a waste of time and effort in a loathsome situation. The proverb warns the son against advancing himself by pushing himself forward as an uninvited guest with an unwilling host.

6 The prohibition *Do not insist on eating* (*tilḥam;* lit. "eat") *the food* (*'et-leḥem;* see 6:8; 23:1) escalates in the essentially synonymous parallel *do not even desire,* and "food" to "delicious morsels" (see 23:3a). *A begrudging host* (lit. "evil eye" > "stingy") is the opposite of the generous person (lit. "good eye"; see 22:9; cf. Deut. 15:9; Sir. 14:10). According to 28:22, he is stingy because he is eager to get rich. But why would such a person invite a guest to his table? A probable parallel in the *Instruction of Any* (8.10-13) suggests that the guest has forced himself on a begrudging host: "Attend to your position, be it low or high; it is not good to press forward, step according to rank. Do not intrude on a man in his house, enter when you have been called; he may say 'Welcome' with his mouth, yet deride you in his thoughts. One gives food to one who is hated, supplies to one who enters uninvited."[15] The host is bound by oriental custom to utter gracious words to his uninvited and unwanted guest who forced himself on him and into his negative attitude.[16] To show that the onus is more on the guest than on the host, "stingy" was rendered "begrudging" and "insist on" was added to the translation.

7 *Because* signals that v. 7 substantiates the admonitions by exposing the begrudging host's hypocrisy. Verset aα presents his reasoning processes during the feast. *As* represents the situation by which to measure him. *He calculates* [see n. 157] *within himself* (*bᵉnapšo;* see I: 90) looks back to the "begrudging host," and the verb's perfective form represents a persistent situation as a single one.[17] *So* introduces the sage's evaluation that his inner thinking exposes his true identity. *He (hû')* refers to the unwilling host but could refer to anyone. Gerard Manley Hopkins noted that one's "inscape" determines his landscape. Verset B dramatically exposes his hypocrisy, contrasting his outward generous invitation with his stingy heart, which confirms the sage's assertion. Verset bα represents the miser's outward behavior. *Eat and drink* represent the two aspects of the banquet (see 9:5; 23:6). His imperatives ostensibly represent his will to fellowship

15. *AEL,* 2:142.

16. D. Römheld, *Wege der Weisheit: Die Lehren Amenemopes und Proverbien 22:17–24:22* (BZAW 184; Berlin: de Gruyter, 1989), p. 7.

17. *IBHS,* p. 487, P. 30.5.1c.

with his guest as symbolized by the meal. *He says* represents the situation as iterative, and *to you* refers to the son as representative of the book's audience. *But* signals the contrast between what he outwardly says with what he thinks and feels in *his heart* (*lēb;* see I: 90). The relatively rare negative *is not* (*bal;* see 10:30) was probably chosen for its broken sequence with *lēb* and its assonance with *'al* ("not") in the Decalogue. *With you* (see 1:15) denotes accompaniment (person with person), here in the sense of fellowship and companionship. Outwardly the host conforms to his social obligation according to oriental rules of hospitality, but inwardly he is revolted by his guest.

8 This verse is linked to vv. 6-7 by continuing the direct address to the son, "you," by the catchword "eat," and by further elaborating the reason not to dine with the begrudging host. Since the verse pictures the son vomiting the food, it represents the subsequent situation when, for having violated social reality, the son's greed backfires against him. Its synthetic parallels represent chiastically the son's loss of food and of words. The outer frame represents the host's delectable food and the son's compliments that accompany it, and its inner core the son's losses. *As for* focuses on *your morsel* (*pitt^{e}kā,* probably a short form for "your piece of food"; see 17:1). *That you will have eaten* (see 1:31) assumes that the son accepted the host's invitation to eat. The dramatic figure *you will vomit it* represents the food as proving itself to be repulsive and indigestible (cf. Lev. 18:25-28; 20:22; Jon. 2:10[11]). *And* (see n. 158) represents a second negative situation of having dined with the miser, not a subsequent one to vomiting. *You will have wasted* means concretely "to make a ruin, thoroughly destroy," with a wide variety of objects such as "all flesh" in the Flood (Gen. 6:17) and in Sodom and Gomorrah (13:10; 19:13). The metaphor does not denote regret. With the object *your words* (see 1:6) it probably denotes "to waste" in the sense of being ineffective, as when Onan "spoiled" his seed on the ground to render it ineffective.[18] *Pleasant* (or gracious; see 22:18) qualifies the words as pleasing to the host and thus compliments, but they are wasted on a person incapable of appreciating them. In sum, the meal is both loathsome and futile, for he will throw away the food and his words.

9. Saying 10 (23:9)

9 In addition to "do not" (vv. 6a, 9a), the tenth saying is connected with the ninth by *dābār* ("word," v. 8b; "speak," v. 9a), by escalating the notion of speaking words from "pleasant" to "prudent," and from wasting them to the injury they will inflict on him. Speaking seriously to a *fool* is as futile and

18. BDB, p. 1,008, s.v. *sḥt; HALOT,* 4:1,470, s.v. *sḥt.*

foolish as speaking to a begrudging host. These two sayings are so closely related that Ibn Ezra combined them,[19] but their admonitions (cf. 23:9a) and motivations (cf. 23:9b) differ. *In the ears* implies the heart, for the ear is the gate to the heart where decisions are made (2:2; 15:31). The phrase connotes that the son's clear insights are spoken to the *fool* (*kᵉsîl;* see I: 109) directly, distinctly, and as Plöger says, "eindringliches Reden" ("emphatic/urgently speaking").[20] *Do not speak ('al-tᵉdabbēr)* refers to the process of a complete address (see 18:23). The parallel shows that its content is moral insight. Woman Wisdom appeals to the *kᵉsîl* to listen but does not pour out her wisdom to him (cf. 1:22, 32; 9:7-8). *Because* signals the motivating reason that assumes the son belongs among the wise (see 1:5). *He will show contempt* [see 1:7] *for your prudent* (*śēkel;* cf. I: 94) *words* (*milleykā,* a poetic equivalent of *dābār* found mostly in Job, another wisdom book). All the well-intentioned son will get for throwing his pearls before the swine (cf. Matt. 7:6) will be a curled lip in contempt for it (cf. 9:18; 17:10; 21:4; 26:4; 27:22). There is a time to keep silent and a time to speak (Eccl. 3:7). However, the proverb must be held in tension with 26:5: a reasoned response to folly is necessary. The proverb implies that the son must take the spiritual measure of a person before responding to him in order to estimate beforehand the effect of his words on him.[21]

10. Saying 11 (23:10-11)

10 The eleventh saying brings the Decalogue to closure in a concluding frame that protects the property rights of the fatherless, which are represented by the ancient boundary stones that protected their fields from encroachment. By repeating *do not move the ancient boundaries* (see 22:28), assumed from known customs to be boundary stones, it is also connected with the fifth saying. In its chiastic parallels, the protective prohibitions comprise its outer frame and the protected spheres its inner core. Verset B escalates "do not move" to *do not enter,* which implies continuance (see 2:10), and "the ancient boundaries" are marked as *in the fields (biśdê) of the fatherless (yᵉtômîm). Śādeh* designates pasture, open fields, and land, including a place for planting a precious vineyard (see 24:30). *Yᵉtômîm* designates children who lost the protection of their father (cf. Job 29:12; Ps. 10:14) and here uniquely typify the special needs of the poor who were too weak to uphold their rights. Throughout the ancient Near East it was the responsibility of the

19. Cohen, *Proverbs,* p. 153.

20. Plöger, *Sprüche,* p. 272.

21. The *Instruction of Ankhsheshonq* (7:4) admonishes, "Do not instruct a fool, lest he hate you" (*AEL,* 3:165).

king and his officials to protect them.[22] To take away their fields, the powerful first secure the sanction of corrupt courts. In Israel the LORD, who owned the fields, granted them as a perpetual usufruct to each Israelite family to guarantee their right to life in the holy land as long as they kept covenant (see 22:28). This lease, which was represented by boundary stones, was to be jealously preserved as the family's permanent inheritance (cf. Lev. 25:23-28; 1 K. 21:3).

11 If the human social network that the LORD established to protect the poor should fail, the LORD himself will protect them by punishing their oppressors. Verset A presents the LORD's role and character, and verset B synthetically adds his function that springs from these. Initial, but medial, *because* again signals the motivating reason for these two admonitions. The LORD himself will become the Father of the fatherless, and he has the strength to plead their case successfully when in faith they appeal to him. *Their Defender* (or Redeemer, *gō'ᵃlām;* lit., "family protector") refers to the LORD, as the parallel frame certifies (cf. 22:23; Gen. 48:16; Exod. 6:6; Job 19:25). The *go'el* is a needy person's nearest relative who is responsible to stand up for him and to protect his property, either his house or real estate (Lev. 25:25-35) or his body from slavery to a foreigner (Lev. 25:47-54), or to avenge the murder of a relative (Num. 35:12, 19-27; Deut. 19:6, 12; Josh. 20:2-3, 5, 9). *Is strong* designates the physical strength that entails securing one's position in a comprehensive sense that a *gō'ēl* must possess to effect his legal sanction. *He* focuses attention on their Redeemer. *Will plead their case* (*yārîb rîbām;* see 22:23) means that at the time of judgment the Father of the fatherless and Defender of widows (cf. Ps. 68:5[6]) will condemn the oppressor and vindicate the innocent (Prov. 14:31; 15:25; 17:5; 19:17; 22:9, 22-23; cf. Job 6:27; 22:9; 24:3, 9; 29:12; 31:16-17, 21). The phrase *against you,* which normally connotes fellowship, with this verb of contending becomes tainted with a hostile, social sense (cf. Gen. 14:2, 8, 9; Num. 20:13),[23] and the pronoun assumes hypothetically that the son has in fact moved the ancient boundary to supplant the fatherless from his source of life to make the point. As verse 23:10 uses a metonymy of effect, 23:11 uses a metonym of cause. The moving of the boundary stones resulted from corrupt legislation and sharp legal practices by powerful and influential neighbors, and the LORD, leaping to the defense of the helpless, guarantees that the oppressors will be evicted and punished and their victims reinstated on their fields.

22. F. Fensham, "Widow, Orphan, and the Poor in Ancient Near Eastern Legal and Wisdom Literature," in *SAIW,* pp. 161-71.

23. BDB, p. 86, s.v. *'et.*

C. SECTION B: AN OBEDIENT SON (23:12–24:2)

12 *Apply your heart to instruction,*
your ear to words of knowledge.
13 *Do not withhold discipline from a youth;*
for if your strike him with a rod, he will not die.[24]
14 *You must strike him with a rod*
and deliver him from the grave.
15 *My son, if your heart is wise,*
my heart will be glad — yes, mine.
16 *And my inward parts will leap for joy*
when your lips speak what is upright.
17 *Do not let your heart be envious of sinners,*
but be zealous for the fear of the LORD all the time.[25]
18 *Surely*[26] *there is a latter end;*
your hope will not be cut off.
19 *Listen, yes you, my son, and become wise;*
direct your heart in the way.
20 *Do not be among those who are drunkards,*
among those who squander flesh for themselves,
21 *because drunkards and profligates become destitute,*
and drowsiness clothes them in rags.
22 *Listen to your father who begot you,*
and do not show contempt for your mother[27] *when she grows old.*
23 *Buy truth and do not sell*
wisdom and instruction and insight.[28]

24. D. W. Thomas ("Some Passages in the Book of Proverbs," *JTS* 37 [1937] 288) et al. think that this is a figure that means nothing more than "he will come to no very great harm." But McKane (*Proverbs,* p. 386) objects: "'[That] death' here is to be taken seriously is confirmed by the opposition of *nepeš* 'life' and Sheol in v. 14b."

25. Verset B cannot be interpreted as a nominal clause, supplying impv. "be," for in that case the impv. form should have been expressed. Rather, the verb of verset A is gapped, though with a different sense. Toy (*Proverbs,* p. 434) et al. gratuitously emend the text to *yĕrā' 'et-YHWH* "fear the LORD!"

26. Gemser (*Sprüche,* p. 87) inserts *tiṣmĕrenna* from the LXX, which reads *ean gar tēr̄ēsẹs auta* ("for if you maintain these things") because the line is too short. This is possible but not necessary. The LXX, having misunderstood *kî 'im,* may have paraphrased the text of the MT.

27. "The logical object of *'al-tābûz* is attracted as subj. of *zāqenâ* (Hitzig)" (Delitzsch, p. 344).

28. Gemser (*Sprüche,* p. 87) with the LXX deletes v. 23 because he thinks it interrupts the connection between vv. 22 and 24. But vv. 22 and 23 are linked by a common

24 *The father of a righteous son surely shouts in exultation,*[29]
and[30] *the one who begets a wise son takes pleasure*[31] *in him.*
25 *Let your father and your mother*[32] *rejoice,*[33]
and let the one who bore you shout in exultation.
26 *Give to me, my son, your heart,*
and let your eyes take pleasure[34] *in my ways.*
27 *Because an unchaste wife*[35] *is a deep pit,*
and the unfaithful woman is a narrow well.

---

syntax and theme. Moreover, the consonance between the verses — *'mk,* the last word of v. 22, *'mt,* the first word of v. 23, *zqnh,* the penultimate word in v. 22, and *qnh,* the second from the beginning in v. 23 — points to an integrity within vv. 22-25. Since it is formulated very differently from 4:5, 7, it could not have been borrowed from those texts. Gemser suggests the possibility of attaching it to v. 19, and Scott inserts it between vv. 21 and 22, but these are not improvements over the noted phonological, grammatical, and contextual links within vv. 22-25.

29. Reading with Q *gîl yāgîl,* not with K *gōl yagûl.* Perhaps misled by K, the LXX reads, "He will raise [his children] well" (< *gaddēl yᵉgaddēl*).

30. Reading with syndetic Q, not with asyndetic K.

31. Reading asyndetic Q with the LXX, Targ., and Vulg., not syndetic K with the Syr. GKC (P. 159-60) explains the syntax of K as a participle used as a casus pendens or as a complete noun clause in the protasis and the *waw* as apodosis *waw* (i.e., "and [as for] the one who begets a wise son, he takes pleasure in him").

32. The LXX and Syr. add "over you" (< *mimmekā),* suggesting to Fichtner *(BHS)* the emendation from *'immekā* to *'immāk,* but all texts and versions attest sensible *wᵉ'immekā.*

33. The ambiguous prefix conjugation is best construed as jussive because of the unambiguously parallel jussive.

34. Reading *tirṣenâ* with K, not *tiṣṣōrenâ* "protect" with Q, LXX, Targ., Syr., Vulg. In the consonantal text the problem is caused by the metathesis of /ṣ/ and /r/; *trṣnh* versus *tṣrnh.* Either reading is possible, and text critics are about equally divided. The root *nṣr* occurs 18 times in this book, but *rṣh* only twice (3:12; 16:7), making K the more difficult reading. Significantly, *derek* is also its object in 16:7. This verb often takes a direct acc. of person or thing (*HALOT,* 2:1281, s.v. *rṣh*). Moreover, the figure of eyes complying with/obeying a way is difficult to comprehend. *Nṣr* does not mean to observe physically (Prov. 3:1; 20:28). By contrast, K seems more cogent. In this saying the father is vying with the adulteress who, according to 6:25, tempts the son with the beauty of her eyes (see v. 27).

35. Although the LXX reads this very differently from the MT, its *allotrios* ("strange," "foreign," "another") represents *zārâ* in its *Vorlage.* The prologue supports this reading because in 5:10, 17; 7:5 *zārâ* stands in parallel with *nokrîyâ* and *zônâ* never occurs as its parallel. In 6:26 the cheapness of a *zōnâ* stands in contrast to the expense of a *zārâ* and in 5:10-11; 6:33-35; 7:22-27 the *zārâ* ruins her victim, the same as in 23:27-28. If *zônâ* is the original reading, she is the *zārâ* of the prologue. Although by itself the argument is not compelling, *zārâ* forms an excellent assonance with *ṣārâ* in 23:27b. In sum, although the external evidence is weak, the internal evidence in favor of reading *zārâ,* not *zônâ,* is compelling.

28 *Indeed, she lays an ambush like a robber,*
and increases the traitors among men.
29 *Who has "Woe!"? Who has "Alas!"?*
Who has bitter conflicts? Who has complaints?
Who has bruises needlessly?
Who has flashing[36] *eyes?*
30 *Those who linger over wine,*
those who come to search out jugs of mixed wine.
31 *Do not look at*[37] *wine when it is an alluring red,*
when it sparkles in the goblet,[38]
when it goes down smoothly.
32 *In the end*[39] *it will bite like a snake,*
and poison like a viper.
33 *Your eyes will see incredible sights,*
and your mouth will speak what is perverse.
34 *And you will become like one sleeping on the high seas,*

36. The root is attested in the adjective *ḥaklîlî* (Gen. 49:12) and in this abstract noun. Both are *hap. leg.*, and both occur with wine. The root is usually identified as *ḥkl,* which in Akkadian means "to be dark" and in Arabic "to hide oneself." Lexicographers often understand the noun to mean "dark" or "dull" in either appearance (i.e., bloodshot, red, etc.) or in a vision from wine. Kapelrud ("Genesis 49:12," *VT* 4 [1954] 426ff.) renders the adjective as comparative "darker than wine." But *HALOT* (1:313, s.v., *ḥkl,* citing Bergsträsser, Bauer, Leander, et al.) think of a metathesis and derive it from *kḥl* "to paint." They suggest the meaning "sparkling" in both texts. The LXX renders the adjective as *chairopoioi* "causing joy," and the noun as *pelidnoi* "livid." Probably one should not emend Gen. 49:12, but we need not decide that text here. "Sparkling," however, in English tends to be *bonum partem;* hence "flashing" to make the eyes *malum partem.*

37. G. R. Driver ("Notes on Proverbs," p. 187) invests *rāʾâ* with the meaning of *rwh* "to drink" (see 17:18), "since 'look not on' is absurd. . . . There is no harm in looking on wine, whatever its color." He validates his interpretation from the LXX *methyskesthe* "to get drunk on." McKane (*Proverbs,* p. 394) grants the lexical possibility of Driver's interpretation, "since *rʾh* is used as a variant of *rwh* in Isa. 53:11 along with *śbʿ* ("to be sated"). But he rejects the interpretation, "since the point of warning is that if you allow yourself to be hypnotized by the rich colour of red wine, in no time at all you will be drinking it." Moreover, *rʾh* is not necessarily a bi-form of *rwh* in Isa. 53:11, and the LXX is a free paraphrase in this verse (A. J. Baumgartner, *Étude critique sur l'état du texte du Livre des Proverbes d'après les principales traductions anciennes* [Leipzig: Imprimerie Orientale W. Drugulin, 1890], pp. 209-10).

38. Q reads *kōs* to correct *kîs* of K.

39. Lit. "its end." Fem. *ʾaḥarîtô* is not the subject of masc. *yiššāk* and *yapriš* (cf. 5:4), but an adverbial acc., and *yāyin* in 23:30 is the pronoun's antecedent. By rejecting the accents of the MT, it could be subject of a nominal clause (i.e., its end is like; cf. Ps. 17:12), but in Prov. 29:21 the expected *yihyeh* is attested.

like one sleeping on top of the mast.[40]

35 *"They hit me, but I am not hurt;*
they beat me, but I do not know it.
When will I wake up
so that I may continue to seek it yet again?"[41]

24:1 *Do*[42] *not envy evil people,*
and do not crave to be with them;
2 *because their hearts ponder violence,*
and their lips speak malice.

An education that sounds very much like the prologues to the book (1:8–9:18) and to the Thirty Sayings of the Wise (22:17-21) marks off the next unit of seven sayings (23:12, 13-14, 15-16, 17-18, 19-21, 22-25, 26-28). Moreover, the seven sayings share the same theme and are entitled "The Obedient Son" by D. Römheld.[43] In addition to the introductory first saying (23:12), the first four proverb pairs admonish the son to heed parental teaching.[44] The second and fourth of these sayings (Sayings 13 and 15) are formulated as negative prohibitions, using *'al* with the jussive: do not withhold the tradition from the next generation (vv. 13-14) and do not envy sinners, who oppose the world-and-life views of the parents (vv. 17-18). The fifth (vv. 19-21) combines the rearing admonition (v. 19) with the prohibition, do not join drunkards (vv. 20-21). The sixth (vv. 22-25), also an admonition to heed parental teaching, is framed among other features by the rare reference to both the mother and the father. The seventh saying (vv. 26-28) combines the admonition to heed parental teaching (v. 26) with the substantiating argument that it functions as a safeguard against the immoral woman (vv. 27-28). To these are appended chiastically two sayings that elaborate on the warning against the drunkard (cf. 23:19-21 and 23:29-35) and the prohibition not to envy sinners/wicked men (24:1-2).

"Heart" runs as a keyword through the sayings (vv. 12, 15-16, 17, 19)

40. LXX *hōsper kybernētēs en pollǭ klydōni* ("like a pilot in a storm") probably represents a creative interpretation of a Hebrew text whose meaning was unknown. Gemser (*Sprüche,* p. 88) et al., however, on its basis emended the text to *ûkērōkēb brā'āš ḥōbēl* ("and like a mariner, who rides in a storm"). Dahood takes *ḥbl* as a metathesis for *ḥlb,* ("mountain"). But H.-J. Fabry (*TDOT,* 4:178, s.v. *ḥōbēl, ḥibbēl*) comments, "This word [in the MT], too, is clearly one of those Phoenician nautical terms whose nuances are still unknown."

41. LXX reads *zētēsō meth' hōn syneleusomai* (< *'ᵃbaqqēš nô'āday*) "I will seek my boon companions" (REB).

42. LXX adds "my son."

43. Römheld, *Wege der Weisheit,* p. 46.

44. The conditional clauses in 23:15 and 16 function as admonitions (see 2:1).

to tightly link the son to the parents. The notion of loyalty between the generations as the son's community boundary colors the entire subunit. His heartfelt loyalty to his parents is matched by his radical separation from sinners. He must neither envy them (vv. 17-18; 24:1-2), nor join profligates such as drunkards (vv. 19-21, 29-35) and prostitutes (vv. 26-28), nor barter away parental wisdom for another world-and-life view (v. 23).

These sayings advance chronologically, spanning one's entire life from *youth* (23:13-14) to a mother grown old (23:22).

There is also an escalation in the imperatives to accept the teaching. In the first (Saying 12), "my son" is not mentioned (v. 12). In the third (Saying 14) this term of endearment is introduced (v. 15). The fifth (Saying 16) adds to "my son" other important terms such as "listen" (v. 19). In the sixth (Saying 17), "listen" is repeated, and in place of "my son" the even more personal terms of intergenerational endearment are used, "the one who begot you" and "the one who bore you" (v. 22). The climactic seventh (Saying 18) uses "my son" and in direct appeal asks the son to give his body parts to his parents' direction (v. 26). This reference to his body parts, "heart" and "eyes," forms an *inclusio* with the twelfth saying that asks him to bring his heart and ears to his parents' wisdom. Their instructions are to be heard and read (see 22:17, 20).

Sayings 17 and 18 implicitly contrast the wise and foolish woman, resembling the great diptychs of these two types of women in chs. 7, 8, 9:1-6, and 9:13-18. Saying 16, in addition to being all about acquiring the parents' teaching and bringing them joy (vv. 22-25), features the godly mother's physical and spiritual role in rearing the son. This life-giving mother functions as a foil to the death-dealing adulteress in the climactic eighteenth saying.

The admonitions to heed parental wisdom have a strong personal reference. "My son" occurs in three of the pairs (vv. 15, 19, 26), "I," "to me," or "father" as a self-reference to the teacher occurs five times (vv. 15, 22, 24, 25, 26), and "mother" twice (vv. 22, 25). Parent and child are also closely linked in this "I-thou" encounter by reference to their body parts. The father speaks of "my heart" (v. 15) and of "my kidneys" (v. 16); he also mentions "my ways" (v. 26). With reference to the son he speaks of "your heart" in four of the five admonitions (vv. 12, 15, 19, 26), of "your lips" (v. 16), and of "your eyes" (v. 26). Saying 18 binds the generations together by speaking of the father and mother as those who begot/bore him (vv. 22, 25).

Their instruction is all about "wisdom" (vv. 15, 19, 23, 24) and its correlative terms (I: 93): "instruction"/"discipline" (vv. 12, 13, 23), "knowledge" (v. 12), "insight" (v. 23), "truth" (v. 23), "what is upright" (v. 16), "the fear of the LORD" (v. 17), and "righteous" (v. 24). In sum, the coloring, verbal links, structure, and other literary features bind this subunit together and almost function as a prologue to the rest of the sayings.

1. Saying 12 (23:12)

Verse 12 has all the marks of beginning a new unit, for it is general in character, has strong affinities both verbally and thematically with 22:17, and its every word is identical with terms of the father's introductory admonitions to his lectures (1:8–9:18; cf. 1:8; 3:1; 4:1; 5:1 passim). At the same time it is linked verbally with the tenth saying (23:9) by "ear" and to the eleventh by *bô'* ("enter," 23:10, and "apply," 23:12). The connection with the "ear" in 23:9 shows that the father does not regard his son as a fool; in Saying 13 he assumes his son will discipline youths in the next generation (vv. 13-14). The proverb pictures the son as bringing his heart and ear to Solomon's insightful and authoritative teachings mediated through his parents (see 1:8). In its complementary parallelism, the imperative *apply* (*hābî'â,* lit. "to cause . . . to participate in entering" [cf. 21:12]) *your heart* (see I: 90) and [apply] *your ear* (see 2:2) (see 2:2; 23:9) form the outer frame. *To the instruction* (see 1:2) and *to words of knowledge* (see 19:27) form the inner core. The heart and ear work in tandem with one another. The inner organ of the heart must open the organ of hearing to allow the outer organ to reshape the inner organ (cf. 2:2; 15:31; 18:15; 19:27). In 2:2 priority was given to the ear; here it is given to the heart. "A listless *heart* . . . produces a careless ear."[45] Solomon brings the two together in his prayer for a "hearing heart" (1 K. 3:9; cf. Prov. 20:12).

2. Saying 13 (23:13-14)

An admonition to the son to become himself an instructor advances the preceding admonition to bring his heart to "instruction" *(mûsār).* As an educator he must not withhold "discipline" *(mûsār)* from a young person. This play on the two meanings of *mûsār* (see 1:2) binds together the two sayings that are addressed to an apprentice in moral education, beginning with his own obedience and climaxing in his being a disciplinarian with a rod (cf. Deut. 6:5-9).[46] But Sayings 12 and 13 essentially differ, contrasting respectively "words of knowledge" for the obedient son's ears with a rod for the back of disobedient youth.

The proverb pair is bound together tightly by developing the protasis of v. 13bα, "strike him with the rod," escalated in a full verset to "you must

45. Bridges, *Proverbs,* p. 429.

46. Ahiqar (6:81-82) says, "Withhold not thy son from the rod, else thou wilt not be able to save [him from wickedness]. If I smite thee, my son, thou wilt not die, but if I leave thee to thine own heart [thou wilt not live]" (*ANET,* p. 428). Similarly the Egyptian *Instruction of Papyrus Insinger* (9:9) states, "A son does not die from being punished by his father" (*AEL,* 3:192).

strike him" in v. 14a. Also, the apodosis ("he will not die") of v. 13bβ is escalated in a full verset to "and deliver him from the grave" in v. 14b.

13 *Do not* [see 22:22] *withhold* [see 3:27; 11:26] *discipline* (*mûsār,* not "instruction" because of the parallel, "rod"; see 1:2) from a youth (see 1:4; 22:6) is explained in verset B as flogging the inexperienced fool on the back because that kind of discipline offers him life. Ambiguous *kî* that introduces the protasis of v. 13bα here plays on both its causal sense "for" (i.e., it gives the reason for heeding the admonition of verset A) and its conditional sense "if." The LXX represents both notions by *hoti ean, for if.*[47] *You strike him* [see 17:10] *with a rod* (see 10:13) refers to a severe, but not fatal, flogging to cleanse the youth and to prevent the repetition of his folly (cf. 17:26; 19:25; 20:30). The elaboration in the proverb pair's outer frame of v. 14b shows that *he will not die* (see 5:23) signifies that because of the flogging he will not die, not that from the flogging he will not die (i.e., he will survive it).[48] Moreover, the parallel in v. 14b also suggests that death refers to an eternal severance from fullness of life that comes from a relationship with the living God (cf. 5:23; 10:21; 15:10; 19:16, 18), not to clinical death. According to v. 14b the disciplined youth can expect clinical death, but the grave will not hold him fast. Severe discipline is not cruel, but to withhold it from callous youth is. Bridges asks, "Is it not better that the flesh should smart, than that *the soul should die?*"[49] (13:24; 19:18; 20:30; 22:6, 15; 29:17). However, the cleansing rod must be applied with warmth, affection, and respect for the youth. Warmth and affection, not steely discipline, characterize the father's lectures (cf. 4:1-9). Parents who brutalize their children cannot hide behind the rod doctrine of Proverbs.

14 The LXX and Syriac assumed that the "for/if" of v. 13bα was elided in v. 14a, but the Targum and Vulgate recognized in the initial, pleonastic *you* an escalation that gives a psychological focus on the son as the disciplinarian.[50] *You must strike him with a rod* chiastically repeats 23:13bα but escalates the "if" clause" to obligation.[51] Cohen paraphrases: "It is obligatory upon thee to beat him."[52] *And* [= "and so"][53] *you will deliver* [see 2:12] *his life* (*napšô;* see I: 90) *from the grave* (see 1:12; cf. 10:2).

47. The parallel in v. 14, "you will save him from the grave," rules out the concessive sense of *kî* (i.e., "although you strike him . . . , he will not die").

48. *Pace* D. W. Thomas, "Textual and Philological Notes on Some Passages in the Book of Proverbs," in *WIANE,* 288-89.

49. Bridges, *Proverbs,* p. 429.

50. *IBHS,* p. 296, P. 16.3.2e.

51. *IBHS,* p. 508, P. 31.4g.

52. Cohen, *Proverbs,* p. 154.

53. An apodosis *waw* after the semantic, not formal, protasis.

3. Saying 14 (23:15-16)

Saying 14 is linked to Saying 12 by "your heart" (vv. 12 and 15) and to Saying 13 by a psychological focus on "you," the first word of v. 14, and on "I," the last word of v. 15. More importantly, both pairs escalated from the son being taught to his becoming a teacher. "And" in v. 16 and a chiastic structure bind together the two verses of this saying. Their outer frame presents the protases representing the son's accepting the father's instruction (vv. 15a, 16b), and their inner core, the father's glad response. The pair chiastically links the father's body parts with the son's: "your heart"/"my heart" (v. 15) and "my inward parts [lit. kidneys]"/"your lips" (v. 16). The Old Testament often mentions "heart" and "kidneys" together (e.g., Ps. 7:9[10]; Jer. 11:20; 17:10; 20:1). By conditioning his joy on the son's wisdom, the father motivates the son to be wise. Verse 16 escalates the persuasion by shifting from their hearts to their outward expressions of joy and wisdom (10:1; 15:20; 17:21, 25; 23:15-16, 24-25; 27:11). Several proverbs ranging over several collections motivate the son to embrace his parents' teaching by impressing on him that he can bring his parents joy or sorrow. This motivation assumes both the parents' and the child's psychological health. The child is dear to his parents, and he desires to please them. A mother gives physical birth in travail, but both parents travail again in spiritual birth (cf. Luke 15:7, 10, 13-24; 1 Thess. 2:19, 20; 3:8-9; 2 Tim. 1:2-5; 2 John 4; 3 John 4). Booker T. Washington argues that the memory white youths have of their ancestry gives them a distinct advantage over black youths who lack this memory. "The very fact that the white boy is conscious that, if he fails in life, he will disgrace the whole family record, extending back through many generations, is of tremendous value in helping him to resist temptations. The fact that the individual has behind and surrounding him a proud family history and connection serves as a stimulus to help him to overcome obstacles when striving for success."[54]

15 Verset A presents the condition, an implied admonition (see 2:1), and verset B the consequence. The versets are arranged chiastically, with "my son" and "even I" constituting the outer frame, and "if your heart is wise" and "my heart will rejoice" forming its inner core. By this balancing chiasm, the father emphasizes the connection between the son's moral health and his psychological well-being. He underscores the connection by drawing the verse to a conclusion: "I certainly will be glad!" *My son* [see 1:8], *if* [see 2:1] *your heart* [see I: 90] *is wise* [see I: 94], *my heart will be glad* [see 5:18]. *Yes, mine* (lit. "I"), the pleonastic pronoun featuring the father, focuses psychologically on his own heart's rapture.

54. Booker T. Washington, *Up from Slavery* (New York: Doubleday, 1902), pp. 36-37.

16 The father continues to motivate the son, now to become an educator himself, by asserting in verset A, the apodosis, his exuberant joy, at a time when the son's speech conforms to the fixed moral order, the protasis of verset B. The two thoughts are joined by conjunctive *and. My inward parts* (*kilyôtāy,* lit. "my kidneys") functions as a synecdoche for the father's emotions. "Of all human organs, the OT associates the kidneys in particular with a variety of emotions. The range of usage is very wide; the kidneys are looked upon as the seat of emotions from joy to deepest agony."[55] Also, both the secret heart and the kidneys designate the whole of the inner person. *Will leap for joy (ta'lōznâ)* denotes the expression of extreme joy through such actions as singing, shouting, and dancing.[56] Since an inner organ of the body cannot express its joy outwardly, it must be a metonymy of source. The father's deep-seated joy will find expression in his mouth. *When*[57] *your lips* [see 4:24] *speak* [see 23:9] *what is upright* (see I: 98; 1:3) is the "evidence of a mind disciplined by morality."[58]

4. Saying 15 (23:17-18)

A prohibition not to envy sinners now complements the proscriptions to embrace the parents' wisdom (vv. 15-16; cf. 1:8-9, 10-19). *Your heart* (*libbᵉkā;* vv. 15, 17) links the two pairs. The reverse side of the coin of the son's heart-loyalty to his parents is his heart-repudiation of sinners. Both sayings substantiate their admonitions in a second verse (vv. 16, 18).

17 The antithetical parallels of v. 17 bring together in a single admonition by a play on *qannē' bᵉ* a prohibition against wrong zeal (v. 17a) and a command to have a rightful fervor (v. 17b). *Do not* [see 23:13] *let . . . be envious of* (*yᵉqannē' bᵉ;* see 3:31) *sinners* (see 1:10), who are here conceptualized as rivals against whom he competes for the same goals. *But (kî 'im)* expresses a contrast after a negative.[59] [*Let your heart be zealous*] *for* glosses the gapped *libbᵉkā yᵉqannē',* with only *bᵉ* expressed. *Qn' bᵉ* in the *Piel* now has its positive sense "to be excited about," "to be zealous for," "to have fervor, ardor for," the well-being of someone or something (cf. Num. 11:29;

55. D Kellermann, *TDOT,* 7:179, s.v. *kᵉlayôt.*

56. *'ālaz* occurs 16 times in the Old Testament, always in poetry. Its meaning can be inferred from its use when the LORD says against Babylon, "I will set out a feast for them and make them drunk, so that that they will shout with laughter [*lema'an ya'ᵃlōzû*]" (Jer. 51:39). The NIV renders it "revel" (Isa. 23:12), "leaps for joy" (Ps. 28:7), "be jubilant" (94:3), and "rejoice" (149:5). It is also combined with *śmḥ* in Jer. 50:11.

57. *IBHS,* p. 603, P. 36.2.1f.

58. Cohen, *Proverbs,* p. 154.

59. *HALOT* 2:471, s.v. *kî 'im.*

25:11, 13; 2 Sam. 21:2). *All the time* [lit. "all the day"][60] *the fear of the LORD* (see I: 100) becomes one's only goal. "There is a right and wrong aspiration or jealousy; the one is a disease and the other a valuable spiritual exercise."[61]

18 *Kî 'im* now binds the admonitions (v. 17) and their substantiation (v. 18). The pun involves moving from its adversative sense (v. 17b) to its asseverative sense (v. 18a). The son's only goal is the fear of the LORD (v. 17), and the outcome of pursuing that goal is an unending beatific future (see vv. 13-14) that is repeated in 24:14 and that can be apprehended only by faith (see v. 14b). The beatific future escalates from "will not die" (v. 13b) to "deliver from the grave" (v. 14b) to "your hope will not be cut off" (v. 18). The faithful person who builds his life on that vision pleases God. The "future" is brought into focus as "your hope," and "there is" is escalated to "will not be cut off." *Surely (kî 'im)* now introduces a positive oath-clause.[62] *There is*[63] *a latter end* (see 14:12-13) here refers to the end that results from constantly fearing the LORD. *And* adds the second situation. *Your hope* (see 10:28) refers to a future when God reverses the present, envious good fortunes of sinners, who took advantage of God-fearers, by punishing the wicked with the loss of everything and rewarding the righteous with prosperity (see I: 104). The metaphor *will not be cut off* (cf. Num. 13:23, 24; 1 Sam. 24:5[6])[64] signifies that the hoped-for abundant life will not be annihilated. The effective motivation to observe both sides of this coin of fervor is the promise that God will fulfill the hope of the righteous for an abundant life both for time and for eternity (cf. Pss. 24:20; 73:17; Jer. 29:11; John 13:7; Rom. 5:5; Jas. 5:11; Rev. 13:10).

5. Saying 16 (23:19-21)

The father's renewed call to hear (v. 19) and the negative command in vv. 20-21 prohibiting keeping company with profligates could be another saying, a construction matching the first two sayings of this subunit (vv. 12, 13-14).

60. A prophetic and poetic equivalent of *kol-hayyāmîm* (BDB, p. 400, s.v. *yôm*).

61. McKane, *Proverbs,* p. 387.

62. *HALOT,* p. 471, s.v. *kî 'im.*

63. *IBHS,* p. 72, P. 4.5b.

64. *Kārat* is also used of "chopping off" a head (1 Sam. 17:51), hands (1 Sam. 5:4), etc., as well as of God's activity. At the time the LORD comes to judge the world, he will "cut off" everything that lives (Gen. 9:1; Zeph. 1:3). At God's eschatological annihilation he will "cut off" (i.e., destroy) horses (Mic. 5:10[9]), the cities of the land (v. 11[10]), and sorcery (v. 12[11]). In the "day of the LORD," money changers and idolaters will "be cut off" [*Niphal*] (Joel 1:4; cf. the *Hiphil* in Ezek. 14:8, 13, 17, 19, 21; 17:17; Zech. 13:2). Israel's "head and tail" will be cut off (Isa. 9:13[14]), and the wicked will be cut off from the land (Prov. 2:22).

But more probably it is a single command like vv. 26-28. "Listen" cries out for an object, and "direct your heart in the way" cries out for definition. Verses 20-21 provide both. If so, the reason for the positive admonition to listen in v. 19 is formulated as the negative command not to keep company with profligates (v. 20) with validation (v. 21).

19 The unexpected, pleonastic addition to *listen* [see 1:8], *yes you* (cf. 23:14, 15) gets the son's attention to focus him on the commands to steer clear of profligates (vv. 20-21). *My son* (see 23:15) connotes warm endearment (see 23:15) and reminds the son of his natural allegiance to the one to whom he owes his life over against a foolish peer group who threaten their relationship. *And* grammatically joins to the command another imperative, *become wise* (*ḥ^{a}kām;* see I: 94), but semantically it indicates result.[65] *And* introduces a parallel result. *Direct* [or "lead"; lit. "make your heart take strides"; see 4:14][66] *your heart* (see I: 90) puts a fine point on the command to "listen." Although "take strides in the way of your heart" is a grammatically tenable gloss, that notion contradicts "folly is bound up in the heart of the youth" (22:15; cf. 23:13). Verses 20-21 will define *in the way* (see 1:15).

20-21 Kidner labels the prohibition of v. 20 with its rationale in v. 21, "from revelry to rags."[67]

20 Drunkards and gluttons epitomize self-indulgence and profligacy. Verset A prohibits becoming identified with drunkards, to whom verset B adds those who flagrantly disregard the value of flesh (cf. 13:20b; 20:1b; 22:24-27; 24:1b, 21b; 29:3b; cf. also vv. 26-28). *Do not be* denotes "to be there or to become in a state of existence" with the connotation "to remain and live" (cf. Ruth 1:2; Jer. 1:3; Dan. 1:21).[68] With *among (b^{e}),* it connotes being in the company of and/or to be identified with a group (cf. 1 K. 2:7; Amos 1:1).[69] *Drunkards (sōb^{e}'ê-yāyin)* means literally, "wine addicts."[70] *Sōbē'* occurs three times (Deut. 21:20; Prov. 23:20, 21) and always with "gluttons" *(zōlēl).* Since the other two texts distinguish them by "and," with *among* they denote two close, but distinct, groups. They represent all the incorrigible, delinquent, and self-indulgent. *Gluttons* glosses *zōl^{a}lê* (lit. "who depise/make light of")[71] *bāśār* ("flesh," i.e., the meat next to the bone full of

65. *IBHS,* p. 653, P. 39.2.5.
66. *HALOT,* 1:97, s.v. *'šr.*
67. Kidner, *Proverbs,* p. 152.
68. *HALOT,* 1:244, s.v. *ḥyh.*
69. BDB, p. 227, s.v. *hāya.*
70. The verb *sāba'* is a denominative of *sōbē',* a kind of liquor (*HALOT,* 2:738, s.v. *sb'*). The nominal cognate in Arabic means "wine," and in Akkadian "a kind of beer." The verbal denominative in Arabic means "to import wine," and in Akkadian "to brew beer." The verb in biblical Hebrew signifies "be a wine bibber," "become drunk" (cf. Isa. 56:12; Nah. 1:10).

blood and the source of energy; cf. Prov. 5:11; 14:30). By itself *zōlēl* denotes a profligate, who makes light of anything that is precious and thus squanders it. But its unique occurrence with "flesh" and its consistent use with drunkards suggest the gloss "glutton." Elsewhere in the book "flesh" refers to one's own body, leading some to draw the conclusion that gluttons are self-destroyers, but the parallelism suggests that flesh refers to the meat consumed at table.[72] *For themselves* denotes that these gluttons gorge themselves on animal flesh without regard to the animal or the need of others[73] (cf. Luke 21:34; Rom. 13:11-14; 1 Cor. 5:11-13; 1 Tim. 3:3; Titus 1:7).

21 *Because* signals the prohibitions' substantiation. The self-indulgent are reduced to destitution (v. 21a) due to the drowsiness that accompanies addiction to wine and overeating (v. 21b). Their full stomachs empty their minds. Moreover, due to their debauchery, they are no longer valiant or vigilant to protect their property and thus become destitute, like the sluggard, without clothing for protection or social status (cf. 6:9-11; 19:15; 20:13). The repetition *drunkard and glutton* (*sōbē' wᵉzōlēl,* assuming *bāśār* is gapped), albeit in the singular, identifies these subjects as the forbidden company of v. 22. *Will become destitute* (see 20:13),[74] and so unable to sustain their lives. *And* compounds the reason. Although *drowsiness (nûmâ)* is a *hap. leg.*, the six occurrences of the verb *nûm* certify its meaning. In contrast to other verbs belonging to the semantic domain of "sleep," *nûm* connotes to stop being vigilant and valiant.[75] Since *will clothe* (*talbîš,* lit. "cause to wear [rags]") always has a personal subject, "drowsiness" is personified. *Lbš* in the *Qal* means, "wear clothing for both physical protection and social acceptance." *Them* (the profligates) is gapped.[76] *In rags (qᵉrā'îm)* is derived from *qāra'* "to rip (in)to pieces"; its three occurrences refer

71. BDB, pp. 272-73, s.v. II *zll; HALOT,* 1:272, I *zll. Zālal* occurs seven times: once in the *Hiphil* and six times as the *Qal* active participle. The latter seems to be used twice in an intransitive sense ("be light/worthless/despised"): of lowly Jerusalem (Lam. 1:11) and of worthless speech in contrast to that which is precious *(yāqār).* In the *Hiphil* it is used of Jerusalem's enemies, who formerly honored her but, having seen her nakedness, "make light of/despise" her (Lam. 1:8). In the other five uses of the active participle, it also seems to mean "to despise/make light of." It is used of the stubborn, rebellious, and disobedient son (Deut. 21:20) and of the opposite of one who obeys the law (Prov. 28:20).

72. Toy, *Proverbs,* p. 435.

73. *IBHS,* p. 207, P. 2.10.d.

74. *IBHS,* pp. 503-4, P. 31.2c.

75. *Nûm* is used in parallel or in association with *yšn* "to sleep" (Ps. 121:3, 4; Isa. 5:27) and *šēnâ* "sleep" (Ps. 76:5[6]); *škb* "to lie down" (Isa. 56:10); *škn* "to lie down to rest" (Nah. 3:18). It occurs only in poetry as a synonym of "to sleep." Three times *nûm* is used of troops or rulers who slumber (Ps. 76:5[6]; Isa. 56:10; Nah. 3:18) and three times of the vigilant and valiant who do not slumber (Ps. 121:3, 4; Isa. 5:27).

76. *IBHS,* p. 438, P. 27.2e.

to torn off pieces of cloth (1 K. 11:30, 31; 2 K. 2:12), which are incapable of providing adequate protection or social acceptance.

6. Saying 17 (23:22-25)

Phonological, lexical, grammatical, and thematic *inclusios* bind together vv. 22-25 into a single saying. Note their threefold assonance of *î/e/ey/kā,* their references to "your father" and "your mother," the catchword *yld* "to beget/to bear," and grammatical expressions appealing to the son's volition in vv. 22 and 25. The logical connection of vv. 22-25 is similar to that of vv. 15-16. The first half (vv. 22-23) presents the admonitions to attain and retain the parents' wisdom, and the second half (vv. 24-25), the motivation (i.e., to give the parents exuberant joy). But Saying 17 remarkably escalates Saying 14 (vv. 15-16).

Its first quatrain (vv. 22-23) is connected by a similar syntax (impv. + *'al* and jussive) and by theme. Both "do not despise your mother when she grows old" and "do not sell wisdom" command the son to hold fast to his parents' teachings. The last two verses are linked chiastically and lexically by *gîl* ("to shout in exultation," vv. 24a, 25b) and *yiśmaḥ* ("to take pleasure in"/"be glad" (vv. 24b, 25a) and also by the merism of "the one who begot" (*yôlēd,* masc., v. 24b) and "the one who bore" (*yôledet,* fem., v. 25b). Instead of substantiating the admonition to heed the parents' instruction (v. 22) by a specific negative command as in vv. 12, 13-14, 15-16, 17-18, 19, and 20-21, the commands to bring the parents joy perform that function (vv. 24-25). The prohibition not to sell the inherited wisdom (v. 25) entails the prohibitions not to be envious of sinners (vv. 15-16; 24:1-2) and not to join the profligates (vv. 20-21, 29-35) and the implicit command not to turn aside to the adulteress (vv. 27-28). Prov. 29:3 also contrasts the son bringing joy to his parents with one who is a companion of prostitutes who squander his wealth (cf. Luke 15:11-32).

The saying camps on the biological and spiritual relationship between the parents and the son. Three times the father mentions that his parents bore him (vv. 22, 24, 25). The saying uniquely stresses the role of the mother in his birth and rearing (cf. 1:8), putting beyond reasonable doubt the home, not a school, as the locus for the Thirty Sayings of the Wise.

22 *Your father* in verset A and *your mother* in verset B exhibit the splitting up in poetry of the prosaic stereotyped phrase "father and mother" (cf. 1:8; 10:1). *Listen* [see 1:8] *and do not show contempt for* [see 1:7; 11:12; cf. Lev. 19:32] *your mother,* which is elided, pertain to both parents. So also the merism the one *who begot you* (see 17:17, 21, 25) and *when she grows old* (see 17:6; 22:6)[77] spans the entire life of both parents in relationship to

77. *IBHS,* p. 492, P. 30.5.3c.

their son, from his birth to their old age. Their gray heads are their crowns for having lived their lives in wisdom (16:31; 20:29), and the child's crowning adornment (17:6b). The command not to show contempt for parents has in view never letting go of their teachings, as shown by the parallels in verset A of this verse, in the rest of this saying (vv. 23-25), and in 30:17[78] (cf. Gen. 22:9; 28:1-5; 48:9-14; Exod. 18:13-24; Ruth 2:22, 23). Disrespect for parents, which leads to all sorts of ungodliness, is one of the signs of the distressing times to come (2 Tim. 3:1-4).

23 The enjambment of v. 23 places the objects of "buy and sell" of verset A in verset B.[79] The commercial figures, *buy* [see 4:5, 7d] *truth* [or reliability; see 11:18] *and,* its antonym, *do not sell (timkōr)* connote that no price is too high to restrain the son from obtaining the parents' wisdom and no offer is high enough to compel his letting go of it (cf. 4:5, 7; 16:16; Matt. 13:45-46). "Truth/reliability" is placed with exceptional emphasis before the verb "to buy," and this is reinforced immediately by the prohibition not to sell *wisdom. . . . Mākar* means to dispose of material goods through a financial transaction. The metaphor connotes a spiritual attitude that counts the world-and-life views of sinners, profligates, the sexually immoral, and the like as better than the inherited wisdom. In this spiritual state, the heir is in danger of losing his precious inheritance. In an enjambment Verset B presents as the objects of "sell" *wisdom and instruction and insight,* the same three that open the book's preamble (1:2).

The four entities point to the totality and comprehensiveness of the persistent values of right living that one can achieve. These inestimable treasures are a free gift. In his famous oxymoron, Isaiah invited Israel to "come, buy wine and milk without money and without cost" (Isa. 55:1).

24 In the synonymous parallelism of v. 24, B paraphrases A: *the father* by *the one who begets* (see v. 23), *of a righteous son* (see I: 97) by *a wise son* (see I: 94) and *surely shouts in exultation* (*gîl yāgîl,* Q; see n. 29) by *takes pleasure* (*yiśmaḥ;* see 23:15) along with the prepositional phrase *in him* (*bô,* i.e., the wise son).[80]

25 This verse reinforces v. 24 by repeating the father's exuberance in a wise son and adding to his joy that of the mother, who is uniquely mentioned in both versets. Verset B again paraphrases verset A: *and your mother* by *the one who bore you* and *rejoice* by *shout in exultation.*

78. Meinhold (*Sprüche,* p. 395) wrongly cites as parallels the Egyptian *Instruction of Any* and the apocryphal book of Sirach (3:11-13). *Any* (7:17–8:2) is concerned with his mother's physical support, and Sirach does not hold the father in the same high esteem as this book. He teaches, "Even if your father is lacking in understanding, show forbearance."

79. Cf. 1:3; 22:4 for similar enjambments.

80. The adjectival substantives "righteous" and "wise" refer to the son because of their connection with "father" and "the one who begets."

7. Saying 18 (23:26-28)

The femme fatale loomed large in the prologue to Proverbs (see 5:1-23; 6:20-35; 7:1-27) and drew its encomiums to wisdom to their conclusion (9:13-18). Solomon's first collection of proverbs remained silent about her until its conclusion (22:14), where she was joined with the sluggard. Now she is encountered in the Thirty Sayings of the Wise as the climactic seventh saying that draws the subunit on the Obedient Son to its conclusion and in connection with profligates (23:19-21). The catchword "your heart" links the unit's seventh saying with its first, third, and fifth (vv. 12, 15, and 19) and "my son" with the last two. Heretofore the receptive organs, heart and ear, played the dominant role, but now the eyes are brought into play because they first perceive the seductive woman (see 6:25).

The saying's first half contains two direct admonitions to the son to give his body parts to the direction of his father (v. 26), and the second half validates them by two metaphors (v. 27) and two insights (v. 28). The depictions of the unchaste wife as a deep pit and as a bandit connote her extreme danger. The father colors her in the same dark tones as in his lectures. She is no ordinary prostitute, who can be had for a loaf of bread (see n. 35). The father's insights represent her as both deadly (vv. 27a, 28a) and deadly effective (v. 28b). She offers the son no benefit and no escape (vv. 28a, b). His only adequate resistance to her gross seductions is a prior commitment of his heart and eyes to God, who is represented by the father. In this light he will uncover her ambush.

26 In the chiastic, synthetic parallels of v. 26, the framing commands of the Hebrew text, *give and* (*w^{e};* see 23:12b) *let . . . take pleasure in* (*tirṣenâ;* see n. 34; 3:12) complement each other. The son gives his body parts to the father: *your heart* [see I: 90; vv. 2, 15, 19] *to me* and *your eyes* [see 20:12] *in my ways* (see 23:19). The first metaphor denotes that the son relinquishes control and possession of his own property and trustingly hands it over to the safekeeping of his wise father. The second metaphor pictures the father's teachings as the road the son travels on (see 23:19). That in which one takes pleasure depends on one's prior spiritual disposition. Accordingly, the heart's commitment (verset A) informs the eyes' pleasure (verset B). To ask the son to give him his heart, which rightfully belongs only to God, implies that the father, with Solomon's inspired teaching in his mouth, speaks as God's surrogate. He depicts his teachings as a path the son delights in to keep from straying into the trap of the huntress.

27 *Because* states explicitly, not inferentially as in the preceding prohibitions, that the reason the son should entrust his heart and eyes to his father is to protect him from an *unchaste wife* (*zārâ;* see n. 35; I: 119). The hunting metaphor *a deep pit* represents either her house (see 2:18; 5:5) or, more aptly, her bodily orifices. In 22:14 her "mouth," which is probably a double entendre (see 30:20) for the orifices of the mouth and of the vagina, is called a deep pit. This smooth-talking beauty (see 5:1-6; 6:25; 7:10-21) engages in sexual intercourse for lust and/or money with no intention and/or capability of a binding and enduring relationship. Once she has trapped her victim, he cannot escape the pit because it is deep. *And* interprets verset B as a synthetic parallel to verset A. *An unfaithful woman* (or "outsider"; see I: 121), the stock-in-trade parallel to *zārâ,* is now compared to *a . . . well (b*ᵉ*'ēr),* having the same extralinguistic referent as "deep pit" (i.e., the vagina). The well is an expected source of refreshing, satisfying water, a common metaphor for sex (see 5:15-18; 9:17). However, the opening to the well is *narrow* (*ṣārâ,* from *ṣrr* "to be restricted"), which connotes that this sexual partner frustrates him. The fornicator came hoping to quench his sexual appetite, but, because he finds her incapable of the intimacy necessary to satisfy that thirst, he cannot penetrate to satisfying water. Moreover, after he has penetrated her, he discovers that he cannot turn and extricate himself from his predicament (cf. Jer. 38:6). In addition to the allusion to her vagina, there may also be one to the grave (see 2:18-19; 5:5; 7:27; cf. Ps. 28:12; Isa. 14:15; 38:18; Ezek. 32:18). In sum, "deep pit" pictures this huntress as a lethal danger (see 22:14), and "narrow well" pictures her as an unexpected source of frustration. Both figures connote that she disguises these dangers from which the victim cannot escape.

28 In the synthetic parallels of v. 28 verset A intensifies the unchaste wife's danger by adding to the metaphor of a passive trap the simile of an active robber. *Indeed* plus the tautalogical pronoun *she* concentrates and expands the application of the metaphors to the adulteress (see 22:19b). *Lays an ambush* (see 1:11) pictures her as coldly digging her concealed trap in order to waylay her victim. The metaphor probably entails her seductive words. *Like a robber* is a *hap. leg.* from a rare verb that means "snatch away" (Job 9:12). The simile of her motives and methods depicts her as conspiring to plunder her victim in a cold, calculating, and ruthless way. To judge from 5:9-10; 6:30-35; 7:19-23, her husband plays a determinative role in the rapine destruction. *And* interprets verset B as synthetic; it intensifies the quantity of men she seduces to abandon their loyalty to God and the covenant community, especially godly parents, by her wiles. *She increases* [cf. 1:5] *the traitors* [or the disloyal; *bôg*ᵉ*dîm;* see I: 110] *among men* (*b*ᵉ*'ādām;* see I: 89). From her hardened point of view, however, she has done no wrong (30:20). To her, such behavior is as natural as eating a delicious meal (9:17).

8. Appendix (23:29–24:2)

The vivid and riveting warning against wine in Saying 19 expands on the warning against drunkards in Saying 16 (23:19-21). The two sayings are connected by "do not" *('al)* in connection with the catchword "wine" (*yāyin;* vv. 20, 31), but shift the danger from keeping company with drunkards to the danger of wine itself. Worse than poverty is lethal, havoc-making addiction. Chiastically, Saying 20 (24:1-2) elaborates on the prohibition against envying sinners in Saying 15 (23:17-18). These obvious elaborations suggest that the next two sayings function as an appendix to the unit on the Obedient Son (23:12–24:2).

a. Saying 19 (23:29-35)

29 The lure of the unfaithful woman (23:26-28) and of charming wine (vv. 29-35) are appropriately juxtaposed. The description of wine by "presents itself as red" and "makes itself go down" (v. 31) represents it as participating in the seduction. Both the vixen and wine are hidden and deadly traps. The preceding saying unmasks the unchaste wife as a triumphant huntress, and this one uncovers wine as a poisonous snake. Hosea (4:11) and Sirach also link women and wine: "Wine and women lead intelligent men astray" (Sir. 19:2). The chiastic catchwords, "your eyes/heart" . . . "your heart/eyes" also link the last of the seven sayings and the first appendix of seven verses (vv. 26, 33). The eyes are the gate by which women and wine seduce the heart (6:25; 23:31; cf. Jas. 1:13-15).

This mocking song drops the themes of loyalty to the parents' teaching and rejection of rival voices. M. E. Andrew analyzes this skillful song with varied subforms as follows. A riddle (v. 29) with an answer (v. 30), a commandment (v. 31) with consequence (v. 31), further consequences in direct address (vv. 33-34), "making the hearer feel as though he were already drunk," and a conclusion in the drunkard's own words (v. 35). The three pairings and conclusions are marked by changes of persons: "anyone" (vv. 29-30), "it" (vv. 31-32), "you" (vv. 33-34), and "I" (v. 35). An *inclusio* of several features frames the masterwork: rare quatrains (vv. 29, 35), questions by the father and by the drunkard, and references to beatings.[81]

At the semantic center of the saying is the command not to yield to wine's temptation. Devastating consequences lampooning addiction surround it. The captivating, introductory riddle points to disastrous social conflicts (cf. 20:1); the graphic consequences that follow, to personal losses. The circle of validating consequences is reinforced lexically by the repetition of the root *'ḥr* in the initial words of the verses surrounding the command (v. 31): "those who linger" (v. 30) and "its end" (v. 32).

29-30 Several features link the two-verse introduction, especially in

81. M. E. Andrew, "Variety of Expression in Proverbs XXIII 29-35," *VT* 28 (1978) 102-3.

the Hebrew text: (1) in literary form, by question (v. 29) and answer (v. 30); (2) in phonology, by the consonance of initial *l* with every clause in both verses; (3) in grammar, by the continued use of the preposition *l* to denote possession, by the interrogative pronouns of v. 29 referring to the relative participles of v. 30 and by eliding the six subjects of v. 29 ("woe," "complaints," etc.), which are also the subjects of v. 30.

29 The riddle coheres by a sixfold striking anaphora *who has (lᵉmî)* in an escalation of the drunkard's social hostility in v. 29a. First, he hears and perhaps hurls — it does not matter which — threatening cries of *"Woe!" (ʾôy).* The onomatopoetic woe-cry uniquely functions as the topic in this indirect discourse, not as, normally, an interjection in direct discourse followed by the topic. If addressed to someone else, it expresses threat and denunciation (cf. Num. 21:29; Jer. 13:27); if expressed to self, it connotes anxiety and despair (Isa. 6:5; Jer. 4:31). The parallels "strife" and "blows" favor the former interpretation. The Masoretic accent *merᵉka* joins to the next "who has" *(lᵉmî), "Alas!" (ʾᵃbôy).* This *hap. leg.* may have been coined to make the intensifying farrago *ʾôy* and *ʾᵃbôy* (cf. Eng. "alas and alack!").[82] The woe-cries escalate with the next two interrogatives *who has (lᵉmî),* along with conflicts and complaints. *Bitter conflicts* (see 6:14, 19) and *complaints (śîaḥ)* denote a person's grievance.[83] The accents mark off the fifth *who has (lᵉmî)* that escalates the conflicts and complaints to *bruises* (see 20:30), probably from blows by floggers and/or in brawls (see 20:30). *Needlessly* (see 1:16) signifies that nothing other than the drunkard's delirium occasioned the strokes and that in his delirium he hoped to gain nothing from the actions that provoked them. Verset B concretizes his pugnacity in his *flashing* [see n. 36] *eyes* (see 23:26), but that meaning is uncertain.

30 In the synthetic parallels giving the riddle's answer,[84] v. 30b juxtaposes and escalates lingering over wine to a diligent and difficult quest to make it a more spicy, potent, and enjoyable drink by mixing it with honey and spices (cf. Isa. 5:11). Woman Wisdom herself prepared mixed drinks in this fashion for her guests, but they did not linger in addiction over them. *Those who linger* (from *ʾḥr* "to be behind") means, in the intransitive *Piel,* "to delay, to hesitate" (cf. Judg. 5:28), but with *over wine* (see 23:20) the

82. *HALOT* (1:4, s.v., *ʾᵃboy*) derives the term either from the interjection I *ʾābî* or from *ʾbh* "to desire" (i.e., "longing" > "uneasiness" [from unrequited desire?]).

83. *Śîaḥ* occurs 14 times, elsewhere always with a pronoun. Lexicographers dispute its meaning in 1 K. 18:27 and 2 K. 9:11. Aside from Ps. 104:34, where it means "meditation" in praise, it always denotes a person's grievance (Hannah's, 1 Sam. 1:16; Job's, 7:13; 9:27; 10:1; 21:4; 23:2) or the psalmist's complaint (Pss. 55:2[3]; 64:1[2]; 102:superscription[1]; 142:2[3]).

84. The initial *lᵉ* that introduces the versets continues to have a possessive force. The answer is marked by the lack of the interrogative pronoun in v. 29.

English idiom prefers "linger." *Those who come* (see 6:11) refers to those who enter into and move within a realm of activity that affects their destiny. *To search out* denotes the activity of a diligent and penetrating probe (see 18:17). "Sample" (NIV) partially connotes the idea but may wrongly connote a small amount. *Jugs of mixed wine (mimsāk)* occurs elsewhere in the Bible only in Isa. 65:11. It derives from *msk* "to mix" (see 9:2, 5). The content "mixed wine" functions as a metonymy for the container(s) as well.

31-32 The cautioning riddle and answer now gives way to the command against giving wine an opportunity to work its charm (v. 31) along with rationale, signaled by "its end" (v. 32). The wordplay on *'ḥr,* "linger" and "end," also unites the riddle and the command. Although vv. 33-35 continue to catalogue the personal danger of wine, the style shifts to the second person. The catalogue of negative consequences is dischronologized: v. 32 threatens death, and vv. 33-35 the delirium tremens before death.

31 The prohibition arms the youth against addiction by nipping the temptation in the bud. As noted at 20:1, the Bible and Proverbs speak both favorably and unfavorably of intoxicants. The issue is how to use them wisely without abusing them. Addiction begins with the first drink. So how does one take any intoxicant without potentially becoming addicted to it? The command resolves the problem by disallowing one to be caught by the enticements of wine. When one is charmed by its color, its sparkle, the goblet's shape, and its delectable taste as it glides down smoothly, he should shove it aside.

The father also forearms the son by calling attention to wine's deception. Like the adulteress, its charm is a hidden trap. The prohibition's synthetic parallels command the son to stop drinking the wine by detailing its tempting allurement to the eyes and palate. Verses 33-35 unmask its pretext. *Do not look at* [see 6:6] *wine* [see 9:2] *when it is an alluring red (yit'addām).*[85] Verset Ba expands on its temptation to the eyes, and Bb adds to its deception its delectable taste. *When* is repeated with its visual danger. *It sparkles* glosses the idiom *yittēn . . . 'ênô.* Normal usage gives the semantically impertinent meaning "gives its eyes." *Nātan* here has its special sense "to give off, to show,"[86] and *'ên* ("eye") has a transferred meaning "gleam, flash."[87] The *'ênô* is its *éclat.*[88] *In the goblet* denotes that the cup is shell-

85. Although the verb *'dm* is often translated as a stative adjective, in its three occurrences, one time each in the *Qal* (Lam. 4:7), *Hiphil* (Isa. 1:16), and *Hithpael* (Prov. 23:31), only the first is truly so. In the internal *Hiphil,* it means "to cause itself to be reddish," a metaphorical sense (*IBHS,* p. 441, P. 27.2g). In the estimative-declarative *Hithpael 'dm* means "present itself [with the connotation of pretext] as reddish" (*IBHS,* p. 431, P. 26.2g).

86. *HALOT,* 2:734, s.v. *ntn.*

87. *HALOT,* 2:818, s.v. *'ayin.*

88. P. Auvray, "Sur le senf dumont *'ayin* en Ezek 1:18 et 10:12," *VT* 4 (1954) 5.

shaped.[89] *When* is gapped in v. 31bβ. *It goes down smoothly* glosses the idiom "walks about in smoothness" *(yithallēk bᵉmêšārîm).*[90] The command is a hyperbole. The English prohibition, "Don't even think about it," entails that one has been thinking about it and means to stop thinking about it. Likewise, the command not to look at wine implies that one has been looking at it, and the qualifying statement, "when it goes down smoothly," entails that one has even begun sipping it. The hyperbole means: "Stop drinking it." The youth must make no provision for his lust.

32 Although this verse lacks the logical particle "because," it functions to validate the command. The deadly end of gazing at wine exposes its true identity. In this synonymous parallelism, "snake" is escalated to "poisonous viper," and "bite" is probably elevated to poisonous strike. Like a poisonous viper, wine's danger is hidden and lethal. *In the end* glosses the temporal sense of *'aḥᵃrîtô* (lit. "its afterward"; see 5:11) and refers to the end result of gazing at wine.[91] *It will bite (yiššāk;* the root is *nšk)* designates a deadly bite. In 11 of its 12 occurrences it is used with poisonous snakes, and in the one exception (Hab. 2:7) it is a play on *nešek* (interest). *Like a snake (kᵉnāḥāš)* completes the simile. *And* interprets the parallels as synthetic. The meaning *poison* (or sting) is uncertain.[92] *Like a poisonous viper,* according to Bodenheimer and Aharoni, refers to *vipera xanthina.*[93]

33-34 These verses are united by the theme of graphically depicting wine's nightmarish effects in direct address (cf. "you"/"your") to the son. Verse 33 presents his wretched state literally; v. 34, by similes (cf. v. 28). By using the second person, the father forces the son to experience firsthand wine's delusions and perversions.

89. *HALOT,* 2:466, s.v. *kōs.*

90. The normal meaning, "walks about in uprightness," is again semantically impertinent. *Ythlk* has its more special sense "to go down" or "to flow [down]" (*HALOT,* 1:247, s.v. *hlk.* The similarity of this passage to Song 7:10 suggests that it has the same meaning in the *Hithpael,* but as a factitive reflexive ("when it makes itself go down/flow down"). Was the *Hithpael* stem chosen for its assonance with *yit'addām* in verset A? For *mêsārîm* see *HALOT,* 2:578, s.v. *mêsārîm;* the preposition *bᵉ* denotes the circumstance in which the action obtains (*IBHS,* pp. 196-98, P. 11.2.5d, e).

91. The pronominal suffix, not translated, is an abstract subjective gen. (i.e., the end that wine effects) (*IBHS,* p. 144, P. 9.5.1e).

92. BDB (p. 831, II *pāraš*) distinguishes between II *pāraš* and I *pāraš* "to make distinct" on the basis of alleged Akkadian and Aramaic parallels, and renders the *hap. leg.* "to pierce, sting (?)." *HALOT* (3:976-77, s.v. *prš*) does not distinguish the roots and offers no certain meaning for *pāraš* in the *Hiphil.* Gemser and Fichtner *(BHS),* on the basis of the LXX's addition *ho ios* and of the Vulg. *venena,* insert *rō'š* ("poison"), explaining its omission as due to haplography. Gemser (*Sprüche,* p. 88) interprets the verb to mean "to insert, inject." He cites Driver that *pûš Hiphil* by itself can have this meaning.

93. Cited by *HALOT,* 3:1,050, s.v. *ṣepa'.*

33 *Your eyes* [see 23:29] *will see* (see 23:31) is a figure of seeing in the mind, as in a vision, dream, or state of intoxication.[94] *Incredible sights* denotes strange visions, but the Hebrew word could denote "disgusting things" (cf. Job 19:17).[95] *And* interprets the synthetic parallel as escalating wine's hallucinatory effects from being unable to see straight (v. 33a) to being unable to speak straight. *Your mouth* [see 23:26] *will speak* [see 23:16] *what is perverse* (see I: 110). Intoxication is folly. Instead of seeing things as they truly are, the inebriated sees an upside-down world. His perversions represent a topsy-turvy moral order.

34 Wine's disastrous effects in both third (v. 32) and second person (vv. 33-34) are underscored by vivid and dramatic similes (vv. 32, 34). *And you will become*[96] *like one sleeping* (*šōkēb;* see 3:24) depicts being completely oblivious to the real world. *On the high seas* ("in the heart of the sea") refers to "the great unknown stretch of the high seas extending beyond the visible horizon"[97] that is characterized by great swelling waves and its ceaseless undulating motion (cf. 30:19). The full simile represents the inebriated as physically nauseated and staggering and as mentally unaware of his peril when he most needs his wits to survive (cf. Prov. 30:19). "His imagination is as uncontrollable as his legs."[98] Verset B escalates his giddiness and danger by comparing him to one sleeping in the crow's nest on top of the rigging where the ship's rocking is greatest. He is *like one sleeping* (*šōkēb,* perhaps repeated to illustrate the up-and-down movement)[99] *on top* [see 8:2] *of the mast* (*ḥibbēl;* see n. 40). Although *hibbēl* is a *hap. leg.* and its meaning is uncertain, it is traditionally thought to be from the root *ḥebel* "cord" (see 1:5), and referred to the corded or roped in lookout basket at the mast head.

35 The mocking song is drawn to a conclusion by having the impenitent and witless drunk express his folly (cf. 5:12-14). The ancient versions add "you will say" to smooth the transition from second to first person. His foolish boast that he has been beaten and felt no pain reveals his insanity. Had he been sober, he would have protected himself. Verset Ab escalates Aa from his being anesthetized to his being totally unaware of the severest beatings. "*They* [indefinite] *hit me* (*hikkûnî;* see 23:35). *But* is inserted to smooth the Hebrew asyndetic clauses. *I am not* (*bal;* see 22:29) *hurt* (*ḥālîtî;* cf. 19:6) expresses his state of bodily malaise and disease and can be greatly extended

94. BDB, p. 744, s.v. *'ayin.*

95. *Zārôt* is parsed as the fem. pl. adj. *zār* (cf. 2:16), but it could be the *Qal* fem. ptcp. of III *zûr* "to be loathsome." See *HALOT,* 1:279, s.v. *zār.*

96. *IBHS,* p. 539, P. 32.2.6c.

97. H.-J. Fabry, *TDOT,* 7:412, s.v. *lēb.*

98. Kidner, *Proverbs,* p. 153.

99. Plöger, *Sprüche,* p. 264.

in sense. "Besides 'bodily debility,' the context can shift the accent to mean 'be in pain, suffer' (cf. 23:35; Jer. 35).[100] *They beat me (hᵃlāmûnî)* occurs eight times, all in poetry, and was probably chosen for its assonance with *hikkûnî.* Nevertheless, its force can be judged by its use: with impersonal objects of a smith striking an anvil (Isa. 41:7), of horse hooves striking the ground (Judg. 5:22), of axe men smashing carved paneling (Ps. 74:6), and of people trampling wine (Isa. 16:8; cf. the sarcasm of wine-trampling men [Isa. 21:8]). With personal objects, it is used of Jael, who with hammer and tent peg in hand struck Sisera the fatal blow (Judg. 5:26; cf. Ps. 141:5). *I do not (bal) know [it]* (see 1:2) shows that the inebriated is the exact opposite of the wise who have their eyes and ears open to know.[101] Verset B escalates his plight; he has learned nothing from his beatings. Instead, he is so addicted that even before he wakes up he craves more stupefying poison, whatever the cost. By asking *when (mātay) will I wake up ('āqîṣ),* the drunkard implicitly likens his inebriated stupor to an unconscious sleep. *So that I may continue*[102] *to seek it* expresses his desire and diligence to obtain the poisonous wine (see 17:9). *Yet again* (see 11:24) underscores that the continued seeking is not an isolated occurrence. "The passage describes more than a night's drinking and a morning's hangover. It describes the increasingly degenerative effects, physical and mental, of the habitual drinker and the alcoholic"[103] (cf. John 8:34-36; 1 Cor. 6:10, 11).

b. Saying 20 (24:1-2)

The next three sayings are linked by the sequence of the alphabet in their initial words: *aleph* (v. 2), *beth* (v. 3), *gimel* (v. 5), covering the seam between the third and fourth units of the Thirty Sayings (24:2 and 3). The second appendix of the third unit (23:12–24:2) elaborates on the prohibition against en-

100. K. Seybold, *TDOT,* 4:402, s.v. *chālāh.*

101. J. Botterweck *(TDOT,* 5:462, s.v. *yāda')* says, "The subject who knows must have the physical ability to apprehend. Eyes are needed (Dt. 29:3 [4]), which must be able to see (. . . Isa. 44:18) and not be blind (. . . Isa. 32:3f.). . . . Ears are needed (Dt. 29:3), which must be opened (. . . Isa. 48:8) and attentive (. . . Isa. 32:3f.). A heart is needed (Dt. 29:3[4]), which must be discerning (Isa. 44:18), not fat (. . . Isa. 6:9f.) or rash (. . . Isa. 32:3f.). One must not sleep (. . . Gen. 19:33, 35; 1 Sam. 26:12), be drunk (Dt. 29:5 [6]; cf. Gen. 19:33, 35), or be blinded (. . . Isa. 44:18)."

102. *Ysp,* when not used in co-ordination with a complementary verbal idea, means "to increase in quantity" (see 1:5). When it is incomplete in itself and receives its necessary complement in the form of a verbal idea, it functions to denote the continuance of the action expressed by the second verb. The connection is normally glossed in these constructions by "to, in order to." With *ysp* the two verbs frequently occur in the imperfect with the same person (see GKC, P. 120a, b, c).

103. Aitken, *Proverbs,* p. 124.

vying sinners (23:17-18; cf. 24:19-20). Both its prohibition (v. 1) and the rationale are double-sided (v. 2).

1 Its synthetic parallels escalate its prohibition not to envy morally repulsive sinners (v. 1a; cf. 3:31; 23:17; 24:19) to not forming cliques with them (v. 1b; see 1:10-14). The prohibition, *do not envy* [see 3:31; 23:17] *evil* [see 1:16] *people* (*'anšê;* see 5:21), assumes a morally topsy-turvy world (see 3:1-12). No one is tempted to join morally repulsive people unless they were successful in their quest for easy money (cf. 1:11-14). *And do not crave* [see 23:3, 6] *to be* [see 23:20] *with them* (*'ittām;* see 1:15; 23:7).

2 Initial, and yet medial, *because (kî)* signals the shift from the double prohibitions to the double rationale validating them. Other sayings motivate youths to use their spiritual energies to serve the community, not to destroy it, by pointing to the punishment awaiting evildoers over against rewards for the faithful (cf. 1:10-15; 3:31-32; 23:17-18; 24:19). But this double-sided rationale moves from describing their wanton violence (verset A) to their mendacious speech (verset B) in order to repulse the son from embracing their wrong attitude toward life and from forming groups to practice violence. *Their hearts* [see I: 90] *ponder* [see 8:7; 15:28] *violence* (*šōd;* see 21:7; cf. the verb in 11:3; 19:26; 24:15). Their inward hearts express themselves in *their lips* that *speak* [see 23:16] *malice* (*'āmāl;* see 16:26). *'āmāl* frequently designates the evil, mendacious, outrageous, violent deeds of the enemy without being specific.[104] Their pondering, wanton acts of destruction, violence, and havoc, veiling their outrageous, horrendous behavior with deceit and treachery, is so repulsive and so outrageous that one intuitively recoils from imitating or joining them (cf. 1:11-14). In the interim, while sinners plunder and deceivers prosper, the righteous live by faith (Prov. 3:5; 2 Cor. 5:7; Heb. 11:1).

104. In designating the unspecified evil activity of enemies against the godly, *'āmāl* stands in connection with *'āwen* "iniquity" (Job 15:11; Pss. 10:7; 55:10[11], *šeqer* "lies" (Ps. 7:14[15]), *mirmâ* "deceit" (Job 15:35), and *ḥāmās* "violence" (Ps. 7:16[17]; cf. Schwertner, *TLOT,* 2:926, s.v. *'āmāl*).

D. SECTION C: STRENGTH IN DISTRESS (24:3-12)

3 *By wisdom a household is built,*
and by understanding it is established,
4 *and by knowledge its rooms are filled*
with all kinds of precious and pleasant wealth.
5 *A wise man*[1] *prevails*[2] *by might;*
a man of knowledge musters strength.
6 *Surely*[3] *by guidance you must*[4] *wage war;*
victory is won[5] *through many counselors.*
7 *Wisdom is too high*[6] *for a fool;*
in the gate he must not[7] *open his mouth.*
8 *As for the one who plans to do evil,*
he will be named "Schemer."
9 *The schemes that come from folly*[8] *are sin,*
and an abomination to humanity is a mocker.

1. The LXX (Syr., Targ.) read *kreissōn* "better" (< *gābar,* not *geber*).

2. The preposition b^e ("by") implies a verb such as "prevail" or "endure" (*IBHS,* p. 224, P. 11.4.3d). The elision confused the LXX translator.

3. If the alternative reading is correct (see n. 1), *kî* has its logical force validating that wisdom is better than strength.

4. The prefix conjugation could signify volition (i.e., "wage war!" *IBHS,* pp. 509-10, P. 31.5) or modality, such as obligation (*IBHS,* pp. 508-9, P. 31.4g [cf. 23:14a]). Its normal habitual sense (*IBHS,* 505-6, P. 31.3b, c) does not work here because history falsifies that notion (cf. Joshua 7–8).

5. See nn. 2 and 4.

6. Gemser (*Sprüche,* p. 89) and Fichtner (*BHS*) suggest emending *rā'môt* to *dimmôtā* ("[if] you keep silent [to a fool is wisdom]") to achieve an "abcd" alphabetic acrostic in vv. 1, 3, 5, and 7.

7. Garrett (*Proverbs,* p. 198) interprets *lō'* as a negative jussive ("let his mouth not open") because "other proverbs teach that the fool's mouth is wide open in court proceedings [cf. 10:11, 18; 15:2; 25:4-5, 7-10; 26:20-28]." In his support, legal literature prescribes penalties for fools who spread slander in the gate (cf. 10:18; Deut. 19:18-19) and historical literature shows the damage their foolish talk inflicts (1 K. 21:8-14). But Garrett's grammatical analysis is questionable. While it is true that *lō'* is rarely used with the jussive, why is *'al,* which is consistently used in "The Thirty Sayings," not used here? A better solution is to interpret the prefix conjugation as signifying a modal obligation (see *IBHS,* pp. 509-10, PP. 31.4d, g). Meinhold (*Sprüche,* 2:403) rules out the notion of capability (i.e., "cannot"): "One can hardly presume a silence out of the fool's helplessness given his predisposition otherwise to speak, for this would presuppose a certain insight."

8. *'iwwelet* is an abstract subjective gen. (*IBHS,* p. 144, P. 9.5.1e). G. R. Driver ("Problems in the Hebrew Text of Proverbs," *Bib* 32 [1951] 196) thinks that it is the abstract form for the concrete (see 23:28). The ancient versions also have "fool."

10 *If you show yourself lax in the time of crisis,*
your strength is meager.[9]
11 *Deliver those being taken to death,*
even hold back[10] *those swaying and being led to slaughter.*
12 *If you say, "We*[11] *knew nothing about this,"*
does not even he who weighs motives discern [the truth]?
As for him who protects your life, does he not know,
and will he not repay a person according to his conduct?

The fourth unit of the Thirty Sayings of the Wise motivates the son to lay hold of the wisdom that will give him strength and strategy in conflict. After the typical introductory educational saying (vv. 3-4), the next saying sounds the theme (vv. 5-6). Its third and fourth sayings motivate him to lay hold of these virtues by sassing the fool's incompetence to strategize wisely (v. 7) and by labeling the fool a social pariah. Its fifth and final saying motivates him to lay hold of wisdom's sinewy strength by shaming the fool if he falters (v. 10) and by threatening him with divine judgment (vv. 11-12). The first four didactic sayings in the third person give way to a didactic saying in the second person that climaxes with an admonition. This admonition forms a transition to the balancing five admonitions of the last unit (vv. 13-14, 15-16, 17-18, 19-20, 21-22).

1. Saying 21 (24:3-4)

The introductory saying also counterbalances vv. 1-2. Wealth must be accumulated by wisdom (vv. 3-4), not by plunder (vv. 1-2). There may be an allusion to the warning against sinners in 1:10-19. They said, "We will fill *(yimmālᵉʾû)* our houses *(bāyit)* with all sorts of precious wealth (*kol-hôn yāqār*" (see 1:13), but this saying asserts that by virtue a house *(bāyit)* is filled *(yimmālᵉʾû)* with all sorts of precious wealth *(kol-hôn yāqār)*." The similarities suggest that Solomon intends to reinforce his contrast between building and furnishing a house by wisdom (24:3-4), not by envying sinners and plunder (vv. 1-2).

The saying marks itself as an introduction by typically commending

9. Gemser (*Sprüche,* p. 89) and Fichtner *(BHS)* add *metri causa bᵉsorkekā* "in your need" (cf. 2 Chr. 2:15). A 3:2 meter, however, is acceptable, and it is questionable in this context to limit the time crisis to one's own need.

10. Fichtner *(BHS)* wrongly alters the "oath" particle *ʾim* (see GKC, P. 149) to *ʾal* on basis of the LXX (Syr., Vulg.): "do withhold [your help]."

11. The LXX (Syr.), followed by Fichtner *(BHS)*, has the facilitating reading *oida* (< *yādaʿtî,* "I did not know").

wisdom, by shifting from an admonition to a statement, by using its second verse to reinforce the first, not to substantiate it, and by exhibiting the unit's catchword "wise" *(ḥkm):* "wisdom" (*ḥokmâ,* v. 3; *ḥākām* "wise," v. 5; *ḥokmôt* "wisdom," v. 7). Its two verses are linked by employing "wisdom," "understanding," and "knowledge," the same agents in the same sequence that the LORD used when he "established" *(kûn)* the world (3:19). This similarity suggests that the microcosm of household and the macrocosm of the world are brought into connection with one another.[12] Initial "and" of v. 4 puts the connection between vv. 3 and 4 beyond question. This saying about material prosperity also exemplifies wisdom's value for spiritual prosperity (see 3:9; 8:18, 21; 14:1; 21:21).

3 The synthetic parallels of v. 3 escalate the making of *a household* (see 11:29) from *is built* (see 14:1; cf. 2 Sam. 7:13) to *it is established* (see 3:19; 8:21).[13] As indicated by the clause-initial words, the focus is on the means, *by wisdom* (see 1:2) and *by understanding* (see 2:2). Unless a household is built on the revealed wisdom upheld by the LORD, "it is only a snow-palace built in the winter, and melting away under the power of the summer's sun."[14]

4 This verse narrows "household" down to its *rooms* (or inner chambers; see 7:27) and "is built" and "is established," to *are filled* (*yimmālᵉʾû;* see 3:10). The focus continues on the agent: *by knowledge* (*daʿat;* see I: 77). In this enjambment verset A is completed by *all sorts of (kol)*[15] *precious* [see 1:13; 3:15] *and pleasant* [see 22:18] *wealth* (see 3:9).

2. Saying 22 (24:5-6)

The second saying of the fourth unit sounds its theme by inferentially calling for wisdom to equip one with strength (v. 5) and with strategy (v. 6). Both are necessary for any undertaking, but especially for war. The repetition of "wisdom" (vv. 3a, 5a) and "knowledge" (vv. 4a, 5b) suggests that the three agents of success in vv. 3-4 are now supplemented by their derivative virtues: "might/strength" (v. 5) and "guidance/many counselors" (v. 6). These derivatives are formally linked by the initial, yet always medial, *surely (kî).*[16] Both the soldier's strength and the general's strategy are indispensable in war. Wisdom provides the full panoply for victory over every enemy who attacks

12. Meinhold, *Sprüche,* p. 401.

13. The rare *Hithpael* was probably chosen instead of the normal *Niphal* for its assonance with *bitᵉbûnâ.*

14. Bridges, *Proverbs,* p. 445.

15. *HALOT,* 2:474, s.v. *kōl.*

16. *IBHS,* p. 665, P. 39.3.4e.

the wise man's household (cf. 11:14; 15:22; 20:18; 21:5, 22). Behind this wisdom stands the LORD himself (16:1, 3, 9; 19:21; 20:24; 21:30, 31). The proverb about war serves as a paradigm for hostile situations.

5 The text of v. 5 is problematic. The LXX, Syr., and Targ. (so also NAB, REB, NRSV), not the Vulg. (KJV, NASB, NJPS, NIV), essentially read: "A wise man is mightier than a strong man, and a man of knowledge than he who has strength" (see n. 1). This alternative reading is attractive because it alleviates the difficulty of the ellipses in the MT (see n. 2) and superficially seems cogent with v. 6. Although 21:22 (cf. Deut. 8:17-18; Isa. 10:13) contrasts the wise and the strong, that proverb represents the wise as attacking and bringing down the strong city of mighty men. This text, however, lacks its crucial verbs "attack" and/or "bring down," and, as will be seen, v. 6 does not validate this alternative reading. In this book guidance/counsel (v. 6) and strength (v. 5) go together (see 8:14). Ringgren says, "MT may be correct."[17] Its synthetic parallels assert that the wise possess a fixed and inviolable security that protects them (verset A) and an inner vital energy that empowers them (verset B). *A wise* (*ḥākām;* see I: 94) *man* (*geber;* see I: 90; 6:34) *prevails by might* (see 8:28). Verset A points to the wise person's fixed and inviolable security; verset B, to his vital energy that empowers him. *A man of knowledge* (*'îš-da'at;* see I: 77), a synonym of *ḥākām, musters* [see 8:28][18] *strength* (i.e., vital energy; see 5:10). The word order keeps the focus on wisdom and knowledge, not on their derivatives, might and strength. The mustering of vital, inner energy to produce something is essential for success in any area (see 31:17), but "to make powerful" is used primarily with war (cf. v. 6) and speech (cf. v. 7).

6 To strength must be added competent counsel to assure success. In the chiastic synthetic parallels of v. 6, the means of victory constitute the outer frame, *by guidance* (see 1:5) escalated to *through many counselors* (see 11:14). The inner core assures their triumph in war. *You must wage* [lit. "to act with effect"; see n. 4; 13:16] *war* (see 20:18).[19] Verset B, which repeats 11:14, qualifies this war as successful, as signified by *victory is won* (see n. 5). The counterargumentation of many counselors, who with a spirit of humility learn from each other, guarantees that the finally agreed-upon strategy will succeed. Conscious ignorance is the first principle of knowledge (1 K. 3:7; 5:12[27]; 10:23-29; 2 Chr. 27:6). Paul prays that Christians "will be

17. H. Ringgren, *TDOT,* 7:125, s.v. *kōaḥ.*

18. The *Piel 'mṣ* means "to have or give strength and power," and the idiom "to make strength powerful" means "to muster strength," "to show superior strength" (see Amos 2:14).

19. The "centripetal" pronoun *lᵉkā* that establishes the son's identity by dissociating him from his familiar surroundings is not translated (*IBHS,* p. 208, P. 11.2.10d).

filled with all spiritual wisdom and understanding" and that they will be "strengthened with all power according to his glorious might so that they [lit. you] may have great endurance and patience" (Col. 1:9, 11).

3. Saying 23 (24:7)

The third saying is connected to the preceding two by the catchword "wisdom" (vv. 3, 5, 7) and functions as a foil to the second saying by noting the incompetence of fools to speak in the gate where public policy is formulated. This saying inferentially commends becoming competently wise by warning against being an incompetent fool. Verset A presents the cause. *Wisdom* [see I: 76] *is too high*[20] *for a fool* (*'ᵉwîl;* see I: 109) means that the incorrigible lacks the wings of piety and humility that soar high enough to attain the heavenly wisdom needed for public affairs (see 8:15-16). Verset B presents the consequence. *In the gate* [see 1:21] *he must not open* [see n. 7] *his mouth* (cf. 16:23) means that the mouthy fool (12:23; 13:16; 15:2, 7) must not be allowed to shape public opinion or policy or settle disputes. Since he is not amenable to being corrected by what is true to creation's design, he never attains the maturity to speak well, authoritatively, and constructively in the gate where matters affecting the community are pondered and debated. If he had any prudence — and he does not — he would keep his mouth shut (17:28).[21]

4. Saying 24 (24:8-9)

The fourth saying also functions as a foil to the second by contrasting the accredited and competent counsel of the wise with the public's condemnation of the self-serving plans of fools. The sage's evaluation that the fool must be silenced (v. 7) is escalated to the public's censure through their opprobrious sobriquet for the self-serving fool of "schemer." Verses 8-9 are linked by a

20. The homonym *rā'môt* may denote black corals (or seashells, or pearls; cf. Job 28:18; Ezek. 27:16). Accepting this meaning, Delitzsch (*Proverbs,* p. 128) et al. assert that wisdom appears too costly to a fool. However, "'wisdom is corals to the fool' is hardly the way to express the idea of an excessive price" (Cohen, *Proverbs,* p. 160). Rather, it is more plausible to take the form with Vulg. as a plene form of the *Qal* act. ptcp. of *rûm* "to be high" (cf. *rā'š,* Prov. 10:4; *qā'm,* Hos. 10:14; the bi-form *rā'ᵃma* for *rāmâ,* Zech. 14:10; and the two forms of the place name Ramoth ["heights of"] Gilead, Josh. 20:8; 1 K. 2:3). As a predicate adjective, its pl. form matches *ḥokmôt.* Because *ḥokmôt* is singular, Driver ("Problems in the Hebrew Text," p. 188) repoints the text as *rā'māt* = *rāmâ,* but that form is unattested. *HALOT* (3:203, s.v. *rwm*) invests the verbal adjective with a comparative degree, comparing a similar use of *niśgab* "too high" (i.e., to attain to) in Ps. 139:6.

21. Sirach (20:6) believes that a fool "keeps silent because he has no answer."

play on *zmm: mᵉzimmôt* ("schemer") and *zimmat* ("schemes"/"villainy"). The divine evaluation that villainy is sin (v. 9) theologically justifies the public's censure (v. 8). The public's disapproval rating of fools escalates from branding them "schemers" (v. 8) to regarding them as repugnant mockers (v. 9). The fool's root problem is his "folly." Instead of adjusting realistically to the community of people, he foolishly overevaluates his own self-importance and so devaluates others.[22]

8 *As for the one who plans* [see 16:9] *to do evil* (see 4:16) focuses on the adept planner who coldly effects strategies that are designed to further his own interest at the expense of the community. His coldly calculated actions to defraud society show that he is neither intellectually dull nor emotionally impulsive. Verset B provides the tragic consequences: the community will see through him, despise him, and tag him with the moniker "Schemer" (cf. 12:5; 20; 16:30; 18:1; 28:5). *He will be named* ["they will give him the name"; cf. 16:21],[23] *"Schemer" (baʿal-mᵉzimmôt,* an alternative of *ʾîš mᵉzimmôt* [12:2]). Other by-names that illuminate a person's social standing are also given in 16:21; 21:24. The loss of a good name and being saddled with a bad one reduce him to becoming a pariah.

9 Whereas the derivatives of wisdom are strength and strategy (vv. 5-6), the derivatives of folly are sin and social disgust (v. 9).[24] Verset A represents antisocial behavior with its cause and true social identity. *The schemes* [or villainy; see 10:23; 21:27] *that come from folly* [see I: 113] *are sin* (see 5:22). Its chiastic parallel represents the antisocial person with respect to his social standing. *And an abomination* [see 3:32] *to humanity* (*lᵉʾādām;* see I: 89) *is a mocker* (see I: 114). The outer frame presents the acts (i.e., crass acts against society that spring from moral insolence) and the actor (i.e., the mocker who debunks wisdom) that disturb and destroy society. The inner core matches these causes with their consequences on society. Villainy is defined for what it is, "sin" (i.e., a transgression against society as ordered by God), and the mocker with his perpetual sneer and his incapability for loyalty to the society that supports him is repugnant to people.

5. Saying 25 (24:10-12)

The topic now reverts from the need of wisdom's competence for good counsel to achieve success in war (v. 6) in contrast to the silence demanded of fools by the sage (v. 7) and by society (vv. 8-9) to elaborate the need for wis-

22. Meinhold, *Sprüche,* p. 403.

23. *Yiqᵉrāʾû* is a shortened form of *qārāʾ šēm lᵉ* and an alternative of *yiqqārēʾ lᵉ.*

24. Five of six words of the verse end with the consonance of a dental */t/ /d/ /ṣ/,* the first four with */t/.*

dom's competence for strength in distress (v. 5). "Strength" *(kōaḥ),* the last word of vv. 5 and 10, binds together the two sayings. If fortified strength is a sign of a person's wisdom (v. 5), then meager strength in crisis signifies a person's lack or loss of wisdom (vv. 10-12). According to Plöger, "The day of distress" (v. 10aβ) finds a concrete situation in people being led away to their slaughter (v. 11), and "if you show yourself lax" (v. 11aα) becomes concretized in the son's self-talk that excuses him from helping (v. 12).[25] The saying is connected with third and fourth sayings that pertain to fools and their antisocial behavior by warning the son against complicity with them by passivity.

10 This verse implicitly calls for wisdom's competence in conflict by censuring reduced strength. The chiastic parallels of v. 10 pit in their outer frame the son's spiritual energies, "you show a lack of courage" and "your strength," and in their inner core the failed help in need, "in time of distress" *(ṣārâ)* and "meager" *(ṣar),* a deliberate paronomasia. *If* represents the hypothetical condition of being discouraged.[26] *You show yourself lax* means "to grow slack" (e.g., the loss of daylight toward evening; Judg. 19:9), entailing cowardice, fear, indolence, and/or carelessness, a lack of resolute strength.[27] *In the time (bᵉyôm)*[28] *of crisis* (see 11:8) refers to the son's own distress or to another's, the focus of the next saying. In Prov. 25:19 the phrase "in time of

25. Scholars differ whether v. 10 is a separate saying from vv. 11-12. Gemser (*Sprüche,* p. 89), Plöger (*Sprüche,* p. 282), and Meinhold (*Sprüche,* p. 404) regard the three verses as a unity. But Römheld argues for the separation of v. 10 from vv. 11-12 on the basis of form and logic. According to him, the development of a truth statement ("Wahrspruch," v. 10) into an admonition (v. 11) with substantiation (v. 12) would be an unusual form. Nevertheless, he concedes that if the equation made by Plöger is valid, then vv. 10-12 is a unity. He denies this connection because the issue of v. 10 is whether the disciple has strength and that at the least it stands in danger of declining, but vv. 11-12 call the disciple to go forth and protect his neighbor, showing that his strength is not circumscribed. According to him, this disparity between declining strength and the call for strength shows that these verses cannot be connected (D. Römheld, *Wege der Weisheit: Die Lehren Amenemopes und Proverbien 22:17–24:22* [BZAW 184; Berlin: de Gruyter, 1989], pp. 41-42). However, the notion that the disciple is in danger of showing himself lax is compatible with the command to show forth his strength. The "Wahrspruch" of v. 10 that shames cowardice, fear, indolence, and carelessness in adversity nerves the son to show himself courageous and deliver the perishing in their time of need. In addition to this common topic, vv. 10-12 use the second person in contrast to the preceding three sayings in the third person.

26. *IBHS,* p. 493, P. 30.5.4.

27. With "hands" as its subject, the idiom means "courage fails," but even without "hands" it can have this meaning (Jer. 49:24). In the *Hithpael* it denotes esteeming or presenting oneself in a state (i.e., "to show oneself lax" [see Prov. 18:9] or "to show oneself without courage"; cf. *IBHS,* pp. 430-31, P. 26.2.f; *HALOT,* 3:1277, s.v. *rph*).

28. BDB, p. 400, s.v. *yôm.*

crisis" is again used with reference to disappointed confidence. Verset B represents the consequences. *Your strength* [see 24:5] *is meager* (lit. "restricted"; see 23:27). The notion may be quantitative as well as qualitative. A person reveals the degree and extent of his strength by his conduct in crisis. "It is when a man is hemmed in and trapped by adverse circumstances that his powers of endurance are stretched and an estimate of his toughness and stamina can be made."[29]

11-12 If the son meets his moral obligation toward a person who is threatened by death, he will show that his mental toughness, his moral courage, and his physical strength are great and large enough to reach out to those in need. Moreover, the admonition escalates his motive for laying hold of wisdom that will fortify him against faltering from shaming him to threatening him. God will not excuse him for his lack of gritty determination, mental toughness, and moral courage to do the right thing.

The admonition is a sober and threatening warning to the son to show courage and to deliver innocent victims from murderers (v. 11), for *(kî)* if he does not, God, who knows this *(zeh),* will repay him in kind (i.e., not deliver him when he is oppressed; v. 12). In terms of determining the destiny of others, the son must overpower the criminals who overpower their victims. The father fortifies him for the task by asserting that the LORD in turn holds power over him to reward or punish him according to his conduct in crisis (cf. Isa. 40:29; 2 Cor. 12:9).

11 The synonymous admonitions "deliver" and "hold back" form the outer frame, and their objects, "those being taken to death" and "those swaying and being led away to slaughter," the inner core. *Deliver* [see 10:2] *those being taken* (see 20:16) by someone or something that has taken possession of them and controls them against their will (see 20:16) *to death* (10:2). *Even* interprets the conjunction as having an epexegetical force. *Those swaying* (see 10:30) signifies that they are rocking and shaking and about to fall off a secure base. *To* implies a verb of motion such as *being led. Slaughter* signifies "the act of killing an enemy." The text assumes that killing is a crime against God (see 1:32). *Hold back ('im-taḥśôk)* interprets *'im* as signifying an emphatic wish, "O that you would hold back!" (see n. 10). The root normally means that the subject of his own free will takes control over an object and holds it back (see 10:19; cf. Gen. 22:12, 16)[30] with the connotation here "to save, spare."[31] The admonitions do not want to narrow down the identity of the victims or the

29. McKane, *Proverbs,* p. 400.

30. Driver ("Problems in the Hebrew Text," 189). Driver holds that the verb here has the sense of Syr. *ḥsak* "preserved, kept safe, defended, "as the Vg.'s *liberare ne cesses* [keep on setting free] suggests."

31. *HALOT,* 1:359, s.v. *ḥśk.*

crisis situation (disease, hunger, war, etc.; cf. 14:25) or the means of deliverance (law, force, ransom, etc.). By the *a fortiori* argument, however, the greater crisis includes the lesser. If the disciple should deliver the wronged from death, how much more in lesser crises. In whatever way or in whatever place the lawless pervert justice, the disciple must show his mettle and intervene and not act cowardly, nor ignore or pass by the wrongdoing (cf. Gen. 37:22, 29; Exod. 1:15-17; 1 Sam. 19:4; 20:26-33; 1 K. 18:4; Esth. 3:6-13; 4:13, 14; 8:4-6; Job 29:12, 13, 16, 17; Jer. 26:24; 38:11-13; 40:3-16; Dan. 2:12-15; Luke 10:25-37; Acts 23:16-22; 2 Tim. 4:16-18).

12 *If* (lit. "for if"; see 23:13) signifies cause and condition. As the former it links v. 12 as the rationale for the admonitions to take control over criminals to protect innocent victims (v. 11), and as the latter it introduces the protasis — the hypothetical lie of being ignorant to excuse oneself from obeying the admonition (v. 12a) — to the apodosis that demolishes the lie with fact that the LORD knows the truth and has power over all human beings to repay them according to their courage and their conduct (v. 12b; cf. 1 K. 20:39, 40; Ezek. 33:8). *You say* represents a hypothetical lie in which a defendant justifies his action to a jury. *"Look"* dramatically represents the defendant inviting the jury to join him in his situation that is represented in his words that follow. By the plural *we knew nothing* (see 23:35; cf. 4:19) he locates himself within a whole community that is claiming ignorance to escape their culpability. Also, it obviates the potential question that if he felt incapable of effecting the rescue by himself, why did he not call on others to help him. Anaphoric *this (zeh)* refers to the situation involving the nouns in v. 12 (i.e., there were "those being taken to death").[32] In sum, to the injustice of not helping the defendant (v. 11), v. 12a adds the injustice of lying. The apodosis in v. 12b presents the consequence of both injustices. Its first half, v. 12bα, presents God's sublime attributes of omniscience (v. 12bα1; cf. 15:3, 11; 16:2; 17:3; 20:27; 21:2; 22:12) and omnipotence (12bα2) that inform his retributive justice (v. 12bβ; see I: 73). The polar rhetorical question of fact *does not* expects an emphatic positive answer (see 14:22). *He who weighs motives* (lit. "who weighs hearts") refers to the LORD (see 16:2). The tautological *even he* focuses on him and emotionally heightens the LORD's involvement.[33] *Discern* (see 1:2; 2:5) governs the unstated object *truth* (i.e., whether "you show lack of courage" or "you did not know"); otherwise why refer to the LORD as the evaluator of motives? Lies cannot hide truth from him. *And* adds his omnipotence to his omniscience. The otherwise precisely parallel syntax between v. 12bα1 and v. 12bα2 suggests that *does not* has been gapped. The description of the LORD as *him who protects* (*nôṣēr;* see 2:8, 11; 3:1) *your life*

32. *IBHS,* p. 311, P. 17.4.2e.
33. *IBHS,* p. 296, P. 16.3.2e.

(*napšᵉkā;* see I: 90), *does he not know* (cf. v. 12a), prepares the way for his just retribution for all. *And* signifies the logical consequence of his knowledge of motives. *He will repay* (*hēšîb;* see 1:23; 12:14)[34] *a person* (*'ādām;* see I: 89) *according to* [i.e., agreement in kind][35] *his conduct* (*poʿolô;* see 20:11). In sum, the omniscient and omnipotent Sovereign will act justly, unlike the passive coward. If the son turns a blind eye to helping victims and does nothing to help them, the Protector of Life will turn a blind eye to him in his crisis. Count on it!

E. SECTION D: PROHIBITIONS AGAINST INVOLVEMENT WITH THE WICKED (24:13-22)

13 *Eat honey, my son, because it is good,*
and honey from the comb is sweet on your palate;
14 *so know*[36] *wisdom*[37] *is like honey for your life.*
If you find wisdom, then there is a blessed future,
and your hope will not be cut off.
15 *Do not lay an ambush as a wicked person*[38] *against*[39] *the dwelling place of the righteous,*

34. BDB, p. 999, s.v. *šûb.*

35. *IBHS,* pp. 202-3, P. 11.2.9b.

36. *Deʿeh* is a long form of the *Qal* impv. of *ydʿ* under the influence of the following *ḥ* (GKC, P. 48.d.l). D. W. Thomas ("The Root *ydʿ* in Hebrew," p. 401, cited by Gemser, *Sprüche,* p. 113) derives the verb from *dʿh,* an Arabic cognate meaning "sought," "desired," "asked," which makes a good parallel to "find." But why read Arabic when the very common Hebrew verb also makes excellent sense and interprets "eat"?

37. Gemser (*Sprüche,* p. 89), followed by Fichtner *(BHS)* and *HALOT* (1:228, s.v. *dʿh*), emends the text to *dēʿâ meṯûqâ lᵉlibbekā wᵉḥokmâ ṭôbâ* "knowledge is sweet to your heart, and wisdom is good." They defend the additions by *metri causa.* Besides this being a questionable method, the four accented syllables of the MT are perfectly acceptable. This and other proposed emendations do not explain from a text-critical point of view how the rare and difficult, but not intolerable, MT reading originated. The parallels "eat honey" and "search for wisdom" form a good analogy.

38. Vulg. and Sym., perhaps misunderstanding the syntax, point the text as *rešaʿ* (i.e., lay an ambush "of wickedness"). But an abstract and/or a direct object with *'rb* would be exceptional. Toy (*Proverbs,* p. 451) and Fichtner *(BHS)* propose to delete what they think is a gloss, but it helps to connect v. 15a with v. 16b and they give no explanation for its origin or insertion. It is best construed as an acc. of state with reference to the subject (*IBHS,* p. 171, P. 10.2.2c; GKC, P. 118q). Delitzsch (*Proverbs,* p. 136), with the Targ. and Syr., interprets it as a vocative, "O wicked man," but these sayings are addressed to the son (22:20), and an admonition addressed to the wicked would be exceptional.

39. *HALOT* (1:83, s.v. *'rb*) renders *lᵉ* unusually by "at," but the parallelism suggests the usual *dativus incommodi* "against" (*IBHS,* p. 207, 11.2.10d).

do not plunder his resting place;
16 *for if a righteous person falls seven times, then he rises;*
but the wicked stumble in calamity.[40]
17 *When your enemy*[41] *falls, do not rejoice;*
when he stumbles,[42] *do not let your heart shout in exultation;*
18 *otherwise the* LORD *will see,*
and it[43] *will be evil in his eyes;*
and he will turn away his wrath from him.
19 *Do not fret because of those who forge evil,*
do not envy the wicked;
20 *for the evil person has no blessed future;*
the lamp of the wicked will be snuffed out.
21 *Fear the* LORD, *my son, and the king;*[44]
with [intriguing] officials[45] *do not get involved.*

40. Or "fall through evil."

41. K = *'ôyebeykā* ("your enemies"), Q = *'ôyibkā* ("your enemy"). The parallel *mē'ālāyw* "from him" favors Q.

42. *bikkāšᵉlô* is the syncope for *bᵉhikkāšᵉlô.*

43. Impersonal subject (*IBHS,* p. 376, P. 22.7b).

44. For the use of *'et* before one direct object of a verb and not before the other see 1 K. 10:4. On the basis of Syr. *w'mlk* ("to give counsel," "to reign," "to make king"), L. Kopf ("Arabische Etymologien und Parallelen zum Bibelwörterbuch," *VT* 9 [1959] 280-83) emended the vowels to an impv. but invested the root with the Arabic meaning "to possess, inherit." Emerton ("Notes and Studies: On Some Passages in the Book of Proverbs," *JTS* n.s. 20 [1969] 210-11) also repoints as impv. but retains the common meaning "to become king/to reign" (= "and thou wilt rule)." However, it is hazardous to build a conjecture on a conjecture. The Syr. more probably means "fear the LORD, give good counsel, and do not meddle with fools."

45. The ancient versions did not understand the difficult Hebrew. The LXX rendered verset B *mētheterǭ autōn apeithēsęs* "do not disobey either of them," which Jaeger retroverted as *'al šᵉnêhem 'al tit'abbār* (= "against the two of them do not flare up"), a reading favored by Gemser (*Sprüche,* p. 89) and Fichtner *(BHS).* Toy (*Proverbs,* p. 50), Meinhold (*Sprüche,* p. 408), et al. (cf. NAB, NJPS, NIV) invest *šnh,* which means "change" (intransitive), with its transitive meaning in the *Piel* "change" (i.e., traditional ideas or systems) or with the meaning "to be different" (Esth. 1:7; 3:8) and extend to either of these meanings the notions of "dissenters" or "rebellious" (cf. Vulg. "detractors"). Either of these linguistic jumps is dubious and arbitrary. D. W. Thomas ("The Root *šnh* = *sny* in Hebrew, II," *ZAW* 55 [1937] 174-76) more plausibly associated *šônîm* with Arab. *saniya* "to be high, exalted in rank" and *sn'* "sublime," "great honor" and renders it "those of high rank (the nobility perhaps)." (Its occurrence in Ugaritic is debated.) He has been followed by G. R. Driver ("Problems in the Hebrew Text," p. 189), Kopf ("Arabische Etymologien und Parallelen zum Bibelwörterbuch," *VT* 9 [1959] 282-83), and *HALOT* (4:1,559, s.v. III *šnh*). The root has been detected in several Old Testament passages (Esth. 2:9; Ps. 68:18; Isa. 11:1; Dan. 7:23; Hab. 3:2). Emerton ("The Meaning of *šēnā'* in Psalm

22 *Because disaster from them*[46] *suddenly appears,*
and who knows what ruin the two of them[47] *can inflict?*

Saying 26 of the Thirty Sayings again encourages the son to obtain wisdom, marking off the last unit of four double prohibitions sharing the same syntax and substance after this introduction. Its five sayings are all proverb pairs consisting of double admonitions in the odd verses (vv. 13, 15, 17, 19, 21) with validation in the even verses (vv. 14, 16, 18, 20, 22). The four prohibitions are all formulated by *'al* plus jussive — only the last contains a positive admonition as well. These negative jussives are stitched together chiastically from Aa in vv. 15 and 19 to Ab or Bb in vv. 17 and 21. The paronomasia of the first prohibition, *'al-t'rb* ("do not lay an ambush," v. 15), and of the last, *'al-tt'rb* ("do not get involved), together with *qûm* ("arises," v. 16b, and "appears," v. 22b) in their validations (vv. 16b, 22a), frames the prohibitions. The endearing term "my son" (vv. 13a, 21a) frames the whole. The prohibitions forbid involvement with the wicked, labeled as such in vv. 15a, 19b-20b, as "your enemies" in v. 17A, as "those who forge evil" in v. 19a, and as "intriguing nobles" (i.e., rebels) in v. 21. The three middle sayings are linked by the catchword "evil": for the deeds and destiny of the wicked outlaw (v. 16), for the LORD's evaluation of gloating as a worse evil (v. 18), and again for the deeds of the wicked (v. 19) and their destiny (v. 20). The stakes in this battle are high. The unit begins with the promise of eternal life for the wise (vv. 14a, 16a) and moves to the eternal death of the wicked (vv. 16b, 20, 22). If you find wisdom, you obtain *'aḥ^{a}rît* "a blessed future" (v. 14a) that never ends (v. 14b). Though the righteous is totally destroyed, he will rise

---

cxxvii 2," *VT* 24 [1974] 25-26) allows only Prov. 5:9; 14:17; 24:21-22, but the first two of these are also questionable. Thomas believes that the admonition means to keep aloof from those who move in higher social spheres, but the following verse implies that in their greed for power, they are undermining the legitimate authority to advance themselves. Gemser acknowledges that *šōnîm* can mean "people of high rank," but holds that it is not as good as retroverted LXX. The NRSV follows the LXX, but curiously in its footnote gives only the meaning "those who change" for *šōnîm.*

46. Or "upon them."

47. The Targ. and Syr. interpret *š^{e}nêhem* as "their years" (cf. Job 36:11). That interpretation, however, is not as good as "the two of them" (so the LXX). After the reference to God and the king in v. 21a of this proverbial pair, this is the most natural interpretation. Moreover, "the disaster of their years" for "the end of their years" seems strained. Thomas and Driver emend to *šônîm* "high officials" (cf. v. 21). In that case the gen. is either agentive ("what ruin such men may cause") or objective (i.e., "what the ruin of such men will be"). But their emendation is improbable from a text-critical point of view, for it does not explain why *h* was added, thereby changing *šnym* to *šnyhm.* Since the antecedent of the "two of them" must be the LORD and the king, the gen. must be agentive, not objective, for nothing can ruin the LORD.

(v. 16a). On the other hand, the fate of the wicked is just as decisive and eternal. They stumble and fall (v. 16b), though this is qualified in v. 18b, and they end in total darkness (v. 20b). They have no *'aḥ^{a}rît* (v. 20a). Disaster comes on the intriguing nobles suddenly (v. 22a) and no one knows its extent (v. 22b). In light of what the sage has already predicated, it must be awful.

1. Saying 26 (24:13-14)

The introductory saying to the final unit consists of two admonitions with reasons: eat honey because it is desirable, beneficial, and sweet (v. 13), and know wisdom because it has the promise of eternal life (v. 14). The comparative particle "so" shows that the first command functions as an analogue of the second. The metaphor of honey for wisdom infers three comparisons. (1) Physically eating is an apt metaphor for spiritually "knowing" (i.e., the internalizing). (2) Wisdom, like honey, has medicinal value but, remarkably, with a sweet taste (see 16:24). (3) The palate, the seat of taste (v. 13b), nicely matches *nepeš* "life" (v. 14b), the seat of passionate vitality. In sum, internalized honey and wisdom invigorate while they give pleasure.[48] But the analogue breaks down in v. 14b, as Malbim notes: "Wisdom has all the immediate sweetness of honey, but also the additional characteristic of a pleasure that lasts for eternity"[49] (cf. 2 Cor. 4:18).

13 In the synthetic parallels of v. 13, "Eat, my son" is gapped in v. 13b; "honey" is escalated to "honey from the comb," and "because it is good" is supplemented by "sweet on your palate." *Eat* (see 13:25) entails a command to have a right relationship with God. Food is God's good gift to faithful Israel (cf. Exod. 16:4ff.; Lev. 25:19; 26:3-5; Deut. 7:11-13; 8:10ff.; 8:16; 12:15; Josh. 5:12), not to unfaithful Israel (Deut. 28:17-18, 31, 33, etc.; cf. Prov. 13:25). Eating and joy go together (Deut. 12:17-18; 14:23). *My son* (see 23:15, 26) presumes the son's faithfulness to the tradition and endears him to it. Though the command functions as a metaphor in this saying, the father also intends his command to eat *honey* (see 16:24) literally *because it is good* (see I: 99), summarizing its healing and delightful properties *And* combines the commands. *Honey from the comb* [see 5:3] *is sweet* [see 16:24] *on your palate* (see 5:3), which is here the seat of taste, not of speech, underscores honey's delightful property.

14 The comparative particle *so* (see 23:7) signals that the father now transforms the command into a metaphor, presenting the admonition in v. 14a and the reason in v. 14b, unlike v. 13, which presented both in both versets. *Know* (see n. 36) has its existential sense of experiencing and inter-

48. God's word is also likened to honey (Pss. 19:10[11]; 119:13; Ezek. 3:3).
49. Malbim, *Proverbs,* p. 248.

nalizing *wisdom* (see I: 76), as in the preamble to Proverbs. *Is like honey* glosses the implied ellipsis. *For* signifies benefit. *Your life* (*napšekā;* see I: 90) refers to his passionate vitality and may connote its meaning "appetite." Verset B essentially repeats 23:18 but transforms that compound sentence into a conditional clause both by adding *if* [cf. 23:15] *you find* (see 3:13) with gapped *wisdom,* which by replacing "the fear of the LORD" links the consequence with the cause, and by adding "then" to *yēš* (lit. *then there is*). The outcome of internalizing the revealed moral order is nothing less than unending eternal delight.

2. Saying 27 (24:15-16)

The unit's first prohibition cautions the disciple not to join the ranks of wicked to take away the abode of the righteous by cunning deceit and violence (v. 15). This prohibition rests on the godly person's faith and conviction that the righteous will recover from their fall and the wicked will finally fall through their evil and never recover from their misery. *For* signals the connection between the admonition (v. 15) and its validation (v. 16), a connection strengthened by the catchwords *righteous* (vv. 15a, 16a; see I: 97) and *wicked* (vv. 15a, 16b; see I: 109). The double prohibition uses imagery from the field of animal husbandry, that is, "pasture" and "bed for animals" (v. 15; cf. Isa. 35:7; 65:10), and the double rationale uses the metaphor of travel ("stumble and fall"; v. 16). The rationale entails that the wicked kill the righteous to plunder them (see 1:10-19) and that they may not get their deserts until the end when the righteous triumphantly rises from his destruction (see I: 107). In sum, the rationale of v. 16 adds to the promise of v. 14 that before the wise/righteous enjoy an eternal future they may first be utterly ruined. It also adds the threat that the wicked are damned. Both promise and threat demand faith that the LORD stands behind this moral order (cf. 3:5-6; 22:23; 23:11; 24:18, 21).

15 *Do not lay an ambush* (see 1:11, 18; 7:12; 12:6) is escalated to *do not plunder* (see 11:3). *As a wicked person* (*rāšā';* see n. 38; 2:22) is a necessary addition to link the fate of the theoretically apostate son with the final doom of the wicked (v. 16b). *Against the dwelling place* (*nāweh;* see 21:20) represents the wicked person's attack against the righteous not as direct but as indirect to include the plunder of his property. The metaphor *his resting place (ribṣô)* refers literally to the abode of animals.[50] Whereas *nāweh* refers

50. The verb *rbṣ* usually refers to the lying down of animals: of flocks (Gen. 29:2), a donkey (Gen. 49:14), a lion (Gen. 49:9 etc.). The nominal form in its two or three other occurrences refers to the resting place for herds (Isa. 65:10) and sheep (Jer. 50:6). The pointing of Isa 35:7 is uncertain but is used of jackals.

to the place of provisioning, *rēbeṣ* refers to the place of repose and of rest from exertion and/or exhaustion.

16 *For if* (see 23:13; 24:12) both signals the rationale for the admonitions of v. 15 and introduces the protasis of v. 16aα. In this antithetical parallelism, a righteous person is juxtaposed over against a company of the wicked (pl.), and his falling and rising with their falling in a final calamity without rising again. *Falls* (see 11:5) could mean merely to "stumble" without falling (Ps. 37:24), but it probably refers to violent destruction.[51] In 1:11-14 sinners plotted to kill the innocent to plunder his property. In the admonition of this saying the wicked lay ambush to plunder his property (v. 15), not merely to trip him up. In the parallel the wicked stumble to fall *(kšl)* into final ruin (v. 15b), and in the next verse "your enemies fall *(npl)*" in ruin (v. 16a). *Seven times*[52] occurs in the Hebrew text emphatically before the verb. The symbolic number (see 6:31; 9:1; 26:16, 25) signifies: (1) a special sacredness (Exod. 23:15; 25:37; 29:30) and/or (2) completeness, the totality of a cycle (6:31; 9:1; 26:16, 25; cf. Gen. 21:28, 30; 29:18; Exod. 20:10). The intensification shows clearly that the life of the righteous does not pass without unmerited suffering (see I: 107). Indeed, it may appear to end in final ruin like the boxer knocked out for the count of ten (i.e., it's over) and like the proverbial cat that used up his "ninth life" (i.e., his last chance). *Then* marks the con(sequence). *He rises* (see 6:9) reverses his prior fall to a violent and final destruction (cf. Jer. 51:64).[53] It is used similarly in opposition to the falling occasioned by an enemy in Pss. 18:38(39); 20:8(9); Mic. 7:8. In the formula *npl-qûm* it acquires the meaning "to recover, to reestablish."[54] Since the righteous rise after a violent and final fall, his recovering points to his resurrection from death. McKane lamely comments that the saying asserts "what will ultimately be seen to be true, and so it becomes difficult to contradict and less difficult to defend."[55] *But* sets up the antithesis for the wicked. *Stumble* (see 4:12, 19) in juxtaposition to *npl* is a metonymy entailing *and fall.*[56] *Bᵉ* denotes sphere and/or agency, and *rāʿâ* (see 1:16) denotes physical evil and/or moral evil, setting up the pun, *in calamity* and *through evil* (see 1:33).

51. *Pace* Gemser, *Sprüche,* p. 89.
52. *HALOT,* 3:1,302, s.v. *šbʿ.*
53. *HALOT,* 3:1,086, s.v. *qwm.*
54. S. Amsler, *TLOT,* 3:1,139, s.v. *qûm.*
55. McKane, *Proverbs,* p. 404.
56. C. Barth, *TDOT,* 7:355, s.v. *kāšal.*

3. Saying 28 (24:17-18)

The promise that the wicked will fall develops (24:16b) into this prohibition not to gloat over their punishment (v. 17). The catchwords "fall" (*npl,* vv. 16a, 17a) and "stumble" (*kšl,* vv. 16b, 17b) strengthen the connection. By its linkage with vv. 15-16 the impersonal representation of the wicked is now personalized as the son's tormentors and their downfall are implicitly personalized as his triumph over them. *Otherwise* (see 5:6) signals that v. 18 validates the prohibition that protects God's holy emotions. The LORD finds gloating so morally repulsive that he would rather turn away from his retributive justice than to look at abhorrent gloating. The catchword "evil" *rāʿâ/rāʿ* links the two substantiations, first for the judgment of the wicked for their evil (v. 16) and then for the LORD's holding back of judgment for a worse evil (v. 18). Conceptually the preceding saying guaranteed the recovering of the righteous; this one aims to circumvent the recovering of the wicked. The son's enemies (v. 17a) are the wicked (vv. 15-16) because v. 18b predicates that his enemies are under God's wrath. In sum, gloating over the disaster visited on the wicked is more wicked than the disaster they inflict on the righteous.

17 *When your enemy* [see n. 41; 16:7] *falls* (*binpōl;* see v. 6a), *do not rejoice* (see 5:18) is essentially repeated in the synonymous parallel, *when he stumbles* (*bikkāšᵉlû;* see 24:16b), *do not let your heart* [see I: 90] *shout in exultation* (see 22:24). But the second prohibition with its focus on the heart is construed as more emphatic by the gloss *indeed* (see n. 42).

18 The reason and purpose of the emphatic prohibition not to gloat is to avoid the necessary negative consequence that, if unheeded, the wicked will get off the hook — at least temporally. The synthetic parallels comprising this theological reason for the prohibition consist of a condition — itself consisting of a condition and a consequence — and a consequence. Each clause of the synthetic parallels presumes a divine attribute, moving from his omniscience (v. 18aα) to his moral sensibility (v. 18aβ) to his righteous and just response (v. 18b). First, *the LORD* [see I: 67] *will see* (see 6:6) *and,* which denotes (con)sequence,[57] *it will be evil* [see 1:16] *in his eyes* (see 3:7). The theological statement entails God's moral sensibility against cruelty, coldness, smug arrogance, faithlessness, and cynicism toward God's image (cf. Obad. 10-12; Zech. 1:15). Subsequently, marked by *and, he will turn away* [see 1:23] *his wrath* [see 15:1] *from him* (i.e., the enemy),[58] a metonymy of effect for the righteous and of cause for the judgment intended for the enemy (see 24:16b). McKane complains, "The absence of every trace of human

57. *IBHS,* p. 531, P. 32.2.3c.
58. BDB, p. 996, *šûb.*

feeling for the enemy who is down and out is uncanny and unpleasant. The attitude which is to be adopted towards him is measured with an eery, impersonal coldness." But he wrongly deconstructs this proverb that prohibits cold and calloused treatment of the enemy. In truth the proverb teaches that the LORD will not promote further moral ugliness by maintaining the situation that exacerbates it. His righteousness demands justice, but his holiness demands that he desist. The two wrongs of the wicked person's action and of the son's reaction offset one another. The proverb censures the pollution of justice and the thwarting of it by another sin. However, the proverb does not address the wrongs done to God. Other texts teach that those sins will be punished (11:21; 16:5). Positively, the son should weep, not rejoice, at the tragic waste and destruction of God's image (cf. Job 10:8-9). One may legitimately hope for God to right wrongs (2 Tim. 4:14) and should celebrate when God's righteousness prevails, but one must not nurse malignant revenge (cf. 2 Sam. 1:10; Job 31:29; Ps. 35:11-14; Luke 19:41-44). Some texts even enjoin positive assistance to the fallen enemy (Exod. 23:4-5; Prov. 25:2; Matt. 5:38-48; Rom. 12:20-21). Woman Wisdom emulated for humanity God's love and his gracious humility by freely extending to those who ignored, despised, and mocked her the offer of life as a free gift (see 1:20-33; 8:1-36). She prepared her feast for simpletons (9:1-6).

4. Saying 29 (24:19-20)

This saying protects the preceding one from the notion that the wicked will enjoy a blessed future because the LORD will turn away his wrath from them in response to cruel and callous gloating over their misfortune. Their bottom line is still zero — they will be annihilated. The LORD's stay of execution is only long enough to deprive the gloaters of their malignant joy. That truth leads to the admonition not to burn with envy at their temporary prosperity. This new saying, in addition to the syntax and style that links together the last five sayings, is linked with the preceding two by the catchwords "wicked" (pl., vv. 16b, 20b) and "calamity/evil" (vv. 18a, 20a) and by the broken sequence of *tṯḥr* ("envy") and *'ḥryt* (blessed future). The stumbling and fall of the wicked (vv. 16b, 17) are escalated to the eternal darkness that befalls them (v. 20). The logical particle *for* links the repeated reasons (v. 20a, b) with the repeated command (v. 19a, b); the *r'* in "forgers of evil" and "evil person" in their A versets and of "wicked" *(rᵉšā'îm)* in their B versets tightens their connection. In 23:18 the positive future prospect of the righteous served as the rationale for not envying the wicked; now the negative prospects of the wicked are indicated.

19 The synthetic parallels prohibit anger, presumably against God, and the envy of the wicked when they prosper. *Do not fret (tiṯḥar)* means not to get burned up emotionally. The verb occurs elsewhere in the *Hithpael* only in the wisdom psalm, Psalm 37 (vv. 1, 7, 8).[59] In both texts the admonition stands in parallel with *do not envy the wicked* (see 3:30 and 24:1) and is substantiated by the ephemeral prosperity of the wicked. The parallels in Psalm 37 and Prov. 23:17 suggest that envy ignites one's internal fury. In other words, the anger is not directed against anyone but is felt as an internal agitation, a fretting, connected with envy that might occasion choosing evil to satisfy one's passions (see 3:31). If this interpretation is right, *because* marks the reason or originating force of an action[60] over against *those who forge evil* (see 17:4). The admonition not to envy entails that they prosper; nobody envies a pauper. Righteous anger is an appropriate response to a violation of one's sense of justice, truth, and/or what is right (cf. Gen. 34:7; 39:17-19; 1 Sam. 11:6; 2 Sam. 13:21). These situations provoke the LORD's righteous indignation (Exod. 22:24[23]; Num. 32:10, 13; Deut. 29:27[26]; 2 Sam. 6:7). "In your anger do not sin" (Eph. 4:26) cautions the apostle Paul. But burning envy of the wicked's success is foolish, for their prosperity is vapid, as the next verse makes clear.

20 *For* signals the rationale for the admonitions: *the evil person has no blessed future* (see 23:18a). *The lamp of the wicked will be snuffed out* repeats 13:9 (see 20:20). When the LORD, as inferred by the divine passive, extinguishes the lamp of the wicked that presently burns so brightly, his wrongly gained property will be righteously redistributed. No sensible person envies property that will destroy him. In sum, keeping the extinction of their lamp in view will extinguish burning envy.

5. Saying 30 (24:21-22)

The last saying builds on the preceding one, pointing to the LORD and his righteous king as the A/agents who uphold the principle of retribution (see I: 73). Its double admonitions in v. 21, to fear the LORD and the king who exercises legitimate authority, are matched by the double reasons in v. 22. The pronoun "their" and "the two of them" in v. 22b look back to "the LORD and the king" in v. 21a. Both the LORD and the king will inflict on intriguing nobles disaster that is so certain, sudden, and extensive that no one knows its

59. *Ḥārâ* normally occurs in the *Qal* with *'ap* as the expressed or unexpressed subject (i.e., "[someone's] nose burned hot"), an idiom meaning "he became very angry." In the *Hithpael* it means "to make oneself burnt up." The *Hithpael* of *ḥārâ* does not refer to passionate anger in contrast to simple anger in the *Qal* (*pace* D. Freedman and J. Lundbom, *TDOT,* 5:176, s.v. *ḥārâ*). In the *Qal* it already has an intensive force; by its nature anger is passionate. The false distinction is based on the mistaken understanding that *Hithpael* is intensive. In fact, it is factitive (= "do not get yourself burnt up") (*IBHS,* pp. 429-31, P. 26.2).

60. *IBHS,* p. 198, P. 11.2.5e.

limits. Several other proverbs represent the king as the guarantor of the social order (see 14:35; 16:10-15; 19:12; 20:2, 8; 22:11; 25:2-5).

21 The positive commandment "fear" and the negative commandment "do not get involved with" constitute the outer frame, and their objects, "the LORD and the king" and "officials" their inner core. *Fear the LORD* [see I: 100], *my son* (see 1:8), connotes that the father's love for his son prompts his admonition to subject himself to God's rule. *And the king* refers to the LORD's anointed regent on earth who effects his rule, dispensing life and death (see 16:10-16). The admonition to "fear" the king as one fears God is unusual (see 1 Pet. 2:17).[61] The identification of the king with the LORD shows that the sage regarded the king's throne on earth as the legitimate representation of God's throne in heaven (cf. Matt. 17:24-27; 22:21; Rom. 13:1-5; Tit. 3:1; 1 Pet. 2:13-17; cf. 1 Sam. 10:27; 2 Pet. 2:10; Jude 8). The parallelism suggests that fearing the LORD and his king entails *do not* (*'al;* see 22:22) *get involved with* (*tit'ārāb 'im;* see 14:10; 20:19) [*intriguing*] *officials* (*šônîm;* see n. 45). To fear the LORD and his king is the opposite of to get involved with nobles. In light of this contrast in v. 21 and of the reason in v. 22, the noblemen in view seek to grab power and advance themselves through intrigue, not by subordination to legitimate authority. In sum, the admonitions imply that the way to advance yourself and not to threaten your career is to revere legitimate authority and avoid becoming involved in plots to undermine them and seize power for oneself.

22 Initial, and yet medial, *because* again signals the motivating reason behind the admonitions. In its synthetic, chiastic parallels, the inner core presents the synonyms, "disaster" and "ruin," that the LORD and the king will inflict. The outer frame represents the merited punishment as coming suddenly and being of unknown limits. The notion that their judgment irrupts intensifies the danger like an incalculable fate (cf. 2 Sam. 18:7, 8; 20:1, 2, 22; 1 K. 2:22-46; Eccl. 8:2-5; Acts 5:36, 37). *The disaster on them* or *from them* (1:26) glosses the ambiguous "their disaster." At first one interprets it as an objective genitive, "the destruction inflicted on them (i.e., the noblemen/rebellious)," but the parallel, "the misfortune of the two of them," forces a reinterpretation to the agentive genitive. The shift in interpretation is probably intentional to allow both interpretations. *Appears* (see 24:16) here has the nuance of "come on the scene."[62] Its personal subjects such as a religious head of a clan (Gen. 37:7), a prophet (Deut. 34:10), or a judge (Judg. 2:16) are all distinguished by their nonhereditary succes-

61. Meinhold (*Sprüche,* p. 408). Meinhold cites the Sumerian-Akkadian proverb: "Once you have seen the gain of adoring (your) god, you will praise (your) god and salute your king."

62. BDB, p. 878, *qûm.*

sion,[63] matching with this impersonal subject "suddenly," which connotes unexpectedly. Crenshaw analyzes the rhetorical question *who knows* into two groups. In its five occurrences in non–wisdom literature (2 Sam. 22:22; Esth. 4:14; Joel 2:14; Jonah 3:9; and [questionably] Ps. 90:11) it leaves a door open to the possibility that the situation will change for human good. Its other five occurrences in Ecclesiastes (2:19; 3:21; 6:12; 8:1) and in Prov. 24:22 close the door to any redeeming situation. In this latter use it serves as strong denial and is equivalent to "no one knows."[64] *What ruin* occurs only two other times, both in Job (30:24; 31:29), and means "disaster," "misfortune," "distress."[65] *The two of them can inflict* glosses the genitive of agency. The two are the LORD and the king (v. 21a). Delitzsch curiously rejects this natural interpretation because it would be "improper to comprehend God and the man under one cipher." Yet the preceding verse comprehends them together with the one command, "fear."[66]

COLLECTION IV: FURTHER SAYINGS OF THE WISE (24:23-34)

23 *These also are sayings of the wise.*[67]
To show partiality in giving a verdict is not good.[68]
24 *As for anyone who says to the guilty, "You are innocent," peoples will curse him,*
communities[69] *will strike him with a curse.*
25 *As for those who establish what is right, it will be pleasant,*
on them will come a blessing that brings good.[70]

63. Coppes, *TWOT,* 2:793, *qûm.*

64. J. L. Crenshaw, "The Expression *mî yōdēaʿ* in the Hebrew Bible," *VT* 36 (1986) 274-88.

65. *HALOT,* 3:925, s.v. *pîd.*

66. *Papyrus Insinger* (4:4) commands: "Do not speak of royalty and divinity with hostility when you are angry" (see *AEL,* 4:4).

67. The Targ. (so also Syr.) adds "I say" and interprets "to the wise" as an indirect object: "I say to the wise." The Vulg. also takes *lḥkmym* as an indirect object, but none of the English versions follows. The other superscriptions (1:1; 10:1; 22:17; 25:1; 30:1; 31:10) suggest that *lᵉ* means "by" or "belonging to."

68. Gemser and Fichtner want to fill out the monostich by a line similar to 18:5; 28:21. However, their B versets do not fit here and interrupt the parallels between vv. 23b and 24 (see the commentary; noted independently from Plöger).

69. Or "nations."

70. Since blessing is good, *ṭôb* is better understood as a gen. of effect (see *IBHS,* p. 146, P. 9.5.2d) than as an epexegetical gen. (= a good blessing).

26 *He*[71] *kisses*[72] *lips*[73] —
the one who gives an honest reply.
27 *Establish your out-of-doors work,*
and prepare it in the fields for yourself!
After [doing that],[74] *then build your household!*
28 *Do not be a witness against your neighbor without reason;*[75]
you would not[76] *convince*[77] *with your lips, would you?*
29 *Do not say, "As he has done to me, I will do to him;*
I will pay the man back according to his conduct."
30 *I passed by the*[78] *field of the sluggard,*
even the vineyard of a man who lacked sense.
31 *And behold, the whole of it had grown up as*[79] *all sorts of nettles,*

71. The LXX, Syr., and Targ. unnecessarily add a subject to the text: "They/people will kiss the lips of those who answer." Rashi (Lyons, "Rashi's *Commentary*," p. 121) renders "lips kiss him," but he too violates Hebrew syntax. The Vulg. and modern English versions rightly interpret verset B as either an independent relative clause and so as the subject (= "the one who kisses lips"), or as a dependent relative clause modifying the 3rd person sing. (i.e., "he kisses the lips who gives"). Though the sense is the same, the second construction better matches the comparative clause.

72. J. M. Cohen ("An Unrecognized Connotation of *nšq peh* with Special Reference to Three Biblical Occurrences," *VT* 32 [1982] 416-24) contends that *nšq* in Gen. 41:40; Job 31:27; and Prov. 24:26 means "seal." He invests that uncertain meaning here by restricting "honest reply" to "just verdicts" and by qualifying "lips" as "cursing/hostile lips." According to him, the verse should be attached to vv. 24-25: "He that gives forthright judgment will silence all cursing lips." His argument is not convincing.

73. Gemser (*Sprüche,* p. 89) unnecessarily adds *k*ᵉ*mērēa'* "as a friend" after *yiššāq.* The syntax and word itself signify the comparison.

74. Not reckoning with the elliptical nature of prepositions, Fichtner *(BHS)* and "many commentators" insert "marry [and build]."

75. Lit. "a witness without cause." The substantive *ḥinnām* is usually an adverb, but here it functions as an attributive gen. (*IBHS,* pp. 149-50, P. 9.5.3a).

76. Delitzsch (*Proverbs,* p. 145) notes *waw* + *he* in 2 Sam. 15:35. The LXX misrepresents the Hebrew as *pseudēs martys* "false witness."

77. The LXX reads *mēde platynou* "do not exaggerate." Although the Greek translator probably mistook the verb as II *pth* "to make wide," he either paraphrased the MT or read *'al-t*ᵉ*pat.* There is no need to alter the more difficult MT according to this retroverted text (*pace* Toy, *Proverbs,* p. 454). McKane (*Proverbs,* p. 574) gives a sharp critique of G. R. Driver's emendation to *wtpthw (= ût*ᵉ*puttēhû)* "and do (not) slander him with your lips." D. J. A. Clines and D. M. Gunn ("'You Tried to Persuade Me' and 'Violence and Outrage' in Jeremiah XX 7-8," *VT* 28 [1978] 21-22) interpret *pth* in the *Piel* here to mean "persuade, convince, or, alternatively, attempt to convince."

78. The article is often omitted in poetry. *Śādeh* is glossed as definite because the sluggard probably had but one vineyard.

79. Accusative of state specifying a feature of the subject (*IBHS,* p. 171, P. 10.2.2d).

its surface was covered over with[80] *all kinds of weeds,*
and its stone wall was thrown down.
32 *And I saw; I paid attention;*[81]
I observed; I accepted a lesson.
33 *A little sleep, a little slumber,*
a little folding of the arms to lie down,
34 *and poverty will come on you like a vagrant,*
and scarcity, like an armed man.[82]

For the structure of this collection, see the Introduction: Structure, I: 24-25.

A. SUPERSCRIPTION (24:23A)

The editorial, prose heading to this second appendix of sayings by wise men to the First Solomonic Collection of Proverbs contains only three words and so is not long enough to justify a separate verse (cf. 10:1). *Also* (*gam;* see 22:6; cf. 14:13) serves as a particle of addition. The deictic, anaphoric, demonstrative pronoun *these ('ēleh)* takes the place of "sayings" *(dibrê). Are by* — an alternative way of expressing authorship to the genitive of authorship (see 1:1; 10:1; 22:17) — *the wise* (*ḥakāmîm;* see 1:6; 22:17aβ; cf. Eccl. 12:11).

B. JUDGING AT COURT (24:23B-25)

The first saying of this collection pertains to giving a fair, objective, just verdict. Terms pertaining to this theme — "in giving a verdict," "innocent," "guilty," etc. — bind its verses together. Verse 24a dramatically illustrates "to show partiality in giving a verdict" (v. 23bα) by quoting an unjust judge in a verdict that acquits the offender. Verse 24b expands "is not good" (v. 23bβ) into "people curse." Though separate, vv. 24 and 25 are antithetical parallels of a quatrain contrasting the responses of the community to an unjust judge and to righteous judges. On the former they pronounce a curse; on the latter, a blessing. The last words, "not good" (v. 23b) versus "good"

80. The same construction, but English idiom demands "with."

81. Short prefix conjugation to represent preterite action (*IBHS,* pp. 497-98, P.31.1.d), judging from the surrounding three suffix conjugations. The short form may have been chosen for its alliteration. After initial *waw* consecutive, the first three words of this verset begin with *'aleph.*

82. See 6:10-11.

(v. 25b), form an *inclusio* around the saying. The contrasting responses of the people — a curse on the unjust judge and blessings on the just — give the reason why it is not good to show partiality in court. In 17:15 the same truth is taught, but the reason is explicitly grounded in God's character. Here the LORD's involvement is implicit. The people must appeal to him to effect their curse and blessing. Although stated as a saying, not an admonition, the intention of the speech act, an admonition not to show partiality, is clear (see 17:15, 23, 26; 18:5; 28:21; cf. Exod. 23:6-8; Lev. 19:15; Deut. 1:17; 16:19).

23b The monostich in a forceful understatement asserts that showing partiality in handing down a judicial sentence is not desirable or beneficial. *To show partiality* glosses the idiom *hakkēr-pānîm.* The *Hiphil* of *hkr* signifies either "to inspect/to look over" (cf. Gen. 31:32; 37:32) or "to pay attention to/to take notice of" (Ruth 2:10, 19). "The potential danger in 'showing attention to someone' is that partiality may result."[83] With *pānîm* "face" as its object it occurs in the context of making such a judgment ("to be a respecter of persons/to show partiality," Deut. 1:17; 16:19; Prov. 28:21).[84] Its synonymous idiom is "to lift up the face" (see 18:5). *In giving a verdict* (*b^e^mišpāṭ;* see 16:11) puts a court situation beyond doubt. *Is not good* (*bal-ṭôb;* cf. 23:7), an equivalent of *lō'-ṭôb,* is a litotes, not to escape censure but as an emphatic understatement (see 16:29; 17:26; 18:5; 20:23).

24 The disjunctive, antithetical *but* (*w^e^*) is exceptional at the beginning of a new verse. The synonymous parallel, verset B, gaps the condition expressed as a nominative absolute, *as for anyone who says* (*'ōmēr;* see 1:11) *to the guilty* (*l^e^rāšā';* see 2:22; 10:2, 3). Though *rāšā'* is usually glossed "wicked," in this juridical context, it denotes one who is guilty of a crime.[85] The direct address, "*you*" (*'āttâ*), dramatically represents the court scene. *Are innocent* (*ṣaddîq;* see 10:2), usually glossed "righteous," has in a juridical context the notion of "persons whose conduct will be checked and found irreproachable."[86] This nominative absolute construction focuses on the corrupt judge and graphically depicts him corrupting the wheels of justice as he acquits the person who disadvantages the community to advantage himself. The main clause repeats itself in the parallelism, which is as precise as possible to emphasize the response of the members of the community's confidence in its integrity and in the rights of each individual under law, by cursing the unjust judge. The plural *peoples* (*'ammîm;* see 11:14) *will curse him* (*yiqq^e^būhû;* see 11:26) is probably a plural of composition, breaking up the

83. M. Wilson, *TWOT,* 2.579-80, s.v. *nkr.*

84. *HALOT,* 2:700, s.v. *nkr.*

85. *HALOT* 3:1,295, s.v. *rāšā'.*

86. *HALOT* 3:1,002, s.v. *ṣaddîq.*

general public who find their protection within a group into its individual parts.[87] *Communities* (*l^e'ummîm;* see 11:26; 14:28; cf. 14:34) is a stock-in-trade parallel to "people." *Strike him with a curse* (*yiz'āmûhû;* see 14:22) connotes that they look to God to effect the curse and bring punishment down on the head of the unjust judge (see 11:26). Note the sequence of *'m* and *'m* in the first and last three words.

25 Again, the condition of verset Aa, another absolute nominative, is gapped in verset B. *As for those who establish what is right* (*lammôkîḥîm;* see 3:12), *it is pleasant* (*yin'ām;* see 15:26). The main clause, "it is pleasant" (verset Ab), is greatly expanded and clarified in verset B. A "pleasant" community is one that mediates the divine life and prosperity on the righteous judges by pronouncing blessings (see 10:6) on them. *On them* (*'^{a}lêhem*) implies that the blessing comes from above (see 10:6). *Will come* (*tābô';* see 6:11) *blessing* (*birkat;* see 10:6; 11:26) *that brings good* (*ṭôb;* see 2:20; 24:23). In sum, their blessings bring on the just judges all they desire and need. By praying God's blessings on those who administer them according to God's law, the people aim to promote the integrity and orderliness of the community.

C. CORRECT SPEAKING (24:26)

Correct judging in the court gives way in the second saying to correct speaking in general, though many restrict the new saying to the court setting. The connection between the two sayings is underscored by the catchword *môkîḥîm,* "those who establish what is right," the first word of v. 25, and "right" or "honest [words]," the last word in the Hebrew of v. 26. In the synthetic parallels v. 26a functions as a comparative clause and as the predicate and the consequence, while v. 26b, *the one who gives* or returns (*mēšîb;* see 24:18) *an answer* or report (*d^ebārîm;* see 18:13) represents the topic and the condition. In 11:22 the comparative clause also comes first. *Honest* (*n^ekōḥîm;* see 8:9) is a geometric term for "straight ahead."[88] Its synonyms are compiled in 8:6-9 — "straight," "fair," "truthful," "righteous," and "upright" — along with its antonyms: "wicked," "deceitful," and "crooked." The one who answers or reports is a person of candor and honesty. The predicate

87. *IBHS,* p. 118, P. 7.3.c.

88. *N^ekōḥîm* occurs eight times: once literally, "the one walks *straight ahead* enters into peace" (Isa. 57:2). Otherwise it is used metaphorically: of "an *upright* land" (Isa. 26:10), of *"honesty"* (Isa. 59:14), of "how to do *what is right*" (Amos 3:10), and of speech. With reference to words it refers to *valid/proper/just* claims in court (2 Sam. 15:3), to *honest* speech (Prov. 8:9), and to *truthful* prophecy, in contrast to illusions (Isa. 30:10).

implicitly compares him either to a close relative or to a devoted friend or a loyal subject who expresses his love and devotion to his covenant partner by a kiss, the symbolic expression of love. *Kisses (yiššāq)* connotes strong bonds of affection and solidarity between the two participants.[89] Its object, *the lips (śᵉpātayim),* is unique in the Bible (cf. Song 4:11; 5:13). Because of its uniqueness, scholars have expressed doubt whether the practice of kissing lips then existed, but Meinhold verifies kisses on the lips in Sumer, Ugarit, and from the New Kingdom period in Egypt.[90] Herodotus (*History,* 1.134) says of the Persians, "When one man meets another, it is easy to see if the two are equals; for then without speaking they kiss each other on the lips; if the difference in rank be but little, it is the cheek that is kissed; if it be great, the humbler bows down and does obeisance to the other." To judge from the use of kiss in the Old Testament, however, it probably intensifies the intimacy, devotion, and love between the two people and is not a greeting of peers. Also, it probably suggests a metonymy with the inquirer's words. The honest answer on the lips of the responder so match the question on the lips of the inquirer that it is as aesthetically satisfying to the emotions of the participants as their lips kissing. According to Prov. 8:9, only the discerning appreciate straight talk. Likewise, this saying implies a discerning inquirer. He lovingly embraces the honest responder. The saying instructs the disciple to express his devotion to his superiors or peers by giving a straightforward, not devious and/or distorted, answer.

D. POSITIVE BEHAVIOR IN WORK (24:27)

The supplementary collection now turns from correct patterns of speaking to correct patterns of working. The saying offers no validation for the pattern of work it admonishes because common sense validates the pattern. Nevertheless, the admonition is needful because human depravity prompts people to

89. Of the 26 occurrences of *nāšaq* in the *Qal,* 15 pertain to family members who symbolize their love, solidarity, and/or reconciliation to one another by a kiss: of a son and his parents and vice versa (Gen. 27:26, 27; 48:10; 50:1; 2 Sam. 14:33; 1 K. 19:20); of affectionate or reconciled cousins and siblings (Gen. 29:11; 33:4; Exod. 4:27; Song 8:1); of intimate in-laws (Exod. 18:7; Ruth 1:9, 14); and of affectionate cousins and siblings (Gen. 29:11; Song 8:1). In the same way it symbolizes the devotion and loyalty of friends (2 Sam. 14:33; cf. 2 Sam. 20:9); of subjects to a ruler and vice versa (Gen. 41:40; 1 Sam. 10:1; 15:5); of devoted worshipers to a deity (1 K. 19:18; Job 31:27; Hos. 13:2); and of lovers (Song 1:2; cf. Prov. 7:13). Once it is used metaphorically to show the close and lovely connection between righteousness and peace (Ps. 85:11). In the New Testament a kiss is a form of greeting (Rom. 16:16; 1 Cor. 16:20; etc.).

90. Meinhold, *Sprüche,* p. 411, citing O. Keel, *Das Hohelied,* pp. 48-50.

violate good sense. Its synthetic parallels admonish the son first to fix and make ready his trade or work out of doors (verset A) and then to bring into existence his household indoors (verset B). Both are essential for the son's well-being. In the synonymous parallels of v. 27a *establish* (*hākēn,* i.e., "make ready and fix"; see 6:8; 8:27; 16:9) *your . . . work* or business[91] (*mᵉla'ktekā;* see 18:9; 22:29) is paired with *prepare it ('attᵉdāh),* a verb that occurs only here in the *Piel* and once in Job 15:24 in the *Hithpael.* Its meaning is derived from the Arabic and Syriac "to be ready" and Jewish Aramaic "to prepare." *Out-of-doors* (*baḥûṣ,* lit. "in the out-of-doors"; see 1:20) is narrowed down to *in the field* (*baśśādeh,* i.e., in the arable land that sustains life; see 23:10). This would include plowing the land and planting gardens and orchards, so that it produces its fruit. *For yourself (lāk)* shows the son's own self-interest to prepare his arable fields to provide food and wealth to sustain his household (verset Ab). Only then, but just as certainly, must he as a craftsman bring into existence his household. *After ('aḥar)* is a temporal preposition that elides something like *doing that*[92] as the *waw*-consecutive *then* implies. With *waw*-consecutive the suffix conjugation has the same value as the preceding imperatives, not a lame permissive sense "you may build." Meinhold's title for the saying, "the right priorities in the things of life," is better emended to "the necessary and right priorities in work." *Build* (*bānîtā;* see 9:1), which entails creative activity, assumes that the craftsman designs that which he brings into existence for a purpose. *Your household* (*bêtekā;* see 11:29) refers to the place of dwelling, its chattel, and its people, including family and servants (Deut. 25:9; Ruth 4:11).[93] Since the household also provides an indispensable basis to sustain his well-being, it entails erecting a domicile to provide him shelter and rest, acquiring chattel including tools and servants, marrying a wife, and producing offspring. In sum, he must first make ready and productive what the Creator has provided to sustain the household, and then he must "create" a household for his prosperity. The saying entails counting the cost before building a household (cf. Luke 6:48; 14:28-30). This ordering of work is necessary because building a house, furnishing it, and sustaining its life consumes wealth. The son by his work must generate the necessary wealth. Otherwise he will take it from someone else or let the household die. Only the first option is righteous. The saying assumes that agriculture formed the economic basis of the society.

91. *HALOT,* 2:586, s.v. *mᵉlā'kâ.*

92. *IBHS,* p. 224, P. 11.4.3d.

93. Parallels in ancient wisdom literature validate this meaning: "When you prosper, found your household, take a hearty wife, a son will be born to you. It is for the son you build a house" (*Hardjedef, AEL,* 1:58]); "when you prosper and found your house, and love your wife with ardor, fill her belly, clothe her back" (*Ptah-hotep* 21 [325-27], *AEL,* 1:69).

People had their houses in the city and their fields outside of it (cf. Ruth 2–3). The saying does not aim to endorse farming over city work as the basis of nourishment, survival, and wealth. Meinhold comments: "*The Teaching of Ani* [6:1-3] considers as the condition for founding a household careful gardening with the making of the cucumber patch and planting of trees and flowers beside plow-land." But Prov. 27:23-27 represents animal husbandry as a person's economic basis. The sayings use farming or raising livestock as an exemplar for any occupation. They admonish all, tradesmen and magistrates alike, to make sure that their sources of food and income out of doors are secure before they take the next, but necessary, step of building a home within doors.

E. WRONG SPEAKING (24:28-29)

Though vv. 28 and 29 constitute one saying, each verse represents a distinct admonition, matching the first two sayings in the first triad of sayings in Collection IV. Verse 28 switches interest from the corrupt judge (vv. 23b-25) to the malicious witness, and v. 29 shifts the topic from good speech (v. 26a) to bad speech (v. 29) by using the catchword *'āmar* "to say," and from giving back what is beneficial (v. 26b) to what is harmful (v. 29b) by using the catchword "return" (*šûb* in the *Hiphil*). Nevertheless, the anaphoric pronoun "to him" and the anaphoric article "the man" in v. 29 have "your neighbor" of v. 28 as their antecedents, showing that these verses constitute a proverb pair. The saying presents two prohibitions: not to be a needless, hostile witness against a neighbor and not to get even with him. The second defines "a witness . . . without reason" as having the wrong motive of revenge.

28 Verset B of this synonymous parallelism concretizes verset A. It replaces the imperative "do not" with the rhetorical question "you would not, would you?" specifies a hostile witness without legal obligation to testify as attempting to persuade the judge with his lips, and gaps "against your neighbor." *Do not be* (*'al-tᵉhi;* see 22:26; 23:20) *a witness* (*'ēd;* see 12:17) *against your neighbor* (*bᵉrē'ekā;* see 3:28) *without reason* (*hinnām;* see 1:11) here signifies to have no legal obligation to testify. The rhetorical polar question *would you (hᵃ)* calls for a negative answer, for the suffix conjugation here expresses a contrary-to-fact situation (cf. Gen. 21:7).[94] *Tempt* (*pittîtā;* see 1:10) elides its object, presumably a judge and/or elders trying the case. The common metonymy *with your lips (biśᵉpāteykā)* probably specifies the body part to make the son recoil from using them for treachery. A firsthand witness to a

94. *IBHS,* p. 493, P. 30.5.4b.

crime has a legal obligation to testify in court (Lev. 5:1; Prov. 29:24), but this "witness without reason" abuses the legal processes to incriminate another as a means of paying off an old personal grudge.[95] Although the saying focuses on the spiteful witness's motives, not on what he says, we may assume that he typically twists the facts to get his revenge (cf. 1 Sam. 21:1-7[2-8]; 22:9, 10; 26:1, 2, 17). According to 26:17, meddling in someone else's dispute is folly. The saying unites in a unique way the repeated prohibitions against being a bad witness (12:17; 14:5, 25; 19:5, 9; 21:28; 25:18) and against revenge (17:13; 20:22; 24:17-18; cf. 16:7; 25:21-22; cf. Gen. 4:23-26; Matt. 5:44; 18:35; Luke 23:34; Rom. 12:19; 1 Pet. 2:21-23).

29 The chiastic, synonymous parallels, apart from the introductory *do not say* or think (*'al-tō'mar;* see 3:28; 20:22; 24:24), represents in the outer frame the comparative past situation *as (ka'ᵃšer) he has done* (*'āśâ;* see 13:16) *to me* (*lî;* cf. 24:27),[96] matching the comparative phrase *according to his conduct* (*kᵉpo'ᵒlô;* see 24:12). The inner core represents the present situation, *so (kēn) I will do to him* (*'e'ᵉśeh-lô;* see 24:29aα), specified as *I will pay back* (*'āšîb;* see 24:26) *to the man (lā'îš). Lā'îš* is used rather than *lᵉ'ādām* (cf. 24:12) because there the form is indefinite and the focus is on humanity in general in contrast to God, whereas here the form is definite and refers back to a specific neighbor (see 8:4; 14:12). The law provided the principle of lex talionis (i.e., "eye for eye") for public justice (Exodus 23–25; Lev. 24:19-20; Deut. 19:19), but not for private revenge. According to the Bible, an injured party must love his neighbor (Lev. 19:18) and commit the injustice to the sublime God and his elect magistrate to adjudicate (see 16:4-7, 10-15). He must neither hold a grudge against his enemy, nor set himself up as a tribunal in the place of God and his magistrate, nor take the sword out of their hands (see cross references at vv. 28-29 above). The saying does not seek to validate its admonitions, perhaps because the other sayings provide the reasons. Meinhold comments, "The principle of personal revenge and of egoism quoted here obviously did not require any additional substantiation according to the sages since the law of the human jungle leads to the absurdum." Nevertheless, Plöger notes, "It is remarkable that a reference to the LORD is avoided" (cf. 24:12b).

95. The Babylonian "Counsels of Wisdom" (before 700 B.C.) instructs: "Seek not the place of a quarrel; for in a quarrel you must give a decision, and you will be forced to be their witness. They will fetch you to testify in a lawsuit that does not concern you" (*ANET,* p. 426).

96. *IBHS,* p. 641, P. 38.5a.

F. NEGATIVE BEHAVIOR IN WORK (24:30-34)

A more extended poem (cf. 23:29-34) about the sluggard is bound with the last saying of the first triad of "More Sayings of the Wise" by the theme of work and the catchword "field" (24:27). The catchword *'îš* (cf. vv. 29b, 30a) connects it with the preceding saying. The concluding saying begins in the form of a graphic autobiographical narrative (cf. 4:1-9; 7:6-23) and ends in direct application. The saying progresses from "I" (vv. 30, 32) to "you" (v. 34) and from an overgrown vineyard to an impoverished existence with needs everywhere. It consists of two proverbial pairs around a single line.[97]

The vigorous sage passes the vineyard of the sleeping sluggard. A hostile creation is also on the move, but it marches to attack the sluggard while he sleeps. Weeds of all sorts have grown up and supplanted the arduously planted and carefully maintained vines of an older generation, and the protective stone wall looks as though an invader tore it down (vv. 30-31). Verse 34 represents the law of entropy as an armed bandit who comes and attacks the sluggard as he lies in bed asleep. If the impersonal creation attacks the sluggard, how much more his spiritual adversaries! The dramatic conjunctive and presentative, "and, look!" — a call to wake up — that initiates v. 31 binds it to v. 30.[98] In verse 32 the sage alertly and cogently engages his *lēb* (i.e., "he pays attention"), in contrast to the sluggard who lacks a *lēb* (i.e., he is brainless; v. 30), to save himself (v. 32). This center line serves as a janus between the two proverb pairs. Its introductory *wā'eḥezeh* "I observed" carries on the narrative begun in v. 30 and begins a new situation. The object of what the father sees in the scene of vv. 30-31 is elided, but the scene of the first proverb pair (vv. 30-31) is clearly implied. From his observation he infers a lesson. The father articulates his *mûsār* "lesson" in the second proverb pair (vv. 33-34). The lesson is driven home using the second person. Untimely naps will allow personified poverty to come — and it certainly will — as a parasitic vagrant and bandit and take away all you inherited (vv. 33-34). Though you remain uncommitted and asleep, your enemy, like it or not, will come and overrun you. The lesson, which is also found in 6:10-11, is bound together by the *waw* consecutive that introduces v. 34.

This last saying in the Solomonic collections has striking affinities with the prologue to Proverbs and with Collection III. The book began with

97. Boström (*Paronomasi i den äldre hebreiske Maschallitteraturen,* p. 200) calls attention to the broken sequence of */h~ḥ, s, r/*: *ḥsr* (v. 30b), *nhrsh* (v. 31b; cf. *mwsr* [v. 32b]), and *mḥsryk* (v. 34b). The first three are final.

98. The sequence *'al* of *'ālâ* "grown up" of v. 31 picks the repeated *'al* "by" introducing both versets of v. 30 along with the broken sequence of *'āṣēl* "sluggard."

Solomon aiming that young people and wise people accept instruction (1:2-3). It ends with Solomon himself taking instruction. The prologue to Collection III challenged the son to pay attention (22:17). The Further Sayings draw to a close with the great sage still paying attention.

The ravaged vineyard serves as an exemplar of any heritage that is lost through negligence.

1. The Sluggard's Vineyard (24:30-31)

The first proverb pair represents the father's laboratory. He passes by the sluggard's vineyard (v. 30) and then asks his audience to join him in his view of it (v. 31).

30 In the synonymous parallels representing the sage's autobiographical encounter, *the field* (*śᵉdēh;* see 24:27) is specified as a *vineyard* (*kerem;* see 31:16; cf. Mic. 1:6) and *the sluggard* (*ʾîš-ʿāṣēl;* see Introduction, I: 114-15) is defined as *a man who lacked sense* (*ʾîš . . . lēb;* see 6:32). *I passed by* (*ʿābartî ʿal;* see 4:15) is gapped in verset B. *Even* glosses the epexegetical sense of *wᵉ*. The sage probably chose the vineyard to illustrate the need for industry because it took painstaking investment, labor, patience, and forethought to prepare and maintain a vineyard. Moreover, because its fruit was so valuable, its owner had to protect it vigilantly (Isa. 5:1-6).[99]

31 The synthetic parallels of v. 31 depict the once productive vineyard as overgrown with inedible growth and its protective stone wall as having been attacked, thrown down, and left in ruins. The replacement of the vines by weeds is underscored by the synonymous parallelism within verset A of "had grown up" and "covered over," though the second is logically subsequent, and by "nettles" and "weeds."

31a *And (wᵉ)* is conjunctive and *hinnēh (behold)* with it is presentative in connection with the verb "to see" (v. 32).[100] *The whole of it*

99. R. K. Harrison and F. N. Hepper (*NBD,* p. 1,225, s.v. "Vine, Vineyard") note: "Its preparation usually involved terracing the hillsides and clearing the stones. A living hedge of boxthorn — in modern times the American cactus was substituted — was planted, or a low wall built and topped with dead spiny burnet to deter animals and thieves. A watch-tower or stone hut served as a cool shelter during the summer when the labourers lived in the vineyards. The enclosed area of ground had been dug over carefully, and when the soil was friable young vines were planted. . . . The vines were pruned each spring by means of pruning-hooks. . . . A covered wooden structure, the watchtower, was erected on an elevation overlooking the vineyard, where the householder and his family kept a watch throughout the vintage period."

100. T. Zewi, "The Particles *Hinnēh* and *Wᵉhinnēh* in Biblical Hebrew," *HS* 37 (1996) 21-38.

(kullô) indicates that the totality of the vineyard *had grown up* (*ʿālâ;* see 15:1).[101] The gloss *as nettles (qimmeśōnîm)* was chosen, not *weeds,* to distinguish it from its synonymous parallel *ḥarullîm,* which KBL glosses as "weeds."[102] In two other occurrences, *qimmeśōnîm* appears in contexts of devastating judgment (cf. Isa. 34:13; Hos. 9:6). *All sorts of* glosses the plural, which is either a countable plural or a plural of extension to signify its density and height.[103] *Its surface* (*pānāyw,* i.e., the vineyard's outer facing; see 8:27)[104] *had become covered over* (*kossû;* see 10:6) with weeds of all sorts. In its two other occurrences *ḥarullîm* also appears in relation to the LORD's devastation (Job 30:7; Zeph. 2:9), making the land unfit for human occupation. If one does not remove weeds from the field in the spring, then nettles and weeds of all sorts spring up from the cursed ground (cf. Gen. 3:17-19) and take over. The heir is required only to preserve what his fathers have bequeathed to him. This son lacks the brains to see that and preserve his life.

31b *And (we)* is again conjunctive. In the phrase *its stone wall (geder ʾabānāyw), geder* refers to a stone wall without mortar, in contrast to *ḥōmâ,* the large protective wall around cities and buildings (see 1:21).[105] The pronominal suffix shows that "vineyard" is the antecedent of these pronouns. *Was torn down* (*neherāsâ;* see 11:11; 14:1) personifies the nettles and weeds as marauders.

2. Center Line: Observation and Reflection (24:32)

The center line forms the transition from the sage's observation (vv. 30-31) to his reflection or lesson (vv. 33-34). The *waw* consecutive *and (wā)* continues the narrative from *ʿābartî* (v. 30). In its synonymous parallel *I saw* (*ʾeḥezeh;* see 22:29), which denotes sharp inspection of something, is paired with *I observed* (*raʾîtî;* see 6:6), and *I paid attention* (*ʾāšît libbî;* see 24:22) with *I accepted* (*lāqaḥtî;* see 1:3) *a lesson* (*mûsār;* see 1:2). It is debatable whether the sage is coining the saying from what he saw, or applying a known saying to it to make it more credible. Its repetition in 6:10-11 favors the latter interpretation. The personal pronoun *I (ʾānōkî)* is tautological and thus conveys a "strong emotional heightening" and "focused attention or deep self-consciousness."[106] The father probably emphasizes that "I" did this to serve as a model to his son whom he instructed in his prologues to do the

101. BDB, p. 748, s.v. *ʿālâ.*

102. *HALOT,* 1:351, s.v. *ḥārûl; HALOT,* 3:1,107, s.v. *qimmôś.*

103. *IBHS,* pp. 119-20, P. 7.4.1a, c.

104. *HALOT,* 3:941, s.v. *pāneh.*

105. Waltke, "Micah," in *The Minor Prophets,* ed. T. E. McComiskey (Grand Rapids: Baker, 1993), p. 757.

106. *IBHS,* p. 296, P. 16.3.2e.

same (see 1:2-3; 22:17). In that light, v. 32 at the end of the sayings of the wise may serve as an *inclusio.*

3. The Lesson (24:33-34)

33 Verse 33 repeats 6:10. In this synthetic parallelism verset A represents the state of taking naps, and verset B the cause, refusing to work in order to sleep, symbolized by the folding of the arms. Isa. 28:24-29 describes how careful, industrious fieldwork looks.

34 Verse 34 repeats 6:11 with three exceptions. (1) It substitutes *mitḥallēk* for *kimhallēk,* an accusative of state specifying the state of the subject[107] for the prepositional phrase and a simile. (2) It uses the durative-iterative *t-stem,*[108] not the frequentative *Piel,* with no difference in meaning. (3) A probably countable plural *maḥsōreykā* "lacks" — "at one time this, at another time that"[109] — replaces the collective singular *maḥsōrekâ.*

V. COLLECTION V: SOLOMON II (25:1–29:27)

For the unity, integrity, and structure of Collection V, see I: 25.

A. SUPERSCRIPTION (25:1)

1 *These also are proverbs*[1] *of Solomon,*[2]
which the men[3] *of Hezekiah the king of Judah copied and collected.*

The editorial prose superscription of 25:1 marks off Collection V. This second collection of Solomon's proverbs, like "Further Sayings of the Wise" (see 24:23), conforms to Kitchen's label, *Type A* (see I: 32).

107. *IBHS,* p. 171, P. 10.2.2d.

108. *IBHS,* p. 427, P. 26.1.2b.

109. Delitzsch, *Proverbs,* p. 148.

1. The ancient versions curiously replace the honorific term *mišlê* with "sayings of." The Targ. and Syr. add "deep/profound sayings." They may have been influenced by the addition of *adiakritoi* to *paideia* in the LXX. It is unclear why the translator uses *paideia* (< *mûsār*) "instructions" instead of the honorific term *paroimiai* "proverbs," as in 1:1.

2. The Targ. omits "of Solomon."

3. Both the LXX and Syr. render "men" by "friends."

The Masoretic accents divide the verse into its two semantic components: its author, Solomon (25:1a), and its compilers, the men in close association with Hezekiah (25:1b). *These also are* [see 24:23] *proverbs of Solomon* (see 1:1; 10:1) suggests that the final editor reckoned this collection an appendix to Solomon's first collection, which Solomon himself authored and presumably compiled (10:1–22:16). *Which the men of ('anšê)* refers Solomon's proverbs to men in close association with[4] *Hezekiah (ḥizqîyâ) the king of Judah (melek-yᵉhûdâ;* cf. 1:1) from 715 to 686 B.C.[5] *Ḥizqîyâ* is a short verbal sentence meaning "The LORD has become my strength," or "The LORD has strengthened me."[6] *Copied and collected* basically means "to cause to advance or move."[7] "Moving" these proverbs entails transmitting and arranging a select number of Solomon's 3,000 proverbs, which were in written and/or oral form, as part of a unified appendix to his original collection (1 K. 4:32 [5:12]).[8] We can infer that

4. Cf. David's men in 1 Sam. 23:3 (*HALOT,* 1:43, s.v. *'îš*).

5. R. Wakely *(NIDOTTE,* 2:84, *ḥzq)* identifies five different forms of the name Hezekiah — the first four usually designate the Judean king: *ḥizqîyāhû* (74x), *yᵉḥizîyāhû* (40x) (= the LORD strenghtens"), *ḥizqîyâ* (13x), *yᵉḥizqîyâ* (3x), and *ḥizqî* (1x), a Benjaminite (1 Chr. 8:17). Hezekiah appears to have assumed a co-regency with Ahaz ca. 729 B.C. and became king ca. 716 B.C. He reigned 29 years until ca. 686 B.C. (cf. 2 Kings 17–20; Isaiah 36–39; 2 Chronicles 29–32). According to Zevit, the shorter theophoric form *yâ* for *yāhû* developed in Judah by the second half of the eighth century (Z. Zevit, "A Chapter in the History of the Israelite Personal Names," *BASOR* 250 [1983] 1).

6. *HALOT,* 1:305, s.v. *ḥizqîyāhû.*

7. *'tq* occurs four times in the *Qal:* twice of eroding rocks that "move" (Job 14:8; cf. 18:4), and twice of advancing in years (i.e., of growing old [Job 21:7 and Ps. 6:7(8)]). In the *Hiphil* it is used three times as a one-place *Hiphil* (i.e., an internal *Hiphil*), lit. "he caused himself to move." With a personal subject in Gen. 12:8; 26:2, it is best glossed as "move." With "words" as its subject in Job 31:15, it means "words move themselves from them" (i.e., "words fail them"). Twice it occurs as a two-place *Hiphil* (i.e., someone causes something to advance/move), once with the object "mountains" (Job 9:5) and once with the object "the proverbs of Solomon."

8. No scientific datum contradicts the book's superscriptions that Solomon authored the proverbs credited to him (see I: 31-36). The additional notice that the men of Hezekiah collected them buttresses that claim. Since no tendentious purpose can be suspected in the mentioning of the otherwise unknown "men of Hezekiah," this is first-rate historical evidence that as early as 700 B.C. Israel associated Solomon with proverbs. Scott argues that the many parallels between Solomon and Hezekiah lend support to the historical credibility of 25:1b. Both kings were sole rulers of all Israel, had peace on every side, had great wealth and nations brought valuable gifts to them (1 K. 4:20-25; 10:1-29; 2 K. 18:7-8; 20:20; 2 Chr. 32:22-23, 27-29; cf. 1 K. 5:1[15], 4[19], 14[29]; 20:21-25), and centralized Israel's worship in Jerusalem (1 Kings 6–9; 2 K. 18:7-8; 20:20; 2 Chr. 29:3-36; 30:13-27). The care to preserve and transmit Solomon's spiritual heritage is entirely consistent with this reforming king. He brought out of obscurity both David's psalms (2 Chr. 29:30) to reform the nation's worship and Solomon's proverbs to reform national character (2 Chr. 31:20-21) (R. B. Y. Scott, "Solomon and the Beginnings of Wisdom in Israel," in *WIANE,* pp. 272-79).

these editors were godly, wise, and literate (see I: 37). At the least, the proverbs in 25:2-15 were originally addressed to budding court officials, a setting matching this superscription. As God's earthly representative (cf. 8:15-16; 16:10-15; 21:10), the king had the task of maintaining order and justice in all areas of his kingdom.[9] But as proverbs, these pedagogic universals now serve as paradigms of many other situations and address all Israel. Jesus may have instantiated vv. 6-7 to guests at a wedding feast (Luke 14:7-11), and Jude applied the image in 25:14 to unproductive people (Jude 12).

B. SECTION C (25:2–27:27)

For an analysis of Solomon II into Solomon IIC and Solomon IID, see I: 15-16.[10]

1. The Court Hierarchy and the Conflict of the Righteous and the Wicked (25:2-27)

2 *The glory of God is to hide*[11] *a matter,*
but the glory of kings is to search out a matter.
3 *As for the heavens with reference to*[12] *height,*
and the earth with reference to depth,
and the heart of kings, there is no searching out [of them].
4 *Remove dross from silver,*
and a vessel comes forth for the silversmith.[13]
5 *Remove a wicked official before a king,*
that[14] *his throne may be established by righteousness.*

9. See Whitelam, in *ABD,* 4:40-47.

10. The exegesis of this section relies heavily on the superb dissertation by R. Van Leeuwen, "Context and Meaning in Proverbs 25–27" (Ph.D. diss., University of St. Michael's College, 1984).

11. The Targ. and Syr. read the infs. of these versets as ptcps.: "The glory of God is he who hides." The LXX has *timai* "honors," having read *hôqēr* (from the verb *yqr*).

12. The LXX leveled the difficult nominative absolute construction of the MT by reading verset A as containing two nominal clauses: "the heaven is high, and the earth is deep."

13. Fichtner [*BHS*] retroverts the LXX *katharisthēsetai katharon hapan* ("purified entirely pure") as *niṣrāp kullô.* This facilitating reading eliminates the metonymy of effect in the MT. Instead of implying the step of manufacturing a vessel as in the MT, it restricts the activity to purification (cf. R. C. Van Leeuwen, "A Technical-Metallurgical Usage of *yṣ*," *ZAW* 98 [1986] 112-13).

14. *Waw* conjunctive + prefix conjugation after an impv. signifies purpose (*IBHS,* pp. 562-63, 650, 33.4b; 39.2.2a).

6 *Do not honor yourself before a king,*
and in the place of great people do not stand.
7 *Better one says*[15] *to you, "Come up here,"*
than one humiliate you before a noble.
What your eyes have seen,[16]
8 *do not bring*[17] *hastily*[18] *to trial,*[19]
lest[20] *— what*[21] *will you do in its end,*
when your peer puts you to shame?[22]

15. The inf. cons. *ʾamor-* is a bi-form of *ʾemor-* ("the saying").

16. The MT connects the relative clause "whom your eyes have seen" to *nādîb* "a noble" in v. 7aβ, but the sense is at best obscure. Delitzsch (*Proverbs,* p. 153) thinks that the MT means "the humiliation which thou endurest is thus well deserved, because, with eyes to see, thou wert so blind." But Garrett (*Proverbs,* p. 205) suggests, "No one wants to have to look at his peers in the face while being publicly humiliated by a superior." The LXX, Syr., Sym., Vulg., NIV, REB, NJPS, and NRSV rightly connect v. 7b to v. 8a, yielding good sense and rhythm. The initial *ʾašer* confused the MT tradition, but the independent relative clause can function as an object (*IBHS,* p. 334, P. 19.3c) before the predicate (cf. Ps. 69:5; Jon. 2:10).

17. Since the MT did not understand verset A as the object of the verb, they pointed *tṣʾ* as in the *Qal,* but the Sym. and Vulg. rightly pointed it as *Hiphil, tôṣēʾ.*

18. The inf. cons. of *māhēr* often functions as an accusative of state modifying the subject of the verbal action (see *IBHS,* p. 171, P. 10.2.2c and p. 602, P. 36.2.1d; *HALOT,* 2:553, s.v. I *mhr.*

19. Symmachus, followed by Toy (*Proverbs,* p. 462) et al., reads *eis plēthos* (< *lārōb* "to what concerns plenty" [i.e., "to the multitude"]. The proverb then demands taciturnity. "If this is correct, the admonition is concerned not with criminal proceedings but with scandal-mongering" (Whybray, *Proverbs,* p. 362). The potential connection with *rîb* in v. 9, however, favors the MT. The Vulg. also reads *rîb.* Finally, *lārōb* means "abundance," never "crowd." McKane (*Proverbs,* p. 580), therefore, renders the clause "do not be in a hurry to broadcast" but fails to document that "to bring forth to abundance" means "to broadcast." The Hebrew has clear ways of expressing that notion (cf. 8:1-3).

20. An anacolouthon. The full thought is either "lest you lose the case. What will you do?" or "lest you do not know what you will do." Toy (*Proverbs,*p. 461) et al., to avoid the anacolouthon, emend *pen* to *kî.* But Meinhold (*Sprüche,* 2:421) rejects the emendation "because of the catchword connection with v. 10 and the facilitating of the reading. Then, of course, the condensed way of speaking has to be developed by connecting the thoughts as ['so that the matter turns out you do not know what to do'], as Rashi attempts to do."

21. G. R. Driver ("Problems in the Hebrew Text of Proverbs," *Bib* 32 [1951] 190); so already BDB, p. 553, s.v. *mâ*) interprets *mah* to signify indefinite "aught" and *bᵉ* to signify price. "Do not blurt out what thou hast seen too hastily in court lest eventually thou dost something that will give the other party a chance to confute thee with ignominy." But his interpretation reads more into the text than the Hebrew warrants. Toy (*Proverbs,* p. 461) earlier rejected a similar proposal by Ewald as unsatisfactory.

22. Lit. "in the putting you to shame of your peer," a broken cons. chain (*IBHS,* p. 140, P. 9.3d; see also pp. 603-4, P. 36.2.2).

9 *Plead your case with your peer,*
but do not divulge a confidence,
10 *lest an arbiter will pronounce you guilty,*
and the accusation against you never depart.[23]
11 *Apples*[24] *of gold in a silver sculpture*
are a decision made appropriate to its circumstance.[25]
12 *A gold earring, even an ornament of fine gold,*
is a wise[26] *arbiter's rebuke*[27] *"on" a listening ear.*
13 *Like the coolness*[28] *of snow at the time*[29] *of harvest*
is a trustworthy messenger to the one who sends him;
he refreshes his master.[30]
14 *Clouds and wind and*[31] *no rain*[32]
is a man who boasts of a gift he does not give.

23. The LXX has a lengthy addition to the saying that it did not understand.

24. Toy (*Proverbs,* p. 466) et al. reverse the consonants to read *pittûḥê* "engravings" or "decoration," but the NIV, REB, NEB, and NRSV rightly reject this emendation.

25. "As pointed in MT it can hardly be a form of *'ôpān,* 'wheel,' which in any case, despite some ingenious attempts to find such a meaning here, makes no sense (for example, that of McKane [and Meinhold], on the basis of the occurrence of what appears to be the same word in the Hebrew of Sir. 50:27)" (Whybray, *Proverbs,* p. 364). If the form is pl., not dual, it may be a countable (i.e., "circumstances") or an abstract (*IBHS,* p. 121, P. 7.4.2b).

26. The Vulg. interpreted "wise" as an acc. case function (reproves the wise), not as attributive.

27. The LXX reads "wise word," and the Targ. and Syr. "reproof/chastisement" (similarly NRSV). These alternative readings may reflect an interpretation of the metonymy in the MT, not a textual variant. The rendering of the participle "rebuker" by a verb is necessary to accommodate the pregnant *'al-'ōzen.*

28. The LXX reads *exodus* (< *ṣē't*). However, a snowfall at harvest is improbable and would be disastrous.

29. The LXX reads *kata kauma* "against burning heat" (< *beḥōm* [?]), which possibly is original (so Gemser, *Sprüche,* p. 91), but this probably represents another of its free renderings (McKane, *Proverbs,* p. 585).

30. Or "those who . . . masters" (so LXX, Targ., Syr., not Vulg.). *Šōleḥāyw* and *'adōnāyw* are probably honorific, not countable, because *'adōnāyw* is typically honorific, and probably one ruler, not several, assigned the one envoy his mission (*IBHS,* p. 123, P. 7.4.3c, e; cf. 1 K. 16:24; Isa. 19:4). Gemser (*Sprüche,* p. 91) thinks that verset B is an addition or, better, that a verset has dropped out. But verset B is essential for the proper interpretation of the proverb and requires no parallel.

31. The *athnach* dictates connecting the predicator with verset A (*IBHS,* p. 661, P. 39.3.3b).

32. The LXX reads *epiphanestata* "are evident," perhaps having read *'yn* "eye," which was invested with the sense of "having considered." According to this reading, rain accompanies the clouds and wind, but the Targ., Syr., and Vulg. read with the MT.

15 *Through patience a ruler is persuaded,*[33]
and a soft tongue shatters[34] *a bone.*
16 *[If] you have found honey, eat what you require,*
lest you have more than enough of it and vomit it.
17 *Make your foot scarce [and turn away] from your neighbor's house,*
lest he have more than enough of you and hate you.
18 *A war club,*[35] *or a sword, or a sharpened arrow*
is a man who testifies against his neighbor as a false witness.
19 *A decaying*[36] *tooth or a turned*[37] *foot*
is reliance[38] *on*[39] *a treacherous person in the time of adversity.*

33. The Syr. points the form as active.

34. The Syr. adds b^e before "tongue" and probably takes the pointed verb as passive: "by a soft tongue a bone is broken."

35. Although all the ancient versions and most modern English versions (NAB, NASV, NJPS, REB, NIV, NRSV, et al.) render *mēpîṣ* as a club of some sort, R. Van Leeuwen (*Context and Meaning in Proverbs 25–27* [SBLDS 96; Atlanta: Scholars, 1988], p. 59) understands it as the *Hiphil* participle of *pûṣ* or an equivalent noun (= "a scatterer with a sword and sharpened arrow"). He validates this interpretation by the use of *pûṣ* with arrows in Pss. 18:14(15) and 144:6 and by the other occurrence of *mēpîṣ* in Nah. 2:1(2). However, in both psalms the object is clearly the collective enemy, and there is no warrant in Prov. 25:18 to add to the text "enemy." The text and meaning of *mēpîṣ* in Nah. 2:1(2) are as debatable as in Prov. 25:18, and so the argument is circular. Therefore it is better to emend the text to *mappēṣ* "mace" with the vast majority of translators or to consider *mēpîṣ* its by-form.

36. *Rōʿâ* is parsed as a *Qal* fem. ptcp. of II *rʿʿ*, an equivalent of *roʿaʿâ* (see GKC, P. 67s), and glosses the verb that means "smash, shatter" (see 18:24; *HALOT,* 3:1,270-71, s.v. II *rʿʿ*) in a way appropriate to a modification of tooth.

37. Parsing *mûʿādet* as a *Pual* ptcp. fem. sing. of *mʿd* without preformative *mem* (see GKC, P. 52s), instead of repointing it as *môʿādet,* a *Qal* fem. sing. ptcp. of that root *(pace HALOT,* 2:609, s.v. *mʿd). Mʿd* occurs four times in the *Qal,* always of turning or slipping in connection with locomotion: of an ankle (Ps. 18:36[37] = 2 Sam. 22:36[37]), foot (Ps. 12:5), steps (Ps. 37:31), and in parallel with "walk" (Ps. 26:1). In the *Hithpael* it may mean "to be bent," of the loins/back (Ps. 69:23), though it is normally glossed "to shake." In the *Pual* it has its factitive meaning "to have been made turned" (*IBHS,* p. 419, P. 25.2a), hence the gloss, "lame."

38. Gemser (*Sprüche,* p. 92) prefers with the LXX to delete *mibṭāḥ* but offers no explanation for its addition in the MT. The LXX in fact, due to other textual corruptions, presents a different proverb: "The way of the wicked and the foot of the transgressor shall perish in an evil day." In spite of *qāmeṣ* the noun is in the cons. state (see *HALOT,* 2:542, s.v. *mibṭāḥ*).

39. Genitive of mediated object (*IBHS,* pp. 146-47, P. 9.5.2d and so most translations and commentators). The grammar allows a subjective gen., "the confidence of a treacherous person" (so Toy, *Proverbs,* p. 466), but one would have expected his ground of hope, such as wealth or power (14:26), to be mentioned. Also, the notion of a failed neighbor better fits v. 18, with which it is probably paired (see vv. 18-19).

20 *One who puts off*[40] *a garment on a cold day,*
[one who pours][41] *vinegar on a wound,*[42]
[is] one who sings songs[43] *to a heavy heart.*[44]
21 *If the one who hates you is hungry, give him food to eat,*
and if he is thirsty, give him water to drink.

40. Interpreting the *Hiphil* ptcp. of *ʿdh,* which in its one other occurrence in the *Qal* means "to walk along" (Job 28:8), to signify "causes his garment to pass along (from him)." The notion of "remove," "put off," is also attested in the causative stems of Aramaic dialects. In the Syriac causative stem it means "to rob, snatch away," and one of its meanings in the Arabic cognate is "to pounce on, attack" (see *HALOT,* 2:789, s.v. I *ʿdh*).

41. The preposition "on" implies a verb of motion (*IBHS,* p. 224, P. 11.4.3c).

42. G. R. Driver ("Problems and Solutions," *VT* 4 [1954] 240-41), followed by the REB and NRSV, derives *nāter* from Arab. *natru(n)* "plunging a weapon deeply in" and *natratu* "a deep wound." The LXX supports him. Plöger (*Sprüche,* p. 296) thinks that *neteq* "scab" is also an option. The traditional interpretation (see Sym., Targ., Vulg., KJV, NIV, NJPS, et al.) renders it as natron (a carbonate of soda), not nitre (nitrate of soda), because in its only other occurrence it is used for soap (Jer. 2:22). Curiously, this is the only meaning given in *HALOT* (2:737, s.v. *neter*), and *NIDOTTE* (3:216, s.v. *neter*). But the meaning "natron" should be rejected. First, the figure of vinegar on natron is ambiguous. Meinhold believes that it signifies the ineffectiveness of singing to a sad heart: "If vinegar were added, it [the natron] was neutralized, dissolved and thereby deprived of its effect. It would be correspondingly senseless and useless, and also tactless, to sing to a burdened mind" (Meinhold, *Sprüche,* 2:429). Others contend that it refers to the resulting effervescence. To Oesterley *(Proverbs)* that connotation signifies to cheer one up; to Scott (*Proverbs,* p. 156), the adding of one bitter thing to another; and to Cohen (*Proverbs,* p. 170), irritation: "Singing songs to a heavy heart throws it into a sour, angry fermentation, as when *natron* is cast into a pot of vinegar (Thomson)." D. Kellermann *(TDOT,* 4:491, s.v. *ḥmṣ)* argues that it means the opposite of that. According to him, as vinegar, an acid, neutralizes soda, this proverb commends the soothing, beneficial effect of singing in the same way that David's playing succeeded in dispelling Saul's "evil spirit" (1 Sam. 16:15-23). But Kellermann's interpretation is incongruous with the first, which should have been "like putting *on* [not *off*] a garment on a cold day." Second, natron, being insentient, would feel no pain, and so it too is not as well suited to the discomfort and insensibility of removing a robe on a cold day, as the sting of vinegar on a wound.

43. Lit. "with the songs." Delitzsch (*Proverbs,* p. 166) thinks that definite songs are in view, but more probably the article is generic (*IBHS,* p. 244, P. 13.5.1f). Driver ("Problems and Solutions," pp. 241-42) emends the text to read *bᵉšārîm* "among the singers." According to him, the meaning of verset B "is that one reveller with a heavy heart spoils good company." His emendation depends on his mistaken emendation of verset A as well.

44. The LXX reads: "As vinegar is bad for a wound, so trouble befalling the body afflicts the heart. As a moth in a garment, and a worm in wood, so the grief of a man hurts the heart." Since only the first clause fits the text of the MT, an original Hebrew *Vorlage* cannot be reconstructed convincingly from the version (so also Gemser, *Sprüche,* p. 92; *pace* Driver, "Problems and Solutions," pp. 240-42).

22 *for burning coals you are taking [and heaping] on his head,*
and the LORD will repay you.
23 *Like a north*[45] *wind that brings forth rain,*
a sly[46] *tongue, a face*[47] *struck by a curse.*[48]
24 *Better is dwelling on a corner of a roof*
than "in" a house shared with a contentious[49] *wife.*[50]
25 *Cold water to a weary person*[51]
and a good report from a distant land.
26 *A muddied spring, a ruined fountain,*
[is] a righteous person who sways before the wicked.
27 *To eat honey excessively*[52] *is not good;*
nor is it honorable to search out weighty matters.[53]

45. Torczyner needlessly emends the text to *ṣᵃpōn* ("hold," i.e., "hold your anger [*rûaḥ*]"), but J. P. M. Van der Ploeg, "Proverbs 25:23," *VT* 3 [1953] 189-91) emends the text to *Qal* passive ptcp. *ṣāpûn* ("the hidden wind"), presumably coming from some hidden or mysterious place.

46. Lit. "that speaks in secrecy," a gen. of location (*IBHS,* p. 147, P. 9.5.2f).

47. Pl. of composition (cf. REB, NJPS), though Delitzsch (*Proverbs,* p. 169; cf. NIV, NRSV) holds that it is a countable pl. because slander affects "the mutual relationships of men."

48. The LXX interpreted *lšwn str* as subject and *pnym nzʿmym* as object but added *erethizei* ("provokes") without warrant. The Vulg., Sym., some early Jewish commentators (not Rashi), KJV (not NKJV), and REB also confounded the subject and object. The Vulg. et al. understood *tḥwll* in verset A to mean "drives away." The REB, probably following Torczyner, emends it to "holds back." With these mistaken understandings of the verb, they take *gšm* as its subject.

49. Q corrects *mdwnym* of K to *midyānîm.*

50. See the notes at 21:19.

51. Or "throat" (see *nepeš;* I: 90).

52. *Harbôt* could be taken as the subject and *ʾākōl* as its object (i.e., "To multiply eating . . ."), but more probably it functions as an equivalent to the inf. absolute *harbēh,* either as an attributive adjective (BDB, p. 915, s.v. I *rābâ*) or as an adverb *(HALOT,* 3:1,177, s.v. I *rbh).* Was it chosen over *harbēh* for its assonance with *ʾākōl?*

53. Prov. 25:27b is notoriously difficult. The MT, which reads "searching out their glory is glory," seems corrupt. The pronominal suffix of *kbdm* has no antecedent; "God" and "king" of v. 2 are too far removed. Also, the relation of MT's versets is unintelligible. The LXX reads *timan de chrē logous endoxous* (< *wḥqr* [*Hiphil* impv. of *yqr* "to be rare/precious"] *dibrê kābôd* = "one must honor glorious words"). Frankenberg (cited by Toy, *Proverbs,* p. 470) et al. (cf. RSV, but not NRSV) interpret the same retroverted text to mean, "so be sparing of complimentary words." However, the track record of the LXX in this book does not inspire confidence in retroverting an original Hebrew text. Moreover, the parallelism is not good. Verset A pertains to self-restraint for one's own good (cf. v. 16), but verset B, according to this alternative, pertains to restraining compliments for the good of others. How would restricting honors to others hurt the speaker? Finally, Frankenberg's interpretation eliminates a probable *inclusio* with v. 2. The Syr. and Targ. read "to search glorious things is not [good]"

Bryce noted that the composition of 25:2-27 has its own special structure and its own particular content.[54] The chiastic *inclusio kbd . . . ḥqr dbr* ("glory . . . to search out a matter," v. 2b) and *ḥqr . . . kbd mikkābēd* ("to search out a weighty matter is without glory," v. 27b) frames the collection. He also noted the chiastic *inclusio dbš . . . 'kl* ("honey . . . eat," v. 16a) and *'kl dbš* ("eat honey," v. 27a), creating the second half of the composition (vv. 16-27). Van Leeuwen further noted

---

(< *ḥqr kebôdîm lō'-ṭôb*), not representing the final *kbwd* of the MT and of the LXX. Since it is unlikely either that *lō'-ṭôb* would be repeated in verset B or that verset B would be retroverted to the metrically implausible *ḥqr kbdm,* it is best not to regard *kbdm kbwd* of the MT as dittography. The Vulg. reads, *Sic qui scrutator est maiestatis opprimitur [a] gloria* "so the one who searches for glory will be overwhelmed/crushed/distressed by glory" (< *weḥōqēr kābôd mkbd*). A. A. MacIntosh ("A Note on Proverbs 25–27," *VT* 20 [1970] 112-13) thinks that Jerome pointed *mkdb* as a *Hophal* participle *(mokbād),* but the *Hiphil* of *kbd* "to cause to be heavy/dull/glorious" never means, "to deal heavily with/oppress," not even in Isa. 9:1 (8:23), and the *Hophal* of *kbd* is otherwise unattested. Driver ("Problems in the Hebrew Text," p. 191) also reads *mekubbād* but retains *weḥeqer* in the sense of either "but the search for or the contempt of honour is honourable [cf. Isa 58:13]." Delitzsch (*Proverbs,* pp. 171-72) a century earlier rejected the alleged Arabic cognate because "it must here remain without example." Moreover, the proverb, like vv. 11-14, 18-20, 23-26, 28, is probably comparative, not a unique antithetical proverb in this chapter. Bühlmann questionably explains the 3rd person pl. suffix of *kbdm* as an impersonal pronoun and understands *kābôd* to mean "burden" with an appeal to Isa. 22:23-24: "The quest for glory is onerous" (REB), but Van Leeuwen ("Proverbs xxv 27 Once Again," *VT* 36 [1986] 110) says, "In the two proverbial instances of a suffix without an antecedent known to me (xiv 26, xx 16), the singular is used in a semantic context adequate for understanding. Such a context is lacking in xxv 27b." Moreover, *kābôd* does not mean "burden" in Isa. 22:23 (cf. NRSV). Delitzsch (*Proverbs,* p. 171) points *kbdm* as *kebēdîm* (i.e., "but as an inquirer to enter on what is difficult is honor"), but an antithetical parallel is unlikely. Van Leeuwen ("Proverbs xxv 27," p. 113) reads *kebēdîm* but regards *lō'* of verset A as doing double duty (= "is not glory") with an appeal to the Syr. and Targ. for gapping *lō',* but they gap *lō' ṭôb,* which is not the same thing. Nevertheless, *lō'* could extend its influence (GKC, P. 152z). The AV, NJPS, NIV, and NRSV seem to have accepted this expedient while retaining the reading *kebôdam* ("nor is it honorable to seek honor"), but in this case it seems "harsh" (Kidner, *Proverbs,* p. 161). Moreover, they run roughshod over the suffix and invest *ḥqr* with a questionable meaning (see the preceding note). The better solution is to read either *weḥeqer kebēdîm mikkābôd,* understanding the second *mem* as dropped by haplography, or to read *weḥeqer kābēd mikkābôd,* with a simple transposition of *mem* and interpreting it as privative = "the searching out of [a] difficult things[s] is apart from/free from/without glory"; i.e., "or is it honorable to inquire into glory?" Sing. *kābēd* is better than pl. because *ḥqr* is used with the sing. *dābār* in v. 2, and this alternative is simpler. In any case, *kābēd* is an adjectival substantive for *dābār kābēd* "weighty matter." Although reading *kbdym,* G. Bryce ("Another Wisdom Book in Proverbs," *JBL* 91 [1972] 150) supports this interpretation from Jer. 17:10, where "examining words" is parallel to eating food, and from the use of *ḥqr* with *dbr* in v. 2. This would also help to explain the LXX use of *logous.* Finally, this interpretation of v. 27b forms an excellent *inclusio* with 27:2.

54. Bryce, "Another Wisdom 'Book' in Proverbs," pp. 145-57.

that the pattern *rš*ʿ . . . *ṣdq* (v. 5) in the second proverb pair (vv. 4-5) chiastically matches *ṣdq* . . . *rš*ʿ in the penultimate verse (v. 26). The contrast between "righteous" and "wicked" occurs in only these two verses in Collection C. Whereas the external *inclusio* pertains to inquiry and glory (vv. 2-3, 27), the second pertains to the righteous versus the wicked (vv. 4-5, 26). Conceptually the two proverbs that occur in the third from the end position liken a refreshing messenger/message to cold snow/water (25:13, 26). The partition of the unit into two halves is strengthened by ending each with a single proverb, each of which stands quite apart in syntax and thought from the preceding proverbs, which mostly occur in pairs. Van Leeuwen also perceived that the second partial unit consists of two parts, marked off by the chiastic *inclusio ʾkl śnʾk* (v. 16) and *śnʾk [h]ʾkl[hû]* (v. 21), dividing this half into vv. 16-22 and 23-27.

The introduction to the composition, which consists of the two proverb pairs (vv. 2-3, 4-5), presents the composition's two themes that set the parameters of meaning within which all its saying are to be interpreted. Verses 2-3 establish the God-king-subject hierarchy, and vv. 4-5 posit the fundamental conflict between the righteous and the wicked that permeates every area of human life. The first half of the body (vv. 6-15) pertains to the first theme, and the second half (vv. 16-27) to the second theme. Each half ends with a unique single-line proverb (vv. 15 and 27). Moreover, the third verse from the end of each section (vv. 13 and 25) uses the imagery of refreshing coolness for the positive effect a message has on a person (Heb. *npš*). Van Leeuwen also observed the matching of positive (+) and negative (-) Sayings (S) and admonitions (A) in the body of the two halves. In sum, he analyzes the composition as follows:

Introduction		S:	+	(vv. 2-5)
Body	I	A:	-	(vv. 6-10)
		S:	+	(vv. 11-15; except for v. 14)
	IIA	A:	-	(vv. 16-17)
		S:	-	(vv. 18-20)
	IIB	A:	+	(vv. 21-22)
		S:	-	(vv. 23-27; except for v. 25)[55]

a. Introduction (25:2-5)

(1) God-King-Subject Hierarchy (25:2-3)

The double lexical links in versets B, "kings" *(mᵉlākîm)* plus the verbal root "search" *(ḥqr),* show that vv. 2-3 are a proverb pair. Its theme pertains to the

55. Van Leeuwen, *Context and Meaning,* p. 64.

glory of God and kings, who are brought into close proximity to God but are clearly subordinate to him (cf. 14:35; 16:1-9, 10-15; 24:22). Both obtain glory by their inscrutability. Their parallel A versets pertain to God, and their B versets pertain to the king. Although v. 3a does not mention God, "heavens and earth" refers only to God's activity. The parallelism between their A and B versets shows that the ambiguous "matter" *(dābār)* in v. 2a refers at least to God's acts in creation and in v. 2b to the king's activity in statecraft. The noun, though repeated, does not cover the same semantic range. The king cannot transgress the boundaries to the hidden things of God. According to their versets B, kings obtain glory by their thorough investigation of a matter (v. 1b), yet their knowledge, motives, and plans remain inscrutable to their subjects (v. 2b). Since their inscrutability refers to matters of statecraft in v. 2b, we may assume that the matter God searches out (v. 1b) also refers to the sphere of his rule. Likewise, since God's acts in creation remain obscure (v. 3a), he obtains glory by concealing this vast and complex activity. God and kings obtain glory *(kābôd)* among their subjects by respectively covering and uncovering a matter (v. 2); both are unfathomable and inscrutable within their own realms (vv. 2-3). The king searches out the affairs of state (v. 2b), but no one, not even the king, penetrates and comprehends the vast extent and complexity of the Creator's acts in the universe (v. 3a). God's inscrutability even to the king sets him high above the king. On the other hand, none of the king's subjects can comprehend his own vast knowledge and penetrate his motives, setting him high above them (cf. Deut. 29:29[28]; Job 26:14; Rom. 11:33-36). In sum, vv. 2 and 3 set up a hierarchy of wisdom, authority, and power: God, king, subjects. The intention of the proverb pair depends to some extent on the addressee. If referred to the king, it stimulates him to rule humbly below God and both to investigate the matters of his realm thoroughly and to play his own cards close to his chest. If referred to his officials and/or subjects, it warns them that the king, who stands next in rank to God, has the capacity to search them out and take appropriate action, while he keeps them in the dark. Both God and the king are awesome and are not to be toyed with.

2 The synthetic parallels of v. 2 begin with "glory" *(kābôd)* plus genitive ("of God"/"of kings") plus infinitive construct ("to hide"/"to search"). This anaphora and the epiphora (see 3:27) couple the glory of kings with that of God but radically contrast the sources of their glory. The singular God stands over against the several kings. *To hide (hastēr)* means to conceal from sight.[56] *A matter (dābār)* may signify a word/speech or thing. The two

56. *Str* occurs 43 times in the *Hiphil.* Twenty-seven times it refers to God hiding his face so as not to look with favor and answer prayer (e.g., Deut. 31:17; Isa 8:17; passim). It is used 11 times with a personal object and means to hide someone for the sake of

can be attenuated from the word/speech to the matter represented by them/it (cf. 11:13; 17:9). Here it has its general sense of "thing."[57] More specifically, the use of the name God, not *YHWH,* and the reference to the heavens and earth in v. 3 of this proverb pair suggest that *dābār* signifies the mysteries in God's acts of creation.[58] *Glory* [see 3:16] *of God* (*'ᵉlōhîm;* see I: 68) means that glory comes to God or is bestowed on him. Solomon's choice of the generic name for God (*'ᵉlōhîm*) instead of *YHWH* is significant because its use here as in 3:5 cannot be explained away as a stock-in-trade parallel (cf. 2:5; 30:9), nor its association with foreigner (2:17). Solomon chose this name because it refers to the transcendent Creator of the vast "heavens . . . and earth" (v. 3a). *And* joins the synthetic parallels. *To search out* (see 18:17) may be to investigate and penetrate human motives and deeds in judical matters (Job 29:16; Prov. 28:11). It has this technical sense in Mishnaic Hebrew. Similarly, *a matter (dābār)* also has this judicial reference.[59] Indeed, the extension of the meaning of *dbr* from thing to matter may have come through the language of law (i.e., the words denoted a case that was handed down in legal proceedings and in popular assemblies).[60] This judicial reference best fits 25:4-5, 6-10; cf. 2 Sam. 14:17; 18:13; 1 K. 3:28; 10:3). *Is the glory of kings* (*kᵉbōd mᵉlākîm;* see 16:10-15). In sum, God obtains his social dignity by hiding his wisdom in his acts of creation,[61] and kings get theirs by searching out the affairs of state (see vv. 2-3). Aitken comments: "The king has a duty to be well on top of the affairs of state, to keep a close eye on how his ministers are carrying out their duties, and to keep himself well-informed about the cir-

---

protection (cf. 22:3; cf. Exod. 3:15; 2 K. 11:2). In its five occurrences with impersonal objects, it means merely to conceal from sight, to prevent from being seen or discovered (cf. 1 Sam. 20:2; Job 3:10; Ps. 119:19; Prov. 25:2; Isa. 29:15).

57. Cf. W. H. Schmidt, *TDOT,* 3:105, s.v. *dābhār.*

58. Van Leeuwen argues: "Job 28, though coming from a different sphere in the wisdom tradition, illumines the language and meaning of our text. Men search (*ḥqr,* Job 28:3) the uttermost recesses of the cosmos for gold, silver, and gems . . . ; that which is hidden (v. 11) man brings to light. But wisdom is hid (*n'lmh*) from the eyes of all living, and concealed (*nstrh*) . . ." (vv. 20-21). God alone understands and knows its place, for he created and 'established' and searched it out (*hkynh . . . ḥqrh,* v. 27; cf. *kwn* in Prov 25:5)." Van Leeuwen also believes that his hidden wisdom comprises God's plans and judgment in history (cf. Gen. 18:17) (*Context and Meaning,* p. 75). Although the verbs "to hide" and "to search out" can be used in this connection, the parallelism between vv. 2a and 3a tends to rule out that interpretation.

59. "The Akkadian expression *amātam amāru* 'to investigate an affair,' which is equivalent to *dīnam amāru* 'to investigate a case,' provides us with the semantic parallel to *ḥqr dbr* as a legal phrase" (Van Leeuwen, *Context and Meaning,* p. 77).

60. Schmidt, *TDOT,* 3:104, s.v., *dābhār.*

61. Cf. Deut. 29:29(28); 1 K. 8:12; Job 11:7-9; 26:14; 28:20-28; Ps. 77:13-14(14-15); Prov. 30:2-4; Eccl. 3:11; 8:17; Isa. 40:12-14; 45:15.

cumstances of the common people."[62] To act as a wise judge is an essential part of the kingly glory, which entails the ability to search out the heart of a matter or conflict *(dbr, ryb)* (cf. 1 K. 3:9, 16-28). Van Leeuwen notes that the shift from the cosmic (v. 2a) to the historical or judicial (v. 2b) is common (cf. Job 11:7-10) and functions to integrate the social order within the cosmic.[63]

As in Prov. 11:22; 24:26; 25:11, 12, 14, 18, 19, verset A presents the things compared, "the heavens . . . and earth," and verset B, the subject, "the heart of kings." In an enjambment, however, they are syntactically combined in a nominative absolute construction glossed by *as for.* The *tertium quid,* the "third thing" in terms of which their likeness or their agreement in kind is proposed, is that "there is no searching." *The heavens* (3:19) here refers to both the visible sphere of the dome of the sky and the air far above the surface of the earth (Gen. 1:6-8), probably not as the home of divine beings (Eccl. 5:2[1]; Ezek. 1:1). The addition *with reference to height* (21:4) emphasizes its highness above human beings, who are restricted to the earth (cf. 30:4). In agreement with one of the ancient Babylonians' views of cosmology, the Hebrews viewed the total universe either tri-partly, as "heaven, earth, and seas" (Exod. 20:11), or bi-partly, as "heaven *and the earth*" (see 3:19; 2:1). The Old Testament frequently uses "the heavens and the earth" as a merism for the vast and complex cosmos (i.e., the organization of everything everywhere). As the sky extends to apparently limitless heights above the surface of the earth, *with reference to depth* emphasizes the apparently limitless extent of the earth far below humankind's feet. The merism suggests that the unfathomable depths below the earth, not the Underworld, is in view.[64] It alludes implicitly to the sovereign Creator who made the profound and complex universe (cf. 30:1-4; Job 26:14; 38:1–39:30; Ps. 115:15-16; Hab. 3:4). No king, no sage, has ever gone up to heaven and come down, nor has one entered the depths of the earth and come back to understand and penetrate the subtle and baffling universe (cf. Job 38:4). All the kings put together succeed only partially in unraveling its mysteries. In the same way none of the king's subjects has penetrated the profundity and inscrutability of his resourceful heart. *And* coordinates *the heart* [see I: 90] *of kings* [see v. 2b]. *There is no* [see 13:4] *searching* (*ḥēqer;* see v. 2b). The parallelism between the vast universe and the immeasurableness of the king's heart takes the breath away. Moreover, Van Leeuwen observes, "The stereotyped expression *'yn ḥqr* is used only of God and of his

62. Aitken, *Proverbs,* p. 216.

63. Van Leeuwen, *Context and Meaning,* pp. 76-77.

64. Normally the Underworld is expressed by *'ereṣ taḥtît* "netherworld" (Ezek. 31:14) or *taḥtîyôt 'āreṣ* "the depths of the earth" (Isa. 44:23), but in some passages *'ereṣ* alone may mean the Underworld (cf. Isa. 26:19; Jon. 2:6[7]).

works in creation and judgment [Job 5:9; 9:10; Ps. 145:3; Isa. 40:28; cf. Job 34:24; 36:2] except in 25:3, where it is applied to the king's heart. This unites the king's glory and wisdom with that of God, but only with respect to those beneath the king."[65] As in 16:10-15, the ideal king is in view. Nevertheless, the spiritual person is even greater than the king (1 Cor. 2:15-16).

(2) The Conflict of the Righteous and the Wicked in Court (25:4-5)

The next proverb pair is linked with the preceding by *mlk* "king" (vv. 2b, 3b, 5a) and by advancing the activity of the wise king in investigating matters of state to his elimination of wicked officials. Initial anaphoric "remove" firmly binds vv. 4-5 together. As the double lexical connection of "glory . . . matter" that linked 25:2a and b prepared the way for the double lexical link of "kings . . . search," binding together vv. 2-3, so also the figurative comparison of the inscrutability of the cosmos (v. 3a) before the real topic of the king's inscrutability (v. 3b) prepares the way for the figurative comment of purifying silver in v. 4 to the tenor of the real topic of purifying the king's officials in v. 5.[66] As the silversmith can only produce a precious vessel with silver that has been purified of dross (v. 4), so a king's throne (i.e., a dynasty) can endure only when wicked officials are removed from the king's presence (cf. 20:8, 26; cf. Isa. 1:21-26; 6:27-30; Ezek. 22:18-22; Mal. 3:2). The conditional protases of their A versets mention only the hard and skillful negative actions of removal of the dross/wicked that a refiner/wise king must undertake to secure their goal. The subsequent manufacture of the vessel is blanked, for the emphasis is on purification, not on manufacturing. The refiner's pure vessel illustrates the king's pure, valuable, and, above all, enduring throne. Removing unscrupulous officials and corruption and replacing them with nobles ready to help the poor and needy is a standard task for all kings, both within and outside Israel (cf. Ps. 101:4-8; Prov. 14:34; Mal. 3:3, 17, 18; Matt. 13:41-43).[67] Perhaps the proverb does not address the king directly so that all servants and officials may feel as though they are also being addressed (cf. 14:35).[68]

65. Van Leeuwen, *Context and Meaning,* pp. 75-76. Van Leeuwen adds: "It is a measure of the collapse of Saul's royal character that he reveals (*glh;* cf. Prov 28:2) and cannot conceal *(ystr)* any matter *(dbr)* from his son Jonathan (1 Sam. 20:20). Jonathan merely has to 'sound out' *(ḥqr)* his father (29:12)."

66. In their A versets "remove dross" = "remove a wicked official," and "silver" = "king." In their B versets "then comes forth" = "is established," "the refiner" = "through righteousness," and "vessel" = "his throne."

67. Van Leeuwen, *Context and Meaning,* pp. 79-80, questionably relates the proverb to Solomon's initial acts as king (1 Kings 2). But 1 Kings 2–3 contrasts Solomon's own acts of wisdom (1 Kings 2) with his need for divine wisdom (1 Kings 3).

68. Cf. Meinhold, *Sprüche,* p. 420.

4 By using the two metallurgical functions of refining the ore and of casting the vessel, these synthetic parallels present the first activity (verset A) as the condition for the consequence of the second (verset B). The silversmith must remove the dross from the silver before he can cast a beautiful and lasting vessel. *Remove* is an elegant equivalent to a conditional clause: "if you remove."[69] *Dross* technically signifies "galina, silver dross."[70] *From silver (mikkāsep)* abruptly shifts to the refined state of the precious metal (see 2:4).[71] *And* represents a subsequent and subordinate situation to the preceding.[72] *Comes forth* (cf. 7:15; 25:8) "serves as a technical metallurgical term to describe the molten metal effluent which 'comes out' of the smelting process as refined and thus ready to cast."[73] The apparent *non sequitur* in Prov. 25:4 is simply due to the immediate connection between the process of refining metal in a crucible or cupel (cf. 17:3; 27:21) and the pouring out or casting of the refined metal into an artisan's mold (cf. Exod. 32:24; Job 23:10b; Isa. 54:16).[74] *For* signifies to the benefit of *the silversmith* (the refiner by smelting gold and/or silver; cf. 30:5). *A vessel* (see 20:15) is not further defined, and they range in size and shape from small flasks to large basins.

5 As with v. 4, this verse's synthetic parallels present first the prerequisite condition that wicked officials be removed from serving the king (v. 5a) and then the consequence that his throne will be firmly fixed through righteousness (v. 5b), which essentially repeats 16:12. The imprecise parallelism that involves "wicked official" and "by righteousness" suggests that

69. II *hgh* is a bi-form of *ygh* (cf. 2 Sam. 20:13), "to separate/remove/expel" (cf. its other use in Isa. 27:8). The *oratio variata* uses the initial inf. absolute as a surrogate for the impv. (*IBHS,* p. 593, P. 33.5.1a).

70. *HALOT,* 2:750, s.v. *sîg.*

71. A. Konkel *(NIDOTTE,* 3:244, s.v. *sîg)* describes the process: "Silver was found bound with lead ores and had to be separated in a two-stage process. The first stage consisted of reducing the lead ore to lead containing the silver. This process contained two steps: the lead ore (commonly galena) was heated leaving lead sulfate and lead oxide (litharge); the mixture was then heated in charcoal at a high temperature in a relative absence of air to reduce it to crude lead. The result of the smelting process was a small amount of silver (in practice usually less than one-half percent) with lead and other metals. . . . The second stage for the metallurgist to extract the silver from the crude lead was refined through a process known as cupellation. The metal was placed in a cupel, a shallow vessel made of a porous substance such as bone ash, and the furnace was heated until the molten lead was bright red; a blast of air turned it into lead oxide, which was absorbed by the cupel, leaving behind the silver."

72. *IBHS,* p. 547, P. 33.1.2f.

73. Van Leeuwen, "A Technical Metallurgical Usage of *ys*'," *ZAW* 98 (1986) 112-13.

74. Van Leeuwen, *Context and Meaning,* p. 113.

righteous officials will replace the wicked and that a self-serving official, like a rotten apple, sours his realm with his wickedness. The adjectival substantive *a wicked* (see I: 109) is glossed by wicked *official* because *before a king* (see 25:2-3) implies the syntagm "to stand before" and means "attend upon, be(come) a servant of."[75] In contrast to v. 4, the (con)sequential connection rests on the lexical connection between *remove* (see v. 4a) and "become fixed," not on the grammatical form of conjunctive *and. His throne* (see 9:14) refers to the king's chair that signified his superiority, honor, and power and symbolized his rule over the realm (cf. 2 Sam. 3:10; 7:13, 16; 14:9). *May be established* (see 16:3, 12) shows that chair functions as a metonymy for his dynasty (cf. 1 K. 2:24, 33; 8:25; 9:5; 2 K. 11:19; 2 Chr. 23:20). *By righteousness* (see I: 97) is the wisdom equivalent of keeping covenant faithfulness elsewhere in the Old Testament (cf. 2 Samuel 7).

b. A Decalogue of Proverbs for Courtiers (25:6-15)

The decalogue of proverbs pertaining to court behavior formally falls into two equal halves: admonitions (vv. 6-10) and sayings (vv. 11-15). Both forms contribute to the courtier's education: (1) humility (vv. 6-7a), (2) thorough preparation (vv. 7b-8), (3) confidentiality (vv. 9-10), (4) appropriate speech and accepting reproof (vv. 11-12), (5) reliability (vv. 13-14), and (6) tactful gentleness.

(1) Admonitions for Courtiers (25:6-10)

Van Leeuwen notes that the proverb pairs of the admonitions in vv. 6-10, like the two pairs in the introduction, have to do first with the hierarchy on the vertical axis of vv. 1-2 and to the opposition of good and evil on the horizontal axis. Verses 6-7a "concern the jockeying for power, position and glory" among the king's men, and vv. 7b-8 and 9-10 "concern legal disputes *(ryb)* among peers *(rʿ)* in which one is declared *sdyq* (in the right) and the other *rsʿ* (in the wrong)."[76]

6-7A Initial, and yet medial, "for" (v. 7a) and the catchword "before" (a king/noble, vv. 6a and 7aβ) bind together the admonition for humility with the prudent reason. The proverb pair cautions the courtier not to cross over on his own initiative into the higher social rank and dignity of the king and his nobles. It is better that superiors elevate him because his aptitude warrants it than that he outreach his limits and risk a reprimand and loss of face that will damage his career prospects (cf. Luke 14:8-11). The proverb

75. BDB, p. 764, *ʿāmad.*
76. Van Leeuwen, *Context and Meaning,* p. 80.

encourages the courtier to advance himself in the right way (cf. 1 Sam. 15:17; 18:18; 1 Kings 1:5, 30; Matt. 18:1-4; John 13:1-15; 3 John 9, 10).

6 This chiastic, essentially synonymous parallelism prohibits an ambitious courtier from hobnobbing with his superiors (cf. Jer. 45:5). The prohibitions in its outer frame present the anabasis of moving from a bumptious attitude of esteeming oneself as deserving deference (verset A) to the action of taking up the higher station (verset B). Its inner core specifies in a katabasis the space, moving from "in the presence of the king" (verset A) to "the place where men of rank and influence meet." *Do not honor yourself* (*tithaddar,* a denominative of *hādār* "splendor, majesty, dignity") distinguishes its possessor and sets him above and apart from his peers (see 20:29).[77] *Before a king* repeats v. 5a. *And (û)* combines two interrelated and overlapping situations. *In the place* has the more restricted sense of the court or some other place where influential people congregate (see 15:3). *Great* refers to *people* of rank and influence (see 18:16). *Do not stand* (see 12:7) cautions the courtier, who alone could face this temptation, not to take up a position with men of rank and influence. Esteeming himself as their equal, on his own initiative he appears with them to join them in their activities. Meinhold represents the situation literally: "It may rather deal with a (standing) audience with the king, which maintained a certain order according to rank of favor for the royal servants and other subordinates or officers with regard to their closeness to the ruler."[78]

7a *For* or "surely" signals that v. 7 substantiates the prohibitions of v. 6 (see 24:20). This comparative proverb contrasts two social situations in the high-low imagery "to come up" versus "to cause to be low." Though framed as a *better . . . than* proverb, verset Aa represents the courtier's promotion as an unqualified good situation, and verset Ab, his demotion as unqualifiedly bad. *He* [i.e., the king] *says* glosses *ʾᵃmor-,* which literally means, "saying" without specifying the speaker of the direct address. *To you* (i.e., the courtier) puts the original court setting beyond reasonable doubt. Spatial *come up* (see 21:22) symbolizes ascending to the higher social position of men of rank. *Here* refers to the "place" in v. 6. If superiors promote a courtier, he can enter their ranks confident that he merits their favor. If not, he anxiously fears the demotion that someone will inevitably inflict on him. The proverb does not address who or how the promotion or demotion will come about. *Than* refers to the situation to which verset A is being compared. *One*

77. This unique *Hithpael* probably has the estimative value of the *Piel,* signifying "esteem or present yourself as being magnificent/having splendor with the expectation that someone else will defer to you" without regard to the question of truthfulness (*IBHS,* p. 429, P. 26.2a; pp. 430-31, P. 29.6.f.).

78. Meinhold, *Sprüche,* p. 420.

humiliate you means literally "cause you to be low" and symbolizes bringing the courtier down to a lower social status because of his unwarranted elevation (see 16:19). *Before* [see 25:5, 6] *a noble* (see 19:6) entails deferring to the noble and yielding to his will.

7b-10 The proverb pairs 7b-8 and 9-10 are closely related to one another: lexically by "case/trial" (*rîb,* vv. 8a, 9a) and "peer" (*rēaʿ,* vv. 8b, 9a), syntactically by the negative admonitions "do not bring forth" (v. 8a) and "do not divulge" (v. 9b), by initial "lest" *(pen)* that introduces the negative consequences (vv. 8b, 10), and conceptually by career loss through shaming (vv. 8b and 10a). The permanency of his shame is expressed by "in its end" (v. 8bα) and "will not depart" (v. 10b). The first pair dissuades the courtier against impetuous litigation. The second urges him to plead (a well-prepared) case but not to breach a confidence to reclaim a right. The imperative "plead your case" of the second pair prevents a misinterpretation of the first. Conflicts have to be resolved but in the right manner; they must be thoroughly investigated (vv. 7b-8) and without gossip. The proverb pair moves from what you have seen as a firsthand witness (v. 7b) to what you have heard as a secondhand witness. Note the change from optical imagery to aural imagery. The catchword *rîb* with its probable sense of "trial/case," not merely strife, and the technical, forensic term "accusation" (v. 10b) points to the legal process as their situational context, not a personal feud. The addressee, "you," is the courtier, and "your peer" is his opposing litigant before "an arbiter" (*šōmēaʿ,* one who hears [the trial]). The reason given is that both impetuous litigation and divulging a confidence will ruin the courtier's career. These court exemplars teach not to jump to a conclusion merely on the basis of what one has seen, and in no quarrel should one breach a confidence. The impulsive and/or the disloyal gossipmonger will end up with a bad name.

7b-8a To humility this pair adds assiduous preparation. Initial "lest" in v. 8b and the address to "you" (i.e., the courtier) bond the proverb pair that admonishes not to rush to court (cf. 24:28). In an enjambment v. 7b presents the object, *what* [see n. 16] *your eyes have seen* (see 20:12), and v. 8a its subject and predicate. *Do not bring* [see n. 17] *hastily* [see n. 18; 1:16] *to trial* (see 3:30). Though one may be an eyewitness to a crime, he may have only a "keyhole" view of the situation and may misinterpret it. It is unclear whether the crime was against the addressee or whether he is a litigant in the case (cf. 18:17; 24:28). *Lest* (see 22:25) points to the potential negative consequences that abort a courtier's career should he lose the case to instill fear in the courtier so as not to be litigious and engage in unnecessary lawsuits (v. 8a; see 22:25). The rhetorical debasing and/or insulting question *what* (20:24) expects a negative answer, such as "I can do nothing!"[79] *Will you do* [see 13:16]

79. *IBHS,* p. 326, P. 18.3f, g.

in the time of *its end* (i.e., of going to court; see 5:11) assumes the disputant's failure. The rhetorical question aims to involve the courtier and to shame him by forcing him to answer that his career will be terminated or thwarted when his opponent exposes that he failed to investigate thoroughly what he saw and/or failed to grasp its import. His case will prove unsound *when* [b^e, introducing a sortal apposition that defines the end] *your peer* [see 3:28; the courtier] *puts you to shame (haklîm).*[80] *Klm* essentially denotes the state of being in public dishonor, ignominy, or shame as the result of a public defeat (18:13).[81] Our Lord advocated going to a brother to correct a wrong first alone, then with a brother, and only then to the church (Matt. 18:15-17). He "turns the whole subject of out-of court settlement into a parable of the fleeting day of grace: Matthew 5:25, 26."[82]

9-10 To thorough preparation, the new pair adds confidentiality. Verse 10 is linked with v. 9 by its initial "lest" *(pen),* by its continued second person address to the courtier, and by looking back to v. 9 for an appropriate object to "hear." The admonition gives priority to confidentiality over winning a case (v. 9; otherwise someone will expose the disloyal courtier and will heap permanent shame on him. Inferentially, the blame for not establishing truth by not supplying crucial information lies with the party with firsthand knowledge. A secondhand informer must not betray his informer.

9 The admonitions to plead a case and not divulge a confidence give priority to confidentiality over reclaiming what is right (see 11:13). *Plead* [see 3:30] *your case* [see 22:23] *with* [see 13:20] *your peer* (see 25:8) denotes persuasion in litigation to reclaim someone's right in a legal process[83] and clarifies not bringing forth evidence hastily in court (v. 8). It makes no difference whether the courtier is representing himself or someone else. *But* presents an exclusion of an overlapping and attendant circumstance, not an antithesis.[84] *Another's* [5:9] *confidence* (see 3:32) designates someone who is assumed to have had a close relationship with the courtier. *Do not ('al) disclose* (see 11:13). One should not smear another's name to clear his own or a

80. *Klm* in the *Hiphil* is glossed "to harm" (1 Sam. 25:7; Ruth 2:15), "to insult" (1 Sam. 20:34; Job 11:3; 19:3), and "to put to shame" (see *HALOT,* 2:480, s.v. *klm*). M. Klopfenstein, *Scham und Schande nach dem Alten Testament* [ATANT 62; Zürich: Theologischer, 1972], pp. 110-16, cited by Van Leeuwen, *Context and Meaning,* p. 57), established the visual component of *klm* in connection with Akk. *kullumu.*

81. For the sour fruit of impetuous strife see Judg. 9:26-40; 2 K. 14:8-12; 2 Chr. 35:21-24. "The considerate Christian will rather concede rights than insist upon them to the hazard of his own soul, and to the injury of the Church (1 Cor 6:1-7)" (Bridges, *Proverbs,* p. 466).

82. Kidner, *Proverbs,* p. 158.

83. BDB, p. 936, s.v. *rîb.*

84. *IBHS,* p. 651, P. 39.2.3b.

defendant's. "There is no success which is achieved at the price of your own integrity or someone else's hurt."[85] Besides, truth is not well served by gossip.[86]

10 *Lest* (*pen;* see 25:9) again signals the substantiation of the prohibition. Verset A represents the judge who hears the case as condemning the betrayer as guilty of disloyalty and spreading gossip, and verset B escalates the betrayer's shame from the moment to an accusation that sticks. *The arbiter* (or "mediator," *šōmēaʿ;* see 1:5; 15:31) invests "hearer" with its forensic sense (Deut. 1:16, 17; Judg. 11:10; 2 Sam. 14:16-17; 1 K. 3:9, 11; Job 31:35; Prov. 21:28) and connotes "who discerns the divulged confidence." According to Whitelam, Absalom was proposing the appointment of such a person during David's reign.[87] The *hap. leg. pronounce you guilty* of disloyalty (cf. Lev. 20:17) is glossed by others as "to shame" (see 14:34).[88] *And* joins the synthetic parallels. *The accusation against you* (*dibbātᵉkā;* see 10:18) glosses the rare root *dibbâ* "injurious report" in this forensic context and interprets the suffix as an objective genitive. The notion of "accusation" or "slander" entails hostility. *Never depart* means literally "will not return" (to the accuser; see 1:23; Isa. 55:11).

(2) Sayings for Courtiers (25:11-15)

The decalogue for proper court decorum now shifts to sayings.

11-12 To confidentiality add appropriate speech and reproof. Kidner captures the thematic connection between the parts of the sixth proverb pair of this unit by his own witticism: "finely said [v. 11], finely taken

85. Plaut, *Proverbs,* p. 258.

86. An Akkadian proverb considers a secret to be safe with children but not with an enemy: "My friend, my secret knowledge is not safeguarded by an enemy: on the contrary, by a son or daughter, my friend, is my secret knowledge safeguarded" (*ANET,* p. 425). Ahiqar (cf. 7.95-110) counseled, "More than all watchfulness watch thy mouth, and over what thou hearest harden thy heart. . . . First count the secrets of thy mouth; then bring out thy words by number." He (cf. 9.123-41) also cautioned, "Reveal not thy secrets before thy friends, lest thy name become despised of them" (*ANET,* pp. 428-29).

87. K. W. Whitelam, *The Just King: Monarchical and Judicial Authority in Ancient Israel* (Sheffield: JSOT, 1979).

88. *HALOT,* 1:336, s.v. I *ḥesed.* It makes little difference here whether negative *ḥesed,* a dominant meaning in Syriac, represents a polar use of positive *ḥesed* or is a homonym of another root (see H. J. Stoebe, *TLOT,* 2:449, s.v. *ḥesed*). The *Piel* is not privative of the positive use (i.e., "to take away kindness") because the negative noun *ḥesed* in Lev. 20:17, where it seems to mean "guilty," calls that interpretation into question. More probably the *Piel* of negative *ḥesed* is declarative estimative or, better, delocative (*IBHS,* pp. 402-4, P. 24.2f-g; so also, independently, Van Leeuwen, *Context and Meaning,* p. 58).

[v. 12]."[89] This proverb pair coheres phonologically *ʿal-ʾopnāyw/ʿal-ʾōzen* ("according to its circumstance"/"upon an ear"), lexically by "gold," syntactically by a double metaphor, each involving a precious metal and ornamentation, and conceptually by "a decision made"/"a wise arbiter." The harmony between a decision and its circumstance bestows beauty and value on the finely crafted mediation (v. 11), and the harmony between the reproving decision and its acceptance enhances its beauty and value (v. 12). The pair moves from the impersonal decision to the arbiter who fashions it, and from the impersonal circumstance for which it was crafted to the personal acceptance of its implicit reproof.

11 Verset A presents the figurative comment, the thing compared, and verset B, the real topic (cf. 11:22; 24:26; 25:3, 4-5). A proper decision is likened to gold apples, and the appropriate circumstance to a silver sculpture. *Apples (tappûḥê)*[90] *of gold* (see 11:22) was preferred to "golden apples" to connote the probability of their metal, not their color, as the parallel in v. 12a shows. *In a sculpture* [or image; see 18:11] *of silver* (see 2:4) means that the artist either engraved a sculptured figure or laid the apples in it. The sage is fond of comparing words with flowers and fruit (10:31; 12:14; 13:2; 17:20). M. Weinfeld comments on the active *dibbēr dābār,* of which *are a decision made (dābār dābūr)* is the passive counterpart: "a thorough examination of all occurrences of the idiom *dibbēr dābār* . . . reveals that in general it does not mean simply 'to speak a word' but rather 'to arrive at a decision through bargaining (usually at a gathering)" (cf. Judg. 11:11; 1 Sam. 20:23; 1 K. 12:7; Isa. 8:10; 58:13; Hos. 10:4).[91] *Appropriate to (ʿal)*[92] *its circumstance (ʾopnāyw)* glosses an obscure *hap. leg. HALOT* glosses it by "proper time,"[93] but Gemser and Van Leeuwen follow Orelli, cited by Delitzsch, in interpreting "proper time" as "the proper circumstance."[94] Orelli says, "A word is commended which is spoken whenever the precise time arrives to which it is adapted, a word which is thus spoken at its time as well as at its place, and the grace of which is thereby heightened."[95] The shape of the apple and perhaps the lovely

89. Kidner, *Proverbs,* p. 158.

90. *Tappûaḥ* occurs four times in Song, once in Joel 1:12, and here. Its attestation in other Semitic languages, both early and late, and in contexts of sauce, cider, etc. favors the fragrant apple or apple tree (Joel 1:12) over other fruit (*HALOT,* 4:1,773-74, s.v. I *tappûaḥ*). In the fortress of Kadesh at Mt. Sinai, more than 200 carbonized apples were found (O. Keel, *Das Höhelied,* p. 82, cited by Meinhold, *Sprüche,* 2:424). Its use in old Israelite place names suggests the antiquity and popularity of the fruit in ancient Israel.

91. M. Weinfeld, "The Counsel," *Maarav* 3 (1982) 43.

92. *IBHS,* p. 218, P. 11.2.13e.

93. *HALOT,* 1:79, s.v. *ʾōpen.*

94. Van Leeuwen, *Context and Meaning,* p. 59.

95. Delitzsch, *Proverbs,* p. 370.

fragrance associated with it refer to the loveliness of a proper decision, and the gold, to its great value. However, like a gold ring in a swine's snout, its beauty and value can be undone without the proper setting. Handing down the carefully crafted decision that in every way is proper to the circumstances of its composition and delivery (i.e., at the right time and in the right way) enhances its aesthetic impression and its moral influence. The proverb has broader application to any fitly spoken word or deed (Job 6:25; Eccl. 12:10; Isa. 40:1-4; 50:4; Luke 14:15; Eph. 5:14; 1 Tim. 6:13; 2 Tim. 2:15).

12 The matching proverb implicitly compares the wise arbiter who reproves the wrongdoer to establish what is right to a gold and ornate earring, and the one who listens, to the ear that wears it. The matching of a wise arbiter who finely crafts his decision with the one who listens and accepts his correction is just as lovely and precious as an exquisitely wrought gold earring on an ear. *A ring of gold* (*nezem zāhāb;* see 11:22) probably designates a man's "earring," not a woman's nose ring. *Even* interprets the conjunctive as epexegetical, because both the ring and ornament of verset A are implicitly pictured in verset B as "on the ear," even though in Hos. 2:13(15) *ḥelyâ,* the feminine doublet of *ḥᵃlî,* is probably distinguished, suggesting that the *nezem* is an earring and *ḥᵃlî,* a necklace. *An ornament* (or jewelry, *ḥᵃlî*) occurs elsewhere only in the plural in Song 7:1(2) to depict the graceful legs of the Shulammite. That text qualifies the noun as "the work of an artist's hands." Of [fine] gold *(ketem)* glosses a poetic synonym of *zāhāb,* to which it is parallel in Job 31:24.[96] *Is* glosses the predicate of this nominal clause. *A wise* [see I: 94] *arbiter* (*môkîaḥ;* see 24:25; cf. Isa. 29:21; Ezek. 3:26; Amos 5:10) glosses the more specific use of *ykḥ* (*Hiphil,* "to establish what is right in a lawsuit," "to reprove"; see 3:12). It can also signify "to decide what is right," "to mediate," "to maintain justice." In his handing down of the decision the mediator implicitly becomes "one that reproves the wrongdoer to establish justice" (Isa. 2:4; Mic. 4:3). This metonymy of cause represents the moral decision that comes *on* [see Deut. 32:2] *a listening ear* (see 15:31), a synecdoche for a person whose heart engages what he hears. This picture of healthy justice stands in sharp contrast to the scene in Amos 5:10.

13-14 The decalogue now adds reliability to confidentiality. The unit's seventh and final proverb pair is linked in its A versets by weather imagery involving unexpected contradictions (snow in harvest; clouds and wind without rain) and by the antonyms *ʾmn* "faithful" and *šqr* "he does not give."[97]

96. *Ketem* may refer either to fine or pure gold or to a place, like the "gold of Ophir" (R. Wakely, *NIDOTTE,* 2:740, s.v. *ketem*).

97. "The root *ʾmn* . . . , be faithful, true, sure, and its derivatives are the most appropriate antonyms to the root *šqr* and its derivatives" (Carpenter/Grisanti, *NIDOTTE,* 4:247, s.v. *šqr*).

Their topic pertains to faithfulness, positively (v. 13) and negatively (v. 14). The reliable envoy, who held a very high position in ancient Near Eastern politics,[98] refreshes his superior, giving him joy (v. 13). On the other hand, the unreliable windbag plays to the gallery and inflates his ego by promising a gift, but he defrauds and disappoints the expectant beneficiary.[99] "These verses return to the courtly hierarchical concern about relations with superiors, first in a positive sense (v. 13) and then in the negative sense of failed upward mobility (v. 14; cf. 18:16; 19:6; 21:14)."[100] Both the positive and negative proverbs admonish truthful words whatever one's socioeconomic status, to refresh another and give him joy and not to wither him and give him bitter disappointment.

13 In this synonymous parallelism, verset A presents both the figurative comment (Aa) and the topic (Ab), and verset B explains the simile of verset Aa.[101] The trustworthy envoy is likened to cold, refreshing drink during harvest. The meaning of the *hap. leg. the coolness* is gathered from Aramaic in this context and in Sir. 43:20 ("the cold north wind").[102] *Of snow* is used in various comparisons.[103] Though the simile is ambiguous, for unseasonable snow may be an unwelcome incongruity (see 26:1),[104] the B verset explains it to mean that the reliable envoy refreshes his master (cf. 13:17; 26:6; Acts 10:4-6, 25; 1 Cor. 16:17, 18; Phil. 2:25-30; 1 Thess 3:1-7). Probably the reference is to drinks cooled with snow. During the hot summers, laborers brought snow and ice from the high mountains and stored them in snow houses or snow caves; they were transported, for example, insulated by jute. The Mari letters (ARM 3.29; 13.32; 14.25, passim) attest to the antiquity of using snow in summer, and the references in Arabic sources to Saladin's Battle of Hattin in Galilee (A.D. 1187) attest to the geographical possibility. A traveler in 1608 first connected the common traditional eastern custom of cooling drinks with Prov. 25:13.[105] Meinhold thinks that "the lux-

98. A. D. Crown, "Messengers and Scribes: The *Sōphēr* and *Mazkîr* in the Old Testament," *VT* 24 (1974) 366-70.

99. Cf. McKane, *Proverbs,* p. 586.

100. Van Leeuwen, *Context and Meaning,* p. 83.

101. Versets Aa and Ab are connected by a chiastic assonance at their center of *qāṣîr* ("harvest") and *ṣîr* ("envoy").

102. *HALOT,* 3:1,037, s.v. *ṣinnâ.*

103. With reference to water, of the fruitfulness and effectiveness of God's word (Isa. 55:10); to melting, of vulnerability (Job 24:19); to flaking, of skin infection (Exod. 4:6; Num. 12:10), to whiteness, of purity (Ps. 51:7[9]; Isa. 1:18); to coldness, of refreshing (Prov. 25:13).

104. The LXX interprets the proverb as a reference to a snowfall in the heat, but this would be an unmitigated disaster.

105. So B. Lang, "Vorläufer von Speiseeis in Bibel und Orient: Eine Untersuchung von Spr 25,13," in *Mélanges bibliques et orientaux en l'honneur de M. Henri Cazelles* (AOAT 212; Neukirchener-Vluyn: Neukirchener, 1981), p. 219.

ury of beverages and other selected delicacies having been cooled in this way might only have been accessible to prominent circles."[106] The Bible (cf. 2 K. 4:18-20; cf. also Jdt. 8:2-3) reports a fatal heat stroke *at the time of* [see 24:10] *of harvest* (see 6:8). *A trustworthy* [or reliable; see 11:13] *envoy* (*ṣîr;* see 13:17; cf. 10:26 — probably chosen instead of its synonym *mal'āk* "messenger" for its assonance with *qāṣîr*) *to the one who sends him* to look into situations (see 10:26). "And" (*w^e*) semantically serves to explain the simile, glossed by *for.*[107] *He* [i.e., the faithful envoy] *refreshes* (*yāšîb nepeš*), that is, "he causes the *nepeš* to return"; see I: 90).[108] *His master* refers to the envoy's earthly, not heavenly, lord.[109] McKane explains: "Just as the cold water revives the stamina of the harvesters, banishing their fatigue and giving them new zest for their work, so a messenger who is completely trustworthy puts new life (*nepeš*) into his master. The knowledge that he counts unreservedly on the loyalty of this man and on the accuracy of his representations in any mission on which he is employed lightens his burden and fortifies him to carry his responsibilities."

14 The complementary proverb pairs the faithful envoy with the unfaithful boaster. Its puts in symbolic parallelism a man who makes himself glorious through a promised gift with clouds and rain, and the gift he promised but does not give with "there is no rain." As in its three other uses, *clouds* (II *n^{e}śî'îm;* cf. Jer. 10:13 [= 51:16]; Ps. 135:7) is a metonymy for thunder and lightning. *And* combines that with *wind* (see 15:4) into one complex thought. The expected climactic third of the meterological trio, *and rain* (*gešem*),[110] is instead climactically excluded by *no* (lit. "there is not"). "Most of the rains are from cyclonic storms traveling the length of the Mediterranean from the Atlantic; when the moist air moves over the land, it is forced to rise rapidly, producing heavy thunderstorms."[111] *A man* (*'îš;* see I: 89) designates an unspecified individual *who boasts* [or praises himself; see 20:14] *of a gift* to bring glory to himself in the eyes of others.[112] *He does not give*

106. Meinhold, *Sprüche,* pp. 425-26.

107. *IBHS,* pp. 649-50, P. 39.2.1c.

108. BDB, pp. 661, 999, s.v. *nepeš, šûb.*

109. "Generally speaking *'ādhôn* seems to mean 'the lord as the master,' while . . . *b'l* means the owners (cf. Ps. 105:21, where Joseph is called lord, *'ādhôn,* of Pharaoh's house, and "ruler" [*mōshēl*] of all his possessions") (O. Eissfeldt, *TDOT,* 1.61-62, s.v. *'ādhôn*).

110. Perhaps *gešem,* a precise semantic equivalent of *māṭār,* was chosen for its assonance with *gārem* in v. 15?

111. M. D. Futato, *NIDOTTE,* 1:901, s.v. *gešem.*

112. *IBHS,* p. 164, P. 10.2.1c. The six occurrences of *mattat* designate a gift in general in contrast to nominal derivatives from *nātan* (e.g., *'etnān* "wages of a harlot," *mattānâ* I "gifts for the sanctuary," etc.).

glosses *šāqer,* which signifies that the gift is in some way fraudulent (see 6:17). He boasts about the gift but intentionally distorts the factual reality to deceive another. The metaphor suggests that the boaster has loudly and with great fanfare promised his gift, exciting great expectations, and then sunk them in disappointment. It also connotes that the gift was essential for the well-being of the deceived. "No rain, no life. It was just that simple in OT times in the Promised Land."[113] Presumably the boaster deceived his victim to get something of value out of him. Instead of giving life, he takes it (cf. 2 Pet. 2:19; Jude 12).

15 This single verse without a counterpart brings the preceding seven proverbial pairs to closure. To the other virtues the pedagogic proverb adds gentleness. It forms an *inclusio* with vv. 2-3, featuring the relation to the superior in a hierarchy on a vertical axis in verset A, and the resolution of conflict by proper speech on a horizontal axis in verset B.[114] The reference to "the ruler" again suggests a court setting for the proverb. Through another figurative comment, it adds gentleness to the education of the young courtier on court etiquette and on how to perform his advocacy within the court.

The proverb functions as a janus between the topics of appropriate speech (vv. 7b-14) and showing restraint (vv. 16-17). "On the one hand it deals with word events like v. 13f.; however, on the other hand, it recommends a kind of restraint which also determines vv. 16ff."[115]

Its emblematic parallelism now matches the topic in verset A and the figurative comment, an unforgettable oxymoron, in verset B. The persuasion of the ruler is likened to the unconventional and difficult shattering of a bone, and the means is escalated from the persuader's inner patience to its outward expression in gentle (i.e., soothing, conciliatory, and non-offending) speech. *Through*[116] *patience* (*'ōrek 'appayim,* presumably a unique variant of *'erek 'appayim;* see 14:29) *a ruler* (*qāṣîn;* see 6:7) *is persuaded* (*y^{e}putteh;* see 1:10), presumably having a positive sense to persuade someone through speech to do the wise, not the foolish, thing. *And* combines two overlapping and related situations. *A soft* [see 15:1] *tongue* (see 6:17) is a metaphor and a metonymy for speech that soothes and comforts the listener's heart and does not hurt or pain him in any way (see 15:1). *Shatters (tišbor)* in the *Qal* signifies to break something to pieces with suddenness or violence, and in the *Piel* "to break up into pieces."[117] *Bone* (*gārem;* see 17:22) may have been chosen

113. M. D. Futato, *NIDOTTE,* 1:901, s.v. *gešem.*

114. Van Leeuwen, *Context and Meaning,* p. 82.

115. Meinhold, *Sprüche,* p. 426. With the preceding proverb pair, their final words share the assonance of *qāṣîr/qaṣîn* and of *gešem/gārem.*

116. *IBHS,* p. 197, P. 11.2.5d.

117. *IBHS,* pp. 396-400, P. 24.1.

because "the bones are the most rigid body parts inside of a person, and fracturing the bones here refers to breaking down the deepest, most hardened resistance to an idea a person may possess."[118] Moreover, the proscription among the Semites not to break a bone (Exod. 12:46; Num. 9:12) suggests the unusual and nonconventional (cf. Prov. 17:22). The courtier can bring another to his way of thinking through a patient, open, and warm disposition and through sensitive, tactful speech (cf. 14:17; 15:1; 16:14; 1 Cor. 9:20-22; Gal. 5:22-24; 2 Tim. 2:24-26). Conceivably, patience could be used in the service of injustice, but that cannot be thought of here. "Since a long-suffering person (14:29a; 15:18b; 16:32a) makes up a positive type of human being, the abstract notion can hardly refer to long-endurance to do wrong."[119]

c. General Human Conflicts (25:16-26)

The *inclusio* referring to the "ruler" in v. 15 (cf. v. 2) separates the unit of 25:2-27 into two subunits: vv. 2-15 and 16-27. The *inclusio* involving "eating" and "honey" (vv. 16, 27a) forms a frame around the second subunit. Whereas the first subunit (vv. 2-15) concerned matters of the royal court, these admonitions and sayings explore human conflict in general, though v. 18 returns to the court in a strict sense. Van Leeuwen notes also that the chiastic *inclusio* *'kl śn'k* (= "eat" and "hate you"; vv. 16-17) and *śn'k [h]'kl[hû]* (= "hate you" and "[give him to] eat"; v. 21) divides the second subunit into two partial subunits, vv. 16-22 and 23-27. "The word pair . . . binds together Admonitions that might otherwise be unconnected in the reader's mind. . . . In verses 16-17 'eating' runs the risk of creating a 'hater,' while in verses 21-22 the problem of the 'hater' is positively resolved by giving him something 'to eat.'"[120] The first partial subunit consists of admonitions (vv. 16-17, 21-22) and of sayings (vv. 18-20); the second, exclusively of sayings (vv. 23-27).

(1) Resolving Conflicts (25:16-22)

Without the positive admonition in vv. 21-22 to resolve conflict, vv. 16-22 present human conflict negatively and without resolution. A play on the *Leitwort* *r'* (*rēa'* ["neighbor"] and *rā'* ["evil"]) in every verse from 25:17 to 21 highlights this theme.

118. Garrett, *Proverbs,* p. 207.

119. Meinhold, *Sprüche,* pp. 426-27. Meinhold notes that *Die Ganze Welt* (58:4) also expresses the conviction that the soft tongue can break strong resistance: "The tongue is without bones, but it breaks bones."

120. Van Leeuwen, *Context and Meaning,* p. 70.

16-17 Admonitions for moderation and restraint in their A versets and the verbatim rationale for not overindulging in their B versets bind vv. 16-17 into a proverb pair. Even things as delightful and desirable as honey and as neighborliness can become loathsome through excess. Although v. 16 is a figurative comment on v. 17, resembling the proverbial pair of vv. 4-5 and the emblematic structure of vv. 11-12, 13-14, and 15, each of these proverbs also stands on its own two legs.

16 To the virtues in vv. 6-15, v. 16 adds moderation and self-control. Verset A admonishes not to overindulge in something even as sweet and beneficial as honey, and verset B substantiates it by asserting the negative consequence of gluttony. Verset Aa represents the good fortune of finding honey, and verset Ab, the admonition to eat (see 24:13) but to restrict the amount to what is agreeably sufficient. *If* [see 24:10] *you have found* (see 24:14) infers that the uniquely sweet and medicinal *honey* (see 5:3) is wild honey that one comes on accidentally without effort (cf. Judg. 14:8-9, 14, 18; 1 Sam. 14:26-27), adding to its pleasure. Meinhold comments: "[Wild honey] was produced by the wild bee *(apis mellifica var. syriaca)* which exited above all in the rocky clefts of the valleys. In Israel and Judah, there was probably not as yet in biblical times any breeding of bees (cf., however, Jeremiah 41:8), even though it is verified in Egypt since the Old Kingdom (5th dynasty, about 2450-2325) and it also occurs in the Hittite laws according to the version of 1400 B.C.)."[121] As the LORD commanded humanity to eat at his banquet table, so the sage commands the son: *eat* the good thing (*'ᵉkōl;* see 24:13; cf. Gen. 2:16), but he qualifies the amount by *what you require (dayyekā).*[122] The Hebrew chiastic construction in verset A contains in its inner core the verbs progressing from "to find" to "to eat," and in its outer core the nouns "honey" and "what is sufficient for you," suggesting that "sufficiency" is relative to "honey." The pronoun "for you" is necessary to show that the amount is relative to each individual. *Lest* (*pen;* see 25:10) signals that verset B presents the rationale. Verset Ba represents the situation, *you have more than enough of it* (see 1:31), having eaten the honey to the point of saturation, and verset Bb the dramatic consequence, *and* then *you will vomit it* (see 23:8). Overindulgence transformed the sweet and healing honey into repulsive and sickening food. Ecclesiastes instantiates the exemplar honey, too. In other words, "too much of anything is bad" (cf. Sir. 37:29).

17 This verse instantiates the principle of moderation and self-control to friendship. Verset A admonishes to make oneself scarce and pre-

121. Meinhold, *Sprüche,* p. 427.

122. *Day* occurs 39 times in the Bible in the sense of being "enough," "sufficient" relative to the situation, restricting the amount here to that which agreeably appeases the appetite.

cious in a neighbor's house, and verset B gives the reason: to avoid being loathed by the neighbor. The admonition entails both seldom to set foot in the neighbor's house, and once there to turn away while the visit is still agreeable. It assumes that neighborliness, like honey, is precious, delightful, and beneficial to both parties and does not aim to chill the flow of neighborly love, or restrain its practical exercise. *Make . . . scarce* (*hōqer;* see 1:13) in the *Qal* expresses a state of small quantity from a root having the basic meaning "to be precious, costly, valuable."[123] In sum, the verb denotes both a small quantity and great value. The synecdoche *your foot* (1:15) graphically depicts the whole person entering and moving around in the neighbor's house. *From the house* [see 12:7] *of your neighbor* (see 3:28) entails the verb "and turn away [from]."[124] *Lest* again signals that verset B gives the rationale. *He have more than enough of you and* repeats v. 16b except for the reversal of subject from second to third person and of object from third to second person. The negative consequence, *hate you* (see 1:22), shows that a lack of prudent restraint in something even so desirable as a loving, enriching friendship can transform it into hurtful hate. Friendship ripens through discreet sensitivity not to intrude on privacy and to allow space for the other person to be a person in his own right, not through self-enjoyment, impetuosity, or imposition. Without that discretion, instead of enriching life, friendship takes away from it.[125] As the son had to learn by experience the limits of his own tolerance for honey, he must also learn by experience his neighbor's level of tolerance for him. In other words, "Familiarity breeds contempt," and "Guests, like fish, stink after three days."

18-20 The next three proverbs are linked by the paronomasia of *rēʿēhû* ("his neighbor," v. 18), *rōʿâ* ("decaying," v. 19), and *rāʿ* ("adversity," v. 20), of *šānûn* ("sharpened," v. 18) and *šēn* ("tooth," v. 19), and of *bwgd bywm* ("on a treacherous person in the time of," v. 19) and *bwgd bywm* ("a garment on a day of," v. 20), by the same syntax (i.e., a figurative comment involving more than one feature in verset A and topic in verset B), and by the theme (i.e., conflict between neighbors). The theme is developed by katabasis, descending from the perjurer (v. 18), to the undependable (v. 19), to the tactless (v. 20), all of whom should be avoided.

18 This proverb denounces the perfidy of a false witness against a neighbor (see 6:19; 14:5; 19:5, 9, 28; 24:18; cf. Exod. 20:16; Deut. 5:17). His perfidy (verset B) is implicitly compared to three deadly assault weapons (verset A). In antiquity the armor bearer carried for the warrior the weapons

123. The other instance of *yqr* in the *Hiphil* represents God as making human beings in Babylon more scarce than fine gold (Isa. 13:12).

124. *IBHS,* p. 224, P. 11.4.3d.

125. McKane, *Proverbs,* p. 587.

he was likely to need for different stages of the battle, like a caddy who carries for the golfer the clubs needed for different stages of the game.[126] *And* connects the three weapons that represent the full panoply of the warrior's assault arsenal, which would also have included the javelin for medium-range fighting. For close-in battle he used the *war club* (or mace;[127] see n. 35), for less close but still hand-to-hand fighting the *sword* (or dagger or scimitar; see 5:4), and for long-distance fighting the bow and *arrow* (*ḥēṣ;* see 5:23).[128] *A man* (*'îš;* see 25:14) *who testifies*[129] *against his neighbor* [see 25:17] *as*[130] *a false* [25:14] *witness* (see 6:19). The sage depicts the false witness as beating out his neighbor's brains with the mace, as piercing his bowels with a sword, and as killing him with a deadly arrow in order to make the son shrink with horror at the thought of perjury (see 12:17).

19 The triplet of proverbs now shifts from the actively treacherous perjurer to a fair-weather friend who passively inflicts destructive perfidy in crisis. One had confidence in this friend, but in distress the friend reneges on his commitment to his needy neighbor (cf. 14:22; 17:17; 19:22; 20:6). This treacherous friend in emergency is as impotent, ineffective, and painfully frustrating as a *crumbling* [see n. 36] *tooth* (see 10:26), on which one cannot bite. *And* adds an overlapping metaphor, a *turned* (see n. 37) *foot* (see 1:15), on which one cannot walk. "The hardest bone of a person, the tooth, is crumbling because of rottenness, and the feet which have to carry the entire burden of the body are staggering."[131] *Reliance* [see 14:26] *on a treacherous person* [see I: 110] *in the time of adversity* (see 24:10) deprives the trusting neighbor of power to defend himself (cf. Pss. 3:7[8]; 58:6[7]) and/or to escape his plight (cf. 2 Sam. 2:18; 4:4; 9:3, 13; Amos 2:15). When danger stalks, a persons needs protection and a way of escape (cf. Judg. 17:7-12; cf. 2 Sam. 16:1-4 with 19:24-28[25-29]; Job 6:14-17; Ps. 55:12-14[13-15]; Acts

126. See *The World of the Bible,* vol. 2: *Former Prophets,* ed. Michael Avi-Yonah et al. (Yonkers, N.Y.: Educational Heritage, 1959), p. 132.

127. In Jer. 51:20 *mappēṣ* is a parallel with *kᵉlê milḥāmâ* "battle weapon." In the same semantic sphere *paṭṭîš* denotes the "blacksmith's hammer" and *maqqebet,* "a workman's small hammer."

128. The entire arrow consisted of a shaft and head. Its light and balanced shaft, which was usually made of wood or reed, had a tail designed with eagle, vulture, or kite feathers to stabilize its flight. Its essential part was its heavy head or blade. There are arrow blades made out of flint in countless shapes dating from the Neolithic Age (7th-4th cent. B.C.) until the early Bronze Age (3150-2200 B.C.) and sporadically thereafter. Later they were made of copper or iron and sharpened to make them more lethal. Frequently they were dipped in poison (Job 6:4).

129. Investing I *'nh* "answer" (see 1:28; 15:18; 18:23) with its more technical sense in legal actions, "to give evidence" *(HALOT,* 2:852, s.v. *'nh).*

130. *IBHS,* p. 171, P. 10.2.2d.

131. Meinhold, *Sprüche,* p. 428.

28:15; 2 Tim. 4:16). The proverb profiles the faithfulness of God, who never fails his servant (e.g., Pss. 46:1[2]; 91:15; Isa. 28:16; Jer. 17:5-8; Matt. 28:20; Heb. 13:5).

20 The triplet now shifts from the lethal talker and silent traitor to the insensitive and inept speaker. The proverb implicitly compares the incompatibility of one singing joyful songs to a sullen heart to the incongruities of putting off a warm garment on a frosty day and to pouring stinging vinegar on a wound. All three foolishly inflict pain with no therapeutic value. *One who removes* [see n. 40] *a garment* [see 6:20] *on a cold* [see 17:27] *day* (*yôm;* see 4:18), which here refers to the daylight hours of a day that is uncomfortably cold in comparison with the other four occurrences of *qārâ* (Job 24:7; 37:9-10; Ps. 147:17; Nah. 3:1). The second metaphor is connected asyndetically: *vinegar* [see 10:26] *on a wound* (*nāter;* see n. 42). *And (wᵉ)* links the topic as an interrelated situation to the two figurative situations. *One who sings*[132] *songs* may underscore the poetic words that accompany the vocal music. Singers with songs aim to heighten feelings of joy, delight, and merriment (cf. 2 Sam. 19:35[36]; Eccl. 2:8; 7:5-6; Isa. 24:9). To sing songs is the opposite of "to sing laments" (2 Chr. 35:25). *To* (*ʿal;* lit. "on") denotes to sing to the heart (Job 33:27; Isa. 40:2; Jer. 6:10; Hos. 2:14[16]) — here *a sullen* [or heavy, *rāʿ* (lit. "bad"/"evil"); see 1:16; 25:19] *heart* (see I: 90).[133] Whereas the figures pertain to senselessly paining the body, the topic pertains to insensitively paining the heart. Seasonable songs can be therapeutic (cf. 1 Sam. 16:15-23; 19:9; Job 30:31; Prov. 12:25), but when sung unseasonably they are painful and damaging to the spirit (cf. Ps. 137:1-4; Sir. 22:6a). The sensitive know how and when to sorrow and to rejoice (Eccl. 3:4; Rom. 12:15; 1 Cor. 12:26; Heb. 13:3).

21-22 The concluding proverb pair of the partial subunit (vv. 16-22) instructs the son on how to resolve conflict with his neighbor that he created through his own folly. "Whereas 'eating' too much causes conflicts in vv. 16-17, giving to eat resolves conflict in vv. 21-22."[134] "For," which introduces v. 22, gives the rationale for the admonitions of v. 21. The LXX glosses *kî* by adding "for by doing this." Meinhold notes that, like vv. 18-20, this proverb pair starts with a person's situation of need, but whereas those verses pertain to actions involving only words, this one, like vv. 11-15, requires concrete deeds. Other proverbs instructed the son not to gloat over a neighbor's misfortune (24:17-18), to overlook injustice (10:12; 17:9; 19:11), and to renounce revenge (20:22; 24:29). This one advances to the positive admonition

132. *Šār,* which often takes *šîrâ* as its objects, here uniquely occurs with instrumental *bᵉ* (cf. Exod. 7:20).

133. *HALOT,* 3:1251; BDB, p. 948, s.v. *rāʿ.*

134. Van Leeuwen, *Context and Meaning,* p. 85.

to show him sympathy and compassion in his plight in the very practical way of feeding him, putting the proverb in the sphere of the commandment to love your neighbor (cf. Exod. 23:4-5; Lev. 19:17-18; Job 31:29-32; Prov. 24:17-18). One must allow God's justice its proper scope.

21 The proverb presupposes that one has a neighbor who hates him (cf. 25:16-17). The context of the admonitions represents the enemy in urgent need, concretized as being hungry (verset Aa) and thirsty (verset Ba), two sides of the same situation. The admonitions urge the son to meet the need immediately, instantiated as to relieve his pangs of hunger by feeding him nourishing food (verset Ab) and to slake his thirst for liquid by giving him water to drink. *If* [see 1:10] *the one who hates you* [see 25:17] *is hungry* [see 6:30; 10:3], *give him . . . to eat* [lit. "cause him to participate in eating/consuming/devouring";[135] see 1:31; 25:16] *food* [see 9:5]. *And if* signifies a hendiadys (cf. 9:5; 23:7). *He is thirsty* refers to the mouth yearning for liquid to ease its unpleasant dryness just as the stomach craves for food to ease its hunger pangs. *Give him . . . to drink* [lit. "cause him to participate in drinking"] *water* (see 9:16; 21:1). The mention of "water," not wine, suggests that the son should meet his basic needs (cf. 9:5, 16; 25:25).[136]

22 Initial *for* signals that v. 22 gives reasons to meet the needs of your enemy. First, *you,* which is tautological and so emphatic, will bring him to godly repentance for hating you (v. 22a), *and* second, *the LORD* (see I: 67] *will repay* [see 6:31] *you.* In verset A the food and water of v. 21 are implicitly compared to *burning coals* (see 6:28), which is placed emphatically before both subject and verb. The meaning of the phrase *are taking* [*and heaping*] *on the head (ḥōteh ʿal-rōʾšô)* is debated.[137] The preposition "on" supports the almost universally accepted interpretation from the days of the

135. *IBHS,* pp. 433-36, P. 27.1; p. 441, P. 27.3a.

136. Meinhold (*Sprüche,* p. 430) comments, "Generally speaking, this admonition means that the enemy ought to be supported in every need one knows him to be in. It is left unsaid that this help will not be given in such a way that will enable him to continue his enmity in a stronger position. Rather, one silently counts on the fact that by giving him help and benefit, his enmity will be overcome and terminated. From the helper's perspective, he has already practically left the enmity behind. The reasons for this action cannot be found in the past but in the future (v. 22)."

137. Driver ("Notes and Studies," *JTS* 32 [1932] 255) identifies two roots of *ḥth,* "kindle" (Prov. 6:27; 25:22; Isa. 30:14) and "destroyed," but with "burning coals" as its object only the former can be in view. Its Aramaic cognate means "to take away (burning coals)," "to rake (out hot coals?)." In the Bible this is its meaning with *min* (Ps. 52:7; Isa. 30:14). M. Dahood ("Two Pauline Quotations from the Old Testament," *CBQ* 17 [1955] 19) curiously argues that *ḥātâ* and *nāśâ* with *min* "make it possible to argue that the expression *ḥātâ ʿal* is identical with *ḥātâ min.*" Van Leeuwen (*Context and Meaning,* p. 60) follows Dahood and appeals to Ps. 81:6 that *ʿal* can mean "from," but the NIV renders that preposition "against."

Septuagint translators down to the NRSV that *ḥth* means "to heap on the head." More specifically it means "to take/carry and [to heap] on his head," the preposition *'al* assuming the elided verb of motion "to put/heap."[138] The parallels in Egyptian instruction literature and in the ritual of repentance substantiate this traditional understanding. However, commentators accepting that meaning of the expression do not agree about its significance. Some think that heaping coals of fire on a person's head is a form of punishment and of appeasing one's need for vengeance, but the parallel, "the LORD will reward you," negates that interpretation.[139] In the book of Psalms, the psalmist prays that the LORD will revenge the wrong, but he never himself pours the coal on his enemy's head. The book of Proverbs rejects any form of personal revenge (17:13; 20:22; 24:17, 18). Both Old and New Testaments instruct the covenant community to love, not hate, their enemies (Lev. 19:17-18; Ps. 35:13; Matt. 5:43). Most interpreters agree that "coals of fire" is a morally good deed, one pleasing to the LORD. The LXX adds to the end of verset B *agatha,* "the LORD will reward you for your *good*." The apostle Paul uses this Septuagint text to reprove taking revenge and abstracts from it the principle to overcome evil with good (Rom. 12:17-21).

Most commentators agree with Augustine and Jerome that "coals of fire" refers to the "burning pangs of shame" that a person will feel when good is returned for evil, his shame producing remorse and contrition. McKane says, "When the enemy has steeled himself to meet hate with hate and is impervious to threats of revenge, he is vulnerable to a generosity which overlooks and forgives, and capitulates to kindness."[140] But heaping coals of fire elsewhere in the Old Testament means to produce terrible pangs of pain as part of God's avenging judgment (cf. Pss. 11:6; 140:10[11] and 4 Esdr. 16:54), not pangs of remorse. However, Morenz validated the majority interpretation from an Egyptian penitential ritual. According to the narrative of Cha-em-wese, the thief Cha-em-wese returned a book of magic stolen out of a grave by carrying a basin of fiery coals on his head. Carrying the fire signified his consciousness and attitudes of shame, remorse, repentance, and ultimately correction. Morenz also thought that the penitential rite was confined to Egypt, but that the metaphor as it exists in Israel should be elucidated by it.[141] The Egyptian background for the forms of other motifs in Proverbs support his view.[142] Whether Solomon and his audience knew the origin of the

138. *IBHS,* p. 224, P. 11.4.3d.

139. Delitzsch, *Proverbs,* p. 167.

140. McKane, *Proverbs,* p. 592.

141. S. Morenz, "Feurige Kohlen auf dem Haput," *TLZ* 78 (1953) 187-92.

142. See, e.g., Christa B. Kayatz, *Studien zu Proverbien 1–9: Eine form- und motivgeschichtliche Untersuchung unter Einbeziehung ägyptischen Vergleichsmaterials* (WMANT 22; Neukirchen-Vluyn: Neukirchener, 1966) and N. Shupak, "Selected Terms

figure is a moot and irrelevant point.[143] "The reward from Yahweh is presumably for achieving reconciliation between the two persons involved. This could only be due to a change of heart on the part of the enemy."[144] Our Lord exemplified and established the precept. Through his life and death for his enemies, he reconciled them to God (Rom. 5:8; 2 Cor. 5:17-21).

(2) Unexpected Conflicts (25:23-26)

The four proverbs of this partial subunit present truths that affect every person by metaphors in their A versets and their topics in their B versets; in each case the first of the pair uses "and" to connect them (vv. 23, 25). They consist of two proverb pairs using weather imagery and two using water imagery respectively. The first pertains to unexpected conflicts due to bad speech, and the second contrasts restoration with ruin, again advocating doing good to restore a conflicted situation (cf. 25:21-22, 25).

23-24 Using the motif of weather imagery, the first proverb pair censures the conflict-arousing, unexpected bad speech of the backbiting tongue (v. 23) and of the nagging wife (v. 24). "Verse 23a pictures bad weather; v. 24a portrays a man in a position where he is exposed to bad weather — which is better than being exposed to the storms of a tempestuous wife, as in the famous story of Socrates and Xanthippe!"[145]

23 The first proverb compares the unexpected damage of a slanderous tongue (v. 23b) to the icy blast of a north wind that unexpectedly brings forth rain (v. 23a). In the chiastic parallels of the comparative proverb, the topics "north wind" and "a sly tongue" form the outer frame, and the objects "rain" and "a face struck by a curse" its inner core. *A north wind (rûaḥ ṣāpôn)* is referred to in the Bible only in Song 4:16. Since rain is associated with the west, not the north, some scholars think that the reference is imprecise and refers to a northwest wind.[146] Morenz thinks that it is an Egyptian-

of Biblical Wisdom Literature Compared with Egyptian Wisdom Literature" (Ph.D. diss., Hebrew University, 1984).

143. Many English speakers know that "Ivy League" designates the football conference of ten eastern universities, but they do not know that it derives from the representation of the league's original four schools by the Roman numeral "IV." Although some wrongly think that the epithet derives from the ivy on their campus buildings, they know that it designates the eastern conference of universities.

144. Whybray, *Proverbs,* p. 368.

145. Van Leeuwen, *Context and Meaning,* p. 85.

146. Cf. Gemser, *Sprüche,* p. 113. Delitzsch believes that the proverb emphasizes the north "because, according to the intention of the similitude, he seeks to designate such rain as is associated with raw, icy-cold weather, as the north wind (xxvii.16, LXX, Sir. xliii.20) brings along with it" (Delitzsch, *Proverbs,* p. 168).

ism.[147] Both explanations fail. The first is too facile and the second is too unlikely, for the proverb would not have currency in a context where it made no sense.[148] More importantly, both explanations fail to reckon with the paronomasia between *ṣāpôn,* whose probable root *ṣpn* means "to hide" (see Prov. 1:11, 18; 2:1), and *seter* "in secrecy." *Ṣāpôn* "north" may mean "the hidden dark region of the world."[149] The people of Israel expect the west wind, not the north wind, to bring rain (1 K. 13:41-46; Luke 12:54). The cold north wind normally cleared the sky and brought good visibility (cf. Sir. 43:20). C. Grave says that the north wind "must have been a constant subject for prayers offered up by merchants and sea-captains in Ugarit, while they were waiting to set out with heavily loaded ships for the main trade targets in the South and Egypt."[150] In sum, the point of comparison is precisely that rain from a north wind is hidden and so unexpected. Hidden slander, like rain from a north wind, brings unexpected damage. *That brings forth* (lit. "to make brought forth through pains of child labor"; see Prov. 8:24) personifies the north wind (cf. Ps. 90:2, where its personified use is parallel with *yullādû*). The advantage or disadvantage of *rain* (see 25:14) and snow depends on the season (cf. Isa. 55:10 with Prov. 26:1, and 25:14 with 28:3). *The tongue* (see 25:15) is explicated by adding *sly* (see n. 46; 9:17). *Brings* [gapped] *a face* (i.e., the outward manifestation of the inner spirit; see 7:13; 15:13) *struck by a curse* (see 22:14; 24:24).[151] Secret speech by nature is malevolent; were it otherwise, why hide it? The damaging effect of the secret speech/curse, which is written all over the face of the victim, assumes that its unsuspecting target suddenly "gets wind" of its circulation. An untimely, icy blast of rain from the north takes the farmer aback and ruins his crop (cf. 26:1; 28:3). So also the unaware victim, when he hears the slander, realizes that the benefits he was about to reap from his work are suddenly ruined.

24 The proverb about the nagging wife repeats verbatim 21:19. There it helped to divide 21:3-29 into subunits and underscored that wicked-

147. "While rain is a source of fructification and blessing in a Palestinian context, it has a negative rather than a positive evaluation in Egypt, where the source of fertility is associated with the inundation of the Nile, and so is an opposite metaphor of slander" (McKane, *Proverbs,* p. 583).

148. Van der Ploeg, "Prov. 25:23," *VT* 3 (1953) 189-91.

149. *HALOT,* 3:1,046, s.v. *ṣāpôn.*

150. C. Grave, "The Etymology of Northwest Semitic *sapanu,*" *UF* 12 (1980) 227-28.

151. The *Niphal* is unique with *zāʿam,* which in the *Qal* and with a human subject means "to curse." "The association with *lᵉšôn seter* (cf. Hos. 7:16; Isa. 30:27) and the use of the word in 22:14; 24:24 support the translation 'struck by a curse'" (B. Wiklander, *TDOT,* 4:108, s.v. *zāʿam*).

ness divides even the closest friends. Here it is connected to the theme of everyday and/or unexpected conflicts. Hostile speech from one's wife is as unexpected and unwelcome as the rain from the north wind and as from a sly tongue. Moreover, there may be a figurative connection between the north wind and exposure on a corner of the roof. "'Better to live in a corner'" of the roof, unprotected from the rain, than to live within the shared house unprotected from her."[152] The nagging wife presents a striking contrast to a sexually satisfying wife (5:18-19).

25-26 The last proverb pair pertains to perseverance, contrasting the restoration of a weary person to persevere by a good word with the ruin of a righteous person by equivocation. The two are linked by the image of precious drinking water that revitalizes life — the first positive, the second negative.

25 This comparative proverb compares hearing tidings of peace from a distant land (verset B) to giving cold water to a weary person (verset A). Giving water to the thirsty in v. 21 is now escalated to giving *cold* [see 25:20] *water* (see 21:1; 25:21), which represents the best remedy. There water was given to restore a hurt person in a relationship; here it is given *to* [lit. "on"][153] *a weary (ʿᵃyēpâ)*[154] *person* (*nepeš;* see I: 90) to enable and encourage him to continue pursuing his goal (cf. Gen. 16:16-19; Exod. 17:1-6; Num. 20:11; Judg. 15:18, 19). *ʿᵃyēpâ* signifies that he is almost completely deprived of energy, especially by hunger and/or thirst, and so unable and/or unwilling to continue to live. Such a person can no longer endure his state of existence and needs to be revived. The presence of water sources, such as cisterns, wells, and all sorts of streams, is essential for life (cf. Exod. 15:22-25; 17:2-7; Num. 20:7-11; 21:16; 24:7; Deut. 8:7-9; 11:11). Cold water could be running water, as from a snow melt, or covered, still water (5:15; 10:11). "Water could be cooled in porous containers made out of clay, for they were able to keep its content at a temperature at least five degrees below that of the storage place."[155] This beneficial physical remedy for the weary functions as a metaphor for the spiritual remedy for a person weary from uncertainty and/or anxiety about the well-being of a situation in a faraway place that he can-

152. Malbim, *Proverbs,* p. 262.

153. *IBHS,* p. 217, P. 11.2.13c.

154. It derives the root *ʿyp,* which is always in the Qal and means "to become tired." In 2 Sam. 17:29 it is associated with exhaustion due to both "hunger" *rāʿēb* and "thirst" *ṣāmēʾ.* In Judg. 4:21 the verb occurs with *wayyāmō̄* "to die" and means "to lose consciousness." Here the weary person needs water to revive him and so refers specifically to exhaustion from thirst (Job 22:7; Ps. 63:1[2]; Isa. 29:8). Although many English versions gloss the adjective "thirsty," *ṣāmēʾ* denotes that notion, and that gloss can do double duty in verset B.

155. Meinhold, *Sprüche,* p. 433.

not control and cannot even reach. *And* [see 25:23] *a good* [see 2:20] *report* (see 15:30) that comes *from* [cf. Isa. 10:3] *a distant* [see 19:7] *land ('ereṣ).*[156] The point of reference, "a weary person," is elided. It can be inferred that the person is psychologically unable and/or unwilling to continue out of exhaustion from his anxiety about a situation in a far-off place (see 13:17; 15:30; cf. Gen. 45:27). In the biblical world news traveled agonizingly slow and was delivered with great difficulty, so that extending the distance to a far-off land heightens the refreshment. "The long interval of these tidings; the lengthened separation from the beloved object; the anxiety necessarily excited by want of intercourse; the uncertainty of his welfare and prospects — all combine to make these *cold waters* specially refreshing *to the thirsty soul*."[157] The "widow's walk" on the top of the house of a sea-faring captain illustrates the thought. "The rabbis ordained a special blessing to be pronounced on hearing good tidings."[158]

26 The perseverance of a weary person is now contrasted with a wavering righteous person's lack of perseverance. The swaying to and fro of a compromised righteous person is compared to trampling feet that muddy a spring, and his imminent fall as he yields before the wicked to the ruined fountain. *A muddied* (see 6:3),[159] bubbling *spring* (see 8:24) depicts a befouled important supply of fresh water (cf. 1 K. 18:5; Hos. 13:15). "To befoul a water-hole on a track across the desert is one unforgivable sin among the Bedouin (E. F. F. B[ishop])."[160] *A ruined* [lit. "was caused to be ruined so as to negatively affect someone"; see 6:32] *fountain* (see 5:18) refers to the destruction of another important source of vital water (cf. Jer. 51:36; Hos. 13:5). The two figures depict the deadly effects of an equivocating *righteous person* (see I: 97) on others and himself; he takes away the life of both. *Who sways* (see 24:11) signifies his moral faltering *before* [with a rare hostile sense][161] *a wicked person* (see I: 109). Proverbs represents the righteous as triumphing over the wicked, never as the wicked forcing or compelling the righteous to yield (11:8; 12:21; 14:19; 16:7;

156. *Rḥq* signifies "to be distant, remote." Its nominal form refers to a place separated by a great distance from someone or something. Of its 18 uses, it occurs six times explicitly as an attributive gen. with "land" *'ereṣ* (see 2:21; cf. Isa. 8:9-10; 13:5; 33:17; 46:11; Jer. 4:16; 6:20; 8:19); sometimes *'ereṣ* is elided (e.g., Isa. 10:23; Ezek. 23:40).

157. Bridges, *Proverbs,* p. 480.

158. Greenstone, *Proverbs,* p. 271.

159. The *Niphal* participle of *rpś,* which in its two occurrences in the *Qal* means to "muddy water by trampling" (cf. Ezek. 32:2; 34:18; cf. the *Hithpael* in Prov. 6:3), is unique.

160. McKane, *Proverbs,* p. 592. Were the wicked the responsible agent, the *Niphal,* not the *Qal,* stem would be used (cf. Ps. 10:6).

161. BDB, p. 817, s.v. *pānâ.*

21:12; 24:15-16).[162] When the righteous person behaves according to his proper character, namely, faith in God (cf. 18:10) and a commitment to serve the community, he is "a wellspring of life" (10:11). But his present commitment and blessing cannot be guaranteed in the future (see 19:27), as Solomon himself tragically illustrates (1 K. 11:1-8; 2 K. 23:13). He, too, may become wearied with resistance, afraid of others or desiring to please man, and have a false love of peace (cf. Gen. 12:18-20; 20:10; 26:10; 2 Sam. 11:2; 12:14; 13:11-14; 16:22; Matt. 5:13-16; Gal. 2:11-14; Philemon 24; 2 Tim. 4:10).[163] His despicable compromise disappoints, deprives, and imperils the many who have learned to rely on him for their spiritual life. All must endure to the end to save themselves and their communities (11:19; cf. 11:31; Matt. 24:13, 42-51).

d. Conclusion (25:27)

Again a single-line proverb draws the subunit to its conclusion (cf. 25:15), but v. 27 also draws the whole unit to its conclusion. Its interpretation is helped by taking note of the chiastic *inclusio*s of "honey . . . eat" (*dbš 'kl,* v. 16) and "eating honey" (*'kl dbš,* v. 27a) and of "searching glory" (*kbd ḥqr,* v. 2) and "searching weighty matters" (*ḥqr k^{e}bēdîm,* 27b). This proverb compares the intellectual searching out of a weighty matter (v. 27a; cf. v. 2) to overeating honey (v. 27a; cf. v. 16; cf. also Jer. 17:10). *To eat* desirable and beneficial *honey* (*d^{e}baš,* 25:16) *excessively* [see n. 52] *is not good* (*lō'-ṭôb;* see 16:29) is again a litotes. *Nor is it honorable* (*mikkābôd;* see n. 53) *to search out* by a cognitive and analytical examination and testing what is difficult to probe (see 25:2).[164] *Weighty matters* (*k^{e}bēdîm;* see n. 53) signifies generally "to be heavy," but here has its specific notion "to be difficult" (cf. Exod. 18:18) or, better, unfathomable,[165] like the hidden things of God and the king (see v. 3).

162. The proverb qualifies 10:30 and 12:3, which, using the *Niphal* of *môṭ,* assert that no external agent can or ever will topple the righteous (cf. Pss. 15:5; 16:8; 55:22[23]). "If it says in 10:30 that a righteous person will not waver forever (cf. 12:3), then this does not mean that he cannot fall by his own fault (cf. Ps. 73:3) and thereby lose his characteristic" (Meinhold, *Sprüche,* p. 433).

163. Delitzsch, *Proverbs,* p. 170.

164. Of 12 occurrences of *ḥeqer,* six are negated, with the sense of "unsearchable, immeasurable," of either God (Job 5:9; 9:10; 36:26; Ps. 145:3; Isa. 40:28) or of the king (Prov. 25:3). Twice it occurs with a similar sense in rhetorical questions (Job 11:7; 38:16). Once each it is used of searching out the heart (Judg. 5:16), of the investigation and findings of the fathers (Job 8:8), and of investigating with reference to judgment (Job 36:26); it means to probe, not to seek.

165. In Ezekiel it is used in conjunction with *'mq* "to be deep" with reference to people whose speech is "unfathomable" (*'mq*) and "difficult" (*kbd*): "whose speech is thick and difficult" (NRSV).

The sage probably chose *kābôd,* not *ʿāmôq,* for its wordplay with *mikkābôd* and to constitute the chiastic *inclusio* with *kbd ḥqr* in v. 2. The introductory proverb (25:2) refers to searching out a matter that is appropriate to divine and human inquiry, but the concluding proverb proscribes humanity's searching out ontological matters that lie beyond its restricted epistemology as eating honey to excess. Investigating profundities that belong to transcendence, such as the complexities of God's universe and of the inspired king's heart (see 16:10-15; 25:3), is not honorable (see I: 78-79).[166] The only proper response to God's transcendence by restricted humankind is to fear the LORD and to depart from evil (Job 28:28) and to accept God's revealed wisdom (cf. Job 28:12-28; Psalm 131; Prov. 30:1-6; Sir. 3:21-22; Bar. 3:29–4:1; 2 Esdras 4). The proverb forms a fitting conclusion to the composition introduced in 25:2.

3. Seven Perverted Types of Humanity (25:28–26:28)

28 *A breached city, which*[1] *has no wall,*
a person whose spirit has no restraint.[2]
26:1 *As snow in summer and rain in harvest,*
so honor is not fitting for a fool.
2 *As a fluttering bird, as a flying sparrow,*[3]
so an undeserved curse does not[4] *come to pass.*
3 *A whip for a warhorse, a bit for a donkey,*
and a rod for backs of fools.
4 *Do not answer a fool according to his folly,*
lest you become like him — even you!
5 *Answer a fool according to*[5] *his folly,*
lest he become wise in his own eyes.
6 *One who chops off*[6] *[his] feet,*[7] *who drinks violence,*[8]

166. Van Leeuwen, *Context and Meaning.*

1. The relative is often gappped in poetry.

2. The LXX reads *ou meta boulēs* < *ʾên môʿēṣâ* (?).

3. Lit. "as the bird with regard to fluttering, as the sparrow with regard to flying."

4. Q (Vulg.) reads *lô* ("to him," i.e., the one uttering the curse?); K (LXX, Targ.) reads *lōʾ,* which is required by the similes in verset A. The subject's image is birds fluttering about, not birds finding a resting place.

5. The LXX renders the *kᵉ* in v. 4 by *pros* and in this verse by *kata.*

6. The Targ. renders *mqṣh* as "he who hastens." The Syr., and possibly the LXX, reads *miqṣēh* "from the end of/under [his feet]." The Vulg. reads *claudus* "lame," probably having pointed the form as the *Pual* ptcp. *mᵉquṣṣeh.* Fichtner [*BHS*] needlessly proposes *miqqāsūy* "from what is cut off."

7. Greek tradition corrupted original *podōn* into *hodon.*

8. The LXX removed the figure, reading *heautou oneidos poieitai* "procures a reproach (< *ḥerpâ;* cf. *BHS*) to himself." N. H. Tur-Sinai (*The Book of Job* [rev. ed.;

is one who sends messages by the hand of a fool.
7 *Legs dangle*[9] *from a cripple,*
and a proverb[10] *dangles*[11] *in the mouth of fools.*[12]
8 *Like one who binds*[13] *a stone in a sling*[14]
is the person who gives honor to a fool.
9 *A thornbush in*[15] *the hand of a drunkard,*

Jerusalem: Kiryat-Sefer, 1967], pp. 259-60), followed by Gemser (*Sprüche,* p. 94; etc.), repoints *ḥāmās* as *ḥōmēs* (see Jer. 13:22) and *šōteh* as *šētō[h]* (see 2 Sam. 10:4; Isa. 20:4), "one who bares his buttock." This also entails repointing *meqaṣṣeh.* But McKane (*Proverbs,* p. 597) finds the emendation philologically "improbable" and sensibly "far-fetched." Plöger (*Sprüche,* p. 310) objects that the new figure makes the stupidity less apparent.

9. The LXX paraphrases *dalyû* by *aphelou* "take away," having parsed the form as impv. An impv., however, is unlikely because initial "and" in v. 7b indicates a simile. Some parse *dalyû* as *Qal,* 3rd masc. pl. perf. = **dālᵉyû* (< I *dlh* "to draw out") and interpret it to mean "take away mobility (lit. 'legs')," but this usage is otherwise unknown. It is better to posit a root II *dll* (= *dallû*) or II *dlh (HALOT* 1:223, s.v. II *dll).* Delitzsch (*Proverbs,* p. 179) rejects this interpretation but achieves the same thought by emending the text to *dillûy* "the hanging down." G. Driver ("Problems in the Hebrew Text of Proverbs," *Bib* 32 [1951] 191) redivides and repoints *šqym mpsḥ* into *šōqê mᵉpassᵉḥîm* "[the dangling of] the calves of those that limp."

10. Greek tradition corrupted *paroimian* "parable" into *paranomian* "transgression."

11. *Dlh/dll* is gapped in verset B.

12. The Targ. (cf. Syr.) paraphrases the proverb: "If you (can) give the ability to walk to a lame man, you will receive a word (of wisdom) from the mouth of a fool," its point being that the two things are impossible to obtain.

13. The *Qal* inf. cons. of *ṣrr* is a homonym with I *ṣᵉrôr* "bag" and II *ṣᵉrôr* "stone/pebble" (so construed by the Targ. and Syr). But a verb is more likely because of the parallel verb *nôtēn,* and II *ṣᵉrôr* would be redundant with *'eben.* The LXX and Vulg. read *ṣôrēr,* facilitating a harmony between *ṣrr* and *nôtēn.* The MT may be due to corruption by metathesis. But in Proverbs the abstract noun in parallel with a concrete noun often has a concrete notion (M. Dahood, *Psalms III: 101–150* [AB; Garden City, N.Y.: Doubleday, p. 411]). The comparative "like . . . so" prevents the gloss: "one who gives honor to a fool is binding a stone in a sling."

14. Jerome renders the verset *"sicut qui missit lapidem in acervum Mercurii,"* pointing *ṣrr* as a participle, investing the common verb with the unique meaning "to cast," and following the Midrash that understood *margēmâ* to refer to a heap of stones consecrated to Mercury. Pagans commonly placed a stone before the idol as a form of petition. But Delitzsch (*Proverbs,* p. 181) rightly objects "that this Graeco-Roman custom . . . cannot be supposed to have existed in the times of Solomon."

15. The KJV renders *'ālâ bᵉ* "goes up into" (= pierce), but the Hebrew idiom will not sustain that meaning (cf. Isa. 34:13; Hos. 9:6). Although *'ālâ* is a common term for the growing up of vegetation, and BDB (p. 748, s.v. *'ālâ*) invests it with that meaning here, the figure of a thornbush growing up in a hand is too harsh and unnecessary. Delitzsch et al. invest *'ālâ bᵉyad* with its sense in Mishnaic Hebrew, "to come into possession of." But why appeal to

and a proverb[16] *in the mouth of a fool.*
10 *An archer who pierces every passer-by,*
and one who hires a fool, and one who hires those who pass by.[17]
11 *As*[18] *a dog returns*[19] *to its vomit,*
so a fool repeats his folly.[20]
12 *Do you see a person who is wise in his own eyes?*
There is[21] *more hope for a fool than for him.*
13 *A sluggard says, "A [fierce] lion is in the way,*

Mishnaic Hebrew? In Biblical Hebrew *ʿālâ* often approximates the meaning of the passive: (a) sacrifices go up onto the altar, meaning they are presented (Lev. 2:12; 1 K. 18:29; Ps. 51:19[21]; Isa. 60:7); (b) *ʿōl* comes up (is put) on to the cow (Num. 19:2; 1 Sam. 6:7; Lam. 1:14); garment onto someone (Lev. 19:19); razor on to one's hair (Judg. 13:5; 16:17; 1 Sam. 1:11); harvest is gathered (Job 5:26)" (*HALOT,* 2:829, s.v. *ʿālâ;* cf. Whybray, *Proverbs,* p. 374). That interpretation best suits this passage, and the verb can be glossed over.

16. The LXX reads *douleia* "servitude," probably in a play on *mōšēl* "dominion," and the Targ. (cf. Syr.) curiously reads *šṭyûtāʾ* "folly" (< *śekel* [?]).

17. The ancient versions did not understand the Hebrew. "All the flesh of fools is greatly distressed, for their excitement is shattered" (LXX). "The flesh of the fool suffers much, and the drunkard passes over the sea" (Targ.). "Judgment determines cases, and he who lays silence on the fool alleviates rage" (Vulg.). D. C. Snell ("The Most Obscure Verse in Proverbs: Proverbs 26:10," *VT* 41 [1991] 350-56) evaluates some of the ancient and several English versions, including the KJV, which reads: "The great God that formed all things both rewardeth the fool, and rewardeth transgressors." He ingeniously reconstructs the text to read: "A great one makes a fool [= *mᵉḥōlēl*] of everyone, but a drunkard is a fool (even of) passers-by," but overlooks that v. 10 is part of a series of comparative sayings in which verset A functions as a metaphor for verset B. Most moderns agree that *rab* means "archer" (McKane, *Proverbs,* p. 599; cf. NAB, NASB, NEB, NIV, REB, NRSV, passim), but Gemser (*Sprüche,* p. 95; cf. NEB, REB, NRSV) alters *wᵉśōkēr* to *wᵉšikkōr* "or drunkard" and transposes *ʿōbᵉrîm* to the end of verset A. The alteration from *wśkwr* to *wškr,* which has the support of the Targ. and Syr., is possible from a text-critical point of view, but the Targ. and Syr. are confused by the Hebrew, and the resulting meter is not good. The transposition of a word from the end of one verset to the other, which has no support, is not textually feasible. The Hebrew syntax does not favor the NRSV ("a passing fool or drunkard") and taking the ptcp. as a dependent relative, not as an independent relative, weakens the proverb. Is it alright to hire a fool or drunkard that is not passing by?

18. The LXX reads *hōsper kyōn hotan epelthę̄ epi ton heautou emeton,* but 2 Pet. 2:22 reads *kyōn epistrepsas epi to idion exerama,* which is much closer to the MT.

19. The participles are best interpreted as signifying the predicate (*IBHS,* pp. 623-24, P. 37.6a, b) because a dependent relative could be misunderstood in a restrictive sense (cf. 15:14).

20. The LXX renders *ʾiwwelet* as *hamartia,* and this becomes a catchword to add to Sir. 4:21 (Plöger, *Sprüche,* p. 308).

21. The English idiom demands that a subject such as *yēš* be added (cf. *IBHS,* p. 72, P. 4.5c).

a lion is in the plaza!"[22]

14 *A door turns on its pivot,*
and a sluggard on his couch.

15 *A sluggard buries his hand in a pan;*[23]
he is too weary to return it to his mouth.

16 *A sluggard is wiser in his own eyes*
than seven men who give a judicious answer.

17 *One who grabs*[24] *the ears*[25] *of a dog passing by*[26]
is[27] *one who becomes enraged*[28] *in a dispute not his own.*[29]

18 *Like a madman*[30] *who shoots*[31]

22. See n. 27 at 22:13.

23. See the note at 19:24.

24. See *IBHS,* p. 440, P. 27.2f.

25. The LXX reads *kerkou* "tail" (< *biznab*). Grabbing a dog's tail is less dangerous than grabbing its ears (cf. Judg. 15:4). Perhaps the translator familiarized the text.

26. A few medieval mss. and perhaps the LXX, Syr., and Targ. omit *ʿōbēr.* The haplography probably occurred through homoioteleuton due to following *mtʿbr.* Delitzsch (*Proverbs,* p. 190) et al. (e.g., REB, NRSV) plausibly conjecture moving the *athnach* to *ʿōbēr.* The MT represents the busybody as minding his own business and either chancing on the dispute (cf. 1 K. 9:8; 2 Chr. 7:21; Jer. 18:16; 19:8; 49:17; 50:13; Lam. 2:15; Zeph. 2:15) or stopping to become involved (7:8; 9:15; 26:10). These other uses of *ʿōbēr* in Proverbs either support the MT or gave rise to its reading. Moreover, the MT displays the nice paronomasia of *lōʾ-lô* at the end of the verset and of *ʿbr mtʿbr* at its beginning. According to the conjecture, the dog was minding its own business and the busybody committed an act of unprovoked transgression against it. In that case, he is more culpable and foolish. The meter and parallelism favor the conjecture. The restored meter is a normal 3 + 3, not an exceptional 2 + 4. Also, both versets now begin with *m* and a participle and end with an asyndetic relative clause. The resulting parallelism is striking and forceful. The paronomasia, which also involves *ʿl-ryb,* tightly binds together the image and topic.

27. The clause of classification, a metaphor, precedes the topic (*IBHS,* p. 132, P. 8.4.2a).

28. The Syr. (and Vulg.?) and Gemser (*Sprüche,* p. 95), and probably the NIV and REB, read "meddle" (< *mitʿabbēr;* see 14:10).

29. Resumptive pronoun with elided *ʾăšer.* The phrase *lōʾ-lô* occurs five times in the Old Testament (Gen. 38:9; Prov. 26:17; Dan. 11:17; Hab. 1:6; 2:6). GKC calls it a "very short form of the relative clause" (P. 155e).

30. The *Hithpael* participle of *lhh* is a *hap. leg.* L. Kopf ("Arabische Etymologien und Parallelen zum Bibelwörterbuch," *VT* 8 [1958] 180-81) suggested the meaning "neglect" on the basis of Arab. *lāhā ʿan.* McKane (*Proverbs,* p. 602) thinks that it means "one who indulges in horseplay" or "one who plays the fool (Barucq)" on the basis of Sir. 32 (35):15, where it stands in contrast to the earnest seeker of Torah, and its parallel *m*^{e}*śaḥēq* "one who is joking" (26:19). If it means "one who plays foolishly," its qualifier, "who shoots deadly arrows," defines him as behaving like a dangerous madman. *HALOT* (2:520, s.v. *lhh*) relate *lhh* to Syr. *mlahlah* "to be confused, filled with consternation" and Arab. *lahā*^{y} "to play" and render the *Hithpalpel* "to behave like a madman." Delitzsch (*Proverbs,* p. 191) says, "He who shoots

flaming missiles[32] *and*[33] *deadly arrows,*[34]
19 *so is a person who*[35] *deceives*[36] *his neighbor*
and says, "Am I not only joking?"[37]
20 *Without wood*[38] *a fire goes out;*[39]
and when there is no slanderer, a conflict calms down.
21 *Glowing charcoal to embers*[40] *and wood to fire,*
and a contentious[41] *person to kindling strife.*
22 *The words of a slanderer are like tidbits;*
so they descend into one's innermost being.
23 *Silver dross*[42] *glazed over a potsherd*

---

every possible death-bringing arrow is thought of as one who is beside himself, one who is of confused mind." Perhaps the lexeme is an onomatopoeia; the *"lah-lah"* sound resembles a madman's uncontrolled speech (cf. "la-la land" in colloquial English).

31. Although the relative participle normally agrees in definiteness, exceptions occur (*IBHS,* p. 621-22, P. 37.5b; GKC, P. 126w).

32. The meaning of the *hap. leg. zēq* is based on Akk. *ziqu, ziqtu* "torch, flaming arrow," Jewish Aram. *zîq,* "comet," *zîqqôt* in Isa. 50:11, referring to something that has been set on fire and gives light, and on archaeology. The burning arrow had holes at its top through which oily threads of tow were pulled and wrappped around. These arrows were shot burning (Meinhold, *Sprüche,* 2:444).

33. Conjunction override (*IBHS,* p. 648, P. 39n. 3; cf. 6:7; 7:17; 21:21).

34. Lit. "arrows and death," a hendiadys like "eyes of green and envy." The Targ. similarly renders "arrows of death."

35. *'ăšer* is elided.

36. II *rmh* occurs eight times, always meaning to design a scheme that will mislead a victim in order to harm him (see 11:1). Its antithesis in 1 Chr 12:17(12:18) is "to come to help" someone. There may be a wordplay with I *rmh* "to cast, shoot."

37. Lit. "Am I not a joker?" (*IBHS,* p. 624, P. 37).

38. Perhaps a plural of composition (i.e., the product or result of splitting the wood; *IBHS,* p. 119, P. 7.4.1b).

39. The LXX presents the truth by a positive equivalent: "With much wood, fire increases." It transformed the synthetic parallelism into antithetic because it either preferred antithetic parallels or read *tirbeh-'ēš* "fire increases" instead of *tikbeh-'ēš* "fire goes out or down."

40. *'ēṣîm* refers to everything in the plant world that is made of wood or has to do with wood. Depending on the context, it is chiefly translated "tree" or "wood." Elsewhere in Proverbs it is always a sing. cons. with *ḥayyîm* (i.e., "tree of life" [3:18; 11:30; 13:12; 15:4]). The pl. of extension (*IBHS,* p. 120, P. 7.4.1c) here refers to sticks of fuel wood (Gen. 22:3; 1 K. 17:12; Zech. 12:6).

41. See 18:19, n. 23.

42. Lit. "silver of dross." *Sîgîm* is a gen. of species (*IBHS,* p. 152, P. 9.5.3g) and a pl. of composition or extension (*IBHS,* pp. 119-20, P. 7.4.1b, 7.4.1c). *Sîg* is a pass. ptcp. of I *sûg* (= "what is cast aside"). In an influential article H. L. Ginsburg ("The North-Canaanite Myth of Anath and Aqhat," *BASOR* 98 [1945] 21, n. 55) repointed the consonants *ksp sygym* to read *kᵉsapsāgîm* (= "like glaze"; so the NEB, JB, NIV, TEV, and REB),

is smooth[43] *lips and an evil heart.*

---

contending that *spsg* in Ugaritic meant "glaze." G. R. Driver ("Problems in the Hebrew Text of Proverbs," *Bib* 32 [1951] 191) substantiated this interpretation, citing Lucas (*Ancient Egyptian Materials and Industry* [London, 1934], p. 106; [1948], p. 193): "Recent research has shown this [the use of silver dross], *spuma argenti* [litargyry or monoxide of lead for glazing] to have been a late discovery in the Middle East." But in 1976 M. Dietrich, O. Loretz, and J. Sanmartin ("Die angebliche Ug.-He. Parallele *spsg// sps(j)g(jm)*," *UF* 8 [1976] 39) and Loretz again in 1983 ("Ugaritische und hebräische Lexikographie (IV)," *UF* 15 [1983] 59-64) dealt the theory what should have been "a death blow" (Van Leeuwen, *Context and Meaning,* p. 111, n. 3) by arguing that the Ugaritic word probably meant "a bowl of fluid clay" and that *sygym* in Prov. 26:23 was derived from a marginal notation, calling attention to similar texts containing *ksp* and *sygym,* e.g., Prov. 25:4; Isa. 1:22). In 1988 Dressler again refuted the Ugaritic evidence, noting that Loretz's article appeared the year Loretz had evaluated his doctoral dissertation on the subject for publication but did not credit his work. In addition to proposing that *spsg* meant "a (glass-) bowl (of fluid clay), Dressler noted that Lucas's work underwent a revision by J. R. Harris in 1962 (A. Lucas, *Ancient Egyptian Materials and Industries* [4th ed. rev. J. R. Harris; London: E. Arnold, 1962], pp. 166-67) that presents a very different picture. In this addition "Lucas gives an example of lead glaze used on faience from the Twenty-second Dynasty (950-730 B.C.), thus entering the Solomonic era" (H. H. P. Dressler, "The Lesson of Proverbs 26:23," in *Ascribe to the Lord: Biblical and Other Studies in Memory of Peter C. Craigie* [JSOTSup 67; Sheffield: JSOT, 1988] 117-25). In sum, there is no reason to deny the traditional interpretation based on well-attested Heb. *sîg* "refuse" that in 26:23 means "silver dross" (L. Köhler, "Alttestamentliche Wortforschung — *Sîg, sîgîm* — Bleiglätte," *TZ* 3 [1947] 232-34). Unfortunately *HALOT* (3:750, s.v. *sapsîg*), later commentaries by Garrett (1993) and Clifford (1999) — but not by Whybray (1994) and Murphy (1998) — and translations such as the NRSV — but not the NJPS and the updated NASB — overlook the studies by Loretz and Dressler.

43. "Smooth" represents *ḥlqym* retroverted from *leia* of the LXX against *dōlᵉqîm* "burning" of the MT. A left vertical stroke is the only difference between *dalet* and *het* in the square script. The verb *dlq* otherwise occurs eight times with the meaning of either "to set on fire" in the *Qal* (Obad. 18) or the *Hiphil* (Isa. 5:11; Ezek. 24:10) or "to [hotly?] pursue" (Gen. 31:36; 1 Sam. 17:15; Ps. 10:2; Lam. 4:19). In Ps. 7:13(14) *dōlᵉqîm* is used of "flaming" arrows. This meaning is consistent with the "fire" images of vv. 18, 20, and 21 and finds a parallel in 16:27, 29, but offers a poor parallel to a "silver leaf" glaze. Van Leeuwen (*Context and Meaning of Proverbs 25–27,* p. 112, n. 4) defends the parallelism with silver dross, pointing out that "the imagery . . . of fire is suitable to the heat-using technologies of metallurgy and ceramic implicit in v. 23a." However, his argument illegitimately extends the image beyond what is stated. "Fervent" (NIV) and "ardent" (NJPS) to signify ardent protests of affection questionably jump from "burning" to an unattested sense. Gemser (*Sprüche,* pp. 95, 113), followed by Meinhold (*Sprüche,* p. 446), interprets *dlq* as meaning "streaming, running, quick" after Arabic I *dalaqa* "to spill," "to make slide." But why posit an otherwise unattested homonym that offers a unique and uncertain meaning when an ancient text offers an excellent parallel to the image of silver leaf glaze, fits the context of "disguising lips" (v. 24) and a "charming voice" (v. 25), and agrees with the use of *ḥlq* in Proverbs (e.g., 5:3)?

24 *With his lips*[44] *an enemy*[45] *dissembles,*
and in his inner being he harbors deception.
25 *If he makes his voice charming,*[46] *do not trust him,*[47]
for seven abominations are in his heart.
26 *His*[48] *hatred is concealed*[49] *by deception;*
his[50] *evil is revealed in a congregation.*
27 *As for the one who digs a pit,*[51] *he will fall into it;*
as for the one who rolls a stone, it will return to him.
28 *The lying tongue hates those oppressed*[52] *by it,*
but the smooth[53] *mouth works ruin.*

Solomon IIC warns against seven morally inferior types of people: the undisciplined (15:28), the fool (26:1-12), the sluggard (vv. 12-16), the busybody

44. K reads *biśpātô* "with his lip"; Q reads *biśpātāw* "with his lips."

45. Lit. "a hater." The hater here stands opposed to the son, as seen in the admonition "do not trust him" (26:25), making him his enemy. This was also the sense of *śōnē'* in 25:21. E. Jenni (*TLOT,* 3:1,278, s.v. *śn'*) notes that "the subst. qal and pi. ptcps. *śōnē'* and *mᵉśannē'* 'hater' usually parallel → *'ōyēb* 'enemy' and other synonyms such as *ṣar.*"

46. The unique *Piel* of *ḥānan* is probably a productive denominative of *ḥen* with its nontheological sense (*IBHS,* p. 413, P. 24.4g).

47. The antecedent of the suffix could be "his voice," but the subject is the personal enemy and its parallel is "in his heart." One trusts words as one gains confidence in a person to make good his word, to uphold it, and to make it true.

48. The pronominal suffix in verset B shows that the concrete noun refers to a person, the personal enemy of v. 24 (cf. Dahood, *Psalms III: 100-150,* pp. 411-12).

49. The LXX reads *ho kryptōn* (< *mᵉkasseh*). The pronominal suffix, "his evil," and *kōreh* (v. 27) probably gave rise to this facilitating reading. Moreover, it destroys the paronomasia with initial *tiggāleh* (G. Boström, *Paronomasi i den äldre hebreiska Maschallitteraturen* [*LUÅ,* N.F., Avd. 1, Bd. 23, Nr. 8; Lund, 1935], p. 50).

50. Although grammatical disagreement is possible, the masc. form is better not referred back to fem. *śin'â.*

51. The LXX adds *tǫ plēsion* "for the neighbor."

52. The LXX, Targ., Syr., and Vulg. read "truth," having thought of the Aramaic abstract noun *dokyā'* (= Heb. *zkh*) "purity." If so, the proverb has an Aramaic source (Driver, "Hebrew Notes on Prophets and Proverbs," *JTS* 41 [1940] 175). Driver ("Hebrew Studies," *JRAS* [1948] 164-68, 168 n. 3) on the basis of Aramaic, emends to *dikkûy* "declaring innocent/acquittal." To fit the sense of the preceding couplet, Gemser (*Sprüche,* p. 95) et al. emend to *'ᵃdōnāyw* or *bᵉ'ālāyw* "its owner," Fichtner (*BHS*) to *yᵉnaśśeh dokyâ* "will lift up its own crashing," and A. B. Ehrlich (*Randglossen zur hebräischen Bibel* [Hildesheim: G. Olms, 1968], Bd. 6) to *yś' dkyw* "will bear his own crashing." Toy (*Proverbs,* p. 481) emends to *yābî' šeber* "brings destruction," and H. Ringgren (*Sprüche/Prediger: Übersetzt und Erklärt* [Göttingen: Vandenhoeck & Ruprecht, 1967]) to *dᵉkî* "collapse," leaving the meaning of the verse open to the destruction/collapse of others and/or of the slanderer.

53. The LXX reads "unguarded"; Targ., "indecisive" (< II *ḥlq* "divide"); Syr., "malicious."

(v. 17), the mischief maker (vv. 18-19), the slanderer (vv. 20-22), and the son's personal enemy (vv. 23-28). Seven symbolizes completeness. If *midḥeh* (= "overthrown") in 26:28 refers to a wall thrust down, the section is framed by an *inclusio* that pictures the ruin of the inferior types of people to a breached wall, escalated from loss of defense (see 25:28) to utter ruin (26:28).

a. Janus (25:28)

This janus proverb is connected syntactically with 25:23-27 by presenting in verset B the topic, a person without self-restraint, and in verset A its comparative image, a breached wall, and thematically with the collection of proverbs about the fool (26:1-12), for the fool is characterized by a lack of self-control (cf. 12:16). *A breached* [see 3:10] *city* (see 1:21), *which has no* (*'ên;* lit. "there is no" [see 21:30]) *wall* (see 18:11) is defenseless (cf. 2 K. 14:13). The decisive characteristic of a city is its protective wall (see 18:11; 21:22); if the enemy razes it to the ground, the city is left defenseless and open to all sorts of villainy. The topic, *a person* (*'îš;* see I: 89) *whose spirit* [see I: 92] *has no* (*'ên;* see verset A) *restraint* (*maʿṣār;* see 14:6),[54] paradoxically presents a person who has uncurbed psychic vitality within as his enemy does from without. His unchecked animal drives plunder him like an attacking enemy for several correlative reasons. First, unless one masters his lust, temper, and evil inclinations of all sorts, sin will overpower him. Freud may have first articulated psychologically that we are not masters in our house, ruled as we are by unruly passions, but he is not the first to discern it. The proverb knows the power of sin that drives one to death as surely as the narrator who represented that power as a crouching lion lying in wait to destroy Cain (Gen. 4:6-7). Second, society will pay the fool back for the unrestrained folly that erupted from within and that he inflicted on them (cf. 10:6; 14:17, 29; 15:18; 19:11, 19; 29:22). Third, he remains defenseless before the wicked and/or temptation from without (see 7:21-22); both can do him great harm (see 1:16). Finally, he is easy prey to an enemy from without who can torment him and/or cause him to act rashly from within (cf. 1 K. 21:1-26; Esth. 3:5, 6; 5:13). The unbridled person is defeated before the contest. His salvation is to embrace the LORD and his wisdom immediately for his defense (see 16:32) and for victory (21:22). Wisdom, which is a divine grace attained by faith, not native power, fortifies the inner self and so safeguards its possessor (see

54. The *hap. leg.* consists of the abstract prefix *mem* plus the verbal root *ʿāṣar* "to prevent someone or something from doing something." It is used of restraining, of limiting, a plague (Num. 16:48), the heavens from giving rain (Deut. 11:17), the womb from giving conception (Gen. 16:2), etc. The by-form *maʿṣōr* in 14:6 is used with *'ên* with reference to LORD's limitless power to deliver (1 Sam. 14:16).

ch. 2; 14:29; 17:27; cf. 3:5; 22:19). For Christians, the fruit of the Spirit yields self-control (Gal. 5:22-23).

b. The Fool (26:1-12)

The keyword "fool[s]" *(k^e^sîl[îm])* occurs in every verse of the new composition (vv. 1-12) except v. 2, suggesting a title for the new poem, "A Mirror of Fools."[55] "Glory," the last word of v. 1, functions as a catchword to the *inclusio* around the preceding unit (25:2, 27). One must neither seek the glory that belongs to God and kings (25:2-27) nor give glory to fools (26:1-12). Formally, the subunit consists of ten sayings (vv. 1-3, 6-12) and two admonitions (vv. 4-5). Apart from the concluding verse, these ten sayings have essentially the same structure. Their A versets present striking negative vehicles from the order of creation (cf. 25:23-28) as images of the fool in the social order. "A Mirror of Fools" develops the theme that it is unfitting, downright dangerous, to honor a fool by educating him with proverbs and entrusting him with responsible service but fitting to punish and rebuke him. Its introduction sounds the theme (vv. 1-3), its body develops both the positive and negative aspects of the theme (vv. 4-10), and its conclusion features its positive aspect (vv. 11-12).[56]

(1) Introduction (26:1-3)

Verse 1 summarizes the negative aspect of the theme: "Honor is not fitting for a fool." Verse 2 functions as a comparison and a contrast with v. 1. Sharing the same syntax as v. 1 ("like" [*ka*] + *"like"* [*ka*] [verset A]) + "so" *kēn* [verset B]), it too pertains to what is unfitting, namely, uttering a curse against an innocent person. However, it principally functions as a contrast. On the one hand, glory is not fitting for a fool because, as v. 1 makes clear and the body will make clearer, giving him social standing will cause great damage. On the other hand, uttering a curse against an innocent person will do no damage because it has no place to rest. A paronomasia with a chiasm assists the contrast. The last word of v. 1b, *kābēd,* the root of "glory" *(kābôd),* means "heavy," and the first word of v. 2b, Heb. *qālal,* the root of "curse" *(q^e^lālâ),* means "light." Indeed, in the Semitic languages it can mean

55. In consonance with the keyword's initial /*k*/, the palatals /*k~q~g*/ predominate and help unify the pericope. Verse 1 sets the stage: *kšlg bqyṣ wkmṭr bqṣyr kn l' n'wh lksyl kbwd.* Apart from the prefixes, every word begins with /*k~q*/ except *lō'-nā'weh* "not fitting."

56. Van Leeuwen (*Context and Meaning,* p. 100) says, "The idea of fittingness is the poem's central concern."

"to be flighty," a notion that gives rise to the image of birds flying about without landing. Verse 3 functions as a climax to the introduction and sounds the positive counterpoint to the negative theme. What is fitting is "a rod for the backs of fools" (v. 3). The assonance between *ṣippôr* "sparrow," *d*^{e}*rôr* "swallow,"[57] and *ḥ*^{a}*môr* "donkey" helps to sound the positive thesis, what is fitting (v. 3), at the same time as the negative, what is unfitting (vv. 1-2). In sum, in v. 1 something good (honor) is unfittingly given to someone bad (a fool). In v. 2 something bad (a curse) is unfittingly given to someone good (an innocent person). In v. 3 something bad (a rod) is fittingly given to someone bad (a fool).[58]

1 *As* (see 11:22) signals that the topic, the incongruity and damage of giving honor (i.e., social weight) to a fool (verset B), is compared to the anomaly and calamity of *snow* [see 25:13] *in summer* (see 6:8), the long, dry season from March to October, *and* [conjunctive] *rain* (*māṭār* is interchangeable with *gešem;* see 25:14, 23) *at harvest* (see 6:8). The main clause, "is unfitting," is elided. Snow could be kept until the time of harvest and could then be used for refreshment (see 25:13), but a snowfall in summer would signal that the times were out of joint and would be catastrophic (cf. 1 Sam. 12:17). Snow or rain ruins the grain harvest by damaging and causing it to rot. *So* [see 11:22] indicates the tenor: *honor* [see 25:2] *is not fitting* [see 17:7] *for a fool* (*liksîl;* see I: 112). The notion of being unfit implies a standard, namely, that which promotes physical life in the cosmic order and social well-being in the social order. The LORD's inspired sages reveal in Proverbs the eternal and life-producing social standard. The fool despises this wisdom, and giving him honor both strengthens him in his folly and encourages the gullible to follow him (cf. 19:10). Elevating him to a position of leadership and/or holding him up as a role model signals a topsy-turvy and damned society (cf. 2 Sam. 15:1-12; 1 K. 12:1-20; cf. Prov. 20:29; 16:31). "Some of the hero worship of the present day falls under the same verdict."[59]

2 People can unfittingly honor a fool (v. 1), but when they curse the wise, the Moral Governor will not fulfill their curse (v. 2). Their unfulfilled, undeserved curse in the social order (v. 2b) is likened to a flitting bird in the created order (v. 2a). *As* (see v. 1) again signals the comparative clause: *a fluttering* (*lānûd,* see n. 2)[60] *bird* (*ṣippôr,* see 6:5) connotes moving about in aimless and/or agitated motion. More specifically, *like a spar-*

57. "Sparrow" and "swallow" are glosses; the precise genre or species of birds is uncertain.

58. So Van Leeuwen, *Proverbs,* p. 224.

59. Aitken, *Proverbs,* p. 105.

60. *Nwd* is used of a head that is moved back and forth (Jer. 18:16), of a person who wanders hither and yon (Gen. 4:12), and here of a bird's fluttering flight.

row (d^{e}rôr) with regard to *flying* (see 23:5). *D^{e}rôr* denotes some kind of bird. In its other biblical occurrence (Ps. 84:3[4]) it is used with the similar-sounding *ṣippôr* with no discernible difference in meaning between them. The predicate, *cannot land,* is elided. *So* (see v. 1) again signals the topic. *An undeserved* [see 1:11] *curse (qillat)* is rooted in the Semitic languages, where it means "to be light, small" and in its factitive and causative stems "to esteem as unimportant, insignificant, to despise, disdain, to hold in contempt, to vilify, to libel, to declare cursed, accursed," the derivative of which means "curse, defamation, slander, vilification." It may have been chosen instead of *'lh, ḥrp,* etc. because the simile works in part by a pun on *q^{e}lālâ,* whose root means "to be light" and so can be used in the Semitic languages in the sense of "to be flighty," matching the fluttering birds. In this respect, it stands in contrast to *kbd* "to be heavy" (see v. 1). The opposite of *q^{e}lālâ* "cursing" (i.e., making one sterile and consigning one to chaos) through a human agent is blessing or *b^{e}rākâ* (i.e., to fill one with the potency for life and victory; see 10:6).[61] All undeserved curses *will not come to pass* (*lō' bō';* see 6:11).[62] As long as a bird is flying hither and yon in an agitated and aimless manner, it remains in the air without landing. Likewise, a groundless curse cannot land in the order of redemption, for a legitimate landing place (i.e., a guilty person) is lacking (cf. Ps. 109:3, 17-19, 28).[63] The deadly effect of a deserved curse (i.e., a word that condemns its victim to sterility, death, and defeat) will come to pass (cf. Deut. 28:15; 29:19[18], 20[19]; Josh. 6:26; 1 K. 16:34; 2 K. 2:24; Prov. 30:10; 1 Cor. 16:22), but not an undeserved curse (cf. Num. 22:6; 23:8; Deut. 23:4[5], 5[6]; 1 Sam. 17:43; 2 Sam. 16:12; Jer. 15:10). Since the Creator and LORD of history is the source of blessing and cursing through a fellow human being, the proverb infers that the undeserved/unfitting curse is ineffective be-

61. *Qll Piel* occurs seven times in opposition to derivatives of *brk.* This opposition to *brk* appears most sharply in connection with the substantive *q^{e}lālâ* with the similarly formed substantive *b^{e}rākâ.* Thanks to this opposition, *q^{e}lālâ* becomes the unique term for the word of cursing by a fellow human being (C. A. Keller, *TLOT,* 2:645, s.v. 1,143-44). Jacob fears that he will bring on himself a *q^{e}lālâ* "curse," not a *b^{e}rākâ* "blessing" (Gen. 27:12), and Balaam's "curse" is transformed into a "blessing" (Deut. 23:6). In Deuteronomy *q^{e}lālâ* expresses curses for disobedience and is often juxtaposed with *b^{e}rākâ.* As the mediated blessing, *b^{e}rākâ* fills one with the potency of life and victory; thus the mediated curse deprives one of blessing. In the era of salvation, people will consider a person who fails to reach a hundred years to have come under a *q^{e}lālâ* (Isa. 65:20).

62. McKane (*Proverbs,* p. 600) weakens the proverb by inserting the restrictive relative *'šer* (i.e., the undeserved curse that does not alight). This allows the possibility that some undeserved curses may be effective, though McKane does not make that point. However, the chiasm with *lō'-nā'weh* in v. 1 and the theology of the book support the traditional syntax.

63. Van Leeuwen, *Context and Meaning,* p. 91.

cause the Sovereign does not back it up. "They may curse, but you will bless" (Ps. 109:28).

3 The introduction now turns from what is not fitting for fools to what is fitting, but again by comparing two things in the created order with the social order. As a whip prods a warhorse and a bit restrains and controls a donkey, so a rod restrains fools from their folly and prods them to conform their lives to wisdom. *A whip* was used as a goad *for a warhorse* (see 21:31) that was attached to a chariot.[64] *A bit,* though often glossed "bridle,"[65] is located in the animal's sensitive lips (2 K. 19:28) and used with *resen,* perhaps the bridle or lead line attached to the bit.[66] Archaeology verifies that bits were placed in the horse's mouth, for at their side are plates with eyes for the rein or bridle. In addition to controlling the charioteer's horse in the open field, a bit also restrains and controls *a donkey,* "the prototypical beast of burden," on an uneven path.[67] Tremendous energy is required to tame the wild spirit of horses and donkeys, and even when tamed, they demand great energy to train them to useful activity. *And* (see 25:20) introduces the topic. *A rod for the back* [see 10:13] *of fools* (*kᵉsîlîm,* I: 109). Both versets elide the predicate "is fitting," to be supplied from v. 1. Brute force, not words, is fitting to goad and govern animals and fools, for it is a language both understand (cf. 10:13; 17:10; 18:6; 19:29; 27:22; Ps. 32:9; Sir. 33:24).

(2) Body (26:4-10)

The composition's seven-verse body consists of two partial subunits: two admonitions that prescribe correction as fitting for the fool (vv. 4-5) and five sayings proscribing honor as unfitting for a fool (vv. 6-10).

4-5 Two admonitions develop the countertheme of what is fitting for a fool and form a relatively smooth transition logically from the introduction into the body. In addition to physical caning to control the fool, without naming who is responsible (v. 3), the wise son/disciple needs to give the fool a verbal answer (vv. 4-5). The pair is firmly linked by their almost verbatim admonitions (verset A), by their identical syntax (impv. [verset A] + *pen* [verset B]), and by the assonance of *pen-tišweh* ("lest you become") and *pen-yihyeh* ("lest he be"). The apparent contradiction between their admonitions, "do not answer a fool" versus "answer a fool," is resolved by clarifying the ambiguous preposi-

64. *Šôṭ* denotes a flexible whip or lash, in contrast to the *šēbeṭ* and *maṭṭeh,* which seem to signify a wooden rod or staff (D. M. Fouts, *NIDOTTE,* 4:64, s.v. *šôṭ*). In its five certain occurrences a *šôṭ* is used to prod (1 K. 12:11, 14 [= 2 Chr. 10:11, 14]; Prov. 26:3; Nah. 3:2) or to punish (Job 5:21; 9:23; Isa. 10:26).

65. *HALOT,* 2:618, s.v. *meteg.*

66. Cf. *HALOT,* 3:1249, s.v. *resen.*

67. M. S. Moore and M. L. Brown, *NIDOTTE,* 2:172, s.v. *ḥᵃmôr.*

tion k^e ("according to") in light of the negative consequence to be avoided in the B versets. The LXX pointed the way by rendering k^e differently in the two proverbs (see n. 5). "In poetry the point of comparison [signified by k^e] may be left vague in order to allow an analogy to open up, inducing the reader to engage the analogy and find not one but many contacts between the things compared."[68] The son's answer must distinguish between what is unfitting (v. 4) and fitting (v. 5). It is unfitting to meet the fool's insult with insult (2 Pet. 3:9). Should the disciple reply vindictively, harshly, and/or with lies — the way fools talk — he too — "yes, even you" — would come under the fool's condemnation. Rather, without lowering himself to the fool's level in a debate, but by overcoming evil with good (25:21-22), the wise must show the fool's folly for what it is. The wise do not silently accept and tolerate the folly and thereby confirm fools in it. Both proverbs are absolutes and applicable at the same time, contrary to the opinion of many commentators, who think they are relative to the situation.[69] To be sure, there is a time to be silent and a time to speak (Eccl. 4:5), but one must always, not in only certain situations, answer a fool to destabilize him, but, always, not sometimes, without becoming like him.

4 The rationale for the admonition not to answer a fool according to his folly (v. 4a) is to avoid the negative consequence of becoming like the fool (v. 4b). *Do not answer* [see 1:28] *a fool* [see v. 1] *according* (*k^e*, in agreement in kind) *to his folly* (see I: 113; i.e., "the fool's malicious and ignorant style").[70] *Lest* [see 22:25] *you become like him* (see 3:15), *even you!* (cf. *'apāttâ* in 22:19), which emphatically focuses the son's attention on himself, who should stand in contrast to the fool.[71]

5 The rationale for answering a fool according to his folly (v. 5a) is to avoid the negative consequence that the fool arrogantly replaces the LORD's heavenly wisdom with his own (v. 5b). *Answer a fool according to his folly* [see 25:4a] *lest* [see 25:4b] *he become wise in his own eyes* (see 3:7). The wise person must expose the fool's distortions to serve his own interests at the expense of the community and must not silently accept it and thereby contribute to establishing his topsy-turvy world against the rule of God. An answer that is in agreement with the LORD's wisdom puts the fool's topsy-

68. *IBHS,* p. 203, P. 11.2.9b.

69. That error began as early as both the Talmud (B. T. Shab. 30b), which applied v. 4 to secular controversies and v. 5 to religious. The Midrash restricted v. 4 to when one knows the fool as such, and v. 5 to when he does not so know him (Delitzsch, *Proverbs,* p. 176). Many moderns (cf. Van Leeuwen, *Proverbs,* pp. 223-24, 227) suggest that the audience must decide which proverb is appropriate to a situation. Whybray comes closer to the true explanation that by the contrary admonitions the editor aims "to demonstrate that no human wisdom can encompass the whole truth" (Whybray, *Proverbs,* p. 372).

70. Clifford, *Proverbs,* p. 231.

71. *IBHS,* p. 663, P. 39.3.4d; pp. 295-96, P. 16.3.2d, e.

turvy world rightside up and and so is fitting. "Granted the discomfort and even danger of such association, someone has to speak up for wisdom."[72]

6-10 The following five sayings return to the introduction's form, using negative images from the created order to answer the questions what is meant by "honor" and why it is "unfitting" for fools (v. 1). However, these verses escalate the images from impersonal weather images (v. 1) to animal images (vv. 2-3) to striking and ludicrous human images, moving from deformed folk (vv. 6-7) to deranged people (vv. 9-10). At the pivot stands the absurd stone-slinger (v. 8). Verses 6 and 7 are sensibly bound by the images of "feet" (Heb. *raglayim*) and "legs" (Heb. *šōqayim*) and syntactically bound by the dual number. Verses 9 and 10 are connected by the paronomasia of *šikkôr* "drunkard" and *śōkēr* "one who hires." Duane Garrett astutely shows that the compilers arranged these sayings in a chiastic structure:

A Committing important business to a fool (v. 6)
  B A proverb in a fool's mouth (v. 7)
    C Honoring a fool (v. 8)
  B′ A proverb in a fool's mouth (v. 9)
A′ Committing important business to a fool (v. 10).[73]

Hezekiah's editors profiled this chiasm by repeating verbatim in its inner core "a proverb in the mouth of a fool," an exaggerated form of catchwords, on either side of the pivot. Its outer core pertains to hiring the fool for a job, of which commissioning him to send messages is one. The pivot is also the center verse of the body and conclusion. In this featured position its final words shout climactically the composition's big idea, "to honor a fool [is unfitting]," repeating verbatim the final words of the summary statement (v. 1). The absurd stone-slinger images the prosaic "not fitting" of the summarization (v. 1). Instead of hurling the stone (i.e., the fool) far from him, the ludicrous slinger (i.e., the one giving the fool honor) binds up "the stone" so that it comes around and whacks him a good one on his own head. Even their syntax of k^e ("like") plus *kēn* ("so") underscores the point. The assonance of *ṣ*^{e}*rôr* ("binding") with *ṣippôr* ("sparrow") and *d*^{e}*rôr* ("swallow") strengthens the pivot's link with the introduction.

The verses surrounding the pivot illuminate how one honors fools. Their inner core points to putting the honored proverbs in their mouths (vv. 7, 9), and their outer frame to commissioning or hiring them (vv. 6, 10). To receive a commission to represent a dignitary was high honor indeed in the biblical world, for the messenger was in fact the sender's plenipotentiary. In

72. Clifford, *Proverbs,* p. 231.
73. Garrett, *Proverbs,* pp. 212-13.

sum, one can glorify a fool by giving him an education and/or by hiring him. Finally, the A versets of the saying around the pivot elaborate why it is unfitting to honor fools. Hiring him and/or educating him is absurd and worthless (vv. 6-7). Worse yet, he is dangerous both to those who honor him (vv. 6-7) and to society at large (vv. 9-10). With respect to the latter, the compilers heighten the images from a brawling drunkard waving his thornbush to a mad archer. This dangerous character, like a modern terrorist, randomly kills all within his sight and range.

6 *One who chops off*[74] *his feet* (or "both legs"; see 1:15) and *one who drinks* [i.e., experiences; cf. 4:17; 23:32; Job 34:7] *violence* (see 4:17; i.e., the violence one suffers [cf. Job 21:20], not what one practices [cf. Job 15:16]) depict *one who sends* [see 22:21] *messages* (*d*^{e}*bārîm;* see 10:19) carried *by the hand* [see 10:4] *of a fool* (see 26:1). The parallels are held together syntactically by independent participles, by a play on feet and hand, and above all by the implied mischief linking the topic and its metaphors. Sending messages by the hand of a fool is as bizarre as chopping off one's feet and as deadly as drinking poison. By infuriating the recipient of the messages rather than gaining a pair of feet to add to one's own, the fool brings about precisely the opposite of what was intended, tantamount to rendering one lame. Instead of bringing healing (see 13:17) and finding refreshment through the communication (25:13; cf. 10:26), one inflicts on himself high-handed injustice and cold-blooded, physical brutality (see 4:17; cf. Num. 13:32; 14:1-4; 1 K. 11:26-40; 2 K. 8:15). By exaggerated sarcasm, the proverb sobers the son to realize that hiring a fool to communicate for him is dangerously unfitting.

7 As a lame person still has legs but cannot use them for walking because they hang loosely and uncertainly from him, so a noble proverb in the mouth of of a fool carries no weight (i.e., authority) and gets him nowhere.[75] *Legs (šōqayim),* when used of human beings, denotes the calves, the shanks, the lower part of the leg from the knees downward in contrast to the thigh (*yārēk;* cf. Judg. 15:8).[76] *Dangle (dalyû)*[77] is used in Job 28:4 of miners who

74. I *qṣh* occurs five times and refers to the diminishing of something. According to *HALOT* (3:1,120, s.v. I *qṣh*), it means "to bring to an end" (Hab. 2:10) in the *Qal*; in the *Piel* it signifies "to break off, cut off piece by piece" (2 K. 10:32) or "to chop off" (Prov. 26:6); and in the *Hiphil* it is used of cutting away the plaster from the inside of walls to rid them of mildew (Lev. 14:41, 43).

75. By adding to the proverb, the Vulg. changes the point from uselessness to being unseemly: "As a lame man has fair legs in vain, so a parable is unseemly in the mouth of fools." But it does preserve the connotation that the problem does not reside in the legs (= proverb) but in the person.

76. V. Hamilton, *TWOT,* 2:912, s.v. *šōq.* When used of animals *šōq* refers to the thigh of the hind legs rather than the shoulders of the fore legs (Hamilton, *NIDOTTE,* 4:70 s.v. *šôq*).

77. From II *dlh* (cf. I *dlh* in 20:5), probably a bi-form of II *dll;* see n. 9.

"dangle, far from people they sway *(nāʿû).*" *From the lame* or the limping *(pissēaḥ)* designates a person whose leg is disabled and unusable for locomotion. *And* (*wᵉ;* see 26:3) *a proverb* (*māšāl;* see 1:1) *dangles in the mouth* (*bᵉpî;* see 14:3) *of fools (kᵉsîlîm).* This proverb entails that it is inappropriate to educate the fool by putting proverbs in his mouth (see 17:16). Fools are morally too dull to utter it seasonably (cf. 25:11-12), and/or they invalidate its effect by their defective character (cf. Matt. 7:3-5; Luke 4:23; Rom. 2:21). The proverb's good message in the flawed messenger falls flat on its face and makes not the slightest impact.

8 The pivot pokes fun at one who gives a fool honor by explicitly comparing him with tying a stone in a sling. *Like* [see 26:1, 2] *one who binds* (*ṣᵉrôr;* see n. 13; 4:12)[78] *a stone ('eben)*[79] *in (bᵉ)*[80] *a sling* (*margēmâ, hap. leg.*[81]). "One could achieve an approximate range of 200 meters by a sling. In this regard, this weapon surpasses a bow to which v. 10a seems to allude (cf. v. 18; 25:18). A sling was made of a leather or textile strip that had been broadened in the middle and into which the stone was placed, but never bound. A person held the ends of the strip together and swung it until he loosened one of its ends so that the stone could fly." *So* [see 26:1, 2] *is the person who gives* [see 22:16] *honor* (*kābôd;* see 26:1) *to a fool.* The proverb escalates v. 1. Giving status and/or fame to a fool is not only unseemly (v. 1) but also absurd, ineffectual, and threatening. A warrior hurls the stone out of the sling to protect himself, and so should a person fling a fool out of society to

78. When geminates are formed like the regular verb, they almost all have an active, not a stative meaning (GKC, P. 67cc).

79. *'eben* is the most common word for "stone" (269x). It could be used of a foundation of several tons (1 K. 5:17[31]) or of a stone the size of a pebble (Exod. 28:9). It was used for a variety of purposes: as building material (Exod. 20:25; 1 K. 5:17-18; Neh. 4:3 [3:35]; Amos 5:12), for vessels (Exod. 7:19), charms (Prov. 17:8), idols (Deut. 4:28), weights (Prov. 20:10), covers for wells and tombs (Gen. 29:2; Josh. 10:18), memorials (Exod. 28:12), writing tablets (Exod. 31:18), and, as here, for a sling stone (Judg. 20:16).

80. Delitzsch (*Proverbs,* pp. 180-81) thinks that *ṣrr* + *bᵉ* means to fit the stone into something, citing Job 26:8; Prov. 30:4, with reference to "wrapping waters in a cloud." According to him, the stone is the fool, and giving honor to the fool is wasteful because it will no more remain on him than a stone in a sling. Although the parallelism equates the stone with the fool, *ṣrr bᵉ* does not mean "to put into something." The metaphor in Prov. 30:4 more probably means to restrain the rain from falling out of the clouds. In 1 Sam. 25:29, Abigail contrasts David, whose life "will be bound (*ṣᵉrûrâ*) in the bundle of the living," with his enemies, whom God hurls away as if from a sling.

81. The LXX (= *sphendonē̜*), Syr., Targ., Rashi, et al. understand it to mean "sling." Although *qelaʿ* is the normal word for "sling," this meaning better fits the parallelism and the 16 uses of the verb *rgm* "to execute by covering with a heap of stones, to stone." The *mem* prefix indicates that it is an instrument for hurling stones (*IBHS,* p. 90, P. 5.6b). Delitzsch (*Proverbs,* 180) cites *raggem* (Targ. Esth. v. 14), of David's slinging stones against Goliath.

protect himself. Whoever gives a fool honor looks as ridiculous as if he tied up a deadly stone in a sling, and instead of advancing his cause by catapulting it, kept whirling the lethal weapon precariously around his own head.

9 The proverb returns to the danger inappropriately educated fools inflict on others by juxtaposing a noxious thornbush in the drunkard's hand with a proverb in the fool's mouth. *A thornbush (ḥôaḥ)*[82] *in* [see n. 15] *the hand* [see 1:24; 19:24] *of a drunkard* [*šikkôr;* cf. 23:29-35; Jer. 23:9] *and a proverb in the mouth of fools* (*kᵉsîlîm;* see I: 109). The abc :: a′b′c′ pattern linking the versets suggests that the thornbush (a) is equated with a proverb (a′), and the hand of the drunkard (b) with the fool's mouth (b′). The incomplete passive construction (see n. 15) does not aim to supply the agent for placing the proverb in the fool's mouth. The drunkard in the Old Testament is no down-and-out bum. Many of its 13 occurrences refer explicitly or inferentially to kings (1 K. 16:9; 20:16; Isa. 28:1, 3) and the wealthy (1 Sam. 25:36), who could afford the quantities required. The staggering drunkard symbolized corruption (Isa. 5:22-23), dereliction of duty (5:11), and, above all, loathsome and deadly folly (1 Sam. 25:36; 1 K. 16:9; 20:16; Job 12:25; Ps. 107:27; Isa. 19:14; 24:20). In 20:1 intoxicants are personified as mockers and brawlers. A thornbush in the hands of a person who does not know where he is going or what he is doing is like the proverbial firearms in the hand of a child. A proverb in the mouth of the wise brings healing, but in the mouth of a fool it wounds and lacerates (cf. 10:32; 11:9, 11; 12:18; 13:16b; 14:3; Job 16:1-4, passim).

10 Whereas vv. 7 and 9 represented the fool as unfit to use even a proverb, this verse shows him unfit for any kind of work. Both in word (vv. 7, 9) and in deed (cf. vv. 6, 10), he inflicts damage. Anyone who hires him hires one who is as berserk and dangerous as a mass terrorist. *An archer*[83] *who pierces*[84] *all* in this context is restricted to *who pass by.*[85] *And* (see vv. 3, 7, 9,

82. *Ḥôaḥ* occurs 11 times and is rendered "a/the thistle" (2 K. 14:9[2x] = 2 Chr. 25:18 [2x]), "brambles" (Isa. 34:13), "thorns" (Song 2:2; Hos. 9:6), and "briars" (Job 31:40) by the NIV. In Song 2:2 it is pl. and probably should be rendered "thornbushes." Twice it is used distinctively of a "hook put into the gills of a sea creature to carry it home" (2 Chr. 33:11; Job 41:2 [40:26]); *HALOT,* 1:296, s.v. *ḥôaḥ*). It is used in conjunction with *sîrîm* and *qimmôš* in Isa. 34:13 (cf. Prov. 24:31).

83. Although *rab* could mean "a great one" of some sort derived from *rbh* or be bi-form I *rbb* (*HALOT,* 3:1,174-75, s.v. I *rbb*), the predicate "pierce" favors interpreting it as a substantive from II *rbb* "to shoot" (Gen. 49:23; *HALOT,* 3:1,173, s.v. III *rab* and 1,175, s.v. II *rbb* "to shoot"; cf. Gen. 49:23; Job 16:13; Jer. 50:29).

84. The *Polel* ptcp. is also a homonym, being derived from either *ḥûl* (= "a master produces" [cf. 25:23]) or *hll* (= an archer who pierces). Since all the A versets in the sayings of vv. 1-12 are negative, the latter is preferable. Also, the notion of wounding links v. 10 with v. 9.

85. "The sense in which *kōl* is to be taken being gathered from the context" (BDB, p. 482, s.v. *kōl*).

10) links the image and the topic, *one who hires* [see 11:18][86] *a fool* (*kᵉsîl;* see v. 1). *And* (*wᵉ;* see 26:1a) compounds the topic. *One who hires those who pass by* (*ʿōbᵉrîm;* see in 9:15; 10:25) by chance (cf. Ezek. 5:14; Mic. 2:8).

(3) Conclusion (26:11-12)

The conclusion to "The Mirror of Fools" inferentially elaborates the positive theme that discipline fits a fool. Verse 11 pillories the fool as incapable of saving himself, but v. 12 speaks of hope for his salvation. According to vv. 3-5, his hope lies in physical punishment and wise answers. The catchphrase "wise in his own eyes" and the use of direct address to the son in vv. 5 and 12 also point to the connection between these verses. The conclusion may be marked off syntactically by *as,* matching the introduction (vv. 1-2) and the pivot (v. 8), and poetically by returning to negative animal images (i.e., sparrow/swallow [v. 2], horse/donkey [v. 3], and dog [v. 11]).

11 This figurative proverb underscores the obduracy of fools, their hallmark, by an intentionally repulsive simile. It juxtaposes a fool with the contemptible dog; his destructive folly with the dog's vomit; and the fool's incorrigibility with the dog's repulsive nature to return to its vomit, to sniff at it, to lick it, and finally to eat it. In the ancient Near East the dog had been a domestic animal for ages, and the Bible speaks of the barking watchdog (Isa. 56:10) and of the sheepdog (Job 30:1). Nevertheless, the 32 occurrences of *a dog (keleb)* hold the animal in contempt (cf. 1 Sam. 17:43). Dogs ate garbage, carcasses, and corpses and licked the blood of the dead, a sort of scavenger (1 K. 14:11; 21:23-24; passim), and were reckoned as unclean and detestable (cf. Exod. 22:31[30]). They appear figuratively for evildoers (2 Sam. 16:9; Ps. 22:16[17]). The metonymy *returns to* (see 1:23) entails that it eats *its vomit* (*qēʾô, qēʾ* being a by-form *qîʾ,* Prov. 23:8).[87] The stomach violently discourages what it has swallowed through the mouth because it proved unpalatable. *A fool* (*kᵉsîl;* see 26:1) *repeats* [see 17:9] *his folly* (see I: 113). In both the image and the topic, the body rejects the repulsive object (i.e., vomit and folly), but the debased spirit craves it! Food poison does not affect the fool's appetite. The New Testament instantiates the proverb in relation to those who "have escaped the corruption of the world" but have become "again entangled in it and overcome" by it (2 Pet. 2:20-22; cf. Exod. 8:8[4], 15[11]; 9:27, 34, 35; 1 K. 21:27-29; 22:8, 37; Matt. 12:43-45; Mark 6:20-27).

12 This verse functions as a janus between "A Mirror of Fools" (vv. 1-12) and "A Mirror of Sluggards" (vv. 13-16). On the one hand it repeats the

86. *Śkr* denotes "granting of payment for labor, service, or almost any type of benefit [see 11:18]" (C. Van Dam, *NIDOTTE,* 3:1,244, s.v. *śkr*)

87. *HALOT,* 3:1,059, s.v. *qēʾ.*

keyword "fool," but on the other hand it drops the structure of the preceding sayings and repeats "wise in his own eyes" at the conclusion of both units (see 26:16). Instead of using negative images drawn from the created order as standards for evaluating the fool, v. 12 sets the fool himself as a standard of comparison for one who is wise in his own eyes. *Do you see a person* [see 22:29] *who is wise in his own eyes* (see 3:7; 26:5)? *There is more hope* [see 10:28] *for a fool* (*kᵉsîl;* see 26:1) *than for him.* The comparison opens the door of hope for the fool's salvation through discipline a bit wider. The sage cracked that door open by suggesting that a rod is fitting for a fool (v. 3), and opened it wider by the admonition to rebut the fool before he becomes "wise in his own eyes." Worse than a fool is a deluded fool. Although the fool cannot learn from his mistakes (v. 11), timely physical and verbal correction can save him from castling himself in his own conceit (cf. Isa. 50:11; Matt. 9:12-13; 21:31; Luke 15:11-18; John 9:40, 41; 1 Cor. 3:18; 8:2). The sluggard is worse off than the non-deluded fool because he is by nature already "wise in his own eyes," which paradoxically is not wise at all.

c. The Sluggard (26:13-16)

"A Mirror of Sluggards" (26:13-16) is connected with "A Mirror of Fools" (vv. 1-12) by the janus of v. 12. The connection escalates the inferior types of men in this unit to a more pernicious stage of adding conceit to folly (cf. 26:5, 12, 16). "A Mirror of Sluggards" (26:13-16) is one of three poems on the sluggard (see 6:6-11; 24:30-34) and the topic of sloth (see I: 114). Several poetic devices unify the composition. First, the keyword "sluggard" is repeated in every verse. Second, the sayings play on the consonance of *mṭtw* ("couch," the final word of v. 14), *ṭmn* ("buries," the initial word of v. 15), and *ṭʿm* ("judicious answer," the final word of v. 16), and on *šûb Hiphil* ("return," v. 15b, and "give," v. 6b). Third, the section is unified by the use of an animal image in vv. 11 and 13. Fourth, in a katabasis of movement the sluggard does not go out of the house (v. 13), cannot even make it off his couch (v. 14), and finally cannot even get his hand from the dish to his mouth (v. 15). Although he cuts a comical figure, the poem climactically represents him as under the illusion that he is wiser than the wisest (v. 16). The poem's frame represents his problem as spiritual/psychological. His irrational fear restricts him to his house (v. 13), and his irrational pride prevents his correction (v. 16; cf. 26:5, 12). The subunit's core deals with the "activities" of sleeping and eating (cf. the same order with the evil men, 4:6-7). He is hinged to his bed because he craves his comfort zone (v. 14) and is unable to feed himself because the very thought of work induces mental fatigue (v. 15). The poem offers no solutions to his fatal lethargy. Perhaps the ludicrous images aim to stir him to action by shaming him (cf. 6:6-11), and unquestionably they warn all that laziness thwarts talent, position, wealth, and power.[88]

13 This proverb is a variant of 22:13, having in its verset A *a ferocious lion (šaḥal),*[89] a synonym for *ʾᵃrî,* and in its B verset *in the way* (*baddārek;* see 1:15) instead of "in the streets." Both proverbs represent the sluggard as suffering from irrational fear. He fantasizes a lion's threatening existence in the marketplace keeping him from work! Instead of "in the midst of the plaza I will be mauled" (22:13b) its verset B reads *a lion* (*ʾᵃrî;* see 22:13) *is within* [lit. "between"] *the plaza* (see 22:13).[90] Both proverbs represent the sluggard as suffering from irrational fear. What better reason could a person have for staying at home and not going to work than have a lion threaten him in the marketplace!

14 Once again the proverb satirizes the topic (v. 14b) with an image in verset A. *A door* [see 8:34] *turns*[91] *on its pivot* (a *hap. leg.* that probably means "hole for door pivot").[92] *And* (*wᵉ;* see 26:3) binds image and topic. *A sluggard* [see I: 114] *on his couch.*[93] Both the door and the sluggard move within a very narrow range. In addition to comparing turning without making progress, the satirical comparison may connote that both are anchored. The sluggard makes no progress because he is fixed firmly to his comfort zone.

88. Van Leeuwen, *Context and Meaning,* p. 108.

89. *Šaḥal* occurs seven times, all in poetry, and connotes a lion of intimidating ferocity. It is parallel to *kᵉpîr*[*îm*] "young lion" in Job 4:10; Hos. 5:14 and to *nāmēr* "leopard" in Hos. 13:7. In Ps. 91:13 the *šaḥal* and *peten* "cobra" are parallel to *kᵉpîr* and *tannîn* "dragon." In Job 4:10 its sound is combined with the roar of the *ʾaryeh* "lion." In Job 10:16 it is said "to stalk" and is parallel to "display awesome power," and in Job 28:8, to *šāḥaṣ* "proud beasts." These contexts suggest some sort of ferocious lion. G. J. Botterweck *(TDOT,* 1:377, s.v. *ʾᵃrî)* thinks that it "may have meant the serpent dragon," but "because of the connection of snake and lion 'in mythopoetical and artistic fancy,' *shachal* was also adopted as a term for 'lion.'"

90. *Rᵉḥōb* occurs 42 times in the Bible, five of which are in Proverbs. Of these latter it occurs four times in in parallel with *ḥûṣ* "without," and only here in parallel with *derek.*

91. *Sbb* has the basic meaning "to go in a circle" *(HALOT,* 2:739, s.v. *sbb),* and its form may be *Qal* "to turn about/around," or *Niphal* "to double back," "to change direction."

92. The upper and lower tenons of an architectural door turned in a pivot made of wood or stone. "In Egypt, the hinge consisted of a socket of metal with a projecting pivot, into which two corners of the door were inserted" (S. Barabas, *ZPEB,* 2:155, s.v. "door").

93. *Miṭṭâ* refers to a stationary or portable piece of furniture — not a sleeping mat — spread with covers, cloth, and pillow for reclining, more specifically for sleeping (Exod. 7:28), for the sick (Gen. 47:31), for resting (1 Sam. 28:23), for the dead (2 Sam. 3:31), or for feasting or carousing (Ezek. 23:41). The word may have been chosen for its chiastic consonance with the dentals of *haddelet tissôb* even as *ʿāṣēl ʿal* offers a chiastic sequence with *ʿal-ṣîrāh* (McCreesh, *Sound and Sense,* p. 118).

The turning of the door on its pivots, however, is profitable because it enables the door to realize its function, whereas the sluggard hinged to his bed is wastefully idle.

15 *A sluggard buries his hand in a pan* repeats verbatim 19:24. The variants in their B versets clarify "he does not return it to his mouth" by *he is too weary to return it to his mouth* (see 19:24). "Weary" signifies to become mentally and spiritually too tired to do something.[94] The sluggard so dislikes any form of work that the very thought of exerting himself exhausts him.

16 The final saying brings "The Mirror of Sluggards" to a climactic conclusion by reversing the sequence of topic and comparison. Moreover, like the conclusion to the "The Mirror of Fools," instead of using a comparative negative image it uses a standard of comparison. But whereas the fool is the standard of the comparison for greater hopelessness of the one who is deluded (v. 12), this conclusion uses seven wise men as the standard of comparison for the utter delusion of the sluggard about his own wisdom. In sum, while there is hope for a fool to be saved from being a deluded fool, there is no hope for a sluggard to be saved from his delusion. *A sluggard is wiser in his own eyes* [see 26:5, 12] *than* [see 25:14] *seven* [see 6:31; 9:1; Ruth 4:16] *men who give* [see 24:26][95] *a judicious* (*ṭāʿam;* see 11:22), a metonomy of adjunct for *answer.*[96] *Seven* symbolizes the perfection of their answer. Probably that is why Artaxerxes had seven advisers (Ezra 7:14). The tradition of the "seven sages" may be due to this symbolic significance (cf. 26:25),[97] not that the proverb is dependent on that tradition.

94. "All the texts have more to do with mental and spiritual exhaustion than with physical fatigue; the word refers to the will and the emotions" (H. Ringgren, *TDOT,* 7:395, s.v. *lāʾâ*), though it can be connected with physical fatigue (cf. Gen. 19:11). In its ten occurrences in the *Niphal,* it connotes with the inf., as here, "to be unable to/cannot/unwilling to [do something]" out of psychological exhaustion caused by dislike. The Egyptians were unable to drink the Nile (Exod. 7:8), and Jeremiah was unable to contain the wrath of the LORD by himself without inflicting others (Jer. 6:11). He wearied himself trying to hold in the word of the LORD, and could not (20:9). The LORD could not bear Israel's festivals (Isa. 1:14). Its five occurrences in the *Hiphil* signify "to make weary to exhaustion." R. Gordis (*The Book of Job: Commentary, New Translation, and Special Studies* [Moreshet series 2; New York: Jewish Theological Seminary of America, 1978], p. 46) argues that *l'h* always means "be unable."

95. The *Hiphil* of *šûb* may signify to "give . . . answer" with a direct object such as *dābār* (see 18:13; 24:26) or *ʾēmer* (22:21) or even absolutely when the context is clear (cf. Esth. 4:13; Job 13:22). Normally, however, in this last use it occurs with an indirect object.

96. Van Leeuwen (*Context and Meaning,* p. 107) compares *mšyby ṭʿm* with *dnyʾl htyb ʿṭʾ wṭʿm lʾrywk,* "Daniel replied with counsel and discretion to Arioch" (Dan. 2:14).

97. Clifford (*Proverbs,* pp. 25-27, 233) renders *šibʿâ* "the Seven," referring to the seven antediluvian sages.

d. Four Kinds of Troublemakers (26:17-28)

Hezekiah's compilers now focus on four malevolent, antisocial types who cause dissension, mostly by their speech (see 6:12-15, 16-19; 16:27-30), escalating from the busybody, who hurts himself (v. 17), to the mischief maker (vv. 18-19), to the slanderer (vv. 20-22), to the son's hateful enemy (vv. 23-28). The busybody and the slanderer are linked by the *rîb* ("dispute"/"strife," vv. 17, 21), and the mischief maker and slanderer by II *rmh* ("deceive"/"deception," vv. 19, 22). Strife is the hallmark of the slanderer (vv. 20-22), and deception that of the personal enemy (vv. 23-25), suggesting that the fight-loving busybody and deceptive mischief maker (vv. 17-19) should be regarded as a unity that introduces the benchmarks of the next two. Van Leeuwen buttresses analyzing vv. 17-28 into four triplets (vv. 17-19, 20-22, 23-25, 26-28). First, three triplets are obviously comprised of a quatrain plus a single line, but vv. 26-27 are phonetically linked to form a quatrain in the last triplet as well. Second, allowing A to stand for the single line and B for the couplet, they are arranged in a stitching pattern: A (v. 17)/B (vv. 18-19); B (vv. 20-21)/A (v. 22); A (v. 23)/B (vv. 24-25); B (vv. 26-27)/A (v. 28). Moreover, lexical *inclusio*s mark off the boundaries of all four triplets: *l'* "not" (vv. 17, 19), *nrgn* "slander" (vv. 20, 22), *lb* "heart" (vv. 23, 25), and *śn'* "enemy/hate" (vv. 26, 28).[98]

(1) The Busybody and the Mischief Maker (26:17-19)

17 The least dangerous of the antisocial troublemakers is the busybody, for he hurts only himself. Verset A typically presents a striking image to illuminate his social folly (verset B). *One who grabs* (see 3:18) is equated with *who becomes enraged* (*mitʿabbēr;* see n. 27), *the ears of a dog* (cf. 26:11) is equated with *in a dispute* (see 15:18), and *passing by* (*ʿōbēr;* see n. 25; 26:10) with *not his own* (*lō'-lô;* see n. 28). The confrontational and outspoken busybody unnecessarily experiences the negative emotions of becoming furious about someone or something and runs the danger of getting hurt. Elsewhere in Proverbs, *mtʿbr* is used of the hothead (14:16) and of a stupid person who angers the king (20:2). The dispute, which itself entails getting hurt (see 17:14), is likened to a semiwild dog. Because of the Hebrews' prejudice that dogs were unclean, most dogs in Palestine were semiwild, like the pariah dogs that still haunt some countries.[99] Its dynamic equivalent would be a jackal. Grabbing it by its sensitive ears connotes the inevitability of getting hurt in the needless dispute. Not even Samson grabbed the foxes by their ears

98. Van Leeuwen, *Context and Meaning,* p. 117.

99. G. S. Cansdale, *All the Animals of Bible Lands* (Grand Rapids: Zondervan, 1970), p. 122.

(Judg. 15:4). The senseless busybody should leave the passing cur alone, and the disciple should walk away from a dispute in which he has no interest.[100]

18-19 The comparative *like* (v. 18) . . . *so* (v. 19) construction is usually found in one verse (see 26:1, 2, 8), but here it spans two that together present the mischief maker as one who causes social havoc by deception. The negative image now takes a whole verse: *a madman* [*mitlahlēah;* see n. 29] *who shoots* [*hayyōreh;* see 1:8] *flaming missiles* [see n. 31], *deadly arrows* (lit. "arrows [see 7:23; 25:18] and death" [see 8:36; 18:21]). Likewise the illuminated topic also takes a verse: *Is a person* (*ʾîš;* see I: 89) *who deceives* [see n. 35; 11:1] *his neighbor* (see 3:28). *And* combines the two related and overlapping situations into one. The rhetorical, polar question *Am I not only joking* (*hᵃlōʾ-mᵉśaḥēq,* lit. "making merry"; see 8:30-31) expects a strong affirmation of assent ("I was joking!").[101] As a cover-up for a deception, *śaḥēq* connotes "to make merry by an unexpected twist." The verb "deceive," however, shows that the jester intends to harm his neighbor. He is a fool for whom villainy is like the pleasure of laughter (10:23); he is not merely a prankster or practical joker. He condemns himself by his self-quotation to explain his behavior, for his question betrays his meanness and cynicism (cf. 6:10; 24:12). The cruel buffoon cannot discern the difference between a joke and cruelty. The comparison of the treacherous clown with an armed and berserk warrior is double. Both cannot distinguish right from wrong and both inflict horrible tragedy on the community. However, the madman is out of his mind and cannot plot evil, whereas the mischief maker is cunning, showing that he is intellectually capable of carrying out a crime. His problem is not intellectual but spiritual; he lacks kind affections. The madman is not culpable for his crime; the mischief maker is.

(2) The Slanderer (26:20-22)

Hezekiah's collectors now ratchet up the section on antisocial types to the slanderer, who destroys the community by inflaming strife (vv. 20-22; cf. 16:28; 18:8). They introduce the slanderer with sayings pertaining to his antisocial behavior. He sustains the strife (v. 20), inflames it (v. 21), and transforms the society into his own image (v. 22). Fire images in their A versets to illuminate the topic of contention in their B versets link vv. 20 and 21. The

100. The Mesopotamian *Counsels of Wisdom* (26-30) also advises people to mind their own business: "Seek not the place of a quarrel; for in a quarrel you must give a decision, and you will be forced to be their witness. They will fetch you to testify in a lawsuit that does not concern you. When you see a quarrel, go away without noticing it" (*ANET,* p. 426).

101. *IBHS,* p. 884, P. 40.3b.

paronomasia of *ʿēṣîm/ʾēš* ("wood"/"fire," vv. 20a/21a), that of *mādōn/ midyānîm* ("conflict"/"contentious," vv. 20b/21b), and the antonyms "calms down"/"set aglow" (vv. 20b/21b) put their connection beyond doubt. The repetition of 26:22 in 18:8, suggesting that it circulated as an independent proverb, frames the triplet (vv. 20b, 22a). The chiastic frame of "slanderer" (vv. 20b, 22a) intimates that "a contentious person" (v. 21b) is co-referential for the "slanderer. Verses 20-21 present two sides of the same coin. The inflammatory speech of the slanderer burns the community down (v. 21), and his absence gives it an opportunity to restore its peace (v. 20). His words are so destructive to the community's well-being because people swallow his inflammatory calumnies like tasty tidbits (v. 22a), making a deep impact on them (v. 22b). The community that tolerates the slanderer is also culpable for the conflicts that tear it apart.

20 Fire going out without fuel (v. 20a) images bitter conflicts dying out without a slanderer (v. 20b). Image and topic are again joined by *and* (see 26:3, 9, 14). The emblematic parallelism is precise right down to the syntax and parts of speech, matching *without* (*bᵉʾepes;* see 14:28) with *when there is no* (*bᵉʾên;* see 5:23), *wood* (see n. 37) with *slanderer* (*nirgān;* see 16:28; 18:8), *a fire* (see 16:27) with [*bitter*] *conflict* (see 6:19), and *goes out* (cf. Lev. 6:12[5]; Isa. 66:24; Jer. 17:27; Ezek. 21:4[9]) with *calms down.*[102] Van Leeuwen defines *nirgān* as the sort of fool who attempts "by verbal calumny to wrongfully attack another's rights, reputation, or authority to secure his own will" (see 16:28; cf. Deut. 1:27; Ps. 106:25; Isa. 29:24). 16:28 labels him "perverse" (i.e., one who turns truth and society upside down and inside out). His tools of trade are innuendoes, half-truths, and facts distorted and exaggerated beyond recognition (cf. 10:18; 11:13, 28; 16:28; 18:8; 20:19). As a storm whips up the sea, this slandering rebel whips up strife so strong that it divides even the closest friends. Without a person seeking to secure his will by attacking the rights of another, even the most bitter conflicts and old hurts calm down (cf. 22:10).

21 This verse reverses the image from burning wood dying out to adding glowing charcoal to embers for fiery missiles and escalates the slanderer's danger from keeping a controversy alive to heating it up to the flash point. *Glowing charcoal* occurs two other times and denotes the "bright, reddish purple, really the color of glowing charcoal (from wood), that produces fire and heat (Isa. 44:12) and can be fanned into a flame (Isa. 54:16)."[103] *To embers* (see 6:18; 25:22; cf. 2 Sam. 14:7; Pss. 120:4; 140:10[11]; Ezek. 24:11) refers to ignited coal. *And* (see 26:1) joins to the first image the em-

102. In its other three occurrences *štq* refers to the sea growing calm (Ps. 107:30; Jon 1:11, 12), and it may be used metaphorically here for calming a quarrel.

103. *HALOT,* 3:924, s.v. *peḥām.*

phatic second image, *wood to fire* (*ʿēṣîm lᵉʾēš;* see v. 20a) to escalate the heat of the fuel and its combustibility to the flash point. *And* (see 26:3, 7, 9, 10) now combines the images and topic — that is, *a contentious person* (cf. 21:9, 19) *to kindling* [i.e., to set aglow][104] *strife* (see 26:17). Inferentially a community must rid itself of the slanderer to have peace.

22 If it does not, the slanderer's yeast will work through the whole batch of dough (2 Cor. 5:6; Gal. 5:9). Verse 22 repeats 18:8 verbatim but functions as a janus between the second and third triples on contention. Looking back, it brings vv. 20-21 to a conclusion by changing the form from image/topic to topic (*the words of the slanderer*)/image *(like tidbits).* The image signifies that the slanderer's audience greedily swallow his inflammatory speech, and the addition, *they descend into one's innermost being,* indicates that, having delighted in them, they make a deep impact on their lives, whether they know it or not. The words now in their hearts will inevitably be on their lips. In sum, the community is culpable for its loss of peace and character by tolerating agitators against all that is right. Looking ahead, the verse anticipates the next trio of verses with their focus on the hidden, inner dimensions of conflict. "*Bṭn* in v. 22 anticipates the terms for the inner man in vv. 23-25 (*lb, qrb, lb* [heart, inner being, heart])."[105]

(3) The Hateful Enemy (26:23-28)

Finally, the compilers narrow the antisocial types down to the son's hateful enemy. The imperative "do not trust him" shows that the son is the hater's target and states the aim of the partial subunit. The first of its triplet of sayings depicts the enemy's deception (vv. 23-25), and the second, his destruction (vv. 26-28). The two triplets are tightly connected in several ways. (1) The keyword "to hate"/"hater" *(śnʾ)* occurs in every other verset A (vv. 24, 26, 28). (2) Metonymies for speech ("lips" [vv. 22, 23], "voice" [v. 24], "tongue" [v. 28a], and "mouth" [v. 28b]) replace "words" (v. 22). (3) "His" in vv. 25 and 26 looks back to the enemy of v. 24. (4) The *inclusio* of "smooth" (*ḥlq,* v. 23b emended, v. 28b) frames the entire partial subunit. (5) Verse 26 functions as a janus; verset A looks back to the enemy's deception, and verset B looks ahead to his destruction. Verse 25a brings the stanza to its climactic admonition: do not trust him or anything he has to say, no matter how attractive it seems.

104. In the *Qal ḥrr* means "to glow" of copper (Ezek. 24:11) and of a body burning with fever (Job 30:30), and in the *Niphal* "to be charred/burnt" (Ps. 102:3[4]; Ezek. 15:4; 24:10). This *Pilpel* is unique.

105. Van Leeuwen, *Context and Meaning,* p. 119.

(a) The Enemy's Deception (26:23-25)

Verse 23 is linked with the proverbial pair of vv. 24-25 by the keywords "lips" (vv. 23b, 24a) and "heart" (vv. 23b, 25b) that give focus to the fourth triplet in 26:17-28. Behind the enemy's attractive veneer (i.e., his speech, v. 23bα, 24a, 25a) lurks an evil heart (v. 23bβ) that harbors deceit (v. 24b) and seven horrors (v. 25b). Verse 23a presents a striking metaphor of the truth, comparing the enemy's dissembling speech to an attractive but cheap glaze of silver dross over a potsherd. Verse 24a presents the subject, a personal enemy whose hatred is the spawning grounds for treachery. Verse 25a brings the stanza to its climactic admonition: do not trust him or anything he has to say, no matter how attractive it seems.

23 The saying returns to the pattern of a metaphor from the physical realm (v. 23a) to illuminate a truth in the social realm. *Silver dross* (see n. 41) refers to the scum or refuse that is thrown off, or falls, in smelting silver (see 25:4). In the process of melting and purifying the ore, the silver, oxygen, and lead are separated, leaving lead monoxide as the silver dross. Because of its silvery gloss, this slag was used as a glaze for ceramics (Sir. 38:29-30). The comparison of *smooth* [see n. 42] *lips* (see 5:21; 7:21) to "silver dross" connotes that flattery is as deceptive and as cheap or worthless as what appears to be expensive-looking, shining silver but in fact is nothing more than lead oxide, a cheap dross (see 25:4). "All that glitters is not gold" (cf. 10:20). The comparison of the *evil* [or depraved, *rāʿ;* see 1:15; 15:26; cf. Jer. 3:17; 11:18; 16:12; 18:12; Ezek. 38:10] *heart* (see I: 90) to *glazed*[106] *over* [see 26:14] *a potsherd*[107] connotes that the reprobate[108] is as worthless as a broken piece of pottery. The combined image implies that an enemy's smooth speech (i.e., flattery and/or hypocrisy for aboveboard honesty and candor) cloaks an evil disposition or a malicious intention (cf. 6:14; 12:20; 26:26; Ps. 62:4[5]; Jer. 9:8[7]; cf. Gen. 37:35; 2 Sam. 15:1-9; Luke 22:47, 48).

106. In the Piel *sph* is used almost exclusively with overlaying the furniture and portions of the tabernacle and temple with gold or bronze, showing that the silver dross is a metonymy for a kind of glaze. Glazing pottery made its first appearance in northern Mesopotamia during the fifth millennium B.C. (Lucas, *Ancient Egyptian Materials and Industries* [4th ed.], p. 464; see also n. 41).

107. *Ḥāreś* denotes burnt clay. It is used nine times as a gen. of material for a whole earthen vessel in the constructions *kly ḥrś* (Lev. 6:21; 11:33; 14:5; 14:50; 15:12; Num. 5:17; Jer. 32:14), *nbly-ḥrś* (Lam. 4:2), and *baqbuq . . . ḥāreś* (Jer. 19:1). In its other six absolute uses, it denotes a potsherd, a piece of a broken earthen vessel (Job 2:8; 41:30[22]; Ps. 22:15[16]; Isa. 30:14; 45:9[2x]; Ezek. 23:34). These 16 occurrences call into question the glosses "earthenware" (NIV, NKJV, NJPS, NEB, NRSV) and "earthen vessel" (NASB), for they connote a whole vessel with functional value, not a broken one.

108. *HALOT,* 3:1,250, s.v. *rāʿ.*

24-25 "Dissembling by his speech" (v. 23b) is now explained by "making his voice attractive" (v. 24a), and "evil heart" (v. 23b) is explained and escalated by "seven abominations in his heart" (v. 24b). The threefold repetition of "his" in v. 25 looking back to the antecedent personal enemy in v. 24 shows that v. 25 could never have existed independently of v. 24. Accordingly, "his lips" and "his voice" are synonyms in their A versets and likewise "in his inner being" and "in his heart" in a chiastic structure in their B versets. Both verses represent the enemy as concealing by his mode of communication the deceit in his heart.

24 The synthetic parallels of v. 24 combine by conjunctive *and* the enemy's outward deceptive speech with his inner and true intention to harm his victim (cf. 10:18). Its halves are linked by: (1) the paronomasia of their initial *b, with/in;* (2) the matching of the external organ *his lips* (see 24:28) and the internal organ *his inner being (qirbô);*[109] (3) the subject *a* personal *enemy* (*śônē',* lit. "hater"; see 25:21) and its pronoun "his"; and (4) the quasi-synonyms *dissembles* (i.e., he disguises the facts, his intentions, and/or his feelings under a false [i.e., foreign] appearance; see Gen. 42:7; 1 K. 14:5, 6)[110] and *he harbors* [lit. "he sets"][111] *deception* (see 11:1). Here the enemy's disguise comes from his speech. What he says is "foreign" to his true intentions, which, as "intends deceit" makes clear, are to mislead his victim in order to harm him (cf. Gen. 3:1-5; 4:8; 34:15-25; 1 Sam. 18:17, 21; 2 Sam. 3:27; 13:22-28; 20:9, 10; Pss. 28:3; 55:21[22]).

25 This climactic verse draws the moral of the triplet — an admonition to see through the enemy's façade of hypocrisy and withhold one's trust from the liar (v. 25a) because he is totally dedicated to deadly foul play that offends the moral tastes of the godly. The versets of v. 25 are held together by a pun on initial *kî* ("if"/"for") and by the paronomasia of final *bô/bᵉ libbô* ("in

109. *Qereb* often refers to the inner organs of the upper half of the human torso, including the heart (1 Sam. 25:37; Jer. 23:9) and stomach (Job 20:14). "As the location of the heart *(lēb),* one's inner being is viewed as the seat of emotions (Pss. 39:3[4]; 55:4[5]; 109:22; Isa. 16:11; Lam. 1:20), thoughts (Pss. 36:1[2]; 64:6[7]), and will (Jer. 31:33)," showing that *qereb* is a metonymy for *lēb* (cf. R. B. Chisholm, *NIDOTTE,* 3:979, s.v. *qereb*).

110. In the *Piel nkr* is glossed "to make strange" (Jer. 9:4), "to misrepresent" (Deut. 32:27; 1 Sam. 23:7), and in the *Hithpael* "to dissemble" (Gen. 42:7; 1 K. 14:5). It may be a denominative of *nokrî* "strange, foreign" (see 2:16; 5:10, 20; 6:24; 7:5; 20:16; 27:13). The reflexive *Niphal* signifies that he disguises himself.

111. The expression "set in one's inner being" is a semantic equivalent of "set the heart" (see 22:17; 24:32; 27:23). The metaphorical use of this verb, which literally describes spatial displacement, with an individual's heart signifies mentally and emotionally focusing on the object in question and paying careful attention to it because of its importance (cf. Ps. 13:2[3]).

him"/"in his heart").[112] The admonition is not given before again underscoring the enemy's deception. The Masoretic accents show that *if* (*kî;* see 23:13) introduces the conditional protasis to the admonition "do not believe him," not a causal protasis giving substantiation to the truth of v. 24. *He makes his voice (qôlô) charming* (see n. 45) is another metonymy for his flattering, inviting speech (see 5:13; 8:4). *Do not trust* (*ta'ᵃmen;* see 14:15) *him (bô),* or "do not rely on him," for your future well-being (cf. Sir. 12:10-18). The admonition entails that the godly must make a judgment about the trustworthiness of a person's character and the truthfulness of his words. *For* (*kî;* see 25:22) signals the admonition's substantiation. *Seven* [see 26:16] *abominations* [see 3:32] *are in his heart* (see I: 90). Seven abominations is an abstraction for the full panoply of his wicked thoughts and deeds that utterly offend the moral sensibilities of the righteous (cf. Matt. 12:45). The son cannot count on even the kisses of an enemy (27:6). Rather, he can count on the fact that his enemy's flattery and eloquence cover up an evil plot to destroy him. Make no mistake, those who hate righteousness will use any deceit to destroy the wise and to overturn God's righteous kingdom (see 3:32; 29:27).

(b) The Enemy's Destruction (26:26-28)

The final triplet brings the partial subunit on seven malevolent antisocial types to a climactic conclusion by predicting the overthrow of the enemy through his own lying tongue. Verse 26a presents the enemy's hate and deception; v. 27a, that his deception will bring him affliction; and v. 28a, that his hatred afflicts others. The triplet's B versets repeat and so underscore that the liar will be punished. Although his enemy may cloak his deception (v. 26a) and oppress the righteous for a season (v. 28a), he will be exposed (v. 26b). The enemy is only contriving his own destruction (vv. 27, 28b). Verses 26-27 are connected both poetically and phonologically. The images of the trapper (v. 27a) and of the stone roller (v. 27b) depict both the enemy's deception (v. 26a) and his destruction (v. 26b). Van Leeuwen notes the "alliterative string (discounting prefixes) that binds these two verses together:

v. 26 t*k*sh *ś*n'h *b*mšwn/t*gl*h . . .
v. 27 *k*rh *š*ht *b*h ypl/w*gl*l. . . ."[113]

26 This verse, like v. 25, cannot stand by itself because "his evil" looks back to the hateful enemy of v. 24. Its antithetical parallels juxtapose the

112. "The sound /*o*-/ at the middle and the end of colon A and at the end of colon B demarcate the sentence and give it a rhythm" (Clifford, *Proverbs,* p. 234).

113. Van Leeuwen, *Context and Meaning,* p. 118.

initial, alliterated antonyms "concealed" *(tikkasseh)* versus "revealed" (*tiggāleh;* see 11:13). *Hatred* (*śin'â;* see 1:22) *is concealed* [see 10:6] *by deception*[114] thematically links the final triplet with the preceding triplet. *Śin'â* ("hatred") and *śônē'* ("enemy," v. 24) link the triplets lexically. The triples by repetition underscore that the son's spiritual enemy will diabolically aim to win his trust by deception in order to destroy him. This hypocrisy is certain, for it is rooted in the enemy's hatred of the son's godly character and of his world-and-life views. Verset B, however, advances the new truth of this final triplet. Semantic pertinence demands that *his evil* (see 1:16) refers to the enemy's immoral deception to ruin the son. *Is revealed* (see 11:13) means that it will be exposed for all to see and so punished. *In the congregation*[115] (see 5:14) refers to a legal assembly convoked to try the enemy's evil deeds and to mete out punishment. In Proverbs justice is meted out in an indefinite future that outlasts death (see 16:4-15), suggesting that the historical legal assembly functions as an exemplar of final justice. Similarly, the prophets speak of an eschatological assembly (Mic. 2:5; 7:18-20), using the language of their culture, which may need to be reinterpreted in light of the New Testament (cf. 1 Cor. 3:13; 4:5; 6:3; 2 Thess. 1:7-10).

27 Perhaps an originally independent proverb (cf. 28:10; Pss. 7:15-16[16-17]; 9:15-16[16-17]; Jer. 18:20, 22) thematically functions as a metaphor to reinforce that the enemy's evil will be punished (v. 26b).[116] The assonance of *tiggāleh* ("is revealed") and *gōlēl* ("the one who rolls") also links the verses. The proverb's synthetic parallels image the enemy as an ill-fated trapper and a doomed stone roller. *As for the one who digs* [see 16:27] *a pit*[117] to trap and kill an animal pictures the enemy's cunning deception and deadly intention, reinforcing v. 26a. Implicitly evil, he *falls into it* (see 11:5), an image reinforcing v. 26b. *As for the one who rolls* [see 16:3] *a stone* (see 26:8) refers to the physical act of moving a stone too big to be carried.[118] The image entails that the stone roller has been rolling the huge stone uphill, depict-

114. The *hap. leg. maššā'ôn* is an abstract nominal derivative (see *IBHS,* p. 90, P. 5.6c) of II *nš',* which in the *Niphal* signifies "to entertain false hopes," and in the *Hiphil,* "to cheat, deceive." It may be coined to conceal the root *śn'* "hate," for "the Hebrew consonants *śin* and *šin* can be considered one letter, as is shown in acrostic poems" (Clifford, *Proverbs,* p. 234).

115. Note the assonance between *glh* "revealed" and *qhl* "assembly."

116. Verset A has an equivalent in *Ankhsheshonq* 26:21, "he who digs a pit [. . .]," and verset B in *Ankhsheshonq* 22:5, "he who shakes the stone will have it fall on his foot."

117. B. K. Waltke, *NIDOTTE,* 4:1,113, s.v. *šaḥat.*

118. It is used of rolling a stone over the mouth of a well (cf. Gen. 29:3, 8, 10) or on the mouth of caves (Josh. 10:18), and to provide an altar (1 Sam. 14:33).

ing his extreme effort to rid his world of the godly. *It will return* [see 1:23] *to him* is a metonymy for "and it will crush him." The image reinforces that the enemy will be crushed to death "in the assembly" (v. 26). By his deception and extreme efforts the enemy has unknowingly set in motion an evil design that assumes a life of its own beyond his control that will destroy him (cf. Num. 22:6 and 24:17; Esth. 3:35 and 7:10; Dan. 6:24). This "poetic justice" is in the hands of the Sovereign (e.g., 10:3, 29; 16:4; cf. Job 5:13).

28 The climactic parallels contrast the painful blows that the lying tongue inflicts on others with the knockout blow it inflicts on itself. The parallels begin by matching the abusive organs of speech, *the lying tongue* (see 6:17) and *the smooth mouth* (cf. 26:22b), both metonymies for the enemy's dissembling (26:23a) and charming speech (26:24a). Then they match the liar's inner motive, *hates* (*yiśnā';* see 26:24, 26; cf. Lev. 19:17), with its outer effect, *works* (see 2:14). Finally, and climactically, they contrast the objects of the verbs. *Those oppressed by it* (see 22:22) refers to the miserable, but not fatally crushed, righteous (cf. Pss. 9:9[10]; 10:18; 74:21).[119] Its parallel, *ruin,*[120] forces the reader to do a double-take. At first it seems to refer to the ruin of the hated, but on reflection it refers to the hater. That interpretation best fits the context of the parallel B versets of the final triplet, best explains the difference between not fatally crushed and fatally ruined, and best fits the optimistic, not pessimistic, theology of this book. In sum, the villain victimizes himself. In the Psalter, God is the refuge and defender of the oppressed (Pss. 9:9[10]; 10:18), and praised by them (Ps. 74:21). Classifying himself among the oppressed, Paul said: "We are hard pressed on every side, but not crushed; perplexed, but not in despair; persecuted, but not abandoned; struck down, but not destroyed" (2 Cor. 4:8-9).

119. The adjective *dak* occurs four times, only here pl., and derives from the hypothetical root *dkk* (*HALOT,* 1:221, s.v. *dk* and H. F. Fuhs, *TDOT,* 3:197, s.v. *dākhā'*).

120. The *hap. leg. midḥeh* consists of the root *dḥh* ("to push/thrust down violently"; cf. *HALOT,* 1:218, s.v. *dḥh*) and a *mem* prefix that may signify an abstraction or an instrument (i.e., it fashions a means whereby to push or trip somebody to fall; cf. BDB, p. 191, s.v. *midḥeh; IBHS,* p. 90, P. 5.6b). The root occurs seven times exclusively in poetic literature. It usually signifies the fatal defeat/ruin of someone "via the imagery of a wall that is pushed so hard that it is falling over (Pss. 36:12[13]; 62:3[4]; 118:13; Prov. 14:32). The imagery is oriented on ANE warfare and is reminiscent of the practice of pushing the battering ram against the walls of a city during the siege" (M. G. Klingbeil, *NIDOTTE,* 1:933, s.v. *dḥh*). In sum, *midḥeh* probably means "calamity," "ruin" (cf. *HALOT,* 2:548, s.v. *midḥeh*).

3. About Friends and Friendship (27:1-22)

1 *Do not boast about tomorrow,*
for you do not know what a day may bring forth.
2 *Let a stranger and not your own mouth praise you,*
an outsider, and let not[1] *your own lips praise you.*
3 *The weight of a stone and the burden of sand —*
but the vexation of a fool[2] *is heavier than both.*
4 *The cruelty*[3] *of wrath*[4] *and the torrents of anger —*
but who can stand before jealousy?
5 *Open rebuke is better than concealed love.*[5]
6 *The wounds of a friend are faithful,*
but the kisses of an enemy are too excessive.[6]

1. In v. 2a, *lō'* with *pîkā* makes "not your mouth" part of the compound subject. In v. 2bα, *yithallelkā* is gapped with the subject *nokrî,* and in 2bβ *'al* governs a gapped *tithallᵉlûkā* (see v. 1a) with *śᵉpāteykā* as the subject. The varied syntax keeps the parallelism from being monotonous (A. Berlin, "Grammatical Aspects of Biblical Parallelism," *HUCA* 50 [1979] 17-43).

2. The gen. can be a gen. of authorship (i.e., the provocation produced by a fool; *IBHS,* p. 143, P. 9.5.1a) or a gen. of inalienable possession (i.e., the irritation inherent to his nature; *IBHS,* p. 145, P. 9.5.1g).

3. The meaning of the *hap. leg. 'akzᵉrîyût* ("cruel," "without compassion") is derived from *'akzārî* (5:9).

4. See n. 2.

5. Fichtner *(BHS)* needlessly emends *mē'ahᵃbâ* to *mē'êbâ* "enmity" to facilitate a simpler antithesis: open rebuke versus enmity endured in silence.

6. The meaning of *n'trwt* is uncertain. Elsewhere *'tr* in the *Niphal* with *lamed* means "to be pleaded with," but the antithetical parallel demands the meaning "deceptive" (cf. Vulg. *fraudulenta*). The Targ. renders the opposition by "good" and "bad." Rashi and Ibn Ezra connect *'tr* with *h'trtm (Hiphil* of *'tr)* in Ezek. 35:13, which Ibn Ezra questionably understood to mean "make 'thick' or 'strong.'" The LXX's rendering *hekousia* "spontaneous" suggests a *Vorlage* with some form of *ndb,* "offer voluntarily." I. Eitan (*A Contribution to Biblical Lexicography* [New York: Columbia University Press, 1924], p. 59) derived the required sense from Arab. *'atara* "to stumble," but it means "to lie" only in the idiomatic expression *'atara lisanahu* "his tongue stumbled," and N. Waldman ("A Note on Excessive Speech and Falsehood," *JQR* 67 [1976-77] 142-73) says, "This cognate equation . . . is rather doubtful." Waldman appeals to Akk. *watāru* "to be excessive, surpass," and *(w)atartu* "excess, exaggeration, lie," but *'tr* cannot be equated with Akk. *watāru* except by way of *ytr* (see 17:7). Fichtner *(BHS)* arbitrarily proposes either *'iqqᵉšôt* ("twisted," "perverted") or, along with Toy (*Proverbs,* p. 485), *nᵉ'ôtôt* (*Niphal* of *'wh* "to be bent, confused"; cf. Prov 12:8), hence "perverted." Kuhn reads *wᵉkattᵉ'ārôt* "as sharp knives" (cited by Gemser, *Sprüche,* p. 96). BDB (p. 801, s.v. II *'ātar*), like the rabbis, thinks of II *'tr* "to be profuse" as an Aramaism — the Hebrew equivalent to Aram. *'tr* is *'šr* (e.g., *'ōšer* "wealth"), which is probably attested both here and in Ezek. 35:13, "to be abundant," "excessive."

7 *A sated person tramples down*[7] *a honeycomb,*
but as for a hungry person, every bitter thing is sweet.
8 *Like a bird that flees from its nest,*
so is a person who flees from his home.[8]
9 *Olive oil and incense*[9] *make the heart glad,*
and the sweetness of one's friend[10] *comes from*[11] *passionate counsel.*[12]

7. Metaphorical *tābûs* is often unnecessarily emended and toned down by the literal *tābûz* "to loathe."

8. Lit. "his place."

9. The LXX adds "wine" (cf. Ps. 104:15), but wine, unlike oil and incense, is drunk, not applied to the body.

10. G. R. Driver ("Suggestions and Objections," *ZAW* 55 [1937] 69) et al. needlessly emend *rʿhw* to *raʿᵃwâ* "friendship" because he wrongly alleges that the pronominal suffix of *rʿhw* lacks an antecedent.

11. The pregnant preposition *min* demands that a verb of motion such as "come" be supplied (*IBHS,* p. 224, P. 11.4d). With varying interpretations, Meinhold (*Sprüche,* p. 454) et al. take the *min* as comparative, but the construction lacks an adjective, *nepeš* does not mean one's own person in contrast to another and the resulting meaning is infelicitous. McKane (*Proverbs,* p. 613, citing Reuss) et al. emend *mēʿᵃṣat* to *mᵉʿammēṣ,* usually in connection with *raʿᵃwâ,* yielding "friendship strengthens the soul." Plöger (*Sprüche,* p. 318) defends the emendation by arguing that "*mēʿammēṣ* [*sic! mᵉʿammēṣ?*] could be somewhat simplified through *maʿᵃṣ(y)m* (pt. ni. [*sic! Hiphil?*] of *ʿṣm*) with the same meaning 'to strengthen.'" His desperate attempt in fact shows that from a text-critical point of view the emendation to *mᵉʿammēṣ* cannot be defended. J. Emerton ("The Root *ʿāṣah* and Some Uses of *ʿēṣāh* and *môʿēṣâ* in Hebrew," in *OTSSWL* 15/16 [Pretoria, 1976], pp. 22-23) circumvents the problem by tentatively postulating the use of the root *ʿāṣâ* in a noun **maʿᵃṣâ.* However, he has to posit for his *hap. leg.* a dubious Hebrew verb *ʿaṣṣ* (cf. Arab. *ʿaṣṣah* "to be hard, firm") and then extend its meaning to "force" or "strength." D. W. Thomas ("Notes on Some Passages in the Book of Proverbs," *VT* 15 [1965] 275) achieves the same sense by juggling the consonants of verset B around to read *waʿᵃṣat rēʿa mamtîqâ* "and the counsel of a friend makes sweet the soul." The only thing to be said in its favor is that it yields a sense very near to the Vulg. *et bonis amici consiliis anima dulcoratur* "and the good counsels of friends are sweet to the soul." In short, the MT, though difficult, is superior to the LXX, the Vulg., and the scholarly emendations.

12. Lit. "counsel of the *nepeš* (see I: 90)." The LXX in verset B reads *katarrhēgnytai de hypo symptōmatōn psychē* "but the soul is torn by trouble" (NRSV) (< *ûmitqārᵉʿâ meʿaṣṣebet* or *mēʿōṣōt*). However, the passive of *grʿ* is otherwise attested in the *Niphal,* not the *Hithpael.* Furthermore, how is the contrast of oil and wine with trouble morally cogent? Driver ("Hebrew Notes," *ZAW* 52 [1934] 54) interpreted the phrase to mean "[more than] fragrant wood," appealing to *bāttê hannepeš* "perfume boxes" in Isa. 3:20. However, the Hebrew word for "wood" is *ʿēs,* and a feminine *nomen unitatis* of the noun (i.e., "piece of wood") is unattested. Driver ("Suggestions and Objections," *ZAW* 55 [1937] 69-70) gave up this interpretation in favor of Rashi's interpretation, without citing him. He gives as an option: "It is sweeter to have a friend whose advice one may take than

10 *Your friend and your father's friend*[13] *do not forsake,*
and the house of your relative do not enter in the time of distress.
A close, next-door neighbor is better than a relative who is far off.
11 *Be wise, my son, and make my heart glad,*
so that[14] *I might answer him who reproaches me.*
12 *A shrewd person, who sees evil, hides himself;*
the gullible, who pass on, are fined.
13 *Take away his garment when one becomes surety for a stranger;*
and for a foreign woman[15] *impound it.*
14 *As for the one who blesses his neighbor with a loud voice early in the morning,*[16]
it will be reckoned to him as a curse.
15 *A leaky roof in*[17] *a cloudburst*[18]
and a contentious[19] *wife are alike.*[20]
16 *Those who shelter her shelter*[21] *wind,*[22]
and oil meets[23] *his right hand.*[24]

---

to be compelled." However, in addition to the lack of a comparative adjective, the parallelism with verset A is inept. Why mention the oil and incense that gladden the heart?

13. K reads *wᵉrēʿeh* and Q reads *wᵉrēaʿ* with no difference in meaning.

14. *Wᵉ* with the cohortative after the impv. normally signifies purpose.

15. The LXX (cf. Vulg.) reads *allotria* (< *nokrîm*), but the MT's *lectio difficilior* is preferable (cf. 20:16).

16. One ms. and some critics omit "early in the morning."

17. *Bᵉyôm,* though it may mean here "on the day of" with reference to a 24-hour day, not just daylight (cf. 25:20), more probably has its vague sense "at the time of," glossed by "in."

18. *HALOT* (2:743, s.v. *sagrîr*) on the basis of an Aramaic cognate and Mishnaic Hebrew opts for the meaning of "cloudburst" for the *hap. leg. sagrîr.* Its Syr. cognate signifies a violent storm.

19. K *mᵉdōnîm;* Q *midyānîm* (see 21:19).

20. The rare *Nithpa'al,* as in other Semitic languages, adds a *t* to the *Niphal* stem to invest it with a reflexive force (see *HALOT,* 4:1,437, s.v. I *šwh*).

21. The basic meaning of *ṣpn* is "to hide or conceal." Its extended meanings in Proverbs are: "to hide in ambush" (1:11, 18), "to save up, store" (2:7; 13:22), "to keep in one's heart" (2:1; 7:1; 10:14). A. E. Hill (*NIDOTTE,* 3:840, s.v. *ṣpn*) uniquely extends its meaning in 27:16 to "hide in the sense of restraining," and Meinhold (*Sprüche,* p. 457) to "hide . . . to protect oneself from shame." *HALOT* (3:1,049, s.v. *ṣpn*) opts for "shelter," a meaning closer to its basic sense and an otherwise attested use (Pss. 27:5; 31:21).

22. The LXX (Targ.) reads, "The north wind is harsh."

23. The ancient versions read I *qr'* ("call"), not II *qr'* ("meet," "encounter," "happen"), leading to nonpertinent meanings (see the next note). Meinhold (*Sprüche,* p. 458) accepts their reading, and, citing M. David, gives the far-fetched interpretation that "Such

17 *Iron is sharpened*[25] *with iron,*
and a person sharpens[26] *the face of his friend.*
18 *He who protects a fig tree will eat its fruit,*
and he who guards his master will be honored.
19 *As, looking in water,*[27] *a face looks to a face,*[28]
so a human being's heart looks to a human being.
20 *The Grave and Abaddon*[29] *are never satisfied,*
and the eyes of humankind are never satisfied.[30]
21 *The crucible is for silver and the furnace for gold,*
and a person is tested[31] *according*[32] *to his*[33] *praise.*[34]

---

a woman cannot be kept hidden from people anymore than the fragrance, if somebody has anointed his hands with perfumed oil. The fragrance wafts like the wind, it makes itself known by itself, it 'calls.'"

24. The ancients invested *qr'* with the meaning "call." The LXX: "But it is called by name propitious." The Targ.: "But she is called the balm of the right hand." The Syr.: "by the name of the right hand." Healey comments: "Context suggests we are still dealing with the contentious wife (who is the husband's right hand?)." The Vulg. is just as confused and difficult: "And shall call in the oil of his right hand."

25. Unless the form should be emended to *yuḥād (Hophal* of *ḥdd),* it is best construed as a one-place *Hiphil,* "causes itself to be sharp" (*IBHS,* pp. 439-40, P. 27.2f). The meaning "be sharp," "sharpen" is assured from an Arabic cognate and its use in the *Hophal* of a sharpened sword (Ezek. 21:14-16). In the *Qal ḥdd* means "to be quick" (Hab. 1:8) and the form would be *yēḥād.*

26. Though the expected form is *yāḥēd, yāḥad* is the *Hiphil* of *ḥdd* due to the guttural (GKC, P. 67v).

27. Lit. "as the water the face to the face." The generic article marks out a class, a use especially common in comparison (*IBHS,* p. 244, P. 3.5.1f). Toy (*Proverbs,* p. 490) corrects the text by the LXX to *k^{e}mô.* The MT is cryptic, but not unintelligible. The pregnant preposition *lamed* demands that an appropriate verb be added (*IBHS,* p. 224, P. 11.4.3d).

28. The LXX (Syr.) reads, "As faces are not like faces." Since this sense cannot be gotten from the MT, Boettcher (cited by Delitzsch, *Proverbs,* p. 407) thinks the LXX probably read *k^e'ên dōmîm.* This misunderstanding, a reversal of the sense of the MT, led to the further translation, "so neither are the thoughts of men." The Targ. read *mayim* but interpreted the verse similarly to the LXX.

29. K = *'^{a}baddōh;* Q = *'^{a}baddô* or *'^{a}baddôn* with no difference in meaning.

30. The LXX adds a proverb: "He that fixes his eye is an abomination to the LORD; and the uninstructed do not restrain the tongue" (P. D. M. Turner, "Two Septuagintalisms with STĒPIZEIN," *VT* 28 [1978] 481-82).

31. The prepositional phrase "according" implies the verb.

32. *L^{e}pî* means lit. "by/to the mouth of," but in 12:8 (see also Exod. 12:4; 16:16; Num. 26:54; 1 K. 17:1; Hos. 10:12) it is an idiom for "according to," an idiom also found in Semitic cognate languages. In 12:8 it also refers to praise as a means of testing.

33. With the verbal noun either an objective gen. and/or a gen. of authorship.

34. *Mah^{a}lāl,* though a *hap. leg.,* is readily decoded by its root *hll* "to praise, extol" (see 27:1, 2) with a *mem* prefix that probably signifies an abstraction. The versions offer

22 *If you grind*[35] *a fool in a mortar,*[36]
in the midst of groats[37] *with a pestle,*[38]
his folly will not depart from him.

Hezekiah's men copied and compiled these 22 proverbs into a literary unit that makes up the fifth of seven units in Solomon II (cf. 25:2-27; 25:28–26:12, 13-16, 17-28; 27:1-22, 23-27; 28:1–29:27). Their collection into a larger unit enriches their individual meanings in the light of their new holistic contexts. The whole is framed by the *inclusio* of "praise" (the first word in v. 1; the last word in v. 21). The *leitwort* synonyms "friend" *('ôhēb),* "neighbor" *(rēa'),* and "next-door neighbor" *(šākēn)* occur in vv. 6, 9, 10, 14, and 17. Other proverbs are paired with these and also pertain to the topic. Verse 22 is a janus (a transition saying, looking backward and forward). The composition's theme, as indicated by the keyword synonyms and the idea that informs the whole, is teachings on friends and friendship. This collection of 22 verses, which is called "alphabetic" because there are 22 letters in the Hebrew alphabet, might well be entitled "A Manual on Friendship." The unit gives insight into the nature of true friendship.

The unit falls into two balanced halves of ten verses each (vv. 1-10, 11-21 [v. 22 is also a janus to the next unit]). The second half begins with a proverb pair that pertains to education, "Be wise, my son" (v. 11), followed by an implied admonition to be "shrewd," not "gullible" (v. 12). Educational proverbs of this sort, which draw their vocabulary largely from the prologue (chs. 1–9), often mark seams in Proverbs. Both halves begin and end with explicit or implicit admonitions in direct address to the son, "you" (vv. 1-2, 11, 22; cf. v. 23), both conclude with an extended proverb, a so-called "tricolon" (vv. 11, 22; cf. v. 27), and both have an essentially alternating ABC/A′B′C′ structure and similar thematic direction.

---

the *lectio facilior, m^ehal^elāyw* ("the ones praising him"), involving an unambiguous objective gen. The LXX adds the moral: "The heart of the lawless seeks evil things, but an upright heart seeks knowledge."

35. The meaning of the *hap. leg. ktš* is based on Arabic and Aramaic cognates meaning "to pound" and the specific application of that sense to a mortar.

36. *Maktēš* etymologically means "pounding place." The oldest mortar found in Israel is dated to the 13th cent. B.C. and is made of basalt.

37. The meaning of *rîpôt* is not beyond reasonable doubt. The Vulg. renders it as "barley groats" (i.e., the trodden barley, separated from the chaff and hull) both here and, with the Syr., in 2 Sam. 17:19. The LXX^{L} rendered it "cakes of preserved fruit," an unlikely meaning because the etymology of *rîpôt* may be traced to Arab. *rafata* "to crumble, break into small pieces." *HALOT* (3:1,227, s.v. *rîpôt*) draws the conclusion: "Barley groats (or barley meal) would be the preferred translation."

38. *'^elî* is the fifth *hap. leg.* of verset A (see *HALOT,* 2:832, s.v. *'^elî*), yet the verset's meaning is not in doubt.

A/A′:	To whom to listen	
	1. Objective friends	1-2
	2. Parents	11-12
B/B′:	Impossible relationships	
	1. Fool, angry, jealous	3-4
	2. Wicked, hypocrite, shrew	13-16
C/C′:	Positive teachings about friendship	5-10, 17-21
	Janus	22

In addition to this structural pattern, the two halves are held together by catchwords and other poetic devices: in their outer frame by "praise" (vv. 2, 21) and in their inner core by "make the/my heart glad" (vv. 9a, 11a). Close to the beginning of each division one finds "stranger" (vv. 2a and 13a) and *nokrî[yâ]* ("outsider"/"foreign"). The need for the reproof of true friends is mentioned in vv. 5-6, 17, 19, and 21. The unexpected false friendship of a shrewish wife, driving a man from his home, may be in view in vv. 7-8 as well as in vv. 15-16.

The conclusion can now be drawn that Prov. 27:1-22 is a relecture of once isolated proverbs. As such, its proverbs can be interpreted both individually and as part of the whole. For example, its frame in light of the whole composition features the necessity of friends praising each another.

a. First Instructions on Friends and Friendships (27:1-10)

1-10 The first half consists of five quatrains linked by catchwords, sense, and/or structure. Its outer frame pertains to receiving praise from others outside the family (vv. 1-2) and the need of a true friend (vv. 9-10). Within that frame, vv. 3-4 pertain to vexing fools, hotheads, and the jealous, and vv. 7-8 probably to a failed marriage, what should have been the closest of friendships. At the center stands the true friend with his rebuke and faithful wounds (vv. 5-6). In sum, the first subunit follows an alternating pattern of positive (+) and negative (-) quatrains about friendship: the need of appropriate praise in friendship (+ vv. 1-2), inferior types who cannot be friends (vv. 3-4), the need of rebuke in friendship (+ vv. 5-6), the causes of failed relationship in friendship (vv. 7-8), and the need of a friend's counsel and help (+ vv. 9-10). The last two quatrains are linked by *nepeš* ("person," word-initial in vv. 7a, b, and "passionate," word-final in v. 9) and the notion of sweetness in their initial verses (vv. 7b, 9b).

1-2 The introductory quatrain begins and ends with "do not praise," moving from censuring self-praise (v. 1) to commending praise from someone outside the family. Self-praise is unfitting because a mortal does not control his own destiny (v. 1). Only the positive evaluation of an outsider is credible and constructive. To judge from vv. 17, 19, and 21, the "outsider" includes the objective friend. Together the proverb pair calls for humility before God and the judgment of the community.[39] This is the kind of person who can be a friend and who should be your friend.

1 Verset B personifies *day* as a parent, and *what* as the offspring. *Tomorrow* refers to the most immediate future and functions as a metonymy for hoped-for experiences and accomplishments such as accumulated wealth, wisdom, and feats of strength like victory in war (cf. Jer. 9:23[22]). If the most immediate and most visible future is not under human control and is uncertain, how much less the distant future. A wise person, says McKane, "must not speak nor plan as if he himself had full disposal of his destiny and power over his future [cf. 1 K. 20:11]."[40] Other proverbs and Scriptures identify God as the Father who "gives birth" to future events. He has the final word, and no human counsel can thwart it. The wise live day by day, trusting the outcome to God and being grateful to God for whatever he grants.[41] Moreover, the wise trust God to shape their destiny in conformity with righteousness and to frustrate human plans that are not conformed to his righteous rule. They boast about knowing the Lord (Jer. 9:23-24[22-23]). This proverb, however, must be held in tension with those that advise one to make plans for the future (11:14; 15:22; 20:18; 21:5; 24:6, 27).

2 The second proverb commends accepting praise from an outsider and forbids self-praise. *Praise (hillēl)* denotes an interpersonal exchange in which one makes a favorable judgment about another's virtue and expresses his admiration by extolling the person and his sublime attribute(s) (cf. 20:14). The one praising does so because he feels that it is the right and proper thing to do and/or the celebration heretofore has been insufficient. Such a person is a friend. *A stranger* refers to someone outside the family, a relationship underscored by its parallel *an outsider.* In the book of Proverbs friends are sometimes compared and contrasted, as we shall see. Commands in direct address, such as in this quatrain, are rare among Solomon's aphorisms. And so are three precisely synonymous parallels like "stranger" and "outsider," *not your own mouth* and *not your own lips,* and praise (repeated twice). The combined effect censures self-praise and commends a friend's praise in a most emphatic way. Since the proverbs aim for piety on the vertical axis and social success on the horizontal axis, it can be inferred that self-praise is unfitting because it destroys one's relationships with God and with people. The Lord detests the proud, and society dislikes and discounts the boaster. Instead of exalting the boaster, self-praise diminishes one's status and suggests that one is proud,

39. Garrett, *Proverbs,* p. 216.
40. McKane, *Proverbs,* p. 607.
41. McKane, *Proverbs,* p. 607.

feels undervalued, and is socially insecure. The admonition protects one against self-deception and flattery. "A person is judged by his praise" (27:21), but to be of value that praise must be credible. Objective friends have no self-interest in either their positive evaluation of a person or in their celebrating his virtue (see v. 21). A German proverb says, *"Eigen-Lob stinkt, Freundes Lob hinkt, Fremdes Lob klingt"* — "self-praise stinks, a friend's praise limps, a stranger's praise rings." McKane comments, "Whereas society will not take the boaster seriously, it has its own way of testing him before according him acclaim and entrusting him with power [cf. v. 21; 25:6-7; Luke 14:7-11; John 12:43]."[42] Moreover, self-promotion through boasting may elevate a person beyond his competence, leading him to fear demotion or in fact to be demoted and shamed. Paul had to make an exception to this conventional wisdom to vindicate his own character (2 Cor. 10:12–11:33; cf. 1 Sam. 12:3; Ps. 7:3-5[4-6]). But, by praising his weakness, he did not negate the proverb's intention. That kind of constrained self-praise is fitting before God and will not deceive others or self. In sum, the proud cannot be true friends and should not be your friend. A true friend is humble and praises others.

3-4 The next proverb pair is linked by exceptional syntax — note the dashes — and by pertaining to irrational and destructive emotional excitements attached to inferior types of people and escalating from "vexation" (v. 3b), to cruel "wrath" (v. 4a) to "jealousy" (v. 4b). Such folk are insufferable (v. 3) and incapable of friendship (v. 4). Their B versets begin with a comparative "but" that moves *a minore ad majus* ("from the lesser to the greater"). Vexation is unbearable (v. 3), but jealousy is even worse! You should avoid such folk to create the spiritual milieu in which friendship flourishes.

3 This implicitly "better . . . than" proverb evaluates material burdens that put a tremendous strain on a person's physical resources to the point of exhaustion and cause intense discomfort and misery as lighter and easier than the immaterial burden of vexation (cf. 15:16, 17). *The weight of a stone* (*'eben;* see 26:8) refers to one that is so heavy that it cannot be lifted, and *and the burden of sand* refers to the sand on the beach (Gen. 22:17; 32:12[13]; 41:49; Josh. 11:4; Judg. 7:12; 1 Sam. 13:5; 2 Sam. 17:11; 1 K. 4:20, 29[5:9]; Pss. 78:27; 139:18; Isa. 10:22; 48:19; Jer. 5:22; 15:8; 33:22; Hos. 1:10[2:1]; Hab. 1:9) and connotes being an immeasurable weight (Job 6:3). But *the vexation* [see 21:19] *of a fool* (*'ᵉwîl;* I: 112) is even more unbearable both in quality and in quantity than these insufferable burdens placed on the physical body. Steer clear of fools because they aim to seduce you to join them (1:10-19; see *'eben* [26:8]).

4 The synonyms *wrath* (see 6:34) *and anger* (see 15:1) occur to-

42. McKane, *Proverbs,* p. 608.

gether 41 times in the Bible. To these unbearable emotions, verset B adds *jealousy* (see 3:31; 6:34; 14:30) as an even more unbearable, damaging emotion. By adding anger's two "sidekicks," *cruelty* and *torrents (šeṭep),* verset A combines anger's unrelenting, merciless, and hard-as-flint cruelty with the overwhelming destruction that it unleashes on the one who arouses it. The six other occurrences of *šeṭep* denote a destructive, overwhelming flood or torrent (Job 38:25; Ps. 32:6; Dan. 9:26; 11:22; Nah. 1:8). The metaphor depicts anger as a spiritual force that is destructive, irrational, and violent. But anger — unlike jealousy — can be withstood. Balaam prophesied against Moab in spite of Balak's anger (Num. 23:10), but David fled from Saul's jealousy (1 Sam. 18:9). Rhetorical *who* asserts emphatically that none *can stand* (*ya'ᵃmōd;* 12:7; 25:6); *'āmad* with *before* "describes more precisely the behavior of servants who stand before their masters and receive orders."[43] The proverb likens the person who arouses jealousy to a servant who is swept away from the presence of his lord (cf. 6:34-35; 16:14; 17:14).

5-6 The responses to the wrongdoing of fools differ from the chosen responses to the wrongdoing of a friend. Friendship with a fool is impossible, but wrongdoing by a friend must be resolved. Verses 5-6 at the heart of this subunit are linked by the chiastically arranged catchword *'hb* ("love" [v. 5b] and "friend" [v. 6a]), by the paradoxes of "open rebuke" versus "concealed love" and of "faithful wounds" versus hypocritical "kisses," and by the teaching that true friendship does not shrink from correcting the beloved.

5 This "better . . . than" proverb represents speaking out and/or taking action against wrongdoing to correct it (verset A) as better than failing to give expression in word or deed of one's love for the beloved. *Open* [lit. "revealed," "disclosed"; see 11:13] *rebuke* [see 1:25] *is better than* [i.e., benefits life more than another; see 12:9; I: 44] *concealed* [or hidden; cf. 22:3] *love* (see 1:22). The imprecise antithesis of open rebuke and secret love suggests that correcting criticism proceeds openly and directly, even severely (cf. v. 6a), but remains caring and is completely concerned with the best interests of its addressee. The juxtaposition also suggests that hidden love entails the failure to rebuke openly. The next proverb validates these inferences. Indeed, hidden love expresses selfishness, for the "lover" cowardly, timidly, and/or lethargically refuses to risk himself in the best interest of the beloved. Secret love is like winking at a girl in the dark; it does neither her nor you any good. Open, loving rebuke is potent; hidden love is impotent. Out of love for their children, parents rebuke them (13:24), even as God out of his love picks up where the parent leaves off and continues to rebuke his children (3:11-12). Love and correction go hand in hand. The command "rebuke your neighbor frankly" (Lev. 19:17) is followed by the command "love your neighbor as yourself" (19:18).

43. S. Amsler, *TLOT,* 2:330-31, s.v. *'md.*

6 The versets of this antithetical proverb present two oxymorons, "friendly wounds" and "wounding kisses." "Wounds," which are normally inflicted by an enemy, when inflicted by a friend symbolize his strong devotion and loyalty to the wounded. Likewise, "kisses," which are normally associated with a loving friend, when multiplied by an enemy are hypocritical and signify his disdain for and infidelity to the one he kisses (see 5:3-4; 7:13; Matt. 26:49).[44] *The wounds* [see 20:30] *of a friend* (*'ôhēb;* see14:20) *are faithful* (i.e., can be relied on to express and to enhance his loyal attachment to the wounded beloved; see 11:13). The "wounds" are a metaphor for the painful and plain words that must be spoken in a true friendship in order to heal the beloved and/or to restore a broken relationship. If one knows the person delivering the painful word truly loves him, he can be confident that the painful words aim to do him good (see 3:11; 13:24). As a lover, a true friend wounds gently. *But* functions to contrast the parallels. *The kisses* [see 7:13; 24:26] *of an enemy* (*śônē';* see 25:21; 26:24) denotes one who emotionally detests, abhors, despises, disdains another.[45] The imprecise antithetical parallels "kisses" and *are excessive* (see n. 6) suggest that the profuse kisses are insincere, hypocritical, deceitful, and/or sycophantic. The deceiving element is already contained in the oxymoron "kisses of a hating one." Meinhold comments, "If already the words of such a person are intended to hide his true mind (see 26:23-28), then even more his kisses. The escalation is also expressed by the multitude . . . of kisses (cf. at 24:26)."[46]

7-8 The next quatrain pertains to gratifying one's appetites in the right way, and to the loss of the most intimate of friendships, that of a husband and a wife. Gratification in the wrong thing leads to contempt of good things (v. 7a), and lack of gratification in good things leads to enjoyment of bad things (v. 7b). Greenstone connects v. 7a with v. 6: "A person who thinks himself fully competent will reject a rebuke even if it be as salutary as the honeycomb." Van Leeuwen joins v. 7b with v. 8: "The satisfied husband is content and does not wander like an errant bird from the nest (see 7:19). People controlled by lust or hunger cannot or do not discriminate."[47] The quatrain is linked stylistically by each having a word repeated with initial *nun* (*nepeš,* "person," v. 7a, b) and *nôdedet/nôdēd* ("flees," v. 8a, b).

7 As antithetic parallels, v. 7a and v. 7b pit the sated appetite against the famished appetite, but as synthetic parallels they present both appetites as

44. The proverb coheres by initial *nun* at the beginning of each verset and in three of its words: *ne'emānîm, na'tārôt, neśîqôt.*

45. E. Jenni, *TLOT,* 3:1,278, s.v. *śn'.*

46. Meinhold goes on to cite two Jewish proverbs: "An honest slap is better than a false kiss"; and "It is better to receive the slap of a wise man than the kiss of a fool" (Meinhold, *Sprüche,* pp. 452-53).

47. Van Leeuwen, *Proverbs,* p. 230.

sick, for they join together an appetite that despises good food with one that craves bad food. *A sated* [19:23] *person* [or "appetite," *nepeš*] *tramples down* [see n. 7] *a honeycomb* (5:3), which in 16:24 connotes what is sweet and healthy. The powerful metaphor "tramples on a honeycomb" depicts despising this delightful and beneficial creation to an extreme degree. A healthy appetite craves it. Overindulgence in honey may make one vomit (25:16), but not so utterly to despise it that one tramples the good honeycomb underfoot. Such a person is sated with something other than what is healthy. Because the parallels are both antithetic and synthetic, conjunctive *waw* can be glossed by *but* or *and. As for a hungry person* (see 6:30) focuses attention on a person who lacks the supply of food and drink that his body demands. The distributive *every* refers to the lack of discrimination — it never means "even" (*pace* NIV)[48] — and *bitter* [*food*] (see 5:4) is a synecdoche for everything that would otherwise be painful and displeasing to the healthy appetite. To this undiscriminating appetite everything that should produce a painful reaction *is sweet* like honey (cf. 5:3-4; Exod. 15:25; Isa. 5:20). Both a person so sated in wrong things that he despises good things and a person so hungry that he perceives *every* bitter thing and harmful thing as sweet are sick. Van Leeuwen instantiates being sated as a protection from an attractive temptation such as a prostitute (cf. 5:3-4b), but one should add that finding gratification in the prostitute may lead a husband to despising his good wife (v. 7a). This interpretation also applies to spiritual conditions. The person who does not find his spiritual craving satisfied in true religion will go after any grievous idolatry and, being sated by it, will despise true religion.

8 This comparative proverb likens a man who unwillingly flees his home to a fluttering bird that flies restlessly, having been driven from the security of its nest (cf. 7:23). For the construction *as, so (ken),* see 26:1, 2. *A bird* (*ṣippôr;* see 6:5) *that flees* (*nôdedet,* lit. "takes flight"; see 26:2) refers to birds taking flight from a distressful situation. In Isa. 16:2 the fluttering birds are pushed from their nest, and in Jer. 4:25; 9:10b(9b) they take flight in disaster (cf. Isa. 10:14). *From its nest (qinnāh)* connotes loss of safety.[49] *A man* (*ʾîš;* see I: 89) *may flee* (*nôdēd,* i.e., in an unwilling flight) in more or less drastic situations.[50] *From his home* (see n. 8) denotes the unique space where

48. See *HALOT,* 2:474-75, s.v. *kōl.*

49. Domeris, *NIDOTTE,* 3:944, s.v. *qnn.*

50. The NIV renders the *Qal* participle as "fugitives" in Isa. 21:14 and as "wanderers" in Hos. 9:17, though the reference is to fugitives. It renders the verb as "flee" in Gen. 31:40 (cf. Esth. 6:1; Pss. 31:11[12]; 68:12[13]; Isa. 21:15; 22:3; 33:3; Nah. 3:7), as "hurry" in Ps. 55:8, and as "wanders" in Job 15:23, though the sense in both cases pertains to flight in distress. In Hos. 7:13, however, the NIV renders it as "stray" in connection with apostate Ephraim. Even here, however, the Ephraimites, like senseless doves (7:11), flee from the Lord under duress.

one ought to be (i.e., his station, his home).[51] The verb "flees" implies a crisis within his home, such as famine, war, exile, or bad fortune, or, to judge from v. 7, a nagging and/or a frigid wife. Cut off from the security of his family and the protection of the community, he is exposed to peril, forfeits his future, and diminishes his own life in essential ways. The proverb does not aim to fault the man as a feckless gadabout but to prompt him to protect his home and to be grateful for it.

9-10 These verses are united by the keyword *rēaʿ* "friend" (*rēʿēhû,* v. 9, and *rēʿᵃka,* v. 10) and by the theme of the importance of friends for giving counsel and support in time of need. The catchword "sweet" (vv. 7b, 9a) connects it to the preceding pair.

9 The first of the pair compares the outward aesthetic agreeableness of glistening olive *oil* (see 5:3; Ps. 133:2) on the face *and* of fragrant *incense (qᵉṭōret)*[52] on the garments (cf. Song 1:3; 3:6; 4:10; Dan. 2:46; John 12:3) with the sweetness of a friend who gives passionate, not disinterested, counsel.[53] *Oil* (*šemen;* 5:3; 21:20) refers to the utilitarian and aesthetic olive oil. The refreshing olive oil *makes the heart glad* (see 10:1). The gladdening oil and incense are similes for the agreeable and delightful counsel of a friend that originates in his very being. Both the outward fragrances and the wholesome counsel produce a sense of well-being. *And* now functions as both a conjunctive and a comparative (see v. 3). The benefit represented by a friend (cf. in particular 17:17; 18:24b; 25:16) is likened to *sweetness* (see 16:21), a metonymy for what is pleasant and agreeable and a metaphor for that which is delightful to the psyche. The gloss of *one's friend* (*rēʿēhû,* i.e., who proves himself a true neighbor by helping another in time of need; see 3:28; 17:17) understands the form as an equivalent of *hārēaʿ,* as in Job 12:4, but the antecedent of the suffix may be "heart," a synecdoche for the person. *Comes from*

51. Cf. Coppes, *TWOT,* 2:794, s.v. *māqôm.*

52. *Qᵉṭōret* is the most common general term for incense. Most of its occurrences in the Old Testament refer to the special incense that was burned on the incense altar (e.g., Exod. 30:1-10). A perfumer blended together fragrant spices — gum resin, onycha and galbanum — and pure frankincense to make it most fragrant (Exod. 30:34). It was a common practice in the ancient Near East to burn the incense in handheld censers that produced a fragrant cloud of incense (cf. Ezek. 8:10-11; Richard E. Averbeck, *NIDOTTE,* 3:914, s.v. *qṭr*). In the sacrificial system, incense functioned as a lovely protective screen veiling off the deity. However, the sage intends no allusion to the cult here. Song 3:6 describes the beloved as "perfumed with myrrh and incense made from all the spices of the merchants."

53. "A faithful friend is a sturdy shelter; he that has found one has found a treasure. There is nothing so precious as a faithful friend, and no scales can measure his excellence. A faithful friend is an elixir of life; and those who fear the Lord will find him" (Sir. 6:14-16).

his passionate counsel (*mēʿᵃṣat-nāpeš;* see n. 12) signifies that the individual's passionate vitality is the source of the counsel (see 1:19).

10 The second of the pair turns from the friend's counsel to his support. The proverb envisions a situation where the son/disciple suffers sudden, calamitous damage, loss, and destruction, and commands him to claim the help of a tried and tested friend of the family (v. 10a) rather than that of a distant blood relative (v. 10b). Such a friend is indispensable in distress. *Your friend* (see v. 9) denotes a socially close neighbor who helps in need. *And* is probably epexegetical, further defining the friend as *the friend of your father,* not conjunctive (cf. "or"; so NRSV), referring to a second friend. His friendship to the family has been tried and tested over two generations. *Do not forsake* (see 2:13) in this book is used in a nontheological sense only here and in 28:13. "In the time of distress" is gapped. *And* now coordinates the two admonitions into a compound sentence presenting two sides of the same coin. *The house* [i.e., the indispensable basis of sound prosperity; see 12:7] *of your* blood *relative* [see 6:19] *do not enter* [i.e., going into a sphere that affects destiny; see 6:11] *in the time* [see 16:4] *of your distress* (*'êdekā;* see 1:26). The B verset gives the rationale for the commands, probably by quoting an otherwise independent proverb. If so, the family friend is also regarded as a close, next-door neighbor, and the relative in view as distant. *A next-door neighbor (šākēn)* denotes "one who resides in some geographically proximate relationship to another and, thus, may designate a next-door . . . neighbor (the neighbor close[st] 'to his house[hold.'"[54] The nearby neighbor is further defined as one who is *close* (see 10:14), probably both literally in space and metaphorically in sympathy and spirit (cf. Lev. 21:3; Ruth 2:20; cf. Ps. 148:14). If this social proximity is not intended, the adjective is tautological with "next-door neighbor" and the truthfulness of the proverb may be called into question, because not all nearby neighbors are friendly (see v. 14). *Better* (see v. 5) refers to the ability to help in crisis. Such a neighbor is better in crisis *than a relative who is far off.* As the antonym of "close, next-door neighbor," the far relative is distant both in space and in thought. "The LORD is *far* from the wicked" entails his unwillingness to draw near to one pleading for help, just as his closeness to Israel entails his helping them (Deut. 4:7). In sum, in crisis the son should turn to a tried and tested friend of the family who lives nearby and is ready to meet his needs, not to a relative who lives far away and/or is not emotionally accessible. The proverb must be held in tension with 17:17: "The neighbor is a friend at all times, and a relative is born for adversity." The tried and tested friend and true neighbor stick closer than a remote brother (18:24).

54. R. H. O'Connell, *NIDOTTE,* 4:112, s.v. *šākēn.*

b. Second Instructions on Friends and Friendships (27:11-21)

The second subunit of sayings on friendship is marked off by the direct address, "My son, be wise." This educational proverb is paired with v. 12, whose initial word, "shrewd," is a co-referential term with initial "wise" in v. 11. They form an *inclusio* with the intractable fool (v. 22) by way of an antonym. Verse 12 also functions as a janus. By implicitly admonishing the son to be shrewd, it looks back to the admonition "be wise." But by also calling on him to avoid evil it looks ahead to relationships to be avoided, namely, putting up security for a stranger (v. 13), the hypocritical friend (14), and the shrewish wife (v. 15). Verse 15 forms a smooth transition to the positive proverbs on friendship (vv. 17-21) by employing the same syntactic structure as vv. 17-21 (i.e., a simile in verset A to illustrate the social truth in verset B, joined by a comparative "and"). In v. 19 the comparative conjunctive is replaced by its equivalent "like . . . so" structure (cf. 26:1-3). Verse 16 is an exception in that it was composed as a pair with v. 15 about the uncontrollable, shrewish wife, who should be closer than the closest friend. Verses 17-21 pertain to true friendship. In an alternating AB/A′B′ pattern, their odd verses assert the values of friends: a friend sharpens one (v. 17) and enables the other to gain a true estimate of himself (vv. 19, 21). These three proverbs are linked by the mention of the body parts of a human being (*'ādām,* v. 19) in their B versets: "face" (v. 17b), "heart" (v. 19b), and "mouth" (v. 21b). Their even verses contain advice for advancement by recognizing boundaries and thus not fracturing relationships: by protecting one's master (v. 18) and by restraining one's appetite (v. 20). Both imply being a reliable friend, loyalty to a master, and not coveting a neighbor's property. Furthermore, every verse of vv. 17-20 repeats the same word or its close synonym twice, "iron" (v. 17a), and "sharp" (v. 17a, b), "protects"/"guards" (v. 18a, b), "face" (v. 19a), "human being" (v. 19b), and "satisfy" (v. 20a, b). Verses 20-21 are linked by the imagery of procedures to test and remove detrimental elements with the help of instruments: "crucible" *(maṣrēp)* and "mortar" *(maktēš).* Verse 21 deals with precious metals; v. 22 with worthless grain.

11 The introductory educational proverb also consists of two admonitions and a motivation clause, linking it syntactically with v. 10. Grammatically, *and* merely combines the commands *be wise* [see 6:6], *my son* (see 1:8; I: 62), and *make my heart glad* (see 27:9), but lexically the second implies a logical result of the first (see 10:1). *So that I might answer* [cf. 16:1] *him who reproaches me* (see 14:31) inferentially binds father and son together against the family adversary. The admonition in verset A reflects an intense sense of family solidarity and mutual pride of the generations in one another (cf. 17:6). The motivation in verset B is based on a healthy culture of shame and honor. United with his son intellectually and emotionally, the father is in a position to refute anyone who denigrates his significance, worth, and ability. What will prove his worth will be the tangible reality of a true son, who through the wisdom he learned prospers, negotiates his way through temptation, and triumphs over death. He will be his father's weapon of defense (cf. Ps. 127:4-5; 2 Cor. 3:1-3; 1 Thess. 2:19-20; 3:8).[55]

12 The second of the introductory pair implicitly defines "be wise" as be "shrewd," not "gullible," This proverb repeats 22:3 with only minuscule stylistic variations without semantic differences.[56] Its asyndetic style, however, makes the manifold paronomasia more striking. Their real difference pertains to their context and function. 22:3 qualifies 22:2, and 27:12 is linked conceptually with 27:11 and with 27:13. Whybray says, "[Verse 12] may be intended to add support to verse 11, as it draws a contrast between the respective fates of the prudent *(ʿārûm)* and the gullible *(pᵉtî)*."[57] Meinhold agrees: "The son is made aware by example that the sapiential rearing and way of life is rewarding."[58] The verse also functions as a janus to the partial unit on evil to be avoided. As in 22:3, "are fined" forms a smooth transition to a following proverb about economics. It connects being gullible with becoming a foolish security.

13 In a katabasis, the introduction retrogresses from the wise and shrewd (vv. 11-12a) to the gullible (v. 12b) to the foolish surety involved with the "unchaste wife" (v. 13). The change from "outsider" (22:1b) to "unchaste [lit. "outsider"] wife" (27:13b) is intentional and significant. The unchaste wife, who is mostly encountered in the book's prologue (see 2:16; 5:10, 20; 6:24), functions as the countervoice to the father's. His voice and teaching aim to overcome her voice and seduction. In that light 27:13 probably functions in this series of educational proverbs as an implicit warning to the son to stay far away from her and the fools that have indebted themselves to her. Verse 13 essentially repeats 20:16.[59] It is also connected with v. 12 by the paronomasia of *ʿrm* ("shrewd," v. 12a), *ʿbr* ("pass on," v. 12b), and *ʿrb*

55. "Should not the children of the Church ponder this deep responsibility, to carry such a profession, as may *answer him that reproacheth,* and stop the mouth, ever ready to open with taunts against the Gospel?" (Bridges, *Proverbs,* p. 512).

56. 27:12a repeats 22:3a but reads *nistār,* not *wayyissātēr* (Q). Consequently "sees evil" is probably an asyndetic relative clause and *nistār* a gnomic perfective. Verse 12b repeats 22:3b except that it reads *pᵉtāʾyīm,* not *ûpᵉtāyîm,* with no difference in meaning and *neʿᵉnāšû,* not *wᵉneʿᵉnāšû,* making *ʿābᵉrû* an asyndetic relative.

57. R. Whybray, *The Composition of the Book of Proverbs* (JSOTSup 168; Sheffield: JSOT, 1994), p. 126.

58. Meinhold, *Sprüche,* 2:456.

59. 27:13a is the same as 20:16a but reads *qaḥ,* not *lᵉqaḥ,* with no difference in meaning; 27:13b is the same as 20:16b but reads "unchaste wife" *(nokrîyâ),* not "outsider" *(nokrîyām).*

("becomes surety," v. 13a). According to this proverb, a foolish guarantor has pledged himself to pay the debt of a foolish stranger, who has indebted himself to the unchaste wife.[60] Both the guarantor and the debtor are in her hands. Probably by her enticements and flatteries, she seduced some male to become indebted to her (see Proverbs 5 and 7). The proverb instructs the disciple to have nothing to do with these fools, neither the guarantor, nor the debtor, nor the creditor (the unchaste wife). His allegiance belongs to his wise father.

14 This proverb picks up the unit's keyword *neighbor* (*rēʿēhû;* see 3:28; glossed "friend" in 27:9, 10), but now within the context of bad friendships (see vv. 13-16). Its verset A represents the blesser as one who, like a priest standing before a large congregation (cf. 1 K. 8:55), greets his neighbor with a loud voice for all to hear. Though *the one who blesses* (see 3:33) probably has its weakened sense "to greet" (i.e., to encounter the neighbor with a *bārûk* [= "blessed be" saying]; cf. 1 Sam. 13:10),[61] its antithetical parallel, "curse," keeps its basic sense to the fore (see 10:6). *With a loud voice* (cf. 1:20) designates his greeting as being more sonorous than normal. *Early* signifies "at rising time" (cf. Hos. 6:4; 13:3), probably with the connotation "insistently" and/or "eagerly" (Jer. 7:13). The meaning is often emphasized by the addition *in the morning* (i.e., the beginning of daylight [cf. Gen. 19:27; 20:8; Judg. 9:33; 19:25-27; Ruth 3:14]), but the qualification can be omitted (Gen. 19:2; Josh. 8:14). His ostentatious manner, enhanced by his eagerly rising early to meet his neighbor at the crack of dawn to pronounce his blessing, aims to make the impression that he has a deep veneration for his neighbor. Verset B, however, presents the way his overdone blessing will be reckoned. His unnatural voice and timing betray him as a hypocrite, and no good will come of it. *It will be reckoned* (see 16:30; 17:28) has as its subject the situation represented in verset A. *As a curse* (see 26:2) turns his hypocritical benediction into a malediction. *To him* could be the neighbor (i.e., the blessing will be reckoned as a curse that will bring something bad on him), but the nominative absolute construction of verset A anticipates the resumptive pronoun so that the blesser is the more probable antecedent. But who is the agent? Is the neighbor reckoning it as a curse pronounced against him? Or is it a divine passive and God reckons the blessing, through which the hypocrite in fact hoped to enrich himself,[62] as a curse and will transform the hypocritical blessing into a malediction against the hypocrite. Probably both are true. The neighbor will not be fooled and

60. See the other "surety sayings" (6:1-5; 11:15; 17:18; 20:16).

61. Keller, *TLOT,* 1:271, s.v. *brk.*

62. Delitzsch (*Proverbs,* p. 209) comments: "The affected zeal is a sign of a selfish, calculating, servile soul."

will reckon instead that the hypocrite holds him in contempt and curses him. And, more importantly, God will not be fooled. Instead of mediating a phony blessing, he will curse the hypocrite, and he will find out what nastiness will come of that. The innocent neighbor, however, has nothing to fear, for an undeserved curse will not land (26:2). Real friendship is expressed in deed and in truth, not in pious pronouncements exceeding the bounds of normalcy (1 John 3:18).

15-16 The next pair turns from the hypocritical neighbor to the shrewish wife. Verse 15 is linked with v. 14 by the temporal nouns "morning" (v. 14a) and "in a day of" (v. 15a; see n. 17) and by the common notion of unanticipated deception. Both the overzealous blesser and the shrew prove false and threaten ruin. The victim should have expected good from the blesser and his wife, but received bad. The pronoun "her" in v. 16 refers to "contentious wife," showing that the verses were composed as a pair.

15 The proverb explicitly equates the quarrelsome wife (verset B) with *a leaky roof* [see 19:13] *in* [see n. 17] *a cloudburst.* In an enjambment, *and* binds "the cloudburst" and *a contentious wife* (see 21:9) with their predicate *are alike* (i.e., "equal to one another"; cf. 3:15). Both are unexpected, deceptive, irritating, and unbearable. The man takes shelter under the roof of his home expecting to find protection from the storm. Instead, he finds that his leaky roof provides him no shelter from the torrential downpour. Likewise, he married with the expectation of finding good, but the wife from whom he expected protection from the rudeness of the world harshly attacks him at home. Both render his home intolerable, and, like a bird that leaves its nest, he flees his home, seeking shelter elsewhere (see I: 118).

16 Linked with v. 15 by "her" and by storm imagery, the second of the proverb pair adds two further metaphors to describe the shrew: a storm "wind," which is impossible to shelter (verset A), and "oil," which is impossible to grasp (verset B). The first escalates the weather imagery from a deceptive and irritating leaky roof (v. 16) to an uncontrollable storm within the home that sets everything within it upside down, and the second reinforces the impossibility of taming the shrew. *Those who shelter her* refers to all the individuals who attempt the task (see 3:18). The singular "his" in verset B also individualizes them. Although *the wind* (*rûaḥ;* see 25:23) might possibly signify a light breeze in Isa. 57:13, in this context it denotes a "storm" (1 K. 19:11). The wind connotes "motion with the power to set other things in motion"[63] (see I: 92). Conjunctive *and* links the compounded metaphors. *Oil* (see 5:3) refers elsewhere in Proverbs to delightful olive oil (see 27:9). *Meets* [see 7:10] *his right hand* (see 3:16), the position of "honor, privilege

63. Albertz/Westermann, *TLOT,* 3:1203, s.v. *rûaḥ.*

and preference."[64] Both metaphors are ironic. The home should have provided her shelter from the storm, but, ironically, she brings the destructive storm into it. Her husband's majestic right hand should have protected her, and she should have delighted her husband as fragrant olive oil. Ironically, her belligerence makes both a frustrating, wasteful incongruity that cannot be resolved.

17 The topic shifts from false friendship back to true friendship (vv. 5-10, 14). This emblematic proverb likens the sharpening of an iron sword or tool by a whetting iron to the sharpening of a man's wit through an authentic friend. *Iron . . . with iron* probably designates the smelted and worked iron from terrestrial ore that was introduced into Palestine about 1400 B.C., not the meteoric iron that was used before that. It is notable for its hardness and strength and used in many types of instruments (cf. Deut. 27:5; Josh. 17:16; Judg. 1:19).[65] Here the genus "iron" is used for the species. The first "iron" is a "sword" or "knife," because "face" is the Hebrew term for a blade's "edge." The second iron is a "sharpening iron," as shown by *with* (or against). *Is sharpened* (see n. 25) is used metaphorically of mouth or tongue (Ps. 57:4[5]; Isa. 49:2), a use that supports *a person* (*'îš,* see I: 89) *sharpens,* which functions as a metaphor for dialogue. The literal sense in verset A is used as a metaphor of the real topic in B, to which it is joined by conjunctive *and. Face* [see 6:35 n.] *of his friend* (or "his neighbor"; see vv. 9, 10, 14) is a pun since the working edge of a sword or knife is called its "face" (see Eccl. 10:10). But it functions as a metonymy for a person's wit and personality that express itself in his face.[66] The analogy infers that the friend persists and does not shy away from constructive criticism. This persistent friend, whose wounds are faithful (v. 6), is the opposite of the fawning neighbor (v. 14) and the cantakerous wife (vv. 15-16), and performs an indispensable task. As a result of his having a "hard" friend — a true one — a man develops the capacity to succeed in his tasks as an effective tool, and in the end he will thank his friend for being hard as flint.[67]

18 This verse matches the style of v. 17 (cf. vv. 9, 20, 21). A true-to-life metaphor in verset A is again paired by simple *and* with the topic. Its em-

64. F. C. Putnam, *NIDOTTE,* 2:467, *yāmîn.* The LORD's right hand is said to be majestic, exalted, supporting, providing refuge, and bringing salvation. These connotations also inform the human right hand.

65. A. H. Konkel, *NIDOTTE,* 1:742, s.v. *barzel.*

66. "Because one's countenance expresses and characterizes one's nature, *pānîm* in an expanded sense can also describe the entire person" (A. S. van der Woude, *TLOT,* 2:1,000, s.v. *pānîm*).

67. "The rabbis applied it to students: 'Just as iron sharpens iron, so does the intellect become keener by contact with other intellects' (Ta'an. 7a; Gen. R. 69:1)" (Greenstone, *Proverbs,* p. 288).

blematic parallels match *he who protects* (*nōṣēr;* see 2:8)[68] *a* precious *fig tree* (*t*ᵉ*'ēnâ, ficus carica* L.) with *the one who guards* (*šōmēr;* see 2:8) *his master* (or "lord," *'ᵃdōnāyw;* see 25:13), a social term for the one having power and authority over others. The honorific plural points to a human master, not God, for no human can protect God. The parallels also match the promises that the former *will eat its* (i.e. the fig's) highly prized, succulent *fruit* (cf. 1:31; 13:2) with the fact that the latter *will be honored,* entailing that he will not be given cheap words but be endowed with the wealth that gives him social dignity and gravitas (see 3:9; 8:18; 13:18; cf. 1 Cor. 9:7; Gal. 6:6; 2 Tim. 2:6). The metaphor implies several truths. First, it suggests that the servant should value his lord as highly as the farmer prizes the fig tree, one of the most highly valued trees in Israel. Second, "to protect" entails careful, precise, and vigilant procedures without transgressing the established orders of creation and of society. Third, it entails patient endurance in the loyal and faithful service of attending to the master's interests (cf. Jas. 5:7-8). Fourth, the fig tree (i.e., the lord) yields its fruit over the course of a number of years, and after it matures over an extended period. Its fruit ripens gradually from the beginning of the harvest in June to its end in fall (see at 6:8; 20:4), not quickly. Fifth, the parallelism between eating the fig's succulent, sweet fruit and being honored implies that social elevation is spiritually invigorating and delightful. Sixth, it also entails that the reward is enduring. "Because of its high sugar content, the fig can be stored dry. In Gezer, a dried fig was found that dated from about 5000 B.C. (Zohary, 58)."[69] The proverb assumes established social boundaries between a master and a slave. The way for the latter to be elevated is not by transgressing these social boundaries, but by honoring them (cf. 17:2; 30:32-33). While there may be some exceptions to the rule of justice on earth, there are no exceptions in heaven (cf. 1 Sam. 2:30; Matt. 25:21, 23; John 12:26; Rev. 22:3, 4).

19 This emblematic parallelism (cf. v. 8) compares a person looking in water as into a mirror to see the reflection of his face (verset A) to a person's heart looking at a human being (verset B), presumably to see its reflection. *As looking in water* (or "as water reflects" [i.e., "as looking in water as a mirror"], see n. 27).[70] Elsewhere in this book water connotes a source of life

68. A. Cohen, "He Who Tends a Fig Tree Will Eat Its Fruit (Prov 27:18)," *BM* 25 (1979) 8-12, on the bases of his experience that fig trees don't require much work and of Jer. 31:5-6, suggests that the root *nṣr* refers to planting figs. But the normal usage of the word for "watchers" and the use of *nṭ'* for planting in that passage undermine the argument. In my own experience, fig trees did not take much care, but it was most difficult to protect their ripe fruit from the birds.

69. Meinhold, *Sprüche,* pp. 458-59.

70. *HALOT,* 2:577, s.v. *mayim.* Water can refer to the abundance of water in a river or sea (8:29; Amos 5:8) or to flowing tears (Jer. 9:18[17]), but here it refers to still, reflecting water in a fountain, well, or cistern (Gen. 24:11; 1 Sam. 9:11; Prov. 18:4).

(30:16), sex (5:16; 9:17), and refreshment (25:25), but the addition "a face looks to a face" (see v. 17), glossed simply by *a face,* shows its reflecting quality since a mirror is in view. *So* (*ken;* see v. 8) *the human heart* (*lēb-'ādām;* see I: 89, 90) *is reflected in a human being* (*'ādām;* lit. "so a human being's heart looks to a human being"). Does a person's heart look to his own person (NIV) or to somebody else (cf. NRSV)? If to oneself, there is a reciprocal relationship between one's heart and his behavior. One can gain an insight into his heart — his thoughts, feelings, and aspirations — by observing his actual behavior (cf. 16:2; Jer. 17:9) According to this interpretation, one can escape his egocentric predicament by paying attention to what he actually says and does, not by justifying his thoughts. More probably, however, in this context about friendship, one can evaluate his character by looking to others. In their behavior, objective compliments (see 27:2) and hard criticisms (vv. 6, 17), and also by their earnest counsel (v. 9), he can get an image of his true character.

20 Once again, as in vv. 17-19, a true-to-life fact represented in the A verset is used as a simile for a social truth in verset B, joined by *and* (see vv. 15-18). It is linked with v. 19 by the catchword *'ādām,* by the connection of *'ādām* with a body part ("heart of a human being" and "eyes of a human being"), and by the sensible connection of looking. The insatiable "appetite" of the human eye is compared with the insatiable "appetite" of the grave. The personification, *the Grave* [*šᵉ'ôl;* see I: 116] *and Abaddon* [see 15:11] *are never satisfied* (see 1:31), represents the destructive realm of death as never spiritually experiencing a state of being satisfied or gratified, not an objective fact of being filled. In the Ugaritic texts, the voracious Monster Maweth ("Death") with gaping throat endlessly devours his victims (cf. 30:15, 16; Isa. 5:14; Hab. 2:5). *The eyes* [see 25:7] *of humankind* (*'ādām;* see v. 19) *are never satisfied* figuratively represents the eyes as having an appetite like a stomach, which, too, can never be finally gratified (cf. Eccl. 6:7-9). The eye is used as a metonymy for that part of the body that awakens the psychic desire, greed, lust, and covetousness to own and possess whatever desirable thing it sees (cf. Eccl. 2:10; 4:8; 1 John 2:16). The comparison of human greed with the ruthless, unsparing, and destructive realm of the dead suggests that its craving is also ruthless, destructive, and insatiable. Consumerism informs both communism and capitalism, and neither economic system can bring peace. Consumerism drives kings to tyranny, nations to war, companies to rape the earth, the irrational adversarial positions of management versus labor, and individuals to lust for each other's homes, spouses, and property. The lust of the eye led Eve and Adam to transgress social boundaries in the first place. It is the bane of humanity, and this truism should drive the son to examine his own lusts and to lead him to the heavenly wisdom that comes as God's good gift to those who seek it and trust him (cf. 28:25; Isa. 55:1, 2). In

Christ, Christians find rest (cf. 4:13-17; Matt. 11:28; John 6:35; 7:37; Phil. 4:11-13).

21 This verse draws the series of comparative proverbs mostly joined by simple *and* to a conclusion. Once again a true-to-fact reality functions as a simile for a social truth. What *a person* (*'îš;* see I: 89) praises and who praises him (i.e., his reputation) are compared with the two images of a *crucible* to test the purity of *silver* and of a small melting *furnace* (or "oven") to try the genuineness of *gold.* The same two images for testing are used in 17:3, but there the LORD tests, whereas here the person is tested by the praise he gives and/or receives. *According to* (see n. 32), if glossed literally "by the mouth of," could signify that one is tested by the character of the one who praises him. But assuming its normal meaning, "according to," *his praise* (see nn. 33, 34) is probably yet another intentional pun. It can mean "the praise given to him," or his reputation is the test of his mettle (3:4; 12:8; Luke 2:52; Acts 2:47; Rom. 14:18; 1 Tim. 3:2, 7). Thus a person can evaluate his character by the measure of public opinion.[71] However, it can also mean a person's mettle is tested by whom or what he praises. Musicians praise their composers; literate people praise their authors; sports fans praise their heroes; and the godly praise the Lord. Likewise, the immoral praise the adulterer and adulteress, and the covetous praise the rich (Ps. 49:18[19]. To honor a fool dishonors oneself. In sum, the saying implicitly admonishes the son to test himself by what he raves about and by investigating his reputation and who it is that praises him (cf. 27:2). Though he may also find himself a lonely minority in a corrupt society, like Jeremiah and our Lord, the opprobrium of sinners is actually the honor of saints.

In sum, the second half confirms the first half and adds to the second truths about being and having a wise and true friend. First, they are loyal to their biblical heritage, if they have one, and avoid fools who are out to make an easy buck or to enjoy easy sex. Moreover, they also avoid the fawning hypocrite and the belligerent. But they do not shy away from giving one another hard criticism. They are loyal to their superiors. Finally, they evaluate their true selves by what they do, by what they praise, and by whom and for what they are praised. But they do not deceive themselves about their endemic greed. Only God can save them from their folly.

71. McKane (*Proverbs,* p. 608) says, "A community has processes for putting a man to the test and trying him thoroughly before it accords him acclaim and preference and entrusts him with power. . . . The processes at the disposal of the community for testing a man's reputation are as rigorous and reliable as those employed for testing silver and gold, and that consequently no one may hope to succeed by pretence or affectation."

c. Janus (27:22)

The extended length of this proverb, matching v. 10 that brought the preceding subunit to its conclusion,[72] and its *inclusio* by way of an antonym with v. 11, suggests that v. 22 draws the second subunit to its conclusion. At the same time, its similar imagery of a crucible and a mortar for the testing, refining, or removing what is useless by a technical process[73] suggests that 27:21-22 draws 27:1-22 to its conclusion. On the other hand, its direct address "you" and its educational vocabulary ("fool" and "folly"), along with its cessation of comparative proverbs with a similar structure in 27:17-21, suggest that it also serves as a seam to the new unit (cf. 27:1, 11).

The janus's topic is the fool and his folly (27:27a, b). *If* (see 2:1) signals the condition that implicitly compares and contrasts disciplining *the fool* (see *hā'ᵉwîl;* see I: 112) to milling grain in a mortar with a pestle. *You grind* [or "pound"] *in a mortar with a pestle* metaphorically depicts severe punishment. *In the midst of* [see 4:21] *groats* implicitly contrasts the fool with dried grain that can be hulled, crushed, and broken into pieces by severe pounding. Verset B, the apodosis, asserts that *his folly* [see I: 113] *will not depart* [see 3:7] *from him* (lit. "from upon him [i.e., the fool]), implicitly likening his folly to a barley's husk. Thus, the intractability of the fool is contrasted with the teachability of the wise (cf. 12:15; 17:10, 16; 18:2; 26:11). Proverbs says a lot about the effectiveness of education (cf. 22:15; 23:13, 14; 29:15, 17), but not for the fool. Bridges comments, "The belief in the necessary working of affliction for our saving good is a fatal delusion."[74] Prisons were made into penitentiaries through the mistaken notion that confinement would bring repentance and effect a cure. Instead, many prisoners become hardened criminals. Divine grace that regenerates the fool is his only hope of being converted into a useful person (cf. 26:11).

4. Caring for "Flocks and Herds" (27:23-27)

23 *Be sure you know*[75] *the condition of your flocks,*
pay attention to [your] herds.
24 *Wealth does not endure*[76] *forever,*

72. This obvious pattern restrains from emending the text to achieve a shorter line.

73. Van Leeuwen, *Context and Meaning,* p. 128.

74. Bridges, *Proverbs,* p. 522.

75. The parallel impv. certifies the use of the impv. as an injunction (*IBHS,* p. 509, P. 31.5b).

76. The preposition "to" has *'ôlām* as its object and demands that a verb of motion be supplied (*IBHS,* p. 205, P. 11.2.10b; p. 224, P. 11.4.3d).

and certainly not[77] *a crown*[78] *from generation to generation.*[79]
25 *If the grass is removed,*[80] *then the new growth appears;*
and if the vegetation of the mountains is harvested,
26 *the young rams will provide*[81] *your clothing,*
and your he-goats, the price of a field.[82]
27 *And you will have*[83] *enough goats'*[84] *milk*
for your food, for the food of your household,[85]
and for[86] *the life of your servant girls.*

77. *'im* glosses the emphatic oath formula construction, "If a crown endures forever, [then may I die?]!"

78. The LXX reads *oude paradidōsin* ("neither does he transmit"), and the Targ. (Syr.) *[m]šlm.* Did they paraphrase *nzr* (*Hiphil,* "to hand over"; cf. Ps. 63 [Gk. 62]:10[11]) or *nṣr* ("to preserve")? Toy, Oesterley, Gemser, Fichtner [*BHS*], Scott, McKane, Ringgren, Plöger, Whybray, and Clifford emend *nzr* to *'ôṣrôt* "treasures" or *'ōšer* "wealth," but not Cohen, Van der Ploeg, Gispen, Barucq, and Van Leeuwen, though Cohen and Gispen interpret *nzr* as a metonymy for wealth (see Van Leeuwen, *Context and Meaning,* p. 134). These emendations and the interpretation of "crown" as a symbol of wealth are unnecessary and show an unawareness of the original royal provenance of wisdom material (see I: 34).

79. K reads *dôr dôr* and Q, *dôr wādôr.* In both the asyndetic and syndetic construction (lit. "to generation [and] generation"), the repetition of the sing. is distributive (*IBHS,* pp. 115-16, P. 7.2.3b).

80. The logical connection between v. 25 and vv. 26-27 suggests that the ambiguous suffix conjugations of v. 25 signify hypothetical situations.

81. Lit. "will be for." The *lamed* of advantage entails a verb of motion (*IBHS,* p. 224, P. 11.4.3d).

82. Gen. of the mediated object, "price paid to buy a field" (*IBHS,* pp. 146-47, P. 9.5.2d). The LXX renders verset B "pay attention to your land that you may have lambs"; the Targ., "the kids for your commerce"; the Syr., "for 'your food.'"

83. Lit. "enough of goats' milk will be for your food." The particle of existence, *yēš,* is elided. *Le* with *leḥem* expresses advantage, not possession.

84. *'ēzîm* is an epicene noun because, though masculine in form, it obviously refers to the female goat (*IBHS,* p. 107, P. 6.5.2a).

85. The omission of *llḥmk llḥm bytk* "your food, food for your household" in the LXX at first (cf. *BHS*) gives the impression that these phrases in the MT are a gloss in an overfull line. However, the LXX has a very free, independent reading with its own overfull line: "My son, you have from me words very useful for life, and for the life of your servants." It is too hazardous to reconstruct its original *Vorlage* from such a free translation, but perhaps its unique omission may be a haplography due to both homoioarcton and homoioteleuton. The omission of *lena'arôteykā* at the end of the verse in Syr. also looks at first like a superior shorter reading. However, its witness to an original text is compromised by its omission of the important word *dê* at the beginning of the line, which is attested in all versions. Furthermore, "servant girls" is attested in all the other versions. The other long lines at the seams of this chapter (vv. 10, 22, 27) support the MT, which also has the support of the Targ. and Vulg.

86. *Le* of verset A is probably gapped.

This brief poem (cf. 23:29-35; 24:30-34), the seventh unit or subunit in Solomon IIC (chs. 25–27; cf. 25:2-27; 25:28–26:12, 13-16, 17-28; 27:1-10, 11-22, 23-27), draws that section to its conclusion. In some ways it matches the poem that ended Collection IV (24:30-34). Both are five verses that end a collection/section, and both refer somewhat chiastically to a field (24:30; 27:26). Meinhold notes that by placing them together one sees a contrast between the sluggard who neglects the good creation and his inherited field and the wise who, by working in harmony with the good creation, produces the wealth that buys a field. Meinhold also observes that it forms an *inclusio* with 25:1-7, for the opening verses to Collection V (= Solomon IIC) explicitly refer to kingship (25:1-7) and this concluding poem implicitly refers to kingship by mentioning its symbol, the crown (27:24).[87] The reference to the crown also forms a janus to Solomon IID (chs. 28–29), which pertains to just rulership. In addition, this conclusion possibly has redactional links with ch. 9, the concluding poem of the prologue to Proverbs (or Collection I), and with 31:10-31, the book's epilogue and the conclusion to Collection VII. Van Leeuwen comments, "In this regard, it is striking that 'servant girls' appears only in v. 27 and in 9:3 and 31:15."[88]

The poem consists of an admonition to take good care of one's flocks and herds (v. 23) and substantiation (vv. 24-27). On the one hand, money and status are depreciating, not self-renewing resources (v. 24). Money vanishes, sometimes flying away unexpectedly and capriciously like a bird (23:4-5). On the other hand, animals are self-renewing and an increasing source of wealth. If given the grasses that the highlands of Palestine naturally provide (v. 25), the he-goats provide clothing and money to purchase arable land, and the she-goats provide enough milk to feed the entire household, including the milkmaids. The list of benefits does not aim to be exhaustive. Flocks were also important for food (Judg. 6:19; Amos 6:4) and for cultic sacrifice (Num. 15:3). Their skins were used for bottles (Gen. 21:14) and fabric (Exod. 35:26), and their horns for vessels (1 Sam. 16:1) or as instruments (Josh. 6:5-16).

The reference to the crown shows that the poem does not admonish a pastoral ideal as a self-contained way of life. At the most, its literal sense assumes that the addressee is a wealthy owner of flocks and herds and "shows the proper interplay between human labor and divine provision."[89] But the reference to the crown in v. 24 points to the poem's original royal provenance and suggests that the pastoral image is a metaphor for an ideal ruler. On the pre-literary level, where the poem circulated in the royal court (25:1), the

87. Meinhold, *Sprüche,* p. 461.

88. Van Leeuwen, *Proverbs,* p. 233.

89. Ross, *Proverbs,* p. 1,101.

good shepherd and his flock is a metaphor for the king's wise care of his subjects (2 Sam. 12:2, 4; 10:21; 22:22; 23:1-6; Ezekiel 34). By promoting their well-being he establishes his crown.[90] On the democratized literary level (see I: 37), however, the crown symbolizes any high social status and authority. By the nature of being a proverb, it has an application beyond its specific, ostensive reference.[91]

a. The Admonition: "Know Your Flocks" (27:23)

The proverb, addressing the son as an owner of flocks and probably a ruler, admonishes him to concern himself intimately and personally with the well-being of his wards. *You know* (see 3:5) instructs him "to be concerned with," to have an intensive involvement with, them that exceeds a simple cognitive relationship with them.[92] *Be sure you know* and its the parallel, *pay attention to* (lit. "set your heart to"; see 22:17), add nothing but emphasis. It takes a lot of effort to provide animals with pasturage and water and to breed them appropriately (Gen. 31:38-42; Sir. 7:22). *The condition* glosses "faces," on the assumption that face(s) here implies that their faces, like a mirror, reflect their condition, the status of their health, though Van der Woude thinks that here it refers to their whole being.[93] *Of your flocks* refers to collections of sheep and goats or only sheep without goats (1 Sam. 25:2), and *your herds* denotes "a group of cattle, sheep, and goats assembled under one shepherd."[94] To involve himself fully and personally with his sources of income will take the energy, discipline, kindness, shrewdness, and other virtues bestowed by wisdom. Moreover, "All should not be left to servants. The master's eye, like that of Boaz, should, as far as possible, overlook the work."[95]

b. Substantiation (27:24-27)

24 *Because* introduces the admonition's negative (v. 24) and positive (vv. 25-27) substantiations. On the debit side, wealth (verset A) and a crown (verset B), the symbols of kingship, are transitory, perishable, and depreciat-

90. "Our stewardship requires that we know intimately those things, creatures, and persons entrusted to our care (27:23). Governments need to understand the people, the land, and justice. Teachers need to know and love their students and their subjects. Workers and artists need to know their materials and their craft. Pastors . . . also need to know and tend their 'flocks'" (Van Leeuwen, *Proverbs,* p. 233).

91. Van Leeuwen, *Proverbs,* pp. 233-34.

92. Schottroff, *TLOT,* 2:514, s.v. *yd'.*

93. A. S. van der Woude, *TLOT,* 2:998, 1,000, s.v. *pānîm.*

94. *HALOT,* 2:793, s.v. I *'eder.*

95. Bridges, *Proverbs,* p. 523.

ing commodities, not self-maintaining resources. Without wisdom's diligence and constant vigilance to preserve and recover them, one loses his wealth and status. *Wealth* [see 15:6] *is not forever* (see 10:25) could refer to an individual's lifetime (cf. Exod. 19:9; 21:6), but the parallel shows that it refers to the farthest, distant time in the sense of unceasing. *And* joins a second, related notion with the first. *Certainly not* (see n. 77) is expressed as an emphatic oath. *A crown,* which was worn on the head by kings (2 Sam. 1:10; 2 K. 11:12) and the high priest (Exod. 29:6), symbolizes kingship (Ps. 89:39[40]). Its exact form is unknown, but David's was resplendent (Ps. 132:18). *From generation to generation* denotes "cycles of time," "life spans." In Gen. 15:16 it is calculated to be a hundred years (cf. Ps. 90:10; Isa. 65:20), but subsequently 40 years.[96]

25 This verse begins the positive argument for taking good care of the flocks. If the agricultural conditions dictated by the order of creation are met (v. 25), then the flocks will richly reward the wise (vv. 26-27). Verset A presents the condition of removing the wild grass that grows in Israel's rainy season, and adds to it the promise that it will replenish itself. *If . . . is removed* (*gālâ;* see 11:13) glosses a root whose basic meaning is "to uncover, to reveal." Intransitively, *gālâ* means "to be removed, to leave, to depart."[97] *Grass (ḥāṣîr)* glosses a term that denotes "wild growth that comes up regularly and abundantly after the winter rains (Ps 147:8) . . . and was valuable as fodder (Ps. 104:14). As quickly as *ḥāṣîr* sprouts in the rain, it withers in drought (Isa. 15:6) or is found along streams at best (1 Kgs. 18:5)."[98] *Then . . . appears* (see 6:6) is a metonymy; its visibility connotes that it is available as food for the flocks. The *new grass (deše')* "refers to the new fresh grass that sprouts after the rains have fallen on Israel . . . and withers in the dry season (Isa. 15:6). *Deše'* can sprout in the steppe . . . , which then serves as pastureland . . . for livestock (Joel 2:21-22)."[99] This promise entails the theological truth that the LORD will bring the rain to renew it. Verset B clarifies that the wild grass in view is the good grass that covers the Palestinian highlands, and that the removal of it entails harvesting it. "Once the first cut of the grass is made (in March), the softer grass follows which was harvested by a second cut at the time of the latter rain (in April)."[100] *And* is conjunctive, adding to the conditions of verset A. *The vegetation ('ēśel)* "is used in some texts in the broad sense of plants (e.g., Gen. 1:11-12). Such plants may grow in the

96. V. P. Hamilton, *NIDOTTE,* 1:931, s.v. II *dôr.*

97. In the intransitive use of *glh,* its subjects are "joy," "glory" (Isa. 24:11), grass (Prov. 25:27), and especially people going into exile (Isa. 5:13; Amos 7:11, 17).

98. M. D. Futato, *NIDOTTE,* 2:247, s.v. I *ḥāṣîr.*

99. M. D. Futato, *NIDOTTE,* 1:999, s.v. *deše'.*

100. Meinhold, *Sprüche,* p. 463.

wild (e.g., Isa. 42:15) or be a product of agriculture (e.g., Exod. 9:22)."[101] The parallel terms suggest that the former is in view. *Of the mountains* also hints at its wild growth, on which the flocks feed. "Because the Palestinian highlands were generally well forested and had good grass cover, they also functioned as a picture of prosperity and fertility (Ps. 72:3; Amos 9:13)."[102] To the Israelites mountains suggest extreme durability and so connote a permanent source of food supply. They are very much a part of the created order (see 8:25). *Is harvested* glosses a word whose basic meaning is "to gather." With words having to do with agriculture it takes on the specific notion "to harvest."[103] The incomplete passive focuses on the fact, not on the agent. The proverb applies to the harmony between the created order to sustain life and human wisdom to utilize it appropriately. The next verse implies that these first and second growths were fed as fodder to the flocks. The condition unites the LORD's good created order, including enduring mountains, good vegetation, and seasonal rain, with human wisdom diligently to reap it at the right time. The combination provides the economic foundation of Israel's animal husbandry.

26 Harvesting the hay will implicitly provide the fodder for taking proper care of the flocks, and they in turn will supply a self-perpetuating form of wealth. Verse 26 points to the riches provided by the males of the flocks, and v. 27 to the wealth from its females. The synthetic parallelism of v. 26 joined by *and* matches *the young rams (kᵉbāśîm),* a species of the "flock" (*ṣō'n,* v. 23), with either *your he-goats*[104] or "male goats and sheep,"[105] which in either case designates another species of the "flock." The former *will provide* (see n. 81) the wool for *your* [sing.; see v. 23] *clothing (lilbûšekā,* the most common term for apparel). *The price* (see 17:16) refers to the money received in exchange for the he-goats, whose proceeds are then used to purchase *a field* (23:10; 31:16). The arable land used for farming, including planting a vineyard, is in view, because the hay and fields in v. 26 are the natural pasturage of Israel's highlands.[106] The livestock provide both usable commodities and money to purchase property. This kind of incremental wealth increases the family's wealth from generation to generation, and with that the family's social status. The proverb does not nuance itself by Israel's laws that the land be returned to its original owners in the year of Jubilee (Lev. 25:23-28).

101. M. D. Futato, *NIDOTTE,* 3.546, s.v. *'ēśeb.*

102. M. Selman, *NIDOTTE,* 1:1,053, *har.*

103. I. Cornelius, A. E. Hill, and C. I. Rogers Jr., *NIDOTTE,* 1:469, s.v. *'sp.*

104. Aitken, *NIDOTTE,* p. 568, s.v. *'attûd.*

105. *HALOT,* 2:903, s.v. *'attûd.*

106. Note the consonance of *k<u>bś</u>ym* and *ll<u>bšk</u>.*

27 Conjunctive *and* links v. 27 as another compound sentence with v. 26 and extends the consequence of taking care of the flocks by feeding them fodder to a sufficient supply of goats' milk. Verset A qualifies that *you will have enough* [see 25:16] *milk,* a comprehensive term for what was considered an indispensable source of nutrition. The milk curds were usually served to guests in bowls from leather bags (Gen. 18:8). J. P. J. Olivier argues that the frequently occurring expression "a land flowing with milk and honey"[107] not only refers to the wealth and natural fertility of the promised land but also reflects the different modes of existence prevalent in ancient Israel. "While 'honey' . . . apparently refers to the best product of the settled farmers, 'milk' designates the main product of pastoralists' herds. Together they allude to the interdependence of and symbiosis between the two major ways of living in the land."[108] The milk is qualified by *goats',* because goats' milk was by far the animal nutrient of choice in the ancient Near East. It is richer in protein and easier to digest than cows' milk.[109] *For your food* (see 6:8) glosses the notion "food to sustain you." *Of your household* (see 11:29) expands the supply of rich food to all the family and personnel attached to one's household, not just oneself (see 11:29). Conjunctive *and* signals that verset B adds milk maidens as an additional beneficiary of the sufficient supply of goat's milk. *Life* (see I: 104) complements "food," the metonymy of cause, with its metonomy of effect.[110] *Of your maidservants* (*naʿarôteykā;* see 9:3) probably uses the genus to refer to the species "milkmaids." They are probably singled out to signify that the abundant, rich goats' milk is totally self-perpetuating. It provides life for those who in turn milk the goats, and that in turn feeds the entire household. If one is wise enough to work in harmony with the good creation, the animals will richly reward one with only a minimum of effort. And if in the social order the king takes care of his subjects, his crown will endure.

107. Cf. Exod. 3:8, 17; 13:5; 33:3; Lev. 20:24; Num. 13:27; 14:8; 16:13-14; Deut. 6:3; 11:9; 26:9; 27:3; 31:20; Josh. 5:6; Jer. 11:5; 32:22; Ezek. 20:6, 15.

108. J. P. J. Olivier, *NIDOTTE,* 2:136, s.v. *ḥālāb.*

109. The Talmud says, "'The goat is for milking, the sheep for shearing, the hen for laying eggs and the ox for plowing'" (cited by M. S. Moore and M. L. Brown, *NIDOTTE,* 3:728, s.v. *ṣōʾn.*

110. Toy (*Proverbs,* p. 494) et al. understand *ḥayyîm* as "maintenance" (cf. Vulg. *ad victum*), but they err in interpreting the metonymy of effect as its meaning. Gemser (*Sprüche,* p. 114), although adopting this meaning, undercuts it with the comment that food and drink sustain and renew life. Probably one should assume that the *lamed* of advantage is gapped (= "and goat's milk . . . for the life of").

C. SECTION D (28:1–29:27)

1 *The wicked flee,*[1] *though*[2] *no one is pursuing,*
but the righteous are confident like a lion.
2 *Because of the transgression of a land, its princes are many;*
but because of a discerning person, one who knows, what is right endures.[3]
3 *A destitute*[4] *man and*[5] *one who oppresses the poor —*
a rain that washes away and there is no food.
4 *Those who abandon instruction praise the wicked,*
but those who keep instruction strive against them.
5 *Evil people do not discern what is right,*
but the one who seeks the LORD discerns everything.
6 *Better a destitute person who walks in his integrity,*
than [one who walks in] the crookedness of double-dealing ways,[6] *though he is rich.*
7 *A discerning son guards instruction,*
but one who associates with profligates puts his father to shame.
8 *The one who increases his wealth by taking interest of any sort*[7] *from the poor*

1. For elegant variation the parallels pair a sing. subject with a pl. verb, a pl. subject with a sing. verb, and a gnomic perfective with a habitual imperfective (cf. GKC P. 145l; *IBHS,* p. 506, P. 31.3e).

2. Interpreting *waw* as concessive (*IBHS,* p. 624, P. 29.1.3B).

3. The LXX read *rîbîm* from *rabbîm,* interpreted *śāreyhā* by Aram. *šr'* "commence," read *yd' kn* as one word, and did not translate *y'ryk,* yielding the translation, "through the sins of the godless, quarrels arise, but a clever man quells them." G. R. Driver ("Problems in the Hebrew Text of Proverbs," *Bib* 32 [1951] 191-92) builds on the LXX and further unnecessarily changes *'rṣ* to *'ārîṣ* and *śryh* to *yiršeh,* appealing to Aram. *rš'* "bring a case against," yielding the translation, "through transgression a violent man raises suits, stirs up strife."

4. The NIV, NRSV, et al. unnecessarily emend *rāš* to *rō'š* ("ruler") or to *'āšîr* "rich." The LXX reads *rāšā'* ("wicked") and combines v. 3b with v. 4. According to Gemser (*Sprüche,* pp. 98, 100), the LXX did not understand the text of 28:9b, 15, 16a, 21b, 22b, 25a, 27b, 28a; 29:2, 5a, 9, 11, 13, 18a, 21a, 26a).

5. The MT accents disallow the reading "a poor man that oppresses the poor" (*pace* Targ., Vulg., KJV). Furthermore, that thought is inapposite. "One does not think of the oppressor of the poor as himself poor" (Delitzsch, *Proverbs,* p. 414). The interpretation that he was formerly poor and subsequently became rich adds too much to the text.

6. Many (see *BHS*) emend the difficult dual to the *lectio facilior* pl. *derākîm* "ways" or *derākāyw* "his ways." But the repetition of the dual with the root *'qš* in v. 18 supports the MT.

7. Q underscores the unity of the phrase *bnšk wtrbyt* by omitting *beth,* unlike K *bnšk wbtrbyt.*

gathers it for one who is gracious to the poor.
9 *As for one who turns his ear aside from hearing instruction —*
even his prayer is detestable.
10 *As for one who misleads the upright into an evil way —*
he will fall into his own pit;[8]
but the blameless will inherit good things.
11 *A rich person is*[9] *wise in his own eyes,*
but a discerning poor person searches him out.
12 *When the righteous triumph,*[10] *the splendor is great,*
but when the wicked rise up, mortals must be searched out.[11]
13 *The one who conceals his transgressions will not succeed,*
but the one who confesses and abandons them[12] *will obtain mercy.*
14 *Blessed is the person who trembles [before the LORD] continually;*
but the one who hardens his heart will fall in calamity.[13]
15 *A roaring lion and a ravenous, charging bear*
is a wicked ruler over a poor people.
16 *A leader who is lacking in understanding multiplies*[14] *extortion;*

8. Some (see *BHS*) plausibly emend the text by dropping 29:10b, supposing that Bb is half a proverb. The LXX has another full proverb at this point, utilizing "good" twice, creating a different antithesis: "The lawless shall pass by what is good *(agatha)* and shall not enter into it *(auta)*." The Syr. and Vulg. support the MT's long but cogent antithesis.

9. So also essentially the NAB, NASB, NJPS, NRSV, and NLT. For the NIV (cf. the REV) "may be" one expects some form of *yihyeh.*

10. A. R. Millard ("*ʿlṣ* 'to exult,'" *JTS* 26 [1975] 87-89) rebuts the existence of an alleged root *ʿlṣ* meaning "to be strong, to prevail" in Prov. 28:12 (see the versions).

11. Though the *Pual* of *ḥpś* is unique, the implication is made explicit in 28:28. *HALOT* (1:341, s.v. *ḥpś*) unnecessarily emends to *Hithpael* "hide themselves." Driver ("Problems in the Hebrew Text," pp. 192-93) unnecessarily proposes an Arabic root meaning "trample upon." The LXX reads *haliskontai* "they are caught" (< *yittāpēś*), reads *bqwm* as *mqwm* "place" and interprets *ʿls* to mean "help." Meinhold (*Sprüche,* 2:472) defends the MT: "Since in the next framing proverb (v. 28) the same subject matter of hiding oneself is dealt with, and, according to 29:2b, the people moan under the rulership of an evildoer, the content intended here is certainly to be perceived by the verb form used. The person does not show up publicly out of his own initiative. The phenotype *(Erscheinungsbild)* of society under a dictator confirms the bitter truth of this half verse."

12. Assuming *pšʿ* is gapped.

13. Or "in [his] evil."

14. Emending *wᵉrab* to *yārēb* (unattested *Hiphil* of *rbb*) or to *yarbeh (Hiphil* of *rbh)* assumes the common scribal confusion of *waw* and *yodh.* The MT, "a leader lacking in competence and great in extortions," leaves 28:16a — assuming with the NRSV (cf. NIV) that it is a nominative absolute — dangling, strangely lacking in 28:16b the expected comment that should predicate something about the nominative absolute. Delitzsch (*Proverbs,* pp. 418-19) proposes reading 28:16a as a vocative, "O prince, devoid," but the expected "you" is missing (cf. 19:27; 20:16; 28:17), and he cites no parallel of direct address to a

those who hate[15] ill-gotten gain prolong days.
17 *A mortal oppressed[16] by shedding the blood of life*
will flee[17] to the pit. Let no one[18] restrain him.
18 *The one who walks as a blameless person will be helped,*
but the double-dealing crook will fall into a pit.[19]
19 *The one who works his land is filled with food,*
but the one who pursues worthless ventures is filled with poverty.[20]
20 *A conscientious person abounds[21] in blessings,[22]*
but one who hastens to get rich will not escape punishment.
21 *To show partiality is not good;*
even for a portion of food a man may commit a crime.
22 *The miser[23] is hasty for wealth,*
but he does not know that poverty will come to him.
23 *The one who reprimands a mortal about his conduct[24] finds favor,*

---

ruler in a proverb. The NRSV (cf. NIV) reads 28:1, 16a as a nominal clause, "A ruler who lacks understanding is a cruel oppressor," but this gloss ignores the *waw.* The LXX reads, "A king in need of revenue is a great oppressor," having read *tᵉbûnôt* as *tᵉbûʾōt.*

15. Q reads the sing.; the more difficult K reads the pl., individualizing the subject to each one.

16. Driver ("Problems in the Hebrew Text," p. 192) emends *ʿāšuq* to *ʿōšēq,* investing it with the Aramaic sense of "busy oneself" or the Arabic, "clung to," both meaning "a man addicted to bloodshed." He has not been followed.

17. Or "as for the mortal . . . , let him flee. . . ."

18. Construing the 3rd pl. as indefinite (*IBHS,* p. 7, P. 4.5a[3]).

19. Reading the Syr. with *HALOT* (1:30, s.v. *ʾeḥād*), BDB, NRSV, et al. as *šāḥat,* even though *ʾaleph* and *shin* are not normally confounded. The MT reads without cogency, "in one." The LXX omits the word. BDB (p. 25, s.v. *ʾeḥād*) originally invested *ʾeḥāt* uniquely with the meaning "at once" (cf. "suddenly," NIV), appealing to Judg. 16:28, but the NIV rejects that meaning in Judg. 16:28. BDB also invests *ʾeḥāt* with the meaning "once for all" (cf. Vulg. *semel*) in Ps. 89:35[36], but there it is lacking the preposition. *HALOT* adds Job 33:14, but there the NIV invests *ʾeḥāt* with the normal meaning, "one." Van Leeuwen (*Proverbs,* p. 239) reads "by one [of his double-dealing ways]," but justice demands that both the injustice and the cover-up be punished.

20. Assuming *rîš* is a by-form of *rēš (HALOT,* 3:1,229, s.v. *rēš).*

21. *Rab* is also a sustantive that designates a "chief"/"commander" in five areas: (a) vocational (e.g., supervisor, foreman), (b) cultic (e.g., chief priest), (c) judicial (e.g., chief magistrate), (d) military (e.g., officer), (e) governmental (e.g., royal officials). However, in all but the cultic *rab* refers only to non-Israelite leaders, ruling out that meaning here. In contrast to abstracts such as *ḥesed* "lovingkindness" (Num. 14:18), *kōaḥ* "strength," and *mᵉʾērôt* "curses" (Prov. 28:27), it means "abounding in."

22. Construing the gen. as a gen. of measure (see *IBHS,* p. 152, P. 9.5.3d, #42).

23. Lit. "a person, an evil eye."

24. The MT reads *ʾaḥᵃray* "after me," but the sage otherwise never introduces himself

not[25] *the deceptive flatterer.*[26]

24 *The one who robs his father and his mother while saying,*[27]
"There is no crime" —
he is a companion to a person who destroys.

25 *The unrestrained appetite stirs up strife,*
but the one who trusts in the LORD will be fattened.

26 *The one who trusts in his own heart — he is a fool;*
but the one who walks in wisdom — he will be delivered.

27 *As for the one who gives to the poor, there is no lack;*
but the one who shuts his eyes abounds in curses.

28 *When the wicked rise up, mortals hide themselves;*[28]
but when they perish, the righteous thrive.

29:1 *As for a person often*[29] *reproved*[30] *[and]*[31] *who hardens his neck,*

---

into his proverb. The LXX reads *hodous* "way" (< *'orḥô*). The scribes confound *waw* and *yodh.* The Targ. curiously reads "in his presence," and the Syr. omits the word. Delitzsch (*Proverbs,* p. 422), cited favorably by BDB (p. 30, s.v. *'aḥ^a ray*), explains it as a noun terminating in *-ay* and meaning "backward," but the form would be unique. G. R. Driver ("Problems in 'Proverbs,'" *ZAW* 50 [1932] 147), cited somewhat favorably by *HALOT* (1:36, s.v. *'aḥ^a ray*), related it to Akk. *'ḫur(r)ū*) "a lowly esteemed person," but Whybray (*Proverbs,* p. 396) deems the proposal implausible. *HALOT,* citing Middle Hebrew, prefers the meaning "legally responsible," but that qualification of *'ādām* is no more called for than "common man." Jerome, followed by the NIV, NRSV, et al., reads *postea* (< *'aḥ^a rît*), but probably refers to God's as well as to mortals' favor, and it is doubtful that wise behavior finds God's favor only in the end. The best solution is to follow the LXX, interpreting *'ādām 'orḥô* as a double accusative involving both the person acted on and the object acted on (*IBHS,* p. 176, P. 10.2.3d).

25. Interpreting *min* as a comparative of exclusion, not a positive comparative (*IBHS,* pp. 265-66, P. 14.4d, e; cf. *HALOT,* 2:598, s.v. *ḥālaq*).

26. Only two words also occur in the B versets of Job 33:1; Ps. 78:3.

27. *W^e* is not a conjunctive joining together two different people because both are antecedents of *hû'* ("he") in verset B.

28. Driver ("Problems in the Hebrew Text," p. 193) suggests that *śtr* is related to *str,* meaning "to demolish" in Akkadian and "cut, abuse, offend" in Aramaic. He has not been followed (cf. Gemser, *Sprüche,* p. 100).

29. "Often" glosses the countable pl. (cf. 6:23). The pl. is not abstract because in this book the abstract fem. noun is sing. (see 1:15, 30; 5:12; 12:1; 13:18; 15:5, 10, 31, 32; 27:5; 29:15).

30. Lit. "a person of reprimands." Although one might expect *'îš tôkāḥôt* to be an attributive gen. (i.e., "reprimander"/"censurer") as elsewhere in this book (see 16:29; 18:24; 21:17; 26:21), semantic pertinence demands that the gen. be understood as an abstract, passive gen. (see *IBHS,* p. 144, P. 5.1e). The Targ. reads: "A man who does not accept chastisement."

31. The Targ. and Syr. also add "and." Plöger (*Sprüche,* p. 340-41) glosses the ptcp. as a predicate: "He who has heard rebukes becomes obstinate," citing 28:14b, but his interpretation has versets Ab and B both presenting consequences of being reproved without a conjunction linking them.

in an instant he will be broken,[32] *and without a remedy.*
2 *When the righteous thrive,*[33] *the people rejoice;*
but when a wicked person[34] *rules, people*[35] *groan.*
3 *A person who loves wisdom makes his father glad,*
but one who associates with prostitutes squanders[36] *[his]*[37] *wealth.*
4 *A king through justice establishes a land;*[38]
but whoever exacts "contributions" or gives them[39] *tears it*[40] *down.*
5 *A man who flatters*[41] *his neighbor*
is one who spreads a net for his feet.
6 *In the transgression*[42] *of an evil person is a snare,*[43]

32. Perhaps a divine passive (cf. *IBHS,* p. 384, P. 23.2.23); the immediate instrument is unspecified.

33. The LXX reads *enkōmiazomenōn* "are praised" (< Heb. *birkôt;* see 10:7; LXX). It is tempting with many (cf. *BHS;* cf. KJV, REB, NRSV) to emend *birbôt* to *birdôt* "when . . . in authority/power." *Rdh* forms a better parallelism with *mšl* than *rbh/rbb,* and scribes commonly confounded *beth* and *daleth.* However, *rbh* occurs in the other three closely related internal framing proverbs (28:12, 28; 29:16).

34. The LXX reads pl.

35. *ʿām* occurs first with, and then without, the article of class because Hebrew parallelism likes elegant variation. The same reason may explain the variation between "righteous" (pl.) and "wicked" (sing.).

36. Lit. "makes perish."

37. The pronominal suffix of v. 3a is probably gapped (see M. Dahood, *Psalms 101–150* [AB 17A; Garden City, N.Y.: Doubleday, 1970], pp. 430-31).

38. Lit. "causes a land to stand/endure."

39. "Contributions" may be either a gen. of the mediated object or an abstract passive gen. (*IBHS,* p. 146, P. 9.5.2e; p. 144, P. 9.5.1e; cf. *ʾîš tôkāḥôt,* 29:1). Probably the ambiguity is intentional. The giver and taker of bribes are inseparable; together they corrupt justice. Since *tᵉrûmâ* is otherwise a cultic term in the Bible, D. W. Thomas ("Notes on Some Passages in the Book of Proverbs," *JTS* 37 [1937] 403) derives the noun from the Arabic root *râma* "to desire eagerly" > "one who is covetous." The LXX *anēr paranomos* "transgressor," the Vulg., *vir avarus* "a greedy man," and the Targ., "wicked man," either reflect guesses or the reading *tarmît* "deceitful" or *tarmôt* (cf. K/Q Jer. 14:14).

40. The 3rd fem. suffix has *ʾāreṣ* as its antecedent.

41. Lit. "deceitfully smooths [his words/tongue] against."

42. S. Pinsker (*Einleitung in das Babyl. u. Hebr. Punktationssystem* [1863], p. 156), followed by *BHS, HALOT* (3:979, s.v. *pešaʿ*), et al., but not by Plöger (*Sprüche,* pp. 343-44), Meinhold (*Sprüche,* p. 480), et al., emend the common noun *pešaʿ* ("transgression") to *peśaʿ* ("step"; 1 Sam. 20:3). The MT has the support of 12:13, which also predicates "in transgression" with "a snare."

43. The Aramaic versions, followed by Driver ("Problems in the Hebrew Text," p. 193), read *mûqāš* "is ensnared."

but the righteous person shouts for joy[44] *and is glad.*
7 *A righteous person is one who knows court decisions*[45] *for the poor,*
but a wicked person does not understand knowing.[46]
8 *Mockers cause a city to pour forth anger,*[47]
but wise people turn back anger.
9 *If a wise person confronts*[48] *the fool in court,*
[the fool] rages and scoffs, and there is no calm.[49]
10 *Bloodthirsty*[50] *people hate the person of integrity;*
and as for the upright,[51] *they seek to kill each*[52] *of them.*[53]
11 *A fool gives full vent to his rage,*
but the wise finally stills it.[54]

44. Pinkser *(Einleitung), BHS,* BDB (p. 943, s.v. *rānan*), et al., but not Meinhold (*Sprüche,* p. 480), *HALOT* (3:1,248, s.v. *rnn*), et al., read *yārûṣ* ("runs"; cf. 4:12; 18:10), not *yārûn* ("give a shout [of joy]") found in the vast majority of the MT mss. and the ancient versions. In favor of the emendation, note that Proverbs seldom duplicates an expression in the same verset, a verb of movement gives a better parallel to "snare," and the form *yārûn* is unattested; it should be *yārôn.* However, duplication does occurs (cf. 27:20); the hendiadys clarifies the meaning of ambiguous *rnn;* parallelism in this section is often imprecise; and the form is not impossible (see GKC P. 67q). Driver ("Problems in the Hebrew Text," pp. 193-94), but not followed by commentators, reads *yādôn* "on the authority of two Hebr. mss. cited by De Rossi," but not by *BHS,* and explains its meaning from Arab. *dâna* (imperfect *yadānu,* "continued").

45. Collective sing., as indicated by the pl. gen. (*IBHS,* pp. 113-14, P. 7.2b).

46. Alleging that the MT is "suspicious," Toy (*Proverbs)* emends *yādîn ʿᵒnî* ("doth not plead for the needy"). D. Winton Thomas ("Notes on Some Passages in the Book of Proverbs," pp. 401-2), followed by *HALOT* (1:229, s.v. II *daʿat*) and Gemser (*Sprüche,* p. 114), who conjectures *dʿtw,* derives *dʿt* from an Arabic root meaning "to seek, desire, demand," and invests it with a uniquely forensic sense, "lawsuit." But they cite no data.

47. "Anger" is gapped in this three-place *Hiphil.*

48. "The tolerative *Niphal* involves the element of efficacy" (*IBHS,* p. 389, P. 23.4g).

49. The Targ. and Syr. pointed the form as *niḥat* (*Niphal* of *ḥtt* "he is [not] broken").

50. The pl. of result (*IBHS,* p. 120, P. 7.4.1b).

51. Confused by the nominative absolute construction and the individualizing sing., *BHS* arbitrarily emends *yšrym* to *rᵉšāʿîm* ("wicked"); Gemser (*Sprüche,* p. 101) emends *bqš* to *bqr* "to attend to"; and G. R. Driver ("Problems in the Hebrew Text," p. 194) derives *bqš* from Akk. *baqāšu* "they magnify/esteem." The NIV (cf. NRSV) legitimately glosses the Hebrew construction by transforming the nominative absolute into the object.

52. The sing. individualizes "the upright people" (GKC, P. 145, 5; see Prov. 28:1, 16)

53. The antecedent of "his" is the upright, not "a person of integrity," because the nominative absolute construction frequently occurs with a resumptive pronoun.

54. The LXX reads *tamieuetai* ("has self-control"). *BHS, HALOT* (4:1,291, s.v. II *šbḥ*), et al. emend *yᵉšabbᵉḥennâ* to *yaḥśᵉkennâ* ("restrains it/holds it back") "because *still* does not accord with the adverb *back*" (Toy, *Proverbs,* p. 512). But Delitzsch (*Proverbs,*

12 *As for a ruler who pays attention to deceptive words,*
all his attendants become wicked.
13 *Poor and oppressor*[55] *meet together;*
the LORD *is the one who gives light to the eyes of both.*
14 *As for a king who judges the poor through truth,*
his throne is established forever.
15 *A rod and reproof give wisdom,*
but an undisciplined youth brings his mother[56] *shame.*
16 *When the wicked thrive, transgression abounds;*[57]
but the righteous will gaze on[58] *their downfall.*
17 *Discipline your son so that*[59] *he will give you rest,*
and he will give delight to you.
18 *Without a revelation*[60] *the people fall into anarchy,*
but as for the one who carefully obeys the teaching, blessed is he![61]
19 *A slave is not disciplined by words;*
though he understands, he does not respond.
20 *Do you see a person who is hasty with his words?*
[There is] more hope for a fool than for him.
21 *[If] one pampers his slave from youth,*

---

p. 430), McKane (*Proverbs,* p. 635), et al. think that the MT can mean "restrain his temper" without emendation.

55. The LXX questionably paraphrases the compound to a more restricted application, "creditor and debtor." The Targ. renders *tᵉkākîm* "intermediary (?)," presumably from mistaking it for *twk* "midst of" (see J. F. Healey, *The Targum of Proverbs* [The Aramaic Bible 15; Collegeville, Minn.: Glazier, 1991], p. 59, n. 5). If so, it read *tᵉwākîm.*

56. The LXX replaces the synecdoche by its intended meaning, *goneis* "parents."

57. The same verb is also rendered "thrives."

58. The LXX reads *kataphoboi ginontai* (< *yîrā'û* from *yārē'* "to fear").

59. *Wᵉ* with the prefix conjugation after an impv. indicates purpose, "so that" (*IBHS,* p. 650, P. 39.2.2.a).

60. The LXX reads *ou mē hyparxȩ̄ exēgētēs* "There shall be no interpreter/exegete." The Targ. (and Syr.) read the first words in an even more different manner, "when the wicked are many."

61. G. R. Driver ("Misreadings in the Old Testament," *WO* 1 [1948] 235) revocalizes *'šrhw* to read *'iššᵉrāhû* "he keeps them (sc. the people straight)," because he believes that *'šrhw* "happy is he" is ungrammatical in form. J. G. Janzen ("The Root *pr,*" *VT* 39 [1989] 396, n. 2) critically appraises the emendation: "The grammatical objection, based on the form *'ašrāyw* in Prov. xiv 21 and xvi 20, is groundless. MT twice displays the form *gibbôrayw* (Jer. xxvi 21; 2 Chron. xxxii 3), but once the form *gibbōrêhû* (Nah. ii 4) — without the *yodh* as *mater lectionis,* just as in *'ašrēhû.* . . . One may note also that Prov. xix 21, xvi 20 and xxix 18 agree in the syntax of their concluding lines: ptcp. + object of ptcp. + suffixed form of *'ašrê.*"

afterward[62] *he will be insolent.*[63]

22 *A hothead stirs up strife;*
a wrathful person[64] *is one who abounds in transgressions.*
23 *The pride of a mortal will bring him low,*
but the lowly in spirit will lay hold of honor.[65]
24 *Whoever is an accomplice with a thief hates his life;*
he hears the divine curse, but will not testify.
25 *Panic induced by a mortal*[66] *lays*[67] *a snare,*

62. Lit. "and [in] the end of him." The *waw* is conjunctive-sequential (*IBHS,* p. 69, P. 39.2.1c, d). J. Reider ("Etymological Studies in Biblical Hebrew," *VT* 4 [1954] 285) thinks that it is due to dittography from *'bdw.*

63. The meaning of *mānôn* is uncertain. The LXX, Targ., and Syr. are not helpful because they interpret the proverb as directed against self-indulgence, not slaves. They read: "He who pampers himself from youth will become a servant, and in the end will grieve over himself [LXX]/will be driven out [Targ.]/will groan [Syr.]." Instead of reading *'bdw* they read *[y]'bd.* A. J. Baumgartner (*Étude critique sur l'état du texte du Livre des Proverbes d'après les principales traductions anciennes* [Leipzig: Imprimerie Orientale W. Drugulin, 1890], p. 238) also holds that they probably read *mnwn* as a contracted form of *m^{e}'unnān, Pual* ptcp. of *'nn,* which in Aramaic means "to sigh" and in Heb. *Hithpolel* "to complain" (Num. 11:1; Lam. 3:39). Frankenberg (cited by Whybray, *Proverbs,* p. 404) arrived at a similar meaning by reading *yāgôn* (cf. "grief," NIV), necessitating reading *mpnq* as passive. McKane (*Proverbs,* p. 634) says rightly of the LXX: "It can only be regarded as an incorrect paraphrase." "Come to a bad end" (NJPS, NRSV) and "grief" (NIV) are probably guesses based on these questionable readings. Meinhold (*Sprüche,* p. 488) and Van Leeuwen (*Proverbs,* p. 245) opt to emend the text to *mādôn,* but Toy (*Proverbs,* p. 516), though he thinks the text is corrupt, rejected this emendation. Plöger defended it by noting that this forms a catchword with v. 22, but one expects *lamed* "have strife" and, from a text-critical point of view, the uncommon confusion of *nun* and *dalet* becomes even more inexplicable in light of the following *mādôn.*

64. A. Hurvitz ("Studies in the Language of the Book of Proverbs — Concerning the Use of the Construct Structure *ba'al-x,*" *Tar* 55 [1985/86] 1-17) notes two features about the construction *ba'al-x.* (1) The construct form of *ba'al* is concentrated in Proverbs and Exodus. (2) Although such constructions became common in the postbiblical period, the biblical authors tend to use other terms (e.g., *'îš*), probably because of their discomfort with the pagan associations of *ba'al.*

65. The LXX paraphrases by adding *kyrios* as subject: "The LORD upholds the humble-minded with glory."

66. Construing the gen. after *ḥerdâ* as a gen. of agency, the same as in 1 Sam. 15:16 (*IBHS,* p. 143, P. 9.5.1b). It is doubtful that the noun can take an objective gen. (*IBHS,* p. 146, P. 9.5.2b). It could also be a possessive gen. (i.e., a person's own panic, not fright before someone else; cf. *IBHS,* p. 145, P. 9.5.1g). In truth there is little difference in meaning. In both cases someone else, either explicitly or implicitly, occasioned the person's fright. L. Kopf ("Arabische Etymologien und Parallelen zum Bibelwörterbuch," *VT* [1959] 257) contends that the phrase means "to seek a refuge in man." He looks to Arabic and other Hebrew constructions involving *ḥrdt* for this meaning. According to him, verset

but the one who trusts in the LORD will be protected.
26 *Many are they who seek the face of a ruler,*
but justice for an individual[68] *comes*[69] *from the LORD.*
27 *An unjust person is an abomination to the righteous,*
but the upright in his way[70] *is an abomination to the wicked.*

The poem of 27:23-27 marks the end of Section C and forms the transition to Collection D. Skehan noted that Section D is drawn to a conclusion with a double *taw:* "The *tô'ᵃbat,* thus a word beginning and ending with *taw,* at the head of each hemistich in 29:27, the final verse, is undoubtedly a signature that this verse is indeed the end of the collection."[71] Malchow broke new ground by analyzing the structure of D. The men of Hezekiah (25:1) organized it by strategically placing proverbs employing *ṣaddîq* ("righteous") and *rāšā'* ("wicked"). The section begins (28:1) and ends (29:27) with antithetical couplets using these words. Within the collection the four proverbs employing these terms (28:12, 28; 29:2, 16) have an integral connection with each other and form a symmetrical pattern. The first and third couplets have similar A versets:

> When the righteous exult, the splendor is great (28:12a).
> When the righteous thrive, the people rejoice (29:2a).

The B verset of the first of these internal proverbs matches the A verset of the second:

B offers no precise parallel like Ps. 118:8-9. In fact, the parallels in Proverbs are often imprecise. Moreover, McKane (*Proverbs,* p. 639) notes that Kopf misses the point that the antithesis is between servility or cowardly fear and trust in Yahweh.

67. Lit. "gives." Although the subject *ḥerdâ* is fem. and the predicate is masc., it is better to take it as the subject, rather than masc. *môqēš* (i.e., "a snare gives fright to a mortal"). This is so because (1) the masc. subject offers a convoluted antithesis to verset B, (2) the so-called masc. is in fact an unmarked form and has a fem. subject elsewhere in this book (see 2:10; 14:6; 26:23), and (3) the meaning of the metaphor "snare" is unclear.

68. Gen. of a mediated object (*IBHS* p. 146-47, P. 9.5.1d). Delitzsch (*Proverbs,* p. 436) thinks that it is a subjective gen. (i.e., "judgment from a person") on the basis of 16:33. This is possible, but the locution for a ruler seems unnatural. In any case, as Delitzsch admits, the meaning remains the same: "It is not the ruler who finally decides the fate and determines the worth of a man, as they appear to think who with eye-service court his favour and fawn upon him."

69. A verb of motion is implied by the preposition *min* (*IBHS,* p. 224, P. 11.4.3c).

70. Epexegetical gen. (*IBHS,* pp. 151-52, P. 9.5.3c).

71. P. W. Skehan, *Studies in Israelite Wisdom* (The Catholic Biblical Quarterly — Monograph Series 1; Washington, D.C.: The Catholic Biblical Association of America, 1971), p. 23.

When the wicked rise up, mortals must be searched out (28:12b).
When the wicked rise, mortals hide themselves (28:28a).

Also, versets B of the second and fourth couplets treat the destruction of the wicked.

When they [the wicked] perish, the righteous thrive (28:28b).
The righteous will gaze on their [the wicked's] downfall (29:16b).

Finally, the B verset of the third couplet is comparable to the A verset of the fourth:

When a wicked person rules, people groan (29:2b).
When the wicked thrive, transgressions abound (29:16a).

"Thus, every one of the eight lines in these four couplets is related to at least one other line outside its own verse, and two lines correlate to two others. The four proverbs as a unity point out the responsibility of a sovereign to reign righteously."[72]

Meinhold independently noted these framing proverbs, but questionably omitted 29:2 from consideration "because of its strong inclusion into the connection of the surrounding verses." He also noted that in the first and last of them "righteous" is plural, whereas "wicked" is singular (28:1; 29:27), but elsewhere, apart from 29:2, the plural form is used for both (28:12; 29:16). Both Malchow and Meinhold omit from consideration 29:7, where both words are singular. Sow-Phen Liew observed that these framing proverbs are stitched together by a chiastic pattern: "wicked/righteous" (28:1), "righteous/wicked" (28:12), "wicked/righteous" (28:28), "righteous/wicked" (29:2), "wicked/righteous" (29:16), "righteous/wicked" (19:27).[73] Moreover, the four internal framing proverbs begin with *b*^{e} plus infinitive construct (= "when"). In addition, each unit within these framing proverbs has its own distinct structure. The framing proverbs 28:28 and 29:2 suggest that Prov. 29:1 is the center verse of the section. If so, it underscores the theme of destruction for refusing to submit to divine instruction. In sum, the structure of D can be analyzed thus:

Introduction: framing proverb (contrasting lifestyles) (28:1)
    First unit (28:2-11)
Janus: framing proverb (28:12)
    Second unit (28:13-27)

72. B. V. Malchow, "A Manual for Future Monarchs," *CBQ* 47 (1985) 239.

73. Sow-Phen Liew, "Social and Literary Context of Proverbs 28–29" (Ph.D. thesis, Westminster Theological Seminary, 1991), pp. 105ff.

Janus: framing proverb (28:28)
 Center proverb (29:1)
Janus: framing proverb (29:2)
 Third unit (29:3-15)
Janus: framing proverb (29:16)
 Fourth unit (29:17-26)
Conclusion: framing proverb (contrasts between adversions).[74]

With regard to the subject matter of Section D, Meinhold observed that "all four sections [or units] shed light, each from a particular primary emphasis, on the structure of connections between a relationship with God, rearing and rulership." He provides these headings to the four units:

I. The relationship to Torah [instruction] as a measure for ruling, in particular that of the rich over the poor (28:2-11).
II. The relationship with God as a measure for ruling and striving for gain (28:13-27).
III. Rearing and ruling that have proved worthwhile in dealing with the poor and humble (29:1-15).
IV. Rearing and relationship with God (29:17-26).

Meinhold notes, "The alternation between righteous and wicked makes it clear from the beginning, and again and again, that submitting [*Bewährung*] or refusal [*Versagen*] in all three levels — in rearing, in the relationship with God, and in rulership — have consequences for the respective person and for the people of the community."[75] The center line supports his conclusion.

Malchow, Meinhold, et al. argue that the section was originally a manual for future rulers, but R. E. Murphy[76]and J. L. Crenshaw[77] have rightly pointed out the fallacy of proceeding directly from the wisdom saying to its life setting. S. Weeks says, "So far as I am aware, nobody has ever ventured to suggest that an obvious interest in sluggards and fools is key evidence for the *Sitz im Leben* of Proverbs." He also notes that king sayings are found in the postexilic books (e.g., Sir. 7:4-5; 10:3, 10; 38:2; 51:6; Wis. 6:24; 11:10; Tob. 12:7).[78] Nevertheless, though this setting cannot be proved, the royal coloring is strong enough in this collection — there are explicit references to

74. Adapted from D. Finkbeiner, "An Analysis of Proverbs 28–29" (paper submitted to Bruce Waltke for Proverbs 813, Westminster Theological Seminary, 1986).

75. Meinhold, *Sprüche,* p. 464.

76. R. Murphy, "Form Criticism and Wisdom Literature," *CBQ* 31 (1969) 481.

77. J. L. Crenshaw, "Wisdom," in *Old Testament Form Criticism,* ed. J. H. Hayes (San Antonio, Tex.: Trinity University, 1974), p. 236.

78. S. Weeks, *Early Israelite Wisdom* (Oxford: Clarendon, 1994), pp. 49, 54.

the ruler (28:2, 15, 16; 29:2, 4, 12, 14, 16, 26) and inferential references to rulership (28:3, 5, 12, 21, 28; 29:7, 14, 16, 18) — to make it probable that its original setting was the Solomonic court. It has been democratized in Proverbs because the behavior of a king is of interest to everybody and the specific content of a proverb serves as an exemplar for many instantiations. Van Leeuwen rightly applies the section "as a penetrating gaze at the interaction of government, money, justice, and poverty."[79] Although these proverbs hope to catch the ruler's ear, he is not their sole audience. Even if the section was originally composed in and for the court, as it now sits in the book of Proverbs it has been democratized for many applications.

1. A Relationship to *tôrâ* as a Measure for Ruling and Gaining Wealth (28:1-11)

a. Introductory Framing Proverb (28:1)

The chiastically arranged antithetical parallels contrast the psychological insecurity of the wicked with the psychological confidence of the righteous. The topics are named in the inner core, and their psychologies in the outer frame. The paranoia of the group hostile to God and the community is implicitly likened to that of warriors or prey fleeing when no enemy or predator is pursuing (see Lev. 26:17, 36; cf. Gen. 3:9-10; Job 15:21). They are presently out of touch with reality. The *wicked* [see I: 109] *flee* [i.e., "remove oneself quickly from a region of danger"],[80] *though* (see n. 2) *no one* [see 21:30] *is pursuing* (see 21:21). By contrast, the inward security of each person who loves God and serves the community is explicitly likened to that of a young lion, the king of beasts (19:12; 30:30), which mauls its attackers and has no reason to fear. *But the righteous* (see I: 97), who are are represented as individuals (i.e., "each one"), not as a class, *are confident* [or secure; see 3:5; 28:25] *like a lion* (see 19:12). Paradoxically, because the wicked do not fear God, they live in fear of people, but because the righteous fear God (1:7), they do not fear people. These different psychologies are due to their consciences, backed up by the threats and promises of God's word. Hostile to God in heaven and to mortals on earth, the consciences of the wicked and the Scriptures condemn them. By contrast, the loyalty of the righteous to God and community, fortified by Scripture, confirms them and enables them to face all kinds of distress in faith. Their loyalty to God assumes their trust in him (3:5; 28:25; 29:25). Both psychologies are grounded in objective reality. God guarantees the safety of the righteous and dooms the wicked to punishment and disaster.

79. Van Leeuwen, *Proverbs,* pp. 245-46.
80. S. Schwertner, *TLOT,* 2:725, s.v. *nûs.*

The rest of the unit is held together by the catchwords "discern" (*mēbîn/bîn;* vv. 2, 5[2x], 7, 11) and "instruction" (*tôrâ;* 4[2x], 7, 9). The former also forms an *inclusio* around the unit. Its theme centers on submitting to the inspired "instruction" in administering justice with particular reference to wealth. The application of justice to wealth brings prosperity to all; its abuse brings disaster. Its mostly antithetical parallels pit the oppressors of the poor (v. 3) against those who contend against the exploiters of the poor (v. 4) and who are kind to the needy (v. 8). Co-references for the oppressors are "the wicked" (v. 4), "evil men" (v. 5), the deceitful "rich" (v. 6, 11), "those who exact interest from the poor" (v. 8), "those who mislead the upright" (v. 9), and those who "abandon instruction" (v. 4, 9). Co-references for their opponents are "the understanding/discerning" (vv. 2, 5, 7, 11), "who walk in [their] integrity" (v. 6), "who keep instruction" (vv. 4, 7), and "who seek the LORD" (v. 5). Although at present the arrogant rich prevail, leaving even strong men without food (v. 3), God's moral order will prevail and the tables will be turned (v. 10). At that time the wicked will find no salvation (v. 9). By contrast, the discerning will prevail and endure (v. 2) and will inherit every good gift (v. 10).

The unit can be analyzed into two equal subunits, vv. 2-6 and 7-11. The first ends with a "better than" saying, which sometimes occurs at the seams of literary units, and the second typically begins with an instructional proverb, motivating the son to embrace the teaching (v. 7). In addition to the factors binding the whole unit together, its two subunits are bound together by the alternating, sequential pattern of keywords: A/A′ (cf. "discerning" or *mēbîn* [vv. 2b, 7a]), B/B′ (cf. "poor" or *dal* [vv. 3a, 8b]), C/C′ (cf. "instruction" or *tôrâ* [cf. vv. 4, 9]), D/D′ (cf. "evil" or *rāʿ* [vv. 5a, 10a]), and E/E′ (cf. "rich" or *ʿāšîr* [cf. vv. 6b, 11a]). Finkbeiner analyzed the unit essentially as follows:

- A Importance of being a discerning person *(mēbîn)* in government (v. 2)
  - B Lack of discernment: oppression of the poor *(dal)* (v. 3)
    - C Basis of discernment: *tôrâ* and social relationships (v. 4)
      - D Basis of discernment: evil *(rāʿ)* people versus seekers of the LORD (v. 5)
        - E Pervasiveness of discernment: poor discerning *(dal mēbîn)* better than rich (*ʿāšîr,* v. 6)
- A′ Importance of discerning person *(mēbîn)* /keeping *tôrâ* in home (v. 7)
  - B′ Lack of discernment: oppression of the poor *(dal)* (v. 8)
    - C′ Basis of discernment: *tôrâ* and God (v. 9)
      - D′ Basis of discernment: evil *(rāʿ)* influence of others (v. 10)
        - E′ Pervasiveness of discernment: poor discerning *(dal mēbîn)* smarter than rich (*ʿāšîr,* v. 11).[81]

81. Adapted from Finkbeiner, "An Analysis of Proverbs 28–29."

b. First Subunit: *tôrâ* and Righteous Government (28:2-6)

After the introductory verse, vv. 3-6 are bound together further by the broken sequence of *rš*ʿ: *rš* ("poor," v. 3), *rš*ʿ ("wicked," v. 4), *r*ʿ ("evil," v. 5), *rš* ("poor," v. 6). The addition of *r*ʿ*h* "companion" in v. 7 helps form a seamless transition.

2 *But (waw)* pits the antithetical parallels, *because of*[82] *the transgression* (*peša*ʿ; see 10:12)[83] *of a land* (a metonymy for the inhabitants of a politically governed area; see 2:22) against *because of a discerning person* (*mēbîn;* see 1:2; 8:9; 17:10), *one who knows* (see I: 77; 1:2) knowledge or wisdom (see 1:7). *Peša*ʿ here is probably "concerned with the *totality* of the crimes of . . . the people, and with the totality of their break with Yahweh. So stated, however, totality is a radical theology of judgment."[84] As a result of the land's total break with the LORD, the people need a large bureaucracy to keep an eye on each other and/or none survives (cf. 1 K. 16:8-28; 2 K. 15:8-15). An Arabic curse says, "May God make your sheiks many."[85] The imprecise juxtaposition of a willfully rebellious citizenry and a discerning leader implies that the country lacks a capable leader who distinguishes right from wrong. In Isaiah's day, the officials loved bribes (Isa. 1:23). Likewise the antithesis pits *its officials* (*śāreyhā,* i.e., the king's advisers and officials who rule the land; 8:16) *are many* (see 7:26) against *what is right* (*kēn,* an adjective indicating the affirmative [see 11:19] and "an indication that something is rightly expected, thus conforming to some known or normal standard"; see 15:7)[86] *endures* (*ya*ʾ*a*rîk; cf. 19:11).[87] This imprecise antithetical parallelism implies that the king's officials do not maintain law and order and are removed, unlike the upholder of law and order who maintains his righteous jurisdiction. To continue in office the son must uphold what is known to be right and not tolerate legal offenses either in himself or in his subjects.

3 The inner core of this chiastic comparative proverb implicitly compares a tyrant, who takes away the produce and labor of the poor, with a driving rain, which sweeps away the soil and the crop. Its outer frame juxtaposes a destitute strong man, an oxymoron, with the lack of food. *A*

82. *IBHS,* p. 198, P. 11.2.5e.

83. The gloss, "when a land rebels," expects the inf. *p*e*šōa*ʿ.

84. R. Knierim, *TLOT,* 2:1,037, s.v. *peša*ʿ.

85. Cohen, *Proverbs,* pp. 185-86.

86. J. P. J. Olivier, *NIDOTTE,* 2:664, s.v. *kēn.*

87. The imprecise parallelism and its polyvalence confused the translators and the commentators. The Vulg. limited the endurance to the stability of the land, paraphrasing verset B, "but by righteous men who know justice its stability shall be prolonged." The Targ. limited the stability to the man of understanding, paraphrasing, "but men who understand knowledge will last." The imprecise parallels imply both senses.

destitute [see 13:23] *man* (*geber;* see I: 89) refers to a strong man who is destitute through no fault of his own (see 13:8). *And* (see n. 5) joins the destitute man together with the tyrant. *One who oppresses the poor* (*ʿōšēq dallîm;* see 14:31) represents a situation where the stronger either directly or indirectly takes away the produce and labor of the weak, giving nothing in exchange. Verset B asyndetically compares this chaos in the social order with that within the cosmos. *A rain* [see 26:1] *that washes away* (or "a sweeping rain" [*sōḥēp*])[88] destroys crops, not promotes their growth, the normal function of rain. *And* again joins the topics. *There is no* (*ʾên;* see 28:1 and note the assonance with *kēn* in v. 2) *food* (see 6:26). The imprecise parallelism suggests that the competent man is starving because the tyrant, probably through corrupt courts, has plundered the food he produced in his strength. Ironically, both the rain and the ruler were expected to nurture and promote what is good and strong (cf. Ps. 72:6), but the betrayers brought ruin and squalor instead.

4-5 These verses are linked by the similar structure of a relative participle with the objects "instruction" (v. 4a, b) and "the LORD" (v. 5b) who revealed the instruction. Murphy says, "One must assume that the will of the LORD stands behind the 'law' [i.e., instruction] which is referred to here."[89] Van Leeuwen agrees, "The search for Yahweh in v. 5 reminds the reader that the norms for human existence cannot be separated from God (v. 9)."[90] The proverb pair also contains a rare repetition of the same words in both versets, "instruction" (v. 4) and "discern" (v. 5). Finally, "justice" (v. 5) entails doing battle against the wicked, not extolling them (v. 4). People who praise those who behave antisocially (v. 4a) are evil and do not have the first clue how to restore a community fractured by the oppression of the weak by the strong (v. 5a; see v. 3; cf. 21:7; 29:7). The pair is linked with vv. 3 and 6 by its identification of the oppressed as the "poor" and by the assonance of *rāš* ("destitute," vv. 3, 6), *rāšāʿ* ("wicked," v. 4), *ʾanšê rāʿ* ("evil people," v. 5).

4 This antithetical parallelism juxtaposes the topics of those who abandon the sage's divinely inspired instruction and of the faithful who keep it. It also contrasts their attitudes and actions toward the wicked. *Those who abandon* [see 2:13] *instruction* (*tôrâ;* see 1:8) refers to apostates from wisdom. Apostates think it right and proper to praise (*yᵉhalᵉlû;* see 27:2) *the wicked* (see I: 109). By contrast, the faithful concertedly do battle against the selfish and greedy. *But* [see 10:1] *those who keep* (*šōmᵉre;* see 2:8) *instruc-*

88. *Sāḥap* occurs elsewhere only in Jer. 46:15. Its meaning, "wash away," is based on these two passages and on Akkadian and Arabic cognates.

89. R. Murphy, "Proverbs," in *Wisdom Literature* (Grand Rapids: Eerdmans, 1981), p. 79.

90. Van Leeuwen, *Proverbs,* p. 237.

tion (tôrâ) strive [see 15:18] *against them* (i.e., the wicked, assuming it is a collective). The proverb divides humanity into two spiritual categories; there is no third. The line dividing humanity is not racial, political, or even religious, but spiritual. That line runs through every human heart. One either strives from his very being against the wicked, or one is against God and from his very disposition praises the wicked.

5 This antithetical parallelism juxtaposes the topics of morally repulsive *evil* [see 1:16] *people* (*'anšê;* see I: 89) and of *those who seek* (*m^e^baqšê,* i.e., whose "goal is not to locate but rather to fulfill a wish or to realize a plan [in which case] the verb acquires an emotional nuance, 'to strive after something, be busy, be concerned' ")[91] *the LORD* (see I: 67-68), including both his person and the wisdom/instruction that comes from him (see 2:5). The LORD is the covenantal name of the majestic God of all wisdom, righteousness, and power (1 Cor. 2:14-15; 1 John 2:20). He is found through the revelation of his sublime character and instruction through the inspired sage. The parallels also juxtapose the predicates. The former, whose moral discernment is jaded by their own evil and rebellion against divine authority, *do not discern* [see *lō' yābînû;* see 1:2; 2:5, 9] *what is right* (*mišpāṭ;* see 1:3). Here *mišpāṭ* refers to a sphere, "that which one is due," "an obligation," "that which one should do," and "what is right and correct" (Exod. 26:30; Judg. 13:2; esp. Job 32:9), not being limited to the legal sphere.[92] In the legal sense they do not realize that divine justice will catch up with them. By contrast, the latter *discern everything* (*kōl,* i.e., all within the parameters of the context). The parallelism suggests everything relative to an obligation, such as taking care of the poor, or, in the case of legal matters, understanding the proper time and procedure (Eccl. 8:5) to restore the community by punishing the rich oppressors and delivering the oppressed poor (vv. 3, 6), and that at the proper time the LORD will reward them. Intellectual clarity and moral discernment hinge on a religious attitude toward the LORD (1:7; 2:1-4, 9). The pious find their abilities to distinguish good from evil and right from wrong and to proceed with equity by seeking the LORD through his revelation. He is the very foundation of their lives.

6 The first subunit is brought to closure by a "better . . . than" saying (see 27:5) that also functions as a janus, a conclusion to vv. 2-5 and a lead into vv. 7-11. "Destitute person" repeats v. 3a and continues the assonance of *rš~rš~r'* in vv. 3a, 4a, and 5a, but "rich" (*'āšîr*) forms an *inclusio* with v. 11b, which is reinforced by the synonyms of "poor," *rāš* and *dal* (v. 11). "As an introductory device . . . the task of the ["better . . . than" proverb] is not simply that of marking a change or transition in the discussion, but the more active

91. Gerleman, *TLOT,* 1:252, s.v. *bqš.*

92. G. Liedke, *TLOT,* 3:1,396.

one of actually setting up the values to be explicated in the remainder of the pericope."[93] Here the superiority of moral integrity to material prosperity is introduced. The next section pertains to wealth and poverty. The true introduction to the new unit, however, is v. 7.

This "better . . . than" proverb asserts emphatically that behaving with integrity, although being destitute, benefits the life of oneself and of others more than acting with duplicity, though being rich. *Better a destitute person who walks in his integrity* repeats 19:1. The person of integrity defines his interest in terms of serving the community in contrast to the perverse, who seeks his own interest and acts apart from or against the community. *Than [one who walks in] the crookedness* [lit. "twisted"; see 2:15] *of double-dealing ways* (*d*^{e}*rākayim;* see n. 6). Some older commentators, and more recently Whybray[94] and Van Leeuwen,[95] think that the reference is to halting between two moral choices, but this interpretation of the dual is inappropriate with the verb "twist."[96] Meinhold points out that "the dual occurs again only in v. 18. . . . One might hardly think of limping on both sides (1 K. 18:21 [cf. Sir. 2:12]), for then the right and the false comportment would be mixed up. Here, however, something that is false in more ways than one is dealt with. The perversion of both ways seems to mean that the rich person acted with intent to defraud and thus commits . . . the first injustice, but then still made his doing appear as impeccable and thus commits a second injustice."[97] *And* combines the double dealer and the rich man into a hendiadys, defining the double dealer more precisely as a rich person. *He is rich* (see 10:15). The double-dealing rich person first defrauds the poor and the humble and then covers over his wrongdoing by making himself appear righteous (cf. 3, 5, 8-9, 11). Actually the poor of v. 6a is the victim of the hypocritical malevolent rich person. This proverb, like 19:11, does not justify its assertion. The reasons can be inferred from others in the unit. The righteous trust in the LORD, confident that he will make the right prevail and endure. When God unleashes his wrath, the rich person's wealth will prove worthless (10:2-3). These "better . . . than" sayings (see 12:9; 15:16-17; 16:8, 19; 17:1; 19:1; 28:6, not 27:5, 10), says Farmer, are "concerned with the hidden costs involved in making choices. Some desirable things come with undesirable conditions attached."[98] The issue confronting the son is whether he is willing to count the cost and live by faith.

93. G. Ogden, "The 'Better'-Proverbs, Rhetorical Criticism and Qoheleth," *JBL* 86 (1977) 504.

94. Whybray, *Proverbs,* p. 390.

95. Van Leeuwen, *Proverbs,* p. 238.

96. Toy, *Proverbs,* p. 497.

97. Meinhold, *Sprüche,* p. 469.

98. Farmer, *Proverbs,* p. 72.

c. Second Subunit: tôrâ and Righteous Government (28:7-11)

The second subunit on righteous government (28:7-11) is marked off by (1) an introductory educational proverb (v. 7); (2) the catchword *mēbîn,* linking it to the preceding introduction (see vv. 2, 7); (3) an initial relative participle, glossed "one who," apart from v. 11; (4) initial *mem* in vv. 8-10 and *mēbîn* "discerning" in v. 7a; and (5) an *inclusio* of "rich" in vv. 6 (a janus verse) and 11.

7 The reference to the "understanding person" *(mēbîn)* links the son (v. 7) with the person through whom what is right and just endures in the land. Its antithetical versets pit *a discerning son* (cf. 13:1; 28:2) against *the one who associates with* [see 13:20] *profligates* (*zôlᵉlîm;* see 23:20). The former is defined explicitly in verset A as one who *guards instruction* (synonym of *šōmrê tôrâ* in 28:4), clarifying the instruction as the parent's wisdom.[99] The son who befriends profligates implicitly abandons his father and his instruction. Indeed, Deut. 21:18-21 equates a *zōlēl* with a son who will not obey his father and his mother. By identifying himself with those who squander all that is precious — life, food, and instruction — the foolish person *puts his father* [see 10:1] *to* public *shame* (see 25:8). This is so because his father cannot defend himself against those who denigrate his significance, worth, and ability by pointing to his son. The missing antithetical parallel to "puts his father to shame" can be supplied from 27:11. Both proverbs aim to motivate the son to embrace his parents' rearing out of his solidarity with the family (cf. 10:1). The Deuteronomistic legislation calls for stoning him.

8 The connection of v. 8 to v. 3 by *dal* (see 10:15) yields the insight that one may oppress the poor by charging them interest. Although grammatically this synthetic parallelism consists of a topic (verset A) and its predicate (verset B), conceptually it is antithetical.[100] The ruthless wealthy person, who in his insatiable appetite for money capitalizes on the misfortune of the poor and needy by charging interest, stands over against the one who freely gives the poor his money and foodstuffs, such as seed for starting a crop. *The one who increases* (*marbeh;* see 6:35) *his wealth* (*hônô;* see 1:13) is a straightforward translation, but *by taking interest of any sort from the poor* glosses one Hebrew term, *bᵉnešek.* In the Bible *nešek* occurs ten times and refers to the charge for borrowed money, which practice in biblical times came to about 30 percent of the amount borrowed. In half of these passages (three in the Pentateuch, Exod. 22:25[24]; Lev. 25:36, 37; and two in Ezekiel based on the Pentateuch, Ezek. 18:8, 13), it explicitly refers to interest from the poor. In Ps. 15:5 and Ezek. 22:12 that precise reference is not as clear, but the latter is

99. Note the assonance of */ō/* in *nôṣēr tôrâ,* and *rōʿeh zôlᵉlîm.*

100. The parallelism is assisted by the paronomasia of *hônô* "his wealth" and *ḥônēn* "the gracious one."

in the context of keeping the Mosaic covenant. According to Deut. 23:20[21], where *nešek* occurs twice, an Israelite could charge interest from a foreigner, even as the Gentiles charged interest from their own poor, but not from a fellow Israelite. The parallel, "poor," in Prov. 28:8 and the context (see vv. 3, 6, 11) strongly favors restricting its meaning to charging interest from the needy. Most scholars agree that all ten passages refer to loans made as "acts of charity for the relief of destitution as opposed to loans of a commercial nature for expanding business."[101] "And" combines *tarbît* with *nešek* into a compound phrase glossed "interest *of any sort*." The parallel "gathers it" treats it as a unity (see n. 7). *Of any sort* is an intentionally vague gloss for *tarbît,* whose meaning is uncertain because it always occurs with *nešek.*[102] *Gathers it* [see 13:11] *for the one who is gracious* [cf. 14:21] *to the poor* (*dallîm;* see v. 3) breaks this cycle of misery. The imprecise parallels implicitly juxtapose the loss of profit for the rapacious rich and the gain of it for the gracious. Had the greedy rich succeeded in depriving the poor, he could have kept them in perpetual servitude. The proverb is based on the conviction that in his secret Providence, the compassionate God protects the vulnerable poor and the just God gives back to them the wealth unjustly taken from them (13:22; Ps. 140:12[13]). The mediator in this divine economy is the gracious human being to whom God entrusts wealth.

9 The connection of *tôrâ* with v. 4 and with the language of worship, "praise," and "prayer" suggests that apostates, the topic of both verses, praise the wicked, not God, and that God stands far off from hearing their prayers. Like v. 8, this proverb asserts the doctrine of reciprocity. "If a man, on his part, is deaf to instruction, then God, on His part, is deaf to prayer."[103] *One who turns aside* (*mēsîr;* see 3:7) *his ear* [see 2:2] *from hearing* [see 1:5] *instruction* (*tôrâ;* see vv. 4, 7)[104] binds ethics to true piety (see 3:27-35). As a consequence of his apostasy, even his prayer in his time of need is so repugnant to God that he keeps himself spiritually so far away that he cannot hear it (cf. 1:23-31; 15:8, 29; 1 Sam. 28:5). *Even* (see 18:9) emphasizes the next word, *his prayer,* which, to judge from the parallels in 15:8, 29, implores God

101. Robin Wakely, *NIDOTTE,* 3:186, s.v. *nšk.*

102. S. Loewenstamm ("*Nšk* and *M/trbyt,*" *JBL* 88 [1966] 79) et al. hold that *nešek* refers to borrowed money, and *tarbît* refers to interest charged on foodstuffs and paid in kind. N. Snaith (cited by Wakely, *NIDOTTE,* 3:187, s.v. *nšk*) believes that the *nešek* type of interest was paid regularly, and in the end the original loan was repaid in a single payment, but in the case of the *tarbît* there was no interim payment of interest, but an increased sum was repaid in the end." Similarly, others think: "*Tarbît* could mean the additional charge which is a supplement to a loan, while what is meant by *nešek* is a loan that is reduced by the payment of interest" (*HALOT,* 4:1,787, s.v. *tarbît*).

103. Toy, *Proverbs,* p. 499.

104. Note the assonance of v. 9a: *mēsîr ʾoznô miššᵉmōaʿ tôrâ.*

to be favorable to him in his need. But if even this prayer *is detestable* (see 3:32), how much more his apostate behavior. Although God is not explicitly mentioned as the indirect object, the reference to prayer demands this understanding. The parallelism shows beyond doubt that God stands behind the instruction.[105]

10 The connection of vv. 5 and 10 by *rāʿ* "evil" suggests that the deceiver misleads the blind to a pit of destruction through his injustice. The antithetical parallels of v. 10 contrast the topics *as for one who misleads* [see 19:27; 20:1][106] *the upright* [see I: 98] *into an evil* (*rāʿ;* see 1:16) *way* (*derek;* see 1:15)[107] and *the blameless* (see I: 98). Implicitly the deceiver aimed to advantage himself and to strengthen himself without regard for the well-being of the upright. Versets Ab and Bb contrast the destinies of these two different lifestyles (i.e., "evil" versus "good"). In poetic justice, the deceiver himself *will fall* [see 26:27a] *into his own pit*[108] (i.e., the evil pit he dug for his upright victim). *He* is emphatic — really "he himself." *But* (see vv. 1, 2, 4, 5, 7) the devoted who resist the seduction *will* receive (see 3:35) as his rightful and permanent inheritance *good things* (i.e., everything that is delightful and desirable; see I: 99; 17:2; 19:4). The deceiver may mislead the upright immediately to their destruction, as, for example, through abusing the judicial system (cf. vv. 5, 6). More probably, he destroys them immediately through enticing them to evil behavior, as, for example, committing perjury or extortion themselves. The upright are corruptible (see 9:15), but they can defend themselves from temptation by hiding God's truths in their hearts (Ps. 119:10). The notion that the deceiver seduced the upright to sin (see 10:17; 12:26) could be an extension of v. 9, explaining why a person apostatizes. The similar syntax involving nominative absolute constructions also favors linking the proverbs. In any case, an earlier uprightness is of no value to the apostate (Ezek. 3:20).

11 This concluding proverb of the unit (28:1-11) and its second subunit (28:7-11) forms an *inclusio* with v. 2 by referring to the discerning person (vv. 2b, 11b) and with v. 7 by the reference to "the rich" (vv. 7b, 11a). The inner core of its antithetical parallels chiastically pits a rich person against the discerning poor person. *A rich person* (see 10:15; 18:11) is now clearly defined as one who *is wise in his own eyes* (see n. 9; 3:7; 26:12). Wealth connected with pride loses its positive value. *But* [see vv. 1ff.] *a dis-*

105. The alliteration of *taw (tôrâ, tᵉpillātô, tôʿēbâ)* assists the connection.

106. *Šgh* in the *Hiphil* is used of leading a blind man astray (Deut. 27:18). The NIV renders it "deceiver" in Job 12:16. In its only other occurrence in this stem, the *Hiphil* is tolerative, "Do not let me stray" (Ps. 119:10).

107. Or "into the way of an evil person" (see 2:16).

108. Presumably *šᵉḥût* is a fem. gender doublet of *šāḥat (HALOT,* 4:1,457, s.v. *šᵉḥût).*

cerning [see v. 2] *poor person* (*dal;* see v. 8) *searches him out.* Through a penetrating probe he uncovers the rich person's deceptive motives and activities (see 18:13; 25:2). Though destitute of earthly wealth, he is rich with heavenly wisdom, having insight into truth by his faith in God and in his revelation. The antithetical predicates in the outer core, "wise in his own eyes" and "searches him out," are not precise, implying that the poor man through the purity of his informed moral discernment can "smell out" the rich person's selfish motives and duplicitous schemes. Paradoxically, according to 26:12 both the ambitious rich person and the apathetic sluggard have less hope of salvation through wisdom than a fool. The latter cannot stir himself to seek it, and the former cannot let go of his riches to find it.

2. The Importance of One's Relationship with God for Ruling and Gaining Wealth (28:12-27)

The unit 28:12-27 is marked off by the single framing proverbs, 28:12 and 28, contrasting the righteous and the wicked. Indeed, 28:12b and 28:28a repeat each other almost verbatim. Every verse between them mentions specific types of wicked people: "the concealer of transgressions, those who harden their hearts, the wicked ruler, the oppressive who hurries to be rich, the partial person, the greedy one (vv. 22, 25), the flatterer, the robber of parents, those who trust in their own minds, and one who raises the eyes to avoid seeing the poor's need."[109] Apart from the frame, the unit begins and ends with sayings pertaining to one's relationship with the LORD (vv. 13-14, 25-26). Though the LORD is not mentioned in vv. 13-14, the notions of "to praise" (v. 13b) and "to tremble" (v. 14a) presume the LORD as their objects.

The introductory pair (vv. 13-14) implicitly instructs the son to be penitent before the LORD and not harden his heart *(libbô).* The concluding pair (vv. 25-26) instructs him to find his security in the LORD, not in his own heart *(libbô).* Muilenburg observed that the divine name often occurs at the beginning or end of a poem.[110] Within that theological frame, apart from vv. 17-18, the unit pertains to proper and improper methods of acquiring wealth, namely, hard work and benevolence versus various get-rich-quick schemes and stinginess. The theological frame prevents reducing the teaching to merely moral instruction; its teaching is based on faith in God who upholds and reveals the moral order, not in self-righteousness and an impersonal ethical code.

After the framing proverb, the unit's 15 verses consist of three units,

109. Malchow, "A Manual for Future Monarchs," p. 241.

110. James Muilenburg, "A Study in Hebrew Rhetoric" (VTSup 1: Congress Volume; Copenhagen, 1953), pp. 97-111.

vv. 13-18 (six verses), 19-24 (six verses), and 25-27 (three verses). The first subunit pertains to God and the ruler, the second to hard work versus the fast buck, and the last to kindness versus stinginess, though the latter is also a false way to get rich (v. 22). Verse 18 functions as a janus between the first and second subunits. Verse 18b pertains to the consequences of oppression, assuming the punishment of God, and v. 18a, to a right relationship with the community, preparing the way for vv. 19-24. Verse 25 similarly functions as a janus: v. 25a to one's relationship with society, and v. 25b to one's relationship with God.

a. Introductory Framing Proverb (28:12)

The single framing represents the fortunes of the people as depending on whether the righteous or the wicked come to power (cf. 11:10-11; 14:34; 28:28; 29:2). Its antithetical parallels pit the causes of their fortunes, *when the righteous* [see I: 97] *triumph* (*baʿᵃlōṣ;* see 11:10) versus *when the wicked* [see I: 110] *rise* to do battle *(ûbᵉqûm). Qûm* means either "to rise to power," "to become powerful"[111] or, more probably, its meaning in military contexts, "to swing into action."[112] This meaning is supported by the military terminology of verset A. The parallels also juxtapose the respectively different consequences, *the* public *splendor* (*tip'āret;* see 4:9), probably a metonymy for the appearance of the people, *is great* (see v. 2) and *mortals* (*'ādām;* see I: 89), who have been hiding themselves, *must be searched out* (see 2:4; 20:29) with lamps (cf. Zeph. 1:12). The last parallelism is imprecise, suggesting that the "great splendor" is a metaphor for the people who come out of hiding. During the reign of the wicked, they "venture not out into the streets and public places (Fleischer), for mistrust and suspicion oppress them all" (cf. 1 K. 17:2, 3; 18:4; 19:1-4),[113] but with the victory of the righteous, they fill the streets with great festivity (cf. Esth. 8:17).

b. The LORD and the Ruler (28:13-18)

This six-verse subsubunit consists of three proverb pairs. The first and last pertain to a guilty conscience under the heavy hand of God (esp. vv. 13 and 17). "Mortal" (*'ādām,* vv. 14a, 17a), "he will fall" (*yippôl,* vv. 14b, 18b), and the paronomasia of *tāmîd* ("completely," v. 14a) and *tāmîm* ("blamelessly," v. 18b) form an *inclusio.* Within this theological *inclusio,* the inner proverbial pair pertains to the tyrant, who gets rich by oppression (v. 15) and corruption

111. So BDB, p. 878, s.v. *qûm.*

112. J. T. Willis, *"Qûmâ YHWH," JNSL* 16 (1990) 207-21.

113. Delitzsch, *Proverbs,* p. 418.

(v. 16). The last two proverb pairs are linked by the root *ʿšq: maʿᵃšaqqôt* "extortions" (v. 16a) and *neʿqaš* "crooked" (v. 18b). The whole subunit is stitched together by the alliteration of *mem* and by the broken sequence of */s~š k~q/: mᵉkasseh* (v. 13a), *maqšeh* (v. 14b), *šôqēq* (v. 15a), *maʿᵃšaqqôt* (v. 16aβ), *ʿāšuq* (v. 17), and *neʿqaš* (v. 18), the last three of which add ʿ to the sequence.

13-14 Verse 14 escalates v. 13. In a chiastic arrangement, v. 13a speaks of the impenitent and v. 14b, of the hardened sinner. Verse 13b teaches forgiveness of sin by giving praise to God through confessing sin and abandoning it; v. 14a, teaches how to avoid sin in the first place by fearing God (cf. 16:6). Van Leeuwen notes, "Together they echo vocabulary and themes from Psalm 32, a psalm that ends in a wisdom instruction."[114]

13 This unique proverb speaks of God's mercy and defines true repentance. The negative of its antithetical parallels speaks of *the one who conceals* [*mᵉkasseh;* see 17:9] *his own transgressions* (see 10:12). It is one thing to cover up the "transgression by a neighbor," and quite another to cover up one's own legal offenses against the personal and property rights of others. Consequently, he *will not succeed (yaṣlîaḥ).* Concretely, *ṣlḥ* in the *Qal* means "penetrate into." Saebø says, "The same concept seems to shine through in uses of the causative hi to state that God causes someone's 'way' *derek* on a journey to 'progress,' 'reach the goal,' i.e., 'succeed.' "[115] The figurative use of the intransitive *Qal* and *Hiphil* means "have success, succeed." *But* (see 28:1, 12) signals the positive antithesis, *the one who confesses (môdeh). Yādâ* occurs 100 times in the *Hiphil,* always with the meaning "to respond to another's action or behavior with public praise." In six passages (1 K. 8:33, 35 = 2 Chr. 6:24, 26; Ps. 32:5; Prov. 28:13) it means "confess (sins)."[116] More specifically, in these passages it means "give God public praise and glory by acknowledging one's need of his forgiveness and deliverance from sin." This entails praising his greatness (i.e,, one cannot hide sin from him), his justice (i.e., he has the right to punish the transgressor), and his grace (i.e., he forgives and delivers; cf. Josh. 1:9). *And (wᵉ)* combines the confessor into a hendiadys with *the one who abandons* (*ʿōzēb;* see 2:13; 28:4). Proper penitence involves a double action: giving God praise and glory by acknowledging sins, and abandoning them.[117] *Them* renders the gapped "his transgres-

114. Van Leeuwen, *Proverbs,* p. 238. They are also connected by a common syntax of *Piel* and *Hiphil* participles in their versets A and B respectively. The connection is assisted by the alliteration of the initial *mem* of these participles in the chiastically arranged assonance of *mᵉkasseh* "one who conceals" (v. 13a) and *maqšeh* "one who hardens" (v. 14b), and by the alliteration and broken sequence of initial *ʾašrê* and *ʾᵃrî.*

115. M. Saebø, *TLOT,* 3:1,078, s.v. *ṣlḥ Piel.*

116. C. Westermann, *TLOT,* 2:507, s.v. *ydh Hiphil.*

117. Cf. J. J. Boda, "Words and Meanings: *YDH* in Hebrew Research," *WTJ* 57 (1995) 277-97, esp. p. 286.

sions." *Will obtain mercy (yeruḥām)* glosses the root *reḥem* "womb." This soft spot became the physical locus for the experience of the strong emotion of pity for the needy. The verb is always used with the emotion of mercy from a superior to an inferior, parents to children, victors to the defeated, and the advantaged to the disadvantaged. The extension of mercy is voluntary, not involuntary. According to H. J. Stoebe, "Four fifths of all occurrences of *rḥm* pi. have God as subj.; God is always the agent of *rḥm* pu. [as here]. The Hos. passages demonstrate that the act of Yahweh described by *rḥm* pi. signifies installation (or the reinstallation) in the child-parent relation (Hos. 1:6; 2:4[6], 23[25]) that is not sentimental but thoroughly real." He also notes, "*Rḥm* pi. stands in exclusive opposition to God's wrath or replaces it because wrath suspends the proper relationship of the people to God." This leads to its use in relation to sin. The verb occurs several times with *ḥnn* "to be gracious." "Thus in a few passages forgiveness, expressed by *rḥm* pi, constitutes the precondition for the reestablishment of the community with God that was lost through sin (Isa. 55:7; Mic. 7:19; cf. also 1 Kgs. 8:50 . . . also Prov. 28:13, where *rḥm* pu. encompasses forgiveness)."[118] The imprecise parallelism entails that the one who covers up his legal offenses refuses both to give God public acknowledgment and to abandon his hostility to the community. Out of his sinful pride he pretends before God and people that he has no need to confess; instead, he seeks to deceive (vv. 6, 18). However, "The intactness of the community requires the confession of unrighteousness that has been committed and the denial that it will be repeated."[119] The imprecise parallels also entail that those whom God restores through the prescribed remedy will succeed (i.e., obtain eternal life, for it is everyone's goal), and those who are not restored will not succeed because they are outside the eternal kingdom of God. The availability of mercy motivates sinners to repent (Ps. 51:13[15]). People may smash their consciences to avoid humbling themselves, but they cannot avoid the reality that God knows and will punish sin. How much better to give him glory by acknowledging this and to experience his mercy (see Ps. 32:3-5; Isa. 1:16-18; Hos. 14:1-3[2-4]; 1 John 1:8-9; cf. Job 31:33-34)! The righteous, who love community, do not repeat a neighbor's transgression (10:12; 17:9) but confront him personally with it (27:5, 6, 9, 17). They allow the transgressor himself to restore his relationship with God's community by publicly acknowledging his having transgressed the personal and property rights of others. That sort of confession restored David (Psalms 32; 51) and Zacchaeus (Luke 19:1-8) to true Israel.

14 This proverb presents the oxymoron *blessed is the person ('ašrê 'ādām;* see 3:13) *who trembles* [see 3:24] *continually* (cf. 5:19), probably an

118. H. J. Stoebe, *TLOT,* 3:1,229, s.v. *rḥm.*
119. Meinhold, *Sprüche,* p. 474.

equivalent of "fear of the LORD." Trembling here refers to the fear of reverence, not of bondage; of caution, not of distrust; of diligence, not of despondency. Instructively this verb in the *Piel* occurs both times (cf. Isa. 51:13) with the person whose inner psyche is fixed in its hostility to God and people, presumably to indulge sinful pride and/or sensual pleasure. His opposite is *the one who hardens (maqšeh)*[120] *his heart* (see I: 90). When one hardens his heart, his psyche can no longer feel, respond, and opt for a new direction. The hardened heart is fixed in unbelief and unbending defiance to God (Exod. 7:3; Ps. 95:8); insensible to admonition or reproof, it cannot be moved to a new sphere of behavior. Durham glosses it "stubborn-minded."[121] The imprecise inner core parallels assume that the trembling heart is one that is open to God and responds to the prompting of his Spirit to redirect his life away from this hostility. In their outer frame, the parallels contrast their fates. The God-fearer maximizes life as God intended and without sin's penalties.[122] Godly fear and true happiness are inseparable. By contrast, the person fixed against God inevitably *will fall,* an important metaphor for defeat/destruction (11:5, 14, 28; 13:17; 17:20; 22:14; 24:17; 26:27; 28:10, 14, 18), *into evil* (*bᵉrāʿâ;* see 17:20), the ruin that belongs to his vile behavior (see 10:27; 14:2, 27; 15:33; 16:20; 19:23; 23:17-18; 29:25; 1 Cor. 10:12; Phil. 2:12; 1 Pet. 4:8). But not every calamity is the manifestation of divine judgment (see Job 1–2; 27:2-6; 42:7). Paradoxically, saints fear God and are bold as lions (28:1).

15-16 These verses chiastically represent a cruel and oppressive tyrant: "a wicked ruler" (v. 15b), "a leader devoid of competence" (v. 16a). Their connection is helped by the consonance of *šqq* in *šôqēq* "charging" (v. 15a) and *maʿᵃšaqqôt* "extortion" (v. 16a). Verse 16 defines the "wicked ruler" as a leader who engages in extortion and other forms of unjust gain.

15 Though a synthetic, single nominal clause, the proverb is semantically a comparative proverb. A wicked ruler over destitute people (verset B) is compared in a single portrait to a hungry lion and a ravenous bear. *A roaring* (or growling, *nōhēm;* see 19:12), hungry *lion* (*ʾᵃrî;* see 22:13) symbolizes strength and ferocity and is seen in figures of lions that guarded temples and

120. A. S. van der Woude *(TLOT,* 3:1,175-76, *qšh)* says, "The verbal and nominal occurrences of *qāšâ* always have a fig. meaning and here refer to the harshness that someone displays in interactions with others. . . . In the *Hiphil* it occurs with *ʿōrep* 'neck' = 'to defy someone.' . . . The image derives from cattle used as draft animals, whose power seems to be concentrated in the neck (cf. Hos 4:16; Jer 5:5). Whoever resists the yoke is 'hard-necked.'"

121. J. I. Durham, *Exodus* (WBC 3; Waco: Word, 1987), p. 84.

122. P. J. Nel (*The Structure and Ethos of the Wisdom Admonitions in Proverbs* [Berlin and New York: Walter de Gruyter, 1982], p. 14) argues that the *ʾašrê* ("blessed") form has an exhortative function.

thrones and in the Sumerian and Akkadian pantheons. Rulers likened themselves to lions and used their images to adorn their gates, temples, palaces and thrones. *A ravenous, charging (šôqēq) bear* (see 17:12) depicts one that charges, assaults, and attacks suddenly.[123] "The threatening element is once witnessed by acoustic sound (growling) and once by motor activity (aggressive movement)."[124] The compound images of the two most savage beasts that roam the forests of Palestine on the prowl for prey (cf. 1 Sam. 17:34) certify and intensify the ruler's ferocity, his surprise attack, and his ravaging destruction. *A wicked* [see 28:12] *ruler* (*mōšēl;* see 6:7) *over* implies dominion over an inferior[125] *poor* (*dāl;* see 28:3, 8) *people* (see 14:28; cf. 29:2, 4, 7). In Collection II the ruler is compared favorably with the lion (19:12; 20:2; 22:13). Ironically, their defender of justice and protector against their enemies turns on them, a vicious beast who greedily mauls and devours his people. "No sentiment of pity softens his bosom. No principle of justice regulates his conduct."[126] He "roars" to keep his "prey" for himself. The portrait is all too familiar in both ancient (cf. Dan. 7:1-8; Luke 22:25) and modern times.

16 The antithetical proverb of the pair pits the morally senseless leader who piles one extortion on top of another against those who hate unjust gain of any sort (see the catalogue in Jer. 22:13-19). Both the etymology and the primary significance of *leader (nāgîd)* has been widely, but inconclusively, debated.[127] *Who is lacking (ḥ*ᵃ*sar)* occurs about ten times with the

123. The verb occurs in the *Qal* four times besides Prov. 28:3. Twice it is used to denote to "pounce on/rush on" something, of people who pounce/rush on spoil (Isa. 33:4) and of locusts who rush/pounce on a city. Twice it is used of a "ravenous" appetite (*nepeš,* Ps. 107:9). In the *Hithpael* the verb is used to denote chariots that "rush to and fro" in the squares of Nineveh. Plöger (*Sprüche,* p. 330) glosses the verb "angriffslustiger (a lusty attack/assault)."

124. Meinhold, *Sprüche,* p. 475.

125. *IBHS,* p. 217, P. 11.2.13c.

126. Paxton, cited by Bridges, *Proverbs,* p. 543.

127. See *HALOT,* 2:667, s.v. *nāgîd;* Hasel, *TLOT,* 9:187-202, s.v. *nāgîd.* The word is found both as a general term for a leader and as a royal designation. As a general term, it is chiefly found in Chronicles, where it may variously denote a tribal chief (1 Chr. 12:27[28]) or temple officials serving in various administrative capacities (1 Chr. 9:20; 2:24; 2 Chr. 31:12; cf. Jer. 20:1). As a royal designation *nāgîd* is only occasionally used of foreign monarchs (Ps. 76:12[13]; Ezek. 28:2). In 1 K. 1:35 it denotes Solomon as the crown prince, appointed by David as his successor (cf. 2 Chr. 11:22). This may been the original significance of the term, according to T. N. D. Mettinger (*King and Messiah: The Civil and Sacral Legitimization of Israelite Kings* [ConBOT 8; Lund: Liberlafomedl-Gleerup, 1976]), pp. 158-62); differently, B. Halpern (*The Constitution of the Monarchy in Israel* [HSM 25; Chico, Calif.: Scholars Press, 1981], pp. 8-11). However, in Samuel-Kings the term is otherwise used theologically to represent the king-designate as the one

genitive *lēb* (see I: 15), once with "food" (12:9) and uniquely here with *understanding* (see I: 96). The antithetical parallel suggests that it, too, entails the inability to survive. *Multiplies (yārēb;* see n. 14) *extortions (ma'ašaqqôt)*[128] occurs elsewhere in the phrase *beṣa' ma'ašaqqôt* "gain from extortion" (Isa. 33:15). *Those who hate* [see n. 15; 1:22] *ill-gotten gain* (< lit. "rip-off"; see 1:19) is probably used as an intended irony with *prolongs (ya'arîk;* see 28:2) *days* (see 3:2), perhaps an intentional pun referring to the ruler's life and/or the life of his subjects (15:27b), and/or his tenure as ruler (see 28:2b; cf. 1 K. 3:14). The imprecise parallelism suggests that those who hate rip-offs are political leaders. The comment that leaders who hate ill-gotten gain prolong days implies that those who exact extortion cut them short, the proof of their incompetence (see 28:2). The honest and honorable leader who does not stoop to corruption has a long and successful tenure of office because the LORD upholds the moral order. The Bible ascribes extending days either to the LORD (Deut. 5:33[30]; 2 K. 20:1-6; Ps. 91:16) or to wisdom (3:16). To pit the ultimate cause against the immediate is mischievous.

17-18 The first subunit concludes with two proverbs that pertain to the consequences of "oppression" *('šq)* and of being a "crook" *('qš;* vv. 17a, 18b) — for the paronomasia linking vv. 16-18 see 28:13-18. The fatal consequence is escalated from fleeing to the edge of the pit (v. 17b) to falling into it (v. 18b; cf. v. 10). Whereas v. 17 pertains to one's relationship with God, v. 18 pertains to one's relationship with society, linking vv. 13-18 with vv. 19-24. The two notions are inseparable; a person's relationship with God is dependent on his relationship to society (see 3:27-35).

17 Although the proverb atypically mixes the syntax of a declarative clause (v. 17a-bα) and an imperative clause (v. 17bβ), it typically reflects the sage's division of thought into cause (v. 17a) and consequence (v. 17b). *A mortal ('ādām;* see 28:14) *who is oppressed ('āšūq;* see 14:31) may refer to his guilty conscience.[129] *'āšaq* refers to inward oppression in Isa. 38:14a. The

---

chosen and appointed by God to rule his people Israel (cf. S. Shaviv, "*Nābî'* and *Nāgîd* in Samuel ix 1–xi 16," *VT* 34 [1984] 111-12). Lipiński, "*Nāgîd* der Kronprinz," *VT* 24 [1974] 497-98) glosses it "crown prince." It has been suggested that this usage represents an early prophetic view of kingship, later taken up in the Davidic theology of the Royal Psalms (V. Fritz, "Die Deutungen des Koenigtums Sauls in den Überlieferungen von seiner Entstehung 1 Sam 9–11," *ZAW* 88 [1976] 352). In related expressions the term is applied to Saul (1 Sam. 9:16; 10:10), David (e.g., 1 Sam. 13:14; 2 Sam. 7:8), Jeroboam (1 K. 14:7), and Baasha (1 K. 16:2).

128. *Ma'ašaqqâ* consists of the root *'sq* "oppress" (see 28:3) plus abstract *mem.*

129. Greenstone (*Proverbs,* p. 300) thinks that the man is charged with willful murder, but the pejorative term "oppress" would not be used of a just legal system. Toy (*Proverbs,* p. 502) believes that the man charged with homicide is fleeing to the city of rescue (Num. 35:31-35), but that meaning cannot be gotten from the Hebrew text.

catchword *'ādām,* and *'ādām* in v. 14 may represent two different responses of unrepentant sinners: one hardens his heart (v. 14), while the other is driven to suicide. Both fall, each in his own way, under the mighty hand of God. *By shedding the blood of life* glosses "by blood" (*bᵉdam;* see 1:11) of life (*nāpeš;* see I: 90), a reference to shedding by violence the blood containing a person's life. The blood is the life (*nepeš;* Deut. 12:23), and the life *(nepeš)* is in the blood (Lev. 17:14).[130] A person who is oppressed by his guilty conscience of shedding the lifeblood of an innocent victim (v. 17a) becomes a fugitive from life (v. 17b). *He will flee (yānûs) to the pit* (*'ad bôr;* see 1:12). *Nûs* occurs elsewhere in Proverbs only in 28:1, also in conjunction with a guilty conscience. As his conscience drove him to flee phantom enemies (v. 1), it now drives him to flee to the entrance of the grave, where he hopes to escape his inward torment (v. 17bα). No one should stay his execution (v. 17bβ). In the negative vetitive *let no one restrain* (*'al*[131]*-yitmᵉkû,* lit. "to lay hold of" and/or "keep hold of"; see n. 18) *him* (see 3:18),[132] whose chiastic antecedent is *'ādām.* In lex talionis, this oppressor himself is oppressed (by his conscience), and, as for the blood he shed, he himself will compensate it by shedding his own blood. His execution from the LORD should not be deflected. The proverb that the son should rescue one heading for death has in view the innocent, not the guilty as here (24:11-12).

18 The antithetical parallels pit *the one who walks* [see 1:11] *as a blameless person* (see 28:10) against *the double-dealing crook* (lit. "the twisted one of double-dealing ways" or "the one who twists himself in double-dealing ways"; see 28:6). These contrasting causes are matched by contrasting consequences. The folk devoted to the LORD and to serving the

130. Malbim (*Proverbs,* p. 285) holds that the man is oppressed by others and that his own lifeblood is in view "when a man is oppressed to his very lifeblood," but for that sense one expects the pronominal suffix.

131. The jussive functions as an "oratio variata" (*IBHS,* p. 570, P. 34.3d).

132. *Tāmak* occurs 20 times in the *Qal* and once in the *Niphal.* In Proverbs, with different objects, it otherwise means to reach out and take hold of: wisdom (3:18), way (4:4), Sheol (5:5), glory (11:16; 29:23), spindle (31:19); of the wicked person in the *Niphal* (5:22). This is also its sense in Gen. 48:17; Isa. 33:15; Amos 1:5, 8. However, it can also connote "to support/assist" (Exod. 17:12; Pss. 16:5(?); 41:12[13]; 63:9; Isa. 41:10; 42:1). The Syr. and some of the Targs. (see Healey, *Targum of Proverbs,* p. 57, n. 10; Gemser, *Sprüche,* p. 98; et al.) invest it with that meaning here. "Let no one support him/offer him assistance" (cf. NIV, NRSV). This is too ambiguous, for that rendering could mean not to help the murderer to evade the authorities or not to save him from his guilty conscience, or not to assist him in his flight to the pit. The Vulg. and the lexicographers (BDB, p. 1069, s.v. *tāmak;* W. Gesenius–F. Buhl, p. 881, s.v. *tāmak*) take it in its consistent sense in this book, not to seize "the one who is burdened with the guilt of murder and is fleeing to the underworld" (*HALOT,* 4:1,751, s.v. *tmk*). Plöger (*Sprüche,* p. 337) comments, "A prohibition not to assist the murderer would be self-evident."

community, including those swindled by the crook, *will be helped* [*by the* LORD] (*yiwwāšēa'*; see 20:22; cf. 11:14). R. Hubbard says, "In general the root *yš'* implies bringing help to people in the midst of their trouble rather than in rescuing them from it. It is almost exclusively a theological term with Yahweh as its subject and his people as its object."[133] Indeed, God is obliged to render help to the blameless. According to the LORD's own law, if one experiences injustice and raises a cry for assistance, those who hear it are obligated to render aid (Deut. 22:27). Since the merciful and just God hears the cry of the oppressed, his effective help is certain (see 18:10). But the double-dealing crook *will fall* (see 28:14) to his final ruin *into a pit* (see n. 19).

c. Wealth by Hard Work versus Haste (28:19-24)

The third subunit continues the topic of proper and improper methods of acquiring wealth, but shifts from the vertical hierarchical axis to the horizontal axis of hard work versus various get-rich-quick schemes. Its three proverb pairs condemn the dreamer (v. 19) and the dishonest (v. 20), greed (vv. 21-22), and false speech (vv. 22-23).[134]

19-20 Verse 18a forms a transition to v. 19a by the similar syntax "the one who walks blamelessly" and "the one who works his land" and by paronomasia of *yiwwāšēa'* "he will be helped" and *yiśba'* "he will be filled." Verses 18-19 contrast the gaining of wealth by just and unjust means. Verse 19a commends industry as the legitimate means for providing food, and v. 20a explains the honest work as coming from a person's inner stability. It also escalates the reward from the basic necessity of food to abounding in all sorts of blessings. The B versets present a person hurrying to get rich, apart from hard work and without character. He is chasing an empty dream, for he will become poor and, more than that, the LORD will punish him. "Blessing" and "not acquitted" implicitly make the LORD the Ultimate Agent behind the truths of this proverb pair.

19 This proverb in verset Bb repeats 12:11, but instead of "lacks sense" (12:11bβ), 28:19bβ reads *is filled* [see 12:11a] *with poverty* (*rîš;* see 10:4, 15). The proverb pits the one who gains a livelihood through honest toil within the God-ordained social structures, such as working the land, against one who engages in dishonest enterprises outside of work and God's established economy. Without attempting a catalogue of the unrealistic and hasty

133. R. Hubbard, *NIDOTTE,* 2:556, s.v. *yš'*.

134. Malchow ("Manual for Future Monarchs," p. 241) thinks that they are also linked by the assonance of *'admātô-'ᵉmûnôt* (vv. 19-20), of the first words in the B verset of vv. 21-22 (*wᵉ'al, wᵉlō'*), and by *lahôn, lāšôn,* and *lᵉ'îš* (vv. 22-24) and by *ḥābēr–rᵉḥab* (24-25).

pursuit of riches, one may think of bribery (v. 21), stinginess (v. 22), deception (v. 23), robbing of parents (v. 24), and greediness (v. 25). The one contributing to the communal wealth is filled with food; the one who unjustly takes wealth from it is ironically filled with a state of deprivation of life's necessities.

20 This antithetical parallelism pits a *a conscientious person* (see 20:6), who is honest, trustworthy, and dependable in both word and deed from his inner stability, against *one who hastens* [see 19:2; 21:5] *to become rich* (see 10:4). "[The conscientious] has sufficient integrity and humanity to enable him to possess wealth without being corrupted by it. It does not destroy his solidarity with his brothers, but rather enables him to give effective expression to his sense of social responsibility."[135] The antithesis is not precise, suggesting that one who is in a hurry to get rich lacks the honesty that comes from inner moral stability. This is certified by the verdict of "guilty" (i.e., "he will not remain unpunished"). The proverb also juxtaposes the different consequences from these two causes. The Author of Life causes the conscientious person to *abound* (*rab;* see n. 21) *in blessings* (see n. 22; 10:12).[136] The affirmation that God "is abounding in unfailing love . . . and truth" (Exod. 34:6) means that he has these virtues to a measure that exceeds human normalcy. The parallelism suggests that the conscientious possesses the potential for life and victory beyond others rather than that he extends them to others. By contrast, the dishonest person, who is not fussy about how he gets rich and who rides roughshod over others to make "the fast buck," *will not escape* [*the LORD's*][137] *punishment* (see 6:29) (i.e., sterility, poverty, and defeat). He misses the way (19:2b), ends up in poverty (21:5b), and is worse off than a fool (29:20; cf. 1 Tim. 6:9-11).

21 Taking a bribe is one quick route to a fast buck. In truth, however, that route ultimately demeans one to taking a bribe for a trifle. Verset A of this synthetic proverb censures showing favoritism to anyone for a bribe; a bribe is neither beautiful nor beneficial. *To show partiality is not good* repeats 24:23 without adding "in giving a verdict." Though not restricted here to the legal sphere, it is used pejoratively for giving honor or showing favoritism to someone that disadvantages others.[138] *Not good (lō'-ṭôb)* is a litotes (see 16:29). *And* joins the two clauses into one thought. Ironically, *even for* [lit. "(reduced) to"; see 6:26] a *portion of food* [i.e., a regular meal; see Gen. 18:5; Judg. 19:5; 1 Sam. 2:36; 28:22; 1 K. 17:11; cf. Prov. 17:1; 23:8] *a*

135. McKane, *Proverbs,* p. 626.

136. Note the alliteration of *'aleph* in the first two words, *'îš 'emûnôt,* and the broken sequence of */b~r/* in the next two words, *rab-berākôt.*

137. So also McKane, *Proverbs,* p. 626; Whybray, *Proverbs,* p. 395; et al.

138. A. S. van der Woude, *TLOT,* 2:1,001, s.v. *pānîm.*

strong, mature *man* (*gāber;* see 28:3), who can work the ground and earn an honest wage, *will commit a crime* (*yipšaʿ;* see 10:12; 28:2). Although the words for "bribe" (see 15:27; 17:8, 23; 18:16 passim) are not used, the parallelism implies that the showing of partiality was in exchange for a gift. The debasing greed and degeneration that go with taking bribes is underlined by the willingness to be corrupted for as little as a meal (cf. 1 Sam. 2:12-16; Ezek. 13:19).

22 This verse adds miserliness to the list of wrong ways of pursuing the fast buck. The opposite of the miser is the generous person (lit. "the good eye"; 22:9). The unethical man hastens to get rich without regard to justice (v. 21); the miser, without regard to compassion (see v. 22; 28:27). Verset A presents the cause, stinginess, and verset B the consequence, want. Verset A defines the stingy man as one who hastens to get rich. *A miser* (lit. "a person of an evil eye"; see 23:6; cf. 22:9) *is hasty* (*nibᵉhāl;* lit. "one who hastens himself"; see 20:21) *for wealth* (*lahôn;* see 3:9). *And* combines the cause and consequence clauses into one thought. *He does not know* (*yēdaʿ;* see 28:2) gives expression to the fundamental moral problem of fools/the wicked; they have not internalized the moral order that matches sin and death. *That poverty (ḥeser)* glosses a noun that occurs only twice, though the verb occurs in 13:25, and the adjective 13 times (see 12:9), mostly in the phrase "lacking moral sense" (see I: 91; cf. 28:16). Job 30:3 uses *ḥeser* for haggard people who suffer from want and hunger in a parched land; they lived on salt herbs and the root of the broom tree. Poverty is a personification of the absence of food; an abstract noun cannot come to someone. *Will come to him* (see 1:26; 10:24) in Proverbs personifies poverty (i.e., the absence of food) to picture the cause-effect nexus, linking bad deeds with bad consequences. The LORD will see to it that only conscientious and compassionate people finally hold wealth in his kingdom.

23 This verse adds deception by flattery to the catalogue of futile "get-rich-quick" schemes. Its antithetical parallels pit the subjects, the causes, *the one who reprimands* [see 9:7] *a mortal* (*ʾādām;* see I: 89; 28:14) *about his conduct* (*ʾorḥô;* see n. 24) against *the deceptive flatterer* (lit. "one who causes his tongue to be smooth"; see 2:16; 5:3). He flatters to set a lethal trap for his victim, not merely to portray his subject too favorably. The latter may find favor with some, but a vicious deceiver finds favor with no one (see 29:5). Meinhold agrees: "With regard to the context, making one's tongue smooth (v. 23) should refer to the hypocritical and deceitful cheating of one's fellow man."[139] The parallels also juxtapose the respective consequences; the rebuker *finds* [see 3:13] *favor* [see 3:4], *not* (see n. 25) the flatterer. However, the proverb leaves open with whom favor is found. To judge from Prov. 3:4,

139. Meinhold, *Sprüche,* p. 478.

the favor is from both the LORD and people, probably including the reproved. But this is not true of the mocker (see 9:7). He may or may not find favor with the one he tries to correct (see 9:7).

24 This saying draws to a conclusion the catalogue of fantasies in regard to quick riches with the most reprehensible of all evils, the unnatural and dastardly robbing of parents. Verset A describes the subject as *the one who robs* [see 22:22] *his father and his mother* (cf. 1:8; 19:26) by forcibly and illegally taking and withholding wealth from them. The circumstantial qualifier that the avaricious offspring disclaims criminal activity, *while saying* [see n. 27], "*There is no*[140] [see 13:3; 28:1, 3] *crime*" (see 28:21), suggests that he is attempting to get hold of their property under some pretext. He may rationalize: "Eventually it all comes to me anyway" (19:14), or "They can no longer manage their finances," or "As a family we own everything in common." 20:21 speaks of a hastily gained inheritance, and 19:26 of driving the parents from their home. The prodigal son wrongly demanded his inheritance before his father's death.[141] The Lord Jesus considered not providing for needy parents under the pretext of devotedness to God as another form of robbery (Matt. 15:5, 6). Verset B, a variant of 18:9b, adds the consequence. The blackguard who feathers his nest without recognizing his parents' need of financial strength and independence belongs to the company of those who devastate people, not to the family "where all the conditions of solidarity of interest are fulfilled."[142] *He* has both participles and their qualifiers as its antecedent. The root of *is a companion (ḥābēr)* means "to join." It can be rendered "united, associate, companion," in either a bad association (Job 34:8; Isa. 1:23) or a good one (Judg. 20:11). *To a person who destroys* (*leʾîš mašḥît,* i.e., brings ruin or devastation; see 6:32).[143] "Children have no more right to their parents' property while they are living than a brigand from outside the family."[144] Implicitly, the LORD will see to it that the unconscionable son will be repaid in kind (22:23).

d. Wealth by Trust in the LORD and Generosity versus Stinginess (28:25-27)

The final subunit, on one's relationship with the LORD as the measure for rulership and striving for gain (28:13-27), returns to the theme of a right rela-

140. Note the alliteration of *ʾaleph* in *ʾbyw [w]ʾmmw [w]ʾmr ʾyn.*

141. Kenneth E. Bailey, *Poet and Peasant and Through Peasant Eyes* (combined version; Grand Rapids: Eerdmans, 1976/1987), pp. 158-206.

142. McKane, *Proverbs,* p. 632.

143. *ʾîš* may have been used instead of *baʿal* for its alliteration with the *ʾaleph* words in verset A.

144. Clifford, *Proverbs,* p. 247.

tionship with the LORD (cf. vv. 13-14). The proverb pair (vv. 25-26) contrasts those who find their security in the LORD (*bôṭēaḥ ʿal-YHWH,* v. 25b) with those who feel secure in their own understanding apart from the LORD (*bôṭēaḥ b*e*libbô,* v. 26a). This close verbal and thematic connection interprets the theology of trust as submission to the sage's teaching (see 3:1-10). Verse 25 links impiety with greed, and v. 26 couples it with divine punishment (cf. 28:20, 22, 24, 27). Thus the poem on ill-gotten gain draws toward a conclusion by tracing the problem back to its source, piety versus impiety. Once again the way the LORD treats mortals depends on the way they treat their neighbors (see 3:27-35).

25 The antithetical parallels juxtapose the two subjects, *the unrestrained appetite* (*r*e*ḥab-nepeš,* lit. "wide of throat/appetite"; see 1:18; 21:4)[145] and *the one trusts in the LORD* (see 3:5; 16:20; 18:10; 28:5; 29:25), and their predicates, *stirs up strife* (see 15:18) versus *will be fattened* (see 11:25). The antitheses are imprecise, suggesting that the greedy are impious and that stirring up strife with others is the opposite of being enriched by others. The greedy person's insatiable appetite brings him into conflict with others, for he transgresses social boundaries. Not content with his portion, he becomes disruptive and destructive, and those whose person and property he violates fight back. This is how wars are started (cf. Jas. 4:1-2). The pious, however, does not transgress boundaries because he relies on the LORD.[146] The pious trust God to uphold his divinely established moral boundaries, which includes honest work, contentment, helping others, and so on. Since the pious depends on the LORD, he is the Ultimate Cause of their "fattening."

26 The proverb juxtaposes the topic *the one who trusts,* or feels secure (see 3:5; 28:1, 15), *in his own heart* (or opinions; see I: 90) with that of *the one who walks* [see 1:15; 28:6, 18] *in* [*the way of*] *wisdom* (see I: 76) — that is to say, who lives and makes his choices in the context of the sage's revealed wisdom. The self-confident lives in a fool's paradise, and no one can tell him otherwise. By contrast, the latter does not trust in his own understanding (3:5, 7) but depends on a heavenly revelation. The topics imply the depravity of the human heart and its need to be redirected by the sage's heavenly teaching. That teaching points the disciple to trust in the LORD who stands behind the doctrine, not in himself (see 3:5; 22:19; 28:14). Indeed, without that teaching and faith a person is brainless (see I: 115) and must acquire one (see 8:5; 15:32; 19:8). The imprecise predication juxtaposes *he is a fool* (*hûʾ k*e*sîl;* see I: 109) with *he will be delivered* (see 11:21), implying that

145. M. Dahood, *Proverbs and Northwest Semitic Philology* (Rome: Pontifical Biblical Institute, 1963), p. 56.

146. "Trust in God frees people from the compulsive drive to find security in material goods and power" (Van Leeuwen, *Proverbs,* p. 240).

the fool will not escape the punishment he justly deserves (11:29; 14:14), but the wise will escape when the Lord punishes the fool (1:32-33; 2:20-22). The fool in view here is not troubled by an evil conscience (see 28:17) but feels totally secure. He is hardened in his sin, and so his judgment is inescapable (see 28:14, 18).

27 The second unit (28:13-27), which pertains to proper and improper means of gaining wealth, is drawn to a conclusion with a proverb that deals with the reciprocity of benevolence and abundance over against stinginess and lack, continuing the teachings of 28:25 (cf. v. 25a with v. 27b and v. 25b with v. 27a). Implicitly, the benevolent trust the Lord to reward them (19:17; 22:9), but the stingy, trusting their own wisdom (v. 26a), selfishly hoard their wealth (cf. Matt. 25:40 with 25:41-46). Its imprecise antithetical topics, *the one who gives* [see 1:4] *to the poor* (see 13:23; 28:3) and *the one who shuts his eyes (maʿlîm ʿênāyw),* suggest that the latter ignores the pleas of the poor and fails to meet their need.[147] The imprecise predicates, *there is no* [see 28:1] *lack* (see 11:24) and *abounds* (*rab;* see 28:12, 16, 20) *in curses* (see 3:33; cf. 10:6), probably mediated through the community's curse formula "cursed be," imply that the benevolent do not lack either the necessities or the luxuries of life (see 10:6). The plural, "abounding in curses," refers to curses that bring a blight on every area of his life (cf. Deut. 27:15-26; 28:15-45). Paradoxically, in God's economy, which is against natural reason, the generous do not lack and the stingy will not escape punishment because the compassionate Lord stands behind the stated principle of reciprocity. When the hardhearted cries out for help, he will justly receive divine curses instead (see 21:13; 28:27b; cf. Zech. 7:9-14). A blind eye and a deaf ear (see 21:13; 24:12) experience the same fate as teeth like swords (30:14).

e. Concluding Framing Proverb (28:28)

This single proverb forms a frame around both 28:12-28, by repeating almost verbatim 28:12b in 28:28a, and the center line, 29:1, by repeating "when the righteous thrive" (28:28b and 29:2a) and by the similar notion in 28:28a and 29:2b of the affliction of humanity when "the wicked" are in power. Delitzsch notes that 28:28–29:3 "form a beautiful square grasp, in which the first and third, and the second and fourth, correspond to one another."[148]

147. *ʿlm* means "to be hidden" 11 times in the *Niphal* and "to hide/conceal" 11 times in the *Hiphil:* five times with the object "eyes," three times to ignore so that a human being does not act appropriately (cf. Lev. 20:4; 1 Sam. 12:3; Ezek. 22:16); once when the Lord does not answer a request (cf. Isa. 1:15); once concealing information (2 K. 4:27), and once of the Lord hiding himself (Ps. 10:1). It has this sense six times in the *Hithpael.*

148. Delitzsch, *Proverbs,* p. 424.

28:28b may also be connected with 28:12a by the root *rbh* (glossed "great" and "thrive"). Like 28:12 and 29:2, this framing proverb asserts the importance for a community of having the right kind of government.[149] The sequence of thoughts could infer their ultimate defeat, but the sequence is reversed in 29:2. Nevertheless, in the end the righteous will hold the reins of government when the nations, especially the poor, will have reason to rejoice (29:6; cf. 2:21-22).

The versets of 28:28 are linked by a paronomasia between the last word of verset A (*'ādām* "mortals") and the first word of verset B *'obdām* "they perish," implying the mortality of the wicked. The versets juxtapose both the cause, *when the wicked rise up* [*to do battle*] (see 28:12b) versus *when they perish* (see 10:28), and the antithetical consequence, *mortals hide themselves* (see 22:3; 27:12) to avoid the terrifying threat from the tyrants versus *the righteous* (*ṣaddîqîm;* see 28:1) *thrive* (*yirbû;* see 4:10; i.e., increase and become powerful, the two meanings of *rbh* also in 29:2, 16).[150] The imprecise parallelism implies that when the righteous increase in number and power, the people come out of their hiding (see 28:12a; 29:2a; cf. 11:10, 11; 14:34; 29:16). This was the case during the reign of Hezekiah, whose men collected these proverbs (25:1; 2 Chronicles 29–30, esp. 30:13-27; cf. Esth. 8:17; Acts 12:23, 24). Meinhold observes, "The proverb admits tacitly — and experience confirms — that the righteous can effectively be hindered. Wise men say: 'Not forever!'"[151] The devastating destruction of the wicked is from the LORD. At the time he judges the tyrants, the righteous take the dominion. This is the hope of humanity. While in the wilderness, the faithful hope for the promised land (see 2:21-22).

3. Center Line: Sudden Death for the Hard-hearted (29:1)

The editors (see 25:1) highlight the importance of heeding correction by placing 29:1 center stage in Section D (chs. 28–29). It stands between the framing proverbs that respectively conclude and introduce the preceding and following units (12:28; 29:2). Malchow calls 28:28–29:2 "the central structural verses in the collection."[152] As its centerpiece, this proverb colors the entire section with the danger of resisting its reproofs (cf. 2 Tim. 3:16).

Verset A presents the topic (i.e., the cause), namely, a person who

149. "When the wicked are in power and control the affairs of state, violence and injustice . . . flourish unchecked (29:16), and the people groan under an intolerable burden of oppression (29:2) and make themselves scarce for fear of life and limb (28:28; 28:12)" (Aitken, *Proverbs,* p. 201).

150. *HALOT,* 3:1,176, s.v. I *rbh.*

151. Meinhold, *Sprüche,* p. 480.

152. Malchow, "Manual for Future Monarchs," p. 241.

again and again defies the parents'/sages' attempts to set him right according to the divinely established order. *As for a person often reproved* [see nn. 29, 30; 1:23; 28:23] *and* [see n. 31] *who hardens* (*maqšeh;* see 28:14b) [*his*] *neck,* a figure of one who defies authority, informs the uniform complaint against Israel (cf. Exod. 32:9; 2 Chr. 36:13-16; Neh. 9:29; Isa. 48:8; Jer. 17:23; Zech. 7:11, 12; Acts 7:51). Verset B presents the predicate (i.e., the consequence), namely, a sudden, final shattering, implicitly from the Lord. *In an instant* [i.e., suddenly] *will be broken and without a remedy* repeats 6:15. When the door of opportunity to repent finally shuts, probably at death, the incorrigible fool is beyond all hope of a cure (see 1:22-32; 28:14, 18; cf. Exod. 9:29-35; 10:27, 28; 14:28; 2 K. 17:7-23; 24:1-4, 18-19; Luke 17:27-29; Rom. 9:22; 1 Thess. 5:3).

4. Rearing and Ruling Proved Worthwhile in Dealing with the Poor (29:2-15)

The fourth unit (29:3-15) is marked off from the center line (29:1) and the fifth unit (29:16-27) not only by the framing proverbs 29:2 and 16 (see 28:1-29:27) but also by two, or possibly three, chiastic *inclusio*s (29:3 and 15; 29:4 and 14; 29:5 and 12-13). The outer *inclusio* (vv. 3 and 15) pertains to rearing the son. It is tightly linked by mentioning only "his father" in 29:3a and only "his mother" in 29:15b. The mention of the mother alone is unique in Proverbs, corroborating the interpretation that the breaking apart of the stereotype compound "father" and "mother" between these two proverbs is deliberate (see 1:8; 10:1). In the second position within that outer *inclusio* is a positive mention of "the king" who through "justice" establishes his "land"/"throne" (vv. 4 and 14). These two references to a just king are unique in this unit. The linking of vv. 3-4 and 14-15 suggests that rearing and righteous ruling go together. Finally, possibly the references to seductive speech (v. 5) and deceptive speech (v. 12, a pair with v. 13) form the third internal chiasm. Moreover, the initial proverb (v. 3) is linked with the first and last verses of the central piece by the catchwords "to destroy" (28:28; 29:3) and *šmḥ* (*yiśmaḥ* "rejoice" and *yᵉśammaḥ* "makes glad"; 29:2, 3). It also belongs to the alternating pattern of framing proverb (28:28; 29:2) plus initial *'îš* (vv. 1, 3). The unit is further linked with the center verse by the catchword "reprove/reproof" in its last verse (29:1, 15).

The unit falls into two subunits, vv. 3-6 and vv. 8-15. Verse 7 functions as a janus between them by mentioning the "righteous," linking it with v. 6, and the "poor" *(dallîm),* linking it with v. 14. Indeed, this janus within the partial section resembles those of the main frame of Section D (28:1, 12, 16; 29:2, 16, 27) by also mentioning "righteous" and "wicked." It may stand apart from the framing proverbs, however, by using the singular for "righteous" and by breaking the stitching pattern of "wicked"/"righteous," "righteous/wicked" (see 28:1–29:27). In addition to the chiastic *inclusio*s noted above, the two subunits are linked by initial "person"/"people" (*'îš/'anšê;* see n. 35 and 29:22-26). The entire unit, like the first two (28:2-27), has a strong coloring of the royal court. Reference is made to the "king"/"ruler"/"attendants" in vv. 4, 12, 14 and effecting justice in vv. 4, 7, 9, and 14 and to judging (*dîn* and *špṭ* in vv. 7 and 9). The other proverbs, mostly about the wise and the fool, probably alert the king to wise court procedures in protecting the poor.

a. Introductory Framing Proverb (29:2)

This single framing proverb also functions as a janus between the center line (29:1) and the third unit, 29:3-15. Once again the framing proverb (see above, pp. 403-4) asserts the importance of righteous versus wicked leadership because of its affect on the citizenry. The proverb imprecisely juxtaposes the topics (i.e., the causes). *When the righteous* [see 28:1, 12; 29:16, 27] *thrive* (*birbôt;* see 28:28), *but* [see 28:28] *when a wicked* [28:28] *person* (*'îš;* see I: 89; 29:3, 4, 8, 9, 10, 20, 22, 27] rules (see 12:24), implies that the flourishing righteous are magistrates who serve their subjects and do not abuse their power to serve themselves. It also juxtaposes the respective predicates, *the people* [see 11:14; 28:15] *rejoice* (see 2:14) with spontaneous shouts of joy for their deliverance from corrupt, autocratic rulers and restoration to prosperity (28:12a, 28b; cf. Isa. 9:3[4]) and *people groan (yē'ānaḥ)* under their wicked rulers (28:12b, 28a). D. Thompson defines *'nḥ* as "an intense, negative response to terrible circumstances, actual or anticipated."[153] In democracies one contrasts statesmen, who use their offices to serve the people, with politicians, who see their offices as prizes they won, often by taking bribe-money from lobby groups.

b. Joy and Stability through Righteousness (29:3-6)

The first subunit is bound together by the catchwords "person" and "to be glad," forming an *inclusio* around the unit. On the one hand, the unit pertains positively to stability: of wealth (v. 3), of a land (v. 4), and of one's self (vv. 5-6). On the other hand, it presents negatively three ways in which wealth can be squandered due to the hostility of others. The prostitute enriches herself through illicit sex (v. 3), the officials through corrupt courts (v. 4), and the neighbor through scams involving seductive flattery (v. 5). The prostitute and the deceitful neighbor use guileful words to disarm their victims (5:3),

153. David Thompson, *NIDOTTE,* 1:455, s.v. *'nḥ.*

and they plunder them while their defenses are down.[154] However, the abuse of wealth is not due entirely to the chicanery of others; their victims are also culpable. The victims of the prostitute and the flatterer are guilty of being gullible, and the one who cooperates with corrupt officials is a villain. Verses 5-6 are a proverb pair, giving the last word to the righteous.

3 A rearing proverb once again begins a new unit. *A lover* [or "friend," *'îš 'ōhēb;* see 1:22] *of wisdom* [see I: 76] *makes his father glad* essentially repeats 10:1; 15:20 (cf. 27:11). Its antithetical parallel, *but one who associates with* (*rō'eh;* 13:20; 28:7) *prostitutes* [see 6:26] *squanders* (*yᵉ'abbed;* see 28:28) *his wealth* (see 3:9), making him "poor" (*dal;* 19:4; 28:8). The imprecise parallel implies that the lover of wisdom in his quest for wisdom keeps himself far from the world-and-life views of women who exploit sex for hire. The imprecise predicates (i.e., consequences) "makes his father [and mother] glad" and "destroys [the family's wealth and health]" entail that the father rejoices in a son who preserves both, and that the one who squanders them by hiring prostitutes brings his parents grief (cf. 31:3; Luke 15:30). It cannot be assumed, however, that this economic benefit is the only reason the parents rejoice in wise children. A wise child "leads to a satisfying child-parent relationship and to the responsible handling of inherited possessions."[155]

4 The next proverb turns from a son who squanders the family fortune (v. 3) to a king who destroys a nation through corruption. It is connected with v. 3 by syntax as well as by the opposition of "to perish" (v. 3b) and its antonym "to stand/endure" (v. 4a) and by the support of its synonym "to tear down" (v. 4b).[156] Its imprecise antithetical parallels juxtapose the topic (the causes) *a king* (8:15) administering his realm *through justice* (or doing what is right; see 1:3; 28:5) with *whoever exacts "contributions" or gives them* (see n. 39). If the "person of 'contributions'" refers exclusively to the king, as Plöger thinks, then the thought must be that he either exacts or accepts corrupt gifts.[157] However, Meinhold contends that someone else is bringing about the downfall of the community.[158] The ambiguous genitive (see n. 39) allows both the giver and the taker of bribes. The antithesis implies that in the exercise of restoring a community to the divine ideal by punishing the oppressor and delivering the oppressed, the king protects the poor and defenseless by a sharp eye that detects and disallows the exchange of bribes and the

154. "The flatterer's words are in the same debased currency of deceit and duplicity as hers" (Aitken, *Proverbs,* p. 136).

155. P. J. J. S. Els, *NIDOTTE,* 1:298, s.v. *'hb.*

156. *'îš* + attributive gen. (initial in v. 3a and in v. 4b).

157. Plöger, *Sprüche,* p. 343.

158. Meinhold, *Sprüche,* p. 483.

like. Since these contributions according to the antithetical parallel distort justice and according to the predicate destroy a nation, the cultic term is probably a metaphor for bribes, blackmail, and all sorts of ill-gotten money. The probable metaphor connotes that both the one who takes and/or the one who gives bribes are blasphemers; the former takes the place of God, and the latter the place of a worshiper (cf. 1 Sam. 12:3).[159] More specifically it connotes that the king rid his realm of godless men who substitute his palace for God's temple in their giving and taking "tithes" from each other. The predicates (i.e., the respective consequences) are precisely antithetical: *establishes* [lit. "causes to stand/endure"; see 12:7] *a land* (see 25:25), a metonymy for its governed citizens, versus *tears it down* (see 11:11), a strong term for a successful attack that destroys its object. A king who governs through social justice creates a nation having an internal solidarity that withstands all kinds of opposition, but a king who governs through corrupt gifts will divide his people, and his realm will eventually splinter apart. The metaphor connotes that godless men who give and take bribes are warriors within his realm who successfully attack his kingdom and bring it to its knees (cf. 16:10-15; 20:8, 26, 28; 28:16; 29:14).

5-6 These verses are a proverb pair because both refer to deceitful people by metaphors involving hunting instruments, "net" (v. 5) and "snare" (v. 6), to signify that they plunder their neighbors. Verse 5 narrows the deceiver to the seductive flatterer, and v. 6 broadens this to any kind of transgression; v. 6 clarifies that in fact they entangle themselves, while the righteous triumph over them.

5 Using the imagery of a hunter trapping a wild animal, the proverb represents the flatterer as seducing his victim into a sense of false security to plunder his wealth (see 1:11-14). The synthetic versets, constituting a single sentence, are also linked lexically by *'al* (not translated in verset A and glossed "for" in verset B), and grammatically by the ambiguous pronoun "his." Verset A presents the topic (the cause). *A man* (*geber;* see I: 81; 28:3)

159. *T^e^rûmâ* occurs 76 times in the Bible and uniquely in this proverb in a non-cultic context. Elsewhere *t^e^rûmâ* refers to contributions to build a temple, to idols (Isa. 40:20), and mostly to priests (Num. 31:29). "The word 'contribution' is . . . used of all kinds of holy gifts given to priests (Num. 5:9; *passim*), including all the grain offerings accompanying the thanksgiving peace offerings (Lev. 7:14); the wave offerings (Num. 18:11-19; e.g., the first fruits of the fresh oil, wine and grain; the firstborn of all animals, etc. . . .); the tithe to the Levites (Num. 18:24; Neh. 10:37) . . . ; the portion of booty given to the priests (Num. 31:29, 41, 52); the half-shekel for the maintenance of the tabernacle service (Exod. 30:13-15); the land for the temple, priests, and Levites in Ezekiel (Ezek. 45:1; 48:8-21); and the portions given to the prince to supply the regular cult of Ezekiel's temple (45:13-17)" (R. E. Averbeck, *NIDOTTE,* 4:335, s.v. *t^e^rûmâ*). In some texts *t^e^rûmâ* is voluntary; in others, involuntary.

is ironic. A strong man should be working and pumping wealth into the economy, not criminally taking it from others by being one *who* deceitfully *flatters* (*maḥᵃlîq*, lit. "one who causes to be smooth," eliding either "tongue" [28:23] or "words" [2:16; 7:5; cf. 5:3; 26:23, 28]) *his neighbor* (*ʿal*[160]*-rēʿēhû;* see 3:29). Verset B presents the predicate (the consequence): *is one who spreads* [13:16] *a net* [for trapping birds or wild animals; see 1:17] *for* (*ʿal*), *his feet* (or steps).[161] The antecedent of "his" is the neighbor and/or the flatterer (cf. 1:16). On first reading it seems that the neighbor's steps are in view, but on reflection the antecedent could also be the feet of the seducer (see "evil" in 1:16).[162] The next verse makes clear that while the net is intended for the neighbor, it actually snares the flatterer (cf. Job 18:7-10).

6 The antithetical parallels of the second proverb about traps juxtapose the topics (the causes) semantically, not grammatically: *in the transgression* [see 10:12] *of an evil person* (cf. 28:5) versus *the righteous person* (see I: 97). To judge from the saying's connection with v. 5 and from the linking of the transgression with "a snare," the transgression in view involves deception, implying some form of scented communication leading to the trap (cf. 12:13). The proverb also juxtaposes the respective consequences: *a snare* (see 12:13) versus *shouts for joy* (*yārûn;* see n. 44). *Rnn* "parallels verbs that indicate a loud cry, a raised voice, or expressions of a more musical nature."[163] It means "call loudly, shrilly" in 1:20; 8:3, but here it signifies loud expressions of joy, as clarified by the addition *and is glad* (see 29:2, 3).[164] The imprecise antithesis implies that the righteous escapes the snare and that in fact the snare destroys the deceiver.[165] Aitken noted that earlier sayings asserted, "The righteous man walks securely through life with unfaltering and unswerving step (10:9 . . . 3:5-8, 21-26; [4:12]) for his uprightness is a guide (11:3; 11:5; cf. 2:9; 6:22) and a guard (13:6; 17:17; 14:32 . . .) against the pitfalls and snares which lurk by the way to impede his steps and trip him up (22:5). Indeed, God himself is his protection (10:29; 18:10 . . . 2:6-8)."[166] But this proverb escalates the thought to "he shouts for joy." The righteous rejoice in their security and in making manifest the connection between crime and punishment.

160. *IBHS,* p. 217, P. 11.2.13c; *pace* Delitzsch, *Proverbs,* p. 426.

161. *HALOT,* 3:952, s.v. *paʿam.*

162. "Whoever allows himself to be flattered is no less in danger of falling than the one who flatters" (Meinhold, *Sprüche,* p. 483).

163. R. Ficker, *TLOT,* 3:1,240, s.v. *rnn.*

164. *HALOT,* 3:1,248, s.v. *rnn.*

165. "If the righteous has a reason for a double portion of joy, then the eventual attack on himself can only have failed, and the evil person may have fallen himself" (Meinhold, *Sprüche,* p. 483).

166. Aitken, *Proverbs,* p. 142.

c. Janus (29:7)

The janus proverb linking the unit's (vv. 3-15) two subunits is joined chiastically with v. 6 by the catchword "righteous" (vv. 6b, 7a) and by the paronomasia of *'îš rāʿ* ("evil person," v. 6a) and *rāšāʿ* ("wicked," v. 7b) and with 29:8-15 by the catchword *dallîm* ("poor," vv. 7a, 14b).[167] Its antithetical parallels precisely juxtapose the topics of *a righteous person* and *a wicked person* (see 28:1, 12, 16, 28; 29:2) and imprecisely predicate one of their essential differences. The former *knows* (i.e., personally involves himself in; see 3:6; 12:10; 27:23) binding *court decisions* (*dîn;* lit. "judgment"; see 22:8 — which may have been chosen instead of its synonym *špṭ* for its assonance with *yābîn*) *for the* powerless *poor* (*dallîm;* see 10:15). The guilty before God in their disregard of anyone's interests but their own *does not understand* (*lō'-yābîn;* see 2:5) *knowing* (i.e., court decisions that affect the economically disadvantaged and oppressed; see 28:5; cf. Luke 18:1-5; Acts 24:26, 27). His ignorance and lack of understanding are not intellectual defects but expressions of his unawareness and insensitivity to the plight of the oppressed and his lack of concern for the poor. The righteous and wicked differ in their religious and ethical affections (4:18-19; 10:32; 12:10; 13:5; 21:10; 23:35; 28:22; 29:10, 27; cf. Gen. 4:8). The former involve themselves in matters that affect the fate and future of the powerless because they recognize the preciousness of life, that all human beings are created in the image of God (22:2) and that God shows compassion to the poor (14:21; 24:12). With them, as with their LORD, it is a matter of justice and mercy, not of a person's economic status. This kind of concern involves an investment of time, patient research, and willingness to risk himself in confronting injustice (cf. Job 29:12-17).

d. Peace through Righteousness (29:8-15)

The catchwords "wise people"/"wisdom" (*ḥᵃkāmîm/ḥokmâ,* vv. 8-9, 15) form an *inclusio* around the second subunit, which pertains to restoring peace and security through righteous courts. Its two smaller subunits of equal length, vv. 8-11 and 12-15, consist of three verses plus a fourth (vv. 8-10 + 11; vv. 12-14 + 15).

8-11 Keeping in mind the royal and court context, vv. 8-10 are linked syntactically,[168] probably with the stitching evaluation pattern of vice (-) and virtue (+): -/+, +/-, -/+. They represent three morally inferior kinds of people: mockers who set a whole community at loggerheads with each other (v. 8); the fool (*'ᵉwîl*), who refuses to listen to reason (v. 9), escalated to murderers who

167. Verset A remarkably alliterates /d/: *yōdēaʿ ṣaddîq dîn dallîm.*

168. Initial *'îš* plus an attributive gen. (vv. 8, 10) or attributive adjective (v. 9) plus a verb plus an object.

seek to kill upright people (v. 10). Verse 11, breaking the syntax and stitching pattern of vv. 8-10, returns to the fool *(k^esîl)*. Nevertheless, it is connected to vv. 8-10 by the *inclusio,* the "wise," in subduing anger and restoring calm (vv. 8 and 11). Synonyms for "anger," a symptom of lacking self-control (see 16:32; 25:28), occur in vv. 8, 9, and 11: "anger" (*'āp;* v. 8), "rage" (*rāgaz;* v. 9; and *rûah,* v. 11). Verse 11 is a necessary corrective to v. 9. In v. 9 the fool is still storming and raging; in v. 12 the wise man quiets him and has the final word. With the exception of the first verb *yāpîḥû,* all the verbs in this section have a sibilant: */š/* in vv. 8b, 9a, 10b, 11b; */ś/* in vv. 9b, 10a; */ṣ/* in v. 11a; and */z/* in v. 9b. A perusal of vv. 8-15 shows that the consonant */š/* predominates. For example, counting words joined by proclisis as one, it occurs with every word in v. 12 and with five of the seven words in v. 13.

8-9 These verses, moving from the group to the individual, are a proverb pair linked lexically by the adjective "wise people/person" and by its antonyms, "mockers" and "fool." They are also connected semantically. In both, the wise are characterized by calmness and the mocker and fool by giving vent to baser passions, such as anger and ridicule. Verse 9 also explicates v. 8. One of the ways the wise can turn back anger (v. 8b) is by confronting the fool in litigation.

8 The antithetical parallels of the subunit's initial proverb juxtapose the topics (the cause): intractable, nonconformist *mockers* (see I: 114) versus educative *wise people* (*ḥ^akāmîm;* see I: 94) They also juxtapose the respective predicates (the consequences). The mockers *incite . . . to anger* (lit. "cause . . . to pour forth anger"), but that gloss is uncertain.[169] The object of the causing is the *city* (see 10:15), and the object of the root is "anger," supplied from verset B. Presumably they pour forth their anger against the mockers and/or each other (13:10; 22:10). The mockers bring a community's inner resentment against social injustices (e.g., cheating, favoritism, and nepotism) to a boiling point by laughing at the moral order, distorting the truth, and arousing people's baser passions through heated rhetoric (cf. 6:13-14;

169. If we exclude from consideration the six occurrences of *yāpîaḥ* (6:19; 12:17; 14:5, 25; 19:5, 9) and the one of *yāpēaḥ* in Hab. 2:3 because they are derived from the root *ypḥ* meaning "witness," as now known from Ugaritic (see 6:19), the verb *pwḥ* occurs seven times: twice in the *Qal* and five times in the *Hiphil.* Its potential Arabic cognates are *fwh* ("pour forth," used for a pot boiling, a wound bleeding, a flower diffusing its odor, and breaking wind") and *fwh* ("to blow"). The latter is clearly in view in its three uses in Song: in the *Qal* the lovers speak of the day "blowing" (2:17 [= 4:6]), and in the *Hiphil* the bride calls the wind to "blow on my garden" (4:16). *Pûaḥ* occurs as a two-place *Hiphil* in Ezek. 21:31(36) and probably in Pss. 10:5 and 12:6. These texts speak of the enemy/the wicked "pouring forth (something [words/anger/ridicule]) against *(b^e* or *'al)* someone." But since this proverb lacks a preposition, it is best to regard *yāpîḥû* as a three-place *Hiphil* (*IBHS,* pp. 441-42, P. 27.3b).

26:20-21; Isa. 28:14; Sir. 28:8-14). By contrast, the wise *turn back* [see 1:23] *anger* (see 15:1) by addressing the issues of the human heart, not by proposing superficial measures that cover over the internal tensions. They call on the community to repent of wrongdoing (28:13), to confront its difficulties while trusting the sovereignty and goodness of God (16:1-3), to seek the well-being of others, not of self (see 29:7), to speak with both calm reason for truth and with grace (12:18; cf. Isa. 28:17), and to act kindly and charitably toward each other (see 11:24-26; passim; cf. Matt. 5:3-10; Jas. 3:17).

9 This synthetic proverb contrasts the behavior of the wise and the fool in court. *A wise person* [see 16:14] *confronts . . . in court* (see 29:14), a gloss of the ambiguous *Niphal* of *špṭ,* "an action that restores the order of a disturbed (legal) community."[170] The wise submits his case to arbitration against (*a fool, 'îš 'ᵉwîl;* see I: 112), confident that he can back up his claim with good evidence and that in the end (cf. v. 11) the fool will be found guilty and sentenced, even though for a time the courts may be corrupt (cf. v. 12). By contrast, the fool flies off the handle and tries to laugh the case out of court. If the proverb had in mind a less-than-real condition, one would have expected a conditional particle, not *then (wᵉ).*[171] The Targum and Vulgate seem to have read the "wise person" as the antecedent of the subject of *rages (rāgaz),* but raging and laughing in court are not appropriate for a wise person affirming his right. Moreover, the wise values and is marked by calmness (Eccl. 4:6; 9:17). *Rāgaz* basically means "to tremble/shake/quake physically." Here "to shake against someone or something is to rebel or rage against [the wise person]."[172] Conjunctive *and* forms the compound predi-

170. G. Liedke, *TLOT,* 3:1,393, s.v. *špṭ*. The *Niphal* of *špṭ* occurs 17 times. When used absolutely or with instrumental *beth,* it means "to be put on trial/to submit to judgment" (see *HALOT,* 4:1,501, s.v. *špṭ*), expecting the verdict "guilty" (Pss. 9:20; 37:33; 109:7; Isa 59:4). It has this same sense, but reciprocal, with *yāḥad* in Isa. 43:26. With *'et,* either the sign of a direct object or a preposition, and with the prepositions *lamed* and *'im* and God as subject, always in prophetic literature, it means "to litigate successfully," "to pass sentence/judgment on someone" (see Isa. 66:16, Jer. 2:35; Ezek. 17:20; 20:35, 36[2x]; 38:22; Joel 4:2). It has this sense also with Jehu as subject and the preposition *'im* in 2 Chr. 22:8 and with *'et* in 1 Sam. 12:7. In 1 Sam. 12:7 the form is cohortative with the preposition *'et;* it probably does not mean, "I will pass sentence against you," but "Let me submit my case against you to judgment." Since Samuel is confident that he will plead his case successfully, the NIV glosses, "I will confront you." That meaning is consistent with its use elsewhere and in this context.

171. *Waw* could have been glossed "but" if the wise person's action of taking his dispute to court were being contrasted with the fool's ranting and raging. However, prefixed to the suffixed conjugation, it more probably functions as an apodosis *waw,* signifying that when the wise takes the matter to court, the fool behaves irrationally (see 9:12; 19:25; *IBHS,* pp. 523-25, P. 32.1.3; pp. 531-32, P. 32.2.3c; pp. 523-25, P. 32.1.3; pp. 531-32, P. 32.2.3c).

172. M. V. Van Pelt and W. C. Kaiser Jr., *NIDOTTE,* 3:1,045, s.v. *rgz*.

cate. Semantic pertinence demands understanding "the fool" as its subject. Presumably the subject of *scoffs* (lit. "to laugh"; see 10:23) is still the fool. "Laughter may have a negative, hostile connotation of derision and ridicule . . . (e.g., 2 Chron. 30:10; Pss. 2:4; 59:8[9]; Prov. 1:26; Jer. 20:7)."[173] *And* adds the third consequential predicate. *There is no* [see 29:1] *calm (nāḥat),* which, apart from the disputed passages in Job 17:16; 36:16, means "quiet/calm, tranquil" (cf. Eccl. 9:17).[174] The verb *nûaḥ* basically means "to land on," from which is derived the idea "to cease activity."[175] The proverb instructs the son to tolerate the fool's irrational response should he become involved in litigation with him.

10 This verse escalates the inferior type of person from the fool to the murderer. By sandwiching it between proverbs pertaining to bringing the raging fool to court and sentencing him, the context suggests that the murderer will be sentenced by the wise through due process of law. Its synthetic parallels escalate the internal revulsion that bloodthirsty people, who disregard the sanctity of human life, feel toward fine, godly people (verset A), to their attempts to murder every person whose life conforms to the established moral order (verset B; cf. 1:10-14; 11:9, 30; 13:2; 16:29; 21:10; 29:27; cf. 1 K. 22:8; Matt. 5:11-12; 27:22-23; John 7:7; Acts 7:52; Heb. 11:36-37; 1 John 3:12-13; Rev. 17:6). *Bloodthirsty people* [see 1:11] *hate* [see 1:22] *the person of integrity* (*tām;* see I: 99). Here it may be a broken hendiadys, "blameless and upright" (i.e., totally upright in his relationship to God and people; cf. Job 1:1; 2:3). *And* combines the clauses into a compound sentence; "bloodthirsty people" is the subject of both clauses. *As for the upright* (see I: 98) must be taken as a nominative absolute with the resumptive pronoun "his" (i.e., the upright's) in connection with the object, "life."[176] *They* [i.e., the bloodthirsty] *seek* (*y^ebaqšû;* see 2:4) *to kill each of them* (*napšô;* see I: 90). *Bqš* occurs as the object of *nepeš* 30 times and "refers primarily to malicious intent"[177] to kill someone.[178] The parallel "bloodthirsty people" validates this meaning. The established meaning of the idiom disallows "the upright" to be the subject. Had the proverb intended that the upright avenges innocent blood by killing the bloodthirsty, it would not have used an idiom connoting maliciousness. Moreover, the consistent use of the idiom disallows investing it with a favorable sense such as "the upright see to their interests" (REB) and "upright men are careful of their life."[179]

173. L. C. Allen, *NIDOTTE,* 3.1:229, s.v. *śḥq.*
174. *HALOT,* 2:692, II *nāḥat.*
175. J. Oswalt, *NIDOTTE,* 3:56-58, s.v. *nûaḥ.*
176. *IBHS,* pp. 76-77, P. 4.7c, nos. 2, 3.
177. G. Gerleman, *TLOT,* 1:252, s.v. *bqš.*
178. Chitra Chhetri, *NIDOTTE,* 1:722), s.v. *bqš.*
179. McKane, *Proverbs,* p. 637.

11 The proverb returns to the wise versus the raging fool but advances beyond v. 9 to the final scene of their conflict.[180] Its chiastic parallels juxtapose the fool and the wise in their inner core. In their outer frame they contrast the former's giving full vent to his rage (cf. 12:16, 23; 14:17, 29; 16:32; 25:28) and the wise person's competence to finally still it (cf. 12:8; 15:1, 18; 26:4-5; 29:9). *A fool* (*k^esîl;* see I: 109) *gives full* [lit. "all of"] *vent* [lit. "brings forth"; see 10:18] *to his anger* (*rûḥô;* lit. "his wind"; see I: 92), investing *rûaḥ* (cf. Ps. 135:7; Jer. 10:13) with its derived meaning of dynamic vitality, more specifically a metonymy for "anger."[181] The dynamic psychic energy finds its expression in words. *But* [see 29:10] *a wise person* (see I: 94) has the last word, not the ranting and raging fool. *Finally* is an uncertain gloss of the otherwise unattested *b^e'āḥôr* (lit. "in the end"; cf. Isa. 42:23).[182] *Stills it (y^ešabḥennâ)* glosses II *šbḥ,* a verb that occurs elsewhere only in connection with the LORD's capacity *to still* the stormy sea (Pss. 65:7[8]; 89:9[10]). That sense also fits here, for the wise still the fool's *rûaḥ* "rage/wind." Meinhold glosses *besaenftigt ihn* ("appeases it").[183] The antecedent of the pronominal suffix is "his anger" (i.e., "the fool's temper"). Grammatically it could refer to the wise person's own temper, but then "in the end" is not semantically pertinent. Moreover, the wise person has a cool spirit at all times and never rages within (17:27).[184] By sound arguments in litigation delivered in a cool spirit with a gentle tongue and by caning (26:3-5; 29:15), the wise finally still the raging of the fool and its detrimental affects on the community. However, one must not suppose the fool's charac-

180. "If the context is still that of v. 9, one can assume he also restores order to the courtroom and brings a case to its proper conclusion" (Garrett, *Proverbs,* p. 230).

181. *HALOT* (3:1,199, s.v. *rûaḥ*) restricts the meaning to "mind," but BDB (p. 925, *rûaḥ*) glosses it as spirit/temper/disposition and more specifically as anger. R. Albertz and C. Westermann *(TLOT,* 3:1,210, s.v. *rûaḥ)* agree: "The original dynamic character of *rûaḥ* is also evident here: directly, *rûaḥ* indicates only impulsive, life-strengthening psychic forces such as anger, rage (Judg. 8:3; Prov. 29:11; Eccl. 10:4; Isa. 25:4; Ezek. 3:14; of God, Zech. 6:8)."

182. *HALOT,* 1:31, s.v. *'āḥôr.* BDB (p. 30, s.v. *'āḥôr*) glosses it by "backward," citing Delitzsch "stilleth it [i.e., the wise man's own anger] when it would break out," but Toy (*Proverbs,* p. 510) thinks that this meaning is improbable. Delitzsch's thought is expressed by the idiom "to turn back" (see v. 8; Lam. 2:3); G. Boström (*Paronomasi i den äldre hebreiska Maschallitteraturen* [LUÅ, N.F., Avd. I, Bd. 23, Nr. 8; Lund, 1928], p. 114) actually emends the text to *y^ešîbennâ.* Moreover, Delitzsch does not adequately answer Hitzig's objection that for this meaning the form should be *b^eqirbô,* not *b^e'âḥôr.*

183. Meinhold, *Sprüche,* p. 481.

184. "The idea of reading the discontent of the wise man himself into the suffix ([stilled] "it") is quite out of the question, since then the wise man would have yielded to anger and not have disciplined himself and tried only afterwards to restrict it" (Meinhold, *Sprüche,* p. 486).

ter, which by definition is intractable, has been changed for the better (26:11).

12-15 In the second partial subunit royal proverbs again come to the fore, forming an *inclusio* with v. 4. More specifically, it gives more specific direction about wise procedures in court. Verses 12 and 14 are connected both by the juxtaposition of a negative image of a ruler (i.e., one who listens to deceptive words) and the positive image of a king (i.e., who establishes justice through reliable words) and by their similar syntax.[185] At the center of vv. 12-14 stands a saying pertaining to the LORD, who grants life to all (v. 13). Behind the royal court stands the LORD (cf. 28:25). Verses 13-14 are linked by the synonyms "poor/destitute" *(rāš)* and "poor/powerless" *(dallîm).* Verse 15, which by the mention of "wisdom" helps form an *inclusio* around vv. 3-6 and 8-15, is connected weakly with v. 14 by the consonantal sequence of *šôpēṭ* ("judges," v. 14) and *šēbeṭ* ("rod," v. 15). It may be connected with v. 13 by the same syntax in verset A (a compound subject + verb). Verse 15, by its connection with v. 17 through the catchword "correction" *(tôkaḥat)* and its synonym "discipline" *(ysr),* after the framing proverb (v. 16), also forms a transition to the fourth unit.

12 Verset A presents the topic (i.e., the cause).[186] *As for a ruler* (*mōšēl;* see 6:7; 29:2, 26) *who pays attention to* [see 1:24; 17:4] *deceptive words* (cf. 6:17) refers to any ruler who through indifference to truth and/or cynicism about God and humanity acts on deceptive testimony to inflict injury on the poor and weak. Verset B presents the comment (i.e., the consequence). *All* probably has its qualitative, not quantitative, sense, for history proves there are exceptions.[187] *His attendants* glosses the *Piel* participle of *šrt,* which "basically means to minister to or wait on another, human or divine"[188] and refers to one of lower rank serving a superior. In royal contexts, *šrt* has reference to personal attendants (2 Sam. 13:17-18; 1 K. 1:4; 10:5; Esth. 1:10) who may also function as political or military officials (1 Chr. 27:1; 28:1; 2 Chr. 17:19). *Become* — a free gloss of the nominal clause — *wicked* (see I: 109) means that all who assist him in governing become guilty before God of antisocial behavior. *Qualis rex, talis grex* ("like king, like people"; cf. Sir. 10:2a). To gain his attention and favor, they inflict injury on each other and others. This is the way to advance in a crumbling kingdom (29:4).

185. A nominative absolute in verset A is connected by a resumptive pronoun with verset B.

186. Note the striking consonance of /m/ and /s/: *mōšēl maqšîb ʿal-dᵉbar-šāqer kol-mᵉšārᵉtāyw rᵉšāʿîm.*

187. For example, Obadiah in the court of Ahab (1 K. 18:3), Ebed-melech in the service of Zedekiah (Jer. 38:7-13), and Daniel in Nebuchadnezzar's court (Dan. 2:48, 49; cf. Dan. 6:1-9).

188. T. E. Fretheim, *NIDOTTE,* 4:256, s.v. *šrt.*

13 The theological proverb sandwiched between the royal sayings (cf. 14:27-28; 16:1-9, 10-15; 25:1-2) is a variant of 22:2, but instead of "rich and poor" it has "poor and oppressor" "to adapt the proverb more closely to the immediate context."[189] Verset A of its synthetic parallels states the *de facto* social unequalities of the oppressed and their oppressors on earth, but verse B asserts their *de jure* social equality in heaven. *A poor person* (*rāš;* see 13:8) *and an oppressive person (ʾîš tᵉkākîm) meet* (see 22:2). On the limited basis of the four occurrences of *tōk* (Pss. 10:7; 55:11[12]; 72:14), I. Swart draws the conclusion that it "can denote the tyrannic and economic exploitation of the socially weak."[190] Verset B presents as their common bond, *the* LORD (see I: 67), who alone has light at his disposal, *is the one who gives light (mēʾîr) to eyes of (ʿênê) both* (see 17:15) In the *Qal ʾûr* means "to be[come] light" (see 4:18), and in the *Hiphil* "to give light" (i.e., to shine; cf. Gen. 1:15-17), "to light up" (i.e., to illuminate; cf. Ps. 77:18[19]), and with *ʿênayim* as object it probably means to illuminate a person within (i.e., to give sight). Giving light (i.e., sight) to the eyes is a metonymy of "to give life" in contrast to death (see Ezra 9:8; Ps. 13:3[4]). In these two passages and here it refers to physical life, but in Ps. 19:8(9) it refers to moral and spiritual illumination from God's word. The positive figure denotes vitality and joy in contrast to death and defeat. Both are indebted to the LORD for being physically lit up within with the joy and delight of seeing the LORD's good creation. As he lit up the darkness at the creation, he gives light in place of darkness to people. The proverb aims to teach both ends of the social extremes: to respect the dignity of others as God's creatures and not to legitimatize oppression (see 1:19; 16:5; 29:6, passim). Though in the end the oppressor will get his just desert, before then both the oppressed and the oppressor are the beneficiaries of God's common grace, a grace that transcends a simple calculus of rewarding good and punishing evil (Matt. 5:44-45).[191] The oppressor should abandon oppressing the poor but value and share with him, recognizing that he himself enjoys life only by God's forbearance (see 14:31). A poor person should not despise or envy his oppressors but recognize that even they are recipients of God's uncommonly common grace and their lives are in God's hands.[192]

14 This verse protects v. 13 against the misinterpretation that since God gives life to the oppressor, a king, who is supposed to represent God's

189. Whybray, *Proverbs,* p. 401.

190. I. Swart, *NIDOTTE,* 4:291, s.v. *tōk.*

191. The LXX brings the proverb closer to a simple theodicy by rendering, "The LORD is the overseer *(episkopēn)* of both."

192. "Both are conditioned by Him, stand under His control, and have to give to Him an account" (Delitzsch, *Proverbs,* p. 450).

rule on earth (see 16:10-15; 24:21-22), may be indifferent to the oppression of the powerless. Quite the contrary. This positive image of a ruler stands juxtaposed to the negative one in v. 12. Its verset A presents the topic (the cause). *As for a king* (*melek;* see 29:4, 12) *who judges* [see 1:3; 29:9] *the poor* (*dallîm;* see 10:15; 29:7) *through truth* (*be'ᵉmet;* see 11:18) refers to a king who reestablishes the disturbed harmony of his realm by punishing the oppressive rich and delivering the powerless and oppressed poor through reliable witnesses and reliable data. In contrast to the ruler who gives heed to deceptive testimony (29:12), he carefully investigates the character of the witnesses to see whether they are firsthand and credible witnesses to the data (see 16:13; 22:11).[193] Verset B presents the comment (the consequences). *His throne is established* [see 16:12; 25:5] *forever* (*lāʿad;* see 12:19). *ʿad* also refers to the perpetuity of God (Ps. 111:3; Isa. 57:15; Mic. 7:18), notably his throne (Exod. 15:18; Pss. 10:16; 45:6[7]). The symbol of the king's authoritative rule will endure into a future whose end cannot be envisioned (cf. 20:28; 25:5; 29:4).

15 The paronomasia of *špṭ* ("who judges," v. 14) and *šbṭ* ("rod," v. 15) signals the shift from the ethos of the state to the home. This rearing proverb and the *inclusio* of "father" and "mother" draw the unit 29:3-15 to a conclusion (see above, p. 430). Its antithetical parallels juxtapose the topics (the causes). *A rod* (*šēbeṭ),* the symbol of chastisement and discipline (see 10:13), *and reproof* (*wᵉtôkaḥat;* see 1:23) could be viewed as a hendiadys meaning "a rod of correction" (so NIV), but to judge from 26:3-5 they are better regarded as compounds of severe discipline, namely, physical punishment and a reasoned, verbal reprimand. Over against these stands *an undisciplined (mᵉšullāḥ) youth* (see 1:4).[194] The antithetical parallels are imprecise, implying that the physical caning and verbal reprimand are the severe means necessary for disciplining a youth (cf. 13:24; 19:18; 20:30; 22:6, 15; 23:14). The parallels also juxtapose the respective predicates (the consequences): *give* [see 1:4] *wisdom* (see I: 76) — "to the youth" is gapped — versus *brings . . . shame* [see 10:5] *to his mother.* No other reason should be speculated on for this unique reference to the mother than that it forms an *inclusio* with v. 3. These imprecise parallels imply that wisdom protects the mother from blush-

193. "The test of a man in power, and his hidden strength, is the extent to which he keeps faith with those who can put least pressure on him" (Kidner, *Proverbs,* p. 175).

194. A rare meaning of *šālaḥ* in Qal is "to release" (cf. Gen. 42:4; 43:8). Most often the *Piel* exhibits a meaning corresponding to this rare meaning. M. Delcor and E. Jenni gloss it "to send forth, conduct forth, release, set free, let flee, permit free movement, dismiss, let move." The *Piel* is used of animals pasturing at liberty (Job 39:5) and the *Pual* of an abandoned pasture. Plöger (*Sprüche,* p. 346) explains this *Pual* participle: "a child lacking rearing, one who simply has been allowed to run free."

ing embarrassment, and a child whose parents let him run wild does not learn to conform to the divinely established moral order.

5. Rearing and One's Relationship with God (29:16-27)

Within the single framing proverbs, 29:16 and 27, the fifth unit in Collection IIID consists of a decalogue of sayings comprised of two equal halves, vv. 17-21 and 22-26. The first half is stitched together through a leapfrog pattern of catchwords and subjects, alternating between the topics of household and public in its aim to instruct the son on the necessity of discipline both in his household and in the nation. Actually this pattern began already in v. 15, linking the fourth and fifth units. Van Leeuwen reflects on the connection between family and society: "In the ancient world, relations in marriage and family, between masters and servants, and in the body politic were generally conceived as parallel hierarchical structures, a fact sill evident in the so-called domestic codes of the New Testament (Rom. 13:1-7; Titus 2:1-2, 8; 1 Pet. 3:13-22)."[195] The second half warns the son against reprobates: the angry (v. 22), the proud (v. 23), and the accomplice of a thief (v. 24). A concluding proverb pair instructs him to trust the LORD (vv. 25-26). In so doing it also implicitly warns him against the cowardly (v. 25a) and those who seek royal favors (v. 26b). Each subunit closes with a proverb whose versets are held together by the consonance of *mem* (see vv. 21 and 26). The whole unit is again drawn to a conclusion by sayings about the LORD, calling for fear of/ trust in the him (vv. 25-26; cf. 28:25; 29:13).

a. Introductory Framing Proverb (29:16)

This single framing proverb separates the last two units of chs. 28–29. It juxtaposes the abounding of transgressions when the wicked abound/thrive (verset A) with the pious and ethical righteous gazing on the sudden overthrow of the wicked (verset B). Verset A continues the same theme as 28:12, 28; 29:2. *When the wicked thrive* [cf. 29:2], *transgression* [see 29:6] *abounds* (*yirbeh;* see 28:28b). But verset B advances beyond them. *But* [see 29:2, 15] *the righteous* [see 29:2, 6, 7] *will gaze on* (i.e., "look at or into something with interest," more specifically "with joy and pleasure"; cf. Ps. 22:17[18]).[196] *Their* [i.e., the wicked's] *downfall* may be a metonymy for what is felled ("a carcass [of a lion]" [Judg. 14:8] and "a felled [tree trunk]" [Ezek. 31:13]) or, more probably, for the verbal action "sudden fall, downfall" (Ezek. 26:15, 18; 27:27; 31:16; 32:10). "This saying carries the theme

195. Van Leeuwen, *Proverbs,* pp. 243-44.
196. BDB, p. 908, s.v., *rā'â.*

further than its companions by its closing assurance. Cf. Habakkuk 2:2-4, 12-14."[197] Verset B logically and chronologically follows verset A. The proverb implies that for a while the impious and unethical and their transgressions abound, but in the end the righteous will survive and see God's moral order worked out (cf. 10:2-3, 24, 28; cf. also Gen. 7:23; 19:28; Exod. 14:30; Pss. 54:7[9]; 112:8; Mic. 7:10; Rev. 11:15). This is not due to some inexorable destiny but to the LORD's intervention (see I: 73). The proverb encourages the son to live by faith until then. Until his judgment falls, however, the proverb also instructs the son to realize that when the wicked increase in numbers and in power, implying the subjugation of the righteous, transgressions against God's moral order will also increase in quantity and quality (cf. Luke 22:53). Implicitly, the wise/righteous must employ all the wisdom of this collection (e.g., 29:5, 12, and 14) to prevent this fermenting corruption of society.

b. Necessity of Discipline (29:17-21)

A rare admonition directly addressed to the son introduces the theme of this unit (v. 17). In addition to the leapfrog pattern of topics, the unit is stitched together by an alternating tandem series of catchwords in every other verset: A: *ysr* "discipline" (vv. 17, 19), *'bd* "slave" (vv. 19, 21), *ḥzḥ* "revelation"/ "see" (vv. 20, 22). Verses 18a and 19b are linked by negative *'ên,* and vv. 19a and 20a by *dbrym* "words."

17 Once again a rearing proverb introduces the unit (cf. 28:7; 29:3), but it escalates the implicit admonitions of 28:2; 29:3 to an explicit imperative and completes the family circle begun in the frame of the fourth unit of "father" (29:3), "mother" (29:15), and now "son" (29:17). It is connected with v. 15 by "discipline" (*ysr;* see 1:2, a synonym of "to reprove/correct" [*ykḥ;* cf. 6:23]) and by the verb *yittēn* "he will give [wisdom/delight]." If not merely a rhetorical variation, the admonition *discipline your son* (see 19:18) points to the home as the life setting for the dissemination of Collection D (see I: 62). The son is mentioned 56 times in Proverbs, with the address "my son" in Collections I (chs. 1–9) and III (22:17–24:22), but in Collections II (10:1–22:16) and V (chs. 25–29) it occurs otherwise only in 19:27 and 27:11. This implicitly conditional clause presents the cause (Aa), and the compound clauses present the consequences (versets Ab).[198] *So that* [see n. 59] *he will give you rest* (*wînîḥekā;* see 29:9) signifies securing the delightful state of being at rest (i.e., undisturbed and quiet) and being free from physical distress and from

197. Kidner, *Proverbs,* p. 175.

198. H. J. Posel, "The Form and Function of the Motive Clause in Proverbs 10–29" (Ph.D. diss., University of Iowa, 1976), p. 81.

emotional anxiety and turmoil (cf. Job 3:26; Ps. 116:7; Isa. 14:3, 7; 63:14).[199] "No admonition in Proverbs exists without any motivation, although some might not be verbally explicit."[200] Verset B underscores and escalates verset Ab. *And (w^e)* introduces the second purpose/result clause. *He will give* [see v. 15] *delight (ma'ᵃdannîm) to you (l^enapšekā;* lit. "to your throat/appetite"; see I: 90, an appropriate noun with *ma'ᵃdannîm). Ma'ᵃdannîm* occurs only three times; in its other two occurrences it refers to delightful food (Gen. 49:20; Lam. 4:5). In this proverb it is probably also a metonymy for emotional luxuries such as peace (29:17), joy (29:2, 12), and honor (29:15) in addition to the rest that accompanies a son's providing the physical necessities of needy, aging parents.[201] Paradoxically, the disciplinarian's rod brings the parents joy and peace (29:17), and its absence, shame and turmoil (29:15). The motivation in all three rearing proverbs is the parents' fulfillment; only in v. 15a is the child's fulfillment in view.

18 This verse, another rearing proverb, turns for a moment from the family and the son to the community's need of wisdom (see 29:3 and 4). J. G. Janzen observes, "In its movement the bi-colon first characterizes the (desperate) situation of a people for whom there is no means to true wisdom [cf. 1 Sam. 3:1; Isa. 8:16; Lam. 2:9; Hos. 4:6; Amos 8:11, 12; Rom. 10:13-17], then identifies the critical issue for the members of a people who possess such a means."[202] Its antithetical parallels imprecisely juxtapose semantically the topics (the causes), the famine of the sage's word of revelation with the one who keeps his teaching (see 2:6). The meaning of *without (b^e'ên;* see 5:23) *revelation (ḥāzôn)* is disputed. *Ḥāzôn* has been rendered "vision" (KJV), "authority" (REB),[203] "prophecy" (Vulg., NRSV), and many other things. The KJV, Vulgate, and NRSV probably based their renditions on the

199. *HALOT* (2:679, s.v. *nûaḥ*) gives three meanings of the *Hiphil* A form of *nûaḥ:* (1) "to cause to rest" (i.e., "to sink" [Ezek. 37:1], (2) "to secure a repose, rest" (Exod. 33:14), and (3) "to pacify and satisfy" (Prov. 29:17; Ezek. 5:13; 16:42; 21:17[22]; 24:13; Zech. 6:8, "to make glad"). This third meaning, however, is uncertain. In the Ezekiel passages the object is "anger/wrath" and the verb means "to subside." In Zech. 6:8 the object is Spirit and the verb means "secure a repose, rest."

200. P. J. Nel, *The Structure and Ethos of the Wisdom Admonitions in Proverbs* (Berlin and New York: Walter de Gruyter, 1982), p. 64.

201. Ancient Near Eastern law mandated that children care for aging parents (J. Greenfield, "*Adi balṭu* — Care for the Elderly and Its Rewards," *AfO* 19 (1982) 309-16.

202. Janzen, "The Root *pr'*," p. 397.

203. The REB emends to *hazzâ,* adopting the proposal of G. R. Driver ("Misreadings in the Old Testament," *WO* 1 [1948] 235), who takes *ḥāzôn* as a *nomen agentis* (cognate with Akk. *ḫazannu,* "magistrate, mayor," and with Aram. *ḥazzan,* "superintendent, supervisor"). However, there is no need to read cognate Semitic languages and not the Hebrew word and its derivatives that occurs 175 times, according to D. Vetter (*TLOT,* 1:400, s.v. *ḥzh*).

noun's consistent association with the prophet who "sees in a vision or hears in an audition" (e.g., Hos. 12:10[11]). Jackie A. Naudé draws the conclusion with most commentators, but not Meinhold,[204] that *ḥāzôn* always refers to "an event through which the Lord spoke to a prophet."[205] But once again a prophetic term seems to take on a different nuance in wisdom literature (cf. *qesem* in 16:10 and *maśśā'* in 30:1; 31:1). Janzen rightly argues, "The use of the verb *ḥāzâ* in xxiv 30-33 to indicate the acquisition of *mûsār* ["instruction"] by observation of social behavior suggests that *ḥāzôn* too is at home in proverbial circles." He adds, "The conviction in Prov. xxix 18a semantically and syntactically parallels that in Prov. xi 14a, 'Where there is no guidance *(taḥbulôt),* a people falls.' There can be no doubt that *taḥbulôt* refers to the guiding power of wisdom received from God (cp. Prov. i 1-7), and as such is generically synonymous with *tôrâ* ("teaching," i 8). Anyone capable of holding the conviction expressed in xi 14a is capable of holding that 'where there is no vision the people fall into anarchy.'"[206] In sum, *ḥāzôn* refers here to the sage's inspired revelation of wisdom (see I: 78). Its imprecise parallel *but as for the one who carefully obeys* (*šōmēr;* see 2:8) *the teaching* (*tôrâ;* see 1:8), which must be regarded in wisdom literature as "a phenomenon independent of priestly and prophetic *tôrâ*,"[207] implies that the "hokmatic" teaching is inspired and that where it is present the critical issue is whether the individuals of the society opt carefully to obey the revelation. The parallels also juxtapose the consequences of a social order giving way to disorder versus an individual's existence becoming worthy of being pronounced blessed. *The people* [see 11:14] *fall into anarchy (yippāra').* This unique *Niphal* of *pr'* (see 1:25; 4:15) has been rendered *defecerit* "fails" (Vulg.), "perish" (KJV), and "cast-off restraint" or its equivalents (REB, NJPS, NIV, NRSV, etc.). The glosses "fail" and "perish" lack lexical authority, and Janzen argues, "The translation 'cast off restraint' is problematic, implying a contrast between keeping *tôrâ* and casting off restraint, for where there is no *ḥāzôn* there is no order or restraint to cast off or ignore." Instead, he argues, 'The *Niphal* verb should be translated, '. . . fall into anarchy,' the point being similar to Judg. xvii 6, xx 25, 'In those days there was no king in Israel, every man did what was right in his own eyes.'"[208] *HALOT,* drawing a similar conclusion, translates "run wild."[209] A nation left to its own devices can run wild just as an individual (see 29:15b). Its imprecise parallel *blessed is he* (see 3:13; 14:21)

204. Meinhold, *Sprüche,* p. 489.
205. J. A. Naudé, *NIDOTTE,* 2:59, s.v. *ḥzh.*
206. Janzen, "The Root *pr',*" p. 396, n. 2.
207. G. Liedke/C. Petersen, *TLOT,* 3:1,416, s.v. *tôrâ.*
208. Janzen, "The Root *pr',*" pp. 396-97.
209. *HALOT,* 3:970, s.v. *pr'.*

implies "People are only truly happy when they earnestly and willingly subordinate themselves to the word of God which they possess and have the opportunity of hearing."[210]

19 The catchword *ysr* returns the theme of rearing back to the household (see v. 17), escalating that theme to the manner of effective rearing and expanding it to include the foolish slave who needs discipline as much as a foolish son. By responding to proper discipline a slave can become wise and displace a disgraceful son (17:2). A slave who flouts the moral order will not be conformed to it by mere words. *A slave* [see 12:9] *is not disciplined* (*lō'-yiwwāser,* i.e., is made admonished/reprimanded; see 19:18),[211] presumably by his "lord" *('ādôn),* though normally the agent of *ysr* is God, the sage, or the parent. Chastisement aims to conform the personal object to the divinely established order. *By words* (*bidᵉbārîm;* cf. 1:6; 15:1; 18:4; 25:11) with *ysr* is a synonym of instructions; in 13:13 it is a parallel of "command" *(miṣwâ).* Implicitly the slave in view is guilty of having violated the moral order. Folly is bound up in the slave's depraved heart as surely as in a youth's (22:15). Words are insufficient to drive his folly from him (13:13). Verset B underscores the point. Concessive *although* (see 6:35) better glosses *kî* than "if/when," for that notion diffuses the meaning by introducing the thought that words may be inadequate because they are not understood. But emphatic "surely" is another possible gloss. *He understands* (see 1:2) entails that the slave has an insight into what is right. "Nevertheless" *(wᵉ), there is no ('ên;* see 29:18) right and proper *response* (*maʿᵃneh;* see 16:1), no repentance and renunciation of his wrongdoing (see 28:13; cf. Isa. 66:3b-4). Implicitly, as with the child, the foolish slave needs a caning to free him from the slavery of his rebellious heart.[212] The master's authority must be maintained, but not "at any cost" (cf. Exod. 21:20-21, 26-27; Deut. 25:3).[213]

20 This verse protects v. 19 against minimizing the power of "words" (cf. I: 101). Used in the service of greed, they damn a person (cf. Jas. 1:19). Verset A presents the topic (the cause). The question *Do you see* (*hāzîtā;* see 22:29) *a person* (*'îš;* see I: 89) by its direct address aims to involve the son in the truth. *Who is hasty* [see 19:2] *with his words* (*bidᵉbārîm,* repeating v. 19)[214] refers to a person who chooses to use his words without regard for their moral effectiveness. McKane observed that words in Proverbs are "transitive and executive." They concern "the outside world and are

210. Delitzsch, *Proverbs,* p. 432.

211. The *Niphal* is the passive of *Piel ysr.*

212. *Papyrus Insinger* (14:11) says: "If the rod is far from his master, the servant will not obey him."

213. *Pace* Bridges, *Proverbs,* p. 578.

214. But with *beth comitantiae,* not instrumental *beth* (*IBHS,* pp. 196-97, P. 11.2.5d).

aimed at the production of social effects."[215] According to the apodosis in verset B, *there is more hope for a fool than for him* repeats verbatim 26:12. The fool's speech is ill considered, rash, and reckless (cf. 12:23; 14:16; 15:2), but a person hasty with his words, like the one hasty to get rich (28:20), misses the way (19:2). He does not passionately blurt out his folly but rationally calculates how to get what he wants when he wants it. His hope for salvation is less than for a fool. The intractable fool is ruled by his passions, but the impious, who is bent on getting what he wants without quibbling about ethics, chooses to be ruled by greed. He "is a fool of the worst kind."[216]

21 The proverb returns to the theme of disciplining *his slave* (see 29:19), tracing his life from his youth (verset A) to his destiny (verset B).[217] But the meaning of the last word *mānôn,* glossed "insolent," is uncertain. Meinhold thinks that v. 19 may be related to v. 20 by the semantic connection between "hope" (v. 20b) and "end/outcome" (v. 21b).[218] Verset A presents the condition (i.e., the cause). *If* is demanded by the syntax (see n. 62). *One pampers* glosses a *hap. leg.* whose meaning is determined by cognate Semitic languages. In Aramaic it means "to pamper," and in Arabic "to let someone lead a pleasant, easy and prosperous life."[219] *From youth* denotes the early, immature but vigorous, trainable stage of life (cf. 1:4; 22:6; Job 33:25; Ps. 88:15[16]). Verset B asserts the consequence, the end, of treating the slave with excessive care and attention so that he can lead a free and easy life instead of training him for the work that he will be required to do when grown up. *Afterward* (lit. "[in] his end"; see 5:11) refers to the temporal and logical end of pampering. "His" has as its antecedent either the master or slave, depending on the meaning of *mānôn* ("insolent"). If *mānôn* refers to the semantic domain of "son," then the antecedent may be the pamperer; if "insolent," its antecedent must be the pampered. *He will be* can also be glossed "become" or "prove to be."[220] *Insolent (mānôn)* is an uncertain gloss of a *hap. leg.*[221] To indulge a slave's baser

215. W. McKane, "Functions of Language and Objectives of Discourse according to Proverbs 10–30," in *La Sagesse de l'Ancien Testament,* ed. M. Gilbert (2nd ed.; Leuven: Leuven University Press/Peeters, 1990), pp. 166-67.

216. McKane, "Functions of Language," pp. 166-67.

217. The versets are held together by the alliteration of *mem,* which is initial in the first two words and in the last word.

218. Meinhold, *Sprüche,* p. 420.

219. *HALOT,* 3:946, s.v. *pnq.*

220. *HALOT,* 1:243-44, s.v. *hyh.*

221. The LXX, Targ., and Syr. are not helpful because they interpret the proverb as directed against self-indulgence, not slaves. They read: "He who pampers himself from youth will become a servant, and in the end will grieve over himself [LXX]/will be driven out [Targ.]/will groan [Syr.]." Instead of reading *'bdw* they read *[y]'bd.* They also probably

passions is no more a kindness to him than to a child. Instead of stimulating gratitude to his owner, diligence in his work, and respect for others, it makes him ungovernable and brings his owner emotional damage, financial loss, and social opprobrium.

c. Spiritually Inferior Types versus Those Who Trust in the LORD *(29:22-26)*

The second subunit of vv. 16-26 warns the son/disciple against spiritual miscreants (vv. 22-24) and instructs him to trust the LORD (vv. 25-26). The subunit begins in v. 22 with a double *'aleph* (*'îš-'ap* "a hothead") and ends in the framing proverb of v. 27 with a fourfold *taw* (i.e., initial *tô'ᵃbat* in each verset). Moreover, there is an alphabetic progression of initial *'aleph, beth,* and *gimel* in the first three versets. The subunit also coheres by beginning and ending with *'îš,* the first word of v. 22 and last word of v. 26. Recall that *'îš* also functioned as a structuring word in 29:1, standing between the framing proverbs 28:28 and 29:2, and that *'îš* helped structure 29:3-15 into vv. 3-6 and 8-10. Meinhold observes that its synonym *'ādām* occurs as an internal frame reinforcing the external (vv. 23a, 25a). Only the center line of the subunit lacks one of the synonyms (v. 24). Meinhold also notes that the second from the last Hebrew word of v. 22 and the first of v. 26 belong to the root "to be many," which occurs both in the inward structure of the framing proverbs (29:16; 28:12, 28) and in a series of verses elsewhere. Finally, Meinhold rightly argues, "The unity of the three proverbs which concern above all representatives of perverted humanity (vv. 22-24) is favored by the fact that the two halves of the JHWH proverb 28:25 are taken up in 22a and 25b with regard to their content, and, therefore, are framing almost the entire passage of

---

read *mnwn* as a contracted form of *mᵉ'unnān, Pual* ptcp. of *'nn,* which in Aramaic and Arabic means "to sigh" and in Heb. *Hithpolel* "to complain" (Num. 11:1; Lam. 3:39). Frankenberg (cited by Whybray, *Proverbs,* p. 404) arrived at a similar meaning by reading *yāgôn* (cf. "grief," NIV). Naturally *mpng* would then have to be read as passive. McKane (*Proverbs,* p. 634) says rightly of the LXX: "It can only be regarded as an incorrect paraphrase." Delitzsch (*Proverbs,* pp. 434-35) derives *mānôn* from the root *nun* or *nin* and in a questionable and circuitous way arrives at the meaning of *bēn* "son" and then "squire" (cf. "son," KJV, NASB; "heir," RSV, not NRSV). Delitzsch believes that it could also be a place or state of growing or increasing, a "nursery." The "master will not be able, in the end, . . . to defend himself against the crowd which grows up to him from this his darling." J. Reider ("Etymological Studies in Biblical Hebrew," *VT* 4 [1954] 286), on the basis of an Arabic cognate *na'na* "to be weak," *muna'na'* "weak," "feeble," and the Talmud, opted for "weakling," but Gemser (*Sprüche,* p. 102) rejected this meaning in favor of *widerspenstig* ("obstinate," "rebellious," "unmanageable") based on Jerome's *contumax* "stubborn" and on Sir. 47:23. *HALOT* (2:600, s.v. *mānôn*) agrees with the glosses "arrogant, insolent, rebellious."

vv. 22-26 [especially since vv. 25-26 are a pair]. Also by that fact the connection between rearing and confidence in JHWH is emphasized"[222] (see I: 82).

22 The first perverted type (the cause) is *a hothead* (*'îš-'ap;* lit. "the angry person"), *a wrathful person (ba'al ḥēmâ)* who *stirs up strife* (see 15:28; 22:24 is similar but reverses *'îš* and *ba'al).* "Anger" describes his outward visage of snorting nostrils, and "wrath," his inner heat of boiling emotions of resentment. The predicate *And . . . is one who abounds in* [see 28:20] *transgressions* (see 29:16), the consequence, complements "stirs up strife." His resentment of others causes him to seek a pretext to transform every difference into a fight, and so he abounds in transgressing God's moral ordering of society. His willingness to pick a quarrel at the drop of a hat shows that in fact he loves transgression (17:19). Seven abominations, including guile (26:24), fill his heart (26:25). Unlike the one who is hasty to get rich or with words, his passions rule him.

23 The next in the series is the arrogant. Its antithetical parallels juxtapose *the pride*[223] *of a mortal* (*'ādām;* see I: 89) with *the lowly in spirit* (see 16:19). "Pride" derives from a root meaning "to be high" and so constitutes a precise antithetical parallel of "lowly." G. V. Smith and V. P. Hamilton comment: "Pride is a fundamental attitude of self-sufficiency because of which a person throws off humility and pursues selfish desires. In pride a person rejects the need for dependence on God or his laws and despises moral or social limitations that regulate behavior according to the highest good for others."[224] His opposite, the humble (Job 5:11; Prov. 16:19; 29:23), has an attitude of dependence on God and of submission to his moral ordering of society. In that upright order one behaves to achieve the highest good of others and bestows on others — not demands for oneself — their rights to life, home, property, and reputation, as mandated in the Ten Commandments (Exod. 20:13-16). The parallels also juxtapose their respective predicates, *will bring him low* (see 16:19; 25:7) versus *will lay hold of* [and hold fast to; see 3:18] *honor* (see 3:16).[225] The imprecise antithesis suggests that the lowly will be exalted and that the proud mortal will lose his social esteem and influence, his property, and all that he gained for the moment by raising his fist against heaven and by transgressing the boundaries of others on earth (see 11:2; 15:33; 16:5, 18-19; 18:12; 21:4; 22:4; 30:21-23; Matt. 19:30; 23:12 [= Luke 14:11; 18:14]).

222. Meinhold, *Sprüche,* p. 490.

223. Perhaps *ga'ᵃwat* is a by-form of the *hap. leg. gē'â* from the root *g'h* (see 8:13; cf. the adj. *gē'eh* in 15:25; 16:19).

224. Gary V. Smith and Victor P. Hamilton, *NIDOTTE,* 1:788, s.v. *g'h.*

225. The versets are tied together with a paronomasia between "brings low *(tašpîlennû)*" and "lowly *(šᵉpal)* in spirit."

24 The catalogue now lists the accomplice of a thief, shifting from a wrong spiritual attitude against God and others to the unethical behavior that results from such a spirit. Meinhold points to 16:19 to establish the logical connection between vv. 23 and 24. "According to 16:19 in the fellowship with the arrogant booty is shared . . . but now the sharing with the thief is talked about."[226] Verset A presents the topic (the cause). *The accomplice* [i.e., one who shares portions according to which one is entitled; see 17:2] *with* [see 3:30; 24:21] *a thief* (see 6:30) agrees to join a thief in his covert stealing in order to have a share in the loot (cf. 1:10-19; Ps. 50:18; Isa. 1:23-24), not a thief who steals because he is hungry (see 6:30; 30:9). Verset Ab presents the predicate (the consequence). The idiom *hates* [see 1:22] *his life* (*napšô;* see I: 90) signifies that he unnaturally does not value his own life and so willingly puts it at risk (cf. 1:18; cf. 8:36). Verset B explains that assertion. *He hears* [see 1:5] *the divine curse ('ālâ) but will not testify* (*yaggîd,* i.e., give personal and important information to someone, presumably a judge; cf. Lev. 5:1). C. A. Keller defines *'ālâ* as being "essentially a judicial term. In contrast to *'rr* 'to curse, place under the ban,' *qll* 'to insult, wish someone ill,' and other expressions of damaging speech . . . , *'ālâ* indicates the curse 'as a legal aid for securing an oath' (Gen. 24:41; Neh. 10:29[30]; Hos. 4:2), contract (Gen. 26:28; Ezek. 17:19), or covenant (Deut. 29:19-20[18-19]; 2 Chr. 34:24), as an ordeal curse (Num. 5:21), and as legal vengeance against unknown thieves, perjurers, and accomplices (Lev. 5:1; Judg. 17:2-3; Prov. 29:24; Zech. 5:3)."[227] The NIV glosses *'ālâ* by "public charge." If a thief heard the curse uttered against him, because there was no other way to pursue punishment (see 26:2) and brings back the pillage, as in the case of Judg. 17:1-3, then the curse will not hit him. On the other hand, if a legal case could not be resolved by other means, and a cursing in public is invoked, whoever knew about the matter but did not make a statement brought the curse on himself (cf. Lev. 5:1). By not contributing to its disclosure, he forfeits his life by the curse (see at 3:33; cf. Zech. 5:3-4). The accomplice lies by his silence (cf. 12:17; 14:25; 19:28), and by his impiety he risks himself to the power of God's curse. The judge's oath brings God himself into the trial; the accomplice will not go unpunished (19:5, 9; 21:28). Paradoxically, the partner joined the thief to satisfy the greed of his swollen appetites, but instead he loses that very life with its drives and appetites.

25-26 These verses are a proverb pair coupled with the catchword "the LORD" and with the teaching to fear and rely on him, not on untrustworthy mortals, drawing the fourth unit to its conclusion before the framing proverb of v. 27. The Sovereign Governor is trustworthy for salvation (v. 25)

226. Meinhold, *Sprüche,* p. 491.
227. C. A. Keller, *TLOT,* 1:113, *'ālâ.*

and for justice (v. 26). Verse 25 contrasts this faith with fear of a mortal, and v. 26, with giving eye service to a ruler.

25 This verse is connected with v. 24 phonetically by initial */ḥ/ heth,* but more importantly by the theme of human behavior as governed by fear of the LORD. The guilty accomplice who refuses to testify under a divine curse shows that he does not fear what the divine curse might afflict on him or, as the next proverb infers, is more frightened by what his accomplice might afflict on him. Both proverbs assert that such a person will not survive the divine vengeance, but this proverb presses on to the solution: trust in the LORD, and experience his protection, and find life. Its antithetical parallels imprecisely juxtapose the topics (the causes), "the panic induced by human threat" with "one who trusts in the LORD." M. V. Van Pelt and W. C. Kaiser Jr. note that typically *the fear (ḥerdâ)* "expresses the terror evoked by an unusual, unexpected event or circumstance."[228] *Of an* earthly *mortal ('ādām;* see I: 89) stands in sharp contrast to the heavenly LORD. The incomplete metaphor *lays (yittēn;* lit. "gives"; see 1:4) *a snare* (see 13:14) represents being caught in a fatal situation. The panic-stricken person does not react reasonably. If he reacts at all, he may do the wrong thing. "Anxiety points to a factor of distress which does not have to claim any ultimate truth with regard to YHWH."[229] Panic-stricken by what others might do to him, he cowardly yields himself to their depraved dictates to please them and thereby incurs God's wrath (cf. 1 Sam. 13:8-14; 15:10-29). By contrast, *the one who trusts in the LORD* (see 1:7; 3:5; 28:25), not in arrogance based on his own understanding (see v. 23), *will be protected* (or "is inaccessible to danger,"[230] *yeśuggāb;* see 18:10-11). "Trust in Yahweh, if it is thoroughgoing and comprehensive, is incompatible with fearfulness, because whoever relies for safety on Yahweh [knows he] is safe indeed."[231]

26 Alden thinks that v. 26 is an illustration of v. 25.[232] Many seek rewards from a mortal ruler, but justice is in the hands of the sovereign God (16:33; 20:22; 21:1; cf. Deut. 1:17; 1 K. 3:28; Pss. 50:6; 75:8[9]; 94:2; 96:13). Its antithetical parallels juxtapose the topics, the many who seek a favorable audience with a ruler through careful court courtesies (see 19:6) over against individuals who seek justice from the LORD.[233] *Many* (see 19:6), especially the rich (see I: 103), *seek the face of* (cf. 2:4; 19:10) signi-

228. M. V. Van Pelt and W. C. Kaiser Jr., *NIDOTTE,* 2:264, s.v. *ḥrd.*

229. Meinhold, *Sprüche,* p. 492.

230. McKane, *Proverbs,* p. 257.

231. McKane, *Proverbs,* p. 639.

232. Alden, *Proverbs,* p. 204.

233. The versets cohere by the consonance of *mem.* If words bound by proclisis are counted as one, it occurs with every word. If counted separately, initial *mem* appears in four of the six words and is final in the first two of verset B.

fies that they are seeking a favorable audience with someone and entails "a sense of a display of courtesy" (see 28:5).[234] The expression *who seek the face of a ruler* (see 6:7; cf. 28:15; 29:2, 12) or its equivalent is found elsewhere only in 1 K. 10:24 (= 2 Chr. 9:23). By contrast, about 30 passages speak of seeking the face of God, which denotes fear, reverence, and trust. Here that spiritual state is transferred to a ruler. The imprecise parallels imply that many fear the mortal who governs their fate and fawn before him to obtain his favor, presumably to intervene in judicial proceedings. "Yet such men are themselves the servants of appetites and pressures (cf. Acts 24:25-27), irrationality (1 Cor. 2:6, 8) and instability (Ps. 146:3, 4), which rob their interventions of all trustworthiness [see 29:12]."[235] The predicate (the consequence) in verset B asserting that *justice* [see 1:3; 16:33; 29:4] *for an individual* (*'îš;* see 29:20) *comes from the LORD* (see I: 73; 29:25) implies that a person should fear and reverence the LORD for justice (Ps. 37:5, 6), not the ruler. Other proverbs clarify that one should fear both God and the king, who ideally mediates justice (see 16:10-15; 25:2-3). Verse 26 does not forbid seeking relief from injustice through the legal system, but it does teach that one should not seek the ruler's favor apart from seeking an audience with the LORD, presumably through reverential prayer (see 28:5). Otherwise, in ways described in 19:6 (cf. 17:8; 18:16), the one using the legal system may himself sin to obtain the ruler's favor and fall under divine condemnation.

d. Concluding Framing Proverb (29:27)

Section D draws to a conclusion contrasting the disdain that the righteous and the wicked feel toward each other's ways. Its antithetical parallels contrast the topics (the causes), the ways of an unjust person who commits crimes and abuses the legal system, and the upright, who does not transgress the boundaries established by God to protect the social, legal, and/or economic rights of others. *An unjust person* (*'îš 'āwel;* cf. see 22:8)[236] is contrasted with *the upright* [see I: 98] *in [his] way* (*dārek;* see 1:15). *'îš 'āwel* denotes a person who acts illegally with reference to crimes of a social, property, or commercial nature and/or with reference to the courts, such as skewing justice by bribery (see 22:8). The preceding proverb suggests the latter notion; the parallel suggests the former. The parallels also juxtapose the predicates (the consequences). The behavior of the former *is an abomination* [see 3:32] *to the righteous,* who serve the community, and that of the latter *is an abomination to the*

234. G. Gerleman, *TLOT,* 2:252, s.v. *bqš.*

235. Kidner, *Proverbs,* p. 177.

236. A gender doublet of *'a/-/vel* (R. Knierim, *TLOT,* 2:850, s.v. *'āwel*).

wicked (*rāsāʿ;* see 28:1, 12, 18; 29:2, 16), who serve themselves. The difference that separates the righteous from the wicked is a matter of the heart. "The conflict of right and wrong, good and evil, is fundamental, uncompromising, and passionate: nothing can mitigate their mutual antagonism and loathing."[237] The proverb implies the need for regenerated religious affections (see 3:32; 11:1, 20; 12:22; 15:8, 9, 26; 16:5, 12; 17:15; 20:10, 23; 21:27; 28:9). It also teaches a right kind of intolerance.[238]

VI. COLLECTION VI: THE SAYINGS OF AGUR SON OF JAKEH (30:1-33)

1 *The sayings of Agur*[1] *son*[2] *of Jakeh.*[3] *An*[4] *oracle.*[5]
The inspired utterance[6] *of the man*[7] *to Ithiel:*[8]

237. Malbim, *Proverbs,* p. 299.

238. "Prov. 28:5 and 29:27 portray the mutual intolerance of the righteous and the wicked. . . . Such sayings portray a world apparently without a middle ground, a world with a fundamental conflict between good and evil. In our tolerant, pluralistic society, such thinking seems troublesome. . . . Should we not rather 'live and let live'? Yet Jesus also spoke in terms of conflict . . . (Matt 12:30). . . . Proverbs reminds us that we may not elevate moral ambiguity and religious mystery to the point of relativism, where the lines between right and wrong, good and evil, true and false, are erased. . . . At that point tolerance is no longer a virtue, but moral indifference in the face of evil. . . . Tolerance is not an adequate response to evil" (Van Leeuwen, *Proverbs,* p. 247).

1. The LXX renders *'āgûr* by *phobēthēti* ("reverence" < jussive of *gzr* "dread, fear"). The LXX rejects /'/ as part of its fiction that Solomon authored these sayings (see I: 4).

2. For the rare pointing, *bin,* see GKC, P. 96.

3. The LXX renders *yqh* by *dexamenos* ("receive" < *lqḥ*) as part of its Solomonic fiction.

4. Interpreting the article to signify class (*IBHS,* p. 244, P. 115.1f).

5. Delitzsch (*Proverbs,* 2:262) et al. think that the prophetic term *maśśā'* is unfitting in wisdom literature, especially in a context where Agur confesses his weakness. They emend the text to either *mimmaśśā'* ("from Massa"), or to *hammaśśā'î* ("the Massaite"), a district in northwest Arabia (K. Kitchen, "Proverbs and Wisdom Books of the Ancient Near East," *TynBul* 28 [1977] 101). But *nᵉ'ûm haggeber* ("the inspired utterance of the man") is also prophetic, reinforcing the MT.

6. *Nᵉ'ûm* ("an inspired utterance") occurs 365 of 376 times in the formula *nᵉ'ûm YHWH* (D. Vetter, *TLOT,* 2:693 s.v. *nᵉ'ûm*). That construction designates that the words that follow originated with the LORD and carry his authority. Once (Jer. 23:31) it occurs absolutely with the same sense (L. Coppes, *TWOT,* 2:541-42, s.v. *nᵉ'ûm*). The other ten occurrences are in construct with a human author to denote the heavenly origin of his utterance and its divine authority: six times of Balaam's oracles (Num. 24:3[2x], 4,

"I am weary, O God,[9] but I can prevail.[10]

15[2x], 16), twice of David's inspired hymns (2 Sam. 23:1), and once of Agur's sayings. Remarkably both Balaam and David use exactly the same formula as Agur: *n^{e}'ûm haggeber* "the oracle of the man." McKane (*Proverbs,* p. 644) dismisses Agur's claim as "very odd," and Whybray (*Proverbs,* p. 407) as "unexplained." P. Franklyn ("The Sayings of Agur in Proverbs 30: Piety or Scepticism?" *ZAW* 95 [1983] 241) forces the interpreter to choose between Agur's sayings as either "part of the formal prophetic tradition, or a self-assertive human revelation in the prophetic mode." J. Pauls ("Proverbs 30:1-6: 'The Words of Agur' as Epistemological Statement" [Th.M. thesis, Regent College, 1998], p. 65) rightly rejects the second option: "Given the explicit claims of vv. 2-3, which denigrate the claims of human wisdom, the second option appears hardly tenable." Moreover, the expression is never otherwise used for "the insight of a 'man,' who is the source of his own wisdom" (*pace* Perdue, *Proverbs,* p. 254). R. Moore ("A Home for the Alien: World Wisdom and Covenant Confession in Proverbs 30:1-9," *ZAW* 106 [1994] 97) draws the right conclusion that in Agur's sayings there is "a striking confluence of sapient and prophetic traditions."

7. E. Lipiński ("Peninna, Iti'el et l'Athlète," *VT* 17 [1967] 73) reads here the personal name Gab(b)ru, according to the Assyrian form of the name, which is also attested in Arabic (cf. *Gaber* in the LXX of 1 K. 4:13, 19). He understands this to mean, "The Athlete." But Franklyn ("The Sayings of Agur," p. 240) objects: "The combination of *n'm hgbr* in Num. 24:3, 15 and 2 Sam. 23:1 decisively overrules a nominal [*sic*! proper noun] usage."

8. Numerous emendations have been unnecessarily proposed. The MT is supported by Theod. and Aquila.

9. Although Targ., Aquila, and Theod. read with the MT, the text should be emended by redividing and repointing *l^{e}'îtî'ēl* as *lā'îtî 'ēl* (cf. Num. 12:13; Ps. 812). C. Torrey ("Proverbs, Chapter 30," *JBL* 73 [1954] 93-103), followed and modified by R. B. Y. Scott (*Proverbs,* p. 176), J. L. Crenshaw ("Clanging Symbols [Prov. 30:1-14]," in *Justice and the Holy,* ed. D. A. Knight and P. J. Paris [Atlanta: Scholars, 1980], pp. 51-64), et al. interpret *l'ytyl* as a scribal coverup in Aramaic for a blasphemy. Torrey (cf. NAB) thinks that the text should read, *l' 'ty 'l* ("I am not God, I am not God"). They essentially read *lā' 'îtay '^{e}lāh lā' 'îtay '^{e}lāh* (cf. Dan. 3:29), "There is no god, there is no god." However, these critics arbitrarily dissect 30:1-6 into the words of skeptical Agur (vv. 1-4) and an orthodox response (vv. 5-6) and overlook or dismiss too easily Agur's claim of inspiration. Finally, one must raise a skeptical eye that either the writer or a scribe inserted Aramaic into a passage otherwise expressed in Hebrew. Scott (*The Way of Wisdom in the Old Testament* [New York: Macmillan, 1971], p. 169) retreated from reading Aramaic and emended the text to *lō' '^{i}ttô* [*sic*! *'ittô*] *'ēl lō' 'ittî 'ēl* "with whom God is not, I have not God." This emendation finds some support in the grammar of the Vulg., *vir cum quo est deus* ("with whom is God"), but not in its content. The LXX also reads a relative clause but with very different content, *tois pisteuousin theǭ* ("to those who believe God"). However, although *n^{e}'ûm haggeber* in Num. 24:3, 15 and 2 Sam. 23:1 is followed by a relative clause, it is not necessary. Moreover, Scott adds consonants to the text in addition to redividing them. Finally, Scott mishandles *n^{e}ûm haggeber* of Num. 24:3, 15 and 2 Sam. 23:1, which support Agur's inspiration. In sum, the proposed and most widely accepted emendation is best from a text-critical,

2 *Surely*[11] *I am too stupid to be a man;*[12]
indeed,[13] *I do not have the understanding of a human being.*
3 *Indeed,*[14] *I have not*[15] *learned*[16] *wisdom,*
but I want to experience[17] *the knowledge of the Holy One.*[18]

---

exegetical, and canonical point of view. In 1669 Cocceius proposed, "I have labored on account of God, and I have obtained" (cited by Toy, *Proverbs,* p. 519). In modern times, he has been accepted by Gemser (*Sprüche,* p. 102). Many favor taking God as vocative (e.g., Plöger [*Sprüche,* p. 354], NEB, REB, NIV [text note], and NRSV). Clifford (*Proverbs,* p. 258) conjectures an earlier and a later stage. According to him, an earlier sage claimed through conventional protestations of ignorance that his message was God's, not his own, and a later sage reread this protestation as a genuine expression of misery that is answered by the assurance that every word of God is true. Clifford's appeal to Psalms 12 and 18 suggests that the later sage is assuring himself, not that a redactor is correcting him. The law of parsimony calls Clifford's interpretation into question.

10. There is little consensus about the meaning of *'ūkāl.*

11. The emphatic adverb *kî* ("surely") should not be separated radically from its logical use, "for" (*IBHS,* p. 665, P. 39.14e).

12. The translation construes *min* as a comparative of capability (*IBHS,* p. 266, P. 14.4f; NRSV). Delitzsch (*Proverbs,* 2:272) understands it as a comparative of exclusion, "not a man" (cf. *IBHS,* p. 265, P. 14.4e), and Franklyn ("The Sayings of Agur," p. 244, n. 24) thinks that the *min* is privative (i.e., "separated from other men by his beastly nature"). All agree, however, that the expression makes a sharp distinction between man and God (cf. Hos. 11:9; see N. P. Bratsiotis [*TDOT,* 1:229, s.v. *'îš*]). The NIV renders it as a superlative, "most ignorant," but the predicate adjective lacks the necessary article for that sense. The LXX supplies the missing element of another superlative construction, *hapantōn anthrōpōn* "of all men" (cf. *IBHS,* pp. 267-68, P. 14.5c).

13. Construing *waw* as epexegetical (*IBHS,* p. 652, P. 39.2.4a).

14. See n. 11.

15. J. Fichtner *(BHS)* attractively but unnecessarily emends the text to *lû,* "would that I had learned." The chiastic structure of the MT with two negatives in the inner core (vv. 2b and 3a) argues against this emendation.

16. The LXX reads *theos dedidaxen me sophian* (< *'ēl limmad 'ōtî hokmâ,* "God taught me wisdom"), which is favored by M. Pope (*El in the Ugaritic Texts* [Leiden: Brill, 1955], p. 14). But Franklyn ("The Sayings of Agur," p. 245) notes, "Most reject the LXX because it imputes more piety into the text than is necessary." The *waw* conjunctive in the MT links v. 3 with v. 2, but the LXX, which omits the conjunctive, puts the verses into tension with each other. The LXX anticipates the resolution in vv. 5-9 (i.e., wisdom is dependent on God's revelation [vv. 5-6] and on piety [vv. 7-9], but provides no transition by way of v. 4 to the resolution of the tension).

17. Lit. "know" in its sense of internalizing "knowledge of the Holy One."

18. Understanding *qᵉdōšîm* as an objective gen. and an honorific pl. (*IBHS,* p. 122, P. 7.4.3; see 2:5; 9:10), not a gen. of inalienable possession and a countable pl. (i.e., "the knowledge that is proper to the holy ones" [*IBHS,* p. 145, P. 9.5.1h]). "The adjective *qādôš* (holy) denominates that which is intrinsically sacred or which has been ad-

4 *Who has ever ascended to heaven and come down?*
Who has ever gathered up the wind[19] *in his fists?*[20]
Who has ever wrapped up the waters in his robe?
Who has established all the ends of the earth?
What is his name? And what is his son's[21] *name?*
Surely you know![22]
5 *Every*[23] *word*[24] *of God*[25] *is purified;*
he is a shield to those who take refuge in him.
6 *Do not add*[26] *to his word,*[27]
lest he convict[28] *you and you be proved a liar.*[29]
7 *Two things I ask of you;*

---

mitted to the sphere of the sacred. . . . It connotes that which is distinct from the common or profane" (T. E. McComiskey, *TWOT,* 2:788, s.v. *qādôš*).

19. The wind has the power to set other things in motion (see I: 92). Here it refers to the thunderstorm.

20. K. Cathcart ("Proverbs 30,4 and Ugaritic *Ḥpn,* 'Garment'," *CBQ* 32 [1970] 418-20) argues that *en kolpǭ* in the LXX does not render *beḥiṣnô* (= "bosom of his garment"), but represents the same reading as the MT — only sing. — because Ugar. *hpn* denotes some sort of garment. This interpretation provides a nice parallel to "robe" in v. 4aβ[1]), but elsewhere the Hebrew word denotes "hollow of the hand" (i.e., "fist") *(HALOT,* 1:339, s.v. *ḥōpen).*

21. The LXX renders by pl. *teknois autou,* apparently to refer to the children of Israel.

22. Rahlfs regards the omission of *kî tēdā'* in the LXX[A,B] as secondary, but they may have been interpolated from Job 38:5. In any case, they do not interrupt the sense.

23. Agur varies David's thanksgiving song (Ps. 18:30[31]) in several ways. (1) He omits David's initial, "As for God, his way is perfect; the word of God . . . ," because David features the reliability of God's word as part of God's protection, but Agur features the reliability of God's word as revelation. (2) By transferring *kol* from verset B (= "to all who seek refuge in him") to "every word of God" in verset A, Agur shifts the emphasis from "from an all-embracing protectorship to a total reliability of divine words" (Crenshaw, "Clanging Symbols," p. 58).

24. "The verb *'mr* [the root here] directs attention to the contents of the speech, whereas *dbr Piel* indicates primarily the activity of speaking" (G. Gerleman, *TLOT,* 1:327, s.v. *dābār*).

25. Ps. 18:30(31) reads *YHWH,* not *'elôah.*

26. The pl. of Deut. 4:2 is replaced by the sing. to accommodate the shift of addressees from all Israel to Ithiel in particular.

27. "The word which I [Moses] am commanding you" (Deut. 4:2) becomes "his word" in order to bind v. 6 to v. 5, to fit the restraints of the poetic line, and to replace Moses' words with Agur's words.

28. *HALOT,* 2:410, s.v. *ykḥ.*

29. Or "be found guilty of a lie" (see Job 41:1 for the other occurrence of *kzb* in the *Niphal*). Agur gaps the other half of the canonical formula, "do not take away from his word," to replace it with a threat for not guarding the sacred word.

do not withhold [them] from me before I die.
8 *A deceitful*[30] *lie*[31] *keep far away from me.*
Poverty or riches do not give me.
Provide[32] *me my quota*[33] *of food;*[34]
9 *lest I be sated and dissemble and say, "Who is the* LORD*?"*[35]
or lest I become poor and I steal, and so do violence[36] *to the name of my God.*
10 *Do not slander*[37] *a slave to his master,*[38]
lest he curse you, and you become liable.
11 *A generation —* [39] *they*[40] *curse their fathers*

30. "Deceit" glosses one of the two senses of *šāwʾ*. J. Shepherd (*NIDOTTE,* 4:53, s.v. *šwʾ*) thinks that the notion of "deceit," "falsehood" derives from its developed sense, "ineffectiveness."

31. The conjunction of *šāwʾ* and *kāzāb* in Ezek. 13:6, 8, 9 with reference to lies spoken by false prophets and diviners suggests that the compound is a hendiadys (i.e., deceit that takes the form of a verbal lie [see 19:22; 21:28; 23:3]).

32. *Ṭrp* in the *Qal* and the cognate languages means "to tear up" with the subject wild beasts. This unique use in the *Hiphil* has a weakened sense "to cause to receive," "to provide anew with" (*HALOT,* 2:380, s.v. *ṭrp*).

33. *Ḥqq* means "carve out, inscribe, dig," from which is derived the meaning, "prescribe, determine" for a particular quantity of grain (Gen. 47:22) or work (Exod. 5:14; Prov. 31:15) and for a "measured quantity of oil" (Ezek. 45:14) and "food," according to God's design to meet basic human need (Prov. 30:8),

34. Toy, Gemser, and Oesterley proposed without justification to delete some parts of the prayer, especially the last line of v. 8, as later glosses. But, "The prayer as it stands has an unusual beauty and carries conviction" (Whybray, *Proverbs,* p. 411).

35. The LXX has *tis me horą̄* (< *mî yeḥzeh ʿōtî* ["who sees me?"]), which is not as good a parallel to verset Bb as the MT.

36. The root *tpś* essentially means "to seize," "to grip." A. H. Konkel *(NIDOTTE,* 4:326, s.v. *tpś)* notes, "When used with the preposition *b*ᵉ, it indicates a certain vigor in the action. . . . The verb is commonly used in relation to war. It describes those taken alive in battle, such as the king of Ai (Josh. 8:23). . . . It also describes the seizure of a city for destruction (Deut. 20:19)." This unique expression, "to seize/to do violence to the name of God," is a metaphor for to profane and misuse God's name (cf. A. S. van der Woude, *TLOT,* 1:1360, s.v. *šēm*). Gemser (*Sprüche,* p. 104) mentions a personal correspondence from G. R. Driver to connect *tpś* with Arab. *tafitha* "to besmirch."

37. *Talšēn* is a unique *Hiphil* denominative of *lāšôn* "tongue" (see *HALOT,* 2:537, s.v. *lšn*). *Lšn* also occurs as unique *Polel* denominative in Ps. 101:5. The meaning "slander" fits the use of the noun. As a metonymy for speech, *lāšôn* more often than not speaks of negative or harmful communication (see 6:17; 12:19; 17:4, 20; 21:6; 25:23; 26:28; cf. 10:20).

38. K reads *ʾᵃdōnô* and Q (cf. Syr.) reads *ʾᵃdōnāyw,* probably an intensive pl. (cf. BDB, p. 11, s.v. *ʾādôn*).

39. *Dôr* (vv. 11-14) is a nominative absolute followed by its resumptive pronoun in the main clause (*IBHS,* p. 76, P. 4.7b, c). The LXX adds a facilitating *kakon* ("wicked")

and do not bless their mothers.
12 *A generation — [they are] pure in their own eyes,*
but are not cleansed from their excrement.
13 *A generation — how*[41] *they raise their eyes!*
And [how] they lift up their pupils!
14 *A generation — their teeth are swords*
and their jawbones are butcher knives
to devour[42] *the poor [and eliminate] them from*[43] *the earth,*
and the needy from humanity.
15 *The horse leech has two daughters: "Give!" "Give!"*[44]
They are three things that[45] *are never satisfied,*
four that never say, "Enough!"[46]
16 *Sheol and the barren*[47] *womb,*
the land that is never satisfied with water, and fire that never says, "Enough!"
17 *As for the eye that mocks*[48] *a father and shows contempt for the gray hair*[49] *of a mother,*

---

to *ekgonon* (= "a wicked generation curses"). Fichtner *(BHS)* facilitates the reading by supplying *hoi* ("Woe to a generation"). Without an article, the form is not vocative.

40. Heb. "it curses." In v. 13 the Heb. uses a pl. verb and a sing. pronoun; the English idiom disallows this incongruity. Here the nonconventional collective "generation" is rendered consistently by the sing. (see *IBHS,* pp. 113-14, P. 7.2.1b, c).

41. Exclamatory *mâ* (*IBHS,* p. 326, P. 18:3f).

42. The gloss "to devour" for *leʾekōl* adds the notion of greedily to the common word "to eat" (see 1:31; 13:2), for that notion is implied "from the earth."

43. The pregnant preposition *min* implies a verb of motion such as "to remove," "to eliminate" (*IBHS,* p. 224, P. 11.4.3d)

44. For this form of *ʿÔlē weyōrēd* see Ps. 68:20. "The upper sign of the *ʿÔlē weyōrēd* often falls away, when the tone is on the first syllable" (W. Wickes, *Two Treatises on the Accentuation of the Old Testament* [New York: Ktav, 1970], p. 55, n. 1).

45. Asyndetic relative construction (*IBHS,* p. 333, P. 19.2g).

46. E. Kutsch *(TDOT,* 2:366, s.v. *hôn)* derives this unique sense of *hôn* (see 1:13) from the root *hwn* "be ready."

47. The meaning of *ʿōṣer,* which occurs elsewhere only in Ps. 107:39 for "oppression" and in Isa. 53:8 for "imprisonment," can be inferred from the use of the verb *ʿṣr* ("to restrain, detain, arrest, imprison") for the womb being withheld from conception in Gen. 16:2; 20:18. Literally, the meaning is "the restraint of the womb," an epexegetical gen. (*IBHS,* p. 151, P. 9.5.3c).

48. Lit. "to stutter in the face of someone." "Eye" is a synecdoche for the person in this mixed metaphor.

49. MT *lîqqahat* (< *yeqahâ* or *yiqhâ* ["obedience"]) is found elsewhere only in Gen. 49:10. The LXX (Syr., Targ.) reads "old age." D. Winton Thomas ("A Note on *lîqqahat* in Proverbs 30:17," *JTS* 42 [1941] 154-155) thinks that the LXX knew a Semitic root *lhq* meaning "old," "to be white [of hair]" (cf. *HALOT,* 2:430, s.v. *yeqāhâ*). He plausi-

the ravens of the wadi will peck it out,
and the vultures will devour it.
18 *They*[50] *are three things that are too wonderful for me;*[51]
and as for four,[52] *I do not know them:*
19 *the way*[53] *of an eagle*[54] *in the sky, the way of a serpent on a rock.*
the way of a ship in the heart of the sea, and the way of a man with[55] *a virgin.*
20 *Thus*[56] *is the way of an adulteress:*[57]
she eats and wipes her mouth, and says: "I have not done iniquity."
21 *Under three things the earth trembles,*
under four it cannot endure:[58]
22 *under an official*[59] *when he becomes king,*
and an outcast[60] *when he becomes full of food;*
23 *under a hated*[61] *woman when she gets*[62] *married,*[63]

---

bly reconstructs an original *l^ehāqat* or *l^ehîqat,* which became corrupted in the MT through metathesis. The parallel of Prov. 23:22b can be used to validate the reconstruction or to explain away the LXX. Some older rabbis, however, invested the MT with the connotation of old age (Delitzsch, *Proverbs,* pp. 459-60).

50. The pronoun is fem. in v. 15b and masc. in v. 18, because the referents are fem. (*rḥm* is fem. in sense) and masc. respectively.

51. Comparison of capability (*IBHS,* p. 266, P. 14.4f).

52. Q *'arbā'â* follows the rule of gender opposition (*IBHS,* p. 277, P. 15.2.2). K *'arba'* contradicts this rule. K may have been influenced by v. 15b, where the same numerals are masc. in gender opposition to *hēnnâ.*

53. The LXX renders the four occurrences of *derek* differently: *ichnē, hodous, tribous,* and *hodous* respectively.

54. The same word is rendered "vulture" in v. 17b.

55. Or "in."

56. The deictic adverb points to what will now be told (*HALOT,* 2:482, s.v. II *kēn;* cf. 1:19).

57. The *Piel* ptcp. with the root *n'p* denotes customary behavior with several different partners (*IBHS,* p. 416, P. 24.5c).

58. Lit. "to bear [the weight]." F. Stolz *(TLOT,* 2:772, s.v. *nś')* thinks that *nś'* here means "produce," but that notion offers a poor parallel to "shake." For "endure" see BDB, p. 671, s.v. *nāśā'.*

59. The precise sense of *'ebed* (= a subordinate of one's lord, "slave, servant, bondman, subordinate, subject, vassal, mercenary, official, minister") is determined by the context (C. Westermann, *TLOT,* 2:821, s.v. *'ebed*). The verb "becomes king" suggests that *'ebed* has its common meaning of "official" *(HALOT,* 2:775, s.v. *'ebed).*

60. See Prov. 17:7.

61. *HALOT* (3:1,339, s.v. *śn'*) defines the term as "not to be able to endure a woman any longer." Van Leeuwen ("Proverbs 30:21-23 and the Biblical World Upside

and a maidservant when she dispossesses[64] *her mistress.*
24 *As for four things, they are small creatures of the earth,*
but they[65] *are extremely wise:*[66]
25 *ants*[67] *are a people without strength,*
and so[68] *they store up their food in the harvest.*
26 *Rock badgers are a people without numerical strength,*
and so they place their houses[69] *in the rocks.*
27 *Locusts*[70] *have no king,*
and so all of them go forth dividing into companies.
28 *A wall lizard you can catch with two hands,*

Down," *JBL* 105 [1986] 602, 608) presupposes "the polygamous situation with a loved and unloved wife in mutual competition" and translates as "despised wife [cf. Gen. 29:31, 33; Deut. 21:15[2x], 16, 17]." But this is not true in Isa. 60:15. Although in its other eight uses the fem. passive ptcp. *śᵉnû'â* (of *śn'* "to hate" [see 1:22]) refers to a married woman, the form does not demand that meaning. If a married woman is in view, the predicate, "when she gets married," is a tautology to a fault. Van Leeuwen ("Proverbs 30:21-23," p. 608) resolves that problem by repointing *tibbā'ēl* as *Qal,* "when she rules," but the *Qal* of *b'l* occurs with a direct object (Isa. 26:13) or with the prepositions *lᵉ* (1 Chr. 4:22) and *beth* (Jer. 3:14; 31:32), none of which occurs here.

62. The parallel prefix conjugations *yimlôk* and *tîraš* ("becomes king" and "dispossesses" respectively) insinuate that the ambiguous prefix conjugation also be interpreted as signifying an incipient situation (*IBHS,* pp. 503-4, 505-6, PP. 31.2.c, 3d).

63. In the *Qal, bā'al* means "to take possession of a woman as bride or wife," and in the *Niphal* "to get married" *(HALOT,* 1:142, s.v. I *b'l).* A married woman is expressed by the *Qal* passive ptcp. The LXX adds gratuitously, "if she should marry a good man."

64. The LXX (cf. Syr.) *hotan ekbalę̄* (if she should cast out) could represent *tᵉgārēš.*

65. *Hēm* replaces *hēmmâ* (v. 18) for stylistic variation *(HALOT,* 1:250, s.v. *hēm, hēmmâ).*

66. The *Pual* of *ḥākām,* also as a ptcp., occurs elsewhere only in Ps. 58:5(6) with reference to a "trained/experienced" enchanter. To judge from the use of the internal cognate acc. with the *Pual* ptcps. in Exod. 12:9, *bāšēl mᵉbuššāl* "thoroughly boiled" (?) and in Ps. 64:6(7), *ḥēpeś mᵉḥuppāś* "well-thought-through plan (?)," *ḥᵃkāmîm mᵉḥukkāmîm* is an idiomatic hyperbole, "extremely wise" (NIV, NRSV; *IBHS,* p. 167, P. 10.2.1g). The reading of the LXX (cf. Syr. and Vulg.) *tōn sophōn* (< *mēḥᵃkāmîm* "than wise men") is due to the exclusive use of *ḥākām* in this book as an adjective, never as a *Pual* ptcp.

67. The small creatures occur alternately with and without the article of class for stylistic reasons.

68. The *waw*-consecutive with the prefix conjugation in vv. 25-27 signifies consequence (*IBHS,* pp. 547-50, P. 312.1).

69. Generic nouns are conventionally expressed in the sing. (*IBHS,* p. 115, P. 7.2.2b).

70. Construed as an article of class with a sing. noun to indicate a group (*IBHS,* p. 114, P. 7.2.2a).

but it lives[71] *in the king's palace.*
29 *They are three creatures that excel*[72] *in their stride,*[73]
and four that excel in their movement:[74]
30 *the lion*[75] *is a hero among animals,*
and does not turn back from the face of anything;
31 *the strutting*[76] *rooster*[77] *or*[78] *the he-goat,*
and a king no one dares to resist.[79]
32 *If you will play the fool*[80] *in exalting yourself,*
and if you scheme to do so,[81] *clap*[82] *your hand over your mouth,*

71. The preposition *beth* demands some such verb (*IBHS,* p. 224, P. 1.4d).

72. Lit. "they make good according to their genre, function, design, and/or situation" (see 15:2).

73. Lit. "of step" (cf. Prov. 4:12; 7:8; 16:9), objective gen.

74. Lit. "make good of going."

75. The Hebrew has many words for lion, but the differences between them is uncertain (cf. *ʾărî* [22:13; 26:13; 28:15]). F. S. Bodenheimer ("Fauna and Flora of the Bible," in *Helps for Translators* [London: United Bible Societies, 1972], 11:50) says that in ancient times African and Persian lions met in the Middle East. The thrice-used poetic term *layiš* (Job 4:11; Prov. 30:30; Isa. 30:16) was probably chosen for its assonance with "he-goat," *tāyiš.*

76. *Motnayim* refers to "the strong set of muscles binding the abdomen to the lower limbs, the outer lumbar region" *(HALOT,* 2:655, s.v. *motnayim).* This attributive gen. is understood to denote "an animal striding proudly" *(HALOT,* 1:281, s.v. *zarzîr).*

77. The meaning of the *hap. leg. zarzîr* is uncertain. Cognates in Akkadian and Arabic point to a cricket; others in Syriac and Arabic, along with the Mishnaic Heb. and Talmud, indicate a "starling." "Rooster" is based on the ancient versions and some rabbis (so *HALOT,* 1:281, s.v. *zarzîr*). Later Hebrew called the cock *geber* because of its manly behavior.

78. To indicate Agur is moving from one figure to another (see Song 2:9).

79. The meaning "no one dares to resist" is uncertain. Some read the obscure *ʾalqûm ʿimmô* in light of the Arabic definite article *ʾal* without being felt as such as in "*al*gebra" and "*al*cohol" and of Arab. *qaum* "levy," yielding "calling up his people/army with him" (cf. "with his army around him" [NIV]). But mixing Hebrew with Arabic is a stretch. The best-suggested emendation is *qām ʿal ʿammô* "standing over (i.e., at the head of) his people" (cf. publicly speaking before a nation in the LXX [cf. Syr., Targ.]; so Plöger [*Sprüche,* p. 355]; Meinhold [*Sprüche,* p. 505, n. 170]; NRSV). The best suggestion without emendation is to etymologize *ʾalqum* into *ʾal* "not" and *qûm* "to rise up" (cf. *ʾal-māwet* in 12:28) and to invest *ʿimmô* with the meaning "against him" (i.e., "secure against revolt" [cf. Eccl. 8:2-4]; so Driver ["Problems in the Hebrew Text of Proverbs," *Bib* 32 (1951), 173-97, esp. p. 194, though he unnecessarily emends *ʾal* to *lōʾ];* so KJV; NIV n.; NJPS, etc.).

80. Perfect of resolve (*IBHS,* p. 489, P. 30.5.1e). This is not an indefinite perfective (i.e., "have played the fool" [so NIV, NRSV]). If it were, then his indiscretion should have already produced strife.

81. Lit. "and if you plan." The conjunction interprets the perfect of resolve.

82. The verb *śîm* should be supplied from the full idiom in Judg. 18:19; Job 21:5; Mic. 7:16.

33 *for [as]*[83] *the churning*[84] *of cream produces butter,*[85]
and as the wringing[86] *of the nose produces blood,*
so the "pressing out" of wrath produces strife.[87]

The chapter as recorded in the MT has integrity as the following outline suggests:[88]

I. Introduction: Agur's autobiographical confession	1-9
A. Superscription	1
B. His confession	2-9
1. His sayings are inspired	2-6
2. His two petitions: for truthfulness and modesty	7-9
II. Main Body: Seven numerical sayings	10-31
A. First unit, without verse-initial title lines	10-16
1. Single-line proverb against disturbing moral order	10

83. Demanded by the asyndetic juxtaposition of the emblematic parallelism of verset A.

84. For this meaning of *mîṣ,* which is based on Akkadian and Arabic cognates and on "the two giants of medieval Bible scholarship, namely, Saadia Gaon and Ibn Janah," see M. Held, "Marginal Notes to the Biblical Lexicon," in *Biblical and Related Studies Presented to Samuel Iwry,* ed. A. Kort and S. Morschauser (Winona Lake, Ind.: Eisenbrauns, 1985), pp. 97-101.

85. So A. Caquot, *TDOT,* 4:390-91, s.v. *ḥālāb;* summarized by J. P. J. Olivier, *NIDOTTE,* 2:166-67, s.v. *ḥem'â.*

86. Held ("Marginal Notes," p. 103) notes that in Akkadian the verbs "to press, to compress" and "to shake, to dislodge" "are not infrequently attested in contexts dealing with pressure applied to various parts of the body, or dislocation thereof."

87. Held ("Marginal Notes," p. 103, n. 35) observes that Alfasi interprets *'pym* to denote "stirring up (of wrath)."

88. By contrast, the LXX divides chs. 30 and 31 into three sections and redistributes them to sustain its fiction of Solomonic authorship (see I: 4). It inserts 30:1-14 between 24:22 and 23 and 30:15–31:9 between chs. 24 and 25, leaving 31:10-31 at the end of ch. 29. In that version, 30:1 reads, "My son, reverence my words and receive them and repent. These things the man says to them that trust in God; and I cease." The "my" refers to Solomon, because 30:1-14 now draws to a conclusion "my [Solomon's] words" in 22:16–24:22. It renders 24:23, "And this thing I [Solomon] say to you that are wise for you to learn." Thus 30:15–31:9, which follows 24:23-34, is also attributed to Solomon. Finally, the acrostic on the valiant wife in 31:10-31 draws Solomon's proverbs collected by the men to Hezekiah (25:1–29:27) to its conclusion. For this translator neither the text of Proverbs nor its canonical shape had been set in stone (see E. Tov, *Of Scribes and Scrolls: Studies on the Hebrew Bible, Intertestamental Judaism, and Christian Origins: Presented to John Strugnell,* ed. H. W. Attridge, J. J. Collins, and T. H. Tobin, S.J. [College Theology Society Resources in Religion 5; Lanham, Md., New York, and London: University Press of America, 1990], pp. 43-56).

After the title in the typical titular form (30:1a), Agur's sayings can be analyzed by form and rhetorical criticism into three sections: an autobiography in direct address (30:1b-9), extended numerical sayings (30:11-16, 18-31) that are introduced by single-line, nonnumerical aphorisms (30:10, 17), and a concluding nonnumerical saying again in direct address (30:32-33). Verse 10 is a janus that, in conjunction with vv. 32-33, forms an *inclusio* around the numerical sayings. All three sections censor greed and hubris, teaching subordination to authority to retain cosmic and social order: to God's word (30:1b-9), in the state and in the home (30:10-16), and so living within boundaries (30:17-31). The concluding command forbids Ithiel from usurping authority (30:32-33). Hubris and greed incur God's wrath (vv. 10, 17) as well as cosmic and social upheaval (vv. 21, 32-33). This is Agur's oracle or burden.

Verse 10 is a janus. Suffice it to note here that, on the one hand, its direct address continues the "I-thou" encounter of the autobiography (cf. in vv. 4b and 6) and that vv. 6 and 10 uniquely share a similar syntax. On the other hand, its lack of the autobiographical form and the catchword "curse" *(qll)* bind it with the first numerical saying (v. 11). The numeral "two" links his confession and numerical sayings. He closes his autobiography with two requests (vv. 7-9), and the first numeral he uses as part of a janus to the titled numerical sayings is "two" (v. 15a). In fact he bangs his audience on the head with that numeral by making it word-initial in v. 7, resembling the titled lines of the numerical sayings. Scholarly differences over the chapter's division attest the chapter's unity, not its disunity.

A. INTRODUCTION (30:1-9)

The introduction consists of a superscription identifying the literary genre, author, and addressee (vv. 1a-bα), followed by the author's autobiography validating his inspiration and authority (vv. 1bβ-9).

1. Superscription (30:1a)

The superscription is craftily sewn into the autobiographical confession in a janus verset (v. 1b) by switching from third person in v. 1bα to first person in v. 1bβ. Furthermore, v. 1bβ summarizes Agur's argument in vv. 2-6 by a prophetic introduction to his autobiography that begins in (v. 1b) and is continued by the medial conjunction "surely" that begins v. 2. In the superscription, Agur claims that his sayings are inspired (v. 1) and then shows the necessity that God reveals truth and how it is attained (vv. 2-6). His vulnerable petitions in vv. 7-9 reveal him as a pure channel of God's revelation. Verset A of the superscription presents the literary genre and author of Collection VI. *Agur son of Jakeh ('āgûr bin-yāqeh),* who is otherwise unknown,[89] represents his *sayings* (*dibrê;* see 1:6) as inspired (i.e., divine-human speech, originating with God and invested with his authority) by placing the prophetic genre term *oracle* (or "burden," *hammaśśā'*)[90] in apposition to the wisdom genre term "sayings."[91] His claim matches Solomon's claim for the inspiration of his words (see 2:6).

89. The Midrash on Proverbs allegorized the name to retain Solomonic authorship: "The words — these are the words of Solomon; Agur — he who girded *('āgûr)* his loins for wisdom; son of Jakeh (Yakeh) — a son who is free *(nāqî')* from all sin and transgression" (B. L. Visotzky, *The Midrash on Proverbs* [Yale Judaica Series; New Haven: Yale University, 1997], p. 117). A. Cohen (*Proverbs,* p. 200) notes that some later Jewish commentators rejected the identification of Agur with Solomon. Ibn Ezra held that Solomon incorporated into his book the words of a contemporary. Jerome interprets the proper names as substantives: *verba congregantis filii vomentis* (= "words of G/gatherer son of V/vomiter"), which Toy (*Proverbs,* p. 518) interprets to mean "the gatherer of people for instruction" and "who pours out words of wisdom." P. Skehan (*Studies in Israelite Poetry and Wisdom* [CBQMS 1; Washington: Catholic Biblical Association of America, 1971], pp. 27-45) interpreted "Agur son of Jakeh" as a riddle. According to him, "Agur" means "I am a sojourner" and Jakeh is an acronym for Yahweh *qādôš hû'* ("Yahweh is holy"). In this way "Agur, in association with Jacob/Israel, is the LORD's son" (see v. 4b). It is best, however, to take it simply as a proper name. The formula, proper noun + "son of" + proper noun, occurs over 1,500 times in the Old Testament. It parallels the superscription in 31:1, which also combines "words of" with a proper noun. In ancient Near Eastern wisdom literature the real author is named (Kitchen, "Proverbs and Wisdom Books," pp. 93, 95). Finally, "Agur" and "Jakeh" show up as proper personal names in the cognate Semitic languages. This may suggest that he is a proselyte to Israel's faith. Even if v. 4 parodies Job 38–41, Agur cannot be dated, for the date of that text is also questionable.

90. F. Stolz *(TLOT,* 2:773, s.v. *nś')* says that *hammaśśā'* is "a prophetic technical term" meaning 'judgment proclamation,'" but he broadens the term to a prophetic address in general in Zech. 9:1; 12:1; Mal. 1:1; cf. Hab. 1:1. The specific genre "judgment oracle" is not inappropriate in connection with the single proverbs that introduce the two parts of the collection of numerical sayings and threaten judgment for violating the established order (vv. 10, 17). Perhaps, however, in wisdom literature the term is modified to mean simply "oracle," even as *qesem* in 16:10 and *ḥāzôn* in 29:18 are nuanced differently from prophetic literature. *Maśśā'* may be a collective for a number of diverse oracles (cf. Prov. 31:1; Mal. 1:1), but the structural analysis of Proverbs 30 suggests that it refers to a unified message as in Hab. 1:1.

91. Agur also infers his inspiration by joining his sayings with God's words to David and to Moses in vv. 5-6.

2. Agur's Autobiographical Confession (30:1b-9)

Many scholars (e.g., Oesterley,[92] Plöger,[93] and Perdue[94]) deny the structural unity of vv. 5-6 and vv. 1-4. Scott[95] and Crenshaw[96] think that the text consists of a dialogue between Agur the skeptic (vv. 1-4) and an orthodox Jew (vv. 5-6). But nothing in the text, or for that matter in the whole chapter, suggests a change of speaker. Rather, one discerns a structural and thematic unity in the verses, confirmed by the structural and thematic parallels in Bar. 3:29–4:1 and Job 28:12-28.

The decision whether or not the text is a unity is decisive for its interpretation. Those who deny its unity interpret Agur's questions in v. 4 as buttressing his skepticism in vv. 2-3 about the inability of humanity to know wisdom. According to them, all his questions about who sustains the universe in v. 4a can be answered by, "No man," and his question "What is his name and the name of his son?" is biting sarcasm. Accordingly, the assertions in vv. 5-6 about the purity and perfection of God's word are out of place, tacked on to correct, or to put into proper perspective, Agur's skepticism.

J. Pauls,[97] however, building on the work of Franklyn,[98] establishes the structural unity of vv. 1-6 as follows:

A Human Confession (vv. 2-3)
  1. Statement #1 (v. 2)
  2. Statement #2 (v. 3)
B Rhetorical Questions (v. 4)
  1. "Who . . . ?" (v. 4a)
  2. "What . . . ?" (v. 4b)
A′ Scriptural Quotations (vv. 5-6)
  1. Counterstatement #1 (v. 5)
  2. Counterstatement #2 (v. 6)

Agur's thematic movement from human ignorance of wisdom to the possession of it follows the same logic as that of Bar. 3:29–4:1 and of Job 28:12-28. All three sages move from confessions that on their own they

92. Oesterley, *Proverbs,* p. 270.
93. Plöger, *Sprüche,* p. 359.
94. Perdue, *Proverbs,* pp. 252-53.
95. Scott, *Proverbs,* p. 176; Scott, *The Way of Wisdom* (New York: Macmillan, 1971), p. 165.
96. Crenshaw, "Clanging Symbols," p. 58.
97. J. Pauls, "Proverbs 30:1-6," pp. 48-51.
98. Cf. Franklyn, "The Sayings of Agur," pp. 238-52.

could not find wisdom (vv. 2-3) to assertions through rhetorical questions that God alone possesses it (v. 4a) and that he has a "son"/*'ādām* whom he teaches (v. 4b). Agur's adaptations of scriptural quotations establish that God's word to Israel is pure (v. 5) and canonical (v. 6). Accordingly, v. 4, instead of being a redundant reinforcement of skepticism, plays a pivotal role and is a janus verse, pointing to a personal relationship with the wise Sovereign as the means to overcome the human predicament of ignorance and death. The "inspired sayings of Agur" (v. 1) are part of the canon and truth not to be tampered with (v. 6).

a. His Inability and Ability to Attain Wisdom (30:1b-6)

After a brief introduction that continues to assert Agur's inspiration, he begins his autobiography by succinctly stating the human tension of inability and ability, of weakness and strength, of incompetence and competence. On his own he cannot attain to wisdom (vv. 1b-4), but by God's revelation of it he can (vv. 5-6). He transforms the human crisis of knowing to a crisis of knowing God in v. 4b.

1b This verset underscores his inspiration by introducing it as *the inspired utterance of the man* (*ne'ûm haggeber;* see n. 6) in apposition to "prophetic oracle." Kosmala[99] notes that *geber* in this formula signifies a man who stands in a special relationship with God (see I: 89). Kosmala also connects Agur's inspired utterances with Agur's assertions about the permanence and sufficiency of God's word in vv. 5 and 6. Agur addresses his inspired saying to *Ithiel (le'îtî'ēl),* but in its canonical context the editor of Proverbs addresses the universal people of God (see I: 37).[100] Finally, verset B summarizes Agur's tension as a sage. He explains his statement, *I am weary, O God* (*lā'îtî 'ēl;* see n. 9)[101] in vv. 2-3 as his quest for wisdom by natural rea-

99. H. Kosmala, *TDOT,* 2:378-79, s.v. *gābhar.*

100. Heb. *le'îtî'ēl* is usually emended in connection with the following words. However, the proper name is attested in Neh. 11:7 and, as documented by Lipiński ("Peninna," p. 72) and Franklyn ("The Sayings of Agur," pp. 241-42, n. 14), has possible analogues in ancient Near Eastern texts. Moreover, it supplies the necessary antecedent to the implied "you" in vv. 4 and 6. Commenting on the addressees in ancient Near Eastern "instructional" texts, Kitchen ("Proverbs and the Wisdom Books," p. 76) says, "Frequently the author addresses his son, the latter often being named." In 31:1, a parallel to this superscription, Lemuel is inferentially the one addressed by his mother.

101. "I am weary, O God" (Heb. *lā'îtî 'ēl*) is an emendation of the MT *le'îtîēl* (see n. 9), which repeats "to Ithiel." The repetition of the addressee's name would be abnormal. Furthermore, if it be a proper name, the conjunction "and" with *'ūkāl* demands that it, too, be taken as a proper name. However, *'ūkāl* is a verb and never attested as a proper name in any Semitic language. Moreover, if *'ūkāl* is a proper name, then we are left with the bizarre situation of an oracle addressed twice to one person and once to another, without

son, and he clarifies its antithesis, *but I can prevail* (*wᵉʾūkāl;* see n. 10),[102] in vv. 5-6 as due to divine revelation. Agur is "weary" humanly speaking (vv. 2-4), but he can "prevail" since God and his canonical word are his refuge (vv. 5-6). Admittedly, an autobiography in a superscription is unusual, but the logical particle "surely"/"for" that introduces his autobiographical confession in v. 2 and that occurs medially in a discourse validates the emendation.[103]

2-3 The initial particles of vv. 2 and 3, respectively, *surely* (or "for," *kî*) and *indeed* (*wᵉ;* n. 11) bind his autobiographical confession to v. 1, and the initial conjunctive of v. 3 binds the autobiography of v. 2 to that of v. 1. The logical particle *kî* suggests that "I am weary, O God," refers to his quest for wisdom.[104] In his quest to know the Holy One and learn his wisdom (v. 3), he failed (v. 2). Agur makes no claim to wisdom *qua* a human being. If he is to know wisdom, he must be taught by God, who alone possesses it. His con-

---

reason. Finally, if these are all personal names, the emphatic and logical particle "surely/because" that introduces v. 2 is nonsensical. The transparent pun *l'yty 'l* and *l'yty'l* readily explains the confusion in the MT. The verbal root has been identified as I *l'h* "to be weary," which is favored by most (see *HALOT,* 2:512, s.v. *l'h*), or II *l'h* "to be strong," which is favored by Dahood (*Proverbs and Northwest Semitic Philology* [Rome: Pontifical Biblical Institute, 1963], p. 57) and Lipiński ("Peninna," p. 74). The second root, however, is otherwise attested only in the cognate languages. Moreover, the notion of weariness, rather than power, better suits Agur's confession of weakness in v. 2, which is syntactically connected with v. 1 by *kî* "surely."

102. The interpretation of *wᵉ* ("but") as an antithetical disjunctive depends on interpreting *'ūkāl* as "I am able" or "I can prevail," the opposite of "to be weary." Without emending the consonants, *'ūkāl* can be read as a defective *Pual* ptcp. of *'kl* (= "and [I am] one who is consumed/destroyed"; cf. Exod. 3:2), but a *daghesh* has to be supplied, and one expects the pronoun *'ānōkî.* Franklyn ("The Sayings of Agur," p. 244) repoints it as *wā'ēkal* (= *waw* consecutive with apocopated short prefix conjunction of *klh*) "and I am spent," which he refers to old age. The LXX probably also read it thus: *kai pauomai,* "and I cease" (i.e., cease speaking); similarly Delitzsch (*Proverbs,* 2:271), "and I have withdrawn" (i.e., from a troubling pursuit of wisdom). Kuhn (cited by Franklyn, "Sayings of Agur," p. 243, n. 18) repointed it as *'ākîl* (defective *Hiphil* imperfect of *kûl* "but I will endure," investing the form with a positive tone, not a negative one). BDB (p. 408, s.v. *yᵉkōl*), Theod., Cocceius, Plöger (*Sprüche,* p. 354), et al. read the MT as a defective form of *'ūkāl* from the root *yᵉkōl* = "I am able/I can prevail." Pauls ("Proverbs 30:1-6," pp. 82-83) defends this reading exegetically, for it holds in tension the notions of human weakness in vv. 2-3 and divine enabling in vv. 5-6. He also supports it textually by noting the defective form of this root in 3rd masc. pl. in Josh. 7:12; Ps. 18:39; Jer. 20:11 and by noting that the root occurs without an object in Exod. 1:23 or a complementary verb in Ps. 101:5; Isa. 1:13. However, the absolute use is unique. Finally, he maintains it lexically by noting that *l'h* and *ykl* are joined together also in Job 4:2; Isa. 16:12.

103. *IBHS,* p. 655, P. 39.14e.

104. Clifford (*Proverbs,* p. 260) validates this interpretation of *kî* from Jer. 1:6.

fession rebuts the rationalism of the so-called "Enlightenment," which contended that unaided human reason can attain truth. Two centuries later its enterprise has proved a colossal failure.[105] Having failed in the enterprise, the Enlightenment's heirs have drawn the perverse conclusion that there are no absolutes, except that one! Agur, however, points the way out of their nihilism. Verse 2 presents the earthbound human predicament of being unable independently to attain wisdom; v. 3 points to "knowledge of the Holy One" as the way out of this ignorance (cf. 3:5-6).

The outer frame of this chiastic quatrain poses the dilemma. On the one hand, Agur is less than human (v. 2a); on the other hand, he wants to know the Holy One (v. 3b). Though using Semitic hyperbole and self-abasement (Job 25:4-6; Pss. 22:6[7]; 73:21-22), he implies that to be truly human entails knowing God. The inner core, linked by *lōʾ,* explains that he is less than human because he lacks both understanding of the divinely established moral order and, though presumably instructed, he had not learned wisdom (see 1:2). He locates his confession within the wisdom tradition by using the same three words Solomon used both to introduce his book, *insight, wisdom,* and *knowledge* (see 1:2), and to conclude his prologue to it, "knowledge of the Holy" (see 9:10). But whereas Solomon made them known, Agur failed to learn them, presumably from his pagan teacher. Although he wearied himself to find wisdom, he came up with what Qoheleth calls *hebel* ("a vapor"; Eccl. 1:2; 12:8). This proselyte to Israel's faith learned them only when he accepted Israel's spiritual and intellectual inheritance from men like Moses, David, and presumably Solomon (cf. 2:6).

2 *Surely, I am too stupid* [or "brutish," *baʿar;* see 12:1] *to be a man* (*mēʾîš;* see n. 12) is hyperbole like David's "but I am worm and not a man" (Ps. 22:5[6]; cf. Job 25:4-6; Ps. 73:21-22).[106] Clifford observes that these examples of "low anthropology," of self-abasement, express reverence.[107] In v. 2b, *I do not have understanding* (cf. 9:10) and *I do not have the understanding of a human being* underscore the self-abasement (cf. Pss. 73:22; 92:6[7]). The parallelism infers that true humanity consists in having insight into the religio-ethical realm. To realize its true identity and destiny humanity requires a divine revelation of the moral order. Meinhold comments,

105. A. MacIntyre, *After Virtue* (Notre Dame, Ind.: University of Notre Dame, 1984).

106. His use of *baʿar* "brutish" with reference to divine thought and ethics (see 12:1) resembles its use in Ps. 73:21-23. Franklyn notes, "The dying psalmist's confession of ignorance [is] followed by immediate affirmation of God's presence and rescue. . . . Here, as in Proverbs, the weary and embittered person confesses ignorance of God and, in the same breath, he seizes the outstretched hand of the divine presence" (Franklyn, "The Sayings of Agur," pp. 244-45).

107. Clifford, *Proverbs,* p. 26.

"These two nominal clauses express at the beginning what Job achieved only at the end of his long wrestling (Job 40:4; 42:3, 6)."[108] Agur begins where Job signed off. "With a mock ruefulness, he observes that others seem to know all about God and to have him completely in their grasp, whereas he, poor fellow, is apparently subhuman, since for him both are shrouded in mystery."[109] Yet, this is his true wisdom. Alden insightfully comments, "A man devoid of intelligence could never have written these words."[110] By confessing that he has no wisdom apart from revelation (vv. 5-6), he displays his wisdom and his becoming a true human being. His confession implicitly polemicizes against sages who claim wisdom through their own efforts (cf. Isa. 5:21; 19:11-12; 29:14; 44:25; Jer. 8:8-9; 9:12[11], 23[22]). In truth, they are so stupid that they do not even know that they fall short of being human. The biblical wisdom tradition often notes the limitations of human knowledge and the need of divine revelation. J. Luyten notes, "In classical wisdom books we meet this theme in the warning against trusting one's insight (Prov. 3:5-7), in sentences on the opposition between man's proposal and God's disposal . . . , and in the saying and poem expressing the transcendence of divine wisdom and man's ignorance (Prov. 30:1b-3; Job 11:[7]-9)."[111] Agur, however, does not relieve his intellectual inadequacy so quickly. Instead he develops step-by-step a way out of the human dilemma.

3 Although taught by a sage, Agur had *not learned* [surprisingly, a unique occurrence of *lāmad* in Proverbs] *wisdom* (see I: 76). *I do have* (lit. "I do not know") or possess the wisdom that can fathom the depths of the enigma with which the Creator confronts the human being (cf. Job 28:12-22). Without that ability to interpret the human situation, he cannot reach certainty about living skillfully. Moreover, the imprecise parallelism between "wisdom" and *knowledge of the Holy One* (see 2:5; 9:10) implies that wisdom as defined in this book is dependent on a personal relationship with God, who stands apart from the restrictions of finitude and depravity (cf. 2:1-5). G. T. Shepherd comments, "Within the presupposition of Wisdom's original status in the heavenly domain of God, the questions of Bar[uch] 3:29-30; Dt. 30:12-13; Prov. 30:3-4 satirize any pretense of grasping her by mere earthly genius and agility."[112] Von Rad rightly remarked that Israel's "thinking had to operate within spheres of tension indicated by the prior knowledge of God."[113] One cannot live in accordance with the divinely established moral

108. Meinhold, *Sprüche,* 2:497.

109. Adopted from McKane, *Proverbs,* pp. 646-47.

110. Alden, *Proverbs,* p. 208.

111. Cited by Franklyn, "The Sayings of Agur," p. 245.

112. G. T. Sheppard, *Wisdom as a Hermeneutical Construct: A Study in the Sapientializing of the Old Testament* (BZAW 151; New York: Walter de Gruyter, 1980), p. 91.

113. G. von Rad, *Wisdom in Israel,* tr. J. D. Martin (London: SCM, 1972), p. 68.

order and find refuge against death (cf. v. 5) apart from empathizing with the mind and will of God. He alone sees "ontologically" (i.e., the whole of what actually is). To be wise, a person must transcend the relativity and depravity of human epistemology. H. Blocher argued, "If the whole of reality comes from one wise and sovereign Lord, who has ordered all things, reality is all of one piece; nothing is independent of God, and nothing can be truly interpreted independently of God."[114] Humanity can know absolutely only if it knows comprehensively. To make an absolute judgment on their own, human beings must usurp God's throne. Van Til said:

> If one does not make human knowledge wholly dependent upon the original self-knowledge and consequent revelation of God to man, then man will have to seek knowledge within himself as the final reference point. Then he will have to seek an exhaustive understanding of reality. He will have to hold that if he cannot attain to such an exhaustive understanding of reality, he has no *true* knowledge of anything at all. Either man must then know everything or he knows nothing. This is the dilemma that confronts every form of non-Christian epistemology.[115]

Earthbound mortals cannot find transcendent wisdom apart from the transcendent LORD. Real wisdom must find its starting point in God's revelation; in his light, we see light (Ps. 36:9[10]).

4 Agur now shifts his attention from his ignorance of wisdom to confront Ithiel, who represents all Israel, to know wisdom. By two sets of rhetorical questions, a form of strong assertion (cf. Ruth 3:1), Agur challenges his audience to bridge the "unbridgeable" gulf between the LORD's knowledge of wisdom and human helplessness by personally identifying itself as a "son" of the Holy One. In verset A, he employs in an anaphora the animate interrogative pronoun *who* (see 23:29) four times, and in verset B, the inanimate interrogative pronoun *what* (i.e., "is his and his son's name?" see 20:24). The answer to the first question is, "No human being, but only God." *All* brings the "who" questions to their climactic conclusion (see 3:15, 17). The answer to the "what?" questions are "the LORD" and "Israel."

The "who" questions exhibit a chiastic pattern. The outer core presents the merism "heaven" (v. $4a\alpha^1$) and "earth" (v. $4a\beta^2$) to denote the cosmos (see 3:19). To ascend to heaven represents its vertical axis, and "ends of the earth" its horizontal axis. The inner core presents the two parts of a thun-

114. H. Blocher, "The Fear of the LORD as the 'Principle' of Wisdom," *TynBul* 28 (1977) 21.

115. C. Van Til, *A Christian Theory of Knowledge* (Philadelphia: Presbyterian and Reformed, 1969), p. 17.

derstorm, "wind" (v. 4aα¹) and "water" (v. 4aβ²) that sustains life on earth (see 3:20). By restraining them, the LORD inflicts a drought. The answer to these questions, standing between humanity's inability to know wisdom (vv. 2-3) and the presence of God's word with his people (vv. 5-6), unravels the paradox of how inaccessible wisdom becomes accessible to earthlings. Striking parallels both in Bar. 3:29-37, which Sheppard has shown reinterprets Deut. 30:12,[116] and in Job 28:12-28 clarify that the first question, *Who has ascended* [see 21:22] *into heaven* [see 25:3] *and come down?* (see 1:12), aims to exclude the earthling from being able to obtain wisdom. Parallels in two ancient Near Eastern texts infer only a god, not even a superhuman being, can ascend into heaven (cf. Gen. 11:7; 35:13).[117] In the hymnic literature, the LORD ascends his throne, perhaps in the symbolic form of Israel's king ascending the throne, to exercise dominion over the earth (Pss. 47:5[6] [cf. Num. 23:21; 2 Sam. 15:10; 2 K. 9:13]; 68:9[10]).[118] In the prophetic literature, the LORD sends to the lowest depths earthlings who in hubris resolve to become God by ascending to heaven to assume dominion (Isa. 14:13-14; Jer. 51:53). The remaining three questions, asking who is sovereign over the cosmic elements, infer that the LORD has access to wisdom. Van Leeuwen comments, "The main value of the topos [of heavenly ascent and descent] is to reaffirm the great gulf that separates humans from the divine realm and the prerogatives of deity, such as immortality, superhuman knowledge, wisdom, and power."[119] He created the *ends of the earth,* implying that nothing is hidden from him (cf. Job 28:23-24), and he controls *the wind* (see 25:14) and *the waters* (see 8:24) that sustain it, implying that nothing is beyond his ability. Grisanti notes that "God's sovereignty is often emphasized by means of his control over water [cf. Gen. 1:9-10; chs. 6–9; Ps. 104:6-7, 10-13; Amos 5:8]."[120] God's total sovereignty over the universe expresses his wisdom. W. Brueggemann, in speaking of Jer. 9:23[22], says that wisdom is not simply about "the power to discern, but the capacity to manage and control."[121] Baruch (3:29-37) develops the same argument:

116. Sheppard, *Wisdom as a Hermeneutical Construct,* pp. 90-99.

117. In the *Epic of Gilgamesh* (3.4 [3]), the heroic superman Gilgamesh asks his counterpart, Enkidu: "Who, my friend, can scale he[aven]? Only the gods [live] forever under the sun" [*ANET,* p. 79b]). In the *Dialogue of Pessimism,* the servant asks his master, "Who is tall enough to ascend to heaven? Who is broad enough to embrace the earth?" (*ANET,* p. 438b).

118. G. Wehmeier, *TLOT,* 2:887, s.v. *'lh.*

119. R. C. Van Leeuwen, "The Background to Proverbs 30:4aα," in *My Sister,* ed. M. Barre (CBQMS 29; Washington: Catholic Biblical Association, 1997), p. 121.

120. M. A. Grisanti, *NIDOTTE,* 2:929, s.v. *mayim.*

121. W. Brueggemann, "The Epistemological Crisis of Israel's Two Histories (Jer 9:22-23)," in *IW,* p. 94.

29 "Who has gone up into heaven and taken her [wisdom],
and brought her down from the clouds?

. . . .

31 There is neither one who knows her way,
nor one who comprehends her path.
32 But he who knows [sees?] all things knows her.
He found her out in his understanding.
He established the earth for evermore;

. . . .

35 This is our God,
with whom none can be compared.
36 He found the way of understanding
and gave it to Jacob his servant
and to Israel whom he loved."

Job 28:12-28 develops the same argument, moving from human inability to obtain wisdom (vv. 12-19) to the LORD's finding and testing of it (vv. 20-27) to his revealing it to human beings (v. 28). Agur's four questions in 30:4a proceed along the same line of reasoning. The first question establishes the unbridgeable gap between the earthling and heaven, presumably where wisdom dwells. The last three establish that God must possess wisdom because he demonstrates it. In Job 38 the LORD asks Job similar questions to Agur's and implies the answer, "Not you, Job, but God" (Job 38:5, 25, 29, 36, 37, 41; 39:5).

Verset Ba asks both for the name of the Sovereign over the cosmos and the name of his son. The inanimate interrogative *What is his name?* (see 18:10) asks not merely for identification but for the circumstances attached to the person's name.[122] From the rest of the Old Testament the answer must be, "the LORD," or its equivalent. The parallel texts in Job 28 and 38 name the LORD. Pauls observes that the question, "What is his name?" resonates with Israel's foundational question, "What is his Name?" (Exod. 3:13) and comments, the question "can produce but one answer — Yahweh."[123] The Midrash also responds, "His name is the Lord."[124] The answer to, "What is the

122. *IBHS,* pp. 319-20, P. 18.2d.

123. Pauls, "Proverbs 30:1-6," p. 117.

124. Visotzky, *The Midrash on Proverbs,* p. 118. Franklyn ("The Sayings of Agur," p. 247), drawing on Crenshaw's *Hymnic Affirmation of Divine Justice* (SBLDS 24; Missoula: Scholars, 1975), pp. 75-92 suggests that the question has a striking affinity with the hymnic refrain, "The LORD [of Hosts] is his name" (cf. Exod. 15:3; Isa. 48:2; Jer. 10:16; 31:35; 32:18; 33:2; Amos 4:13; 5:8, 27; 9:6). "Accordingly," he suggests, "the answer to the first *mah* . . . would most appropriately be 'Yahweh is his name' or 'Yahweh of Hosts is his name.'"

name of his son?" must be based on the lexical foundation that in Proverbs "son" always elsewhere refers to the son whom the father teaches (see 1:8). In the Old Testament, the LORD brought Israel into existence and named his firstborn (cf. Exod. 4:22; Deut. 14:1; 32:5-6, 18-19; Isa. 43:6; 45:11; 63:16; 64:8[7]; Jer. 3:4, 19; 31:20; Hos. 11:1).[125] The LXX reads "his son" as plural, "his children," apparently interpreting "his son" as "the children of Israel." This is also the interpretation in the Midrash Yalkut Shimoni.[126] The striking parallel in Bar. 3:37 confirms the interpretation. Sheppard, commenting on Bar. 3:37b, says, "In the end the author concludes that created humanity can know the way only if God gives it by his elective will and that he has so chosen Israel (v. 37b)."[127] If one object that the answer "Israel" (see 1:1) is derived from outside the wisdom tradition, note Agur's use of intertextuality or *relecture.* The question in v. 4b, "What is his name?" probably echoes Exod. 3:14; v. 5 cites Ps. 18:30(31), and v. 6 alludes to Deut. 4:2 and 12:32(13:1), just as *n*^{e}*'um haggeber* echoes Num. 24:3-9 and 2 Sam. 23:1-7.[128] Bar. 3:29-30 is based on Deut. 30:12, and although neither Agur nor Baruch explains how the LORD "gave wisdom," we may assume that the LORD mediated it through prophets, including his inspired sages (see v. 1; cf. Exod. 24:1, 9-12; Isa. 6:1-11; 40:1-3; Dan. 7:13-14, 27).

In the New Testament Jesus Christ fulfills typical Israel, for a Gentile tyrant threatened his life at birth; he, too, returned from exile in Egypt, suffered in the wilderness, and taught on a mountain. Unlike Israel, he perfectly obeyed his Father (Matt. 2:15; Heb. 5:7-10). But he is more than a son (see I: 131). He identifies himself as the Son of Man who comes on the clouds, the biblical symbol of divine transcendence. In Luke he is the incarnate Son of God by the virgin birth (Luke 1:29-33), and in John he is the eternal Son of God (John 17). As such he speaks with an immediate authority (cf. Matt. 7:28; 9:1-8; 12:8, 42; Heb. 3:3-6; Rev. 5:1-14), and through the Holy Spirit he guided his apostles into all truth (John 16:12-15).

In v. 4bβ Agur escalates his implied challenge that Ithiel embrace his opportunity to possess wisdom by asserting in direct address, *Surely you know!* In addition to forming an *inclusio* with "I do not know" (v. 2), his assertion echoes God's challenge to Job in a similar context (Job 38:3). Both assertions challenge the son to name the LORD as the Sovereign over creation and to receive from him his inheritance. Pauls says, "The second question represents a dramatic shift in our text. It is hardly a sarcastic comment about the 'unbridgeable gulf' between men and God, but rather, a small part of a

125. Cf. G. Fohrer, *TDNT,* 8:351, s.v. *huios.*

126. Visotzky, *The Midrash on Proverbs,* p. 118.

127. Sheppard, *Wisdom as a Hermeneutical Construct,* p. 91.

128. Clifford, *Proverbs,* p. 258.

larger invitation to bridge that very gulf. It does not merely assert impossibility but affirms possibility in that [the] wisdom [of the LORD] is accessible [to the son]."[129] Pauls then draws the conclusion: "It is in this dual movement of the text — inaccessible/accessible, impossible/possible, hidden/made known, despair/hope — that Agur's opening words — weary/able — gain substance."[130] Moreover, Pauls notes that by asking the questions "Who?" and "What is his name?" not "How do you know?" Agur "radically reshapes the crisis of knowing . . . as a crisis of relationship. The preeminent rhetorical question, 'No one but Yahweh' and the dual request for personal names, shapes the passage in a radical way, suggesting that the resolution to the epistemological crisis is defined in relational rather than intellectual categories. True wisdom is found in a responsive and receptive relationship with Yahweh, who is wisdom's sole possessor."[131] Similarly, Job's epistemological angst was relieved only when he humbled himself before the transcendent Sovereign. He replaced his prior state of being "without knowledge" with "I know that you can do all things" (Job 42:2-3).

5-6 These verses are united by "his words" in v. 6a, having as its antecedent "every word of God" in v. 5a, and the threat of death in v. 6b complements the promise of life in v. 5b. The Holy One and his wisdom, who is otherwise unknown and which is unaccessible through general revelation (vv. 2-4), is known through his inspired special revelation. Childs remarks, "As an answer to the inquirer's despair at finding wisdom and the knowledge of God, the answer offered is that God has already made himself known truthfully in his written word."[132] R. Moore agrees: "Knowledge of the Holy One depends not on a human search for truth but a humble acceptance of the divine disclosure through inspired spokespersons."[133] Agur has brought his audience back full circle to the claim of the superscription, namely, his sayings (or "words") are a *maśśā'* ("an oracle"). "The sayings *(dibrê)* of Agur" (30:1) are "his [God's] words" (*d^ebārāyw,* 30:6a).

In v. 5 Agur cites David's confession of the reliability of God's word (v. 5), and in v. 6, Moses' assertion of its canonical status (Deut. 4:2; 12:32[13:1]). Agur's line of reasoning again follows that of Moses and Baruch. After rejecting the notion that Israel needs to ascend into heaven to obtain the law, Moses asserts, "No, the word is very near you; it is in your mouth and in your heart so you may obey it" (Deut. 30:14). Likewise, after

129. Pauls, "Proverbs 30:1-6," p. 122.

130. Pauls, "Proverbs 30:1-6," p. 122.

131. Pauls, "Proverbs 30:1-6," p. 124.

132. B. Childs, *Introduction to the Old Testament as Scripture* (Philadelphia: Fortress, 1979), p. 556.

133. Moore, "A Home for the Alien," pp. 100-101.

saying that the LORD found wisdom and gave it to Israel, Baruch immediately adds, "This is the book of the commandments of God and the law which endures forever" (Bar. 4:1). So also Agur implicitly admonishes his audience to seek their refuge in God by appropriating God's word, including his own sayings. Agur makes no attempt to validate by human reason Scripture's absolute claim for its reliability and canonical authority and perfection. If such an attempt were made, it would make limited human reasoning the final arbiter of truth, turning the argument back on itself and of necessity once again ending in skepticism. The finite mind can neither derive nor certify infinite truth. Certain truth is found in the Scriptures themselves as the Holy Spirit certifies them to obedient children (cf. Matt. 11:25-27; 16:13-17; John 5:45-47; 8:47; 10:2-6; 2 Cor. 3:14–4:6; 1 Thess. 1:5).

5 This verse is an adaptation of David's victory song, celebrating his escape from his enemies and death (2 Sam. 22:31 = Ps. 18:30[31]); see n. 23; cf. also Pss. 105:19; 119:4). Agur's changes of David's text suggest that he is employing the trope of metalepsis, a rhetorical and poetic device in which a later text alludes to an earlier one in a way that draws on resonance of the earlier text beyond the explicit citation.[134] Immediately after the text quoted by Agur, David gives God's name: "Who is God but the LORD?" (Ps. 18:31[32]), the anticipated answer to Agur's question in verse 4b. Also, David celebrates the LORD as the one who soars on the wings of the wind and who makes the dark rain clouds his covering (Ps. 18:10-11[11-12]), a thought similar to Agur's in v. 4a. The synthetic parallels the *word of God* (cf. 2:5) in verset A and *he* (a reference to God himself) in verset B imply that God and his word are inseparable. In verset A, the refiner's imagery of *purified* (see 25:4) precious metal asserts the truthfulness of God's teachings (cf. Pss. 12:6[7]; 19:9b[10b], 10a[11a]; 105:19b; 119:140).[135] All of God's inspired teachings perfectly represent the divinely established nexus of cause and effect (see "knowledge," I: 77). In verset B, the imagery of God as a *shield* (see 2:7) represents him as a warrior who protects his faithful ones from all their enemies, including death. The imprecise parallelism implies

134. For a discussion of the trope in ancient and modern literature, see J. Hollander, *The Figure of Echo: A Mode of Allusion in Milton and After* (Berkeley: University of California, 1981); for the Old Testament, see M. Fishbane, *Biblical Interpretation in Ancient Israel* (Oxford: Clarendon, 1985); for the New Testament, see R. B. Hayes, *Echoes of Scripture in the Letters of Paul* (New Haven and London: Yale University, 1989), pp. 14-21.

135. Purified *(ṣᵉrûpâ)* implicitly likens God's word to a precious metal, such as silver or gold, from which dross has been removed. The purified, molten precious metal is now ready to be poured from the crucible or cupel into a cast. Free from impurities, the cast figure both endures and radiates beauty. The removed dross in this metaphor refers to falsehood.

that *those who take refuge in him* do so by committing themselves to his inspired words (see 3:5-6), even in death (see 14:32). The revelation aims to promote trust in the Speaker, not to give bare knowledge.[136] God's revealed word and the disciple's humble trust in God to keep it are fundamental aspects of "fear of the LORD" (see I: 100).

6 In v. 6a, a variation of Deut. 4:2 and 12:32(13:1), Agur asserts the canonical status of his sayings (see Rev. 22:18-19). Since the Hebrew canon was not completed until ca. 165 B.C., Agur refers to them as part of a developing canon.[137] *Do not add* [see 1:5] *to his words* (see 2:1), the so-called canonical formula,[138] "was intended to prompt Israel's obedience . . . , not simply to define the canonical status of divine utterances."[139] The formula emphasizes the authority of Agur's sayings, reinforces their purity, and safeguards them against an apostate form of human authority by tampering with them. Anyone who alters them by adding to them is not seeking refuge in the LORD but arrogantly conforming the LORD to his own inspiration (cf. 1 Cor. 4:6).[140] Verset B provides the motivation for recognizing the canonical status of Agur's sayings. Since a human being by nature cannot know wisdom (vv. 2-3), anyone who adds to them will falsify them. In contrast to an empirical epistemology that is accustomed to proving everything else by human experience, Agur argues it is *our word,* not God's, that finally must be proven.[141] God will *convict* (see 3:12) the offender. It can be inferred that the crime of adulterating Agur's sayings is a capital offense, since those who trustfully obey his word find salvation from death. That interpretation is validated by its metalepsis with Deuteronomy 4. To the canonical formula in Deut. 4:2, Moses attached life for obedience to God's word and death for disobedience in 4:3. To this promise and threat Moses added the further motivation that observance of his words will establish Israel, God's son, as a wise and understanding people, set apart in the sight of all nations (4:6-8). Agur's intention for "the son" is the same.

136. Kidner, *Proverbs,* p. 179.

137. R. T. Beckwith, *The Old Testament Canon of the New Testament Church and Its Background in Early Judaism* (Grand Rapids: Eerdmans, 1985).

138. André, *TDOT,* 6:122, s.v. *yāsap.*

139. A. E. Hill, *NIDOTTE,* 2:476, s.v. *ysp.*

140. Van Leeuwen (*Proverbs,* p. 252) thinks that v. 5 [better, vv. 4-6] aims to exclude apocalyptic speculation. Pseudepigraphical Enoch claimed, "I know everything; either from the lips of the Lord, or else my eyes have seen from the beginning even to the end. . . . I know everything. . . . I measured all the earth . . . and everything that exists. . . . And I ascended to the east, into the paradise of Eden (i.e., into heaven)" (2 Enoch 40, 41).

141. Moore, "A Home for the Alien," p. 101.

b. Agur's Petitions for Truthfulness and Modesty (30:7-9)

Agur's exemplary prayer in vv. 7-9, the only prayer in Proverbs, continues his autobiography and functions as a janus to his numerical sayings. On the one hand, his petition to God mediates his word through a prayerful and pure channel, and Agur's inspired words are trustworthy because he depends on God to keep him from "lies." Moreover, his petition to keep him from lies (v. 8a) and his assertion that anyone who adds to God's word will be proved a liar (v. 7) imply that his words are from God and therefore truthful. The connection between his confession and his prayer is strengthened by the catchwords "who" (vv. 4a, 9a) and "name" (vv. 4b, 9b), both terms referring to "the LORD," the implied answer to his questions in v. 4. Agur's sayings will be received by those cast from the same spiritual mold as he. On the other hand, "Two things I ask of you" resembles the title lines of the main section's numerical sayings by the cataphoric use of a numeral. *From me (mimmenni)* forms a lexical link between the numerical heading (v. 7b) and the petitions (v. 8a), assisted by its connection with the negative and positive synonyms, "do not withhold from me," and "keep far away from me." As his first petition is connected with his confession, his second petition, for modesty, is connected lexically by the catchword *śbʿ* (vv. 9a and 15aβ) and thematically by the notion of modesty versus greed. He motivates God to answer his petitions in order that he might not become insubordinate to God by deserting him and desecrating his name. In addition to providing a thematic linkage with the main body and conclusion, his petition points to God, not human effort, as the savior to overcome human greed (vv. 10-16), breaking of boundaries (vv. 17-31), and insubordination (vv. 32-33). In sum, Agur overcomes the epistemological problem of ignorance and the moral predicament of greed through dependence on God and a desire for God's fame. His unified petition can be analyzed thus:[142]

I. Introduction (heading line of the numerical petition)	7
II. Petitions	8
A. Two negative petitions	8a
1. Regarding words: deceit and lies	8aα
2. Regarding money: poverty and wealth	8aβ
B. Positive petition: daily quota of bread	8b
III. Reasons for petitions regarding money	9
1. Danger of wealth (sated > dissemble): desertion from the LORD	9a
2. Danger of poverty (poor > steal): desecration of LORD's name	9b

142. Adapted from Meinhold, *Sprüche,* p. 499.

R. Byargeon argues that the exemplary Lord's Prayer in Matt. 6:9-13 echoes in its structure and theology Agur's Prayer. He notes the following *chiastic* structural similarities:

Proverbs 30:7-9	Lord's Prayer
Keep deception and lies far from me	Sanctify your Name
Feed me only my quota of bread	Give us this day our daily bread
Profane the name of my God	Do not lead us into testing[143]

7 *I ask* (see 22:17) looks back to Agur at its antecedent (see 1:1, 2-3), but semantic pertinence rules out Ithiel as the antecedent of *you* (lit. "from with you"). Only the LORD can satisfy Agur's spiritual and physical needs. In verset A he introduces his prayer for these *two things* (see 24:22), and in verset B he underscores his urgency in three ways: (1) by shifting from the indicative mood to the imperative; (2) by escalating "I ask of you" into *do not withhold from me* (see 1:15); and (3) by adding *before I die* (see 5:23; 10:21), inferring that his clinical death is fast approaching and the time for fulfillment is immediate.[144] He prays "with all the intense earnestness of a dying sinner."[145]

8 In this synthetic parallelism, Agur presents in verset A two negative petitions: *keep far away from me* [better than "remove from me"; see 4:24; 5:8] *deceitful lies* (assuming literal "deceit[146] and a word of deception" is a hendiadys; see 14:5; 19:22; 23:3) and *do not give me* (see 1:4) either the economic extremes of *poverty* [or being destitute; see 10:4, 15] *or riches* (see 3:16; 11:28). In verset B he presents the second petition positively, *provide me* [lit. "cause me to devour"; cf. 31:15] *my quota of food.* "Food" functions as a synecdoche for all of one's needs, and "my quota" (cf. 8:29) depends on one's calling and circumstances (cf. Exod. 16:18; e.g., whether one is single or married, a public person or private citizen, etc.). By placing this second petition in the emphatic second position (see 6:16-19), by presenting it alone both negatively and positively (v. 8bα, β) with rationale (v. 9), he underscores his peti-

143. Rick W. Byargeon, "Echoes of Wisdom in the Lord's Prayer," *JETS* 41 (1998) 353-65.

144. Franklyn ("The Sayings of Agur," p. 249, n. 43) writes, "The combination of the verb *mwt* and *bᵉṭerem* is found in four other texts. At Ps. 39:13[14]; Job 10:21 and Gen. 45:28 the speaker expects the assault of death in the very near future. In Jer. 38:10 the king commands Ebed-melech to remove the prophet from the cistern before he dies *(bᵉṭerem yāmût)* of hunger." He also comments, "It might seem strange that he would be concerned about either wealth or poverty in the future but compare the psalmist's request for just a little happiness before death (Ps. 39:13)."

145. Bridges, *Proverbs,* p. 596.

146. J. F. A. Sawyer, *TLOT,* 1:1304, s.v. *šāw'.*

tion for modesty. The petitions for truthfulness and modesty, however, are integrated. He prays to be protected from telling lies, either out of fear of greed or of poverty, by praying only for sufficiency (cf. Matt. 6:11; Luke 11:3; 1 Tim. 6:8).[147] Agur's ideal is the golden mean because he is keenly alert to the spiritual and moral damage that either extreme economic state produces. "We might expect the prayer: 'Teach me to use . . . riches aright,'" says Toy,[148] but he knows his frailty. His prayer that God not give him riches stands in tension with the promise that riches are wisdom's fruit (3:16; 8:18; 22:4) and the crown of the wise (14:24). But the paradox is not a contradiction. The prayer not to be given riches lest one become independent from God (v. 9) expresses true wisdom. God can safely entrust wealth to be used in the service of society to such a wise person (see 11:28; cf. Phil. 4:11, 12).

9 The synthetic parallels of v. 9 state the reason or goal of Agur's petition for the golden mean. In versets Aa and Ba, he sets forth the negative situations of his being sated or destitute, and in versets Ab and Bb their respective negative consequences of becoming a scoffer or a blasphemer, behavior that is not tolerated by God in any setting. In sum, the glory of God, not his personal need, motivates Agur's requests. On the one hand, if he became sated — *lest I be sated* (see 5:10) — he would become a scoffer. The normally positive good of being sated (see 12:11) becomes negative when one is sated beyond his allotted portion. Without a need for God's intervention to give him his allotted food, even Agur will *dissemble (wᵉkiḥaštî).* In contrast to *kzb* and *šqr,* which are in the semantic domain of "lies," *kḥš* "denotes the disguising, concealment or denial of a given situation contrary to better knowledge; it thus also represents a deliberate accountable act."[149] *And say* (see 1:11) gives concrete expression to his faithless dissimulation. The rhetorical question *"Who* [see 9:4] *is the LORD*?" (see I: 67) betrays a scoffing haughtiness. Moses also cautioned Israel against the moral jeopardy of apostasy when one is too comfortable (Deut. 8:12-14). On the other hand, if he became destitute — *lest I become poor* (see 20:13) — he would *steal* (6:30). This entails that *I will do violence* (see n. 36), a metaphor for to defame or besmirch *the name of* [see v. 4b] *my God* (see v. 5), that is, *Yahweh,* as the parallel shows. Stealing may convince others that the LORD "is of no help or that his laws are impossible to keep."[150] It may also suggest that God's worshipers are hypocrites. Stealing not only involves a transgression of the eighth commandment but also may lead to the suspected thief taking oaths of innocence and abusing God's name and thereby violating the third com-

147. Meinhold, *Sprüche,* p. 500.

148. Toy, *Proverbs,* p. 525.

149. K.-D. Schunck, *TDOT,* 7:133, s.v. *kḥš.*

150. Garrett, *Proverbs,* p. 238.

mandment.[151] Stealing and lying are among the actions that demonstrate that Israel does not know God.[152] Finally, hunger may prompt one to curse God and the king (Isa. 8:21). Because the name of God is holy, serious warnings are issued against misuse of God's name for any reason.[153]

B. MAIN BODY: SEVEN NUMERICAL SAYINGS (30:10-31)

Agur's numerical sayings exhibit both a structural and a thematic unity. A preliminary overview of Agur's numerical sayings reveals an alternating AB/A′B′ pattern:

A	Single-line saying proscribing overturning the social order	10
B	Three verse-initial untitled sayings proscribing greed	11-16
A′	Single-line sayings proscribing overturning the social order	17
B′	Four verse-initial titled sayings proscribing breaking boundaries	18-31

Two single-line sayings (vv. 10, 17) are followed by three verse initially untitled numerical sayings (vv. 11-14, 15a, 15b-16) and four verse initially titled numerical sayings, assuming that the saying about the awful way of the adulteress in v. 20 stands in opposition to the four awesome ways in vv. 18-19. The janus quality of v. 10 was noted above. Verse 17 is implicitly a typical introductory saying, calling for submission to parental authority.[154] Verse 10 condemns slander, and v. 17 the haughty eye. Significantly, the two notions are placed in parallel also in Ps. 101:5. Agur's numerical sayings contain seven — the number of completion — carefully structured sayings (vv. 11-14, 15a, 15b-16, 18-20, 21-23, 24-28, 29-31), introduced and divided into two units by single-line introductions (vv. 10, 17). Each of the two numerical units begins with a fourfold anaphora, employing *dôr* in vv. 11-14 and *derek* in vv. 18-20 (esp. v. 19). In fact, the second saying of the second unit also uses a fourfold anaphora of *taḥat* (vv. 21-23). In sum, three numerical sayings use a fourfold anaphora.

The macrostructure of the sayings as three and four matches the microstructure of the numerical echelon "three . . . four" in the title lines (vv.

151. Meinhold, *Sprüche,* p. 500.

152. Van Leeuwen, *Proverbs,* p. 251.

153. J. A. Soggin, *TLOT,* 3:1,360, s.v. *šēm.*

154. R. N. Whybray (*The Composition of the Book of Proverbs* [JSOTSup 168; Sheffield: JSOT, 1994] independently reached the conclusion that educational proverbs introduce units.

18, 21, 29).[155] The fourfold introductory anaphora of *dôr* and *derek* complement the threefold anaphora of *mîṣ* in the conclusion. In the first unit of the main section, the first two subunits are untitled (vv. 11-14, 15a) and its third is titled, but not as an initial verse (v. 15b), unlike the second unit (vv. 18, 21, 24, 29). The numerical sequence of vv. 15 and 16 functions as a janus. On the one hand, by tucking away the title line of verse 15b, Agur groups the initially untitled sayings of vv. 10-16 together. On the other hand, the non-initial title line of v. 15b leads into the four initially titled sayings.

The section's structural unity serves as a handmaid to its thematic unity. These seven numerical sayings essentially aim to preserve social order by implicitly calling Ithiel to renounce hubris and greed. In an *inclusio,* his first introductory saying instructs him as a lord to uphold it by noble treatment of his wards (v. 10), and his last saying, also his conclusion, commands him to preserve it by not plotting revolution against his lord (vv. 32-33). His structuring single-line sayings (vv. 10, 17) warn that the LORD will hand down a death sentence for provoking insubordination by the ruler or by the ruled (cf. Deut. 21:18). The first introduction commands the ruler not to provoke a subject through slander to the point of calling down the LORD's curse, which will overthrow the ruler (v. 10). The second introduction (v. 17), which occurs exactly at the midpoint of all of Agur's sayings, threatens the arrogant child with a humiliating death from birds in the sky. To judge from the figure itself and from the reference to the LORD in v. 10, the carrion birds symbolize a heavenly visitation. The first preserves order by instructing the leader; the second preserves order by instructing the led. These two introductions provide the penalties that are glaringly absent in the numerical sayings that follow them. In sum, the basis for social order is the fear of the LORD.

The numerical sayings that follow the introductory single lines implicitly condemn greed and hubris, the complementary conditions that disturb peace. The three sayings (or subunits) of the first unit pertain to curbing greed to gratify one's appetites to excess (i.e., beyond its necessary quota of food) and greed for power to gratify pride. Greed drives humankind to throw off God's established restraints, which seem a galling bondage to the self-ambitious.

155. Steinmann, "Three Things," p. 61. But Andrew J. Steinmann, "Three Things . . . Four Things . . . Seven Things: The Coherence of Proverbs 30:11-33 and the Unity of Proverbs 30," *Hebrew Studies* 42 (2001) 59-64, is not convincing that "three" *(šlwš/šlš)* occurs four times (vv. 15, 18, 21, 29) and "four" occurs three times (vv. 15, 18, 21) because "four" also occurs in vv. 24 and 29. Perhaps I am missing something. I did not find convincing his matching the opening fourfold *dôr* with the closing threefold *mîṣ* (vv. 32-33) until I noted the threefold anaphora of *mîṣ* in the conclusion in connection with the fourfold anaphora that open the two units of the numerical sayings.

1. First Unit: Renouncing Greed (30:10-16)

Agur's command not to slander the underprivileged (v. 10) stands appropriately after his petition not to defame God's name and before his condemnation of a generation that curses their parents (v. 11). His command leads thematically to the greedy generation (vv. 11-14), the "greedy leech" (v. 15a), and "the four cosmic insatiables" (vv. 15b-16). The unit ends, however, on a positive note by citing the barren womb and the earth that thirst for life in contrast to the greedy grave and consuming fire. In sum, the unit has as its theme that social order triumphs over anarchy through living within boundaries and through curbing appetites.

a. Single-Line Proverb: The Slandered Slave's Curse (30:10)

In addition to the already observed features linking v. 10 with vv. 7-9, the topic of "lies/deceit" (v. 8) and "slander," which is a clandestine lie (v. 10), and the syntax of an imperative followed by negative reasons (i.e., "lest"; vv. 9, 10b) bind them together. As Moses' initial law in the Book of the Covenant protected the slave (Exod. 21:1-6), Agur's first oracle protects the slave against the abuse of slander (cf. Deut. 23:15). *Do not slander* (see n. 37) focuses the many proverbs and sayings against slander (cf. 16:28; 18:8; 25:23; 26:20, 28) to this prohibition not to defame *a slave* or *official* — perhaps an intentional pun on *ʿebed* (see 11:29) — *to his master* (see 25:13; cf. Deut. 15:9; 23:15[16]). The slave/official resorts to a curse because he feels that he has no other recourse to defend himself in court.[156] *Curse* is the most common word for reviling speech by a wronged, weaker party to elevate himself above his oppressor through threatening the evildoer's life (see 20:20).[157] Agur's verdict, *you become liable,*[158] entails that God will uphold the demeaning word (see 26:2) and exact righteous retribution. Agur's introduction preserves the social order by forbidding rulers by calumny to provoke the ruled to overturn it.

b. Three Numerical Sayings without Verse-Initial Title Lines (30:11-16)

The three numerical sayings without verse-initial title verses escalate from one subject with four characteristics to several subjects with one characteristic in an echelon escalating from one (a leech), to two (its daughters), to three and four cosmic insatiables. The numerical sequence, says Glück, "creates a

156. Meinhold, *Sprüche,* p. 501.

157. E. Jenni, *TLOT,* 1:1,143, s.v. *qll.*

158. R. Knierim defines *ʾāšam* as "a situation in which someone is or becomes obligated to discharge guilt by giving something" *(TLOT,* 1:192, s.v. *ʾāšam).*

cumulative effect, a feeling of growing intensity."[159] All four sayings pertain to greed, the climactic vice of the evil generation, the proverbial leech and the four insatiables, which "never say, 'Enough.' Probably the leech and the insatiables are linked by the consonance of their final *hab* ("Give!" v. 15a) and *hôn* ("Enough!" vv. 15b, 16), both of which occur twice. Obviously, the leech serves as an exemplar of human greed.

(1) The Greedy Generation (30:11-14)

The catchword "curse" (vv. 10, 11) links the numerical sayings to the introduction, and the catchwords "father" and "mother" in the initial line of the first unit of numerical sayings connect it with the introduction to the second unit of numerical sayings (vv. 11, 17). By beginning with children cursing their parents, it parallels the second introduction (v. 17). This connection is reinforced by the threefold reference to their haughty "eyes" (vv. 12, 13, 17). The intentional absence of a title line identifying several independent sayings within its unity unifies the four characteristics as belonging to one generation.[160] The initial anaphora of *a generation (dôr)* in each verse compensates for the lack of a title line. Gerleman refers *dôr* broadly here to "a collective group of people living at a particular time,"[161] but Freedman and Lundbom refer it to "family" or "children."[162] Although the reference to the father and mother favors the latter interpretation, Agur's aim to maintain both political and domestic order suggests that he attenuated the two meanings. "Generation," however, here designates a distinct sort of children, not the entire contemporary generation, because they envision evil children oppressing their peers. The sayings' four verses also cohere by their common syntax and by the logical development of their common theme. The outer frame portrays their behavior and features their greed in the home (cursing parents, v. 11; see Exod. 21:17; Prov. 20:20) and the public arena (devouring the poor, v. 14). Their inner core, which is linked by the catchword "its eyes," portrays their spiritual attitude, escalating their arrogance from their self-delusion and incorrigibility (v. 12) to their despising others (v. 13).

11 This verse typically breaks apart the stereotyped phrase for parents into its parallels, *their fathers* and *their mothers* (see I: 43). The generation not only fails to honor their parents (cf. Exod. 20:12; Deut. 5:16; cf. Lev.

159. J. J. Glück, "Proverbs xxx 15a," *VT* 14 (1964) 368.

160. W. M. W. Roth, *Numerical Sayings in the Old Testament* (VTSup; Leiden: Brill: 1965), p. 7, believes that the initial title line is implied, but he fails to note that this saying presents one subject with varying characteristics, not two or more with a common characteristic.

161. G. Gerleman, *TLOT,* 1:334, s.v. *dôr.*

162. D. Freedman and J. Lundbom, *TDOT,* 3:173-74, s.v. *dôr.*

19:3), but they even *curse* them (see v. 10), a capital crime in the Mosaic law (Exod. 21:17; Deut. 27:16; cf. Prov. 5:14). Solon, when asked why he had made no law against parricides, replied that he could not conceive of anyone so impious and cruel. Bridges comments, "The divine law-giver knew his creature better, that his heart was capable of wickedness beyond conception (Jer. 17:9)."[163] These foolish rebels (cf. 10:5; 13:1; 15:5; 19:26; 23:22; 28:7, 24) *do not bless* (or do not mediate through their prayers the divine blessing that enriches with life and prosperity; see 3:33; 10:6) those to whom they owe their very lives, Instead, they demean and defame them to obtain their inheritance faster (cf. 20:21) and to relieve themselves of responsibility to care for them (Matt. 15:3-6). Although the parents may be wise, these fools "reward" their parents with heartache, not joy (cf. 10:1; 15:20; 17:21, 25; 23:15, 16, 24, 25; 27:11; 29:3). The fools will suffer the same fatal fate as those who blaspheme God, their Creator and the teacher of wisdom (20:20; 30:17; cf. Job 15:2-3).

12 Nevertheless, the perverse *generation* deludes itself into thinking that it is ethically pure and acceptable to God (16:2). The antithetical parallels of v. 12 juxtapose *pure* [a metaphor for being free of ethical contamination that renders one pleasing and acceptable to God; see 15:26; 20:9] *in their own eyes* (see 3:7) and *not cleansed* [i.e., by being doused with water and rinsed off] *from their excrement* (see Isa. 4:4; 28:8; 36:12 [= 2 K. 18:27]). The latter metaphor refers to gross iniquities that defile a person and render him totally offensive to God and implicitly offers him cleansing by turning to God. The self-deluded generation's epistemology is relative and wrong because, having adopted their own evil nature as their standard (cf. 4:16-17), they consider wrong as right. In that way "they take part in the incorrigibility of the fools (3:5b; 26:5b, 12, 16; 28:26a)."[164] Anyone who thinks that he is pure apart from God's divine cleansing conceals an unsuspected depth of depravity (3:7; 12:15). Jesus condemned the self-righteous Pharisees of murder and of belonging to this generation (cf. Matt. 6:22-23; 23:25-27; Luke 16:15; 18:9-14; John 8:44; 9:40, 41; cf. also Rev. 3:17, 18).

13 This verse further indicts the defiled generation as being superciliously arrogant. In the verses' synonymous parallelism, the subject *a generation* is gapped in verset B, and the predicate *they raise their eyes* (see 6:17) is emphatically restated by its semantic equivalent, *and lift up their pupils* (see 4:25). The predicated metonymies signify an attitude of being superior to God's revealed teachings and of self-exaltation over another person, thereby violating the fundamental equal honor of each individual. The outward visage of their eyes reveals the inner disposition of their insubordinate

163. Bridges, *Proverbs,* p. 600.
164. Meinhold, *Sprüche,* p. 502.

hearts (cf. Ps. 131:1; Prov. 21:4; 23:6, 7; 30:17). Exclamatory *how* (see n. 41) vents the sage's amazed indignation at proud sinners (cf. Esth. 5:11; Isa. 16:6; Jer. 48:29; Ezek. 28:2; Dan. 11:36; Acts 12:21-23; 2 Thess. 2:4)!

14 The arrogance of the *generation* escalates into unethical exploitation of the weak and defenseless poor. Verset A of this climactic verse grotesquely represents the generation's *teeth* (see 10:26) and *jawbones*[165] — unique metonymies for speech in this book — by the metaphors *swords* [see 5:4] *and butcher knives*[166] respectively (i.e., cruel, insensitive, and lethal). Verset B expands and inferentially explains the metaphor. Their speech cuts up *to devour* [i.e., to cannibalize; see 1:31] *the* wrongly oppressed *poor* [see 3:34(K); 15:15; 22:22] *and the needy* [see 14:21; Deut. 24:14] *and* so *eliminate them from the earth* (cf. Job 29:17; Pss. 14:4; 57:4[5]; Mic. 3:1-4). The metaphor signifies that they gratify their insatiable greed by robbing the needy poor and/or by withholding from them what is their due. Presumably the evildoers give false testimony in court (Prov. 22:22) to confiscate the property of the poor and/or to vindicate not paying them their rightful wage. As a result the poor lose the land that sustains their lives and, without the means adequately to feed themselves and their families, die prematurely (see 28:3; cf. Ps. 10:8, 9; Eccl. 4:1; Isa. 3:15; Amos 2:6, 7; 4:1; 8:4; Mic. 2:1, 2; Hab. 3:14). The LORD will punish such a generation (cf. Prov. 14:21, 31; 15:25; 17:5; 22:16, 23; 23:11).

(2) The Leech (30:15a)

The evil generation's greed is followed immediately by a reference to the blood-sucking leech (v. 15a) that appropriately introduces the four other insatiables (v. 15b). The LXX and the Syr. represent the leech as having three "beloved" daughters and make the verse into an integrated whole, but the MT and the Targ. treat these verses as containing two numerical aphorisms.[167] By joining the leech with the four insatiables Agur also achieves a contrast. The four insatiables of v. 16 cannot be avoided or eliminated, but the son/disciple can take precautions against the insatiable horse leech.

15a Implicitly, just as the parasitical, loathsome leech must be quickly eliminated from doing more damage, so also the wise must either exercise precaution to avoid the greedy or take quick and decisive action to get rid of them and so preserve their life and health (cf. 2 Thess. 3:10). Verset A

165. *HALOT,* 2:654, s.v. *m^{e}tall^{ʿe}ōt, M^{e}tall^{ʿe}ōt* is parallel with "teeth" also in Job 29:17 ("fangs," NIV); Ps. 58:6(7).

166. In its other two uses (Gen. 22:6, 10; Judg. 19:29), *maʾ^{a}kālôt* denotes a knife large enough to dissect the human body.

167. Roth, *Numerical Sayings,* p. 28, n. 1.

personifies the blood-sucking *horse leech,*[168] which had two sucking organs at each end (one to suck blood, the other to attach itself to its host), as a mother of *two* [see v. 7] *daughters.*[169] This leech "could be found in all stale waters of Palestine and attached itself above all in the nostrils and palate of drinking horses. The Talmud warns people against drinking water from rivers or ponds by the mouth or from the hollow of one's hand (tract. Avoda Zara 12b)."[170] Verset Ab names its sucking organs as *Give! Give!*[171] to warn the disciple against this dangerous parasite. The double-sucking leech symbolizes either an individual's inordinate lusts (such as substance or process addictions) or a wicked person (such as a crook or a welfare loafer), both of whom take life and wealth from a society rather than enriching it.

(3) Four Insatiables (30:15b-16)

The structure of vv. 15b-16, consisting of the title line (v. 15b) and the list of four insatiables (v. 16), shows that its collective verses belong to one saying. It is the first explicit numerical saying, though it has been anticipated in vv. 7, 11-14, and 15a. When numbers in the title line are set in synonymous parallelism, as here, according to the rules of Semitic and Homeric poetry, the second unit is one unit higher and contains the real number (x-1//x; see I: 43). The title line and the list are also linked by the consonance of initial *šālôš (three)* and *šᵉʾôl (Sheol)* in their A versets and the consonance of *ʾrbʿ (four)* and *ʾrṣ (earth)* in their B versets. Moreover, "The *title line* describes or alludes to that feature or those features which the items listed have in common."[172] This title line personifies the insatiables' essential feature by the catchwords *are never satisfied* (v. 5bα, 16bα; cf. v. 9) and *never say, "Enough!"* (the adverbial meaning of *hôn,* vv. 15bβ, 16bβ; cf. 1:13). Within the title line *they (hēnnâ),* the second word, shares a consonance with *hôn,* the last word. Agur divides the four insatiables into two pairs (vv. 16a and b). Their pairing is signified by the Masoretic accents, by the use of the conjunction *and,* by their syntax (i.e., two nouns versus two nouns with qualifying clauses), and by pairing the extremes of human existence with extremes in the inanimate realm. *Sheol* (see I: 116) ever yearns to end life, *and the barren womb* (see n. 47) ever yearns to produce it (cf. Gen. 30:1; 1 Samuel 1; Luke

168. The meaning of the *hap. leg.* *ʿᵃlûqâ,* though disputed (Glück, "Proverbs xxx 15a," *VT* [1964] 367-70), is confidently based on unambiguous Aramaic, Arabic, and Ethiopic cognates *(HALOT,* 2:831, s.v. *ʿᵃlûqâ).* The LXX and the Vulg. specify it as the horse leech.

169. Fem. *laʿᵃlûqâ* guided the poet's imagination (*IBHS,* p. 100, P. 6.11e).

170. Meinhold, *Sprüche,* p. 506.

171. *HALOT,* 1:236, s.v. *hab.*

172. Roth, *Numerical Sayings,* p. 5.

1:5-25). Likewise, the arable *land is never satisfied* with enough *water* (see v. 4) to produce crops that sustain lives, *and fire* (cf. 26:20-21) ever destroys them (cf. 26:20-21). Moreover, fire and water extinguish each other and so oppose each other. The chiastic parallels place in the outer frame the insatiable end makers. The grave *(Sheol)* implicitly craves bodies, and fire craves combustibles. In the inner core stand the insatiable life makers: the barren womb implicitly craving seed and the arable soil craving water. But what is the point? Although the sage practiced keen observation of the natural order and stood in awe of what he observed,[173] nevertheless his interest lay in discovering moral parables (see 1:6). "The [numerical] sayings . . . never press their lesson, but leave it to the reader to ponder and tease it out," says Aitken.[174] Probably Agur intends the son to compare these four insatiables, which represent life and death, engaged in unending battle as long as the earth endures. Until God separates the wheat from the chaff (see 2:20-22), greedy tyrants (cf. vv. 11-14, 15a) never say, "Enough!" (cf. 27:20) and the righteous ever strives to produce life.

2. Second Unit: The Wisdom of Living within Boundaries (30:17-31)

After the introductory saying that infers an admonition to heed the teaching (v. 17), the second half presents four numerical sayings with the echelon *three (š*^{e}*lōšâʾ* or *šālôš) . . . and*/or *four (w*^{e}*ʾarbāʿā* or *w*^{e}*ʾarbaʿ)* in their title verses (vv. 18, 21, 24, 29).[175] The first two sayings contrast the amazing created order, both by God and by man (vv. 18-19), with social disorder (vv. 21-23). The first saying pertains to the four creatures/creations whose behavior within the created order amaze Agur, climaxing in human, erotic love (vv. 18-19). His awe of human "eros" with a virgin stands in contrast to the adulteress's, who sees nothing wrong with demeaning her sexuality with another sexual partner to nothing more than eating a meal (v. 20). Her breach of marital fidelity forms a transition to four upside-down things in the social order (vv. 21-23). The last two sayings escalate from wise creatures overcoming their weakness by wisdom (vv. 24-28) to those fearlessly ruling their realms (vv. 29-31). The first of these sayings names four extraordinarily wise beasties, climaxing in the lizard living in a king's palace (vv. 24-28). This reference to the king forms a transition to the fourth saying, which pertains to regal striders and climaxes in the

173. Toy's comments, particularly of vv. 16, 18-19, that the sayings are simply a record of observations and a lesson in natural history and physics, without ethical meaning or application, are woefully inadequate (*Proverbs,* pp. 529, 531).

174. Aitken, *Proverbs,* p. 232.

175. Three have the echelon pattern, "three . . . four" (vv. 18, 21, 29). The third (v. 24) stands apart, simply stating the numeral "four."

stride of the king, whom no one dares to resist (vv. 29-31). The probable reference to the queen mother in the climax of the second saying (see v. 23) and the certain references to the king in the climaxes to the third and fourth point to a court relevance for the last three numerical sayings (vv. 22, 28, 31). In sum, the titled numerical sayings move from order within the home, to within society, to within the state. This escalation prepares the way for Agur's concluding exhortation to his son not to usurp his superior's authority (vv. 32-33).

a. Single-Line Proverb: The Ignominious End of the Rebellious Child (30:17)

The catchwords "father" and "mother," "eye" and "devour" link the introduction to the second unit of numerical sayings with the first unit's first saying (v. 11). Haughty children, represented by their eyes, despise their parents (v. 11) and devour others (v. 14), and heavenly scavengers devour the haughty child's eye. His *eye* reveals his inner cast of mind (see v. 13). Two synonymous parallels disclose his arrogant rebellion: *mocks* (*til'ag l^{e};* see 1:26) *a father* and . . . *mother* [see I: 43; cf. 1:8; 10:1; 30:11] *and despises* (see 1:7) their *gray hair* (see n. 49), symbolizing their wisdom (cf. 16:31; 20:29). Verset B presents his judgment in two complementary parallel metaphors, both using unclean (cf. Lev. 11:15) carrion birds (cf. Isa. 34:11; Jer 16:3-4), whom the LORD feeds (Job 38:41). *The ravens* will *peck it out,*[176] and *the vultures* (lit. "members of the vulture family who have a certain destiny")[177] *will devour it* (see v. 14). The defiant child's unburied carcass symbolizes his tragic and dishonorable end. The thoroughness with which the carnivores (cf. Gen. 8:7) rid the earth of the symbolic eye is connoted by the two species acting in concert, by the plural number for both, and by locating the ravens in *the wadi,* which is devoid of other food (cf. 1 K. 17:4, 6).

b. Four Numerical Sayings with Verse-Initial Title Lines (30:18-31)

The four sayings (or subunits) of the second unit (vv. 18-31) pertain to living within boundaries, climaxing with a king striding regally. More specifically, the "four awesome ways" (vv. 18-19) condemn the awful way of the adulteress who refuses to live within the constraints of marriage to gratify her sexual

176. The verb *yiqq^{e}rûhā* is used of digging out/gouging out eyes as a severe form of disabling and punishment of living persons in Num. 16:14; Judg. 16:21; 1 Sam. 11:2.

177. Cf. *HALOT,* 1:138, s.v. *ben. Nešer* can also mean "eagle." Eagles are more solitary; vultures more gregarious. The visual image is that of a swarm of vultures stripping a carcass (see G. Cansdale, *All the Animals of the Bible Lands* [Grand Rapids: Zondervan, 1970], p. 142).

greed (v. 20). Implicitly, this first saying, which combines greed with insubordination, forms a janus between the untitled and titled numerical units. Moreover, the earth cannot endure under the four upstarts that turn the social order upside down (vv. 21-24). But the four extremely vulnerable creatures triumph over their limitations by being extremely wise, which by definition entails living within boundaries (vv. 22-28). The four vulnerable creatures are matched by the four invulnerable, their sequencing suggesting that through humbly recognizing incompetence one becomes competent. Climactically, the wise king not only survives but, by being fearless like the three leaders in animal husbandry, he walks with a regal stride (vv. 29-31).

(1) Four Awesome Ways and the Awful Way of the Adulteress (30:18-20)

Verses 18 and 19 of the first saying are united by a title line (v. 18) introducing the four wonderful "ways" named in v. 19. Verse 19a features two ways in the animal realm (eagle and snake), and verset B profiles two ways in the human (ship and potent man); v. 19aα features the expanse of the sky above and v. 19b of the sea below, the merism representing the cosmos. The ways of all four wonders move in and cleave to their appropriate and difficult environments according to an invisible course in an easy, intriguing, gracious, undulating manner, without leaving a trace and without being taught, and yet reaching their goals. Although the first two pertain to animals and the last two to man's creation (the ship) and his behavior, the prepositions "in"/"on" emphasize their topoi: the first three have their "way" in the cosmic dimensions of sky, rock/land, and sea (see Genesis 1). The fourth way stands apart from the three cosmic domains, referring instead to the social dimension of a man in a virgin. Thus, the virtuous sex act stands dramatically apart from the first three as a climactic fourth, as in the creation narrative of Genesis 1. "Using delicate imagery for love," comments Van Leeuwen, "his small poem sings implicit praise to God for the glories of creation, especially for sexual love."[178] The *Leitwort* "way" contrasts the unconscionable *way* of an adulteress (v. 20), who, unlike the virgin, is characterized by a number of sexual partners, with the four *ways* Agur admires. Agur's amazement at the created order's breathtaking ways, especially in proper sex, stands in contrast to the adulteress who, without wonder, regards sexual intercourse with a number of partners as nothing more than wiping "her mouth" after a meal (cf. 9:16-17).[179] Also, her sexual activity that breaks the bonds of marriage contrasts with the propriety of virginal sex. As

178. Van Leeuwen, *Proverbs,* p. 254.

179. Clifford (*Proverbs,* p. 266) notes: "In the Talmud, 'to eat' can mean 'to sleep with' (*b. Ketub.* 65.13-23), and 'mouth' can refer to the vulva (*b. Sanh.* 100a; *b. Menah.* 98a)."

with the four incomprehensible ways, the undulating adulteress leaves no trace, but unlike the other ways, which enhance life, her way is contrary to the created and social order and threatens to undermine it. This is the saying's "burden."

18 The feature *too wonderful for me* (see n. 51) unites the four ways. Measured by the standards Agur is accustomed to or what he normally expects, these ways appear extraordinary and wonderful, evoking a reaction of astonishment and praise from him.[180] *I cannot not empathize with them* (lit. "do not know them"; see 29:7) defines an aspect of wonder. Job's (42:3) use of the same expression in his repentance for hubris in questioning the Creator suggests that the four breath takers so humble the beholder that he does not defy the created order (i.e., God's wisdom).

19 The catchword *eagle* (or "vulture," *nešer;* see n. 54) connects the first wonder with the introduction to the second collection (v. 17). Other biblical authors stand in awe of the eagle's swiftness in its dive (cf. 2 Sam. 1:23; Jer. 48:40; Lam. 4:19; Hab. 1:8). But *the way* (*derek;* see 1:15) that impresses Agur is the artless, yet so artful, soaring, seemingly endless, circling high *in the sky* (see 23:5) of one of Palestine's heaviest birds. With the largest wingspan of any bird, the eagle defies gravity. *The serpent* (*nāḥāš* — note its consonance with *nšr;* see 23:32) is a general term for the 30 species of snakes — six of which are poisonous — in Palestine.[181] Its gliding movement over smooth rock, though it has no legs (Gen. 3:14) and nothing to hang onto, unlike its way in a tree, is most impressive. *On a* large *rock* (or "boulder"), not in the grass, sand, or dust, was probably also chosen because there the serpent leaves no visible sign of its action. Agur probably chose *a ship* (see 31:14), not a fish, both to turn attention away from animal skills to human skills and for its rocking motion in common with the other three things. *In the heart of the sea* (or high seas; see 23:34), which refers to the remote open seas and trade routes away from coastal areas (e.g., Ezek. 27:4, 25-27), connotes the ship's defiance of the unfathomable, hidden depths. *Of a man* (*geber;* see I: 89) *with* (or more probably "in"),[182] refers to sexual inter-

180. "In the large, major category of its usage, the root *pl'/plh* indicates an event that a person, judging by the customary and the expected, finds extraordinary, impossible, even wonderful. *Pele'* never hinges on the phenomenon as such but includes both the unexpected event and one's astonished reaction. Consequently, the language of *pele'* is the language of joyous reaction (praise). The wonder, the astonishment, includes the recognition of the limits of one's own power to conceptualize and comprehend" (R. Albertz, *TLOT,* 2:982, s.v. *pl' Niphal*).

181. See R. C. Stallman, *NIDOTTE,* 3:85, s.v. *nāḥāš.*

182. Since the other two uses of *beth* ("in the sky . . . in the . . . sea") are clearly spatial, as is *'ᵃlê* ("on"), and since the common denominator is a rocking motion within an area, the spatial sense of *beth* is preferred to its concomitant sense (see *IBHS,* pp. 196-97, PP. 11.2.5b, d).

course. The NIV renders *ʿalmâ* in its other six occurrences by *virgin* twice (Song 6:8; Isa. 7:14), by "maiden" thrice (Gen. 24:43; Ps. 68:25[26]; Song 1:3), and by "girl" once (Exod. 2:8). In every occurrence *ʿalmâ* is at the least a maiden who has not yet borne children; in two nondebatable texts she is a virgin (Gen. 24:43; Exod. 2:8); in none has she demonstrably experienced sexual intercourse; and, leaving aside the highly controversial Isa. 7:14, in the others she is probably a virgin.[183] If so, virgin here refers to her initial sexual encounter. This is the goal of the mysterious, magnetic attraction of romantic love. The habit of intercourse in marriage would be expressed by *bᵉʾištô* ("in his wife"; cf. "woman" in v. 20). A "virgin," symbolic of sexual purity, stands in marked contrast to the adulteress.

20 *Thus* focuses the son's attention on the *way* [see v. 19] *of an adulteress* (see n. 57), a married woman who forms a sexual liaison with more than one man (cf. 2:16). She is not a person of integrity, leads her victims to economic ruin, and shatters the network of family relationships, which are God's foundation stones for an ordered society. The metaphor *she eats* (see 9:17) depicts her sexual activity. Agur links her activity with the preceding numerical saying (v. 19) by adding to the metaphor *and she wipes* [see 6:33] *her mouth* (cf. 5:3), signifying that she leaves no visible trace of her sexual congress. Her self-condemning quote, *and says* (see 30:9), *"I have not done* [see 16:4] *iniquity"* (see 6:12), vividly dramatizes her greed and insubordination. In her amoral world-and-life view she has not executed violence and deceit against society (see 6:12; 10:29; 21:15). She is as morally blind as the foolish generation (30:12; cf. 5:6). The adulteress lacks any conscience about smashing the very foundations of an ordered society because, for her, gratifying her sexual appetite is no different from gratifying her gastronomic appetite. Besides, no one observes her violence and deceit.

(2) Four Upside-down Social Situations (30:21-23)

The adulteress's refusal to observe the proper sexual boundary, which is symbolized by the man in his virgin, not in a number of sexual partners, functions as a janus to four intolerable, topsy-turvy social situations where inferiors do not remain in their assigned places. The catchwords *gbr* (*geber* "man"; v. 19bβ and *gᵉbîrâ* "mistress"; v. 23b) and *mlk* (*yimlôk* "becomes king"; v. 22 and *melek* "king"; vv. 27a and 28b) link the new subunit with the first and third subunits of numerical sayings respectively. Toy,[184] McKane,[185]

183. The LXX, however, has *neotēti* "young woman."

184. Toy, *Proverbs,* p. 532.

185. McKane, *Proverbs,* p. 659.

Whybray,[186] et al. contend that this second numerical subunit is a humorous or whimsical social comment on people who become too big for their own britches. But Roth,[187] Van Leeuwen,[188] Bridges,[189] et al. interpret it as a sober social commentary on a world upside down. The former commentators also think the four items listed are an arbitrary selection. In fact, the quatrain pertains to men in society (v. 22) and to women in the home (v. 23). The outer frame of its chiastic arrangement presents threats to the king (v. 22a) and perhaps the queen (v. 23b) by the "male slave" and the "female slave" respectively within the social structure.[190] The inner core presents those who threaten the social order from without, the outcast man and the rejected woman. Moreover, the saying infers judgment against hubris. The human quest for dominion prompted Adam and Eve to reject God's rule and spurs fools on to reject their rulers. The resulting upheaval in the social order leads to upheaval in the cosmic order (v. 21). The earth cannot bear up under arrogant fools. The sober saying motivates the son to govern wisely in order to forestall upstarts from seizing control and to preserve the creation (cf. v. 10).

21 The title line introduces the four upstarts. As in 29:4, *the earth* (see 30:4) functions as a metaphor and a metonymy for the planet's social order (cf. 1 Sam. 2:10; Amos 7:10). The earth's breakup escalates from *trembles* (see "rages"; 29:9) to *cannot endure* (lit. "bear"; see 6:35; 9:12). But instead of quaking from an earthquake beneath its crusts, it first trembles and then collapses *under*[191] the weight of scamps and scoundrels in the political and domestic hierarchies.[192] The earth's shattering depicts the collapse of its social order.

22 Turning to the threat to society from within, a society collapses *under* the control of *an official* (*'ebed;* see n. 59) *when he becomes king* (see 8:15). Although *'ebed* has its normal domestic sense elsewhere in this book (11:29; 12:9; 14:35; 17:2; 19:10; 22:7; 29:19, 21; 30:10), it probably functions here, as in the historical books, as a litotes for a high official. An official could more readily usurp the reins of government than an indentured slave. Unlike the household slave, "the king's *'ebed* is a freeman who held a high position. His fundamental requirement is loyalty to the king (2 Sam. 15:21),

186. Whybray, *Proverbs,* p. 417.

187. W. Roth, "NBL," *VT* 10 (1960) 403-4.

188. R. C. Van Leeuwen, "Proverbs 30:21-23 and the Biblical World Upside Down," *JBL* 105 (1986) 599-610.

189. Bridges, *Proverbs,* p. 608.

190. The word pair "slave . . . maidservant" occurs 21 times according to R. Schultz, *NIDOTTE,* 4:212, s.v. *šiphâ.*

191. *Taḥat* in this figure has both its literal, spatial sense and its abstract notion ("under the authority of someone"; *IBHS,* p. 220, P. 11.2.15).

192. The LXX destroys the chiasm by reversing the versets of v. 21.

upon which the king depended (1 Sam. 27:12)."[193] The official here, however, presumably betrayed that trust by usurping the throne through intrigue, not through divine election (cf. 1 K. 16:9-20; 2 K. 8:7-14). In the ancient Near East kings ruled by divine right in dynastic succession, and in Israel this was signified by prophetic designation.[194] The proverb does not have in view a slave like Joseph who rose to power through wisdom (Gen. 41:41). The parallel to *'ebed,* an "outcast," supports the interpretation. A nation cannot survive under the rule of an impious usurper to the throne; such a faithless ruler will prove to be a pompous tyrant over those under him. In a democracy a nation should look to God for a worthy ruler. Society also collapses *under* a social *outcast* (*nābāl;* see n. 60). The elevation of a man whom society regards as a scamp because he behaves in an utterly unruly fashion is signified by *when he becomes full of food* (cf. 9:5; 30:9, 15, 16). The sacrilegious fool has food beyond his divinely ordained lot, which should have been a starvation portion. If fed, thereby destroying the proper moral order by rewarding vice, he becomes more arrogant and dangerous and eventually will dismantle the society that tolerates him.

23 The topsy-turvy social order now moves from the body politic to the home (cf. vv. 10, 17). First, the home is threatened when from without it comes *under* the control of *a hated woman* (see n. 61). The chiastic parallel, "a churlish outcast," points to an odious, quarrelsome, unlovable woman whom society rejects, the opposite of a prudent wife (12:4; 18:22; 31:10). *When she gets married* (see n. 63) connotes that the hateful woman, who cannot rule her own tongue, now rules the home (see 12:4; 19:13; 21:9, 19; 25:24; 27:15), or at the least that portion under the wife's normal supervision (see 31:27). Having rightly been shunned by society, she now gets even with it from the security of her elevated place within society. The home can also be ruined by an uppity *maidservant (šipḥâ),* the female equivalent of *'ebed* (see n. 193).[195] The maidservant served the woman of the household most directly "and thus is used with mistress *gᵉbîrâ* more often than with master."[196] *When she dispossesses*[197] entails that she takes possession over the home by

193. Westermann, *TLOT,* 2:822, s.v. *'ebed.*

194. Tomoo Ishida, *The Royal Dynastics in Ancient Israel* (New York and Berlin: Walter de Gruyter, 1977), pp. 7-25.

195. According to Schultz *(NIDOTTE,* 4:212, s.v. *šipḥâ),* "That *šipḥâ* denotes a lower status as laborer, while *'āmâ* indicates a higher status and a more personal relationship, is suggested by Ruth's use of the former to describe herself in 2:13 when she compares herself with Boaz's female slaves but the latter in 19 when marriage to Boaz is attainable."

196. Schultz *NIDOTTE,* 4:212, s.v. *šipḥâ.*

197. N. Lohfink *(TDOT,* 6:371, s.v. *yāraš)* notes that with personal objects the central idea of *yrš* is "legal succession." In parallel with the uppity slave, the profligate

driving out *her mistress (gᵉbîrâ),*[198] the social opposite of the "slave" (cf. Gen. 16:1ff.; Ps. 123:2: Isa. 24:2). Before the *gᵉbîr* ("lord, master"), the masculine equivalent of *gᵉbîrâ,* slaves bow (Gen. 27:29, 37). Its chiastic parallel, "becomes king," suggests that the queen mother may be in view. J. Kuehlewein observes, "*Gᵉbîrâ* is an honorary title at the royal court either for the queen (1 Kgs. 11:19) . . . or the king's mother (1 Kgs. 15:13) [cf. 2 K. 10:13; 2 Chr 15:16; Jer. 13:18; 29:2]." The queen mother, who is almost always mentioned in the book of Kings, influenced the policy and theological stance of the king (cf. 1 Kings 1–2, 11; 16:31; 21:25; Matt. 14:8).[199] The rebellious maidservant presumably first stole the affections of her mistress's husband. To retain the stability of his home a man must marry wisely and then remain true to his wife.

(3) Four Wee but Wise Beasties (30:24-28)

The third subunit is connected with the preceding by the catchwords "four" and "earth" in their title lines (vv. 21, 24), by "food" in their second verses (vv. 22, 25), and by "king" in vv. 22, 27 and v. 28. The syntax of a *waw* disjunctive ("but") plus pronoun ("they" and "it") introducing the B versets of vv. 24 and 28, in contrast to *waw* consecutive ("and so"), forms an *inclusio* around the unit. More importantly, the four wee beasties have the divine wisdom that enables them and the cosmic order to survive, to succeed, and to be secure. The subunit's four small creatures in natural theology display divine wisdom in the created order and stand in contrast to the preceding saying's four upstarts who overturn the social order. The saying's moral, "brains over brawn," takes the form of a parable from which the son ought to draw conclusions for his own comportment;[200] the small creatures are not merely "a bit of natural history," as Toy thinks.[201] The four examples can be analyzed in several ways. In vv. 25-27, verset A identifies the creatures' severe limitations;

---

scamp, and the rejected woman *HALOT* (2:441, s.v. *yrš*) define *yrš* here: "to be heir to someone, oust someone from his possessions (Prov. 30:23 = to dispossess . . .)." The ancient Israelite inheritance law did not provide for a slave woman to become the real heir of her mistress. The Sumerian law code of Lipit-Ishtar (P. 26; *ANET,* p. 160) provided for the sons of a slave woman who had taken the position of a deceased wife, and the Code of Hammurapi (P. 146; *ANET,* p. 172) made provision for a child-bearing female slave who claims equality with a barren wife. These laws, however, are not parallel because the proverb does not envision sons.

198. *Gᵉbîrâ* derives from a root whose basic meaning in the *Qal* is "to be/become superior."

199. J. Kuehlewein, *TLOT,* 1:301, s.v. *gbr.*

200. Meinhold, *Sprüche,* p. 511.

201. Toy, *Proverbs,* p. 534.

verset B their compensating wisdom,[202] as signified by "and so."[203] Verses 25-26 are coupled together in their A versets by the metaphor "people" *(ʿam)* in relation to "people without" and by superficial synonyms for "strength." In fact, however, the apparent synonyms distinguish them. Ants lack "brute strength" *(ʿaz),* not numerical strength; the rock badger lacks both *(ʿāṣûm).* Verses 27-28 are coupled together by the *inclusio* "king," which in the Hebrew text is the first word of v. 27 and the last word of v. 28. In an alternating pattern, vv. 25 and 27 are linked by swarming animals (ants and locusts), and vv. 26 and 28 by more isolated animals (rock badgers and the lizard). A negative *(lōʾ* and *ʾên)* in verset A represents the limitation of the first three wee beasties, and an initial, alogical *waw*-consecutive ("and so") in the B verset introduces their compensating virtues: timely industry (v. 25), seeking shelter (v. 26), and working in unity with strict discipline (v. 27). Verse 28 stands apart by not using a negative and by not mentioning a compensating virtue but simply infers wisdom's reward of gaining "a free run"[204] of the royal palace (cf. 8:15-16).

24 The title line identifies the unifying features of these four beasties as being "small" but "exceedingly wise" (see v. 18). The saying devotes one verse to each of the four animals, defining more specifically how *they are small creatures of the earth* in the sense of being severely limited.[205] *But they are wise* (see I: 94) uniquely uses "wise" for animals to denote their skill to cope and their masterful cunning to survive in spite of their severe limitations, which expose them to threats that endanger their very existence. *Extremely* (see n. 66) signifies that they are masters in its exercise. Since human beings did not train these four creatures, we may infer that the all-wise God taught them their survival skills (see I: 76).

25 By personifying the harvester *ants,* who store their food in their nests, as *people* (or "a nation," *ʿam;* see 6:8; 11:14; 14:28), Agur infers that he intends the natural order to serve as a parable for the social order. Though unified, ants suffer the severe limitation of being *without strength* (see 10:15; 21:14) to either overcome their enemy by physical force or defend themselves by irresistible strength. To compensate for this weakness, they *store up their food in the harvest* (see 6:8). Their exceptional achievement, which is

202. D. Daube ("A Quartet of Beasties in the Book of Proverbs," *JTS* 36 [1985] 380). Daube notes, "The theme of wisdom compensating for smallness permeates the Scriptures" (cf. Gen. 25:29ff.; 27:1ff.; 30:25ff.; 31:1ff.; 32:1ff.; 33:1ff.; 1 Sam. 17:38ff.; 18:1ff.; Eccl. 9:13ff.).

203. *IBHS,* p. 547, P. 311.2a.

204. Van Leeuwen, *Proverbs,* p. 255.

205. Whybray (*Proverbs,* p. 418) cites Exod. 18:22; 1 Sam. 15:17; Isa. 60:22; Amos 7:2, 5 to document that *qāṭôn* "small" can mean weak or insignificant, not necessarily physically small.

out of proportion to their seemingly inadequate size and power, provides a model for God's people to exercise prudent foresight, discipline, and industry in a timely manner (see 6:6-8). For example, the disciple should show prudent forethought to lay up the sage's teachings, which will speak to him in testing (6:22) and enable him to outlast death.

26 As the ant prepares its food for survival, the vulnerable *rock badger (šᵉpannîm)* knows how to reside in security. This yellow and brown Syrian coney *(procavia syriacus)*[206] lives among rocks from the Dead Sea valley to Mt. Hermon. About the size of a hare and with a short tail, but with small ears, it is admirably suited for its habitat. "It has no hoofs but broad nails. The toes, four on the forelegs and three on the back limbs, are connected with skin almost like a web. Under its feet it has pads like sucking-discs which enable it keep its footing on slippery rocks."[207] This *people* is *without numerical strength (lōʾ-ʿāṣûm).* Commentators often disagree whether to gloss *ʿāṣûm* as "strong" or "numerous." The two notions are attenuated (see 7:26; cf. Num. 22:6; Ps. 35:18). To compensate for their vulnerability *they place* [see 23:2] *their houses* [or "dwellings"][208] *in the rocks (selaʿ),* making them inaccessible to predators (Ps. 104:18). *Selaʿ* is used of rocks where wild animals live (Job 39:1; Ps. 104:18) and fugitives hide (Judg. 20:47; 21:13; 1 Sam. 13:6-7; 23:15; Isa. 7:19; Jer. 16:16; 48:28) and "lend themselves to the building of fortifications and strongholds (Jer. 49:16; Obad. 3)."[209] The son by himself is vulnerable to greedy men and wanton women, but he can find security from the wicked predators by seeking shelter in God and his inspired sages' teachings (see 3:5; 22:19). Christians find their safety in the Rock, Christ Jesus.

27 The first two "beasties" make up for their weaknesses by prudent provision and prudent shelter. *Locusts*[210] model prudent unity. They are well known for their amazing ability to form gigantic swarms that can wreak devastation of a scale almost beyond imagination. Highly reliable eyewitness accounts of modern locust plagues border on the incredible (cf. Exod. 10:14; 1 K. 8:37; Pss. 78:46; 105:34).[211] The parable of locusts is par-

206. *HALOT,* 4:1,633, s.v. *šāpān.*

207. Bodenheimer, "Flora and Fauna," pp. 69-70.

208. See BDB, p. 109, s.v. *bayit.*

209. A. E. Hill, *NIDOTTE,* 3:267, s.v. *selaʿ.*

210. The *ʾarbeh* is the sexually mature adult; it is also the generic word for locust.

211. Jerome describes his observation of locusts: "When the swarms of locusts came, and filled the lower region of the air, they flew in such order, by the divine appointment, and kept their places as exactly, as when several tiles or party-coloured stones are skillfully placed in a pavement, so as not to be an hair's-breadth out of their several ranks" (cited by Delitzsch, *Proverbs,* p. 465). Assurbanipal's library yielded a prayer to ward off locust invasions. Ancient Near Eastern literatures use locusts to describe armies. The

ticularly apt for the swift destructive power of armies (Judg. 6:5; 7:12; Jer. 46:23; Nah. 3:15).[212] However, they are limited by their mode of government; they *have no king* (see 14:28; 30:22, 31; cf. Hab. 1:14) to give them leadership. *And so,* to compensate for this lack that normally leads to anarchy (cf. Judges 17–21; esp. 17:6), *all of them* (see 3:15) together *go forth* to battle (cf. 7:15),[213] *dividing into companies*[214] (or "swarming groups"). "They maintain perfect marching orders" (cf. 1 Sam. 11:6-15; Joel 2:7).[215] How much more should God's people under God's king (see 16:10-15) advance God's kingdom by fighting in unison against the enemy, not themselves, each one doing his part within his own rank of peers with the strictest discipline (cf. Numbers 2).

28 The meaning of the *hap. leg. wall lizard (śᵉmāmît)* is disputed. *HALOT* and others identify it "as a type of lizard: gecko, *hemidactylus turicus,*"[216] but the Committee on Translations of the United Bible Societies and others prefer "spider."[217] The four-legged wall lizard runs over the walls and ceilings of Palestinian houses by means of sucking discs on its toes. It is so small and vulnerable that it *can be caught* [see v. 9b] *with two hands* (see 6:5). Verset B, instead of presenting a compensating wisdom for its vulnerability signified by the "and so," draws the saying to its conclusion by asserting, *but it lives* (see n. 71) *in the palace* (*hêkᵉlê;* cf. 1 K. 21:1; Ps. 45:15[16]; Dan. 1:4; Amos 8:3; Nah. 2:6[7]) *of the king* (see v. 27). The plural *hêkᵉlê* signifies the inherent spaciousness and/or complexity of the palace.[218] This conclusion points to wisdom's reward of living in a luxurious royal palace. If the son, whom wicked men and women want to capture, exercises caution, though as vulnerable as a lizard, he too will live in the chief residence of the realm (cf. Psalm 45). Paradoxically, the people of God who are foolish by the world's standards live in heavenly places (Eph. 2:6; Col. 3:1).

Ugaritic *Legend of KRT* likens the king's army to locusts. The Egyptian inscriptions of Rameses II (ca. 1250 B.C.) and Merneptah (ca. 1225 B.C.) compare defeated armies to locusts, emphasizing both their multitudes and their weakness. Assyrian royal annals compare the destructive power of invading armies to these insects. See Daube, "A Quartet of Beasties," pp. 380-86.

212. In the Apocrypha, locusts are the basis of comparison for a huge crowd (Jdt. 2:20), myriad numbers of snowflakes (Sir. 43:17). In the Apocalypse, the fifth angel's trumpet brings hordes of stinging locusts that are described in frightening detail (Rev. 9:3-11).

213. *HALOT,* 2:425, s.v. *yṣʾ.*

214. *HALOT,* 1:344, s.v. *ḥṣṣ.*

215. V. P. Hamilton, *NIDOTTE,* 2:247, s.v. *ḥṣṣ.*

216. *HALOT,* 3:1,338, s.v. *śᵉmāmît.*

217. Bodenheimer, "Fauna and Flora," p. 78.

218. Pl. for a complex inanimate noun (*IBHS,* p. 120, P. 7.4.1e).

(4) Four Stately Marchers (30:29-31)

Agur balances his four vulnerable but wise creatures with four creatures who stride in majestic dignity over their spheres of influence. The wise, knowing how to compensate for their vulnerability, march with their heads held high, fearing no one but God. The catchword "king" connects this fourth subunit with the preceding two (vv. 22, 27, 28, 31) and connotes its royal interpretation. After the title line, the outer frame of the saying elaborates on the lion and the king. Both owe their stately carriage to their being fearless. Within that elaborated frame, one should interpret the significance of the proudly striding cock and he-goat. All four leaders stride regally because they cringe before nothing. The first three animals, the supreme leaders of their realms, lead up to the fourth, the stately king in the human sphere (cf. v. 27). The connection to the king and the personification of the lion as a "hero" infer that the three animals function as a parable for human rulers. The son likewise should walk in a stately fashion, cowering before nobody, knowing that the LORD establishes his step and protects the wise (*ṣā'ad,* 16:9; cf. Neh. 6:1-14; Prov. 3:21-26).

29 The title line identifies the unifying feature of the sayings' four figures as *excel* (see n. 72) in their *stride* (see n. 73) — that is, *in their movement* (see n. 74; cf. Prov. 4:12).

30 The first stately marcher, *the lion* (*layiš* [cf. 19:12; 28:1, 15; see Job 4:11; Isa. 30:6], probably chosen for its alliteration with *tayiš* in Prov. 30:31) is one of the largest and strongest carnivores, dangerous not only to domestic cattle but also to humankind (cf. 1 K. 13:24; 20:36; Mic. 5:8[7]). "Its majestic appearance is heightened by its movements and fearlessness, and also by its mane."[219] Here it is uniquely personified as *a hero* (*gibbôr,* an intensive form of *geber* [see 30:1], and whose basic meaning is "strength"),[220] presenting a striking contrast to the preceding animals without strength (see 16:32; 21:22) and again inferring its parabolic function. *Among animals* (see 12:10) is added because a hero surpasses his peers in its strength and capability to accomplish great feats. The heroic force of the king distinguishes him from the rest of humanity. *Gibbôr* is used of the Messiah in Isa. 9:6(7) (cf. Ps. 45:3[4]). Verset B defines its heroism as its fearlessness expressed by *and does not turn back* [see 1:23] *from the face of anything* (cf. Gen. 49:9-10).

31 The second stately marcher, *the strutting rooster* (see nn. 76, 77), unfortunately is a guess. The LXX (cf. Syr.) paraphrases, "when he [the cock] walks around courageously[221] among the hens." On two seals

219. Bodenheimer, "Fauna and Flora," p. 50.

220. J. Kuehlewein, *TLOT,* 1:300, s.v. *gbr.*

221. Probably a guess at Heb. "girt loins."

dating from the seventh and sixth centuries B.C. a cock can be discerned in an attacking position.[222] *Or the he-goat ('ô-tāyiš),* who also belongs to small livestock (7:23-27), also strides proudly. The LXX paraphrases "a he-goat leading the herd." Many, varied interpretations have been given of the obscure phrase modifying *king* [see v. 28], *no one dares to resist* (see n. 79).

C. CONCLUSION: A WARNING NOT TO UPSET THE DIVINE ORDER (30:32-33)

Lest Ithiel, whom God has not elected for royal birth (see 30:1), think that striding like the king of the realm has a carte blanche of irresistibility, the last saying cautions him not to play the outcast by promoting himself as supreme, If he has, he should shut up immediately. Otherwise the political climber will so irk the community that they will eventually bloody his nose and perhaps end up at loggerheads among themselves. Verse 32a presents the foolish situation of plotting one's self-exaltation through boasting, and v. 32b posits the solution of shutting up at once. Verse 33 gives the reason. Thus the proverb, a climactic conclusion to Agur's numerical sayings, aims to maintain legitimate authority and to protect the son and the community from usurpers and from conflict (cf. also 6:16-19; Rom. 13:1, 2).

32 *If you will play the fool* (*nābaltā;* "being an outcast"; see v. 22) points to one's resolve to commit an inappropriate and unruly act that will demean others and disrupt the social order. *In exalting yourself* (cf. Num. 16:3; 23:24; 1 K. 1:5; Prov. 19:18; "raise," 30:13) specifies self-promotion, which involves boasting, according to verset Bb, that makes one an outcast. *And if you scheme to do so* (cf. 1:4) clarifies that the unruly self-exaltation is part of a planned coup (cf. 24:9).[223] *Clap your hand over your mouth* (lit. "hand to mouth") signifies "keep immediate and absolute silence" (Judg. 18:19; Job 21:5; Mic. 7:16] and symbolizes respect for a superior (Job 40:3-5).

33 *For* introduces the reason to stop the revolt immediately. Verset A presents two asyndetic similes as the standards by which to measure the social tension and ultimate conflict occasioned by obnoxious self-exaltation. The first comparison, *as the churning* [*mîṣ,* lit. "pressing"] *of cream* [see 27:27] *produces* (*yôṣî';* see 10:18) *butter,* signifies the inevitability of churning's outcome, not its beneficial effect. If the milk were sentient, its churning

222. See *ANEP,* p. 85, no. 277.

223. *Zāmam* means "to plan." Context invests it with the pejorative sense "to scheme."

would be as painful as wringing the nose. The second protects the first against a positive interpretation. *And as the wringing (mîṣ) of the nose ('ap,* see 11:22) *produces (yôṣî') blood* (see 1:16). Both comparatives speak of a sustained and strong pressure from without that inevitably reaches a point changing something's very nature. Verset B clarifies the significance of the metaphors by partially continuing them — *so* [lit. "and"] *the pressing out... produces (mîṣ . . . yôṣî')* — in connection with a pun on — *of wrath ('appayim;* see 14:17; 15:1, 18).[224] The metaphor "pressing out of wrath" probably pictures the pretender as so disdainfully pressing down a community in his self-ambitious rise to the top that the people's anger finally gets squeezed beyond its limits and breaks out literally in *strife* (see 26:21; cf. 29:22). The conflict is either between the community and the pretentious fool alone or as part of a political faction in a long, bitter, and costly struggle for control.

VII. COLLECTION VII: THE SAYINGS OF LEMUEL (31:1-31)

A. THE SUPERSCRIPTION (31:1)

1 *The sayings of Lemuel, a king*[1] —
an oracle[2] *that his mother taught*[3] *him.*

Both the form and content of v. 1 mark it off as a superscription, presumably for the entire chapter (cf. 1:1; 10:1; 25:1; 30:1a). However, many scholars credit only the poem "The Noble King" (vv. 2-9) to Lemuel's mother. They exclude the poem "The Valiant Wife" (vv. 10-31) because of its distinct form and structure, its separation from vv. 1-9 in the LXX, and an endemic scholarly skepticism about the Bible's own claims to its authorship. If Lemuel is

224. *'ap/'appayim* mean lit. "nostril(s)," to gesture, or snorting.

1. "The appositive after a name (usually a *personal name*) serves to identify the bearer of the name by office or relationship" (*IBHS,* p. 231-32, P. 12.3e). Were it a title (i.e., King Lemuel), it should have the article.

2. Many scholars emend the text to "king of Massa" (cf. 30:1). Although *maśśā'* here lacks validation by *n^{e}'ûm* ("the inspired utterance") as in 30:1, it finds confirmation in that parallel. Delitzsch (*Proverbs,* p. 317) grants that this sing. is more appropriate here than in 30:1, "for the maternal counsels form an inwardly connected compact whole."

3. See 1:3 for the meaning of the root *ysr* ("to teach").

not the author of "The Valiant Wife," it is a unique orphan in Proverbs — that is, it lacks a superscription ascribing its authorship. To be sure, the former poem consists of admonitions addressed to the king and the latter of sayings in the form of an acrostic, and the valiant wife's husband is not the king, for her husband sits in the gate, not on a throne (v. 23). However, diverse poems with unique forms do not prove different authorship. In fact, sages in both Egypt and the Bible compose unified pieces in diverse forms.[4] Agur skillfully mixed autobiographical confession and numerical sayings of varying types into a unified whole. The LXX of Proverbs is clearly secondary; its translator reinterpreted 31:1[5] and relocated 30:15–31:9 between 24:33 and 25:1 as part of his fiction that Solomon authored the whole book (see the Introduction, I: 4).

In comparing the two poems in ch. 31 with Egyptian analogies, Kitchen summarizes the case that the superscription refers to the entire chapter:

> The subject matter of verses 10-31 . . . is wholly consistent with the reputed origin of the work . . . both being feminine. . . . Conversely, if verses 10-31 be excluded from Lemuel, then (i) the resulting first "work" of only 9 verses becomes ludicrously brief, and (ii) the supposed second "work" of vv. 10-31 becomes an isolated poem with no title and falls outside the instructional literary genre altogether. It would then be an anomalously foreign body in the Proverbs.[6]

Further, M. H. Lichtenstein cited verbal and thematic data to demonstrate that one ordering mind integrated the formally distinct poems into a unity.[7] Both poems begin with specific references to women (vv. 3, 10) and show concerns for *ḥayil* ("strength" [v. 3]/"valiant" [v. 10]), to "open your/her mouth" (vv. 8, 9, 26), and to protect the poor and needy (vv. 9, 20). The superscription credits that ordering mind to Lemuel.

Verset A identifies the genre as "*sayings* [of the wise]" (*dibrê;* see 1:6; 22:17; 30:1) and their author as *Lemuel* (*lᵉmû'ēl,* probably an other-

4. Cf. Kenneth Kitchen, "Proverbs and Wisdom Books of the Ancient Near East: The Factual History of a Literary Form," *TynBul* 28 (1977) 100-101.

5. The LXX reads, "These words of mine have been dictated by God. They are the prophecy of a king whom his mother instructed." 31:10-31 also concludes the book of Proverbs in the LXX, but by attaching it to 29:27 it subsumes it under its superscription "the miscellaneous instructions of Solomon" in 25:1. Without syntactic warrant it also rendered *melek maśśā'* as "oracle of a king."

6. Kitchen, "Proverbs and Wisdom Books of the Ancient Near East," p. 101.

7. Murray H. Lichtenstein, "Chiasm and Symmetry in Proverbs 31," *CBQ* 44 (1982) 202-11. His arguments, based on the alleged similarity of style and structure of vv. 2-9 with vv. 10-31, are less convincing.

wise unattested long form of Lael; Num. 3:24), which means "belonging to God" or "dedicated to God" (cf. "son of my vows," v. 2).[8] Since such a king is unattested in Israel's history, he is probably a proselyte to Israel's faith. The inspired editor of the book of Proverbs added Lemuel's wisdom to the developing canon of Scripture (see I: 36-37; cf. 30:1-6). Ancient Near Eastern wisdom was certainly well known in Israel (see I: 30; cf. 1 K. 5:1; Job 2:11; 15:1, 10, 18-19; Lam. 4:21).[9] Delitzsch emends the text to "the king of Massa" because he believes that taking *a king* (*melek;* see 30:31) as an apposition to "sayings" is impossible.[10] However, the apposition identifies the sayings as "royal instruction," a well-known, longstanding literary genre current in the ancient Near East (see n. 1).[11] Lemuel's sayings (see esp. vv. 4, 8-9) resemble the Egyptian and Babylonian wisdom literature, which also aims to equip rulers to discharge their duties as wise and just kings (see 1:1).[12] Verset B qualifies the royal sapiential genre as also a prophetic *oracle* (*maśśā';* see 30:1) and modifies Lemuel's burden as that which *his mother* (*'immô;* see 1:8; 30:11a) *taught him* (*'ᵃšer-yissᵉrattô;* see 9:7; 19:18; 29:17, 19; cf. Ps. 2:10). *Yāsar* means, "to communicate knowledge in order to shape specific conduct."[13] Queen mothers influenced the policies and theological stance of the king (see 30:23), but no parallel exists in ancient Near Eastern literatures of a mother's wise sayings to her son (see 1:8; 4:3; 6:20).

B. THE NOBLE KING (31:2-9)

2 *Listen,*[14] *my son!*[15] *Listen, son of my womb!*[16]

8. See *HALOT,* 2:532. This meaning finds support in the variant *lᵉmô'ēl* in v. 4.

9. Gemser, *Sprüche,* p. 108.

10. Delitzsch, *Proverbs,* p. 315.

11. R. N. Whybray, *The Composition of the Book of Proverbs* (JSOT 168; Sheffield: Sheffield Academic, 1994), p. 153.

12. For Egyptian examples, see *The Instruction Addressed to King Merikare* (end of 22nd cent. B.C.) for his successor (*ANET,* p. 414) and *The Instruction of King Amenemhet* (ca. 1975 B.C.) for his son (*ANET,* p. 418). For a Babylonian example see *Advice to a Prince* (ca. 1000-700 B.C.) in W. G. Lambert, *Babylonian Wisdom Literature* (Oxford: Clarendon, 1960), pp. 110-15.

13. R. D. Branson, *TDOT,* 6:129, s.v. *yāsar.*

14. The meaning of the thrice-repeated *mah/meh* is uncertain. Elsewhere it means "what"/"why"/"how," but those senses do not fit here. The NIV glosses it by an exclamation and the NRSV by "No!" However, the interrogative has a negative connotation in questions that demand a negative answer, and the NRSV gloss leaves the perplexed reader asking, "No to what?" The LXX, followed by Gemser (*Sprüche,* p. 107) and Fichtner (*BHS*), suggests, "What my son, what Lemuel, my firstborn, am I to say to you?" But in

Listen, son of my vows!
3 *Do not hand over*[17] *your strength to women,*
and your sovereign power[18] *to those who destroy*[19] *kings.*[20]
4 *It is not*[21] *for kings, Lemuel,*[22] *not for kings to drink wine,*
nor for rulers[23] *to crave*[24] *intoxicants;*[25]

Proverbs a parent/teacher does not ask the son/student what to say, and this suggestion does not match the certitude of the admonitions that follow. Probably *mah* here is cognate to an Arabic equivalent, "take heed"/"listen." This felicitous meaning matches the typical introductory calls in wisdom literature to give concentrated attention and receptivity to the teaching (see 1:8; 2:1; passim). The use of an Arabic loanword is consistent with this probably non-Israelite author's use of other forms of non-Israelite origin (see n. 40). This proposal by E. ben Yehuda ("The Edomite Language," *JPOS* 1 [1920/21] 114) is followed by McKane (*Proverbs,* pp. 408-9) and Plöger (*Sprüche,* p. 371).

15. The Aramaic term for "son" (*bar;* cf. Ps. 2:12; Ezra 5:1) is used all three times.

16. F. Deist ("Prov. 31:1. A Case of Constant Mistranslation," *JNSL* 6 [1978] 3) thinks that Lemuel is addressing his son, principally on the basis of Job 19:17. However, the mention of "mother" in v. 1 makes his suggestion of an exceptional meaning for *beṭen* seem far-fetched.

17. A gloss of *nātan* "to give" (cf. Num. 21:3; see BDB, p. 679, s.v. *nātan*).

18. *Drk* means "might" (*HALOT,* 1:232); cf. Hos. 10:13 and a Ugaritic cognate. But if *drk* means "ways," it refers to his whole way of life (see 1:15).

19. Heb. *lam^{e}ḥôt* could be a *Hiphil* inf. cons. of I *mḥh* (cf. the apheresis in Num. 24:17) and mean "the wiping out of kings" (so Vulg.), but the parallel "to women" is poor. The versions read the word differently. The LXX reads "remorse" (< *l^{e}naḥ^{a}môt* or *l^{e}nōḥām);* Targ., "daughters" (< *l^{e}'amḥôt*); Syr. "fat dishes" (an incomplete metaphor for fat concubines?) (< *l^{e}meḥôt*). Modern conjectures are *lōm^{e}ḥôt* "those who steal glances," after an Arabic cognate (E. ben Yehuda [p. 14]); *l^{e}māḥôt* "the amusement/pleasure" (Gemser, *Sprüche,* p. 108); *laḥ^{a}nôt,* from an Aramaic cognate for "concubine" (Ehrlich, cited by Greenstone, *Proverbs,* p. 330) and, with more probability, *l^{e}mōḥôt* "those who destroy women" (Gesenius; Delitzsch [*Proverbs,* pp. 318-19]; BDB [p. 561, s.v. *māḥâ*]). Reider ("Etymological Studies," *VT* 4 [1954], 287, citing Muehlau) finds the same meaning without emending the MT by interpreting it as an abbreviated form of the Aram. *Peal* ptcp. *limmaḥôt.* This seems best in light of the other Aramaisms in this subunit, including the next word. Reider, however, gratuitously emends the next word to Aram. *milkîn* "counsel."

20. *M^{e}lākîn* is Aramaic.

21. *'al* with the indicative expresses emphatic negation (GKC, P. 107p; *HALOT,* 1:48, s.v. *'al*).

22. *L^{e}mô'ēl* is a variant form of *l^{e}mû'ēl* (see 31:1).

23. The repetition of "not for kings" and the direct address add emphasis. The term "ruler" adds further dignity, weight, and gravitas to the parallel, "king" (see 14:21).

24. The form and meaning of *'ēw* are uncertain. K reads *'ô* (= "or strong drink for rulers"), but the syntax is strange. Q reads *'ēy* (see BDB, p. 32, s.v. *'ay*), to which one must supply "to ask" (= "for rulers to ask 'Where is beer?' "). D. W. Thomas ("*'ēw* in Proverbs xxxi.4," *VT* [1962] 499-500) reconstructs *r^{e}'ô/rā'ô* "being/to be sated/drunk" (inf. cons./absolute < *r'w/rww*), and G. R. Driver ("L'interpretation du texte masoretique à la lumière

5 *lest he[26] drink [them] and forget what is decreed,*
and lest he change a verdict[27] for every oppressed person.
6 *Let intoxicants be given[28] to the one who is perishing,[29]*
wine[30] to those who are bitter;[31]
7 *let him drink and[32] forget his poverty,[33]*
and remember no more his misery.[34]

---

de la lexicograhie hebraique," *ETL* [1950], [337-53] 35a) refines this to *r'h* because in several places verbal or nominal forms of *rwh* may be restored *mutatis mutandis* from *r'h* (e.g., Job 10:15; Prov. 23:31). Plöger suggests the negative *'î* (= "and for rulers [there must be] no beer"). Later G. R. Driver ("Problems in the Hebrew Text of Proverbs," *Bib* 32 [1951] 195) regarded the form as defective spelling, *'awwô,* for *'awwo,* "to desire," or an Aramaic nominal form (cf. BDB, p. 16, *'āw*). Possibly it is an apocopated *Piel* inf. cons. < *'awweh* [cf. GKC, P. 75k, bb). There is little difference in sense between "to ask for" and "[to] desire." Moreover, rulers obviously desire it in order to drink it. In sum, there is little sensible difference between the variants.

25. *Šēkār* denotes any inebriating drink with about 7-10 percent alcoholic content, not hard liquor, because there is no evidence of distilled liquor in ancient times (see V. P. Hamilton, *"shēkār," TWOT,* 2:927; R. L. Harris, *"yayin," TWOT* 1:376). It was made from either fruit and/or barley beer (see P. P. Jenson, *"škr," NIDOTTE,* 4:113).

26. The sing. breaks down the pl. "kings"/"potentates" to the individual king.

27. S. M. Paul ("Unrecognized Biblical Legal Idioms in the Light of Comparative Akkadian Expressions," *RB* 86 [1979] 231-39) explains the *hap. leg.* from the Akkadian — *shn dyn* (= change a verdict).

28. The probably indefinite pl. impv. "you" is rendered as an indefinite passive to distinguish it from the 2nd masc. sing. imperatival commands in vv. 3, 4, and 8 (cf. *IBHS,* p. 71, P. 4.5a).

29. Or "dying" (cf. Num. 17:12 [17:27]; Job 29:13). The verb is used mostly of the devastating, destructive end that God inflicts on the wicked. In Proverbs it is otherwise always used of the wicked. However, since the verb may be used without a specific reference to the wicked (cf. Job 6:18; 29:13; Jer. 40:15), that connotation is best not insisted on here.

30. In all but two of its 22 instances *šēkār* occurs with *yayin* "wine," but only here is *yayin* in the second position, perhaps to form a chiasm with the occurrence of these two words in v. 4.

31. Lit. "bitter ones in soul." *Nepeš* is a gen. of location (*IBHS,* pp. 147-48, P. 9.5.2f) and designates their emotional state due to deprivation (see B. K. Waltke, *"nāphash," TWOT,* 2:589). It matches *'w* in v. 4. Against Kutler ("A 'Strong' Case for Hebrew MAR," *UF* 16 [1984] 111-18), who argued that *mar* here means "strong," cf. the critique of the alleged root in D. Pardee (*UF* 10 [1978] 249-88).

32. The conjunctive *waw* with the prefix conjugation after the jussive signifies purpose/result (*IBHS,* p. 650, P. 39.2.2).

33. The parallel escalates his inebriation from being knocked out for the moment to a permanent stupor.

34. *'āmāl,* often "toil," but here "trouble, misery" (i.e., "his emotional misery"; see 16:26).

8 *Open your mouth*[35] *for the mute;*
to give[36] *judgment for everyone fading away.*[37]
9 *Open your mouth, judge righteously,*
and issue edicts[38] *for the poor and needy.*[39]

The admonitions regarding "the Noble King" exhibit the following structure:

I. Introductory admonition to hear	2
II. Admonitions to show restraint	
A. With regard to women: not to waste national strength	3
B. With regard to intoxicants: to protect the poor	4-7
1. Not to become drunk and forget edicts that protect the poor	4-5
2. To give intoxicants to the poor to forget their misery!	6-7
C. Admonition to give new edicts for the poor	8-9

The queen's admonitions primarily urge her royal son to preserve the current statutes that protect the poor (vv. 4-5) and to produce new statutes to protect them (vv. 8-9).

2 This verse reinforces verset B of the superscription and contains the parent's/teacher's typical admonition to the son to hear. The use of foreign loanwords in this poem, including *mah,* which is glossed *listen* (*mah* — see n. 14), lends credence to the conviction that Lemuel and his mother are proselytes to Israel's faith (cf. v. 30).[40] The godly mother's endearing epithets — *my son* (*b*ᵉ*rî;* see 1:8), *son of my womb* (*bṭn;* see 13:5), *son of my vows* (*bar-n*ᵉ*dārāy;* see 7:14; 20:25) mirror their close relationship. She traces his close connection to her backward from the present to his gestation in her womb and to her vows before pregnancy. The latter epithet probably refers to a vow she made that, if God gave her a son, she would dedicate him to live according to

35. A vivid metonymy for "to speak up" (NIV).

36. *'el* signifies the goal (*IBHS,* pp. 193-94, P. 11.2.2a).

37. So *HALOT* (1:321, s.v. I *ḥlp*), who derive *b*ᵉ*nê-ḥ*ᵃ*lôp* from *ḥlp* "to take over from each other by turns," "to pass on," "to fly along" (cf. Ps. 90:5-6; Isa. 2:18). Cf. McKane (*Proverbs,* p. 411), who says the needy "have been treated unkindly by fate or worsted by circumstances over which they have no control."

38. *Dîn* is the verbal homonym of the noun *dîn* "judgment" of v. 8 (*HALOT,* 1:22). It differs from *špṭ* by signifying legal binding decisions in contrast to nonbinding arbitration (G. Liedke, *TLOT,* 1:336, s.v. *dîn*).

39. "The poor and needy" is a hendiadys (see 30:14) to designate the powerless and disadvantaged poor (see 14:31; 31:20).

40. For example, Aram. *bar* (v. 2), *m*ᵉ*lākîn, limmaḥôt* (v. 3), *'ēw* (v. 4); Arab. *mah* (v. 2); and Ugar. *drkyk* (v. 3).

God's wisdom (cf. 1 Sam. 1:11). Appealing to Lemuel's finer feelings, she motivates him to embrace her teachings. He immortalized her life and teachings by passing them on to others, and the Holy Spirit through the community of faith canonized them (cf. Ps. 116:16; Eph. 6:4; 2 Tim. 1:5; 3:15). Her sayings through Lemuel still instruct the people of God.

3 She first cautions Lemuel against unrestrained sexual gratification, but she is not advocating celibacy. *Do not hand over* (*'al-tittēn;* see n. 17) *your strength (ḥayil)* could be a metonymy for virility (see 12:14) and its parallel *and your might* (*ûdᵉrākeykā;* see n. 18) could be interpreted narrowly as metonymies for sexual vigor. But the qualification that these women will destroy him suggests that they are metonymies for all that contributes to making him a strong king (see 13:22; 31:10). *Women* (*nāšîm;* cf. 7:10) here are defined more narrowly as *those who destroy* (*lamᵉḥôt;* see n. 19; 6:33) *kings (mᵉlākîn),* a reference either to women who provide sex outside of marriage (2:16-19; 5:1-23; 6:20-35; 7:1-27; cf. 2 Sam. 12:9, 10) and/or to a large harem of concubines (1 K. 11:11; Esth. 2:10-14; cf. Deut. 17:17). Obsession with such women corrupts the king's sovereign power, including wasting his money. Gratification of lust distracts his attention from serving the people, blunts his wit, undermines his good judgment, exposes him to palace intrigues,[41] and squanders the national wealth (see 13:22) better spent to promote the national good.[42] David's lust for Bathsheba made him callous toward justice and cost Uriah his life, and Solomon's many sexual partners made him callous toward pure and undefiled religion and incapable of real love. In other words, obsession with women has the same effect as obsession with liquor (v. 5).

4-5 The motherly instruction now turns to a warning not to succumb to drunkenness and so distort justice (cf. 20:1; 21:17; 23:20, 29-35). As v. 3a qualified v. 3b, so also the absolute prohibition not to drink wine in v. 4 is qualified in v. 5 to mean drinking to the point of inebriation (cf. 23:29-35). Likewise, the command to give beer and wine to the perishing in v. 6 means that they drink to oblivion to forget their pain (v. 7). A total prohibition, says Ross, "would be unheard of in the ancient courts,"[43] and v. 6 assumes that the king has wine cellars.[44] Other texts caution that liquor will befuddle the king's mind, weaken his will, and drive him to plunder his subjects to pay for his expensive addiction (cf. 1 K. 16:9; 20:16; Eccl. 10:16; Esth. 1:10, 11; Isa. 5:22-23; 28:7; 56:12; Hos. 7:5; Mic. 2:11; Mark 6:21-28; 1 Tim. 3:3; Titus

41. Meinhold, *Sprüche,* p. 517.

42. McKane (*Proverbs,* p. 409) says that unrestrained sexual gratification will "undermine the foundations of his personal authority and the principles of sound government, thereby bringing him into contempt."

43. Ross, *Proverbs,* p. 1128.

44. Meinhold, *Sprüche,* p. 518.

1:7). To these the queen mother adds that debauchery will undermine the just decrees already enacted to protect the poor.[45] The king must practice temperance to uphold the laws that protect the miserable poor who are too socially weak to have a voice.

Verset B escalates *lest* (*pen;* see 30:9) *he drink* (*yišteh;* see 9:5) *and forget* (*w^e yiškaḥ;* see 3:1) *what has been decreed* to establish justice (*m^e ḥuqqāq*)[46] *and lest* [gapped] *he change* (*wîšanneh* — note the alliteration with *yišteh;* cf. 24:21) *a verdict* (*dîn;* cf. 20:8). What earlier had been decreed (i.e., the verdict) had favored *every oppressed person* (*kol-b^e nê-ʿōnî;* see 3:34), who, by definition, is in a condition of inflicted pain, suffering, and anguish.[47] Instead of forgetting them, the king must speak up for them (cf. vv. 8-9, 20; Ps. 72:1-4, 12-14; Prov. 16:12; 24:10-12; 29:4, 7, 14; Jer. 22:16).

6-7 The command *let him drink* (*yišteh;* v. 7) further develops v. 6. This second proverb pair warning against intoxicants also consists of both a "command" (this time positive, v. 6) and a reason (v. 7).[48] Kings have no reason to desire intoxicants (v. 4), but the perishing, who are bitter from lack of food, may have reason to want it. Nevertheless, the command to give intoxicants to all who are dying of hunger to anesthetize them permanently is sarcastic,[49] not a proposed welfare program to provide "free beer . . . as an opiate to the masses."[50] The indefinite plural *give* (*t^e nû*) shows that the queen mother is not giving her son a specific command as in vv. 3, 4, and 8. If taken literally, her command to give *intoxicants* (*šēkār;* see 20:1) *to the one who is perishing* (*l^e 'ôbēd;* see 10:28) *and wine* (*w^e yayin;* see 20:1) *to those who are bitter* (*l^e mārê nāpeš;* see n. 31) would be completely out of harmony with wisdom. The perishing and miserable in v. 6 are defined in v. 7 as suffering from grinding poverty. Drowning one's sorrows in drink solves nothing; its anesthetic effects merely deepen the drinker's inability to face his problems (see 20:1; 23:29ff.). Instead, the following proverb pair specifically commands the king to deliver the poor from their miserable poverty. To offer

45. Meinhold (*Sprüche,* p. 518) comments: "to change their right . . . is the easiest thing to do, since they lack other strong protection."

46. From its basic graphic meaning "carve out, inscribe" (see 8:27) the *ḥqq* develops in the legal realm the meaning "to establish justice" (see 8:15).

47. Cf. Paul Wegner, *NIDOTTE,* 3:451, s.v. II *ʿnh* I.

48. The switch from negative to positive commands also occurs in 26:4-5.

49. The command in 19:27 is also sarcastic. Meinhold (*Sprüche,* p. 519) indirectly supports a literal interpretation from a stipulation in the Babylonian Talmud to offer wine mixed with myrrh to those who have been sentenced to death so that their conscience will be dulled, and the pain of dying will be weakened (Sanhedrin 43a; cf. Mark 15:23 passim). However, it is one thing to stupefy the dying, and quite another to knock out the living to forget the misery of grinding poverty (v. 7).

50. Garrett, *Proverbs,* p. 246.

drink without that material help would be cynical. The sarcastic command aims to debunk intoxicants as useless. Their only possible value is to knock out the poor and to keep the addicts permanently in a drunken stupor. To make the point by negatives, the mother is not recommending intoxicants as either medicine,[51] or a reminder to show love,[52] or a stimulant,[53] or to bring conviviality and cheerfulness to the dying.[54]

8-9 Verses 4-7 negatively warned the king against intoxicants that dismantle just decrees that protect the poor. By contrast, vv. 8-9 positively command him to enact righteous decrees to protect them. The two instructional sets are connected by their common theme and by the catchwords *dîn* ("verdict"/"judgment"/"issue edicts") and *ʿōnî/ʿānî* ("poor") (vv. 5b, 8b, 9b). The repeated initial commands *open your mouth (pᵉtaḥ-pîkā),* a metonymy for "speak up," in versets A of vv. 8 and 9 and the repeated initial homonyms in verset B, *dîn* ("judgment"/"issue edicts") (i.e., give just and righteous verdicts) bind vv. 8-9 together. What follows "open your mouth" clarifies its sense, that is, to *judge righteously* (*šᵉpāṭ-ṣedeq;* see 1:3; 29:14) in v. 9a escalated to *issue edicts* (*wᵉdîn;* see 31:5) in v. 9b. The otherwise synonymous, escalating parallelism strongly supports interpreting *everyone (kol) fading away* (*bᵉnê ḥᵃlôp;* see n. 39) in v. 8b as *the poor and needy* (*ʿonî wᵉʾebyôn,* 22:22; 30:14) in v. 9b.

The description of the fading poor and needy as *mute* (*lᵉʾillēm,* lit. "to have the lips tightly closed")[55] in v. 8a is a metaphor for their lack of a voice to defend themselves in the court unless the king speaks up for them (cf. 16:10; 20:18; 25:5; 29:4a, 14; Ps. 72:12-14; Jer. 22:15-19).[56] They are socially and economically too weak to defend themselves against the rich and powerful. The poor may be defenseless against them because they are too ignorant to counteract the obstructionist tactics of the legally savvy, too inarticulate to state their case convincingly, too poor to produce proper evidence, and/or too lowly to command respect. Furthermore, the rich and powerful can bribe witnesses to accuse them falsely. In sum, the king must be accessible to the people (e.g., 2 Sam. 15:3; 1 K. 3:16ff.; 2 K. 6:26ff.) and champion the cause of one who cannot otherwise get a fair hearing. What is said here of the king, says Meinhold, "is valid for each person in his sphere of activity."[57]

51. *Pace* McKane, *Proverbs,* p. 410.

52. *Pace* Bridges, *Proverbs,* p. 618.

53. *Pace* V. P. Hamilton, *TWOT,* 2:926, s.v. *shēkar.*

54. *Pace* P. P. Jenson, *NIDOTTE,* 4:114, s.v. *škr.*

55. J. N. Oswalt, *NIDOTTE,* 1:412, s.v. *ʾlm.*

56. McKane (*Proverbs,* p. 411) thinks that the referent is literal, but Toy (*Proverbs,* p. 540) objects that if it were literal, "The mute would not depend on the king, but on his nearest friend or his legal representative."

57. Meinhold, *Sprüche,* p. 519.

C. THE VALIANT WIFE (31:10-31)

10 *aleph* *A valiant wife*[58] *who can find?*[59]
Her price is far beyond corals.
11 *beth* *The heart of her husband*[60] *trusts*[61] *in her;*
he does not lack "spoil."[62]
12 *gimel* *She does*[63] *him good and not evil*
all the days of her life.[64]
13 *daleth* *She selects diligently*[65] *wool and flax,*[66]
and works[67] *with her glad palms.*
14 *he* *She becomes like trading*[68] *vessels;*
she brings her food from afar;[69]
15 *waw* *and*[70] *she arises [like a lioness] while it is still night,*

58. *'ēšet* "wife/woman" is the initial word in this *'aleph* line. Hereafter the initial Hebrew word will be cited, allowing the reader to match its initial consonant with the acrostic. The last word in verset A is *māṣā',* making its initial and last letter *'aleph.*

59. Imperfect of capability (*IBHS,* p. 322, P. 18.2g).

60. Outside of Proverbs *'îš* ("man") is mostly used for "husband" (81 times), but in Proverbs *ba'al* ("lord," "owner") is used for that notion and always in relationship to *'ēšet-ḥayil* (12:4; 31:11, 23, 28). In 31:11 the choice serves the consonance of *beth* in every word of verset A of this *beth* line *(bṭḥ bh lb b'lh)* but not in 12:4.

61. Heb. *bāṭaḥ* "trust" is word-initial.

62. *Šālāl,* which occurs 75 times in the Old Testament, always refers to plunder, booty, or spoil, and the LXX, Targ., and Vulg. accept that sense here; but cf. Syr. ("her food supplies never diminish"); *HALOT,* 4:1418 (*Gewinn* "gain"). J. L. Kugel ("Qohelet and Money," *CBQ* 51 [1989] 46) thinks that *šll* means "wealth" in Ps. 119:162 and Prov. 1:13, which he arbitrarily alleges are late, but the NIV rightly judged that it meant "spoil" in these two texts as well. The proposal by Clifford (*Proverbs,* p. 275) that *šll* "may be vernacular" is arbitrary and overlooks Wolters' study.

63. Heb. *gāmal.*

64. Reading pronominal suffix with most mss. and editions.

65. Heb. *dāraš* (see 11:27). Aside from the last word, *kappeyhā* "her palms," the sibilants */š~ś~ṣ/* occur unexpectedly in every word of this *daleth* line.

66. Lit. "stalks of flax."

67. *'āśâ* with *beth* attached to an abstract noun signifies "to act in the manner of" (BDB, p. 794, s.v. *'āśâ*).

68. Understanding the *Qal* ptcp. as a substantive and an attributive gen. (so *HALOT,* 1:71, s.v. *'ᵒniyyâ*). It could also be rendered "a fleet belonging to a merchant/trader."

69. In its other 17 occurrences, apart from Ps. 138:6, *merḥāq* refers to other countries.

70. Initial *waw*-consecutive subordinates v. 15 to v. 14, filling in "particulars or details, [a] component or [a] concomitant situation" (*IBHS,* p. 551, P. 33.2.2a). Cheryl Julia Dunn ("A Study of Proverbs 31:10-31" [M.A. thesis, Talbot School of Theology,

and provides "prey"[71] *for her household,*
and[72] *the quota [of food] for her servant girls.*[73]
16 *zayin* *She considers*[74] *a field and purchases*[75] *it;*
from the fruit of her palms she plants[76] *a vineyard.*
17 *heth* *She girds*[77] *her loins*[78] *with strength;*
she strengthens her arms for the task.[79]
18 *teth* *She perceives that her trading is good;*
her lamp [of prosperity] does not go out at night.[80]
19 *yodh* *Her hands she holds out to the doubling spindle;*[81]

1993], pp. 47, 51) notes that all three clauses begin with *waw* (*wattāqom . . . wattittēn . . . wᵉḥōq* in this *waw* line, and the final word of each begins with the alliteration of *lamed* and ends with the assonance of */â/āh/hā (laylâ . . . lᵉbêtāh . . . lᵉnaʿᵃrōtêhā).*

71. The 25 occurrences of the verb *ṭrp* signify to tear into pieces by animals of prey, and of the 22 occurrences of the noun *ṭerep,* according to *HALOT* (2:380), 18 designate prey and four "what has been torn > of food" (Job 24:5; Ps. 111:5; Prov. 31:15; Mal. 3:10), but see 30:8. Getting up while it is still dark to provide the *ṭerep* suggests that the poet is using an incomplete metaphor for a lioness, which hunts its prey at night. If so, one need not amend *ḥōq* to *tôrâ* ("quota of work; *pace* Kuhn [cited by Gemser (*Sprüche,* p. 108), McKane [*Proverbs,* p 668], Fichtner [*BHS*]). Gemser himself, however, defined *ḥōq* here as "quota of food."

72. Fichtner *(BHS),* Whybray (*Proverbs,* p. 427), Van Leeuwen (*Proverbs,* 5:261), et al. suggest omitting verset B. Meinhold argues, "Only here in this poem three versets occur; . . . the term quota cannot be grasped without ambiguity. . . . There is a question whether and — if yes — how the food for the whole day has been distributed already in the morning" (*Sprüche,* p. 524). However, it is hazardous to emend the text *metri causa,* and his other objections are based on a failure to understand *ṭerep* as an incomplete metaphor.

73. Cf. V. Hamilton, *NIDOTTE,* 3:126, s.v. *naʿar.*

74. Heb. *zāmam.*

75. Lit. "takes." Delitzsch (*Proverbs,* p. 330) notes that in Aramaic, Arabic, and postbiblical Hebrew "taking" and "giving" (see v. 24b) denote buying and selling respectively, and Meinhold (*Sprüche,* p. 525) cites the same phenomena in Ugaritic.

76. *Qere* (and probably the versions — the LXX has *katephyteusen*) reads *nāṭᵉʿā, Qal* perfective 3rd fem. sing., but *Kethib* probably reads either *nᵉṭōaʿ, Qal* inf. cons., meaning either "to plant" or "planting of" or *nᵉṭaʿ,* cons. of *neṭaʿ,* also meaning "planting of."

77. Heb. *ḥāgar.*

78. The muscular middle portion of her anatomy that connects its upper and lower portions (V. P. Hamilton, *NIDOTTE,* 2:1,150, s.v. *motnayim*).

79. "For the task" is based on the LXX's addition *eis ergon* < *laʿᵃbōdâ (BHS)* or *lᵉmaʿᵃśeh* (so L. H. Brockington, *Hebrew Text of the Old Testament* [Oxford: Oxford University; Cambridge: Cambridge University, 1973], p. 168). The haplography in the MT was caused by the homoioteleuton of final *h.*

80. Qere reads the expected *balaylā* "at night," but the Kethib *layl* is also attested in Isa. 16:3.

81. Following Al Wolters, "The Meaning of *Kîšôr,*" *HUCA* 65 (1994) 91-104.

her palms grasp the spindle.
20 kaph *Her palm*[82] *she spreads out to the poor,*
and she holds out her hands to the needy.
21 lamedh *She is not*[83] *afraid for her household on account of*[84] *snow,*
for all her household is clothed with scarlet.[85]
22 mem *Coverlets*[86] *she makes for herself;*
her clothing is fine linen and [wool dyed with] purple.[87]
23 nun *Her husband is respected*[88] *at the city gate*
when he sits with the elders of the land.
24 samekh *Garments*[89] *she makes and sells [them];*
sashes she supplies to the merchants.[90]
25 ʿayin *Strength*[91] *and majesty is her clothing,*[92]

82. Heb. *kappāh* "her palm." Perhaps the sing. *kap* is used to avoid confusion with the idiom "to spread the palms *prś kpym* (in prayer [for]"; cf. Exod. 9:29; 2 Chr. 6:12; Ezra 9:5; Job 11:13; *HALOT,* 2:492, *kap*). Moreover, it allows opportunity for an escalation to the pl. in verset B. *Kappāh* is best understood as the object and not the subject in spite of the syntax of the parallel v. 19b because "palm" is a normal object, not subject, of the verb *prś* (V. P. Hamilton, *NIDOTTE,* 3:700, s.v. *prś*).

83. Initial *lōʾ* "not" begins the *lamed* line. If the cons. phrase *lbš šnym* be counted as one word, every word except *kî* contains *lamed: lʾ . . . lbyth mšlg . . . kl . . . lbš.*

84. *Min* denotes cause (*IBHS,* p. 213, P. 11.2.11d).

85. *Šānîm* is either a bi-form of *šānî* (cf. Isa. 1:18) or a dittography from following *marbaddîm.* G. R. Driver ("On a Pronoun in the Baal Epic (IVAB iii.24) and Proverbs xxi.21," *BASOR* 105 [1947] 11), followed by Gemser (*Sprüche,* p. 110), derives *šānîm* from *šᵉnayim* "double" (i.e., double clothing for warmth) on basis of the LXX and of Vulg. "duplicibus" (also found in several of the Midrashim [A. J. Baumgartner, *Étude critique sur l'état du texte du Livre des Proverbes d'après les principales traductions anciennes* (Leipzig: Imprimerie Orientale W. Drugulin, 1890), p. 245]). However, the Syr. and Targ. retain the more difficult MT reading. The MT reading nicely combines the notions that her household is warmly and splendidly clothed in wool (cf. Meinhold, *Sprüche,* p. 526). It also matches "the purple dyed wool" (i.e., warm and splendid clothing) in v. 22.

86. Heb. *marbaddîm* (see 7:16).

87. Meinhold (*Sprüche,* 2:526) says that this Hittite loanword *(ʾargāmān)* refers to fine clothes made with dye of this color.

88. *Nôdāʿ* "known/respected" is word-initial.

89. Heb. *sādîn.* The gnomic perfective verb *ʿāśᵉtâ* (*IBHS,* pp. 487-88, P. 30.5.1c) necessitates that the sing. indefinite nouns *sādîn* and *ḥᵃgôr* be rendered as pls.

90. Heb. *kᵉnaʿᵃnî* "Canaanites." The Canaanites were so well known for their trading that "Canaanite" became synonymous with trader (cf. Isa. 23:8). Their name derived from *kᵉnaʿan,* the red purple obtained from the purple shellfish of the Phoenician coast, mainly for export *(HALOT,* 2:485, s.v. *kᵉnaʿᵃnî).*

91. Heb. *ʿōz.*

92. The definite noun is probably the subject (*IBHS,* p. 132, P. 8.4.2a).

and so[93] *she laughs at the coming days.*
26 *peh* *Her mouth*[94] *she opens with wisdom,*
and loving teaching[95] *is on her tongue;*
27 *ṣadeh* *one who watches over*[96] *the affairs;*[97]
the food of idleness she does not eat.[98]
28 *qoph* *Her sons*[99] *arise*[100] *and pronounce her blessed;*[101]
her husband [rises] and praises her:
29 *resh* *"Many*[102] *daughters do valiantly,*[103]

93. *Waw*-consecutive to signify logical succession (*IBHS,* p. 547, P. 33.1.2.1a).

94. Heb. *pîhā.*

95. The ambiguous gen., *tôrat-ḥesed* is interpreted as an attributive gen., like "true [not false] instruction," in Mal. 2:6. Possibly it is also an objective gen., "instruction about lovingkindness," and/or a genitive of species, "the law, kindness."

96. Heb. *ṣôpîyâ.* The consonance of the dentals /*ṣ~t*/ echoes throughout the line, occurring in every word except *leḥem* "food" and *lō'* "not." Al Wolters (*"Ṣôpîya* as Hymnic Participle and Play on *Sophia," JBL* 104 [1985] 577-87) explains with erudition its unexpected morphology, *ṣôpîya,* as due to a clever bilingual pun on Gk. *sophia* (pronounced *sopia* in Greek). If so, the pun allows the translation "all her household is wisdom." Using Wolters' reasoning, Claire Gottlieb ("The Words of the Exceedingly Wise: Proverbs 30–31," in *The Biblical Canon in Comparative Perspective,* ed. K. L. Younger, Jr., W. W. Hallo, and B. F. Batto [ANETS 11; Lewiston/Queenston/Lampeter: Edwin Mellen, 1991], p. 290) thinks that the pun is closer to Egyp. *sbȝyt,* meaning "instruction" or "wisdom." If so, it may be a triple pun. G. Rendsburg ("Bilingual Wordplay in the Bible," *VT* 38 [1988] 354-56) points out other examples of bilingual wordplays in this poem (e.g., v. 27b) and in the Hebrew Scriptures besides those given by Wolters.

97. *Hᵃlîkôt,* from *hlk* "to go/walk," is rendered elsewhere as "advance" in the NIV (Nah. 2:5[6]), "orbits/pathways" (of the stars), "caravans" (Job 6:19), "procession" (Ps. 68:24[25]). Here the metaphor means "the orderly affairs [of her household]." An Akkadian equivalent means "lifestyle" (G. Sauer, *TLOT,* 1:368, s.v. *hlk*).

98. The gen. of material personifies the food by the human characteristic of sluggishness. The *hap. leg.* *'aṣlût* is the abstract nominal form of *'āṣēl,* "sluggard." The clause could be read: "idleness [i.e., the abstract noun for the concrete "idler"] does not eat food." Meinhold (*Sprüche,* p. 528) understands the syntax, against the Masoretic accents, in this way: "The consequence from the observations in her household is that laziness is not rewarded by bread with her . . . (cf. 2 Thess 3:10)."

99. Preferred to "children" because elsewhere in this book *bānîm* refers to sons and because the poet may intend a play with "daughters" in his pairing of this verse with v. 29.

100. Heb. *qāmû* is word-initial.

101. Construed as a delocutive *Piel* (see *IBHS,* p. 403, P. 24.2g).

102. Heb. *rabbôt.*

103. Lit. "to do valor." *'āśâ* "to do, make, produce" with an abstract noun as object may denote behavior and is therefore glossed by an adverb (cf. 12:4, 22; 21:3, 7, 15; 31:10). With *lamed* the phrase is used for producing wealth and person (*'āśâ lî ḥayil* "made for me wealth," Deut. 7:17, 18; cf. v. 3) and is so understood here in all the ancient versions, but that construction does not occur here. It *may* refer exceptionally to procreative strength in Ruth 4:11.

but you surpass all of them."

30 *shin* *Charm*[104] *is deceitful*[105] *and beauty is fleeting;*
as for a woman who fears the LORD, *she should be praised.*[106]

31 *taw* *Extol her*[107] *for the fruit of her hands,*
and let her works praise her in the gates.

The poem "The Valiant Wife" is structured as an acrostic (i.e., the initial consonant of each verse follows the order of the Hebrew alphabet), and, like the acrostic poem in Sir. 51:13-20, draws the book to its conclusion. By describing the capable wife within such a rigorous structure, the poet and his audience experience in a most memorable way the catharsis of having fully expressed themselves ("everything from A to Z"), even though in truth the whole cannot be stated.[108] Unfortunately, this obvious structure has obscured for many its other embroidered structures. K. C. Hanson, however, defended the thesis that all the alphabetic poems in the Hebrew Scriptures and the three in the Dead Sea Scrolls[109] "employ a variety of interactive structures."[110] In

104. Generic article. The syntax unambiguously points to "charm" *(ḥēn)* and "beauty" *(yōpî)* as subjects and "deceitful" and "fleeting" as classifying their qualities (see *IBHS,* p. 132, P. 8.4.2a). *Ḥēn* (see 1:9) refers broadly to the distinctive that makes someone or something visually acceptable or attractive to another. Here visual attractiveness, not spiritual graciousness, is in view because it is compounded with "and beauty" (*yōpî* [see 6:25]).

105. Heb. *šeqer* is the initial word of this *shin* line.

106. An imperfect/nonperfective of obligation (*IBHS,* p. 508, P. 31.4g). Although exceptional with *hll,* the *Hithpael* expresses the passive voice (*IBHS,* p. 431-32, P. 2.3a), not the reflexive (cf. 27:2). Also, the sense cannot be, "As for woman, let her boast in the fear of the LORD," for that would require *byr't.*

107. The root is *tnh* "to recite, commemorate," not *ntn* "to give," because (1) it offers a better parallel with *hll* in verset B; (2) *ntn* demands supplying an object; and (3) in its other two occurrences *tnh* also has a human (not a divine) object (Judg. 5:11; 11:40). If so, the form probably should be repointed to *Piel tannû.* This root is proposed by G. R. Driver and followed by B. Gemser (*Sprüche,* p. 110); A. Wolters ("Proverbs XXXI 10-31 as Heroic Hymn," pp. 449-50, n. 24); Whybray (*Proverbs,* p. 431); L. C. Allen (*tnh, NIDOTTE,* 4:311), Van Leeuwen (*Proverbs,* p. 263), et al. and is found in the NEB and NJPS.

108. N. K. Gottwald (*Studies in the Book of Lamentations* [SBT, 1st series, 14; rev. ed.; London: SCM, 1962], p. 32) argues that the purpose of the acrostic structure is primarily to achieve a sense of totality and that memory is its secondary goal.

109. Psalms 9/10, 25, 34, 37, 111, 112, 119, 145; 155; Prov. 31:10-31; Lamentations 1, 2, 3, 4; Nah. 1:2-8; Sir. 51:13-30; Apostrophe to Zion.

110. K. C. Hanson, "Alphabetic Acrostics: A Form-Critical Study" (unpub. Ph.D. diss., Claremont Graduate School, 1984), p. ii. There has been no consensus, however, concerning what structures lie within the acrostic. Lichtenstein ("Chiasm and Symmetry in Proverbs 31," pp. 202-11) finds an alternating pattern of A/A′ nine-verse units (vv. 10-18, 21-29); B/B′ two-verse codas (vv. 19-20, 30-31). The abiding value of his work is his

addition to being an acrostic, this eulogy to the Valiant Wife is arranged logically. Its broad thematic divisions are:

I.	Introduction: her value	10-12
	A. Her general worth inferred from her scarcity	10
	B. Her worth to her husband	11-12
II.	Body: her activities	13-27
	A. Her cottage industry	13-18
	B. Seam (or janus)	19
	C. Her social achievements	20-27
III.	Conclusion: her praise	28-31
	A. By her family	28-29
	B. By all	30-31

The acrostic's rhetorical artistry reinforces its thematic unity. The introduction and conclusion progress logically from her blessing of her husband to his praise of her. The conclusion is connected chiastically with its introduction by the three catchwords *'iššâ* "wife/woman" (vv. 10, 30), *ḥayil* "valiant/valiantly" (vv. 10, 29), and *ba'al* "husband" (vv. 11, 28). This seven-verse frame consists of two chiastically matched parts: the wife's worth/praise generally (vv. 10, 30-31) and her worth/praise with reference to her family (vv. 11-12, 28-29). The itemization of her activity proceeds logically from her income based on her skill in weaving and expanded through trading (vv. 13-19) to her accomplishments on that economic base (vv. 20-27). Verse 27 is joined with v. 26 by its initial qualifying participle, making them one sentence. Counting the seam (or janus) in v. 19 with the first half of the body

---

identification of the two-verse chiastic unit (vv. 19-20). K. C. Hanson ("Alphabetic Acrostics") restricts himself to a thematic and form-critical analysis. The abiding value of his work is the identification of the unity of the praise conclusion. T. McCreesh ("Wisdom as Wife: Proverbs 31:10-31," *RB* 92 [1985] 25-46) observes verbal repetitions such as *'iššâ, ḥayil,* and *ba'lāh* in vv. 10-11 and 28, 29, 30 (so also Meinhold, p. 529), and of *lbš* in vv. 21, 24, and 25. Meinhold (*Sprüche,* pp. 521-22) analyzes the poem into seven divisions (v. 10, vv. 11-12, vv. 13-18, vv. 19-20, vv. 21-25, vv. 26-27, and vv. 28-31). An abiding value of his work is his isolation and summarization of vv. 13-18. By form criticism Wolters ("Proverbs XXXI 10-31 as Heroic Hymn," pp. 446-57) identifies an introduction announcing the celebrant (vv. 10-12), a body that enumerates her praiseworthy attributes (vv. 13-27), and a concluding exhortation to give her praise (vv. 28-31). Garrett (*Proverbs,* p. 228) analyzes the whole poem as a chiasm with a pivot on the husband in v. 23. The abiding value of his work is his recognition of the chiasm in vv. 21-27. W. G. E. Watson (*Classical Hebrew Poetry: A Guide to Its Techniques* [JSOTSup 26; Sheffield: JSOT, 1984], p. 194) arbitrarily analyzes it into two halves (vv. 10-20, 21-31), and Van Leeuwen (*Proverbs,* p. 262) supports him by noting an *inclusio* of *yr'* in vv. 21 and 30. No one has published a thorough syntactic, poetic, and thematic analysis.

and v. 27 as a grammatical unity with v. 26, the two halves of the main body also consist of seven sentences each.

Two preliminary issues require comment. First, what is the poem's genre? Al Wolters argues that this panegyric to the valiant wife belongs to the genre of praise hymns found in the Psalter, especially Psalm 112. Both are acrostics, use the so-called "hymnic participle," and celebrate a person who fears the LORD (31:30; 112:1), itemizing their God-fearing works, their wisdom (31:2; 112:5), wealth (31:16, 18, 29; 12:3), compassion and liberality to the poor (31:20; 112:4, 5), and fearless attitude to the future (31:25; 112:7, 8).[111] Several things, however, undermine this thesis. First, the introduction of Psalm 112 begins with the essential hymnic motif of praise psalms, a call to praise the LORD, but that motif is lacking in this introduction. Second, "the hymnic participle" usually begins and dominates the body of praise psalms, but its one occurrence in v. 27 draws the main body to a conclusion and functions to qualify v. 26, not v. 10. Finally, lexical similarities in themselves do not establish a formal identity between this poem and Israel's hymns.

Wolters, however, is on more solid ground when he classifies Prov. 31:10-31 as belonging to Israel's heroic poetry, characterized by recounting the hero's mighty deeds, usually his military exploits.[112] He concludes that

111. Wolters, "Proverbs XXI 10-31 as Heroic Hymn," pp. 446-57. He argues that both the praise psalms and this "song" share (1) the same structure: an introduction, a body, and a conclusion that calls for praise; (2) a call on inanimate objects to praise (v. 31; Ps. 145:10); (3) the so-called hymnic participle (v. 27; Ps. 145:10); (4) an ascription of "strength and honor" (v. 25; Pss. 93:1; 104:1); and (5) the theme of incomparability (v. 29). *[Wî]halᵉlûhā* "praise her" in the conclusion (v. 31; cf. v. 28) is strikingly similar to *halᵉlû-yāh* "praise Yah" in the Psalms (e.g., Ps. 105:48).

112. He noted several similarities between the Song of Deborah (Judges 5), the women's songs for Saul and David (2 Samuel 18 and 21), and David's elegy for Saul and Jonathan (2 Samuel 1) and this poem. (1) *'ēšet-ḥayil* (v. 10) may be translated "valiant woman," for *ḥayil* is frequently found in military contexts. (2) The term forms an *inclusio* around the poem (vv. 10, 29). (3) The repetition of *ḥayil,* which essentially means "power" or "prowess," compounded with two occurrences of its synonym *'ōz* "strength" (vv. 17 and 25) gives a remarkable emphasis to her strength. (4) A number of terms have a military connotation: "plunder" (v. 11); "prey" (v. 15); "you ascend above," which is usually used of going out to battle (v. 29); "she stretches out her hand" (v. 19), which, according to the Egyptologist Paul Humbert, elsewhere always occurs in an aggressive context; Humbert, however, excluded this poem ("Entrendre la Main," *VT* 12 [1962] 187). (5) *Tnh* "extol" (v. 31, i.e., sing a responsive victory song) elsewhere occurs only in heroic poetry (Judg. 5:10; 11:40). (6) Like heroic poetry, the poem is characterized by action, not by inner feelings or physical appearance. (7) Heroic poetry celebrates members of the aristocratic class, to which this wealthy woman obviously belongs (cf. vv. 15, 16, 20, 22, 23). To these three more similarities can be added: (8) "Laughs [in victory]" is a warlike term (v. 25). (9) "Girds her loins with strength" (v. 17) is a masculine and heroic image. (10) "Watching over" glosses the normal Hebrew term for "to reconnoiter" and "to spy" *(HALOT,* 3:1,044, s.v. I *ṣph).*

this heroic poem functions as a polemic first against the praise of women in ancient Near Eastern literatures. It counters that writing's preoccupation "with the physical charms of women from an erotic point of view" with celebration of "her activity in the ordinary affairs of family, community and business life."[113] In fact, King Lemuel's mother debunks physical beauty as praiseworthy (v. 30). Also, more subtly and indirectly, this heroic poem critiques "the intellectual ideal of Hellenism,"[114] for the eulogy aims to praise not an abstract theoretic wisdom rooted in impartial rationality but "concrete practical wisdom rooted in the fear of the LORD."[115] It may also be a polemic against the ideal wife's counterpart in the Greek literature of the Classical and Hellenistic periods. Maryse Waegeman[116] finds that this Greek literature prizes the silent, "homebody" spouse, unlike the ideal wife in this Hebrew heroic poem, who is diligent, "takes charge," is engaged in profit-making ventures, and is also a wise teacher and philanthropist. Following R. G. Marks, Wolters holds that the heroic poem, as in rabbinic literature, redefines *g^ebûrâ* from "heroic prowess" to "academic and moral victories":[117] "Heroism of the battlefield is transposed in this case . . . to a woman's *vita activa* in home and community."[118] Erika Moore insightfully adds that the poem's use of military imagery in the domestic sphere presents the godly wife "as a spiritual heir of Israel's ancient heroes" and "a champion for those around her by her diligent application of wisdom." In short, "the valorous wife is a heroic figure used by God to do good for His people, just as the ancient judges and kings did good for God's people by their martial exploits."[119]

The second preliminary issue concerns whether the valiant wife personifies wisdom, like "Woman Wisdom" in the prologue (cf. 1:20-33; 8:1-36; 9:1-6), or models an ideal for a real wife who incarnates wisdom. If she is an allegory for wisdom, then the son through embracing her as a wife obtains the strength to provide for the family (cf. 4:4-9). On the other hand, if she represents a woman as real as Ruth, who is praised in the gate as "a valiant woman" (*'ešet ḥayil;* Ruth 3:11; cf. 2:10), she emerges as an important contributor to the economy of the family and of the community. By her economic contributions she frees her husband to play a prominent public role. McCreesh rejects

113. Wolters, "Proverbs XXXI 10-31 as Heroic Hymn," pp. 456-57.

114. Wolters, "Proverbs XXXI 10-31 as Heroic Hymn," p. 457.

115. Wolters, "Proverbs XXXI 10-31 as Heroic Hymn," p. 457.

116. Maryse Waegeman, "The Perfect Wife of Proverbia 31:10-31," *Goldene Apfel,* pp. 101-7.

117. Richard G. Marks, "Dangerous Hero: Rabbinic Attitudes toward Legendary Warriors," *HUCA* 54 (1983) 181-94.

118. Wolters, "Proverbs XXXI 10-31 as Heroic Hymn," p. 457.

119. Erika Moore, "The Domestic Warrior" (unpubl. paper submitted for OT 813, Proverbs, to Bruce Waltke, Westminster Theological Seminary, 1994), p. 18.

a literal interpretation because "the husband is left with little or nothing to do!"[120] He argues for a symbolic interpretation by noting the valiant wife's correspondence to the sapiential values. Certainly, like Woman Wisdom and the values she represents, the wife is valiant (v. 10; 14:1), rare (conveyed by Heb. *mî ymṣ'* [v. 10; 1:28; 3:13; 4:22; 8:17, 35]), precious (v. 10; 3:13; cf. 12:4; 16:16; 18:19; 21:15), trustworthy (v. 11; 3:1-6; 4:6, 8, 9, 12; 10:9), energetic, not a sluggard (cf. vv. 13, 27b; 6:6-11; 26:13-16), resourceful (conveyed by Heb. *zmm* [v. 16; 1:4]), strong (v. 17; 24:5), ever prosperous and wealthy (v. 18; 3:10; 13:9), kind to the poor (v. 20; 3:27; 11:24-25; 14:21), fortified (v. 21; 1:26-27; 30:25), a wise and loving teacher (v. 26; 8:14, 32), and pious (v. 30; 1:7).[121] However, although these similarities show that this heroine incarnates wisdom, they do not establish that she is fictitious. The echoes of Woman Wisdom, who is portrayed on the purely symbolic register in the prologue, in this portrait of the valiant wife are wholly compatible with an ideal wife on the historical register. Finally, McCreesh's argument for the wife as a symbol from the poem's words and phrases is not convincing.[122]

The exegesis that follows validates the traditional interpretation that the valiant wife belongs in the historical, not the allegorical, realm.[123] Whybray finds support for the symbolic interpretation in the unmistakable return in the book's conclusion to the prominent role of the feminine figure in the prologue.[124] To be sure, this *inclusio* is no coincidence but intentionally func-

120. Thomas P. McCreesh, "Wisdom as Wife: Proverbs 31:10-31," p. 27, following E. Jacob, "Sagesse et Alphabet: A propos de Proverbes 31:1-31," in *Hommages à Andre Dupont-Sommer,* ed. A. Caquot and M. Philonenko (Paris, 1971), p. 288.

121. Cf. H. Ringgren, *Sprüche/Prediger* (ATD 16/1; Göttingen: Vandenhoeck & Ruprecht, 1967), p. 121; Whybray, *Proverbs,* pp. 160-62; Jutta Hausmann, "Beobachtungen zu Spr 31,10-31," in *Alttestamentlicher Glaube und Biblische Theologie: Festschrift für Horst Dietrich Preus zum 65,* ed. Hausmann and Zobel (Stuttgart: Kohlhammer, 1992), pp. 21-77.

122. McCreesh ("Wisdom as Wife," pp. 28-30) assumes that Woman Wisdom's call to the gullible in ch. 9 to make their home with her "is completed by the portrait of the woman settled down with her own in chapter 31." If this is an argument to support the thesis, it begs the issue. To be cogent, he must first establish that the acrostic represents a figurative personification of Wisdom, which is unambiguously the case in 1:20-33; 8:1-36; and 9:1-6.

123. Andre Barucq, *Le Livre des Proverbes* (Domais biblique; Paris: Gabalda, 1964, cited by McCreesh, "Wisdom as Wife," pp. 28-29, n. 11) interprets *yir'at-YHWH* in v. 30 as a noun, not as an adjective, yielding the meaning "the woman, the fear of the LORD." Although grammatically possible, lexicographers, ancient and modern translators, rabbis, and commentators almost universally understand the term as an adjective. The symbolic interpretation cannot rest securely on an ambiguous point of grammar.

124. Whybray, *The Composition of Proverbs,* pp. 154, 158, following C. V. Camp, *Wisdom and the Feminine in the Book of Proverbs* (Sheffield: Almond, 1985), pp. 183-91; cf. E. Jacob, "Sagesse et Alphabet," p. 291; Meinhold, *Sprüche,* p. 26.

tions as the book's frame. However, it does not follow that because the feminine portrait in the prologue is symbolic, the feminine portrait in this climactic culmination cannot be real. Woman Wisdom in 9:1-6 is purely symbolic, but the foolish woman in 9:13-18 incarnates folly.

With the Protestant insistence on the *sensus literalis* the valiant wife has been traditionally interpreted as a real wife.[125] In the second half of the twentieth century most scholars agree that she incarnates wisdom's ideals, without removing her from the historical realm. Had the author intended an identification with figurative Woman Wisdom, it is unlikely that he would have referred to her as "a valiant wife," which denotes a real woman in its other occurrence (12:4). Indeed, in every other occurrence in Proverbs *'iššâ* "woman" refers to a real woman (see 14:1; 18:22; 31:3). Also, McCreesh undermines his own argument by noting in his conclusion that the valiant wife of this poem has striking parallels with Ruth, a real woman, called *'ēšet-ḥayil* (Ruth 3:11). The differences, which Hawkins notes, between the two female portraits in the book's frame support the traditional view: (1) Woman Wisdom is never clearly pictured as a wife or a mother, unlike the valiant wife. (2) Woman Wisdom is presented as a composite figure (prophet, teacher, and mediatrix), whereas the capable wife is exclusively a homemaker.[126] Finally, against McCreesh, one must grasp the concentrated way in which the authors in this book represent truth.[127] This panegyric portrays lopsidedly only the valiant wife as the family's breadwinner, just as the rest of the book lopsidedly spoke only of sons, never of daughters. The full truth is obtained in this sort of literature by collating all the proverbs and poems into a coherent montage. Surely it is wrongheaded to think that only the wife engages in philanthropy (v. 20) and speaks with wisdom (v. 26). In fact, the preceding pericope prevents such a misinterpretation (cf. vv. 8-9). So also it is wrongheaded to think that the valiant woman alone tends to the domestic sphere, leaving the husband nothing to do. Earlier proverbs warn the son against being a slug-

125. See Jana K. Reiss, "The Woman of Worth: Impressions of Proverbs 31:10-31," *Dialogue: A Journal of Mormon Thought* 30 (1997) 141-48. For bibliography up to 1985 see McCreesh, "Wisdom as Wife," p. 26, n. 4. Since then she has been understood as a real wife either explicitly or implicitly by Plöger (*Sprüche,* p. 376), Meinhold (*Sprüche,* p. 521), Garrett (*Proverbs,* p. 248), and Van Leeuwen (*Proverbs,* p. 264). Whybray (*Proverbs,* p. 160), however, equivocates. Ellen Lyons ("A Note on Proverbs 31:10-31," in *The Listening Heart: Essays in Wisdom and the Psalms in Honor of Roland E. Murphy, O.Carm.,* ed. K. G. Hoglund, E. F. Huwiler, J. T. Glass, and R. W. Lee [Sheffield: Sheffield Academic, 1987], p. 287) thinks that the valiant wife is akin to the matriarchs in premonarchic Israel.

126. Tom R. Hawkins, "The Wife of Noble Character," *BSac* 153 (1996) 12-23.

127. McCreesh ("Wisdom as Wife: Proverbs 31:10-31," p. 29) wrongly thinks, "The entire domestic operation of the household is in her hands."

gard and portray him as gathering the harvest (6:6-9; 10:4-5), laboring in the vineyard (24:30-34), and caring for his flocks (27:23-27). The paean of praise to the valiant wife assumes that the husband has founded the home on a sound economic foundation (24:27); within that context his wife can settle down and function to her maximum capacity.

In conclusion, this valiant wife has been canonized as a role model *for all Israel* for all time. Wise daughters aspire to be like her,[128] wise men seek to marry her (v. 10),[129] and all wise people aim to incarnate the wisdom she embodies, each in his own sphere of activity.[130] One should avoid emphasizing one of these applications at the expense of another, forgetting that by nature proverbial material sets forth exemplars, asking audiences to make the appropriate application to their own spheres.

1. Introduction (31:10-12)

This three-verse paragraph runs smoothly into the three-verse paragraphs that comprise the next subunit (vv. 13-15, 16-18).

10 Placing the direct object as the poem's initial words, the sage brings immediately into focus his celebrant, *a valiant wife* (*'ēšet-ḥayil;* also 12:4). *Ḥayil* elsewhere denotes "competent strength"[131] (Prov. 12:4; cf. Ps 84:7[8]) and connotes wealth (cf. 2 K. 15:20)[132] and membership in a select group (cf. Gen. 47:6; Exod. 18:21), including a warrior class (2 K. 24:14 and 16).[133] "Valiant" satisfies these notions and fits the present heroic form (cf. the LXX's *andreios* "manly, courageous"). Metlitzki, who opts for "women of strength" or "woman of valorous virtue," notes that Jerome rendered the phrase *mulier fortis* ("strong woman") and that Jewish translators into English commonly have "a woman of valor."[134] She points out that the etymology of traditional "virtuous" (KJV) is Lat. *virtus* — "manly excellence" (cf. *vir* "man"), a sense that nicely fits the heroine's description as one who "girds

128. Margaret B. Crook, "The Marriageable Maiden of Prov. 31:10-31," *JNES* 13 (1954) 140; Roland E. Murphy, *Wisdom Literature: Job, Proverbs, Ruth, Canticles, Ecclesiastes and Esther* (FOTL; Grand Rapids: Eerdmans, 1981), p. 82.

129. Garrett, *Proverbs,* p. 228.

130. Dorothee Metlitzki, "A Woman of Virtue: A Note on Eshet Ḥayil," *Orim: A Jewish Journal at Yale* (1986) 26; Antonio Bonora, "La donna eccellente, la sapienza, il sapiente," *RivB* 36 (1988) 138.

131. H. van der Sluis–van der Korst and D. van der Sluis, "De deugdelijke huisvrouw in opspraak: een interpretatie van Spreuken 31:10-31," *Schrift* 69 (1980) 94.

132. Hence a parallel to "price" here.

133. See Gottlieb, "The Words of the Exceedingly Wise: Proverbs 30–31," pp. 282-92.

134. Metlitzki, "A Woman of Virtue," pp. 23-26.

her loins with strength and strengthens her arms for the task" (v. 17).[135] The itemization of her deeds in the body of the poem defines specifically what *ḥayil* means.

The rhetorical question *who* (*mî;* see 30:4, 9) *can find* (*yimṣāʾ;* see 3:13) aims to awaken within the audience the desire to find such a wife or to be like her. The parallel verset B implies a relative, not an absolute, negative answer, "Almost no one" (cf. Ps. 90:11; Isa. 53:1; Hos. 14:9[10]).[136] It also clarifies the meaning of the rhetorical question and equates the valiant wife with a treasure. From the assertion *her price* (*mikrāh;* cf. 23:23) *is far beyond* (*rāḥōq mip-;,* lit. "more than beyond"; see 7:19; 15:9) *corals* (*pᵉnînîm;* lit. "more than beyond corals"; see 3:14), it becomes clear that she is rare, exceedingly precious, and attractive. The figure is based on the ancient Near East practice of obtaining a wife by means of a "bride-price" (see 4:5-7). She is precious because she uses her strength, ability, wisdom, and valor so totally and selflessly for others. Such a wife is a gift from God (19:14) and must in part be sought by faithful prayer (15:29; 16:3; Jas. 1:6).

11-12 The pronouns in the expressions "in her" *(bāh),* "her husband" *(baʿlāh)* and "her price" *(mikrāh)* link vv. 11a and 10b, and the pronoun "him" in v. 12, looking back to "her husband" in v. 11, links those two verses. Verses 11-12 focus the valiant wife's value to her relation to her *husband* (*baʿlāh;* see 12:4). The verses are also bound together by the symmetry of a positive statement (vv. 11a, 12aα) reinforced by a negative (vv. 11b, 12aβ).

11 The statement, his *heart* (*lēb;* see I: 90; cf. 2:2) . . . *trusts* (*bāṭaḥ;* see 3:5) *in her (bāh),* which entails that his well-being stands or falls on her reliability, is remarkable. Outside of this text and Judg. 20:36, Scripture condemns trust in anyone or anything apart from God/the LORD (cf. 2 K. 18:21; Ps. 118:8-9; Isa. 36:5; Jer. 5:17; 12:52; 18:10; 48:7; Ezek. 33:13; Mic. 7:5). As E. Gerstenberger observed, "One can successfully place confidence only in Yahweh, . . . no other entity can be an ultimate object of trust."[137] The present exception elevates the valiant wife, who herself fears the LORD, to the highest level of spiritual and physical competence. The claim implies that this husband and wife enjoy a robust spiritual relationship. Verset B presents the cause of his trust: *he does not lack* (*lōʾ yeḥsār;* see 13:25) anything necessary. The surprising object, *spoil* (*šālāl;* see n. 62), a military metaphor, implies

135. Wolters ("Proverbs XXXI 10-31 as Heroic Hymn," p. 455), citing the *Oxford English Dictionary,* observes that "virtuous woman" at the time of the KJV would have meant "heroic woman."

136. E. W. Bullinger, *Figures of Speech Used in the Bible* (Grand Rapids: Baker, 1968), p. 950.

137. E. Gerstenberger, *TLOT,* 1:229, s.v. *bṭḥ.*

that the woman has to win essentials like food and clothing through strategy, timely strength, and risk in this fallen world (see 24:30-34).

Verse 12 functions as a seam between the introduction (vv. 10-12) and the main body of the poem (vv. 13-27). "All" (*kōl;* see 3:15) commonly occurs in summations, and the generalizations of vv. 10-12 prepare the reader for the specifics of vv. 13-27. In this verse, her value to her husband and why he trusts in her are defined by the extent (verset A) and duration (verset B) of what *she does for him* (*gᵉmālathû,* i.e., her deliberately performed duties; see 3:30; 11:17). *Good* (*ṭôb;* see I: 99; 2:9) is a metonymy for all that is spiritually and physically desirable and beneficial to life, escalated to the litotes *not evil* (*lōʾ-rāʿ;* see 1:16). The body of the poem defines "good" primarily in terms of her economic benefits. *All the days of* (*kōl yᵉmê;* see 21:26; 23:7) *her life* (*ḥayyeyha;* see 2:19) means that at each point along the continuum of her life with her husband she never fails. Her commitment to her husband's wellbeing is true, not false; constant, not temperamental; reliable, not fickle; and discerning.

2. Body (31:13-27)

The poem now praises the "valiant wife" by itemizing her deeds and thereby defines *ḥayil* ("valiant"). This itemization extends her value to her entire household and to the community, including its poor and needy. Indirectly, by contributing to the household's economy she empowers her husband to provide leadership for the entire land (v. 23). Thematic, syntactic, and poetic factors combine to show that the body consists of two halves (vv. 13-18, 20-27), with v. 19 functioning as an almost invisible seam stitching them together. Thematically, the first half itemizes her contribution to the family economy by the trade of her surplus textiles; the second half itemizes mostly her palpable contributions to her family and community on that economic base. Syntactically, an initial verbal form (i.e., "she does X")[138] begins each verse in the first half, but an initial nonverbal form is used in the second half. The initial verb reappears in the conclusion (v. 28). Poetically, the first half is developed according to an alternating structure, and the second according to a chiastic structure.

a. Her Sources of Revenue (31:13-18)

Repetition of key terms exposes the alternating structure and reinforces the argument that her "cottage industry" provides the economic basis for her trading to enrich the household.

138. A *Qal* perfective 3rd fem. sing. in each verse apart from v. 15, which begins with a *waw*-consecutive, 3rd fem. sing.

A	Her palms *(kappeyhā)* work the raw textiles	v. 13
B	She trades *(sḥr)* to enrich the table	v. 14
C	She arises at night *(laylâ)* to seek "prey"	v. 15
A′	She invests in a vineyard from the earning of her palms *(kappeyhā)*	v. 16
B′	She gains strength from her trading *(sḥr)*	vv. 17-18a
C′	Her lamp does not go out at night *(laylā)*	v. 18b

A/A′ feature the income her palms produce, supplementing her income from her surplus textile production to that from the vineyard she purchased from the earnings of her weaving. The initial verbs in vv. 13a and 16a entail thoughtful evaluation behind these activities. B/B′ mention her trading, first to enrich the family table and then, assuming a logical connection between vv. 17 and 18a, as a source of her spiritual strength. C/C′, using figurative language, begins the day with her rising while it is still night and ends it with her light not being extinguished at night.

13-15 Positive emotions drive her work in manufacturing thread from the raw materials of animals *(wool, ṣemer) and* of vegetation (*flax, pištîm,* ready to be made into linen thread), synecdoches for her weaving skills (v. 13). Meinhold writes, "The flax plant grows to a height of ca. 50 cm, has slim leaves and blue blossoms and develops a fruit capsule with several oily seeds. Both products, fiber and oil-fruit, were probably used already in the 10th century B.C. The flax was pulled out with the root and dried on the roof (Joshua 2:6). The tools mentioned in v. 19 for spinning and the various articles referred to in vv. 21f, 24 allow the conclusion that flax served here for the purposes of clothing."[139] The collective plural of composition indicates that it has been gathered, measured, and dried and so is ready for sewing.[140] Meinhold also describes the procedures: "The wool had to be weighed, combed and washed. After the flax had been pulled out, it had to soak in water and then be dried. Pieces of bark and wood were removed. The fibers obtained were pulled by crooked, blunt hooks (heckling) to split and arrange them. Short fibers were removed as tow. Verses 19, 21f, 24 talk about further particular procedures."[141] *And she works* (*watta'aś;*[142] see 21:25) *with her glad palms* (*b^eḥēpeṣ*[143] *kappeyhā*[144]) signifies

139. Meinhold, *Sprüche,* p. 524.

140. *IBHS,* p. 119, P. 7.4.1a.

141. Meinhold, *Sprüche,* p. 524.

142. *'āśâ* with *beth* attached to an abstract noun signifies "to act in the manner of" (BDB, p. 794, s.v. *'āśâ*).

143. The attributive gen., *ḥēpeṣ* indicates "a subject's feeling: delight as a psychic attitude" (see 3:15; G. Gerleman, *TLOT,* 2:467, s.v. *ḥpṣ*).

144. The analysis of the acrostic's poetics necessitates distinguishing *yodh* ("hand," the appendage from the elbow to the fingertips) from *kaph* ("palm," the append-

a succession situation. The goal of her work is to produce clothing, a symbol in the Bible of "industry, intelligence, and, when worn, of the glory."[145]

14 Verses 14-15 link her manufacture of textiles to her trade. Her weaving industry provides the economic foundation for her trade for exquisite food from far-off places. Claire Gottlieb documents that in ancient societies women who had acquired skills in spinning and weaving were greatly admired and desired.[146] In Elephantine a good woolen garment would cost over two months' wages and an inexpensive linen one half of a month's wage.[147] Verset 14a depicts the heroine as a merchant fleet, and verset B interprets the figure. *She becomes* (*hāyᵉtâ;* see 5:14) *like trading vessels* (*kā'ᵒniyyôt sôḥēr;* see n. 68) signifies trading that is prudently planned, diligently executed, and enterprisingly ventured; the plural suggests the multitude of her purchases.[148] *Brings* (*tābî';* see 21:17) *her food* (*laḥmāh;* see 9:5) *from afar* (*mimmerḥāq;* see n. 69), though purchased from the local merchants, connotes an atmosphere of faraway countries; that is, beyond the usual nourishment from fields or trades, she provides tasty foreign delicacies (cf. v. 24). Her bounteous table replicates in miniature that of fabled King Solomon (cf. 1 K. 4:21-23[5:1-3]).

15 Syntactically subordinate to v. 14, the following figure of a preying lioness supplements the preceding figure of a trading fleet.[149] *And she arises* (*wattāqom;* see n. 70; see 6:9) *while it is still* (*bᵉʿôd;* cf. 2 Sam. 3:35) *night* (*laylâ;* see 7:9) belongs to the preying imagery and should not be interpreted literally; a lioness hunts food by night,[150] but not an aristocratic woman! The figure connotes that in keeping with her character she puts the well-being of the household before her own comfort. The incomplete metaphor of a predator, she provides (*wattittēn;* see 1:4) *prey* for its young (*ṭrp*) is

---

age from the wrist to the fingertips). According to Delitzsch (*Proverbs,* p. 331), *kaph* "denotes the hands when the subject is skilful, successful work."

145. Van Leeuwen, *Proverbs,* p. 261.

146. Gottlieb, "Proverbs 30–31," pp. 286-87.

147. Bezalel Porten, *Archives from Elephantine: The Life of an Ancient Jewish Military Colony* (Berkeley: University of California, 1986), tables, 2, 75.

148. See *ANEP,* pp. 31-33, nos. 108, 111. Ezek. 27:17 and Ezra 3:7 do not include linen or woolen products among the items used in Israel's trade.

149. The parallelism of v. 15 consisting of Aa and Ab + B, usually designated by the misnomer "tricola," may separate v. 15 from v. 16. W. G. E. Watson noted: "In the main, though, the tricolon does have the function of *demarcating stanzas* (or segments of poetry), coming either at the beginning or at the end, and sometimes in both places. It can also mark a climax" (*Classical Hebrew Poetry,* p. 113). Kugel (*The Idea of Biblical Poetry,* pp. 26-27), however, disagrees in the light of Ugaritic poetry. He considers the role of the tricola to be "repetition and restatement, an emphatic, elevating function quite independent of symmetry, parallelism, or even poetic structure."

150. *Encyclopedia Britannica* (1929), s.v. "lion."

so shocking that most translators and the LXX, which reads *brōmata,* opt to render *ṭerep* "food."[151] McCreesh, however, does not flinch, commenting: "At the very least, this word represents provisions acquired only after the exercise of great strength, prowess, and ingenuity and would seem to commend the extraordinary ability of the wife in providing for her household even against great odds. Both *ṭerep* and *šālāl,* therefore, illustrate in a very dramatic way the wife's ability to provide for those in her charge."[152] The preying metaphor must not be pressed to signify unethical activity; this woman fears the LORD (v. 30). The parallel *and the quota [of food]* (see 30:8) for *her servant girls* shows that *bētāh* means *to her house* (*lᵉbêtāh;* see 27:27).

16-18 Verse 16 escalates her economic base and her table fare to the purchase of a field where she plants a precious vineyard.[153] Such activity demands tremendous physical (v. 17) and psychic energy (v. 18). Verse 18 draws the unit to a conclusion. Like v. 12, it too is an extended line, and for the first time since v. 12b the "valiant wife" is not the subject of the clause in v. 18b.

16 *She considers* (*zāmam,* i.e., she puts together a plan or strategy to act on; cf. 30:32)[154] *a field* (*śādeh;* see 23:10; 24:30), probably on a fertile hillside (see Isa. 5:1). After carefully considering it from all angles, *she* boldly executes her plan and *buys it* (*wattiqqāḥēhû;* see n. 74). Her revenue to buy it derives from the *fruit* (*mippᵉrî,* see 1:31) *of her palms* (*kappeyhā;* see v. 13), a metonymy for the textiles she made with her palms (cf. v. 24). *She plants* (*nāṭᵉʿā;* n. 76; cf. Gen. 2:28) *a vineyard* (*kārem;* see 24:30) assumes that she dug up the field and cleared it of stones before planting it with choicest vines, and afterward built a watchtower in it and cut out a winepress (see Isa. 5:2).

17 This verse represents this wealthy woman, who has servant girls (v. 15), as herself having the capacity to do the required, sustained manual labor to plant a vineyard in addition to manufacturing textiles, though undoubtedly she employed male slaves to do much of the work. Sarah (Gen. 18:6-8), Rebekah (24:18-20), and Rachel (29:9, 10) show that women of high social rank and wealth were not above manual, even menial, labor (cf. Exod. 2:16; 2 Sam. 13:5-9). In this complementary parallelism, which features her strong body parts, "loins" and "arms," both versets represent her spiritual preparation for hard work and her physical competence to accomplish it. *She girds* (*ḥāgᵉrâ,* i.e., binds around) *her loins* (*motneyhā;* see n. 78) metaphorically

151. See n. 71.

152. McCreesh, "Wisdom as Wife: Proverbs 31:10-31," p. 41.

153. "Plant" in verset B assumes that the field had been purchased (verset A). Unlike the distinction between "fields" and "vineyards" in 1 Sam. 22:7; Neh. 5:4; Ps. 107:37, the parallelism in Prov. 24:30 and here suggests that "vineyard" specifies the kind of field in view.

154. John E. Hartley, *NIDOTTE,* 1:1,112, s.v. *zmm.*

pictures her putting on *strength* (*bᵉʿōz,* "with strength"; see 10:15). Meinhold comments, "If, like a belt, strength is tied around this part, then the entire body stature is strengthened (v. 25a)."[155] The idiom "to bind the loins" means to get ready for some "kind of heroic or difficult action,"[156] such as hard running (1 K. 18:46; 2 K. 4:29), escape from Egypt (Exod. 12:11), or physical labor (Prov. 31:17). The metaphor points to her psychic and spiritual motivation and preparation that equips her powerful body. Thus girded mentally and spiritually, *she strengthens* (*wattᵉʾammēṣ;* see 8:28; 24:5) *her arms (zᵉrōʿôteyhā),*[157] signifying that she both resolves to make her arm strong and that she has the strength and endurance to complete *the task* (*laʿᵃbōdâ,* LXX; see n. 79) to which she commits herself after prudent evaluation.[158]

18 This verse points to the source of her psychic and spiritual energy, drawing to a conclusion the section on her gains by trading her surplus textiles. Verset B clarifies that to experience "good" (verset A) means to enjoy enduring wealth. The beneficial reward prompts her continued activity. *She perceives* (*ṭāʿᵃmâ,* i.e., learns by experience and evaluation; cf. 11:22; 26:16)[159] *that (kî) her gain* (*saḥrāh,* that is, the profit from her trading, such as the food on her table and the wine from her vineyard; see 3:14) *is good* (*ṭôb,* i.e., beneficial to life and so desirable and valuable; see 3:27; 11:23). The meaning of v. 18b is disputed. *Her lamp* (*nērāh;* see 6:23; 20:27) *does not go out* (*yikbeh,* see 26:20) *at night* (*laylā;* see n. 90) is usually taken to mean that she works "till far in the night."[160] C. Gottlieb recalls a parallel incident from Livy in which Collatinus unexpectedly arrived home late at night and found his wife Lucretia "in the hall of her house, surrounded by her busy maid-servants, still hard at work by lamplight upon her spinning."[161] In this way, Lucretia won the prize for womanly virtues. However, it is not wise to be active until late at night (cf. Ps. 127:2), especially if one arises while it is still dark (v. 15). Moreover, if taken at face value, not as hyperbole, the verse

155. Meinhold, *Sprüche,* p. 525.

156. Van Leeuwen, *Proverbs,* p. 261.

157. *Zᵉrōaʿ* probably includes the shoulders (cf. BDB, p. 285, s.v. *zᵉrōaʿ*). A. S. van der Woude, *TLOT,* 1:392, s.v. *zᵉrōaʿ,* M. Dreytza *(NIDOTTE,* 1:1,146, s.v. *zᵉrōaʿ),* and *HALOT* (1:280, *zᵉrōaʿ*) think especially of the forearm, but the citations are not convincing, and *yodh* refers to that part of the arm.

158. Whybray (*Proverbs,* p. 428) thinks that *ʾmṣ Piel* means "summons the strength of her arms," citing Amos 2:14; Nah. 2:1(2), but there the idiom is *ʾimmēṣ kōaḥ* (see 24:5).

159. *Ṭāʿam* literally means "to try and evaluate with the tongue the flavor of food" (1 Sam. 14:24, 29, 43). From the notion of "tasting" with the tongue (2 Sam. 19:35[36]) develops the notion of testing words (Job 12:11; 34:3) and finally the idea of evaluation and perception.

160. For example, Delitzsch, *Proverbs,* p. 331; Meinhold, *Sprüche,* 2:525; et al.

161. Gottlieb, "Proverbs 30–31," p. 286.

asserts that her lamp *never* goes out. Probably the clause is an incomplete, idiomatic metaphor meaning that she enjoys enduring wealth. To judge from a Middle Eastern proverb, "he sleeps in the dark," or "he has not another penny in the house,"[162] "her lamp never goes out at night" means that there is always money in the house. Toy, following Wildeboer, reached a similar conclusion from references to "lamp" in the Old Testament: "In a well-ordered house the lamp burned all night . . . as a sign of life; its extinction marked calamity (Jer. 25:10; Job 18:6)."[163] In sum, her lamp burning all night signifies her enduring prosperity (cf. Prov. 13:9; 20:20; 24:20).

b. Janus (31:19)

Verse 19 functions as a seam uniting the two sections of the acrostic's main body — that is, her income (vv. 13-18) and her production. On the one hand, it thematically forms an *inclusio* with v. 13, bringing closure to the unit on her textile manufacture (vv. 13-18). The janus develops the valiant wife's selection of the raw wool and flax for her textiles (v. 13) to the actual making of thread by reference to the spindle, a metonymy of instrument, the thematic connection strengthened by the lexical *inclusio kappeyhā* (vv. 13b, 19b). On the other hand, it is linked syntactically with the second half by the line-initial, nonfinite verbal forms that characterize vv. 20-27 and by its double chiastic structure with v. 20:

v. 19 A her hands she extends *(yādeyhā šilleḥâ)* to the doubling spindle,
       B her palms *(kappeyhā)* grasp the spindle.
v. 20 B′ her palm *(kappāh)* spreads out to the poor,
     A′ her hands she extends *(yādeyhā šilleḥâ)* to the needy.

The outer frame, *her hands* (*yādeyhā;* see n. 82) *she holds out* (*šilleḥâ;* see 6:14, 19), surrounds the inner core, "her palm[s]" *(kappeyhā/kappāh).* This connection is further strengthened lexically by the initial synonyms "hands" *(yādeyhā),* introducing the *yodh* ("hand") line of the acrostic, and by initial "palms" *(kappeyhā)* in its *kaph* ("palm") line. That phenomenon occurs elsewhere only in v. 26, where *pîhā* "her mouth" introduces the *peh* ("mouth") line. Van Leeuwen comments, "The hands that grasp to produce open wide to provide [v. 20]."[164]

162. Gemser, *Sprüche,* p. 110.

163. Toy, p. 545. Similarly, Selman *(NIDOTTE,* 3:160, s.v. *nēr)* says that the lamp symbolized a prosperous household, as in 13:9, and *HALOT* (2:457, s.v. *kbh*) interprets the extinguishing of the lamp at night as "a sign of poverty."

164. Van Leeuwen, *Proverbs,* p. 262. Cf. Eph. 4:28.

According to Wolters, *the doubling spindle (kîšôr)* was grasped "either for re-spinning or for doubling, that is, for making two-ply or three-ply yarn out of previously spun threads."[165] The spinner passes a thread drawn out but only slightly twisted through a ring or over a forked stick or other support and spins it as thread onto a large spindle grasped in both hands.[166] *Her palms* [see vv. 13, 16] *grasp* [see 3:18; 11:16] *the spindle* or spindle whorl[167] reinforces the picture of her skill and industry.

c. Her Production (31:20-27)

The second half of the poem's body (vv. 20-27), in addition to shifting from the syntax of line-initial verb to line-initial non-verb, itemizes her mostly palpable contributions to the household and community in a chiastic structure:

A	Spreads palms to the poor	v. 20
B	No fear of snow	v. 21a
C	Household clothed in scarlet	v. 21b
D	She makes *(ʿāśᵉtâ)* coverlets and clothing for herself	v. 22
X	Husband respected at the gate	v. 23
D′	She makes *(ʿāśᵉtâ)* garments and sashes for merchants	v. 24
C′	Wife clothed with strength and dignity	v. 25a
B′	Laughs at the future	v. 25b
A′	Opens mouth with wisdom, looking after her household	vv. 26-27

Apart from the janus (v. 19), A/A′ uniquely feature her body parts in relation to the body parts of the acrostic.[168] The wise words of her mouth inform the deeds of her hands and, *mutatis mutandis,* the wise deeds of her hands give credibility to the wise teachings of her mouth. The alliteration of /*p*/ and the assonance of /*â~ah*/ in initial *kappāh pārᵉśâ* "she spreads out her palm" (v. 20) and initial *pîhā pātᵉḥâ* "she opens her mouth" (v. 26) reinforce the frame. B/B′ refer to her confidence or certitude in facing the future by means of negative and positive synonyms. BDB states that *śḥq* "to laugh"

165. Wolters, "The Meaning of *Kîšôr,*" p. 103.

166. Grace Crowfoot, *Methods of Hand Spinning in Egypt and the Sudan* (Bankfield Museum Notes, Second Series, no. 12; Halifax [England]: Kings & Soins, 1931), repr. in Grace M. Crowfoot and H. Ling Roth, *Hand Spinning and Woolcombing* (McMinnville, Oreg.: Robin and Russ Handweavers, 1974), p. 14, cited by Wolters, "The Meaning of *Kîšôr,*" p. 101. See *ANEP,* nos. 142, 631, and esp. 144.

167. *HALOT,* 3:933, s.v. *pelek.*

168. Other body parts in the acrostic that could have been played upon are *ʿayin* "eye," *resh* "head," *qoph* "scalp," and *šîn* "tooth."

plus *l* (v. 25a) is the equivalent of the negative "have no fear" of v. 21a (Job 5:22; Prov. 31:25; Hab. 1:10).[169] C/C′ explain the reasons for her confidence. She has protected her household against the snow without (v. 21b) and fortified herself with strength within (v. 25a). Within the macro-chiasm the poet structures a micro-chiasm (vv. 21a-25b, 25a-21b). D/D′ uniquely mention the specific textile items she makes, two for herself (coverlets and clothing of linen, probably white linen undergarments and wool dyed purple for outer wear) and two for the merchants (garments and sashes). The connection is reinforced by repeating the verb "she makes" *(ʿāśᵉtâ),* the second of three words in both A versets. X highlights by means of the pivot the poem's central message. The valiant wife's accomplishments empower her husband to lead the nation in righteousness and justice. This message is further enhanced by a hierarchical escalation, ascending from her contributions to the poor (v. 20), to the household (v. 21), to herself (v. 22), to her husband (v. 23). The pivot is further accented by three other framing techniques. First, vv. 19-20 and vv. 26-27 form two balanced pairs of verses around the core, vv. 21-25. This inner core in turn is chiastically framed by the root *lbš* (*lābuš* "clothed," v. 21b and *lᵉbûšāh* "clothing," v. 25a) and the antonyms "does not fear" (v. 21a) and "laughs" (v. 25b).

20 Pride of place is given to her ministry to the afflicted and destitute in the community (cf. Job 29:12-17; Acts 9:39). The stereotypical phrase "poor and needy" (see v. 9), perhaps a hendiadys used for the powerless and disadvantaged poor (see v. 9), is here broken apart in the parallelism (see I: 42-43; cf. Pss. 9:18[19]; 72:4, 12; Prov. 30:14).[170] Whereas the king opens his mouth to defend their interest in court, the valiant woman is openhanded to meet their palpable needs. *She spreads out* (*pārᵉśâ;* see 13:16) *her palm (kappāh)* means either to invite home or to give material aid (22:9).[171] Either way, she gestures to help. *To the poor* (*lᵉʿānî;* see 3:34) denotes those who, suffering from some kind of disability or of distress through no fault of their own, cry out for help. *And her hands* (*wᵉyādeyhā;* see v. 19) she holds out (*šillᵉḥâ;* see v. 19) *to the needy (la'ebyôn),* referring to the destitute who live daily from hand to mouth, is either a metonymy of cause (i.e., to give to them what they need) or a metonymy of adjunct (i.e., to invite them to her home by gesture).

21 The list returns to the splendid clothing she manufactured, this time not for trade to enrich the household's table but to protect each family

169. BDB, p. 965, s.v. *śḥq*.

170. Cf. S. Gillingham, "The Poor in the Psalms," *ExpTim* 100 (1988) 15-19; R. N. Whybray, "Poverty, Wealth and Point of View in Proverbs," *ExpTim* 100 (1989) 332-36.

171. *HALOT,* 3:976, s.v. *prś.*

member from the snowy cold. Verset A presents her confident psychological state. *She is not afraid* (*lōʾ-tîrāʾ;* see 3:25) means that anticipated danger does not strongly agitate her. *Of snow* (*miššāleg;* see 25:13), which falls in Palestine in the winter rainy season (i.e., from November to February), is a metonymy for the freezing weather that threatens their lives (cf. 25:13; 26:1). *All her household (kol-bêtāh)* in verset B escalates *for her household* (*lᵉbêtāh;* see v. 15) in verset A. *Is clothed* (*lābūš;* see 27:26) *in crimson (šānîm),* the color of the thread, is a metonymy for costly wool (see v. 22; cf. 2 Sam. 1:24; Jer. 4:30).[172] Linen does not readily accept dye.[173]

22 The woman also uses her splendid weaving talents *for herself (lāh).* In the Hebrew text, the outer frame of the chiastic parallelism (v. 22) mentions the woven products *she makes* (*ʿāśᵉtâ;* see 8:26; 31:13), coverlets for her bed (verset A) and clothing for her dress (verset B). Though the data are meager, probably both occurrences of the word *bed covers* (*marbaddîm;* see Prov. 7:16) pertain to making the bed soft, comfortable, and attractive. *Her clothing* (*lᵉbûšāh;* see 27:26) is made of the finest textiles from agriculture and animal husbandry. Verset B escalates v. 13a from linen to *fine linen (šēš),* which was normally imported from Egypt (cf. Gen. 41:42; Ezek. 16:10, 13; 27:7), and from wool (v. 13a) to *wool dyed with purple (ʾargāmān),*[174] also a traditional import. To produce this red dye was costly because it comes from a seashell off the Phoenician coast and so connotes wealth and luxury (cf. Judg. 8:26; Song 3:10; 7:5[6] and Ezek. 27:7, 16; Acts 16:14).[175]

23 *Her husband* (*baʿlāh;* see v. 11) *is respected* (*nôdāʿ;* lit. "known," probably "renown")[176] for several reasons. McKane reasons that the absence of domestic worries and his prosperous household can build his reputation.[177] Since *ydʿ* means to know through personal contact, *nôdāʿ* may infer that the other dignitaries are familiar with his own judicious wisdom and so respect him. The apparel with which she adorns him (see v. 21b) also enhances his prestige. Finally, her own character and genius, which are praised in the gate (see 31:31), are a crown on his head (see 12:4). *In the gate* (*bašᵉʿārîm;* see 1:21; cf. Job 29) symbolizes the city's collective authority and power. *When he sits* (*bᵉšibtô;* see 9:14) on the bench is a metonymy for opening his mouth to give authoritative counsel and teaching (cf. Gen. 19:1; 2 Sam. 18:24; 19:8[9]; 1 K. 22:10). *With the elders* (*ʿim-ziqnê;* see 17:6; 20:29) numbers

172. See R. Alden, *NIDOTTE,* 4:193, s.v. *šānî.*

173. *The New Encyclopedia Britannica* (Micropaedia; Chicago: Helen Hemingway Benton, 1973-74), s.v. "flax."

174. *HALOT,* 1:84, s.v. *ʾargāmān.*

175. R. Alden, *NIDOTTE,* 1:498, s.v. *ʾargāmān.*

176. Although Job 29:7-17 does not use the verb, it undoubtedly describes what it means to be known in the city gate.

177. McKane, *Proverbs,* p. 669.

him among the highest local authorities from time immemorial in the ancient Near East. Prior to the monarchy, their authority guarded the internal order of the community (Ruth 4:1-12) and represented the community to the outside world (Judg. 8:14, 16; 1 Sam. 11:3). During the monarchy the elders of the capital city and of other major cities became members of a nation's aristocracy. Their primary duty was to furnish counsel, just as the wise did (cf. Ezek. 7:26 with Jer. 18:18; also Job 12:20; Ezek. 27:9).[178] *Of the land* (*'āreṣ;* see 28:2), the parallel to (city) gates, suggests that their authoritative influence extended beyond the city to larger jurisdictions.[179]

24 *She makes* (*'āśᵉtâ;* see vv. 13, 22) continues to itemize her profitable contribution to the household and perhaps just as importantly to empower merchants to produce wealth. The precise species of *linen garments (sādîn)* — probably an Egyptian loanword — is uncertain.[180] The narrative *and sells* [*them*] (*wattimkōr;* see 23:23) completes the thought. *She supplies* (*nātᵉnâ;* lit. "she gives to"; see v. 16) is a synonym for "sell." A visual depiction of a *sash (ḥᵃgôr),* the noun related to the verb "girds" *(ḥāgar)* in v. 17, may be preserved in the "Black Obelisk" of Shalmaneser III (858-824 B.C.), where Jehu is shown wearing a fringed outer garment.[181] In Isa. 3:24 it refers to an article of fashionable women's dress. Perhaps "[under]garments" and outer "sashes" are a merism for all kinds of fine apparel.[182]

25 She is not only "not afraid" (v. 21a), but she even laughs at any tide of adversity that may come (v. 25b). She clothed her household in scarlet (v. 21b; cf. v. 22), but even more important, *her clothing* (*lᵉbûšāh;* see v. 22) is strength and honor, the abstract qualities that make the real clothing possible and enable her to overcome any foe. In the Old Testament, to put on clothing is to show one's true colors or to display one's true character.[183] *Strength* (*'ōz;* see v. 17) denotes effective and enduring energy, while *and majesty* (*wᵉhādār;* see 20:29; 25:6) signifies the magnificence that sets her apart from and above her peers. The praise of the woman can hardly be higher: it attributes to her the advantages of both youth and old age (i.e., "power and splendor"; 20:29).[184] Like a conqueror who derides his enemy (see 1:26; 29:9), *so she laughs* (*wattiśḥaq;* see 1:26) *at* her metaphorical enemy, *the coming day* (*lᵉyôm 'aḥarôn;* lit. "days in the future"; see 27:10, 15),

178. See J. Conrad, *TDOT,* 4:128, s.v. *zāqēn.*

179. M. Dahood (*Proverbs and Northwest Semitic Philology* [Rome: Pontifical Biblical Institute, 1963], p. 63) points to Phoenician inscriptions showing a semantic transition from "land" to "city-state" that exercised dominion over a larger territorial area.

180. *HALOT,* 2:743-44, s.v. *sādîn.*

181. *ANEP,* p. 122 (#355).

182. I. Cornelius, *NIDOTTE,* 2:669, s.v. *kᵉna'an.*

183. Whybray, *Proverbs,* p. 429.

184. Meinhold, *Sprüche,* p. 527.

the indefinite future, with all its possible alarming prospects or circumstances.

26 The itemized list now reaches a climax, turning from her down-to-earth accomplishments to her speaking out the moral and spiritual values that inform them.[185] *She opens her mouth* (*pîhā pātᵉḥâ;* see v. 8) is a Hebraism meaning to speak at length or with great solemnity or freedom.[186] That she speaks *with wisdom* (*bᵉḥokmâ;* see 1:2; cf. 3:19; 24:3; 28:26) implies that she already possesses it and that wisdom shapes what she has to say and how she says it. Specifically, *loving teaching* (*tôrat-ḥesed;* see n. 95; cf. 1:8; 3:3; 5:13; 13:14) *is on her tongue* (*ʿal-lᵉšônāh;* see 21:23) probably signifies that her teaching is informed by her own lovingkindness. If so, her generous sacrificing of herself to help those in need models her instruction (cf. 13:14). Without that sublimity, notes Delitzsch, her industry is without virtue.[187] But the phrase could also be rendered "the law of kindness" as either a reference to a particular body of teaching about kindness or as a metonymy of adjunct for all her speech.[188] Her teaching is informed by the content of Proverbs.

27 Verset A asserts the teacher's vigilance over her household, and verset B reinforces it by asserting her unstinting diligence.[189] The initial participle *one who watches* vigilantly *over* (*ṣôpîyâ;* lit. "keep a lookout"; see n. 96) links v. 27 with v. 26,[190] explaining that as a teacher she keeps a sharp lookout over the *affairs* (*hᵃlîkôt;* see n. 97) *of her household* (*bêtāh;* see v. 21) promptly to right any irregularities (see 15:13) and to maintain its orderly arrangement. With regard to the children, the aristocratic wife turns over to her servant girls much of the routine work in rearing the children but assumes responsibility for their instruction and retains final authority (see 1:8). Her wise husband celebrates her wisdom (cf. vv. 28-29, 30-33), and,

185. Possibly v. 26 is linked with v. 25 by the chiastic syntax of a nominal clause in the outer frame (vv. 25a, 26b) and a verbal clause in the inner core (vv. 25b, 26a). The chiastic parallelism of this verse matches in its outer frame the synonymous metonymies for her speech, "she opens her mouth" and "is upon her tongue"; in its inner core it pairs the manner and/or content of her speaking, "with wisdom" and "loving instruction." Note, too, that the organs of speech (i.e., "mouth" *peh* and "tongue" *lašôn*) are both masculine nouns, and the terms denoting the content (i.e., "wisdom" *hokmâ* and "teaching" *tôrâ*) are both feminine.

186. Bullinger, *Figures of Speech,* p. 842.

187. Cf. Delitzsch, *Proverbs,* p. 338.

188. Bridges (*Proverbs,* p. 625), interpreting the phrase as a genitive of species, comments: "The same love that binds her heart, governs her tongue, not with the caprice, but with *the law, of kindness.*"

189. In the inner core *hᵃlîkôt bêtāh* (feminine-masculine nouns) stands over against *leḥem ʿaṣlût* (masculine-feminine).

190. Keil and Delitzsch (*Proverbs,* p. 339) also noted the connection of v. 27a to v. 26.

like Adam who celebrated his wife's equality with him,[191] encourages her to share her loving and wise teaching with him (cf. Eph. 5:21). The metaphor *she does not eat* (*lōʾ tōʾkēl;* see 1:31) is the negative match of "watches over" in verset A. *The food* (*wᵉleḥem;* see v. 14) *of idleness* (*ʿaṣlût;* see 19:15) signifies that she does not indulge in the habits, excuses, or miseries of the sluggard (cf. 24:30-34; 26:13). On the other hand, by a clever pun, verset A also means, "All the affairs of her household are wisdom and/or instruction."[192] Read in these two ways, v. 27 offers a summarization of the character of her contributions to her household rather than a specific item, and verset B reinforces her general character and behavior. Her very way of life teaches wisdom — so deeply rooted is it in her person.

3. Conclusion (31:28-31)

The poet concludes his encomium by rewarding her with praise, first by citing her household's praise of her (vv. 28-29) and then by calling on the community to praise her (vv. 30-31; cf. 27:2). He marks off the conclusion by returning to the syntax of an initial finite verb — also perfective (so vv. 11-18, unlike vv. 19-27) — and by repeating the keyword "praise" *(hll)* in the B verset of three of the four verses (vv. 28, 30, 31). The stylistic contrasts between the conclusion and the preceding poem are striking.[193] The introduction and main body of the poem emphasize the blessings she bestows on her husband (*baʿlāh;* vv. 11-12, 20, 23) and her household (*bêtāh,* vv. 15, 21), but the conclusion emphasizes the reciprocal good they do her. She has done such good that now he praises her to give her public honor. In v. 24 she gives (*nātᵉnâ,* glossed "sells") her works to others; in v. 31 her works extol *(tᵉnû)* her. In v. 16 "from the fruit of her hands" *(mippᵉrî kappeyhā)* refers to the income she invests to enrich her household; in v. 31 to the praise that the investment brings to her (cf. "her hands" [*yādeyhā*] in vv. 19a and 20b). As she "rises" (*qûm,* v. 15) to pursue her ceaseless industry for her household, now they all "rise" (*qûm,* v. 28) to give her public honor (cf. v. 23). The city gate, site of her good works (vv. 23-24), becomes the place where her works praise her (v. 31). In sum, the woman so concerned for others now becomes the central concern and praise of others.[194] Note, too, that the woman who otherwise does "not fear" (*lōʾ-tîrāʾ* [v. 21]) "fears the LORD" *(yirʾat-YHWH).*

191. Adam's only words prior to the fall celebrate his wife's equality apart from their sexuality: "bone of my bone; flesh of my flesh."

192. See n. 96.

193. McCreesh, "Wisdom as Wife," pp. 35-36.

194. McCreesh, "Wisdom as Wife," p. 36.

28 The passing reference to *her sons* (*bāneyhā;* see 1:8; 4:13; 8:32 — it is unclear whether many siblings and/or more than one generation is in view — in the conclusion suggests that this wife finds fulfillment less in having given birth to sons and raised them than in maximizing her opportunities on behalf of *her husband* (*ba'lāh;* see vv. 11, 23), who with their sons now *arise* (*qāmû;* see v. 15), presumably in her presence, to symbolize their respect for her (see Job 29:8; Isa. 49:7).[195] *And pronounce her blessed* (*way^{e}'aššᵉrûha,* see n. 101; also 3:13; 8:32, 34), signifying that they esteem her and declare her to be living life optimally, as the Creator intended, and so endowed with wisdom's benefits. *And praises her (way^{e}hal^{e}lāh)* sounds very similar to *way^{e}hal^{e}lûyāh,* "and praise Yah."

29 The husband's praise, which is based on years of experience. as indicated by the maturity of their children, is now cited verbatim. His quotation is set apart syntactically by following a verb of speaking (i.e., "praise") with the second feminine singular of address. He expresses his praise in a comparative superlative,[196] naming in verset A the *many* (*rabbôt;* see 7:26; 19:6) *daughters (bānôt),* all of whom she is judged to surpass in verset B. Commentators differ on the reason for the poet's choice of *bānôt.* Lange's opinion that by the diminutive the husband puts himself above his wife rings a sour note in this paean of praise.[197] Toy pontificates that it reflects an age "when a woman, even after marriage, remained always a member of her father's family, and was defined as his 'daughter,'"[198] not noting that the term is used as a synonym for "women" only in poetry (cf. Gen. 30:13 ["women" in the NIV, NRSV]; Song 6:9), a fact that undermines his claim. More plausibly, Delitzsch suggests that it is "a more delicate, finer name for women,"[199] and Van Leeuwen implies that it completes a parallelism with *bānîm* in v. 29.[200] Moreover, it probably implies that these virtuous women embraced their parents' wisdom when they were daughters (see 1:8). Amazingly she ascends above those who *do* (*'āśû;* see 2:14) *valiantly* (*ḥāyil,* v. 10), the very quality that the poet said was most rare among women (v. 10). Indeed, she is so exceptional that by comparison such women are plentiful! The expression "to do valiantly" is used mainly in the realm of heroic warfare (i.e., to triumph and be victorious; 1 Sam. 14:48; Ps. 60:12[14]; par. 108:13[14]; 118:15). The husband's praise, *but you* (*w^{e}'at;* see 23:14; 25:22) *surpass* or advance against (*'ālît;* see 2 K. 20:22) *all of them (kullānâ)* must be hyper-

195. So Meinhold, *Sprüche,* p. 529.
196. *IBHS,* p. 269, P. 14.5.
197. Lange, *Proverbs,* p. 259.
198. Toy, *Proverbs,* p. 248.
199. Delitzsch, *Proverbs,* p. 340.
200. Van Leeuwen, *Proverbs,* p. 263.

bole, for the valiant wife serves as a model for all the daughters of Israel, and one cannot surpass the other in the same virtue.

30 The shift from "you" back to "she" signals that the poet takes over from the husband. *Charm* (*ḥēn;* see 1:9) and *beauty* (*hayyōpî;* see 6:25) are abstractions for a charming and beautiful woman who stands in an implicit antithetical parallelism with "a woman who fears the LORD." According to the Masoretic accents, "charm . . . beauty" stand together with "deceitful . . . fleeting" in an implied contrast with "should be praised." A charming and beautiful woman, in contrast to one who fears the LORD, is not praiseworthy, for her virtue is aggressively *deceitful* (*šeqer;* see 6:17). Just as "charm" is more narrowly defined as "beauty," so "deceitful" is more narrowly specified as *fleeting* (*hebel;* lit. "a puff of air" and metaphorically "ephemeral and transitory" [see 13:11; 21:6]). In short, "charm" deceives because it promises a lifetime of happiness that it cannot deliver.[201] As Toy comments, "Beauty is said to be deceitful because it passes away, and with it passes the hope of happiness based on it."[202] However, this truth about beauty's deceit must be held in tension with the father's prayer that God give his son a wife with sex appeal (5:19) and the Song of Solomon's celebration of erotica within marriage. The antithetical parallelism, *as for a woman* (*'iššâ;* see 7:10; 14:1) *who fears the LORD* (*yir'at-YHWH;* see I: 100; 1:7), *she (hî') should be praised* (*tithallāl;* see 31:28),[203] also implies that inner spiritual beauty does not deceive, "for what is seen is temporary, but what is unseen is eternal" (2 Cor. 4:18). As part of the poem's climactic conclusion, this vertical virtue with Israel's covenant-keeping God provides the necessary theological base for her horizontal social virtues.[204] Although questioning the text's originality, Meinhold also notes that the phrase at the end of the book connects wisdom and fear of the LORD (vv. 26a, 30b), a connection made also at its be-

201. The four other occurrences of the two words together also assert that deceit is worthless because it is futile (i.e., it perishes and/or does not profit [Prov. 21:6; Jer. 10:14, 15 (= 51:17, 18); 16:19]).

202. Toy, *Proverbs,* p. 548.

203. The conjunction is jarring; elsewhere those who fear the LORD praise him (cf. Pss. 22:25, 27[24, 26]; 40:5[4]), not receive praise.

204. The introduction of her piety this late in the poem causes some (e.g., Toy, *Proverbs,* pp. 548-49; Whybray, *Proverbs,* p. 430; et al.) to suggest or imply that the original text read "an intelligent woman" and that a later scribe substituted "fear of the LORD" to supply the otherwise missing piety to the poem. Some base their emendation on the double reading of the LXX: "False are allurements, and vain the beauty of a wife. For a woman of understanding *(synetē)* is blessed. Let her therefore praise the fear of the LORD." Note, however, that both the MT and the LXX — though its syntax is faulty — contain *yir'at-YHWH,* the point at issue. In sum, emending verset B to *'ešat bînâ/nᵉbōnâ hî' tthll* "an insightful woman is to be praised" is arbitrary.

ginning (1:7; 9:10) and in its middle (15:33).[205] By definition, the fear of the LORD means in part living according to the wisdom revealed in this book. This woman's itemized, self-sacrificing activities for others exemplify the fear of the LORD (see 1:7).

31 In this synonymous parallelism, whose repetition adds emphasis, the verbs *extol* (*tᵉnû;* see n. 107) *her* (*lāh;* see v. 22) and *let praise* (*yᵉhalᵉlûhā;* see v. 28b) are volitive plurals. The poet changes from the imperative of direct and personal address, "you," in verset A to the jussive of indirect and impersonal address, "let them," in verset B. This variation suggests that in verset A he addresses the responsible citizens *in the gate* (*baššᵉʿārîm;* see v. 23a; cf. Ruth 3:11), which must be supplied from verset B. The final word, *her works* (*maʿᵃśeyhā;* see 16:11),[206] a parallel that defines *the fruit of her hands* (*mippᵉrî yādeyhā;* see v. 16b), climactically summarizes her many splendid accomplishments itemized in the poem.[207] Of course, her works praise her to the extent they are publicly acknowledged and acclaimed. Thus, as a fitting climax to his eulogy, the poet and sage shifts from recording the wise family's spontaneous accolades (vv. 28-29) to obliging all in the gate to extol her (see v. 23). Not to adore and praise "true" beauty is wrong, he implies. C. S. Lewis said, "If we do not admire [what is praiseworthy], we shall be stupid, insensible, and great losers."[208]

205. Meinhold, *Sprüche,* p. 530.

206. The nominal form of *ʿśh* "to do/make/produce" (see vv. 13b, 22a, 24).

207. One often finds *maʿᵃśeh yᵉde[y]hem* "the work of their hands" for the product of one's labor or character of one's activity (cf. Deut. 2:7; 14:29; 16:15; 24:19; 28:2; 30:9; 2 K. 22:17; Pss. 28:4; 90:17; Jer. 32:30; Lam. 3:64 [cited by Dunn, "Studies in Proverbs 31:10-31," p. 178, n. 502]).

208. C. S. Lewis, *Reflections on the Psalms* (New York: Harcourt, Brace & World, 1958), p. 92.

INDEX OF SUBJECTS

INDEX OF AUTHORS

INDEX OF SCRIPTURE REFERENCES

INDEX OF SELECTED HEBREW WORDS AND PHRASES